MW00769703

THE WORKS OF

JOHN WESLEY

General Editor: RANDY L. MADDOX

THE WORKS OF
JOHN WESLEY

Volume 30

——

Letters

VI

1782–1788

EDITED BY

RANDY L. MADDOX

Abingdon Press

Nashville

THE WORKS OF JOHN WESLEY VOLUME 30:
LETTERS VI: 1782–1788

Copyright © 2024 by Abingdon Press

All rights reserved.

ISBN: 9781791031978

MANUFACTURED IN THE UNITED STATES OF AMERICA

THE BICENTENNIAL EDITION OF
THE WORKS OF JOHN WESLEY

This edition of the works of John Wesley reflects the quickened interest in the heritage of Christian thought that has become evident during the last half century. A fully critical presentation of Wesley's writings had long been a desideratum in order to furnish documentary sources illustrating his contribution to both catholic and evangelical Christianity.

Several scholars, notably Professor Albert C. Outler, Professor Franz Hildebrandt, Dean Merrimon Cuninggim, and Dean Robert E. Cushman, discussed the possibility of such an edition. Under the leadership of Dean Cushman, a board of directors was formed in 1960 comprising the deans of four sponsoring theological schools of Methodist-related universities in the United States: Drew, Duke, Emory, and Southern Methodist. They appointed an Editorial Committee to formulate plans and enlisted an international and interdenominational team of scholars for the Wesley Works Editorial Project.

The works were divided into units of cognate material, with a separate editor (or joint editors) responsible for each unit. Dr. Frank Baker was appointed textual editor for the whole project, with responsibility for supplying each unit editor with a critically developed, accurate Wesley text. The text seeks to represent Wesley's thought in its fullest and most deliberate expression insofar as this can be determined from the available evidence. Substantive variant readings in any British edition published during Wesley's lifetime are shown in appendices to the units, preceded by a summary of the problems faced and the solutions reached in the complex task of securing and presenting Wesley's text. The aim throughout is to enable Wesley to be read with maximum ease and understanding, and with minimal intrusion by the editors.

This edition includes all of Wesley's original or mainly original prose works, some select examples of his extensive work as editor and publisher of extracts from the writings of others, and one volume devoted to his *Collection of Hymns* (1780). An essential feature of the project is a complete bibliography of the works published by Wesley and his brother Charles, sometimes jointly, sometimes separately. An index is supplied for each unit and a general index for the whole edition.

The Delegates of the Oxford University Press agreed to undertake publication, but announced in June 1982 that because of severe economic problems they would regretfully be compelled to withdraw from the enterprise with the completion in 1983 of volume 7, the *Collection of Hymns*. Abingdon Press offered its services, beginning with the publication of the first volume of the *Sermons* in 1984, the bicentennial year of the formation of American Methodism as an autonomous church. The new title now assumed, however, refers in general to the bicentennial of Wesley's total activities as author, editor, and publisher, from 1733 to 1791, especially as summarized in the first edition of his collected works in thirty-two volumes, 1771–74.

Dean Robert E. Cushman of Duke University undertook general administration and promotion of the project until 1971, when he was succeeded as president by Dean Joseph D. Quillian Jr. of Southern Methodist University, these two universities having furnished the major support and guidance for the enterprise. Subsequent presidents of the project include: Dean James E. Kirby Jr. of Southern Methodist University (1981–90), Dean Dennis M. Campbell of Duke University (1990–2003), Dean Russell E. Richey of Emory University (2003–06), Dean William B. Lawrence of Southern Methodist University (2006–16), Dean Craig C. Hill of Southern Methodist University (2016–22), and Dean G. Sujin Pak of Boston University (2022–).

During the decade 1961–70, the Editorial Committee supervised the task of setting editorial principles and procedures, and general editorship was shared by Dr. Eric W. Baker, Dean William R. Cannon, and Dean Cushman. In 1969 the directors appointed Dr. Frank Baker, early attached to the project as bibliographer and textual editor for Wesley's text, as editor-in-chief also. In 1986 the directors appointed Richard P. Heitzenrater to succeed Baker as general editor, beginning with the Journal and Diaries unit. At that same point the directors named Randy L. Maddox as associate general editor, to work alongside Dr. Heitzenrater. Most recently, in 2014, Randy L. Maddox stepped into the role of General Editor, upon Dr. Heitzenrater's retirement from that capacity.

Other sponsoring bodies have been successively added to the original four: Boston University School of Theology, the Conference of the Methodist Church of Great Britain, The General Commission on Archives and History of The United Methodist Church, The United Methodist Board of Higher Education and Ministry, and the World Methodist Council. For the continuing support of the sponsoring institutions the Directors express their profound thanks. They gratefully acknowledge also the encouragement and financial support that have come from the Historical Societies and Commissions on Archives and History of many Annual Conferences, as well as the donations of private individuals and foundations.

On June 9, 1976, The Wesley Works Editorial Project was incorporated in the State of North Carolina as a nonprofit corporation. In 1977 by-laws were approved governing the appointment and duties of the Directors, their officers, and their Executive Committee.

The Board of Directors

PREFACE AND ACKNOWLEDGMENTS

I again wish to express my sincere thanks to the staff of the many libraries and archives who have assisted me in verifying the location of surviving letters and obtaining copies in order to ensure accuracy of transcription. I also gratefully acknowledge the assistance of my wife, Aileen Frances (Chadwick) Maddox, in proofreading and standardizing the final text.

Randy L. Maddox

CONTENTS

CONTENTS

EDITORIAL GUIDELINES

Readers of this volume are strongly encouraged to read Dr. Frank Baker's excellent introductory essay in vol. 25, which places John Wesley's correspondence in historical context, describes previous editions of Wesley's letters, and elaborates the editorial principles adopted for this edition. But it may be helpful to distill the most important principles here, including a couple of slight changes adopted in this volume.

One set of principles concerns the sources privileged in preparing the text of Wesley's letters. We present the text of the actual letter that Wesley sent (the holograph) whenever it has survived. In the absence of a surviving holograph, on a few occasions we have either Wesley's working draft or a final copy that he made and retained for his records. Typically, no manuscript version survives for letters that Wesley sent to newspapers and journals for publication, or those that he published in the *Arminian Magazine*, because the manuscripts were discarded after publication. In such cases the original published transcription must serve as source. Finally, there are several instances where previous editors and researchers had access to holographs that no longer survive or are in undiscovered private hands. In this situation we are dependent upon either the earliest (or most complete and detailed) published transcription, or on a manuscript transcription in surviving records. In every case we identify the type of item that is serving as our source.

A second set of principles relates to the presentation of Wesley's text. After describing problems with previous editions in this regard (25:120–23), Baker depicted the approach of this edition of Wesley's letters as a careful balance between historical accuracy, showing Wesley 'warts and all', and modern readability (25:123–28). We continue Baker's practice of retaining Wesley's colloquialisms, contractions, and outdated grammatical usages. But, like Baker, we routinely expand Wesley's abbreviations (whenever clear), including abbreviated names and his frequent use of the ampersand. We also silently update archaic spellings (though retaining typical British spellings). Likewise we have followed Baker's precedent in imposing modern practices of capitalisation and punctuation. We keep editorial additions to Wesley's text at a minimum, and clearly identify them with [square brackets]. A few of the manuscript sources have been damaged or have obscured text. In these cases we have reconstructed the missing text as much as possible, placing the reconstructed text within ⟨angled brackets⟩.

Instances of emphasis deserve special notice. In manuscript materials Wesley usually showed emphasis by underlining. We have generally rendered such material in *italics* (as the modern parallel). But, as was typical in the eighteenth century, Wesley also often used underlining in his manuscripts to identify direct quotations from Scripture. We have rendered these instances within quotation marks, unless there was some ambiguity about whether he was intending *emphasis* as well. These principles have their parallel in cases where the source is a published transcription of a Wesley letter. Eighteenth-century printing conventionally placed direct quotations of Scripture in *italics*, which we have altered in all clear instances to standard font and quotation marks. Similarly, printed works of this period typically italicise proper names of people, places, languages, and the like; all of which we render in standard font, unless there is reason to assume that emphasis was intended.

The most noticeable changes in presentation of Wesley's text adopted in this volume (in comparison to the prior two volumes) involve standardising the format of letters. For example, Wesley fluctuated some in where he positioned on his letters the current date and the place from where he was writing. He also occasionally omitted one or the other of these details. We present this material consistently at the top of the letter, listing place of origin on one line and date on the next. We also reconstruct missing place or date information, placing it in [square brackets], drawing in particular on Wesley's *Journal*. Another change from Baker's practice is that the header line for female recipients now identifies them by maiden and married names (if known). Thus, for example, 'To Mrs. Mary Wesley' becomes 'To Mary (Goldhawk/Vazeille) Wesley'. Finally, while limitations of page size and other factors often led Wesley to vary the format of his closing line and signature, we render them in a uniform format.

The third set of editorial principles guiding this edition of Wesley's letters focus on the information given at the end of holograph letters. Four types of information are potentially listed:

Address:	Giving the address exactly as written (usually by Wesley), without expanding abbreviations or correcting spelling.

Postmark:	Some holographs have only the 'Bishop Mark' indicating the month and date of posting. Others have as well a stamp of the town where the letter was posted. A few contain more than one listing because the letter was redirected. All marks that are legible are indicated.
Charge:	This is the recorded charge paid when the letter was delivered (it became common only near the end of the eighteenth century for the sender to pay the charge). Often only a squiggle is made to indicate payment, without listing the amount.
Endorsement:	Many of the holographs have annotations of when they were received, and sometimes short summaries of their contents or the recipient's response. There are also later cataloguing remarks on some letters. We generally present here only annotations that appear to be contemporary to when the letter was received. These can usually be presumed to be in the hand of the recipient. We note this as the case only when it is in a hand that we could verify (such as that of Charles Wesley).

The final set of principles for this edition relates to annotation of the letters. Our goal is to aid in understanding the letters. We privilege original sources in documenting quoted material in Wesley's letters and in providing background information, in part because these older sources are increasingly available over the web. For example, transcriptions of the original editions of the various collections of hymns and poems published by John or Charles Wesley (from which John frequently quotes in his letters) are available through the Center for Studies in the Wesleyan Tradition, Duke Divinity School (https://divinity.duke.edu/initiatives/cswt). We identify whenever possible both Wesley's correspondents and other persons mentioned in the letters. More detailed biographical information is given on the first occasion a name appears, which can be located through the name index on the Wesley Works website (www.wesley-works.org). Finally, we identify all quotations from Scripture, as well as significant allusions to Scripture, using 'cf.'

and 'see' in the specific manner described under 'Signs, Special Usages, and Abbreviations'.

Readers will notice again the absence in this volume of 'in-letters', or surviving letters that were addressed to John Wesley. This decision was made by the Board of the Wesley Works Editorial Project in order to provide readers with *more* access to in-letters. To keep the first two volumes within a manageable size, Dr. Baker included only select in-letters, and frequently abridged them. The Board decided to make *all* of the known in-letters available *in their entirety*, but to do so *online*, on an internet site dedicated to the project: www.wesley–works.org. This is where (under the tab titled "Online Resources") readers will find the letters addressed to Wesley that are mentioned in footnotes or appear in the cumulative correspondence list in the Appendix. Readers can also find there a complete list of surviving Wesley letters that gives holding information. Finally, a chart appears there that lists where published transcriptions of letters are found in this and previous editions of collected letters, as well as journals and other locations.

SIGNS, SPECIAL USAGES, ABBREVIATIONS

[ ] Square brackets enclose editorial insertions or substitutions in the original text, or (with a query) doubtful readings.

⟨ ⟩ Angle brackets enclose conjectural readings where the original text is defective or obscured.

... An ellipsis indicates a passage omitted by the preparer of the original source—for this purpose Wesley generally employed a dash.

[...] An ellipsis within square brackets indicates a passage omitted silently by Wesley from a text he was quoting, to which the present editor is drawing attention.

(()) Double parentheses enclose words that have been struck through by the author in the original manuscript (particularly drafts), to indicate their omission.

[[ ]] Double square brackets enclose passages supplied from shorthand or cipher, from an abstract or similar document in the third person, or reconstructed from secondary evidence.

/ A solidus or slant line marks the division between two lines of text in the original manuscript.

a,b,c Small superscript letters indicate footnotes supplied by Wesley.

1,2,3 Small superscript numbers indicate footnotes supplied by the editor.

Cf. Before a scriptural or other citation by Wesley, indicates that he was quoting with more than minimal inexactness, yet nevertheless displaying the passage as a quotation.

See Before a scriptural citation indicates an undoubted allusion or a quotation that was not displayed as such by Wesley, and that is more than minimally inexact.

Wesley's publications. Where a work by Wesley was first published separately, its title is italicised; where it first appeared within a different work such as a collected volume, the title appears within quotation marks.

Book-titles in Wesley's text are italicised if accurate, and given in roman type with capitals if inaccurate. If a title consists of only one generic word that forms a major part of the original title, it is italicised; but if it is inaccurate (such as 'Sermons' for a volume entitled *Discourses*), it is printed in lower case roman.

Abbreviations. In addition to common abbreviations like c[irca], ed[itio]n, n[ote], orig[inal], and st[anza], the footnotes in this volume utilise the following abbreviated forms for items referred to repeatedly:

AM	*Arminian Magazine* (London, 1778–97).
Asbury, *Journal*	Elmer T. Clark (ed.), *The Journal and Letters of Francis Asbury*, 3 vols. (Nashville: Abingdon, 1958).
Atlay, Letters	John Atlay, *Letters that Passed between the Rev. John Wesley and Mr. John Atlay, relative to the People and Preaching House at Dewsbury* (London: J. Matthews, et al., 1790.

Atmore, *Memorial* — Charles Atmore, *The Methodist Memorial: bring an Impartial Sketch of the Lives and Characters of the Preachers* (Bristol: Edwards, 1801).

Ball, *Memoir* — John Parker (ed.), *Memoir of Miss Hannah Ball, of High Wycomb[e], in Buckinghamshire* (London: John Mason, 1839).

Batty, Scotland — Margaret Batty, *Scotland's Methodists, 1750–2000* (Edinburgh: John Donald, 2010).

BCP — *The Book of Common Prayer* (London, 1662).

Beinecke Library (Yale) — Beinecke Rare Book and Manuscript Library, Yale University, New Haven, Connecticut.

Bennis, *Correspondence* — Thomas Bennis (ed.), *Christian Correspondence; being a Collection of Letters written by the late Rev. John Wesley, the late Mrs. Eliza Bennis, and others* (Philadelphia: B. Graves, 1809).

Bennis, *Journal* — Rosemary Raughter, *The Journal of Elizabeth Bennis, 1749–79* (Dublin, Ireland: Columba Press, 2007).

Benson, *Works* — Joseph Benson (ed.), *The Works of the Rev. John Wesley*, 2nd edn., 16 vols. (London: Cordeux, 1813).

Bibliography — Forthcoming bibliography in this edition (vol. 34), which has a different numbering system from Richard Green's *Wesley Bibliography*.

Bradburn, *Memoirs* — Eliza Weaver Bradburn (ed.), *Memoirs of the late Rev. Samuel Bradburn* (London: Richard Edwards, 1816).

Bretherton, *Chester* — F. F. Bretherton, *Early Methodism in and around Chester* (Chester: Phillipson & Golder, 1903).

Bridwell Library (SMU) — Bridwell Library, Perkins School of Theology, Southern Methodist University (Dallas, Texas), Special Collections.

Bristol Directory (1775) — *Sketchley's Bristol Directory* (Bristol: James Sketchley, 1775).

Bulmer, *Mortimer* — Agnes Collinson Bulmer, *Memoirs of Mrs. Elizabeth Mortimer, with Selections from Her Correspondence* (2nd edn.; London: John Mason, 1836).

Byrth, 'Memoir' — Thomas Byrth, 'Memoir', in Thomas Tattershall, *Sermons* (London: Hatchard, 1848), pp. v–lxxvi.

CCEd — Clergy of the Church of England database (online).

Clarke, *Life* — *An Account of the … Life of Adam Clarke*, edited by J. B. B. Clarke (London: T. S. Clarke, 1833).

Clarke, *Memoirs* — Adam Clarke, *Memoirs of the Wesley Family*, enlarged 2nd edn., 2 vols. (London: Tegg, 1836).

Coates, *New Portrait* — Edward Coates, *A New Portrait of Methodism: being a Circumstantial Account of the Dispute between the Rev. John Wesley and the Trustees of Millbourn Place Chapel at North Shields* (Leeds: J. Heaton, 1815).

Cocking, *Grantham* — Thomas Cocking, *The History of Methodism in Grantham* (London: Simpkin, Marshall, & Co., 1836).

Cooney, 'Dublin Society' — Dudley Levistone Cooney, 'Dublin Methodist Society Membership 1788', *Bulletin of the Wesley Historical Society in Ireland* 10 (2004/5): 44–62.

Cory Library (South Africa) — Makandha (Grahamstown), South Africa, Rhodes University, Cory Library, Archives, Methodist Church of Southern Africa Collection.

CPH (1741)	John and Charles Wesley, *A Collection of Psalms and Hymns* (London: Strahan, 1741).
CPH (1743)	John and Charles Wesley, *A Collection of Psalms and Hymns* (London: Strahan, 1743; 2nd edn. of 1741, with additions).
Crofts, *Satan's Throne*	Bruce Crofts (ed.), *At Satan's Throne: The Story of Methodism in Bath* (Bristol: White Tree, 1990).
Crookshank, *Ireland*	Charles H. Crookshank, *History of Methodism in Ireland*, Vol. 1 (Belfast: Allen, 1885).
Crookshank, *Irish Women*	Charles H. Crookshank, *Memorable Women of Irish Methodism in the Last Century* (London: Wesleyan-Methodist Bookroom, 1882).
CW	Charles Wesley (1707–88).
CW, *Journal Letters*	Randy L. Maddox, et al. (eds.), *The Journal Letters and Related Biographical Items of The Rev. Charles Wesley, M.A.*, Enlarged 2nd edn. (Nashville: Kingswood Books, 2023).
CW, MS hymn collections	https://divinity.duke.edu/initiatives/cswt.
CW, *MS Journal*	MARC, DDCW 10/2; transcription published as S T Kimbrough Jr. & Kenneth G. C. Newport (eds.), *The Manuscript Journal of the Rev. Charles Wesley, M.A.*, 2 vols. (Nashville, TN: Kingswood Books, 2008).
Dale, *Letters*	Helen Pelham Dale (ed.), *The Life and Letters of Thomas Pelham Dale*, 2 vols. (London: G. Allen, 1894), 1:1–26.
DEB	Donald Lewis, ed. *Dictionary of Evangelical Biography, 1730–1860*. 2 vols. (Grand Rapids: Baker Academic, 2004).
Drew, Methodist Archives	Drew University (Madison, New Jersey), Methodist Library, Archives.
Duke, Rubenstein	Duke University (Durham, North Carolina), David M. Rubenstein Rare Book and Manuscript Library.
Dunn, *Clarke*	Samuel Dunn, *The Life of Adam Clarke, LL.D* (London: William Tegg, 1863).
Dyson, *Isle of Wight*	John B. Dyson, *Methodism in the Isle of Wight* (Ventnor, Isle of Wight: George M. Burt, 1865).
Eayrs, *Letters*	George Eayrs (ed.), *Letters of John Wesley: A Selection* (London: Hodder and Stoughton, 1915).
EMP	Thomas Jackson (ed.), *Lives of Early Methodist Preachers*, 4th edn., 6 vols. (London: Wesleyan Conference Office, 1871).
Everett, *Sheffield*	James Everett, *Historical Sketches of Wesleyan Methodism, in Sheffield and its Vicinity*, 2 vols. (Sheffield: James Montgomery, 1823).
Fletcher, *Second Check*	John William Fletcher, *A Second Check to Antinomianism; occasioned by a Late Narrative. In Three Letters to the Hon. and Rev. Mr. Shirley* (London: New Chapel, 1771).
Forsaith, *Labours*	Peter S. Forsaith, *Unexampled Labours: Letters of the Revd. John Fletcher to Leaders in the Evangelical Revival* (Peterborough: Epworth, 2008).
Foundery Band Lists	Manuscript notebook of JW containing lists from 1742–46; MARC, MA 1977/503, box 1, book 2.
Funeral Hymns (1746)	[CW,] *Funeral Hymns* [(London: Strahan, 1746)].
Garrett-Evangelical	Garrett-Evangelical Theological Seminary (Evanston, Illinois), Library, Special Collections.

Hastling et al., *Kingswood*	A.H.L. Hastling, W.A. Willis, and W.P. Workman, *The History of Kingswood School* (London: Charles Kelly, 1898).
Hopkins, *Life*	Benjamin Hopkins, *The Life of Rev. Robert Hopkins* (Sheffield: J. C. Platt, 1828).
HSP (1739)	John and Charles Wesley, *Hymns and Sacred Poems* (London: Strahan, 1739).
HSP (1740)	John and Charles Wesley, *Hymns and Sacred Poems* (London: Strahan, 1740).
HSP (1742)	John and Charles Wesley, *Hymns and Sacred Poems* (Bristol: Farley, 1742).
HSP (1749)	Charles Wesley, *Hymns and Sacred Poems* (Bristol: Farley, 1749).
Huntington Library	The Huntington Library (San Marino, California), Manuscripts Collection.
Jackson, *EMP*	Thomas Jackson (ed.), *Lives of Early Methodist Preachers*, 4th edn., 6 vols. (London: Wesleyan Conference Office, 1871).
Jackson, *Works* (3rd)	Thomas Jackson (ed.), *The Works of the Rev. John Wesley, A.M.*, 3rd edn., 14 vols. (London: Nichols for Mason, 1829–31).
Jones, *Glenorchy*	Thomas Snell Jones, *The Life of the Right Honourable Willielma, Viscountess Glenorchy* (Edinburgh: W. Whyte, 1824).
JW	John Wesley (1703–91).
JW, *Christian Library*	*A Christian Library: Consisting of Extracts from, and Abridgements of, the Choicest Pieces of Practical Divinity which have been Published in the English Tongue*, 50 vols. (Bristol: F. Farley, 1749–55.
JW, MS Poetry Miscellany	A manuscript notebook in which JW transcribed (c. 1725–30) poetry from various sources; MARC, MA 1977/503, Box 1, Vol. 1. (transcription available at https://divinity.duke.edu/initiatives/cswt)
JW, *Works* (1771–74)	John Wesley, *The Works of the Rev. John Wesley, M.A.*, 32 vols. (Bristol: Pine, 1771–74).
Lovely Lane Museum	Baltimore, Maryland, Lovely Lane Museum Library, United Methodist Historical Society of the Baltimore-Washington Conference.
Lyth, *Methodism in York*	John Lyth, *Glimpses of Methodism in York* (York: W. Sessions, 1885).
Manchester, Rylands	The John Rylands Library, University of Manchester, Manchester, England (for materials outside of the MARC collection)
MARC	Methodist Archives and Research Centre, The John Rylands Library, The University of Manchester (Manchester, England).
Maxwell, *Life*	John Lancaster (ed.), *The Life of Darcy, Lady Maxwell* (New York: Mason and Lane, 1837).
Melbourne, Queen's College	Queen's College Library, University of Melbourne (Melbourne, Australia), Sugden Collection.
MHS Ireland Archives	Edgehill College (Belfast, Ireland), Methodist Historical Society of Ireland Archives.

Minutes (post-Wesley)	*Minutes of the Methodist Conferences.* Vol. 1, 1792–98 (London: John Mason, 1862) Vol. 2, 1799–1807 (London: Thomas Cordeux, 1813) Vol. 3, 1808–13 (London: Thomas Cordeux, 1813) Vol. 4, 1814–18 (London: Thomas Cordeux, 1818) Vol. 5, 1819–24 (London: J. Kershaw, 1825) Vol. 6, 1825–30 (London: John Mason, 1833) Vol. 7, 1831–35 (London: John Mason, 1838) Vol. 8, 1836–39 (London: John Mason, 1841) Vol. 9, 1840–43 (London: John Mason, 1845)
MM	*The Methodist Magazine* (1798–1821).
Moore, *Mary Fletcher*	Henry Moore, *The Life of Mrs. Mary Fletcher*, 3rd edn. (London: Cordeux, 1818).
Moorhouse, *Defence*	*The Defence of Mr. Michael Moorhouse*, written by himself (Leicester: Ann Ireland, 1789).
MSP (1744)	John Wesley (ed.), *Collection of Moral and Sacred Poems*, 3 vols. (Bristol: Farley, 1744).
Myles, *Chron. History*	William Myles, *A Chronological History of the People Called Methodists*, 4th ed., (London: Conference Office, 1813).
NT Notes	John Wesley, *Explanatory Notes Upon the New Testament*, 3rd corrected edn. (Bristol: Graham and Pine, 1760–62).
ODNB	*Oxford Dictionary of National Biography* (2003).
OED (1989)	*The Oxford English Dictionary*, 2nd edn. (New York: Oxford University Press, 1989).
OT Notes	John Wesley, *Explanatory Notes Upon the Old Testament* (Bristol: Pine, 1765).
Pawson, *Letters*	John C. Bowmer and John A. Vickers (eds.), *The Letters of John Pawson*, 3 vols. (Peterborough: Methodist Publishing House, for WMHS, 1994–95).
Rankin, MS Journal	Typescript copy by Francis Tees of Thomas Rankin's manuscript journal; Garrett Evangelical Library, BY429.R21 A3.
Redemption Hymns (1747)	Charles Wesley, *Hymns for Those That Seek and Those That Have Redemption in the Blood of Jesus Christ* (London: Strahan, 1747).
(Roe) Rogers, *Experience*	Hester Ann (Roe) Rogers, *The Experience of Mrs. H. A. Rogers; to which are added some Select Letters written to her by the Rev. John Wesley*, 2nd edn. (Bristol: R. Edwards, 1796).
(Roe) Rogers, *Extracts*	Rogers, Hester Ann. *Extracts from the Journal of Mrs. Hester Ann Rogers* (London: James Rogers, 1818).
Rowley, *Knapp*	Edith Rowley, *Fruits of Righteousness in the Life of Susanna Knapp* (London: Hamilton, Adams & Co., 1866).
Scripture Hymns (1762)	Charles Wesley, *Short Hymns on Select Passages of the Holy Scriptures*, 2 vols. (Bristol: Farley, 1762).
Seymour, *Huntingdon*	Aaron Crossley Hobart Seymour, *The Life and Times of Selina, Countess of Huntingdon*, 2 vols. (London: W. E. Painter, 1839).
Stamp, *Bradford*	William W. Stamp, *Historical Notices on Wesleyan Methodism in Bradford and its Vicinity* (London: Mason, 1841).
Stamp, *Orphan House*	William W. Stamp, *The Orphan House of Mr. Wesley* (London: Mason, 1863).

Stevenson, *City Road*	George John Stevenson, *City Road Chapel London and its Associations* (London: Stevenson, 1872).
SW Jr., *Poems* (1743)	Samuel Wesley Jr., *Poems on Several Occasions*, 2nd edn. (Cambridge: S. Bentham, 1743).
Taft, *Holy Women*	Zachariah Taft, *Biographical Sketches of the Lives and Public Ministry of Various Holy Women*, 2 vols. (London: Kershaw, 1825–28).
Taft, *Original Letters*	Zachariah Taft, *Original Letters, Never Before Published, on Doctrinal, Experimental, and Practical Religion* (Whitby: George Clark, 1821).
Telford, *Letters*	John Telford (ed.), *The Letters of the Rev. John Wesley, A.M.*, 8 vols. (London: Epworth, 1931).
Tyerman, *Fletcher*	Luke Tyerman, *Wesley's Designated Successor: the Life, Letters, and Literary Labours of the Rev. John William Fletcher* (London: Hodder and Stoughton, 1882).
Tyerman, *John Wesley*	Luke Tyerman, *Life and Times of the Rev. John Wesley*, 2nd edn., 3 vols. (New York: Harper and Brothers, 1872).
Tyerman, *Oxford Methodists*	Luke Tyerman, *The Oxford Methodists* (London: Hodder and Stoughton, 1873).
UCC Maritime Conference	Sackville, New Brunswick, Maritime Conference of The United Church of Canada, Archives.
Upper Room Museum	The Upper Room (Nashville, Tennessee), Museum of Christian Art [Wesley items now held in Bridwell Library (SMU)].
Vickers, *Dictionary*	John Vickers (ed.), *A Dictionary of Methodism in Britain and Ireland* (London: Epworth, 2000).
Wellcome Institute	London, Wellcome Institute for the History of Medicine, Archives.
Wesleyan University Library	Middletown, Connecticut, Wesleyan University, Library, Literary and Historical Manuscripts Collection
Wesley's Chapel (London)	London, England, Wesley's Chapel & Leysian Mission, Museum of Methodism, Archival Material.
Whitehead, *Life*	John Whitehead, *The Life of the Rev. John Wesley*, 2 vols. (London: Couchman, 1793–96).
WHS	*The Proceedings of the Wesley Historical Society* (England, 1898–).
WHS Ireland Archives	Belfast, Edgehill College, Wesley Historical Society of Ireland Archives.
WHS Library	Library of the Wesley Historical Society, Oxford Centre for Methodism and Church History, Oxford Brookes University.
WMC Museum	World Methodist Council Museum (Lake Junaluska, NorthCarolina)[WesleyitemsnowheldinBridwellLibrary(SMU)].
WMM	*The Wesleyan Methodist Magazine* (London, 1822–1913).
WTS (DC), Archives	Wesley Theological Seminary (Washington, DC), Library, Archives.

To Ellen Gretton

London
January 5, 1782

My Dear Sister,

It is a true word, 'Gold is tried in the fire, and acceptable men in the furnace of affliction.'[1] But we know the exhortation, 'Despise not thou the chastening of the Lord' (count it not an insignificant or accidental thing), 'neither faint when thou art rebuked of him', but receive it as a token of his love.[2]

I do not despair of seeing you again in Lincolnshire and taking another little journey with you. This will be, if it is best; and it is not impossible that I should see you in London. Perhaps it may be (if we should live so long) at the time of the Conference. That might be of particular service to you if providence should make a way for you. In the meantime let brother [Robert] Derry and sister Fisher[3] and you do all the good you can.

I am, dear Nelly,

Your affectionate brother,

J. Wesley

Address: 'To / Miss Gretton / At Mr. [Robert] Derry's / In Grantham / Lincolnshire'.

Postmark: '5/IA'.

Source: holograph; Drew, Methodist Archives.

[1] Ecclus. 2:5.
[2] Prov. 3:11; Heb. 12:5.
[3] Mrs. Dorothy Fisher (c. 1733–1806), a widow (maiden name unknown), had been converted to Methodism in London after hearing JW preach. In 1779 she resided in Muston, Leicestershire, about 10 miles from Grantham, and by 1781 had moved to Grantham to support Robert Derry in the face of the opposition he was receiving to his Methodist meetings. When JW preached at Grantham on July 9, 1781 (see *Journal*, 23:216 in this edn.), it was in a yard or paddock behind the premises occupied by Mrs. Fisher. She continued to support Methodists there and in Lincoln (where she moved in 1787) until her death. See Cocking, *Grantham*, 217–26.

1

To Joseph Thompson

London
January 5, 1782

Dear Joseph,

It gives me pleasure to hear that you are not weary of well doing, but are diligent in advancing the cause of religion. There is one means of doing this in which it will be worth your while to take some pains. I mean in *recommending the [Arminian] Magazines.* If you say of them in every society what you may say with truth, and say it with an air of earnestness, you will produce several new subscribers.

I am, dear Joseph,

Your affectionate friend and brother,

J. Wesley

Source: published transcription; *Christian Witness* 18 (1861): 133.

To James [?][4]

London
January 6, 1782

Dear James,

You may meet with brother Alderman, Highland,[5] or any other leader you choose. But I am willing to hear what objection you have to James Dewey[6] and the two other leaders you refer to. You may know them better than I do.

I am,

Your affectionate brother,

[J. Wesley]

Source: published transcription; Telford, *Letters*, 7:97–98.

---

[4] This person was clearly related to City Road Chapel, in London. He may have been requesting to meet with a specific class leader.

[5] Loftus Highland (1736–1805), a native of Ireland, was introduced to Methodism there, and drawn back into the movement in 1762, after moving to London. Loftus became a leader at the Foundery, and later at City Road Chapel, where he is buried. See Stevenson, *City Road*, 526–28.

[6] James Dewey (c. 1744–1807), a London weaver, was one of the original trustees of City Road Chapel, and is buried there. See Stevenson, *City Road*, 534.

To Thomas Tattershall

London
January 11, 1782[7]   5

Dear Tommy,

I think gentle electrifying might help you much.[8] And you would do well to take, every morning, a teaspoonful of flour of brimstone and honey, or treacle.[9] Much prayer should be made that God would continue the health of the preachers. Perhaps we have been   10
wanting in this.

You need not pay for Mr. [John] Fletcher's works. Mr. [John] Atlay will send them with the other books.

The following receipt has never failed to cure an ague (after a little vomit and a purge): Mix two grains of white arsenic with two   15
scruples of Castile soap. Divide this into eight pills and take one pill every four hours, between the fits.[10] It is quite safe.

I am, dear Tommy,
Your affectionate brother,

J. Wesley   20

Address: 'To / Mr. Thos. Tattershall / At the Preaching house / In Doncaster / Yorkshire'.
Source: published transcription; Byrth, 'Memoir', xxxii.

25

To Hester Ann Roe

30
London
January 17, 1782

My Dear Hetty,

In the success of Mr. [John] Leech's preaching we have one proof of a thousand that the blessing of God always attends the publish-   35

---

[7] Byrth misread the month as 'June'; a common error in transcribing JW's abbreviation 'Janu'.

[8] Tattershall was currently assigned to the Epworth circuit (which apparently included Doncaster). His letter, to which JW was replying, is not known to survive.

[9] This was JW's common remedy for an ague.

[10] This receipt does not appear in either JW's early *Collection of Receipts or the Primitive Physic*; in a later letter he calls them 'Dr. Sanders pills'; see JW to Charles Atmore, May 28, 1782.

ing of full salvation as attainable now by simple faith. But there is a danger here which is to be carefully guarded against—namely, lest the other preachers should be jealous of his success. This has been a very common case. And you can hardly conceive what a grievous hindrance it has always been to the work of God. Both he himself, therefore, and all that love him should do everything that is in their power to prevent it; he especially, by an humble, condescending, obliging behaviour to his fellow labourers. And it will be prudent for you all not to speak too strongly in commendation of him in *their* hearing, for you know, 'the spirit that is in us lusteth to envy'.[11]

I have never at all repented of my late journey to Chester.[12] A flame was kindled both there and at Wrexham, which I trust will not soon be put out. I do not know that I have spent a day at Chester with so much satisfaction for many a year.

This afternoon I was agreeably surprised by a letter from our dear Miss Ritchie.[13] It really seems as if God, in answer to many prayers, has lent her to us yet a little longer. He bringeth down to the grave and bringeth up again.[14] Wise are all his ways![15]

I am not assured that there is not something preternatural in those pains which you frequently experience. Not improbably they are caused by a messenger of Satan, who is permitted to buffet you. But all is well. You find in this and all things his grace is sufficient for you.[16]

I always am, my dear Hetty,

Most affectionately yours,

J. Wesley

Source: holograph; British Library, Department of Manuscripts, Add. MS. 42711, fol. 123.

[11] James 4:5.
[12] The most recent time that JW recorded being in Chester was c. Apr. 16, 1781; see *Journal*, 23:199 in this edn.
[13] Ritchie to JW, Jan. 10, 1782; see JW's reply on Jan. 19.
[14] See 1 Sam. 2:6.
[15] See Milton, *Paradise Lost*, iii.680.
[16] See 2 Cor. 12:9.

To Ann Loxdale

London
January 18, 1782 5

My Dear Miss Loxdale,

I did not receive yours till a day or two ago, or you would have heard from me sooner.[17] Indeed the rather, because you do what I desired—you write to me without reserve. Surely he that withholds from us no good thing,[18] will in due time give us to meet together. I 10 should feel a degree of impatience for it, but that I know

His manner and his time are best.[19]

You must not measure your letters by the length of mine, because 15 I have a thousand things to do. But write all that is in your heart. I shall never be tired with reading anything that comes from *you*. I cannot tell you how near and dear you are to me. But you may judge by what you feel in your own heart. You see, I am as open to you as 20 you are to *me*; although I wonder at myself, considering I have never seen you. I cannot say I ever found anything like this in all my life before! I think a wise providence will explain it by and by.

I advised formerly my dear Jenny Cooper, and so I advise *you*, frequently to read and meditate upon the thirteenth chapter of the 25 First of Corinthians. There is the true picture of Christian perfection! Let us copy after it with all our might! I believe it might likewise be of use to you to read more than once the *Plain Account of Christian Perfection*. Indeed what is it more or less than humble, gentle, patient love? 30

Pray much for, my dear Nancy,
    Your ever affectionate,

J. Wesley

Postmark: '19/IA'. 35
Endorsement: by Loxdale(?), at top, '6th'.
Source: holograph; Bridwell Library (SMU).

[17] Loxdale's letter to JW is not known to survive.
[18] See Ps. 84:11.
[19] Cf. CW, 'Groaning for Redemption', Pt. III, st. 3, *l.* 5, *HSP* (1742), 107.

To John Francis Valton[20]

London
January 18, 1782

5 My Dear Brother,
   I have received the first two sheets of your life.[21] Be not afraid
of writing too much. I can easily leave out what can be spared. It
pleased God to lead John Haime and you a long way through the
wilderness. Others he leads through a shorter and smoother way;
10 and yet to the same point. For we must not imagine that *such a degree* of suffering is necessary to any degree of holiness. In this God
does certainly act as a sovereign—giving what he pleases, and by
what means he pleases. I believe the holiest man that ever lived was
the apostle John, yet he seems to have suffered very little.
15   You should take care never to write long at a time, and always to
write *standing*; never on any account leaning on your stomach. God
gives me just the strength I had thirty years ago.
      I am,
         Your affectionate friend and brother,
20   J. Wesley

Source: published transcription; *Wesleyan Methodist Magazine* 37 (1824):
   306–07.

25

To the Rev. Thomas Davenport[22]

London
30   January 19, 1782
Dear Sir,
   Many years ago I saw a condemned person in the Castle at Oxford two or three hours before his execution. When I asked him,

[20] The published transcription in *WMM*, conveyed through Thomas Marriott appears
to merge two distinct letters, which had been the property of Rev. John Waterhouse, and later
came into the possession of Robert Young (this duplication is carried over into the editions of
Jackson and Telford). It also misreads the date of the first letter as 'June' (which Jackson retains,
but Telford corrects). JW was in London in January, but not in June. We have moved the later
section of the transcription in *WMM*, which composes the text of a letter of June 23 in the record of Robert Young, to that date. See Robert Young, *The Southern World* (London: Hamilton,
Adams, and Co, 1854), 377–78, 433.
   [21] I.e., the autobiographical account Valton was preparing for JW to publish in *AM*.
   [22] JW was replying to Davenport's letter of Jan. 15, 1782.

'Whither are you going?' he said, 'To hell, to be sure.' And on my remarking, 'But you seem to have no fear, no sorrow, no concern', he coolly replied, 'I have none at all. And why should I tell a lie?' I said, 'I cannot understand this.' He said, 'I will tell you how to understand it. Some told me five months ago, "Mr. Pope, make the best of your time, for the *day of grace* may end before the day of life ends." And so it is with me.'

But it is not so with *you*. If it was, you would have no fear, no trouble, no uneasiness, but would be just as easy and careless and unconcerned as that poor creature was.

It is, I believe, near forty years ago that a friend recommended to me Mr. Marshall's *Gospel Mystery of Sanctification*.[23] A few passages I found scattered up and down which I thought leaned towards antinomianism. But in general I approved of it well, and judged it to be an excellent book. The main proposition, that inward and outward holiness flow from a consciousness of the favour of God, is undoubtedly true. And it is a truth that should always be before our eyes.

I commend you to him that loves you more than you are sensible of; and am, dear sir,

Your affectionate friend and brother,

J. Wesley

Address: 'To / the Rev. Mr. Davenport / At Allexton / Near Uppingham / Rutlandshire'.

Charge: '4'.

Source: holograph; MARC, MAM JW 2/81.

To Elizabeth Ritchie

London
January 19, 1782

It seemed a little strange to me, my dear Betsy, that I did not hear from you for so long a time.[24] But I imputed your silence to your bodily weakness, of which several of our friends sent me word.

---

[23] (London: Thomas Parkhurst, 1692). See the more negative letter JW printed in his *Journal* (Nov. 20, 1767; 22:110–11 in this edn.) warning that this book contained 'much poison mixed with food'.

[24] JW was replying to Ritchie's letter of Jan. 10, 1782. The most recent prior known letter was Jan. 16, 1781.

From our brethren in various parts of England and Ireland I have very pleasing accounts of the uncommon blessings which many received at the time of renewing their covenant with God.[25] I am glad to hear that you at Otley had your share.

5   That point, entire salvation from inbred sin, can hardly ever be insisted upon, either in preaching or prayer, without a particular blessing. Honest Isaac Brown firmly believes this doctrine, that we are to be saved from all sin in this life.[26] But I wish, when opportunity serves, you would encourage him: 1) to preach Christian per-

10   fection constantly, strongly, and explicitly; 2) explicitly to assert and prove that it may be received now; and 3) (which indeed is implied therein) that it is to be received by simple faith.

In every state of mind, in that of conviction or justification or sanctification, I believe every person may either go sensibly back-

15   ward, or seem to stand still, or go forward. I incline to think all the persons you mention were fully sanctified. But some of them, watching unto prayer, went on from faith to faith;[27] while the others, being less watchful, seemed to stand still, but were indeed imperceptibly backsliding. Wishing you all may increase with all the

20   increase of God,
       I am,
          Ever yours,

                                              J. Wesley

25   *Source*: published transcription; Benson, *Works*, 16:251.

30   To Richard Rodda[28]

                                            London
                                        January 24, 1782
       Dear Richard,

35   Nancy Bolton had done more good in Witney than all the other women in the society put together. Not one of them is to be com-

---

    [25] It had become standard Methodist practice to observe their 'covenant renewal' during a watch-night service on New Year's eve.

    [26] Brown was the Assistant assigned to the Keighley circuit, which included Otley.

    [27] See 1 Pet. 4:7 and Rom. 1:17.

    [28] Richard Rodda was the Assistant for the Oxfordshire circuit, which included both High Wycombe and Witney. His letter to JW that drew this response is not known to survive.

pared to her either for grace or understanding. Give her all the employment she can undertake. I know few such jewels in the three kingdoms. You have done exceeding well in changing the men-leaders. It will much tend to enliven the people.

You would do wisely to give Hannah Ball and her sister [Ann]   5
as much employment as they can possibly attend to. There [are] exceeding few in Wycombe that are like-minded, nor indeed in all the circuit.

I do not take any thought so long beforehand concerning stationing the preachers. Sufficient for the day is the care thereof.[29] Mr.   10
[John] Atlay tells me, he has no sets of the two last years' *[Arminian] Magazines*.

I am, with love to sister [Elizabeth] Rodda, dear Richard,
        Your affectionate friend and brother,
                                            J. Wesley   15

Address: 'To / Mr Rd Rodda / At Mrs. Haws' / in / High Wycombe'.
Postmark: '24/IA'. *Charge*: '3'.
Source: holograph; Boston University School of Theology, Library, Archival Collections, New England Conference Commission on Archives   20
    and History.

                                                            25

To Francis Wolf

                                            London
                                    January 24, 1782   30
My Dear Brother,

You have much reason to bless God, both on your own account and on account of the people. Now see that you adorn in all things the doctrine of God our Saviour.[30] See that your conversation be in grace, always seasoned with salt,[31] and meet to minister grace to the   35
hearers. And let none of you preachers touch any spirituous liquors upon any account!

[29] See Matt. 6:34.
[30] See Titus 2:10.
[31] See Col. 4:6.

I am sorry for poor Joseph Batten. The loss of that excellent woman will be a loss indeed! But there is one who is able to turn all to good.

I am, dear Franky,

Your affectionate brother,

J. Wesley

Address: 'To / Mr Francis Wolf / In Redruth / Cornwall'.
Postmark: '24/IA'. *Charge*: '4'.
Source: holograph; Wesley's Chapel (London), LDWMM 1997/6775.

To Samuel Bardsley[32]

London
January 25, 1782

Dear Sammy,

I am glad you had no reason to complain of our northern brethren. Many of them are as sincere and affectionate as any in England. And the way to do them good is to observe all our Rules at Inverness just as you would at Sheffield; yea, and to preach the whole Methodist doctrine there as plainly and simply as you would in Yorkshire. But you have not sent me (neither you nor Peter Mill) any plan of the circuit. This should be done without delay. See that you both do all you can for a good Master! Lose no time! Peace be with all your spirits!

I am, dear Sammy,

Your affectionate brother,

J. Wesley

Address: 'To / Mr Sam. Bardsley / At Mr. [Robert] McComie's / In Inverness'.
Postmark: '26/IA'. *Charge*: '6'.
Source: holograph; MARC, MAM JW 1/22.

---

[32] JW was replying to Bardsley's letter of Jan. 10, 1782.

Circular on Tract Society

London
January 25, 1782

I cannot but earnestly recommend this institution to all those
who desire to see true, scriptural Christianity spread throughout
the nation. Men wholly unawakened will not take the pains to read
the Bible. They have no relish for it. But a small tract may engage
their attention; and may, by the blessing of God, prepare them for
going forward.

John Wesley

Proposals for Establishing a Society to Distribute Religious Tracts

I. Our design is to distribute religious tracts among the poor, particularly among soldiers and sailors, in every part of Great Britain
and Ireland.

II. For this end, to desire each subscriber to subscribe half a guinea, a guinea, or more yearly.

III. To receive everyone as a Governor that subscribes a guinea
or more, who may have yearly a guinea's worth of books or more at
prime-cost, in proportion to his subscription.

IV. To select seven of these as a Committee, to meet every Sunday
morning at seven o'clock wherever the preachers in London meet.

V. To appoint a Secretary, who is to keep an account of money
received and books sent to subscribers or others.

Some of the tracts distributed will be:
Allein[e]'s *Alarm*,[33] Baxter's *Call*,[34] Law's *Later Works*
abridged (2 vols. duodecimos),[35] Morgan's *Crucified Jesus*,[36] *The Heavenly Footman*,[37] *The Nature and Design of
Christianity*.[38]

[33] JW's abridgement of Joseph Alleine, *An Alarm to Unconverted Sinners* (1782; *Bibliography*, No. 428).

[34] JW's abridgement of Richard Baxter, *A Call to the Unconverted* (1782; *Bibliography*, No. 429).

[35] JW, *An Extract from the Rev. Mr. Law's Later Works* (1768; *Bibliography*, No. 312).

[36] James Morgan, *The Crucified Christ* (1772; sold at Foundery, 1777; *Bibliography*, No. 557).

[37] John Fletcher, *A Race for Eternal Life*; being an extract from *Heavenly Footman, a sermon ... by [John Bunyan]* (1777; *Bibliography*, No. 535).

[38] *Nature and Design of Christianity* (1740; JW's extract of first two chapters of William Law, *A Practical Treatise upon Christian Perfection*; *Bibliography*, No. 41).

Sermons on: The Important Question, Awake Thou that
Sleepest, The Almost Christian, Original Sin, Salvation
by Faith, The New Birth, The Good Steward, The Great
Assize.[39]

5   *Instructions for Children, Tokens for Children, Lessons for
Children.*[40]

A Word to: a Sailor, a Soldier, a Common Swearer, a Drunk-
ard, a Sabbath-Breaker, a Street-Walker, a Condemned
Malefactor, a Freeholder, a Smuggler.[41]

10

N.B. The Society intends to add several other tracts for the ensuing year, if not for the present.

Source: printed circular; *Bibliography*, No. 425.[42]

15

To Thomas Hanson[43]

20

London
January 30, 1782

Dear Tommy,

25   There were certainly false musters.[44] This ought to be observed if
we live to see another Conference.

I never was fond of multiplying circuits without an absolute necessity. Your remark is unquestionably true, that this is oftener proposed for the *ease* of the preachers than the profit of the people. But

30   it is clear to me that many of the preachers have already rather too
little exercise than too much.

If you are not yet recovered from the disorder in your mouth, I
wish you would consult the *Primitive Physic* or John Floyde.

---

[39] See respectively Sermons 84, 3, 2, 44, 1, 45, 51, and 15 in this edn. These were all
published as individual tracts.

[40] See *Bibliography*, Nos. 101, 117–20, and 175 (in vol. 16 in this edn.).

[41] These tracts are collected above in vol. 15 of this edn.

[42] No copies of the original circular are known to survive. The text here comes from the
A State of the Society for Distributing Religious Tracts among the Poor, for the Year 1782 (1783),
where it was reproduced (See Appendix B of vol. 15 of this edn.). Cf. JW's report on the progress of the society in his letter to Rev. Thomas Davenport, Dec. 28, 1782.

[43] Hanson was currently Assistant for the Colne circuit.

[44] I.e., lists of the members of societies and circuits.

I am, dear Tommy,
   Your affectionate friend and brother,

J. Wesley

Source: holograph; Toronto, Canada, United Church of Canada Archives.

5

To Ann Tindall

10

London
February 1, 1782

Dear Nancy,

   As doctors differ, so do counsellors. Several years ago I had the
advice of a counsel here, who said it was quite sufficient for the
remaining trustees to endorse the old deed, in the form specified
in the *Minutes*,[45] provided you have three new stamps added; otherwise the court will set it aside.[46] Certainly the steward of the society
for the time being should always keep the deeds. The Scarborough
deed you may as well keep for the present as another.

   I am glad you have made so great an advance towards clearing [the
cost of] the preaching-house.[47]

   If you first seek the kingdom in good earnest, all other things
must be added unto you.[48] I hope our preachers strongly and explicitly exhort you to go on to perfection.[49] Then the work of the
Lord, in every branch, will prosper in their hands.

   I am, dear Nancy,
      Your affectionate brother,

15

20

25

J. Wesley

30

Address: 'To / Miss Ann Tindall / in / Scarborough'.
Postmark: '1/FE'. *Charge*: '4'.
Endorsement: by Tindall, 'Feb. 1. 1782'.
Source: holograph; British Library, Department of Manuscripts, Add.
   MS. 43695, ff. 63–64.

35

---

[45] See 'Large' *Minutes* (1763), §67, 10:868–70 in this edn.
[46] The person who gave this opinion was Martin Madan; see JW to Thomas [Taylor],
Feb. 21, 1786.
[47] Tindall's letter reporting this, and raising the question of a deed, is not known to
survive.
[48] See Matt. 6:33.
[49] See Heb. 6:1.

To Alexander Suter[50]

London
February 9, 1782

My Dear Brother,

You see the wisdom of that advice, 'O tarry thou the Lord's leisure!'[51] And there is great reason that we should trust the invisible God farther than we can see him.

There will need the greatest care and attention possible both in you and John Moon at Exeter.[52] For Satan will surely endeavour to lay stumbling-blocks in the way of the people. It is your part to prevent or remove them as quick as possible.

I am,

Your affectionate brother,

[J. Wesley]

Source: published transcription; Telford, *Letters*, 7:104.

To Ellen Gretton

Lambeth
February 12, 1782

My Dear Sister,

If it pleases God to visit us with adversity, undoubtedly he will send a blessing with it. It will be for our profit, a means of weaning us from the world and uniting us more closely to him. And if afterwards he changes it for prosperity, this also will be for good. It is our wisdom to improve the present state, be it one or the other. With what *will be* we have nothing to do. We need take no thought for the morrow.[53]

[50] Alexander Suter (1756–1817), was converted in London by Thomas Olivers, and soon appointed by JW as a class leader there. He was admitted 'on trial' as an itinerant at the 1779 Conference (see 10:484 in this edn.). He would serve diligently for 33 years, before settling in Halifax, Yorkshire, where he died. See *Minutes* (post-Wesley, 1817), 4:292–93.

[51] Ps. 27:4.

[52] John Moon (1752–1801) was converted in his mid-teens and admitted 'on trial' as an itinerant at the 1774 Conference (see 10:427 in this edn.). He served for 27 years, until his death in Bristol in Feb. 1801. See *Minutes* (post-Wesley, 1801), 2:83–84. Moon was currently Assistant for the Tiverton circuit (which included Exeter), with Suter serving alongside him.

[53] See Matt. 6:34.

As yet I do not see my way clear, but wait for farther evidence, before I can determine whether I should put out toward Ireland or Scotland. If I do set out for Ireland and am driven back again,[54] I shall say, 'Good is the will of the Lord.'[55]

'With good advice make war.'[56] Do not hastily engage in anything 5 so far that you cannot retreat. One would be particularly wary in that circumstance, which, as Prior observes

> ... is joy [...] or strife,
> Is all the colour of remaining life!"[57] 10

Concerning this especially be much in prayer, and the unction of the Holy One will guide you.[58]

I am, my dear Nelly,

Yours very affectionately, 15

J. Wesley

My kind love to sister [Dorothy] Fisher and brother [Robert] Derry.

Source: holograph; Pitts Library (Emory), John Wesley Papers (MSS 20 153), 3/25.

To John Bredin 25

London
February 20, 1782

My Dear Brother,

It was a good providence that none of your bones were broken.[59] 30 God gave his angels charge over you. So far the old murderer could go, and no farther.[60]

---

[54] This had happened the previous year; see JW to Thomas Rutherford, May 8, 1781 (29:644).

[55] Cf. 2 Kings 20:19; Isa. 39:8; and JW's use in *The Character of a Methodist*, §7, 9:36 in this edn.

[56] Prov. 20:18.

[57] Prior, *Solomon*, ii. 234–35.

[58] See 1 John 2:20.

[59] John Bredin's last regular appointment was to Athlone in 1780. He was now appearing in the *Minutes* as an 'invalid' receiving support from the Conference.

[60] See Job 38:11 and John 8:44.

It is well if these headstrong Volunteers do not soon get their own necks into an halter.[61] The southern Volunteers have absolutely refused to join them in any such measures.

This is not my year for Ireland. But whether I shall go westward or northward, I have not yet determined. You say 'Pray deliver the enclosed';[62] but you do not say to whom. I suppose you mean to Mr. [John] Abraham.

I am,
Your affectionate friend and brother,

J. Wesley

Source: holograph; MARC, MA 1983/027 (Mather scrapbook).

To Joseph Benson[63]

London
February 22, 1782

Dear Joseph,

Who Mr. Tyndall is, I know not.[64] But he is just as sound a divine as Mr. Madan. I regard no authorities but those of the Ante-Nicene fathers; nor any of them in opposition to Scripture. And I totally deny that (supposed) matter of fact: that polygamy was allowed among the primitive Christians, or that the converts 'who

[61] On the Irish Volunteers, see the note on JW to James Creighton, May 8, 1780, 29:570 in this edn. Many of them were now agitating for greater autonomy, leading in 1782 to the repeal of the Declaratory Act of 1720 and providing greater legislative initiative to the Irish Parliament.

[62] Bredin's letter to JW, which included this note, is not known to survive.

[63] In his letter to Benson of May 21, 1781 (29:646–47) JW had approved Benson's proposal to write an extended critique of Martin Madan's *Thelyphthora* (1781), which argued for biblical and historical warrant for polygamy in certain cases. Benson had just sent JW the critique in manuscript, fashioned as several letters to JW; see Benson to JW, c. Feb. 18, 1782. Within a month JW would review the manuscript and move it toward publication; see JW to Benson, Mar. 30, 1782.

[64] Telford (*Letters*, 7:106) cites a manuscript copy of Benson's Life (p. 1175), written by Benson's son, as recording that Benson read the works of William Tyndale (1494–1536) in Jan. 1782, and commented favourably about Tyndale's stress on 'justification by faith, and the proper fruit and evidence of this in love and obedience', etc. [unfortunately, the location of this manuscript is now unknown]. In the letter which accompanied the manuscript Benson was sending JW (a letter not known to survive), he apparently cited a text in Tyndale that suggested a position like that of Madan.

had many wives, were not required to put any of them away'. I have not yet time to read over the manuscript. When I do, I must read it all in a breath.

Having talked with my friends, I judge it will be expedient to visit the north this year. I expect to be at Manchester on Wednesday, the 5 10th of April, and in Yorkshire in the beginning of May.

I have no objection to your printing a few copies of those two sermons to oblige your friends in the neighbourhood.[65] I doubt we are not explicit enough in speaking on full sanctification either in public or private.   10

I am, with kind love to sister [Sarah] Benson, dear Joseph,
    Your affectionate brother,

                                                        J. Wesley

Address: 'To / Mr Benson / At the Preachinghouse / near / Leeds'.   15
Postmark: '23/FE'. *Charge*: '4'.
Endorsement: by Benson, 'Feb 22 1782'.
Source: holograph; Pitts Library (Emory), John Wesley Papers (MSS 153), 3/26.   20

To William Watters[66]

25

London
February 22, 1782

My Dear Brother,

You send me an agreeable account of the work of God in Ameri-   30
ca.[67] It is amazing that any good should be done in a time of so much hurry and confusion, when one would imagine man would think of nothing but the works of the devil. I wish you would send me whenever you have an opportunity a particular account of what is doing throughout the province. Formerly we had some societies in   35

---

[65] I.e., Joseph Benson, *Two Sermons on Sanctification* (Leeds: J. Bowling, 1782).

[66] William Watters (1751–1827) was appointed to a circuit at the first Conference of Methodist preachers in North America in Philadelphia in 1773. This made him the first official itinerant who was American-born. Watters assisted Francis Asbury in preserving the movement in face of the departure of most of the British-born itinerants during the Revolutionary War. He was ordained with the founding of the Methodist Episcopal Church and served (usually as a located elder, due to his health) until 1805.

[67] Watters's letter is not known to survive.

North Carolina and likewise in Maryland. I hope they still subsist
and are growing in grace as well as increasing in number. It is a
great blessing that there is an end of that unhappy dispute, which
otherwise would have torn you all in pieces.[68] Again and again it has
been set on foot in England and Ireland, but it never came to any
height.[69] We always took care to suppress it at the very beginning,
so that it could not do much mischief.

   I hope Mr. Jarratt is not weary of well doing, but goes on with his
labour of love.[70] Now and then I suppose you can contrive to send
a letter to New York and thence to your friends in England. The
word of God has free course throughout these kingdoms and sinks
deep into many hearts. I have pleasing accounts from various parts
where many are justified and many sanctified, and so it is wherever
our preachers strongly and explicitly exhort all the believers to go
on to perfection.[71]

   Peace be with all your spirits. I am, my dear brother,
      Your affectionate brother,

                                                    [J. Wesley]

Source: published transcription; Telford, *Letters*, 7:106–07.

To 'A Respectful Reader'[72]

                                                  [London]
                                          February 23, 1782

   I have answered simply to your questions, whether they be proposed out of good or ill will.

                                                        J. W.

---

[68] British troops had been driven down into the Carolinas and Georgia (from where they
would withdraw fully later this year). The formal end of the war, with the Treaty of Paris, would
come on Sept. 3, 1783.

[69] That is, the anti-monarchial efforts of the English 'patriots' and the Irish 'volunteers'.

[70] Devereux Jarratt (1733–1801), a native of Virginia, had been ordained in the Church
of England in the early 1760s. He was one of the few Church of England clergy in North
America supportive of the Methodist work. See his introductory letter to JW, June 29, 1773,
which JW published in *AM* 9 (1786): 397–99. JW had published earlier [Devereux Jarratt,] *A
Brief Narrative of the Revival in Virginia*; in a letter to a Friend (London: R. Hawes, 1778); see
Bibliography, No. 399.

[71] See Heb. 6:1.

[72] JW published his replies interspersed among the queries, so we reproduce the whole.

February 13, 1782

Reverend Sir,

I am, as you are, an Arminian. I am well acquainted with your religious tenets, and have read most, if not all of your works. And though I do not entirely fall in with you in *every* article of your 5 creed, yet I have much respect to your character, great reverence for your principles in general, and an entire affection for your person. Depending upon the acknowledged candour of your disposition, and your uniform zeal for the truth, I expect your attention and answers to the following questions: 10

Is it your wish that the people called Methodists should be, or become, a body entirely separate from the Church [of England]?
Answer. No.

15

If not, where (that is, how often), and where (I mean, upon what description of teachers, of the establishment) are they to attend?
Answer. I advise them to go to Church.

More particularly, if the fall, the corruption, and natural impo- 20 tence of man, his free and full redemption in Christ Jesus, through faith working by love, should be taught and inculcated, and offered to the attention of *all*, at the [established] Church of the parish where they reside, are they *then* in your opinion bound in con- science *to hear*, or may they, at their own option, *forbear*? 25
Answer. I do not think they are bound in conscience to attend any particular church.

Or if they are at liberty to absent themselves, are they at liberty— that is, have they a *Christian privilege*—to censure this doctrine in 30 the gross, to condemn such teachers, and boldly to pronounce them 'blind leaders of the blind'?[73]
Answer. No; by no means.

Lastly, whenever this happens, is it through prejudice or rational 35 piety? Is it through bigotry or a catholic spirit? Is it consistent with Christian charity? Is it compatible with a state of justification? Or is it even allowable in the high habit of evangelical perfection?
Answer. I think it is a sin.

---

[73] Matt. 15:14.

Your unequivocal answers to these interesting queries, in the *Arminian Magazine*, will oblige, reverend sir,

A Respectful Reader

Source: published transcription; *Arminian Magazine* 5 (1782): 374–75.

To Joseph Algar[74]

London
February 24, 1782

Dear Joseph,

Your builders should consider 1) that the Conference can allow them nothing, and 2) that they cannot expect to collect anything in the circuit. Then, if they *will* build, let them observe the advices given in the *Minutes* of the Conference.[75]

Barely by not 'going on to perfection'[76] all believers will grow dead and cold. And then they are just ripe for levity, tattling, and evil-speaking, which will soon destroy all the life of God out of their souls. Therefore you have need on this very account to preach perfection in the most strong and explicit manner possible. Without this you can never lift up the hands that hang down and strengthen the feeble knees.[77]

And what you preach to others you have particular need to apply to your own souls. Fly on, and take the prize.[78] It is received by simple faith. Believe, and enter into rest![79]

I am, dear Joseph,

Your affectionate brother,

J. Wesley

---

[74] Joseph Algar (1757–1804) apparently entered itinerant ministry between the 1781 and 1782 Conference, as he first appears in the *Minutes* as already 'on trial' in 1782 (see 10:519 in this edn.). Algar was one of the preachers who protested the Deed of Declaration at the 1784 Conference, but did not join those who withdrew from the connexion (see 10:548). He shows up in appointment lists through 1803, is missing in 1804, and the only comment about his death in the 1805 *Minutes* is: 'After travelling many years, we trust he died in the Lord.' *Minutes* (post-Wesley, 1805), 2:271. JW was replying to a letter from Algar that is not known to survive.

[75] See *Minutes* (1765), QQ. 13–14, 10:309 in this edn.

[76] Cf. Heb. 6:1.

[77] See Heb. 12:12.

[78] See Phil. 3:14.

[79] See Heb. 4:3.

Address: 'To / Mr Joseph Algar / At Mr Henry Jone⟨s's⟩ / In Swansea /
    South Wal⟨es⟩'.
Postmark: '26/FE'.
Source: holograph; MARC, DDWes 9/8.

5

To Ambrose Foley

10

London
February 26, 1782

Dear Sir,

On Saturday, March 23, I hope to be at Birmingham to open the
new chapel and to spend a few days there.[80] About the middle of the   15
ensuing week I shall be willing to give you a sermon at Quinton. I
am glad to hear that our labour there has not been in vain and that
you are not 'ashamed of the gospel of Christ'. It will be a particular
pleasure to me to see Mrs. [Jane] Foley, and I hope to see her happier than ever she has been yet.   20

Peace be with your spirits. I am,
    Your affectionate brother,

J. Wesley

25

Address: 'To / Mr Foley / At Quinton, near / Birmingham'.
Postmark: '24/FE'. *Charge*: '4'.
Source: holograph; MARC, MAM JW 3/4.

30

To Ann (Turner) Knapp

London   35
February 27, 1782

My Dear Sister,

If ever I observe you in any fault, I shall certainly tell you of it,
because I love you much; and I am persuaded you would not be

---

[80] JW's plans were revised by various factors. He ended up opening the Cherry Street
Chapel in Birmingham on July 7, 1782; see *Journal*, 23:245 in this edn.

angry but rather pleased with my plain dealing. I wrote word to brother [John] Knapp that I hoped to be with you on the 20th of March. I am pleased with any opportunity of spending a little time with you. And when I am at Worcester, let me have a few minutes
5   with you alone, that you may be able to speak freely. I want you to be 'all praise, all meekness, and all love'.[81] You know that's your calling.

 I am, my dear sister,
  Your affectionate brother,

         J. Wesley
10

Source: published transcription; Rowley, *Knapp*, 3–4.

15

To Elizabeth (Nangle) Bradburn

            London
20   February 28, 1782
My Dear Betsy,

 You did exceeding well to write.[82] You should always permit those you love to share both in your joys and your sorrows. The account you give brings strongly to my mind the words of the angel to the
25   hermit:

   To all but thee *in fits* he seemed to go,
   And 'twas my ministry to deal the blow.[83]

30   I am much inclined to think this was an instance of the same kind. Our Lord saw good to take the little one into Abraham's bosom. His angel came with a commission to fetch him. But it was not seen good to remove him at one stroke, lest you should be swallowed up of over much sorrow. A reprieve was given for a few days, that you
35   might be more prepared for the great trial and more determined to say, 'It is the Lord. Let him do what seemeth him good.'[84]

 [81] CW, Hymn on Ezekiel 36:26, last line, *Scripture Hymns* (1762), 2:49.
 [82] See Elizabeth's letter of Feb. 24, 1782, informing JW of the death of her and Samuel's first child, Ebenezer Bradburn (1779–82), on Feb. 17.
 [83] Thomas Parnell, 'The Hermit', ll. 230–40; retained by JW in his abridged version in *MSP* (1744), 1:275–76.
 [84] 1 Sam. 3:18.

I expect to be at Manchester on the 12th of April, and about the beginning of May in Yorkshire. But I believe I had better take Blackburn, Preston, and Colne (to save time) in my way thither.

Sammy Bradburn does right in giving himself directly to the work of God. It is far better and more comfortable for him than to sit musing at home. May God enable him and you to do and to suffer his holy and acceptable will![85] So prays, my dear Betsy,

Your ever affectionate brother,

J. Wesley

Source: published transcription; *WHS* 9 (1913): 70.

To Robert Costerdine[86]

London
March 2, 1782

Dear Robert,

I have now before me a particular account of the behaviour of William Goodrich toward Sally Phipps and others.[87] I am greatly surprised at the partiality of brother [Joseph] Harper. Besides, he had no authority to administer an oath to any one. I forbid William Goodrich to preach any more in any of our societies. And I beg of Joseph Harper not to say anything in his defence either in public or private. Brother Whitehouse informs me you have heard the case at large and do not lay any blame on Sally Phipps.

I am, dear Robert,

Your affectionate brother,

J. Wesley

Source: published transcription; *WHS* 26 (1948): 125–26.[88]

---

[85] See 1 Pet. 4:19.

[86] Costerdine was currently assigned to the Leicester circuit, where Joseph Harper was the Assistant.

[87] The specific society within the circuit where these two and brother Whitehouse resided is unclear. Goodrich was apparently a local preacher, never appearing in the *Minutes*.

[88] This corrects the transcription in *WMM* 68 (1845): 580 [reproduced in Telford, *Letters*].

To Mary (Franklin) Parker[89]

London
March 2, 1782

My Dear Sister,

I do not wonder at the obstinacy or bitterness of those that have separated themselves from you; it is the natural consequence of the dreadful opinions which they have drank into. Whatsoever may be the case with those who have been bred up therein, those who are converted to them are generally more bitter of spirit than Jews or Mahometans. And what is religion without love?

I wish the preachers who are in your circuit, Mr. Wood in particular,[90] would consider the reasons which you assign for making an exception from our general rule at Fakenham;[91] and whatever they determine will be acceptable.

My dear sister,
    Your affectionate brother,

J. Wesley

Source: published transcription; New Zealand Branch insert in *WHS* (Sept. 1937) 21.3.

To Ann Bolton

Bristol
March 8, 1782

My Dear Nancy,

I came hither from Bath this afternoon, and just snatch time to write two or three lines. It gave me pleasure to see your letter dated from Caerleon,[92] as I know your spending a few days there would not be in vain. You will give and receive a blessing. Iron sharpeneth

---

[89] Mary Franklin (b. 1754) of Wood Dalling, Norfolk, whom JW wrote in 1772, married Franklin Parker of Fakenham in Sept. 1779.

[90] James Wood was currently the Assistant for the Norwich circuit.

[91] This was likely a rule about not starting new preaching points too near to existing ones.

[92] Ann Bolton to JW, Feb. 23, 1782.

iron, and the countenance of a man his friends.[93] Not only the conversation, but the very countenance, as I have often found when I
looked upon *you*. But much more your words shall (by the grace of
God) convey health to the soul. You will comfort and quicken my
dear Sally, and not suffer her hands to hang down.[94] I can say noth-   5
ing of *Sir Charles Grandison*, because I never read a page of his.[95] On
Monday, the 18th instant, I hope to have the pleasure of meeting
you at Stroud. On Tuesday I have promised to dine with that amiable woman Mrs. Wathen at New House.[96] But I should not desire
it unless *you* was there.   10

     Peace be with all your spirits. I am, my dear Nancy,
       Yours most affectionately,

                        J. Wesley

Address: 'To / Miss Bolton / At Miss [Sarah] James' / in / Caerleon / +p   15
     [i.e., crosspost] Gloster'.
Postmark: 'Bristol'.
Endorsement: by Bolton, 'Mar 8th 1782'.
Source: holograph; MARC, MAM JW 1/93.

                                     20

To Robert Carr Brackenbury

                                     25

                             Bristol
                     March 9, 1782

Dear Sir,
     The letter you refer to as giving me an account of Mrs. Bracken-
bury's illness I have never seen.[97] I did not hear anything of it till I   30
received Mr. [Brian] Collins's letter from Raithby.

---

[93] See Prov. 27:17.

[94] See Heb. 12:12.

[95] Bolton had told JW that Sarah James was reading to her in the evenings from Samuel
Richardson (ed.), *A History of Sir Charles Grandison, in a series of letters*, 7 vols. (London:
Richardson, 1754).

[96] Anne (Iles) Wathen (1739–1803), sister of John Iles of Stroud, had become the second
wife of Joseph Wathen (c. 1723–86), the owner of Thrupp mill, in 1760. Their manor home,
called 'New House', was later renamed Brimscombe Court. JW would visit Anne again the year
after she was widowed; see JW, *Journal*, Mar. 20, 1787, 24:9 in this edn. Cf. *WHS* 5 (1906):
251–53.

[97] See the note on JW to Brackenbury, Nov. 19, 1781 (29:699). Robert's wife Jane had died
on Mar. 3; Brackenbury's letter with this information is not known to survive.

What a comfort it is that we know the Lord reigneth, and that he disposes all things in heaven and earth in the very manner which he sees will be most for his own glory and for the good of those that love him. I am firmly persuaded the present dispensation, severe as
5   it may appear, will be found in the event a means of greater blessings than any you have yet received. Even already you find the consolations of the Holy One are not small with you. And he enables you to make the right use of this providence by devoting yourself more entirely to his service.
10   I am glad you have such a friend as Mr. Collins with you. I will write to Dr. [Thomas] Coke and desire him to look out for such a family near London as you want. I am not afraid of *your* speaking too little, but of your speaking too much. Stay! A thought just comes into my mind. On April the 4th I expect to be at Manchester, in
15   order to visit the societies in Lancashire, Cheshire, Yorkshire; and thence to proceed (if God permit) to Scotland. Perhaps it would be of use if you took part of the journey with me. You may let me know your thoughts by a line directed to Manchester. Let Mr. Collins and you strengthen each other's hands in God.[98]
20   I am, dear sir,
        Your ever affectionate friend and brother,

                                                              J. Wesley

25   *Address*: 'To / Robert Brackenbury, Esq / At Raithby, near Spilsby'.
     Postmark: '11/MR'. *Charge*: '8'.
     Endorsement: by Brackenbury, 'receiv'd March / 18'.
     Source: holograph; MARC, MAM JW 1/106.

30

To Ann Loxdale

35   Bristol
                                                      March 9, 1782
My Dear Miss Loxdale,
    'Gold is tried in the fire, and acceptable men in the furnace of adversity.'[99]

---

[98] See 1 Sam. 23:16.
[99] Ecclus 2:5.

You say, 'I know not where I am going.'[100] I will tell you where.
You are going the straight way to be swallowed up in God. 'I know
not what I am doing.' You are suffering the will of God and glorifying him in the fire. 'But I am not increasing in the divine life.'
That is your mistake. Perhaps you are now increasing therein faster   5
than ever you did since you were justified. It is true that the usual
method of our Lord is to purify us by joy in the Holy Ghost and
a full consciousness of his love. But I have known several exempt
cases, and I am clearly satisfied yours is one; and

                                                                            10

      Far, far beyond thy thought
        His counsel shall appear,
    When fully he the work hath wrought
      That caused thy needless fear.[101]

                                                                            15

If it be possible, meet me at Madeley on Saturday; then you may
talk more largely with, my dear Miss Loxdale,
    Yours most affectionately,

                        J. Wesley

                                                                            20

Source: published transcription; *Methodist Magazine* 31 (1808): 328–29.

                                                                            25

To Hannah Ball[102]

                           Bristol
                 March 10, 1782   30

My Dear Sister,
    I would not willingly grieve you. I love you too well, and have
done for many years. I was disappointed both last year and this: last
year your preachers did less than I expected; and this year they have
done more than I expected.[103] Yea, and I trust you shall see greater   35

---

[100] Excerpts from Loxdale's letter to JW, which is not known to survive.

[101] Paul Gerhardt, 'Trust in Providence', st. 14 (as translated by JW), *HSP* (1739), 143.

[102] While the address portion is missing and no name is used, the holograph was part of
the papers of Hannah Ball, and the letter is transcribed in her *Memoir* (p. 155). Ball's letter to
JW, which drew this response, is not known to survive.

[103] The previous preachers had been George Story and John Acourt; those assigned at
the 1781 Conference were Richard Rodda, Thomas Warwick. See JW to Ball, Nov. 17, 1781
(29:698).

things than these.[104] The work of God has wonderfully revived in many parts of the nation. And I do not know why it should not revive among *you* also. Certainly you should look and ask for it.

5   I am glad to hear so good an account of your sister [Ann]; the more active she is the more her soul will live. I wanted to know what was become of those little maidens,[105] and trust some of them will bring forth fruit to perfection. As you have a peculiar love for children and a talent for assisting them, see that you stir up the gift of God which is in you.[106] If you gain but one of them in ten, you
10   have a good reward for your labour.

I am, my dear sister,
Yours affectionately,

J. Wesley

15   *Source*: holograph; MARC, MA 2008/013.

20   To Thomas Brisco

Bristol
March 12, 1782
25   My Dear Brother,
On Thursday, April 4, I expect to be at Manchester. The plan of my journey through Yorkshire I have sent to brother [Alexander] Mather, from whom you may have a copy if you have it not already. I desire no better lodging than either that at Birstall or Dawgreen.
30   You have done well in changing the hours of preaching at Morley.[107] I would encourage all persons to go to Church as much as they possibly can.
The meeting the children, whenever there is an opportunity, is a point of the utmost importance. By earnest exhortation we may
35   prevail upon their parents in all our larger societies to send them, and some of them will second the advices which their children receive from the preachers.

---

[104] See John 1:50.
[105] The girls in the school which Hannah and Ann ran in High Wycombe.
[106] See 2 Tim. 1:6.
[107] Brisco's letter is not known to survive, but he had clearly moved the preaching away from the time of scheduled services in the Church of England parish.

I hope you give sister [Ann] Brisco full employment.[108] She may be of great use. I am,
    Your affectionate friend and brother,

                    J. Wesley

Source: holograph; MARC, MAM JW 2/15.

To Robert Costerdine

                               Worcester
                        March 22, 1782
Dear Robert,
    I think you have acted exceeding right in the case of William Go-odrich.[109] I cannot in any wise consent to his preaching in any of our societies. But does not one more thing lie upon you, namely, to talk plainly and fully with Joseph Harper? Otherwise I cannot say that you are clear of his blood.
    I am, dear Robert,
        Your affectionate brother,

                    J. Wesley

Address: 'To / Mr Rob. Costerdine / At Mr Tho Hefford's / in / Leicester'.
Postmark: 'Birmingham'. *Charge*: '4'.
Source: holograph; privately held (WWEP Archives holds photocopy).

To Ann Tindall

                               Worcester
                        March 22, 1782
My Dear Sister,
    I exceedingly approve of the method you have entered upon for paying off the debt upon the [preaching-]house.[110] It will oppress no one, and will be lessening and lessening your burden, till it is

---

[108] Thomas Brisco married Ann Bignell (b. 1738) in Portsea, Hampshire, in Feb. 1771.
[109] See JW to Costerdine, Mar. 2, 1782.
[110] See JW to Tindall, Feb. 1, 1782.

quite removed. I will subscribe toward it for a year, half a crown a week, beginning from the first of April. John Fenwick may pay twenty shillings for my first eight weeks (out of the book money) when you receive this.

5   I am glad to hear that brotherly love continues among you. Probably I shall be able to call upon you either in May or June.

On Saturday next, I am to be at Madeley. Saturday sennight, at Warrington. Saturday, April 20th, at Colne.

I am, dear Nancy,

10   Yours affectionately,

J. Wesley

Address: 'To / Miss Ann Tindal / in / Scarborough'.
Postmarks: '27/MR' and 'Gloucester'. *Charge*: '8'.
Endorsement: by Tindall, '22 March 1782'.
15 *Source*: holograph; British Library, Department of Manuscripts, Add. MS. 43695, ff. 66–67.

20

To John Francis Valton

Madeley
March 24, 1782

25 My Dear Brother,

I have no objection to your proposal.[111] Let the trustees give such a bond as you mention; and see that the scarecrow house[112] be made as handsome and convenient as the house at Leeds is. In particular, I beg all the windows may be sashes opening downward.[113] Do not
30 spoil the house to save a little expense.

[111] Valton was currently the Assistant for the Birstall circuit. Growth of the society in Birstall made necessary a rebuilding of their preaching house. While Valton's letter to JW is not known to survive, it apparently conveyed an initial proposal that £350 be borrowed from eight intended new trustees; who in turn would receive interest and eventual repayment from rents and profits from the pews and seats. JW agreed to this proposal—see *WHS* 35 (1957), 32–34. However, a clause added subsequently gave the trustees and certain class-leaders authority to appoint preachers after the death of JW and CW. This challenged the connexional nature of Methodism. For JW's summary of the resulting debate, see his letter to CW of May 28, 1782; and 'The Case of Birstall House', 9:504–09 in this edn.

[112] JW was using the term in a derogatory manner, implying that the old preaching house was rough and shoddy, like a scarecrow. Cf. JW to Charles Atmore, Oct. 15, 1785.

[113] As stipulated in *Minutes* (1765), Q 13, 10:309 in this edn. On the reasons for this style, see *Methodist History* 36 (1998): 128–29.

I think you: have my plan: Huddersfield, April 23; Halifax, Wednesday, [April] 24; Keighley, Saturday, 27; Bingley, Sunday, 28; Yeadon, Monday, 29; Otley, Wednesday, May 1; Friday, [May] 3, Bradforth; Saturday, 4, Wakefield; Sunday, 5, Birstal [at] noon [and] evening [at] Bradforth; Monday, [May 6], Daw Green; Tuesday, [May 7], Leeds.

I am,

> Your affectionate friend and brother,

> > J. Wesley

Address: 'To / Mr Valton / At Birstal near ~~Bradforth~~ / Leeds[114] / Yorkshire'.
Postmark: 'Newcastle under Line [i.e., Lyme]'. Charge: '4'.
Endorsement: by Valton, 'March 24, 1782'.
Source: holograph; Bridwell Library (SMU).

To Joseph Benson[115]

> Macclesfield
> March 30, 1782

Dear Sir,

Many have inferred from my not answering Mr. Madan's book that I was of the same judgment with him. But it was owing to another cause, my want of time. I am glad you have supplied my lack of service; and that you have done it with temper, though not with that complaisance which is quite unseasonable on such an occasion. I have read over your remarks with attention and believe they will satisfy any impartial reader. I commend you and your labours to the God of truth and love.

I am,

> Your affectionate friend and brother,

> > John Wesley

Source: published transcription; *Arminian Magazine* 6 (1783): 37.

[114] The change from 'Bradforth' to 'Leeds' is in another hand.
[115] This letter is a formal endorsement of the extended critique of Martin Madan's *Thelyphthora; or, A treatise on female ruin* ... (London: J. Dodsley, 1780–81), that Benson had prepared with JW's encouragement (see JW to Benson, May 21, 1781, 29:646–47 in this edn.). Benson had sent JW the manuscript a month earlier (see JW to Benson, Feb. 22, 1782). The letter stands at the beginning of a series of twenty-four monthly installments publishing Benson's extended manuscript, which Benson styled as a series of letters to JW; see Benson to JW, c. Feb. 18, 1782.

To Thomas Carlill[116]

near Manchester
April 3, 1782

Dear Tommy,

Be of good courage. You have had a token for good at Lynn, where it was supposed the case was desperate. And I do not doubt but you will see good days in and about Fakenham, though the people as yet do not know much of discipline—and no wonder, if they have never yet had the [General] Rules of our Societies. First explain them at large, and afterwards enforce them, very mildly and very steadily. Molly Franklin[117] and sister Proudfoot are good women.[118] Deal very gently with them, and lovingly labour to convince those whom it concerns of the evil of buying or selling on the Lord's Day.

I am, dear Tommy,

Your affectionate friend and brother,

J. Wesley

Source: holograph; privately held (WWEP Archive holds digital copy).

To John Atlay

Stockport
April 4, 1782

My Dear Brother,

I think two thousand more of the *Hymns for the Nation* may be printed as soon as is convenient, leaving out the 2nd, 3rd, 8th, 12th,

---

[116] JW was replying to Carlill's letter of Mar. 26, 1782.

[117] JW was forgetting to use her married name.

[118] Carlill's concerns may have been that both Mary (Franklin) Parker and Mrs. Proudfoot (fl. 1780–90) had preached in public settings—see JW, *Journal*, Oct. 29, 1781, 23:226 in this edn.; and J. B. B. Clarke, *The Life of Adam Clarke* (London: T. S. Clarke, 1833), 1:216.

16th, 21st, and 22nd.[119] When these seven are omitted (which are not of so general use), the remainder will be large enough for a threepenny book. Five hundred of these I would have sent to Sheffield (over and above the five hundred sent to Leeds), and five hundred to Newcastle upon Tyne. I hope they will be at Sheffield before the 9th of May.

I am poorly provided with fellow travellers. To save John Broadbent's life,[120] I take him with me for a month while George Whitfield supplies his place.[121] But he and Thomas Simpson together are but half a man.[122] So that it is well I have learnt to serve myself. Do not boast of your riches to Thomas Olivers; it is enough to make him stark mad.[123]

I am,

  Your affectionate brother,

                                          J. Wesley

---

[119] This collection was begun by CW in reaction to the surrender of General Cornwallis at Yorktown, in the Battle of the Chesapeake, on Oct. 19, 1781. As news of this decisive defeat reached England, George III lost control of Parliament to the peace party and staunch royalists (like CW) were deeply disheartened. CW issued an initial pamphlet of *Hymns for the Nation* in 1782, with nine hymns, in fall 1781. Shortly after he printed a pamphlet with the same title, with the addition of 'Part II', comprised of eight new items. And before 1781 was over he printed an edition that combined the seventeen hymns. Then on Jan. 20, 1782, George III called for a public fast to be observed on Feb. 8. CW rushed into print a pamphlet containing fifteen new hymns, titled *Hymns for the National Fast*. As soon as the fast day was past, a new edition of *Hymns for the Nation* in 1782 was released that appended these fifteen to the prior seventeen hymns, with a total of 32. JW was calling for one more printing (it would be the last), which removed those hymns that were most focused on the rebellious North Americans.

[120] John Broadbent had been serving as Assistant for the Staffordshire circuit. He would be assigned to London in the coming year (to continue recovering his strength).

[121] George Whitfield (1753–1832), while he shared a nearly identical name with the famous Calvinist Methodist preacher, had from a young age been part of Wesleyan Methodism and by 1779 was serving as JW's Book Steward in London and often accompanying JW on journeys. Whitfield was listed among the itinerants from 1784 (see 10:552 in this edn.), but appointed to London, continuing as Book Steward and assisting JW in other administrative roles. On his death he was buried at City Road Chapel. See Stevenson, *City Road*, 279, 516.

[122] Thomas Simpson had been struggling with spiritual doubts (see his letter to JW, Feb. 12, 1782). This led JW to relieve him for a time of his duties at Kingswood school, and bring him on the current preaching tour.

[123] Olivers served as supervisor of JW's printing operation in London, and apparently thought that he was not receiving sufficient compensation; see JW to Atlay, Apr. 13, 1782.

If you print 2,000 *Estimates of the Manners of the Times* for 2 pence and send me 500 of them to Leeds as soon as you can, and 500 to Sheffield with the *Hymns [for the Nation]*, I can sell them.[124]

Address: 'To / Mr Atlay / City Road / London'.
Postmarks: '8/AP' and 'Manchester'. Charge: '4'.
Endorsement: by Atlay, 'Mr Wesley April 8[125] / 1782'.
Source: holograph; New Room (Bristol), NR2001.225.

To Francis Wrigley[126]

[Manchester]
[April 4, 1782[127]]

My Dear Brother,

I have no objection to the judgment of the rector of Trowbridge.[128] And it seems this would stand between you and blame—as no one could condemn *you* without first condemning *him*.

I do not know anything that is amiss in the behaviour either of brother Fowler or his wife. But I do not know that he is called to preach.[129] Certainly he should not go where they are not willing to hear him.

I am,

Your affectionate friend and brother,

J. Wesley

Address: "To / Mr. Wrigley / At the Preaching-house / In Bradford / Wilts."
Postmark: "Manchester." Charge: '4'.
Source: holograph; Duke, Rubenstein, Frank Baker Collection of Wesleyana, Box WF 1.

[124] JW, *An Estimate of the Manners of the Present Times* (1782; *Bibliography*, No. 426; vol. 15 in this edn.). While the opening section of this tract gives voice to JW's concerns about a regimen of diet and exercise, its primary focus is on the 'ungodliness' rampant in British society, to which JW attributes the recent failures of British forces on sea and at land.

[125] The date he received the letter.

[126] Wrigley's letter to JW is not known to survive.

[127] The location and date are cut off from the holograph now at Duke. Telford gives this location and date with no hint of speculation, which fits both when JW was in Manchester and when Wrigley was Assistant of the Sarum circuit (which included Trowbridge).

[128] Rev. John Ekins (1732–1808) was currently rector of Trowbridge; the specific judgment referenced is unknown.

[129] John Fowler, of nearby Bath, whom JW visited several times in the 1780s. See JW's later, and very different evaluation of Fowler in JW to John Valton, Oct. 9, 1786.

To John Bredin

Manchester
April 6, 1782   5

My Dear Brother,

It is probable I shall be able to hold a little conference in Dublin before the middle of July.[130] But you will hear more before that time. The four volumes of *Sermons* with the *Notes on the New Testament* (small edition) are the best books for Mr. Hezlet.[131] Any other of   10
our books you may *give* to him or Mr. [John] Dillon in my name. If Adam Clarke can come to London at the Conference, I will send him to Kingswood directly.[132] You may take those three volumes of *[Arminian] Magazines* with as many as make up the set. You may likewise have the *History* of England and of the Church.[133]   15

John McKenny must take his choice.[134] If he will refrain from going to that house, it will remove the offense. But if he *will go*, he does thereby put himself out of our society.

I am,

Your affectionate friend and brother,   20

J. Wesley

Address: 'To / John Bredin / In Coleraine / Ireland'.
Source: holograph; MARC, MAM JW 2/5.

---

[130] JW's intended visit this year to Ireland was overridden by demands in Britain; so he sent Thomas Coke in his place, who met with the preachers in Ireland in late June 1782.

[131] Orig., 'Haslett'. Rev. Robert Hezlet (d. 1821) was curate, then rector of Killowen parish 1767–1821. He was supportive of the Methodists in Coleraine, often attending weekday meetings. See G. B. Johnson, 'Methodism in Coleraine', *Irish Christian Advocate,* May 3, 1935, p. 7.

[132] Clarke set out from Ireland for Kingswood in Aug. 1782 (see the letter by John Bredin that he took with him, dated Aug. 13, 1782, in-letters file). But after only one month there it became clear he would gain little benefit and he began serving as an itinerant, being formally admitted at the 1783 Conference; see Adam Clarke, *Life*, 1:159–69.

[133] I.e., JW's four-volume sets: *A Concise History of England* (1776) and *A Concise Ecclesiastical History* (1781).

[134] John McKenny was a contemporary of Adam Clarke during his time in Colermaine in 1781–82; see Crookshank, *Ireland*, 356. His son, of the same name (c. 1748–1847), would become a Wesleyan Methodist missionary South Africa and Sri Lanka. Lacking Bredin's letter to JW, nothing can be said concerning the nature of the offending situation.

To Samuel Mitchell[135]

Manchester
April 6, 1782

5   My Dear Brother,

Joseph Pilmore did not let me know that you had sent a plan of the circuit to Dublin. Otherwise George Whitfield need not have wrote.

It is very probable I may get as far as Dublin, in order to hold a little conference, about the beginning of July.[136]

10   As it was so greatly wanted and the people were so willing, you did well to begin the preaching-house, and as far as circumstances will admit let it be built accordingly to the directions laid down in the *Minutes*.[137]

If you strongly and explicitly encourage all the believers in every
15   place to expect *present* and *full* salvation from *all* sin, the work of the Lord will prosper in your hands.

I am, dear Sammy,

Your affectionate friend and brother,

J. Wesley

20
You will contrive to send brother Foster's letter to him.[138]

Address: 'To / Mr Sam. Mitchell / In Clones / Ireland'.
Postmarks: 'Manchester' and 'AP/11'.
Source: holograph; Lovely Lane Museum Library.

25

To John Bredin

30
Liverpool
April 10, 1782

My Dear Brother,

I have a letter from Mrs. Davenport,[139] informing me that Hugh Moore has offered marriage to Kitty Davenport without the con-

---

[135] Samuel Mitchell was admitted 'on trial' as an itinerant in 1779 (see 10:484 in this edn.). He was presently the Assistant for the Clones circuit. Mitchell served only in his native Ireland, and withdrew from the connexion in 1791 (10:765).

[136] See the note on JW to John Bredin, Apr. 6, 1782.

[137] See *Minutes* (1765), QQ. 13–14, 10:309 in this edn.

[138] Henry Foster was currently Assistant for the Charlemont circuit. JW had surely included a page for Foster as a typical double letter. It is not known to survive.

[139] This letter is not known to survive.

sent of her parents.[140] Pray write to him strongly upon the head, and show him the sinfulness of such a proceeding—reminding him withal that if he married a person without the consent of her parents, he would thereby exclude himself out of the Methodist connexion. Let him remember the exemplary behaviour of John Prickard on a like occasion.

If he will seriously promise entirely to drop the affair, he may come to Coleraine as usual.[141] If he will not, he must come thither no more. I am,

Your affectionate friend and brother,

J. Wesley

Address: 'To / Mr. John Bredin / in Coleraine / Ireland'.
Postmark: 'Liverpool'.
Source: holograph; MARC, MAM JW 2/6.

To Thomas Taylor

Liverpool
April 12, 1782

Dear Tommy,

I find the difference between us is very small, for most of what you say I subscribe to.[142] That 'the war has been ill-conducted', that 'millions of money and thousands of lives have been thrown away', that 'numerous families have been ruined, trade much hurt', that we are 'in danger of losing all North America, if not the East Indies too', 'that our commanders both by sea and land love robbing and plundering far better than fighting', are melancholy truths which no man that has any knowledge of public affairs can deny. But you do not know half yet. If we live to meet, I can tell you stranger things than all these.

---

[140] Hugh Moore was currently the Assistant for the Londonderry circuit.
[141] The marriage apparently never took place; JW records visiting K[atherine] Davenport in Coleraine on June 7, 1787 (see his diary, 24:211 in this edn.).
[142] Taylor's letter to JW is not known to survive.

I have changed the plan of my journeys. From Leeds I go to Lincolnshire, and thence by Hull and Scarborough to Newcastle. So that I shall not be at York till the latter end of June.[143]

I am, with love to sister [Ann] Taylor, dear Tommy,

5   Your affectionate friend and brother,

J. Wesley

Source: holograph; MARC, MA 1992/035.

10

To John Atlay[144]

15   Liverpool
                                              April 13, 1782

My Dear Brother,

By all means send what remains of the former edition of the *Hymns [for the Nation]* before you send the new. You may likewise
20   send to Sheffield an hundred of each of Mr. Galloway's tracts.[145] Let us shut the stable door, though the steed is stolen.

As Thomas Olivers has the interest of five hundred pounds besides my allowance, I do not see how he can possibly be in want, unless there be a marvellous want of economy. However, be it as it may.
25   I am at a point: I will give him forty pounds a year and no more.

I am,
          Your affectionate brother,

J. Wesley

30   *Source*: holograph; MARC, MAM JW 1/3.

---

[143] Taylor was Assistant for the York circuit.

[144] The recipient is clear from the continuity with JW's prior letter to Atlay of Apr. 4, 1782; Atlay's response to this earlier letter is not known to survive.

[145] The extracts JW published of four of Joseph Galloway's publications critical of how British forces had performed in the Revolutionary War; see *Bibliography*, Nos. 405–06, 415–16.

To Hester Ann Roe[146]

[Wigan]
April 15, 1782   5

You should always have in readiness that little tract the *Plain Account of Christian Perfection*; there is nothing which so effectually stops the mouths of those who call this a 'new doctrine'. All who object to it are really (though they suspect nothing less) seeking   10
sanctification by works. If it be by works, then certainly there will need *time* in order to the doing of those works. But if it be by faith, it is plain, a moment is as a thousand years.[147] Then God says (in the spiritual as in the outward world) 'Let there be light, and there is light.'[148]   15

As his own soul is much quickened, I am in great hopes John Sellers will be a blessing to many in Chester.[149] A few witnesses of true love remain there still, but several are gone to Abraham's bosom.

You will encourage those at Macclesfield that enjoy it to speak explicitly what they experience, and to go on till they know all that   20
love of God which passeth knowledge.[150] Give all the help you can, my dear Hetty, to them and to,

Yours affectionately,

J. Wesley

25

Source: manuscript copy for records: MARC, MA 1977/295 (transcribed by Roe in her ms journal, on Apr. 18).[151]

---

[146] JW was replying to Roe's letter of Apr. 7, 1782.

[147] Cf. 2 Pet. 3:8.

[148] Cf. Gen. 1:3.

[149] Orig., 'Sellars'. John Sellers (1758–90) was a schoolmaster, who served as a class-leader and local preacher in the Methodist society in Chester; see Bretherton, *Chester*, 149.

[150] See Eph. 3:19.

[151] Additional secondary transcriptions: MARC, MA 1977/485; and Duke, Rubenstein, Frank Baker Collection of Wesleyana, VOLS 7, Letter book 10 (by James Little), p. 17.

To Thomas [Lewis][152]

near Colne
April 21, 1782

Dear Tommy,

So let what is past be forgotten. With regard to Molly Maddern, I believe, from what I hear on all sides, that she has (perhaps innocently) prejudiced many of the people against the preachers, and thereby hindered their usefulness.[153] I believe too that the preacher's wife may fully supply the place of an housekeeper. But sister Maddern must not want. Let her be allowed, weekly or quarterly, whatever *you* judge proper.

I am, dear Tommy,
    Your affectionate brother,

J. Wesley

⟨Molly? is a⟩ good servant. If she chooses to go away, let her go; but I desire she should not be put away.

Source: holograph; MARC, MAM JW 6/50.

To Zachariah Yewdall

Otley
May 1, 1782

My Dear Brother,

I see no reason yet why you may not spend the next year in Cork and Bandon.[154]

---

[152] While the address portion is torn away (affecting one line at the bottom), this letter was almost certainly sent to Thomas Lewis, General Steward for the Bristol society. If so, it was JW's last letter to Lewis, who was buried in Bristol on Apr. 28, 1782.

[153] JW had placed Mary (Francis) Maddern as the housekeeper at the New Room in Bristol after she was widowed. But she had recently quarrelled with itinerants assigned to Bristol; see John Pawson to Joseph Benson, May 2, 1782, Pawson, *Letters*, 1:22–23.

[154] Yewdall was currently serving the Waterford circuit. He was named Assistant for the Cork circuit at the 1782 Conference.

If nothing unforeseen prevent, I shall be at Dublin the beginning of July.

If you desire to promote the work of God, you should preach abroad as often as possible. Nothing destroys the devil's kingdom like this.

You may have the *History* of the church;[155] money is nothing between you and me. Be all in earnest!

I am, dear Zachary,
    Your affectionate brother,

              J. Wesley

Source: holograph; Huntington Library, Manuscripts, HM 57049.[156]

To [Elizabeth Woodhouse?[157]]

              Bradford
            May 5, 1782

My Dear Sister,

I snatch a few minutes to inform you that I shall be at Epworth, if God permit, on Saturday next. And I expect to stay there till the Wednesday following, when I am to be at Gainsborough.

In every temptation God will make a way for you to escape, that you may be able to bear it.[158] He is faithful. You remember the true remark: Man's extremity is God's opportunity. So you will find. He will come and will not tarry![159]

I am, my dear sister,
    Yours affectionately,

              J. Wesley

Source: holograph; Huntington Library, Manuscripts, HM 57050.[160]

[155] I.e., JW's four-volume *Concise Ecclesiastical History.*

[156] MARC, MA 1977/485, p. 256 is a 19th-century transcription by James Everett.

[157] Woodhouse was the woman living in Epworth with whom JW corresponded most frequently, though the last clear surviving letter is in late 1780.

[158] See 1 Cor. 10:13.

[159] See Heb. 10:37.

[160] There is no address portion. On the back of the letter is copied a 'Hymn for Christmas' in an unknown hand, and of unknown authorship (it is not a CW hymn).

To Mrs. Nuttal[161]

Leeds
May 7, 1782

Dear Mrs. Nuttal,
   When I was at Preston,[162] I was much pleased with your spirit, and found a tender concern for you. I saw you had real desire to be a Christian, and this endeared you much to me. I saw likewise a good deal of affection in your behaviour, which united me to you the more. But as you are weak and inexperienced you have need of much prayer and much watchfulness. And you have great need that others who have more experience should watch over you in love. Therefore it is highly advisable for you to join the society. Yet do not imagine that all in the society are angels. They are weak, fallible creatures like yourself. But weak as [they are] they may be helpful to *you*. If I could help you in any respect, it would be a peculiar satisfaction to, my dear Mrs. Nuttal,
         Your affectionate servant,

J. Wesley

Address: 'To / Mrs Nuttall / At Mr [Roger] Crane's / In Preston / Lancashire'.
Charge: '3'.
Source: holograph; Pitts Library (Emory), John Wesley Papers (MSS 153), 3/27.

To Ann (Dupuy) Taylor

Thorne
May 14, 1782

My Dear Sister,
   I will certainly rather encourage than discourage the sale of Mr. [Thomas] Taylor's *Concordance*.[163] And I have no objection to rec-

---

[161] Mrs. Nuttal, a lady of independent means, lived at Walton-le-Dale. She was one of the earliest Methodists in the neighbourhood. See Richard Allen, *History of Methodism in Preston and its Vicinity* (Preston: Toulin, 1866), 35.
   [162] JW had been there most recently on May 24, 1781 (see *Journal*, 23:205 in this edn.). JW would visit her on Apr. 17, 1784, when she was apparently near death (23:303).
   [163] For details see JW's letter of endorsement below, May 21, 1782.

ommend it as far as I can upon a slight perusal; but I have by no means time to read it over. I hope to be at York about the middle of June, but I cannot fix the day yet.[164] Peace be with you and yours!
I am,
Your affectionate brother,

[J. Wesley[165]]

Source: holograph; MARC, MA 1992/035.

To William Petty, Earl of Shelburne[166]

Scarborough
May 21, 1782[167]

My Lord,
If I wrong your Lordship, I am sorry for it. But I really believe your Lordship fears God. And I hope your Lordship has no unfavourable opinion of the Christian revelation. This encourages me to trouble your Lordship with a few lines, which otherwise I should not take upon me to do.

Above thirty years ago a motion was made in Parliament for raising and embodying the militia, and for exercising them (to save time) on Sunday. When the motion was like to pass, an old gentleman stood up and said, 'Mr. Speaker, I have one objection to this: I believe an old book called the Bible.' The members looked at one another, and the motion was dropped.

Must not all others who believe the Bible have the very same objection? And from what I have seen, I cannot but think these are still three-fourths of the nation. Now, setting religion out of the question, is it expedient to give such a shock to so many millions

---

[164] Thomas Taylor was currently the Assistant for the York circuit.

[165] The place where JW's signature would have appeared has been neatly cut out.

[166] Sir William Petty, 1st Marquis of Lansdowne and 2nd Earl of Shelburne (1737–1805) had been installed Home Secretary by George III on Mar. 27, 1782. In this capacity he issued a circular letter, dated May 7, 1782, in response to the threatened invasion by French and Spanish forces, directing mayors in the most populous cities to form militias and instruct them in 'military exercise' 'without interruption of labour'. See *Morning Chronicle* (May 11, 1782), p. 2. This led to debate over holding this training on Sundays.

[167] A transcription of this letter was published in Whitehead, *Life*, 2:399–400, where the date suggested was Dec. 1782, from London. All prior collections repeat this date, not having seen the holograph.

of people at once? And certainly it would shock them extremely. It would wound them in a very tender part. For would not they, would not all England, would not all Europe, consider this as a virtual repeal of the Bible? And would not all serious persons say, 'We have little religion in the land now, but by this step we shall have less still. For wherever this pretty show is to be seen, the people will flock together, and will lounge away so much time before and after it that the churches will be emptier than they are at present!'

My Lord, I am concerned for this on a double account. First, because I have personal obligations to your Lordship,[168] and would fain, even for this reason, recommend your Lordship to the love and esteem of all over whom I have any influence. Secondly, because I now reverence your Lordship for your office sake, and believe it to be my bounden duty to do all that is in my little power to advance your Lordship's influence and reputation.

Will your Lordship permit me to add a word in my old-fashioned way? I pray him that has all power in heaven and earth to prosper all your endeavours for the public good; and am, my Lord,

Your Lordship's willing servant,

John Wesley

Source: holograph; privately held (WWEP holds digital image).

For Thomas Taylor[169]

Scarborough
May 21, 1782

Mr. Cruden's Concordance is undoubtedly the best which hath yet been published in the English tongue.[170] But abundance of peo-

---

[168] Lady Arabella (Fitzmaurice) Denny (1707–92) was the aunt of William Petty. She was also a friend of JW, who visited her on May 6, 1783 (see *Journal*, 23:268 in this edn.), and likely on Apr. 21, 1758 (ibid, 21:142).

[169] The itinerant Thomas Taylor had prepared *A New Concordance to the Holy Scriptures* (York: R. Spence, 1782), an abridgement of the standard work by Cruden. Taylor's wife apparently sent JW a copy to solicit his support; see JW to Ann (Dupuy) Taylor, May 14, 1782. This is JW's resulting letter of endorsement, which appears in most (but not all) surviving copies of this volume.

[170] Alexander Cruden (1699–1770), *A Complete Concordance to the Holy Scriptures* (London: Midwinter et al., 1737).

ple who want a concordance cannot go to the price of it. I am in hopes this small, cheap, and portable one may answer the same intention. I therefore recommend it to all lovers of the Bible.

John Wesley

Source: published transcription; Thomas Taylor, *A New Concordance to the Holy Scriptures* (York: R. Spence, 1782), [i].

To Samuel Tooth

Yarm
May 23, 1782

Dear Sammy,

I advise you immediately to have Counsellor Parker's opinion concerning this intricate affair. He is just now in town, and lodges in Lamb's Conduit Street, at No. 29.[171]

I am, dear Sammy,
Your affectionate brother,

J. Wesley

Address: '⟨… Me⟩rchant / ⟨… R⟩oad / ⟨… Lo⟩ndon'.[172]
Endorsement: 'The Rev Mr J Wesley's / Letter about Mr / J Crotland's(?)[173] Affair / May 1782 / To Samuel Tooth'.
Source: holograph; MARC, MAM JW 5/17.

To Samuel Bardsley[174]

Sunderland
May 24, 1782

Dear Sammy,

I hope to be at Edinburgh on Thursday next, the 30th instant; on Monday at Dundee; Tuesday, Arbroth; Wednesday, Aberdeen.

---

[171] This is apparently Thomas Parker Esq., Counsellor-at-Law, whose office was on Red Lion Square, very near Lamb's Conduit Street.

[172] The left half of the address portion is missing.

[173] The name might begin 'J G…' or be something like 'Hartland' instead. Nothing has been found to confirm either the spelling or the nature of the affair.

[174] While the address portion is missing, Bardsley was the only 'Samuel' currently stationed in Scotland. He was assigned to the Aberdeen circuit.

I do not know that I can go any farther north. My time will not permit.

Peace be with all your spirits! I am, dear Sammy,

Yours affectionately,

J. Wesley

Source: holograph; Drew, Methodist Archives.

To Martha Chapman

Sunderland
May 25, 1782

My Dear Sister,

Some fault we may allow to be in the heart of that poor creature. But undoubtedly the main fault lies in her head. It is as manifest a case of insanity as ever came under my notice.

With regard to *you*, it is the wise providence of God. For the present it is not joyous, but grievous; yet by-and-by you will find all these things working together for good.[175] I advise you all to let her say whatever she has a mind to say. But answer her not one word either bad or good.

I am, my dear Patty,

Your affectionate brother,

J. Wesley

Address: 'To / Miss Patty Chapman / At Wattleton[176] / Near Nettlebed / Oxfordshire'.

Postmarks: 'Sunderland' and '28/MY'.

Endorsement: by Chapman, '12th 1782'.

Source: holograph; MARC, MAM JW 2/28.

[175] See Rom. 8:28.
[176] I.e., Watlington.

To Captain Thomas Webb[177]

Sunderland

May 25, 1782   5

My Dear Brother,

Explain to our brethren wherever you go your conversation with
Colonel Barré,[178] and enforce the proposal as far as you can. Then
you will [be] the better able to judge what number of soldiers you
may reasonably expect to raise among the Methodists.   10

I wish you would tell Mr. [William] Moore I desire he would not
converse *at all* with the separatists at Bath.[179] If he does, I shall look
upon it as an open declaration that he has no regard for me.

If twenty people pledge themselves for Mr. [John] Walker, they
may.[180] But I have nothing more to do with him. I will give him one   15
more guinea, and that is all.

I am,

Your affectionate brother,

J. Wesley

20

Source: holograph; Drew, Methodist Archives.

---

[177] Thomas Webb's proposal in 1779 to raise a militia among Methodists for the defence
of England was not accepted; see the proposal, dated Oct. 24, 1779 in in-letters; JW's endorsement of the same date; and JW to Ann Loxdale, July 24, 1782. The proposal of William Petty,
as Home Secretary, in early May 1782, to raise militias in the larger cities of Britain resurrected
Webb's interest in efforts among Methodists; see JW to William Petty, May 21, 1782. Webb's
letter to JW on this matter is not known to survive.

[178] Colonel Isaac Barré (1726–92), M.P. for Calne (1774–90) had served with Webb in
North America and was now closely connected with William Pitt. Barré was appointed in Apr.
1782 (briefly) as Secretary at War, making him the natural person for Webb to approach in his
renewed efforts; cf. JW to Joseph Benson, Aug. 3, 1782.

[179] The unrest fomented by Alexander M'Nab in late 1779 about the preeminence of
ordained clergy over lay preachers in JW's connexion had centered in Bath, and resulted in
a small group who separated from the society there. See JW to M'Nab, Oct. 19, 1779, 29:515
in this edn.; and JW to John Francis Valton, Feb. 9, 1780, 29:546–47. William Moore was currently assigned to the Bristol circuit, which included Bath.

[180] Walker had been assigned to the Gloucester circuit by the 1781 Conference, but was
now apparently in Bristol, where Webb resided, and would be set aside by the 1782 Conference (see 10:520 in this edn.). See JW to William Tunney, Jan. 22, 1781, 29:624–25 in this edn.

To Charles Atmore[181]

Alnwick
May 28, 1782

Dear Charles,

Agues this year spread all over the kingdom, and they are far more stubborn than usual. If you have not tried Dr. Sanders pills, you should (after taking a little vomit). They are entirely safe, as has been proved in a thousand instances. Take Castile soap, two scruples; *arsenicum album*, two grains. Mix thoroughly, and make into eight pills. Take one every four hours between the fits.[182] It very seldom fails. I am considered at present an invalid too; yet I trust we shall both recover our strength.

I am, dear Charles,
Your affectionate brother,

J. Wesley

Source: published transcription; *Wesleyan Methodist Magazine* 68 (1845): 9–10.

To the Rev. Charles Wesley[183]

Alnwick
May 28, 1782

[[Dear Brother,]]

The history of the matter is this: When I was at Dawgreen, near Birstall, the trustees for Birstall house brought me a deed, which they read over and desired me to sign. We disputed upon it about an hour. I then gave them a positive answer that 'I would not sign

---

[181] This is the first letter for which there is surviving text from JW to Charles Atmore (1759–1826), who had just entered itinerancy at the 1781 Conference. The biographical account in which it appears indicates that Atmore's battle with the ague led him to take leave from his preaching for a few months, but he was appointed again the following Conference and had a long career.

[182] See the note on this receipt in JW to Thomas Tattershall, Jan. 11, 1782.

[183] Concern over revisions proposed by the trustees in Birstall to the deed for their preaching-house was heating up; see the note on JW to John Valton, Mar. 24, 1782. CW had written JW about it, in a letter not known to survive.

it'; and, leaving them abruptly, went up to my room. About noon I preached at Horbury. In the evening I preached and met the society at Wakefield. At night, a little before I went to bed, the trustees came again, got round, and worried me down.[184]

But I think they cannot worry *you*. May not you very properly 5
write to Mr. Valton: 'If the trustees will settle the Birstall house on the Methodist plan, I will sign their deed with all my heart; but if they build an house for a Presbyterian meeting-house, I will not, I dare not, have anything to do with it'?[185]

I never yet sent a letter of attorney on such an occasion, nor wrote 10
in any other form than this: 'Its receipt shall be your discharge.' If the executor says, 'I will not pay it on such a receipt', then I will send a letter of attorney.

The beginning of Rodney's account is utterly unfashionable.[186] I wonder how it entered into his head. We 'get God on our side' by 15
the continual prayer of thousands. You may send me Cicero, and Fabritius and the American War,[187] together with the next *[Arminian] Magazines*, to York. I expect to be ten or twelve days in and near Edinburgh, and about the 17th of June at Newcastle.

Peace be with you all! 20

[[Adieu!]]

Address: 'To / The Revd Mr C. Wesley / City Road / London'.
Postmarks: '31/MA' and 'Alnwick'.
Endorsement: by CW, 'B[rother] May 28. 1782 / of the Deed'. 25
Source: holograph; MARC, DDWes 3/52.

[184] The events summarized here are on May 9, 1782; JW's *Journal* account does not mention the debate (see 23:238–39 in this edn.).

[185] John Valton was currently the Assistant of the Birstall circuit (see 10:522 in this edn.), and had apparently written CW seeking advice about the brewing disagreement. CW indeed refused to sign the deed JW signed on May 9; see Joseph Benson to JW, Dec. 14, 1782.

[186] Admiral George Rodney (1718–92) was commander of the British fleet that defeated a French fleet in a celebrated battle in the Caribbean, Apr. 9–12, 1782. A public letter from Rodney announcing the victory appeared in British papers on May 20, 1782 (e.g., *Public Advertiser*, pp. 1–2). Rodney opened the letter proclaiming that God had granted the victory 'out of his divine providence'.

[187] From Dec. 1781 through Apr. 1782 Joseph Galloway published, under the pen name 'Fabricius', a series of public letters criticizing the conduct of British military leaders in the war with the American colonists. These were gathered into a pamphlet, which CW had apparently mentioned to JW.

To Mary Clark[188]

near Edinburgh
June 1, 1782

5 My Dear Sister,

I am glad to hear that the select society increases, and that you meet it constantly. The prosperity of the whole society greatly depends on that little number. If these continue steadfast and alive to God, they will enliven the rest of their brethren.

10 I love your little maidens, and wish they knew how well our Saviour loves them.[189] If they did, they would certainly love him! And then, how happy they would be!

I am, my dear sister,

Your affectionate brother,

15 J. Wesley

Address: 'To / Mrs. Clark / At Mr. [John] Knapp's / Glover / In Worcester'.

Source: holograph; Wisbech, Cambridgeshire, Wisbech and Fenland Mu-
20 seum, WISFM 2003.35.341.1.

To Samuel Bradburn[190]

25

Aberdeen
June 7, 1782

Dear Sammy,

30 Cannot you give part of John Hodgson's class to the other leader? Let each person meet with which he chooses. Let Henry Atkinson and Thomas Haigh be the stewards for the ensuing year.[191]

---

[188] On Mary Clark, see the note on JW's earlier letter of Mar. 21, 1776, 29:236 in this edn. Her letter to JW that drew this reply is not known to survive.

[189] It is possible Clark was conducting a private school for girls, but this was more likely a class for young girls preparing to join the society; cf. JW's induction of several young members on his next visit to Worcester, *Journal*, Aug. 26, 1783, 23:287 in this edn.

[190] JW was replying to a letter that is not known to survive.

[191] Henry Atkinson was a 'stuff maker' living in Manningham who had been a trustee of the chapel built in Bradford in 1765; see Stamp, *Bradford*, 45. Thomas Haigh (1730–1798), an umbrella maker, appears on a 1781 list as a class leader, circuit steward, and local preacher in Bradford; ibid, 62–64.

I see no reason why brother Proctor should not remain in the circuit till the Conference.[192] But whenever you have the opportunity earnestly exhort him to be serious and to be jealous for God.

Whoever is pleased or displeased, the preaching at Greetland and at Halifax must remain as it is. Our yea is yea, and our nay is nay.

I have little objection to John Oliver's request; it seems reasonable enough.

I am glad to hear my poor Betsy gathers strength.[193] I love her well. Peace be with both your spirits!

I am, dear Sammy,
    Your affectionate friend and brother,

                             J. Wesley

Address: 'To / Mr Bradburn / At the Preaching-house / In Bradforth / Yorkshire'.

Source: holograph; privately held (MARC, MAM JW 1/117 is a photocopy).

To Jonathan Hern

                             Alnwick
                      June 16, 1782

Dear Jonathan,
    I have made all the haste from the north of Scotland which I reasonably could. But still my time falls short. I shall not be able to reach York before the 27th instant. And I shall then have all the Midland societies to visit. So that I cannot get any time for Ireland this summer. For before I have well done my business in the country, the Conference will call me to London. Peace be with you and yours! Be zealous for God!

I am,
    Your affectionate friend and brother,

                             J. Wesley

Address: 'To / Mr Jon. Hern / At the Octagon / In Chester / crosspost'.
    Postmark: 'Alnwick'.
Source: holograph; MARC, MAM JW 3/44.

---

[192] Stephen Proctor was currently the Assistant at Glamorgan. His connection to Bradburn is unclear; but Proctor was recognized at the 1782 Conference as having ceased to travel (see 10:520 in this edn.).

[193] I.e., Elizabeth (Nangle) Bradburn; see JW's letter to her of Feb. 28, 1782.

To Thomas Tattershall

Newcastle

June 20, 1782

Dear Tommy,

Watch and pray, that you enter not into temptation! Probably this illness was sent as a means of preserving you from greater evils.

Your reasons for desiring to be in another circuit are certainly of weight; and I do not yet see any reason why you cannot be in the circuit with Joseph Harper. But no circuit must be left without preachers during the Conference. I am, dear Tommy,

> Yours affectionately,

J. Wesley

Address: 'To / Mr. Tattershall / At Mr. [William] Hutton's / In Epworth / Near Thorne / Yorkshire'.

Source: published transcription; Byrth, 'Memoir', xxxii.

To Ellen Gretton

Newcastle

June 22, 1782

My Dear Miss Gretton,

But that I am in hopes it may be some comfort to you, I should not put you to the expense of a letter.[194] I want to help you, not to hurt you, because I feel a great affection for you. God has chosen you in the furnace of affliction. And when you have been tried, you shall come forth as gold.[195] You know and feel that all this is for your profit, that you may be a partaker of his holiness. Let all of you that are in one house be of one heart and one mind, striving together for the hope of the gospel![196] You have already two or three in Grantham that both love and fear God.[197] And God does not

---

[194] Remember that recipients paid the postage charge for letters.

[195] See Job 23:10.

[196] See Phil. 1:27.

[197] Robert Derry, Dorothy Fisher, etc.

despise the day of small things.[198] Though as yet it is but the dawn of the day, yet we are sure the sun of righteousness will rise upon you, with healing in his wings.[199] You know not but a little one will become a thousand! The Lord will hasten it in his season.

I am, my dear Nelly,   5
    Yours affectionately,

                                                                    J. Wesley

Address: 'To / Miss Gretton / At Mr. [Robert] Derry's, Shoemaker / In
    Grantham / Cross post Lincolnshire'.   10
Source: holograph; Bridwell Library (SMU).[200]

                                                                    15
To Hester Ann Roe[201]

                                                        Darlington
                                                     June 25, 1782   20
My Dear Hetty,
    It is certain there has been for these forty years such an outpour-ing of the Spirit and such an increase of vital religion as has not been in England for many centuries. And it does not appear that the work of God at all decays. In many places there is a consider-   25
able increase of it. So that we have reason to hope that the time is at hand when the kingdom of God shall come with power,[202] and all the people of this poor heathen land shall know him, from the least to the greatest.[203]
    I am glad you had so good an opportunity of talking with Mr.   30
[John] Sellers.[204] Surely, if prayer was made for him, so useful an in-strument as he was would not be suffered to lose all his usefulness.

---

[198] See Zech. 4:10.
[199] See Mal. 4:2.
[200] Held previously in the Upper Room Museum, L-167.
[201] JW was replying to Roe's letter of June 13, 1782.
[202] See Mark 9:1.
[203] See Jer. 31:34; Heb. 8:11.
[204] Sellers had heard JW preach in Apr. 1781 and Roe conversed with him after JW left Chester; see (Roe) Rogers, *Extracts*, 188.

I wish you could make such little excursions oftener, as you always find your labour is not in vain.[205]

Take particular care, my dear Hetty, of the children. They are glorious monuments of divine grace; and I think you have a particular affection for them and a gift to profit them.

I always am, my dear friend,
>Yours most affectionately,

J. Wesley

Source: published transcription; Benson, Works, 16:264–65.

To John Francis Valton[206]

Leeds
June 29, 1782

My Dear Brother,

I cannot allow Joshua Sc[h]olefield to be any longer a leader. And if he will lead the class, whether I will or no, I require you to put him out of our society. If twenty of his class will leave the society too, they must. The first loss is the best. Better forty members should be lost than our discipline lost. They are no Methodists that will bear no restraints. Explain this at large to the society.

>Your affectionate friend and brother,

J. Wesley

Address: 'To Mr. John Valton / At Birstal / Near Leeds'.
Source: published transcription; Robert Young, *The Southern World: Journal of a Deputation from the Wesleyan Conference to Australia and Polynesia* (London: Hamilton, Adams, and Co., 1854), 433.

---

[205] The transcription published in Benson gives a paragraph here that was actually part of JW's letter to Roe on Jan 17, 1782, about receiving a letter from Elizabeth Ritchie.

[206] This is the second letter that was merged into that of Jan. 18, 1782 (see above) in the published transcription in *WMM* 37 (1824): 306–07. Young's transcription dates the letter 'June 23', but JW's manuscript '9' and '3' can be similar, and JW did not arrive in Leeds until June 29 according to his Journal. The address for the letter comes from the *WMM* transcription, reflecting that Valton had been moved mid-year from Manchester to Birstall.

To John Bredin

Birmingham
July 8, 1782   5

My Dear Brother,

Your letter reached me this morning.[207] I know not whether it would not be best for you to spend the ensuing year in London. There you might have the best medical advice, and might preach more or less as your strength allowed.   10

Adam Clarke may easily get over to Liverpool or Chester. But ships sometimes go from Newry to Bristol, and very frequently from Dublin, especially at this time of the year. My kind love to Alleck Knox.

I am,   15

Your affectionate friend and brother,

J. Wesley

Address: 'To / Mr. John Bredin / At Mr. McKean's / in / Londonderry'.
Postmark: 'Birmingham'.   20
Source: holograph; Wesley House (Cambridge University), Archives, 9/8/5.

25

To Mary (Bosanquet) Fletcher[208]

Birmingham   30
July 12, 1782

My Dear Sister,

I was much pleased with the thought of meeting Mr. [John] Fletcher and you here. But the will of the Lord be done!

It gives me satisfaction to hear that the work of our Lord prospers   35
in your hands. That weak young man (whether with design or with-

---

[207] This letter is not known to survive.
[208] JW was replying to her letter of July 7, 1782.

out) had damped it sufficiently.[209] I trust the flame will now revive
and increase on every side.

It seems to have been the will of God for many years that I should
have none to share my proper labour. My brother never did.[210]
Thomas Walsh began to do it; so did John Jones. But one died and
one fainted. Dr. [Thomas] Coke promises fair; at present I have
none like-minded.

When a lot is cast, I have no more to say. Peace be with your
spirits!

I am, my dear sister,
Your ever affectionate brother,

[J. Wesley]

Address: ' To / Mrs Fletcher / At Madeley near Shifnal / Salop'.[211]
Postmark: 'Birmingham'.
Source: published transcription; Telford, Letters, 7:128.

To Ann Loxdale

Birmingham
July 12, 1782

My Dear Miss Loxdale,

It raised some wonder in me that I had not a line from you in so
long a time.[212] I began to be almost afraid that your love was growing cold. And it would not be at all strange if it did—it is more
strange if it does not, especially while you have an affair in hand
that naturally tends to engross the whole thought. Whoever follows
the few plain directions which are given in the sermon on enthusi-

[209] Rev. Alexander Benjamin Greaves (c. 1751–1834) was Fletcher's curate at Madeley
1777–81, serving the church alone most of this time while Fletcher was in Europe. Fletcher
heard of problems while he was away, and was dismayed by the lack of spiritual life in the parish
on his return. See Fletcher's letter to Greaves, May 31, MARC, MAM Fl. 18/3.

[210] This judgement is coloured by the alienation between the brothers after CW's marriage and his interference in JW's relationship with Grace (Norman) Murray. Prior to that CW
shared very actively alongside JW.

[211] The address portion, separated from the letter, originally held at Upper Room Museum, L-141, is now at Bridwell (SMU).

[212] JW was replying to Loxdale's letter of June 1, 1782, which lamented her delay in
writing.

asm will easily and distinctly see what is the will of God concerning any point in question.[213] That is, provided the eye be single, provided he has one design and one desire. But it is a just observation, 'As a very little dust will disorder the motion of a clock, and as a very little sand will hinder the sight of the eye, so a very little desire or selfish design will greatly obstruct the eye of the soul.'[214] By experience, the strongest of all arguments, you have been once and again convinced that salvation from inbred sin is received by simple faith, although it is certain there is a gradual work both preceding and following.

Is it not, then, your wisdom not willingly to converse with any that oppose this great and important truth? If you play with fire, will you not be burnt sooner or later? Nay, have you not been burnt already? I remain,

My dear Nancy,

Yours most affectionately,

J. Wesley

Source: published transcription; *Methodist Magazine* 32 (1809): 348.

To Penelope Newman

[Birmingham]
July 12, 1782

My Dear Sister,

I do not yet see any reason why Jonathan Coussins should not labour next year in the Gloucestershire circuit. But I do not use to determine things of this kind absolutely before the Conference.[215]

---

[213] Sermon 37, 'The Nature of Enthusiasm', 2:46–60 in this edn.

[214] One of JW's maxims from Jean Duvergier de Hauranne, Abbé de Saint-Cyran, included in 'Farther Thoughts upon Christian Perfection', II.7, 13:128 in this edn.

[215] Coussins, currently in the Sarum circuit, was appointed to Gloucestershire at the 1782 Conference. Newman's letter requesting this is not known to survive. Newman and Coussins would be married in Oct. 1782.

Afflictions, you know, are only blessings in disguise.[216] 'He prepares occasions of fighting that thou mayest conquer.'[217] Whenever you have an opportunity of making a little excursion it will be for good.

5   I am, dear Penny,
    Your affectionate brother,

[J. Wesley]

Address: 'To / Miss P. Newman / In Cheltenham / Gloucestershire'.
Source: published transcription; Telford, *Letters*, 7:129.

10

To Ellen Gretton

15

London
July 23, 1782

My Dear Miss Gretton,
    We are frequently called to give up our own will, not only when it
20 is contrary to the will of God, but when it *seems* to us we desire to do this or that purely to promote his glory. And in cases of this kind we are required (in a sense) to give up our understanding as well as our will. By making this sacrifice we profit much. We die to ourselves and advance in the life of God.
25   But I do not apprehend you are at all obliged to make a sacrifice of all your religious friends, all the opportunities of doing good, and all the means of grace which you now enjoy, if there be any possibility of avoiding it. You have undoubtedly returned your thankful acknowledgments both to your father and your brother for their kind
30 offer.[218] But I should think it was your best way neither to accept nor refuse it for the present.
    I commend you to his care who loves you, and am, dear Nelly,
        Yours affectionately,

J. Wesley

[216] See the note in JW to Ann Tindall, Apr. 23, 1776.

[217] Thomas à Kempis, *Imitation of Christ*, I.xi.4 (I.ix.4 in JW's abridged version). For instances where JW gave this maxim without indicating it was a quotation, see his letters to Damaris Perronet, Mar. 30, 1771, 28:365 in this edn.; Elizabeth Briggs, Apr. 14, 1771, 28:370 in this edn.; and Mary (Edwin) Savage, May 6, 1774, 29:29–30 in this edn.

[218] Gretton's family was trying to draw her away from Methodist influence. See Cocking, *Grantham, 181.*

I know not but I may find a way for your coming to Conference.

Source: holograph; privately held (MARC, MA 1985/002; a photocopy).

5

To Ann Loxdale

London   10
July 24, 1782

My Dear Miss Loxdale,

Two or three years ago, when the French were expected to land, I made an offer to the Government.[219] It was not accepted, so I thought of it no more. But some months since, Captain [Thomas] 15 Webb renewed it to Colonel [Isaac] Barré. I knew nothing of the matter. But I would not oppose it, as neither did I forward it. I barely gave him leave to inquire what number of the Methodists were willing to embark with him.[220] But I suppose the whole is now at an end, as Colonel Barré is out of place.[221] 20

I wish you to retain a close acquaintance with Mr. ____.[222] He is an upright man. And I am in hopes we may now set his head right, as he that confounded his intellect is gone to another world.

There is no danger of your taking any step that is materially wrong if you continue instant in prayer.[223] But I know so little of the 25 thing you refer to that I can say little about it. Only, do not expect that any creature will increase your happiness any farther than it increases your knowledge and love of God.

I am, my dear Nancy,
Yours affectionately,   30

J. Wesley

in another hand on back: 'To Miss Loxdale'.

35

Source: holograph; New York, Pierpont Morgan Library, MA 516.12.

---

[219] See JW's endorsement of a proposal by Thomas Webb to raise a Methodist militia, Oct. 24, 1779, 29:518–19 in this edn.
[220] See JW to Thomas Webb, May 25, 1782.
[221] Barré had now been moved from Secretary at War to Treasurer of the Navy.
[222] The name has been cut out.
[223] See Rom. 12:12.

To Thomas Rutherford

London
July 29, 1782

5 Dear Tommy,

I doubt not but the work of God will revive in Dublin; for brother [Andrew] Blair and you will not only preach the full Methodist doctrine, but enforce our discipline in every point, and preach abroad at every opportunity.[224]

10 Pray tell Richard Calcut I thank him for his letter. I have a letter likewise from George Pellat, of Eyrecourt, and am glad to hear his daughter is so well married.[225]

Now I speak a word to *you* in your ear. Thomas Bethell has been basely used.[226] James Deaves is deeply prejudiced against him, and 15 has prejudiced many others. Do all you can, by little and little, to remove that prejudice. He is a downright honest man, and 'a troublesome man' only to mongrel Methodists. I thank nobody for hindering his prayer-meeting, which was a direct affront to *me*. Give him the note which I have enclosed.[227]

20 I am, with love to sister [Isabella] Rutherford, dear Tommy,
Your affectionate friend and brother,

J. Wesley

Source: holograph; MARC, WCB, D6/3/1/10.

25

To Alexander Knox

London
30 July 30, 1782

Dear Alleck,

There is no great danger that I should neglect to answer any letter which I receive from *you*. I do not remember to have received

---

[224] Rutherford and Blair were appointed to the Dublin circuit when the Irish preachers met with Thomas Coke in June 1782; an appointment formally listed in the *Minutes* of the Conference in London, Aug. 6, 1782 (see 10:523 in this edn.).

[225] Neither of these letters are known to survive.

[226] Bethell had confronted Joseph Pilmore, the previous Assistant for the Dublin circuit, over actions that Bethell judged would split the society, earning him disdain from many itinerants. Matters did not resolve, so JW assisted Bethell in relocating to London in 1784, where continuing resistance by John Atlay and others led Bethell to move into Baptist circles. See Thomas Bethell, *A Letter to Mr. John Atlay* (London: for Bethell, 1788), 10–13.

[227] This note is not known to survive.

any letter from you when I was in Edinburgh.[228] Neither have I received fifteen guineas, or any sum that I recollect, from any person
of the name of Harvey;[229] except five guineas which were given me
by Miss Harvey of Hertfordshire, for a poor woman in London.[230]

There is no doubt but there is a natural disorder in your body,   5
which (for want of better language) we call weakness of nerves.[231]
And there is a disorder in your mind which is surely natural, namely unbelief. But without question there is something preternatural
too, for Satan knows whereof you are made and will not fail to press
every advantage which bodily weakness gives him.   10

I have known never two experiences more exactly resemble each
other than yours and that of George Clark (now printing in the *Arminian Magazine*[232]). He was for many years thoroughly miserable.
About twenty years ago he was perfected in love, and has been ever
since one of the happiest of men. Such, I expect, will Alexander   15
Knox be! What a miracle of mercy!

> Let the Spirit now come down!
> Let the blessing now take place![233]
                                                                         20
Look up! Look up! The Lord is at hand![234] Let him take you all
together!

I am,

   Ever yours,

                       J. Wesley   25

---

[228] JW had been in Edinburgh in early June 1782, and again the middle of that month.

[229] See JW to Knox, Sept. 3, 1781, 29:681–82 in this edn.; and Apr. 5, 1783.

[230] Elizabeth Harvey (1744–1807) was a sister of Rev. Edmund Harvey (1739–1823), rector of Finningley, who invited JW to preach in his church on July 11, 1770 (see *Journal*, 22:240
in this edn.). Edmund's first appointment in 1763 was as curate to Rev. John Rooke, vicar of
Willian and Hinxworth, Hertfordshire. Edmund married the vicar's daughter Mary Rooke
(1742–75) and appears to have remained in Hinxworth after receiving the living at Finningley.
His sister Elizabeth came to reside in Hinxworth, and became a strong supporter of the Methodists, building chapels at Baldock, Biggleswade, and Stevenage, as well as a residence for the
preachers of that circuit; see *WMM* 52 (1829):291. JW had been at her home on July 19, 1782
(see *Journal*, 23:247 in this edn.).

[231] See JW, 'Thoughts on "Nervous Disorders"' (1786), with introductory comment,
32:607–21 in this edn.

[232] George Clark (1711–97) was converted at the age of thirty-five after hearing JW
preach, and became a key leader at the Foundery, and later City Road Chapel. He was among
those who testified clearly to Christian perfection. An abstract of his journal appeared in *AM* 5
(1782):298–301, 351–55, 404–408, 465–68, 519–24, 575–80, 639–41.

[233] CW, 'The Salutation', st. 1, *HSP* (1742), 157 (JW added the emphases).

[234] See Phil. 4:5.

Pity but Adam Clarke had come over with Dr. [Thomas] Coke.[235]

Address: 'To / Mr Alexr Knox / in Londonderry'.
Postmarks: '31/IY' and 'AU/6'.
5   *Endorsement*: by Knox, 'From the Rev. Mr Wesley / London July 31st
          1782'.
      Source: holograph; Bridwell Library (SMU).[236]

10

To Mrs. Nuttal

                                                            London
15   July 31, 1782
My Dear Sister,
      You judge right that preaching abroad is an admirable means of
increasing the work of God, as many will then have opportunity of
learning the truth that otherwise would never have heard it. Let not
20   the stewards therefore, or any other persons, discourage the preachers from doing it. Rather let all who wish religion to flourish exhort
and encourage them to it.
      You would do well during this fine season to make every oppor-
tunity of hearing the good word. Otherwise there will be a danger
25   that your desires of being altogether a Christian should faint and
die away.[237] And, indeed, the staying always at home may gradually
impair your bodily health. For exercise in the open air is absolutely
necessary to this. Therefore on a very fair day, if you can go no farther, you should walk half an hour or an hour in your garden. In the
30   meantime, let it be your great desire and care to exercise yourself
unto godliness.[238] Be a Christian indeed! Be all alive to God! And
you will give more and more satisfaction to,
      My dear sister,
          Yours very affectionately,
35
                                                            J. Wesley

---

[235] See JW to John Bredin, Apr. 6, 1782. Clarke would come over in early Aug.
[236] Held previously in the Upper Room Museum, L-30.
[237] See JW, *The Almost Christian* (1741), 1:131–41 in this edn.
[238] See 1 Tim. 4:7.

Address: 'To / Mrs Nuttal / to be left at Mrs Warmsley's / Proud Preston'.[239]

Postmark: '2/AV'. *Charge*: '4'.

Source: holograph; Pitts Library (Emory), John Wesley Papers (MSS
153), 3/28.

To Catherine Warren

London
July 31, 1782

My Dear Sister,

It pleases God to give me much better health in general than I
had at five-and-twenty. For many years also I was frequently weary, but I know not now what weariness means. I have just strength
enough for what I am called to do; and at the end of my work I feel
just the same as at the beginning.

Till very lately I had hopes of paying you a short visit after the
Conference. But I find it cannot be. I *must* see them in the west of
Cornwall, where there is a great revival of the work of God. And
before I can return thence there will hardly so much time remain as
will be due to the Bristol circuit.

Thomas Tennant writes to me and desires he may not continue
any longer in Pembrokeshire.[240] However, I will tell him the desire
of his friends in Wales, and then leave him to his choice. Mr. [Sam-
uel] Randal has been there two years already. So it is time for him
to remove.

You are exactly in your place. If you desire it, you shall have more
employment. But you would be a loser if you had less. Peace be with
all your spirits!

I am, my dear Kitty,

Your ever affectionate brother,

J. Wesley

[239] Preston, Lancashire was called 'Proud Preston' because of its abundance of gentry.

[240] Thomas Tennant was admitted 'on trial' as an itinerant at the 1770 Conference (see
10:380 in this edn.). He served for 22 years, though his efforts were hindered at times from a
nervous disorder. See *Minutes* (post-Wesley, 1793), 1:276. He did return to Pembrokeshire for
the coming year.

Address: 'To / Miss Warren / in / Haverford West'.
Postmark: '1/AV'. Charge: '4'.
Source: holograph; MARC, MAM JW 5/44.

5

To Joseph Benson[241]

near London
10   August 3, 1782
Dear Joseph,
    Do not you know that all the preachers cannot leave a circuit at
once? Therefore, if you left it, brother [Christopher] Hopper could
not.[242] Perhaps, likewise, I can depend upon your judgment more
15 than that of another man.
    Two or three years ago, when the kingdom was in imminent dan-
ger, I made an offer to the Government of raising some men.[243] The
Secretary of War (by the king's order) wrote me word that 'it was
not necessary; but if it ever should be necessary, his Majesty would
20 let me know.'[244] I never renewed the offer, and never intended it. But
Captain Webb, without my knowing anything of the matter, went
to Colonel [Isaac] Barré, the new Secretary of War, and renewed
that offer.[245] The Colonel (I verily believe, to avoid his importunity)
asked him how many men we could raise. But the Colonel is out of
25 place.[246] So the thing is at an end.
    I read over both the sermons; but I did not see anything materi-
ally wrong in either.[247]
    I am, with love to sister [Sarah] Benson, dear Joseph
        Your affectionate brother,
30   J. Wesley

We will consider what you propose.

[241] Benson's letter that drew this reply is not known to survive.
[242] Benson and Hopper were serving the Leeds circuit, with Alexander Mather as
Assistant.
[243] See JW's endorsement of a proposal by Thomas Webb to raise a Methodist militia,
Oct. 24, 1779, 29:518–19 in this edn.
[244] See Charles Jenkinson to JW, Nov. 10, 1779.
[245] See JW to Thomas Webb, May 25, 1782.
[246] Barré was moved from Secretary at War to Treasurer of the Navy in June 1782, became
Paymaster of the Forces in Aug. 1, 1782.
[247] The manuscripts for Joseph Benson, *Two Sermons on Sanctification* (Leeds: J. Bowling,
1782).

Address: 'To / Mr Benson / At the Preachinghouse / near / Leeds'.
Postmark: '3/AV'.[248] Charge: '4'.
Endorsement: by Benson, 'Aug 3 1782'.
Source: holograph; Bridwell Library (SMU).

5

To Ann Bolton[249]

near London   10
August 3, 1782

My Dear Nancy,

I thought you had known the truth of the old saying, 'a friend is made for adversity.'[250] Very probably you have suffered more by keeping your sufferings to yourself. But still we know the Lord is   15
king and ruleth all things both in heaven and earth.[251]

I am glad your brother's distresses are a little relieved. I shall not be sorry when he is entirely quit of Finstock.[252] I never expected great things from it, but I thought he knew better than me.

I believe, if you feed the poor man three or four weeks with ab-   20
solutely nothing but bread and milk, it will totally restore his sens-es.[253] I have known it tried here, and the patient recovered entirely.

Miss [Elizabeth] Ritchie is just alive; she is still hovering between life and death.[254]

I have divided Nottingham circuit into two, and stationed brother   25
[Thomas] Warrick in the Derby part of it.[255]

Do not, my dear Nancy, again delay so long writing to

Yours most affectionately,

J. Wesley

30

Address: 'To / Miss Bolton / In Witney / Oxfordshire'.
Postmark: '3/AV'. Charge: '3'.
Endorsement: by Bolton, 'Augst 3d 1782'.
Source: holograph; MARC, MAM JW 1/94.

[248] It was first stamped '3/IY', a mistake, then stamped correctly on top of the first mark.
[249] Bolton's letter to JW is not known to survive.
[250] See JW to Hannah Ball, June 28, 1781; and JW to Bolton, July 17, 1781.
[251] See Ps. 103:19.
[252] Referring to the business Edward Bolton Jr. set up in Finstock, which was failing; see JW to Ann Bolton, May 13, 1774 (29:34–35 in this edn.); and Feb. 20, 1781 (29:628).
[253] This is a cure for 'raging madness' in *Primitive Physic*; see 32:204 in this edn.
[254] Ritchie was recovering; see her letter to JW of Aug. 15, 1782.
[255] While Derby was created as a distinct circuit from Nottingham at the 1782 Confer-ence, Warrick was stationed to Leicestershire; see 10:521 in this edn.

To Hannah Ball[256]

London
August 4, 1782

My Dear Sister,

I almost wondered that I did not receive a line from you for so long a season. I could not easily believe that your love was grown cold, and I am glad to hear it is not.[257] But it is a discouragement to see one month pass after another without any perceptible fruit of our labour, without any discernible outpouring of the Spirit, either in his convincing or converting influences. But beware you do not cast away hope! He will come, and will not tarry.[258] You know not how soon he may send on all around you

> A kindly, gracious shower
> Of heart-reviving love![259]

Look for it, my dear Hannah! Pray for it! Expect it soon! And you will not be disappointed. Peace be with all your spirits!

I am, my sister and friend,
Your affectionate brother,

J. Wesley

Source: holograph; MARC, MA 2008/013.

To John Bredin

London
August 4, 1782

My Dear Brother,

In your present state you must not attempt to travel. It is as much as your life is worth. You may be a supernumerary in whatever place

---

[256] While the address portion is missing, her first name is used and the holograph was part of the papers of Hannah Ball, transcribed in her *Memoir* (p. 156). Ball's letter to JW, which drew this response, is not known to survive.

[257] The last documented exchange of letters between JW and Ball was Mar. 1782.

[258] See Heb. 10:37.

[259] CW, 'Psalm 133', st. 9, *HSP* (1742), 175.

you judge most advisable; and the little salary, the £12, we will allow
from hence.[260]

I do not understand what is the accusation against Hugh Moore.
Simply administering an oath is a folly, but I know not that it is contrary to any law.[261] If he is afraid of staying at Coleraine (although I   5
know not why), let him change with a Sligo or Castlebar preacher.[262]

I am,
    Your affectionate friend and brother,

                            J. Wesley
                                     10

Source: secondary manuscript transcription; Drew, Methodist Archives.

                                             15

To Ann Tindall

                                     London
                            August 5, 1782   20

My Dear Sister,

If you continue at peace and unity with each other, you will surely
increase in number. For the God of peace will be in the midst of you
and will enlarge your borders.[263]

That is as easy and ready a method as can be taken. Let sister   25
Burn pay you the two [shillings] and sixpence a week, and charge it
to John ⟨At⟩lay's[264] account. By even a small contribution, you will
be g⟨etti⟩ng forward, if it be but slowly.

I hope you do not grow weary of your labour of love. Speak as
freely to brother [William] Dufton or his fellow labourers, as you   30
used to do to John Fenwick, of anything which you think may either
further or hinder the work of God.[265] The more you exert the zeal
which has [been] given you, the more it will increase.

---

[260] Bredin's name appears among the located ministers receiving support starting with
the 1782 *Minutes*, 10:527 in this edn.

[261] It is unclear whether this relates to the matter discussed earlier in JW to Bredin, Apr.
10, 1782.

[262] In Conference a few days later it was decided to transfer Hugh Moore from Ireland to
Aberdeen, Scotland; see 10:522 in this edn.

[263] See Zeph. 3:17 and Exod. 34:24.

[264] A small hole is torn away by the wax seal, affecting two lines.

[265] Dufton (as Assistant), Lancelot Harrison, and Charles Atmore were assigned to the
Scarborough circuit at the 1782 Conference.

I am, dear Nancy,
    Yours affectionately,

J. Wesley

5   *Address*: 'To / Miss Tindall / in / Hull Scarborough'.
Endorsement: by Tindall, '5 Aug 1782'.
Source: holograph; British Library, Department of Manuscripts, Add.
    MS. 43695, ff. 69–70.

10

To Francis Wolf

15

London
August 6, 1782

My Dear Brother,
    Necessity has no law. Till your strength is restored, do all the
20 good you can as a local preacher.[266]
    According to my last regulations, pray inform the preachers and
Captain [Richard] Williams my plan is this: Taunton, Thursday,
August 15; Exeter, Friday, [August] 16; Plymouth, Monday, [August] 19; St. Austell, Wednesday, [August] 21; Helstone, Thursday,
25 [August] 22; Penzance, Friday [and Saturday], [August] 23 and 24;
St. Just, Sunday, [August] 25; and in the west, St. Ives, Thursday,
[August] 29; Redruth, Saturday, [August] 31; St. Anne's, Redruth,
Gwennap, Sunday, September 1.
    I am,
30   Your affectionate brother,

J. Wesley

Address: 'To / Mr Francis Wolf / In Redruth / Cornwall'.
Postmark: '6/AV'. Charge: '4'.
35 *Source*: holograph; MARC, MA 1998/016.

---

[266] Wolf desisted from travelling in 1782 and settled in Redruth, where Wolf ministered locally until his death in 1807; see *MM* 31 (1808): 585.

To Jasper Winscom

London
August 10, 1782   5

Dear Jasper,

That the work of God has not prospered in the Salisbury circuit for several years is none of your fault. I am persuaded you have his work at heart and will do all that is in your power to promote it. So will Mr. [John] Mason; so will the other preachers.[267] Look for   10
happy days!

    I am,

        Your affectionate brother,

J. Wesley

15

Address: 'To Jasper Winscom'.[268]
Endorsement: by Winscom, 'J. Wesley Aug 10 1782'.
Source: holograph; Bridwell Library (SMU).

20

To William Sagar

25

London
August 11, 1782

My Dear Brother,

    Certainly nothing can more effectually stop the work of God than the breaking in of Calvinism upon you. I hope your three preach-   30
ers will calmly and diligently oppose it;[269] although not so much by preaching as by visiting the people from house to house, dispersing the little tracts as it were with both hands.

        Your affectionate brother,

J. Wesley   35

Source: published transcription; Moore, *Burnley*, 37.

[267] Mason had just been assigned as the Assistant for the Sarum circuit, alongside William Hoskins, William Moore, and Nathanael Ward.

[268] The letter was likely personally delivered to Winscom by Mason.

[269] The three preachers just assigned to the Colne circuit, in which Sagar resided, were Thomas Hanson (Assistant), Thomas Johnson, and David Evans.

To Harriett Cooper

London
August 12, 1782

My Dear Harriett,

Take place on the coach, and I will pay the expense. Make no delay, but come away immediately to

Yours affectionately,

[J. Wesley]

Come straight to my house in the City Road, near Moorfields.

Address: 'To / Mrs. Harriet Cooper / Liverpool'.
Source: published transcription; Telford, *Letters*, 7:136.

To Robert Hopkins

London
August 13, 1782

Dear Robert,

I am very well satisfied with your letter.[270] I could take your word in a greater matter than this. The whole seems to have arisen from a misapprehension of your words, so the matter is at an end.

I am,

Your affectionate brother,

J. Wesley

Source: published transcription; Hopkins, *Life*, 9.

---

[270] Hopkins had been serving at Norwich for the appointment year just ending. His letter is not known to survive, which leaves unclear the matter that had been reported.

To the Rev. Thomas Davenport

Bristol
August 14, 1782

Dear Sir, 5

It would have given me a good deal of satisfaction to have had a little conversation with you.[271] But I do not stay long in one place. I have no resting-place on earth:

> A poor wayfaring man, 10
> I dwell awhile in tents below,
> Or gladly wander to and fro,
> Till I my Canaan gain.[272]

You would have been very welcome at our Conference. Mr. Pugh 15
and Mr. [William] Dodwell were present at it, and I believe are more determined than ever to spend their whole strength in saving their own souls and them that hear them.[273]

I believe one of our preachers that are stationed in the Leicester circuit will call upon you at Allexton. And I make no doubt but 20
some of the seed which you have been long sowing will then grow up. No one should wish or pray for persecution. On the contrary, we are to avoid it to the uttermost of our power. 'When they persecute you in one city, flee unto another.'[274] Yet, when it does come, notwithstanding all our care to avoid it, God will extract good out 25
of evil.

Tomorrow I am to set out for Cornwall. In about three weeks I expect to be here again. In the beginning of October I generally move towards London, in the neighbourhood of which I usually spend the winter. 30

I am, dear sir,
Your affectionate friend and brother,

J. Wesley

Address: 'To / The Revd Mr Davenport / near Uppingham / Rutlandshire'.
Source: holograph; privately held (WWEP holds photocopy). 35

---

[271] Davenport had apparently written, expressing regret that he and JW had not gotten together when JW was in the Leicester area in mid-July 1782. The letter is not known to survive.
[272] CW, 'The Pilgrim', st. 6, *Redemption Hymns* (1747), 67.
[273] Rev. John Pugh (1742–99), a graduate of Hertford College, Oxford, was vicar of North and South Rauceby from 1771 till his death.
[274] Matt. 10:23.

To Ellen Gretton[275]

Bristol
September 7, 1782

5 My Dear Sister,

It pleases God to lead you in a rough path for the present. But it is enough that all will end well. I never knew any disorder in the bowels which might not be speedily cured by drinking plentifully of lemonade;[276] unless in a few peculiar constitutions, which could not
10 bear lemons. And the drinking nettle-tea (instead of common tea) will commonly perfect the cure.

If occasion require, she should certainly return to some place where she is not known. And I hope God will incline his heart to allow her what is necessary.[277]

15 The fearing lest we should be called hence before we are perfected in love is one species of taking thought for the morrow.[278] You have nothing to do with this. Live today! And

> Be *now* willing to receive
20 > What his goodness waits to give.[279]

I am, my dear Nelly,
Yours affectionately,

J. Wesley

25 *Source*: holograph; Bridwell Library (SMU).

To Richard Rodda[280]

30

Bristol
September 9, 1782

Dear Richard,

You should take particular care that your circuit be never with-
35 out an assortment of all the saleable books, especially the *Appeals*,

---

[275] While the address portion is missing, the letter fits a rhythm of JW's current correspondence with Gretton, and he addressed her as 'Nelly'. Gretton's letter to JW is not known to survive.

[276] Cf. the remedy for a 'bilious colic' in *Primitive Physic*, 10:151 in this edn.

[277] The reference is apparently to a young woman for whom Gretton is caring.

[278] See Matt. 6:34.

[279] An adaptation of CW, Hymn on Jeremiah 17:9, st. 10, *HSP* (1742), 41.

[280] Rodda was currently Assistant for the Oxfordshire circuit.

the *Sermons*, Kempis,[281] and the *Primitive Physic*—which no family should be without. Send for these, and (according to the rule of Conference[282]) take them into your own keeping. You seem to be remarkably diligent in spreading the books; let none rob you of this glory. 5

I am glad you have talked with Mr. Atkins. You should give him a set of *Appeals* in my name. If Mr. Hawes can procure the church, well.

I expect to [be] on Monday, October 14, at Wallingford; Tuesday, [October] 15, Witney; Wednesday, [October] 16, Oxford; Thurs- 10 day, [October] 17, [High] Wycombe.

Order the quarterly meeting how you please.

I am, dear Richard,
    Your affectionate friend and brother,

J. Wesley 15

Address: 'To / Mr Rd Rodda / At the Preachinghouse / In High Wycombe / Bucks'.
Postmarks: 'Bristol' and '10/SE'.
Source: holograph; Black Forest, South Australia, South Australia Synod 20 Uniting Church History Centre.[283]

To Joseph Taylor[284] 25

Bristol
September 9, 1782

Dear Joseph,

You will now have full scope for the exercise of every talent that 30 God has given you. And you have fellow labourers after your own heart. See that no strangeness creep in between you! If you continue instant in prayer, I trust there will be such a work in Cornwall as never was yet.

---

[281] I.e., JW's *Extract of the Christian Pattern; or, A Treatise of the Imitation of Christ* (1742).

[282] E.g., 'Minutes' (1749), Q. 7, 10:234 in this edn.; *Minutes* (1767), Q. 27, 10:350; *Minutes* (1768), Q. 23, 10:360–61; and *Minutes* (1774), Q. 21, 10:435 in this edn.

[283] Held previously at Parkin-Wesley Theological College.

[284] Joseph Taylor (1752–1830) was admitted 'on trial' as an itinerant in 1777 (see 10:464 in this edn.). He had just been appointed for the first time as an Assistant, in the western Cornwall circuit. Taylor would serve for 44 years, before settling in Derby. He was one of three preachers JW ordained for Scotland in 1785, and he was elected President of Conference in 1802. See *Minutes* (post-Wesley, 1830), 6:555–56; and Vickers, *Dictionary*, 345.

You remember the rule of Conference that every Assistant should take my books in his own hands, as having better opportunities of dispersing them than any private person can possibly have.[285] I desire you would do this without delay. The *Primitive Physic* should be in every family. So should the *Christian Pattern* if possible. Of
5   the *[Arminian] Magazines* I need say nothing. Herein I am persuaded you will tread in James Rogers's steps, and go beyond him as far as you can.[286]

The children will require much attention; and the bands too, or they will moulder away.
10 I am, dear Joseph,
Your affectionate friend and brother,

J. Wesley

15 *Address*: 'To / Mr Jos. Taylor / At the Preachinghouse / In Redruth / Cornwall'.
Postmark: 'Bristol'.
Source: holograph; MARC, MAM JW 5/2.

20

To the Rev. James Creighton

25   Shepton Mallet
September 10, 1782
Dear Sir,
You have sufficient indication of providence, that you are at present just in your place. So long as it is the design of our great Shep-
30 herd that you should remain in your curacy, he will continue to put a bridle in the mouth of the Archdeacon and all your *small friends*.[287] But if he should at any time see you would be more useful elsewhere, you will have a clear and full discharge.

The present phenomenon of Methodism is utterly new—one has
35 never appeared before upon earth. I do not read of any other reformers for these thousand years who have spent their whole time and strength in reforming first the tempers and then the lives of

---

[285] See the annotations on the letter to Richard Rodda of the same date.
[286] Taylor had served under James Rogers (as Assistant) in Sheffield the previous year.
[287] While Creighton retained his curacy, he was now preaching in several surrounding settings, which drew reprimand from his superiors; see Creighton to JW, Jan. 20, 1785.

themselves and those that heard them. All others (who had really the power of God attending their ministrations) spent a part, perhaps the greatest part, of their time and strength in reforming men's opinions or modes of worship. The Methodists let those stand as they are. They let every man abound in his own opinion,[288] and employ their whole force in destroying both the outward and inward works of the devil and promoting the kingdom of God among men—righteousness and peace and joy in the Holy Ghost.[289]

It is an amazing instance of divine providence that they are permitted to do this, to range up and down the three kingdoms uncontrolled and overturn Satan's kingdom. It would almost induce one to think that he is bound already;[290] otherwise he would fight, that his kingdom might not be delivered up. If any are weary of thus labouring in our Lord's vineyard, and seek to *settle* in the world, it is certain their love is grown cold and they are already settled upon their lees. They are relapsed into the love of ease, of honour, or money. It is well if their end be not destruction.[291]

If you observe any of our young men near you who are tempted to depart from the work, a word from *you* may have more weight than from another and make them sensible of the blessings they enjoy.

May *you* never be weary of well doing. In due time you shall reap, if you faint not.[292] I am, dear sir,

Your affectionate friend and brother,

J. Wesley

Address: 'To / The Revd Mr Creighton / Near Belturbet / Ireland / +p [i.e., crosspost] Gloster'.
Postmarks: 'Frome' and 'SE/16'.
Endorsement: by Creighton, 'Septm 10. 1782' and 'Twenty first Letter'.[293]
Source: holograph; Bridwell Library (SMU).

---

[288] See Rom. 14:5.
[289] See Rom. 14:17.
[290] See Rev. 20:1–3.
[291] See Phil. 3:19.
[292] See Gal. 6:9.
[293] The sixteenth through twentieth letters are not known to survive.

To William Roberts[294]

Frome
September 12, 1782

I was much concerned when I saw your last.[295] And as 'life for delays [...] no time will give',[296] especially *my* life, which is far spent, I take the first opportunity of speaking once for all. You are in a large way of business, wherein I suppose you clear one (if not two or three) hundred [pounds] a year. Over and above that you have an estate which, if you gave above thirty years' purchase, is an hundred a year. You have neither son nor daughter. And yet you *cannot afford* sixpence a month for the *[Arminian] Magazine*! Nay, you could not afford to give a guinea in a pressing case, even at the instance of an old tried friend!

Are you then in more *debt* than you can pay? Or is your trade gone, so that it will no more than *keep your house*? Do you *clear nothing* in the year? If so, you may still lay up the annual income of your estate. (What you could sell it for is nothing to the purpose; you do not need to sell it.) Are you not then 'laying up treasures upon earth'?[297] And how is this consistent with Scripture? Surely no more than living in adultery or habitual drunkenness.

Those words of St. Paul have for some time past been much impressed on my mind, 'If any man that is called a brother be a fornicator, or covetous, with such an one, no not to eat.'[298] Now, I cannot clear you of covetousness, deep uncommon covetousness, such as I very rarely meet with. I do not know that in forty years I have *asked* a guinea of any other man that has denied me! So I have done! I give you up to God. I do not know that you will any more be troubled with
Your former friend,

John Wesley[299]

Source: holograph; Oxford, Lincoln College, Archive, MS/WES/A/2/1.

---

[294] This is the first surviving letter of JW to William Roberts [or Robarts]. Roberts had served as an itinerant preacher in the early 1750s, then married and settled into a career in business in Tiverton, where he continued to support Methodist work.

[295] JW had written Roberts (apparently in Aug. 1782, the letter is not known to survive) requesting some financial assistance for the movement. Roberts had replied (in another letter not known to survive) declining this request, because his business had run into financial troubles.

[296] Cf. Abraham Cowley, 'Martial, Book II, Epistle 90', *l.* 5.

[297] Cf. Matt. 6:19.

[298] 1 Cor. 5:11.

[299] Note the formal use of his full name; instead of 'J. Wesley'.

To Ann Bolton[300]

Bath
September 15, 1782 5

My Dear Nancy,

Be so kind as to inform brother [Richard] Rodda that, if God prolong my life and strength, I shall be at Wallingford on Monday, October 16; at Oxford on Tuesday, [October] 17; at Witney, Wednesday; and at High Wycombe on Thursday. 10

As I hope to see you in a short time, I do not now inquire into the particulars of your afflictions, although it is pity but you had used the privilege of a friend and told me them all just as they occurred. But it is enough that God drew good out of evil,[301] and commanded all things to work together for good.[302] He has proved you in the 15 furnace of affliction.[303] And when you have been tried, you shall come forth as gold.[304]

In many parts of the kingdom there has been a considerable increase of the work of God. And why should there not be the same with you also? It will if our brethren be instant in prayer.[305] 20

One effect of your trials is to unite *me* more closely to you as 'pity melts the mind to love'.[306] Indeed, you long have been exceedingly near to, my dear Nancy,

Yours most affectionately,

J. Wesley 25

Address: 'To / Miss Bolton / In Witney / Oxfordshire'.
Endorsement: by Bolton, 'Sept 15th 1782'.
Source: holograph; MARC, MAM JW 1/95.

---

[300] JW was replying to Bolton's letter of Sept. 9, 1782.
[301] See Gen. 5:20.
[302] See Rom. 8:28.
[303] See Isa. 48:10.
[304] See Job 23:10.
[305] See Col. 4:2.
[306] John Dryden, 'Alexander's Feast', *l.* 78.

To William Roberts[307]

Bristol
September 19, 1782

5

Strange! Have you not an estate? Does it bring you in nothing? Have you not a large trade? Do you gain nothing thereby? Then how can you avoid 'laying up treasures on earth'?[308] I want to know.
10 I desire to justify you.

Source: holograph; Oxford, Lincoln College, Archive, MS/WES/A/2/2.

15

To Joseph Taylor

Bristol
September 24, 1782

20 Dear Joseph,
Joseph Andrew writes to me about his keeping the books still.[309] I answer, 'It was determined at the Conference that the books all over England should be kept by the Assistant in each circuit.'[310] I believe he has discharged this office well, but I believe *you* will discharge
25 it better. Yet do not expect to do your duty without giving offence!
Recommend the *[Arminian] Magazines*, Kempis, and the *Primitive Physic* in earnest. And take care of the bands and the children.
I am, dear Joseph,
Your affectionate friend and brother,

30   J. Wesley

Address: 'To / Mr Jos. Taylor / At the Preachinghouse / In St. Ives / Cornwall'.
35 *Postmark*: 'Bristol'.
Source: holograph; MARC, MAM JW 5/3.

[307] Roberts replied on Sept. 16 to JW's letter of Sept. 12, drawing this response.
[308] Cf. Matt. 6:19.
[309] Joseph Andrew was a grocer and member of the society at Redruth; cf. Francis Wrigley to JW, Nov. 1, 1786.
[310] JW had written Taylor on Sept. 9, 1782, instructing him to take charge of the books in his circuit, which drew a letter of protest from Joseph Andrew—the person previously with that responsibility. Neither Andrew's letter to JW nor JW's reply to him are known to survive.

To an Unidentified Man[311]

Bristol
September 30, 1782

My Dear Brother, 5

You well know the regard I have for *you*, and that I would do anything in my power to oblige you. But you cannot desire that I should
act contrary to the clear dictates of my conscience.

Upon your letter as follows:[312]

10

Honoured and Dear Sir,

You was deceived. You did not imagine when you consented
that the old deeds were so abominable. Whatever promise
therefore you made under that deception is absolutely null
and void. It is not *your* hurt as an individual, but highly prej- 15
udicial to the Methodist cause and the Church of England.
And as an *impartial* man before God, you tie your hands in
future if you suffer the present case to pass.

In short, I am fully persuaded that, though the whole su-
perintendency of the work has been laid upon you by God 20
himself, yet you have not the shadow of a right to sacrifice the
work itself to your own tender feelings. The present case has
been discussed and determined by yourself in Conference.[313]
It is therefore the touchstone of your mind and future conduct, because actions speak louder than words. And you can 25
meet with no case ⟨of th⟩e[314] kind which requires redress more
than the present.

This is exactly my own sentiment. I am,
Your affectionate friend and brother,
30
J. Wesley

Postmarks: 'Bristol' and '3/OC'.[315]
Endorsement: 'Septem 30 1782'.
Source: holograph; privately held (WWEP Archive holds photocopy).

---

[311] Whoever the correspondent, the letter JW received (and quotes) concerned the debate
about the revision proposed by the trustees of the Birstall preaching-house to their deed; see
JW to CW, May 28, 1782.

[312] About three words between 'letter' and 'as' are so obscured as to be indecipherable. It
is unclear whether this was by JW or another hand.

[313] See *Minutes* (1782), Q. 22, 10:529 in this edn.

[314] A small portion is torn away.

[315] The remainder of the address portion is missing.

To William Ripley

c. October 1782[316]

5   You have great reason to praise God on behalf of your son who
has so happily finished his courses.[317] I hope all your children ⟨who
remain⟩ will closely follow after him.[318] It would be a sad thing for
any of them to be found on the left hand, when he is on the right of
the great Judge!
10   I am, with love to sister [Dorothy] Ripley, dear Billy,
    Your affectionate brother,

J. Wesley

Source: holograph; Oxford, Bodleian Library, MS Autogr. c. 24, f. 288.

15

To Penelope Newman[319]

Bristol
20 October 1, 1782
My Dear Sister,
    I have often been concerned at your being cooped up in a corner.
Now you are likely to have a wider field of action. Only the danger
will be lest, when you have more opportunity, you should have less
25 desire of doing good. This is the case of many pious persons when
they marry, and I do not wonder at it. I should rather wonder it is
not the case of all.
    I am,
        Your affectionate brother,
30 [J. Wesley]

Source: published transcription; Jackson, *Works* (3rd), 13:137–38.

---

[316] The holograph does not include an address portion to show the postmark. A second-ary hand has written '1783' on it; but it is unlikely that Ripley would wait that long to inform JW of this death, or JW to reply. JW was travelling most of Sept., but was in Bristol in early Oct. and London the middle of the month, where he would have received mail being held.

[317] Ripley had married Dorothy Johnson in 1761. Their son William Ripley Jr. (b. 1763) died Aug. 27, 1782; see Dorothy Ripley, *Memoirs of William Ripley, Minister of the Gospel* (Phil-adelphia: J. H. Cunningham, 1827), 63.

[318] A portion affecting 2–3 words has fallen off along a fold mark. The Ripleys had five daughters and a son who survived William Jr.; ibid., 81.

[319] JW had received word that Newman was marrying the itinerant preacher Jonathan Coussins. They were wed Oct. 17, 1782. There is no known further correspondence between JW and Penelope, but she is mentioned in JW's letters to her husband.

To Hester Ann Roe[320]

Bristol
October 1, 1782   5

My Dear Hetty,

I received yours two days after date, and read it yesterday to Miss Stockdale,[321] and poor Peggy Roe, who is still strangely detained in life. But she is permitted to stay in the body a little longer that she may be more ready for the Bridegroom.   10

You did exceedingly well to send me so circumstantial an account of Robert Roe's last illness and happy death. It may incite many to run the race that is set before them with more courage and patience.[322]

The removal of so useful an instrument as your late cousin in   15
the midst, or rather in the dawn, of his usefulness (especially while the harvest is so great and the faithful labourers so few), is an instance of the divine economy which leaves our reason behind. Our little narrow minds cannot comprehend it. We can only wonder and adore.[323]   20

How is your health? I sometimes fear lest you also (as those I tenderly love generally have been) should be snatched away. But let us live today.

I always am,
    Affectionately yours,   25
                    J. Wesley

Source: published transcription; Benson, *Works*, 16:265.

---

[320] JW was replying to Roe's letter of Sept. 28, 1792, which distilled the journal of her cousin Robert Roe, and gave an account of his death.

[321] Jane Stockdale (1742–1804), who never married, was the youngest sister of Robert Roe's mother Mary (Stockdale) Roe (1729–63).

[322] See Heb. 12:1. To this end JW serialized the account in fifteen installments in *AM* 6–7 (1783–84).

[323] See CW, Hymn 57, st. 4, ll. 7–8, *Hymns on the Lord's Supper* (1745), 41.

To Thomas Rutherford

London
October 19, 1782

5

Dear Tommy,

I allow you to give any books you please to any preacher, to the value of forty shillings. I have hope for Thomas Bethell. Watch over him and he will reward your labour.[324]

10   I think you have determined right concerning Waterford and concerning brother Christie.[325]

Send me *the substance* of the quarterly plans.

Cannot you find an easier circuit for John Crook?[326]

We cannot receive John M'Burney.[327]

15   I like your prayer-meetings well. If you judge it right, let there be one on Thursday too. But I hope you do not discontinue morning preaching.

There is something very awful in the sudden removal of that good man Richard Boardman.[328] But what can be done to supply

20 his place? Cork is of very great importance. Can anything better be done (at least for the present) than to cut off your own right hand— to send Andrew Blair thither, and to keep John Mealy in Dublin?[329]

I am, with kind love to sister [Isabella] Rutherford, dear Tommy,
       Your affectionate friend and brother,

25
                         J. Wesley

Source: holograph; MARC, WCB, D6/3/1/11.

[324] See JW to Rutherford, July 29, 1782.

[325] James Christie had been admitted 'on trial' at the 1779 Conference (see 10:484 in this edn.); but age or possibly health problems consigned him to support from the preachers' fund in 1784 (10:562).

[326] Crook was the Assistant of the Lisburn circuit.

[327] John M'Burney, a devoted young Irishman, was admitted 'on trial' as an itinerant in 1772, and appointed to the Enniskillen circuit (see 10:406–08 in this edn.). On Mar. 4, 1773, while preaching near Aghalun, he was beaten severely by six ruffians; see Crookshank, *Ireland*, 271. M'Burney never fully recovered from this beating. He was reappointed to Enniskillen by the 1773 Conference (10:418), left unassigned in 1774 (10:427), returned to appointment in 1775 (10:443), is not mentioned in 1776 or 1777, is shown on disability in 1778 (10:482), and appears under appointment one last time in 1779 (10:488). Either his physical condition or something in his behaviour now ruled out another attempt of appointment.

[328] Boardman died of a stroke on Oct. 4, 1782, in Cork.

[329] Blair had been scheduled to assist Rutherford in Dublin, while Mealy (JW spells: 'Mayly') was to go to the Clones circuit.

To Joseph Taylor

London
October 19, 1782   5

Dear Joseph,

Those tracts that are in any degree damaged you will do well to sell at half price. And those of them that are greatly damaged you may give away as you see proper. But I apprehend it would be best, when a proper occasion is, to send the *[Arminian] Magazines* by sea   10 to Bristol or London.

Where they have preaching only one night in a week, you may meet the bands and the society by turns.

I am, dear Joseph,
    Your affectionate friend and brother,   15
                J. Wesley

Address: 'To / Mr Jos. Taylor / At the Preachinghouse / In Redruth / Cornwall'.
Postmark: '19/OC'.   20
Source: holograph; MARC, MAM JW 5/4.

25

To James Rogers

London
October 20, 1782   30

Dear Jemmy,

I am glad you have furnished the house and made an alteration in the circuit, which I doubt not will be for the best.[330] And the house at Burslem will be very convenient. You must mend or end Sam[uel] Roebotham—only as gently as you can.[331]   35

Nothing can be done at Mob[b]erley till after the Conference. We have work enough in hand at present.

---

[330] Rogers was now the Assistant for the Macclesfield circuit. His letter to JW is not known to survive.

[331] This was apparently a local preacher.

I have a particular account of the death of that blessed young man.[332] I hope you love my Hetty Roe.

I am, with kind love to sister Rogers,[333] dear Jemmy,

Your affectionate friend and brother,

J. Wesley

Source: holograph; Wheaton College, Billy Graham Center Archives, Ephemera of John Wesley, Collection 31.

To Zachariah Yewdall

Sevenoaks
October 21, 1782

My Dear Brother,

Undoubtedly you are to act as Assistant.[334] And if you carefully read the great [i.e., 'Large'] *Minutes* of the Conference, and keep close to them in every point, assuredly you will see the fruit of your labour. But whom can you get to help you? I know none, unless you can persuade brother [Thomas] Rutherford to spare you Andrew Blair, and to take a poor invalid, John Mealy (who is now at Dublin), in his stead.[335] You know we have no preachers to spare. Every one is employed. And we can neither make preachers nor purchase them. God alone can thrust them out into his harvest.[336] All you can do, till help comes, is to divide yourself between Cork and Bandon.

I am,

Your affectionate friend and brother,

J. Wesley

Address: 'To / Mr Yewdall / At the New Room / in / Cork'.
Postmarks: '23/OC' and 'OC/28'.
Source: holograph; MARC, MA 2008/016.

---

[332] Robert Roe; see JW to Hester Ann Roe, Oct. 1, 1782.

[333] Rogers had married Martha Knowlden in 1778; after her death Hester Ann Roe would become his wife.

[334] Yewdall had been appointed as Assistant for the first time, of the Cork circuit, with the Richard Boardman serving alongside him. With Boardman's sudden death, Yewdall had clearly queried JW whether he could fulfill this role. The letter is not known to survive.

[335] JW again spells 'Mayly'. See JW to Rutherford, Oct. 19, 1782.

[336] See Matt. 9:38.

To Alexander Knox

near London
October 22, 1782   5

My Dear Alleck,

You judge exactly right. That whole affair entirely slipped my memory. So entirely that I do not remember to have once thought of it from that time till I read your last.[337]

The epidemic distemper has had the same effect on many in vari-   10
ous parts of England; especially where the Peruvian bark has been given in any considerable quantity.[338] This has turned the fever in a few days or weeks into a true, pulmonary consumption. And I do not recollect any instance wherein a consumption caused by the bark has been cured. But I trust all this will be mercy to her and   15
hers.[339] For I doubt not she will witness a good confession, before her spirit returns to God that gave it. O how ready he is to save! To save both her and you! Yea and to save you to the uttermost![340] Look up! All is ready!

Peace be with all your spirits! I am, dear Alleck,   20

Yours most affectionately,

J. Wesley

Address: 'To / Mr Alexr Knox / in / Londonderry'.   25
Source: holograph; Bridwell Library (SMU).[341]

[337] This letter is not known to survive.

[338] A major flu epidemic that began in Asia reached Great Britain in early summer 1782. Peruvian bark (the natural source for quinine) would not have been effective in treating this.

[339] Knox's second sister (not Sarah) was sick, and would soon die; see JW to Knox, Dec. 2, 1782.

[340] See Heb. 7:25.

[341] Held previously in the Upper Room Museum, L-31.

To Duncan M'Allum[342]

near London
October 24, 1782

Dear Duncan,

Epworth, I believe, is not supplied. I think it will be a comfortable place for Peter Mill, and I trust he will be more useful than ever. Yet I was afraid he would be straitened for money, so I have drawn a little note on Mr. [John] Prickard in his favour, who keeps the money of the Contingent Fund in Dr. [Thomas] Coke's absence. If he wants anything, he shall have it.

I am, dear Duncan,
Yours affectionately,

J. Wesley

Source: manuscript transcriptions (19th century), MARC, MA 1977/485, 312–13; and Duke, Rubenstein, Frank Baker Collection of Wesleyana, VOLS 7, Letter book 10, p. 11.

To Ellen Gretton

London
October 26, 1782

My Dear Sister,

For about a fortnight, I shall be out of town [i.e., London]. I shall then stay in town a fortnight. Afterwards I shall only be in town on Saturdays and Sundays, till about the middle of December. Then I shall hope to see you. You must strive, or you cannot conquer! Wherever you are, you will be under the shadow of the Almighty.[343] And consequently will be just as safe as if you was sitting in your own apartment. Praise him, praise him evermore!

Peace be with all your spirits! I am, dear Nelly,
Your affectionate,

J. Wesley

Source: holograph; privately held (transcription provided to Frank Baker).

---

[342] This note is a bit puzzling. There were three preachers assigned to Epworth at the 1782 Conference; and Duncan McAllum was Assistant for the Newcastle circuit, with no direct responsibility for Epworth. But Peter Mill, assigned to Dundee by the 1782 Conference, did not move there and was listed in Epworth the following year.

[343] See Ps. 91:1.

To Elizabeth (Nangle) Bradburn[344]

Yarmouth
October 30, 1782

My Dear Betsy,

My disorders are seldom of long continuance; they pass off in a few days, and usually leave me considerably better than I was before. We are always safe while we are either doing or suffering the will of him that orders all things well.[345]

I do not doubt but you will find both profit and pleasure in the conversation of my dear Miss [Elizabeth] Ritchie. I had marked her out for your acquaintance, or rather friendship, before you set out for England. You are two kindred souls, and I almost wonder how you could be so long kept apart from each other. Her conversation, I doubt not, will quicken your desires of being all renewed in the image of him that created you.[346] But let those desires rise ever so high, they need not lessen your thankfulness. Nay, the strongest hunger and thirst after righteousness are found in those that in everything give thanks.[347]

I am glad to hear the little jars that were in Bradford are at end.[348] Let them all die and be forgotten. But let brotherly love continue. Peace be with both your spirits!

I am, my dear Betsy,

Yours most affectionately,

J. Wesley

Source: holograph; MARC, MAM JW 1/108.

---

[344] While the address portion is missing, the identity of the recipient is clear from the first name and that Elizabeth's husband Samuel was currently stationed in Bradford.

[345] See Eph. 1:11.

[346] See Col. 3:10.

[347] See Matt. 5:6 and 1 Thess. 5:18.

[348] The tensions in Bradford likely related to the debate over the deed for the preaching-house in nearby Birstall.

To Samuel Bradburn

London
November 9, 1782

Dear Sammy,

I abhor the thought of giving to twenty men the power to place or displace the preachers in their congregations.[349] How would he then dare to speak an unpleasing truth? And if he did, what would become of him? This must never be the case while I live among the Methodists. And Birstall is a leading case; the first of an avowed violation of our plan. Therefore the point must be carried for the Methodist preachers now or never. And I alone can carry it; which I will, God being my helper.

You are not a match for the silver tongue, nor brother [Christopher] Hopper.[350] But do not, to please any of your new friends, forsake

Your true old friend,

[J. Wesley]

Source: published transcription; Jackson, *Works* (3rd), 13:99.

To Thomas Hanson

London
November 9, 1782

Dear Tommy,

Indeed you have had an hard part to act. I fear you have to do with one that will neither lead nor drive.[351] But Mr. [William] Sagar writes he 'will undertake for the pay of four preachers, provided *we* will provide for sister Evans'.[352] So we will do it out of the con-

---

[349] JW was surely aware that Bradburn had been approached by the trustees of a Congregational chapel recently erected in Little Horton Lane in Bradford to become their pastor, and had refused (he refused a similar offer from the trustees of the Independent White Chapel in Leeds, in Dec.). See Bradburn, *Memoirs*, 86, 90–91.

[350] The 'silver tongue' was likely James Carr, the attorney for the trustees of the Birstall preaching-house; see his letter to one of the trustees in Tyerman, *John Wesley*, 377–78.

[351] Hanson had been appointed in Aug. as the Assistant for the Colne circuit, along with Thomas Johnson and David Evans. Prior to his arrival William Sagar had written JW about Calvinist influence (or preachers) negatively impacting the circuit (see JW to Sagar, Aug. 11, 1782). Sagar was likely pushing Hanson to counteract this influence quickly.

[352] This letter is not known to survive.

tingent fund, or out of my pocket. I have wrote for a preacher now at Sheffield to go to Colne without delay. Do not envy delicate and self-pleasing preachers. You and I are happier than they. The more self-denial, the more blessing; so I have found for near these four-score years.

    I am, dear Tommy,
        Your affectionate friend and brother,

                                  John Wesley

Address: 'To / Mr Hanson / At the Preachinghouse / In Coln / Lanca-shire'.[353]
Postmark: '9/NO'. *Charge*: '4'.
Source: holograph; Wesley's Chapel (London), LDWMM 1994/1929.

To Zachariah Yewdall

                                  London
                          November 12, 1782

My Dear Brother,
    Before this time I suppose you have my last.[354] I have wrote to Thomas Rutherford to send Andrew Blair. The leaders, I find, were unwilling to part with him; but I think he will be guided by me rather than by them. Till I have done meeting the classes, I shall have little leisure to write either prose or verse, being fully taken up from morning to night.[355] After this I may get a little time. O let us work while the day is! The night cometh, wherein no man can work.[356]

    I am,
        Your affectionate brother,

                                  J. Wesley

Source: published transcription; Jackson, *Works* (3rd), 13:13.

---

[353] Hanson inscribed a list of abbreviated names on the address panel, and on the left margin of the letter he added an apparent narrative using both abbreviated words and scattered shorthand marks. The narrative cannot be expanded with any confidence.

[354] JW to Yewdall, Oct. 21, 1782.

[355] Yewdall had written JW requesting some text for Richard Boardman's tombstone. While Yewdall's letter is not known to survive, see JW's subsequent letter of Nov. 21, 1782.

[356] See John 9:4.

To Zachariah Yewdall

On The Death of Mr. [Richard] Boardman

With zeal for God, with love of souls inspired,
Nor awed by dangers, nor by labours tired,
Boardman in distant worlds proclaims the word
To multitudes, and turns them to his Lord.
But soon the bloody waste of war he mourns,
And, loyal, from rebellion's seat returns;
Nor yet at home, — on eagles' pinions flies,
And in a moment soars to paradise![357]

London
November 21, 1782

My Dear Brother,

I believe you need not be ashamed to inscribe the lines above on Richard Boardman's tombstone.[358] I doubt you do not find any account of himself among his papers.

I am,

Your affectionate brother,

J. Wesley

Address: 'To / Mr Z. Yewdall / At the New Room / in / Cork'.
Postmarks: '21/NO' and 'NO/26'.
Source: holograph; MARC, MAM JW 6/39.

To Joseph Benson[359]

London
November 29, 1782

Dear Joseph,

I am well pleased that it is *you* who give me an opportunity of considering this important question, because you are able to bring

---

[357] The title and text are in CW's hand. JW added his note below and sent it to Yewdall. CW's epitaph also appears in his MS Funeral Hymns (1756–87), 112.

[358] Likely because of its strong loyalist tone (against the rebellious colonists), CW's epitaph was passed over for another on Boardman's tomb; see Crookshank, *Ireland, 365*.

[359] JW was replying to Benson's letter of Nov. 16, 1782, wherein Benson showed sympathy for the Birstall trustees and complained about how Thomas Coke had handled matters.

the whole strength of the cause—so that in answering *you* I may answer all.[360]

I will first endeavour to state the case, and then argue a little upon it.

When our Lord preached on the mountain, or St. Paul by the riverside, there was no such thing as *patronages*. But as soon as Christians grew rich, some of them built preaching-houses afterwards called churches; and those who built were called *patrons*, and appointed whom they pleased to preach in them. When revenues were annexed to these houses, they disposed of houses and revenues together. Indeed, the patrons generally gave the lands from which the revenues arose. At the Reformation many rich men built new churches, and still claimed the disposal of them. And many Presbyterians and Independents built preaching-houses at their own expense, and placed in them whom they pleased. But others entrusted their powers with a few friends whom they could confide in.

I built the first preaching-house which was built for the people called Methodists, namely at Bristol, in the year 1739. And knowing no better, I suffered the first deed of trust to be drawn in the presbyterian form. But Mr. [George] Whitefield, hearing of this, wrote me a warm letter asking, 'Do you consider what you do? If you let the trustees name the preachers, they may exclude you and all your brethren from preaching in the houses you have built. Pray let the deed be immediately cancelled.' To which the trustees immediately agreed.

Afterwards I built the preaching-houses in Kingswood and at Newcastle upon Tyne. But I took care that none but myself should have any right to name preachers for them. About this time a preaching-house was built at Birstall, by contributions and collections. But John Nelson, knowing no better, suffered a deed to be drawn without my consent or knowledge, giving twelve or thirteen persons a power not only of *placing* but even of *displacing* the preachers *at their pleasure*. Had I then known of this, I should have insisted on having it altered as that at Bristol.

Soon after this I was informed that the houses at Bristol, Kingswood, and Newcastle were *my* property, and as such liable to descend to my heirs. I immediately procured a form to be drawn up by three of the most eminent counsellors in London, whereby not only these houses but all hereafter to be built might be settled on

---

[360] Compare this initial draft to the printed circular *The Case of Birstall House*, which JW circulated among his preachers in early Jan. 1783.

such a plan as would infallibly secure them from the heirs of the proprietors, for the purpose originally intended.

In process of time, Birstall house being too small for the congregation, it was moved to build a new one. And a new deed was pre-
5   pared which, like the old, gave a few people the power both to *place* and *displace* preachers *at pleasure*. When I heard this, I vehemently objected to it, and positively refused to sign it. But in the evening several came and strongly urged me to sign, averring that the old deed *could not be altered*; on which consideration, at length I unwill-
10 ingly complied.[361]

This was mentioned at the ensuing Conference and it was asked, What can be done with regard to the preaching-house at Birstall? The answer was, 'If the trustees still refuse to settle it on the Methodist plan: 1) let a plain state of the case be drawn up; 2) let a collec-
15 tion be made throughout all England in order to purchase ground, and to build another preaching-house as near the present as may be.'[362]

'But why should not all our houses be settled like that at Birstall?' Because, if the trustees have a power to place and displace preach-
20 ers, then: 1) Itinerant preaching is at an end. When the trustees in any place have fixed a preacher they like, the rotation of preachers there is at an end, at least till they pick a quarrel with him and turn him out. 2) While he stays, how he will be gagged, since if he displeases the trustees he will lose his bread! And how will he dare
25 to put a trustee out of the society? 3) If any beside the Conference name the preachers, surely it should not be twenty or thirty men, but all the society! Unless you would say all the congregation. 4) The power of these trustees is greater than that of any nobleman; yea, or of the king himself. He can put in a preacher where he is
30 patron, but he cannot put him out.

'But since this power will not commence till after your death, why should *you* oppose it?' Because none else can oppose it so effectually. I have more influence than any other person is likely to have after me. And everyone sees I am not pleading my own cause (as they
35 would say the other preachers were). I am pleading not for myself, but for every preacher who desires to act on the old Methodist plan. I am pleading for Mr. [Christopher] Hopper, Mr. [Samuel] Bradburn, Mr. [Joseph] Benson, that you may not be liable to be turned out of all or any of our houses without any reason given, *at the plea-*

---

[361] See JW's longer account in his letter to CW, May 28, 1782.
[362] *Minutes* (1782), Q. 22, 10:529 in this edn.

sure of twenty or thirty men.[363] I say 'or any', for I see no sufficient reason for giving up any house in England. And if one were given up, more would follow. It would be as the *letting out of water*.[364]

'But you did consent to it with regard to this house.' Yes, I was worried into an unwilling consent. And even this was grounded on the positive assertion that the deed *could not be altered*; whereas it was actually altered in the second deed, not in one but in twenty places.

The plain conclusion is, if the trustees will not alter the deed, they must keep their house and we must build another. 'But then you occasion endless strife, animosity, confusion, and destroy the work of God.' No, not I. It is these trustees that cause all the strife, animosity, and confusion. I go on in the old way. It is they that, by going out of it, hinder, yea destroy, the work of God. I sit down with the loss, leave them the house, and go on as if they were not in the world. It is they who do the wrong, who bawl with all their might and pour out bitter words. But let them take care, for God heareth. And he will arise and maintain his own cause.

I am,

Your affectionate brother,

J. Wesley

Source: holograph; Toronto, Victoria University, Emmanuel College Library, Wesleyana Collection, No. 369a, item 1.[365]

To a British Officer

London
November 30, 1782

Sir,

I am informed by some of my friends in Lowestoft that they have been frequently disturbed at their public worship by some officers quartered in the town.[366] Before I use any other method, I beg of

---

[363] JW lists three preachers closely involved with this debate; Hopper was currently stationed in Birstall, while Benson and Bradburn were in nearby Bradford.

[364] See Prov. 17:14.

[365] The text of the letter is in the hand of John Atlay, but JW has added his signature.

[366] JW had preached in Lowestoft on Oct. 31, 1782; see *Journal*, 23:258 in this edn.

you, sir, who can do it with a word, to prevent our being thus in-
sulted any more. We are men. We are Englishmen. As such we have
a natural and a legal right to liberty of conscience.

   I am, sir,

5   Your obedient servant,

                                              John Wesley

Address: 'To / The Commanding Officer / in / Lowestoft'.[367]
Source: holograph; Haverford, Pennsylvania, Haverford College, Library,
10   Charles Roberts Autograph Letters Collection.

15   To John Bredin[368]

                                          near London
                                    November 30, 1782

My Dear Brother,

20   Medicines, I think, will be of no service to you—unless it were
a course of tar-water.[369] But very probably change of air might be
of service. It might be of service to spend, suppose, a week or two
at Liverpool; afterwards a week or two at Chester or Parkgate; and
perhaps [a week or two] at Manchester. Your diet in the meantime
25   should be chiefly milk and vegetables, of which I judge turnips, po-
tatoes, and apples to be the best. Preach as much as you *can* preach,
and no more.

   I am,

      Your affectionate brother,

30   J. Wesley

Address: 'To / Mr Bredin / At the Preachinghouse / in / Whitehaven'.
Postmark: '30/NO'. *Charge*: '8'.
Source: holograph; Manchester, Rylands, English Ms 345/122.

[367] The letter was likely hand-delivered by one of the preachers on the Norwich circuit.

[368] Bredin had increasing health issues during his recent assignment in Ireland. JW suggested in a letter of July 8, 1782, that he consider coming to England for better medical care.
He was placed on disability by the 1782 Conference, and was currently on the western coast
of England.

[369] This treatment had been championed recently by Bishop George Berkeley. It appears
several times in *Primitive Physic*, along with directions on how to make it; see 32:83 in this edn.

To [John Watson Jr.][370]

near London
November 30, 1782

My Dear Brother,   5
I am glad to hear you are better. Probably in a little time you
may be able to act as a travelling preacher. It was not at all proper
that you should stay longer at Arbroth. You could be of little use
there. But perhaps you might be able to do that easy work, to supply
Dunkeld and Perth. Then John Ogylvie may have opportunity of   10
going north, which will be best for him also.[371] If you can undertake
this, the sooner the better. And write word of it to Mr. [William]
Thompson at Dundee.[372]
I am,
Your affectionate brother,   15
J. Wesley

Source: holograph; Bridwell Library (SMU).

20

To Hannah Ball[373]

London   25
December 1, 1782

My Dear Sister,
It is hard if we cannot trust the invisible God farther than we can
see him! We do not yet see the fruit of our labours. But we can trust

[370] While there is no address portion, this letter was most likely to John Watson Jr.—cf.
WHS 33 (1961): 15. After being stationed by the 1781 Conference in Belfast, the younger
Watson does not appear among the stations in the 1782 Minutes. This would be explained by
illness (as would his spending time recuperating in the seaside town of Arbroth, Scotland). He
would be stationed in Glamorgan, Wales by the 1783 Conference. See JW's letter to the same
correspondent, Apr. 25, 1783.
[371] John Ogylvie / Ogilvie (d. 1839) had just been admitted 'on trial' as an itinerant at the
1782 Conference and stationed on the Dundee circuit (see 10:520, 522 in this edn.). He served
until 1821, when poor health required him to retire to Cornwall, living with his children. See
Minutes (post-Wesley, 1839), 7:420.
[372] Peter Mill had been assigned as Assistant for the Dundee circuit but did not assume
this role; see JW to Duncan M'Allum, Oct. 24, 1782. This led JW to transfer William Thompson from his assigned circuit of York to Dundee; see JW to Thompson, Mar. 6, 1783.
[373] While the address portion is missing, the holograph was part of the papers of Hannah
Ball, transcribed in her *Memoir* (pp. 156–57).

him that hath promised, 'He will fulfill the desire of them that fear him.'[374] He hath already done great things. But he will do greater things than these. Only 'hold fast the beginning of your confidence steadfast unto the end'.[375]

5 You do well, whenever opportunity offers, to step over to Watlington.[376] It will be a means of increasing life both in them and yourself. I only wish you could see our friends at Oxford too, that iron might sharpen iron.[377]

I hope you do not drop the select society. If Mr. [Richard] Rodda
10 strongly and explicitly preaches perfection, he will see more and more fruit of his labour.

I am, with love to my dear Nancy,[378]

Your affectionate brother,

J. Wesley

15

Source: holograph; MARC, MA 2008/013.

20

To Ann Loxdale

London
December 1, 1782

25 My Dear Sister,

I did not know that you had been ill till you sent me the welcome news of your recovery.[379] I do not doubt but exercise and change of air have generally contributed to it. And if you desire the continuance of your health, you must still continue to use all the ex-
30 ercise you can. What a comfort it is that our trials work together for good?[380] They must do so, as long as we can say 'Father not as I will, but as thou wilt.'[381] This is the essence of holiness, a loving resignation to the will of God. See that you hold fast what he has given you! And after you have suffered a while he will not only make

---

[374] Ps. 145:19.
[375] Cf. Heb. 3:14.
[376] The hometown of Martha Chapman.
[377] See Prov. 27:17.
[378] Hannah's sister Ann.
[379] Loxdale's letter to JW is not known to survive.
[380] See Rom. 8:28.
[381] Matt. 26:39.

you perfect, but 'stablish, strengthen, settle you thereby,[382] and pre-
serve you unblamable in holiness unto the coming of our Lord Jesus
Christ![383] I am, my dear Nancy,
　　Yours very affectionately,

　　　　　　　　　　　　　　　　　　　　　J. Wesley　5

My kind love to your sister [Sarah] and Suky Eden.[384] I am glad she
is with you. See that you do her good!

Address: (not in JW's hand) 'To Miss Loxdale'.
Postmark: '2/DE'.　　　　　　　　　　　　　　　　　　　　10
Source: holograph; MARC, WCB, D5/33/1.

To Alexander Knox　15

　　　　　　　　　　　　　　　　　　　St. Neots
　　　　　　　　　　　　　　　　　December 2, 1782

My Dear Alleck,

　I am glad you have favoured me with so circumstantial an account　20
of your sister's death.[385] When we lay all the particulars together,
there is no room for any doubt, of her spirit's being removed by the
ministering spirits into Abraham's bosom. And it is highly probable, as you observe, that longer life would not have been a blessing
to her. So we have another proof that all things are ordered well.　25
I hope my dear Sally and George will profit by this providential
dispensation![386] Peace be with all your spirits!

　I am, my dear Alleck,
　　Yours most affectionately,

　　　　　　　　　　　　　　　　　　　　J. Wesley　30

Address: 'To / Mr Alexr Knox / in / Londonderry / +p [crosspost] Port-
　patrick'.
Postmarks: 'St Neots' and '4/DE'.
Source: holograph; Bridwell Library (SMU).[387]

---

[382] Cf. CW, Hymn for Believers #15, st. 7, *HSP* (1749), 1:219; 'Settle, confirm, and 'stablish me'.

[383] See 1 Thess. 5:23.

[384] Susannah Eden Jr., of Broad Marston.

[385] This letter is not known to survive, leaving the name of Alexander's second sister unknown.

[386] Alexander's other two siblings.

[387] Held previously in the Upper Room Museum, L-32.

To John Francis Valton[388]

St. Neots
December 3, 1782

5   My Dear Brother,
    You are thoroughly satisfied that there is nothing wherein conscience is not concerned which I would not do for *your* sake. But here conscience is very deeply concerned. What I do, I do unto the Lord. The question is, in the last resort: Methodism or no Meth-
10   odism! A blow is struck at the very roots of our whole discipline, as appears by the short state of the 'case' which I have sent to Joseph Benson.[389] And if this evil is not obviated while I live, probably it never will be. None can stem the tide when I am gone. Therefore I must now do what I can, God being my helper. And I know the
15   fierceness of man shall turn to his praise![390]
        I am,
            Your affectionate friend and brother,

J. Wesley

20   *Address*: 'To / Mr John Valton / at Birstal, near / Leeds'.
    Postmark: 'St. Neots'. *Charge*: '4'.
    Endorsement: 'Der 3 1782'.
    Source: holograph; MARC, MAM JW 5/30.

25

To Zachariah Yewdall

London
30   December 7, 1782[391]

My Dear Brother,
    I do not see that you can fix upon a more proper person than either George Howe or Laren Wright.[392] You should endorse it on the back of the deed, only taking care to have fresh stamps.

---

[388] Valton was currently the Assistant for the Birstall circuit; thus in the center of the controversy over the Birstall preaching-house.

[389] See JW to Joseph Benson, Nov. 29, 1782.

[390] See Ps. 76:10.

[391] Jackson dates the letter Dec. 1 in *Works* (3rd), but changes to Dec. 7 in *Works* (4th).

[392] George Howe (c. 1744–1831) was converted in his late teens and became a member of the Methodist society in Cork, remaining active in this role (particularly in visiting prisons) until his death. See Crookshank, *Ireland*, 153; and *WMM* 10 (1831), 207.

Those who will not meet in class cannot stay with us. Read the *Thoughts upon a Single Life* and weigh them well. You will then *feel* the wisdom of St. Paul's advice (especially to a preacher, and to a Methodist preacher above all), 'If thou mayest be free, use it rather.'[393]

I hope Andrew Blair is now with you. Brother [Robert] Swindells is dead, and John Trembath is alive again.[394]

I am,

> Your affectionate friend and brother,

> > [J. Wesley]

Source: published transcription; Jackson, *Works* (3rd), 13:14.

To Robert Hall Jr.[395]

London
December 19, 1782

My Dear Brother,

The Conference *gives nothing* toward building houses, but they may give you more circuits to beg in. And if you had Joseph Bradford to beg for you, you would succeed well.[396] The Londoners are a princely people; they are never weary of well-doing. You want only a zealous and skilful advocate, and perseverance in prayer. God will do great things. If I live till March, and your 'house' be then ready, I might open it.

I am, dear Robert,

> Your affectionate brother,

> > John Wesley

Source: published transcription; G. Packer, ed., *Centenary of the Methodist New Connexion* (London: G. Burroughs, 1897), 95.

[393] 1 Cor. 7:21.

[394] The obituary for Swindells appeared in the 1783 *Minutes*, 10:532 in this edn. The comment on Trembath reflects his letter to JW, Oct. 4, 1782.

[395] Robert Hall (1754–1827) was born in Nottingham, where his father (of the same name) was a prosperous merchant and manufacturer. The younger Robert was converted to Methodism at seventeen and active in the movement from that time. He was currently seeking assistance from Conference toward building a preaching-house. While close to JW, after the latter's death Hall came to side with the Methodist New Connexion. See *OED*, and 'Memoir of Robert Hall', *New Methodist Magazine* (Jan.–Feb. 1828).

[396] Bradford was currently Assistant for the Leicestershire circuit.

To Jonah Freeman[397]

City Road [London]
December 20, 1782[398]

5   My Dear Brother,
      That you have received a considerable blessing from God is be-
yond all dispute. Hold fast whereunto you have attained and do
not *reason* about it. Do not concern yourself whether that it should
be called by this, or another name. It is right as far as it goes. And
10   whatsoever is yet lacking, God is able and willing to supply. I am,
           Your affectionate brother,

                                                            J. Wesley

      Address: 'To / Mr. Jonah Freeman / At Mr. [George] Clark's, Hosier / In
15   Fann's Alley / Aldersgate Street'.
      Source: holograph; North Pararmatta, New South Wales, Australia, Cam-
          den Theological Library.

20

To William Petty, Earl of Shelburne

City Road [London]
December 21, 1782

25   My Lord,
      Will your Lordship excuse my intruding upon your leisure, at so
very busy a time as this? Indeed I should not have done it, but that
I was afraid lest my solicitation should have come too late. Michael
Mangham, the writer of the letter enclosed, is one I have known
30   about thirty years. He is an honest, industrious man, and does work
when he can work. If your Lordship would please to recommend
him, it would much oblige, my Lord,
           Your Lordship's obedient servant,

                                                          John Wesley
35
      Endorsement: '21 Decr 1782 / Revd Jn. Wesley / The case of Michael
          Mangham, who asks for the King's bounty; or yearly pension'.[399]
      Source: holograph; Drew, Methodist Archives.

      [397] Jonah was likely an apprentice to George Clark—a setting in which there would have
been ready encouragement to seek Christian perfection.
      [398] Telford, *Letters*, 4:197, misread the year as '1762'.
      [399] This request was apparently not granted; see JW to Petty, Jan. 25, 1783.

To an Unidentified Man

London
December 23, 1782   5

My Dear Brother,

Many years since, when I read those words in the Lesson for the day, 'Son of man, I take from thee the desire of thine eyes with a stroke',[400] I was so affected that it was not without difficulty I could speak a word more.[401] But it was not long before he enabled me to   10
say, 'Good, is the will of the Lord.'[402] I trust he has taught you that great lesson, which reason alone cannot teach. He has always one end, whether in his pleasing or painful dispensations: to wean us from all things here below and to unite us to himself. You see the present dispensation of his providence in a true light. He is vindi-   15
cating his right to your whole heart and claiming you for his own. And he can make you large amends for all he has taken away by giving you himself.

Let not this medicine be without its full effect. 'It is a great loss to lose an affliction.'[403] Now is the time that you are loudly called   20
to give up yourself wholly to God. It would be your wisest way to select two or three for your intimate acquaintances who are deeply alive to God, and to have no farther intercourse with those who know not God than necessary business requires. If you form this resolution and keep steadily to it, you will meet our dear friend   25
again in a little time. May God enable you so to do! His grace is sufficient for you.

I am,
Your affectionate brother,

[J. Wesley]   30

Source: published transcription; Telford, *Letters*, 7:155–56.

[400] Ezek. 24:16; the lesson assigned for the eighth Sunday after Epiphany.
[401] JW was likely referring to the role of this passage in his surrender of a claim to Sophy Hopkey; see JW, Manuscript Journal (commenting on Mar. 4–12, 1738), 18:469–70 in this edn. Ezek. 24:16 would have been the lesson on Sunday, Feb. 27.
[402] Cf. 2 Kings 20:19; Isa. 39:8.
[403] A saying of Philip Henry; see JW to Mary Bishop, Sept. 13, 1774, (29:72–73 in this edn.).

To Matthias Joyce[404]

[London]
c. December 25, 1782[405]

Dear Brother,

Not only Mr. [Edward] Smyth but several others gave a satisfactory account of you at the Conference. Mr. [Richard] Watkinson writes me word that, as Robert Blake has left him, he is in great want of help.[406] I have no objections, if your wife is willing, for you to go upon trial to Limerick.[407]

Source: published transcription; *Arminian Magazine* 9 (1786): 532.

To the Rev. Thomas Davenport

London
December 28 [1782]

Dear Sir,

I believe Mr. [Vincent] Perronet laboured about thirty years in the parish of Shoreham, and that with all his might, before there appeared the least fruit of his labour. He then broke through, and in spite of reproach accepted the assistance of the poor Methodists. Immediately the seed which he had been so long sowing began to grow up. And for several years the largest and most lively society in all the circuit is that of Shoreham. I should not wonder if it should be the same case at Allexton. God is able out of the stones to raise up children unto Abraham there also.[408] But I do not know which of our circuits borders upon it, otherwise I would write to the Assistant of that circuit to pay you a visit at the first opportunity.

---

[404] Matthias Joyce (1754–1814) set out in response to this letter for Limerick on Jan. 11, 1783. He was admitted 'on trial' as an itinerant at the Irish Conference in Apr. of that year (see 10:968 in this edn.) and served for thirty years. See Jackson, *EMP*, 4:228–73 (cf., in-letters, Oct. 14, 1785); and *Minutes* (post-Wesley, 1814), 4:7.

[405] *AM* reads '1783', but this is a mistake. Joyce began itinerating in Jan. 1783.

[406] Watkinson was Assistant for the Limerick circuit. His letter to JW is not known to survive. On Blake, see JW to Zachariah Yewdall, Dec. 31, 1782.

[407] Joyce had married Alice Burrowes in Dublin, on Dec. 26, 1776.

[408] See Matt. 3:9.

Our little society for dispersing religious books among the poor has now spread them through all England.[409] Two of the books which they disperse are Alleyne's *Alarm* and Baxter's *Call to the Unconverted*. Any person that subscribes half a guinea or a guinea yearly will have four times as many books sent down as he could otherwise purchase with that sum. It seems this is one of the most excellent charities that we can be concerned in.

One of our society here went to rest on Tuesday last, and another on Wednesday.[410] They had both walked in heaviness for many years, but God did not forsake them at the last. The sting of death was taken away, and they calmly fell asleep.[411]

But there is not any need for you to stay so long before your spirit rejoices in God your Saviour.[412] He is not far from you now![413] All things are ready.[414]

> Lo! on the wings of love he flies,
> And brings redemption near![415]

I am, dear sir,
　Your very affectionate brother,

J. Wesley

Address: 'To / the Revd Mr Davenport / At Alexton / Near Uphingham / Rutlandshire'.
Postmark: '28/DE'.
Source: holograph; Bridwell Library (SMU).[416]

---

[409] See JW to Potential Subscribers, Jan. 25, 1782.

[410] The first of these was sister Gant, whom JW buried on Dec. 27; the second was Thomas Forfitt, whom he buried on Dec. 29 (see JW, Diary, 23:434). Forfitt (1706–82) was connected with the Foundery society much of his life and a trustee of City Road Chapel for three years; see Stevenson, *City Road*, 181, 250, 557.

[411] See 1 Cor. 15:55–57.

[412] See Luke 1:47.

[413] See Jer. 23:23.

[414] See Luke 14:17.

[415] CW, 'Hymns for Those Who Wait for Full Redemption, #31', st. 1, *HSP* (1749), 2:188.

[416] Held previously in the Upper Room Museum, L-164.

To Ellen Gretton

London
December 31, 1782

My Dear Sister,

You do not consider the slowness of the by-posts. A letter could not be wrote on the receipt of yours so as to reach Skillington by Wednesday, January the 1st.[417]

The thing seems to be altogether providential. It was no way of your own contriving. There is not only a fair prospect of a sufficient provision for yourself (which a Christian should not despise), but of being an instrument of good to others, which is highly desirable.

One that fears God and is waiting for his salvation is not such an unbeliever as St. Paul there speaks of.[418] Proceed with much prayer, and your way will be made plain.

I am, my dear sister,
Your affectionate brother,

J. Wesley

Address: 'To / Miss Gretton / At Mr. [Robert] Derry's, Shoemaker / In Grantham / Lincolnshire'.
Postmark: '1/IA'.
Source: holograph; Wellcome Institute, Archives, MS 6810/5.

To Zachariah Yewdall

London
December 31, 1782

My Dear Brother,

You fear when no fear is. I have appointed Mr. [Andrew] Blair to labour with you at Cork and Bandon, and shall not alter that appointment without stronger reasons than I am likely to see. If I live, I shall probably see Ireland in summer; if I do not, I expect Dr. [Thomas] Coke will.

---

[417] Gretton's letter to JW is not known to survive. In the letter she had informed JW of William Christian's proposal of marriage. They would be wed on Feb. 25, 1783.

[418] In 2 Cor. 6:14, 'Be ye not unequally yoked together with unbelievers.'

Robert Blake may go just where he will. I have nothing to do with him. Three times he left his circuit without the consent of his Assistant. He has stupidly and saucily affronted almost all the leaders. His high spirit, I fear, will destroy him. Till he is deeply humbled, I disclaim all fellowship with him.[419]

I am,

Your affectionate friend and brother,

J. Wesley

Source: published transcription; Jackson, *Works* (3rd), 13:14.

---

[419] Robert Blake (c. 1752–89) had been admitted 'on trial' as an itinerant in 1778 (see 10:474 in this edn.). He served appointments in Wales and Cornwall before crossing over to Ireland, where he served four more years (currently assigned to Limerick), before desisting from travel before the 1784 Conference (see 10:553, 971).

To Abraham Orchard[1]

1783

Dear Brother,

You have reason to be thankful to God for enabling you to set out in his good way. And if you would go on therein, remember that you cannot walk alone. Therefore your wisdom is, not to think much of shame or the fear of any temporal matter, to connect yourself in the closest manner you can with those you believe to be the children of God. A form of prayer used in private may be of considerable use; only now and then, at the beginning or middle or end of it, you may break out a little and speak a few words, just according to the present temper of your mind. When your sins are forgiven, you will surely be sensible of it. And 'everyone that seeketh findeth.'[2] But it will be given you without money and without price.[3] You know not how soon! Perhaps now!

I am,

Yours affectionately,

[J. Wesley]

Source: published transcription; Jackson, *Works* (3rd), 12:507.

Printed Circular Letter on Birstall House

London
[January 3,] 178[3]

The Case of Birstall House

[I.] 1. As many persons have spoke much upon this subject, without well understanding it, I believe it is my duty to throw all the

---

[1] Abraham Orchard (1753–93) married Martha Bishop (1759–95) in 1775. Martha was the niece of JW's friend Mary Bishop. Abraham was a solicitor with an office on Chapel Court in Bath. He was secretary of the Sunday School Committee in Bath, and one of the executors for Rev. Walter Chapman in 1791.

[2] Cf. Matt. 7:8.

[3] See Isa. 55:1.

light upon it that I can. In order to this: I will first endeavour to state the case; secondly, argue a little upon it.

2. In order to state the case fully I must look back to ancient times. As soon as the heat of persecution was over, and Christians increased in goods, some built preaching-houses, afterwards called churches. In following times those that built them were called patrons, and appointed whom they pleased to preach in them. And when they annexed lands to them, they disposed of houses and lands together.

3. At the Reformation many rich men built new churches, and disposed of them at their pleasure. And when many Presbyterians and Independents in England built preaching-houses, they placed in them whom they pleased; which power they entrusted when they died to a few friends they could confide in.

4. I built the first Methodist preaching-house so-called at Bristol, in the year 1739. And knowing no better, I suffered the Deed of Trust to be drawn up in the presbyterian form. But Mr. [George] Whitefield, hearing of it, wrote me a warm letter asking, 'Do you consider what you do? If the trustees are to *name* the preachers, they may exclude even *you* from preaching in the houses you have built. Pray let this deed be immediately cancelled.' To this the trustees readily agreed. Afterwards I built the preaching-houses in Kingswood and at Newcastle upon Tyne. But none beside myself had any right to appoint preachers in them.

5. About this time a preaching-house was built at Birstall, by con-tributions and collections. And John Nelson, knowing no better, suffered a deed to be drawn in the presbyterian form, giving twelve or thirteen persons power not only of *placing* but even of *displacing* the preachers *at their pleasure*. Had Mr. Whitefield or I known this, we should have insisted on its either being cancelled, like that at Bristol, or so altered as to insure the application of the house to the purpose for which it was built, without giving so dangerous a power to any trustees whatever.

6. But a considerable difficulty still remained. As houses at Bris-tol, Kingswood, and Newcastle were *my* property, a friend remind-ed me that they were all liable to descend to my heirs. (Pray let those consider this who are so fond of having preaching-houses vested in them and *their heirs* forever.) I was struck, and immedi-ately procured a form to be drawn up by three of the most eminent counsellors in London, whereby not only these houses, but all the Methodist houses hereafter to be built, might be settled on such a plan as would secure them, so far as human prudence could, *from the heirs* of the proprietors, for the purpose originally intended.

7. In process of time the preaching-house at Birstall became abundantly too small for the congregation. It was then proposed to build a new one. And a new deed was prepared which, like the old, gave a few people the power of *placing* and *displacing* preachers
5   *at their pleasure.* This was brought and read to me at Dawgreen. As soon as ever I heard it, I vehemently objected to it, and positively refused to sign it. I now thought I had done with it. But in the evening several persons came again and importunately urged me to sign—averring that it was the same in effect with the old deed,
10 and that the old deed *could not be altered.* Not adverting that it *was altered* in the new one, I at length unwillingly complied.[1]

But observe. Whether I did right or wrong therein, or in any other instance, it does not affect the merits of the cause. The dwelling upon this is mere finesse to divert us from the one question, 'Is that
15 deed right or wrong?'

8. These things were mentioned at the ensuing Conference and it was asked, What can be done? The answer was, 'If the trustees still refuse to settle it on the Methodist plan, if they still insist that they will have the right of *placing* and *displacing* the preachers *at*
20 *their pleasure,* then: First, let a plain state of the case be drawn up. Secondly, let a collection be made throughout England, in order to purchase ground and to build another preaching-house, as near the present as may be.'[2]

9. This I take to be a plain state of the case, separating it from all
25 unimportant circumstances of what this or the other person said or did, all which only puzzle the cause. Now this, neither more nor less, being the naked fact, I proceed,

[II.] Secondly, to argue a little upon it.
30 1. If it be asked, Why should not the Birstall house, or any other, be settled according to that deed?

I answer, because if the trustees have a power to place and displace preachers, then 1) itinerant preaching is no more. When the trustees in any place have found and fixed a preacher they like, the
35 rotation of preachers there is at an end—at least till they are tired of their favourite preachers, and so turn him out. 2) While he stays, is not the bridle in his mouth? How dares he speak the full and the whole truth, since whenever he displeases the trustees he is liable to

---

[1] See JW's longer account in his letter to CW, May 28, 1782.
[2] See *Minutes* (1782), Q. 22, 10:529 in this edn. JW has added to the text in the *Minutes* the clause 'if they still … at their pleasure'.

lose his bread? How much less will he dare to put a trustee, though ever so ungodly, out of the society? 3) But suppose any beside the Conference (who as long as they subsist will be the most impartial judges) name the preachers, should it be thirty or forty men, or the whole society? Nay, why not the entire congregation? Or at least all the subscribers? 4) The power of the trustees is greater than that of any nobleman; yea, or of the king himself. Where he is patron, he can *put in* a preacher, but he cannot *put him out.*

[2.] But you ask, 'Since this power will not commence till after your death, why should *you* oppose it? Why should not you keep yourself out of the broil, and let them fight it out when you are at rest? Why should you pull an old house upon your head when you are just going out of the world? Peace will be in *your* days. Why should you take upon yourself the burden which you may leave to your successors?'

I answer, in this respect I have an advantage which my successors cannot have. Everyone sees I am not pleading my own cause. I have already all that I contend for. I am pleading for Mr. [Christopher] Hopper, Mr. [Samuel] Bradburn, Mr. [Joseph] Benson, and for every other travelling preacher, that you may be as free after I am gone hence as you are now I am at your head; that you may never be liable to be turned out of any or all of our houses without any reason given but that so is *the pleasure* of twenty or thirty men. I say *any*, for I see no sufficient reason for giving up *any* house in England. Indeed, if one were given up, more would follow; it would be 'as the letting out of water'.[3]

I insist upon that point, and let everything else go. No Methodist trustees, if I can help it, shall after my death, any more than while I live, have the power of *placing* and *displacing* the preachers.

Observe. *Placing* and *displacing* the preachers! This is the one point. Do not ramble from the question. Do not puzzle it by a multitude of words. If the trustees will not give it up, we must proceed by the Minute of the Conference.

[3.] 'But why should we not wait till another Conference?'

First, because that will not alter the merits of the cause. To lodge the power of *placing* and *displacing* the preachers in trustees would be as wrong then as it is now.

Secondly, because you cannot ensure my life till another Conference. Therefore whatever is to be done should be done quickly.

---

[3] Cf. Prov. 17:14.

[4.] 'But then, it is said, you occasion endless strife, animosity, confusion, and destroy the work of God.' No, not I. It is these trustees that occasion all the strife, animosity, and confusion by insisting upon a right to *place* and *displace* preachers. I go on in the old way, as I did at Bristol, Kingswood, and Newcastle. It is they that, by obstinately going out of it, hinder, yea destroy, the work of God. And I charge *them* with the blood of all those souls that are destroyed by this contention. I sit down with the loss, leave them the house, and go on as if it were not in the world. It is they who do the wrong that will *place* and *displace* the preachers, who bawl with all their might and pour out bitter words. But let them take care, for God heareth. And he will arise and maintain his own cause.

J. Wesley[4]

Address: 'To / Mr [Joseph] Thompson / at the Methodist Chapel / in / Hull'.
Postmark: '6/IA'. *Charge*: '4'.
Source: printed circular; Duke, Rubenstein, Frank Baker Collection of Wesleyana, BX8483.B57 W475 1782.

To Ann Bolton[5]

London
January 5, 1783

I thought it long since I heard from my dear Nancy.[6] But I hoped 'no news were good news', and that this was a token of your not having had any fresh embarrassment. Undoubtedly you have your hands full of business. But it will not hurt you while your heart is free. As long as this is given up to God all these things must work together for good.[7] But I wanted to know whether the clouds begin

---

[4] The signature is in JW's hand.

[5] JW was replying to Bolton's letter of Jan. 3, 1783.

[6] We have placed the letter of Bolton to JW in *AM* 13 (1790): 667–68, dated Dec. 27, 1782, in 1781 instead. It is a fitting reply to JW's of Dec. 2, 1781. And if Bolton had written on Dec. 27, 1782, this opening sentence in a reply to her letter of Jan. 3, 1783 makes little sense. With this adjustment, Bolton's most recent surviving letter to JW (prior to Jan. 3) was Sept. 9, 1782.

[7] See Rom. 8:28.

to disperse? Whether you have an hope of seeing better days? Do Neddy's difficulties increase or lessen?[8] Has he a prospect of getting through his troubles? If his income is now superior to his expense, he has ground to believe all will end well. And how does he bear up under this burden? Does it drive him from or lead him to God? It 5 is enough if it

> Keeps him dead to all below,
> Only Christ resolved to know.[9]

10

I have likewise great hopes that you will see a good increase of the work of God in Witney. I suppose the prayer meetings still continue! In many places they have been of more use than even the preaching. And in them the flame first broke out which afterwards spread through the whole people. You have, I hope, more than one 15 or two at those meetings who use the gift which God has given them. And if they pray for the *whole gospel salvation*, God will send a gracious answer down. I shall hope for the pleasure of seeing you in March. But do not stay till February before you write to, my dear Nancy, 20
       Yours most affectionately,

                       J. Wesley

Address: 'To / Miss Bolton / In Witney / Oxfordshire'.
Postmark: '6/IA'. 25
Endorsement: by Bolton, 'Jan 5 1783'.
Source: holograph; privately held (WWEP Archive holds photocopy).

30

To Robert Carr Brackenbury

                   London 35
            January 10, 1783
Dear Sir,
    As I expect to remain in London till the beginning of March, I hope to have the pleasure of spending a little time with you before

---

[8] Her brother, Edward Bolton Jr.
[9] CW, Hymn on John 16:24, st. 4, *HSP* (1739), 220.

I set out on my spring and summer journeys, which I shall probably continue as long as I live. And who would wish to live for any
meaner purpose than to serve God in our generation?[10] I know my
health and strength are continued for this ⟨one⟩[11] thing. And if ever
5   I should listen to that siren song 'Spare thy life', I believe my Master would spare me no longer, but soon take me away. It pleases him
to deal with *you* in a different way. He frequently calls you not so
much to *act* as to *suffer*. And you may well say,

10   O take thy way! Thy way is best.
                    Grant or deny me ease.
                This is but tuning of my breast
                    To make the music please.[12]

15   I am glad you are still determined to do what you can, and to
do it without delay. But others are not of this mind. I have just
received a letter from Mr. [James] Oddie, formerly one of our travelling preachers, informing me whereas it has pleased God to take
away his dear partner, 'he is resolved again to give up himself to the
20   work'—after he has settled his worldly business, which he thinks
will take but sixteen or seventeen months![13] Would one think he had
ever read the ⟨Epistle⟩ of St. James? or that he had ever heard those
words, 'What is your life? It is even a vapour, which appeareth and
vanisheth away?'[14] Commending you to him who is able to save you
25   to the uttermost,[15]
       I am, dear sir,
          Your affectionate friend and brother,

                                                    J. Wesley

30   *Address*: 'To / Robert Brackenbury Esq / At the New Room / in / Bris-
       tol'.
     Postmark: '11/IA'.
     Source: holograph; Drew, Methodist Archives.

[10] See Acts 13:36.
[11] A small portion is torn away by the wax seal, affecting one word on each side of the page.
[12] George Herbert, 'The Temper', st. 5, as adapted by JW in *HSP* (1739), 54.
[13] This letter from Oddie is not known to survive. He married Sarah (Holehouse) Thompson in 1761, and decided to locate in Yarm in 1771. In fact, Oddie did not return to itinerant ministry; instead marrying in 1784 Sarah (Flesher / Sharp) Colbeck, the widow of Thomas Colbeck.
[14] James 4:14.
[15] See Heb. 7:25.

To Elizabeth Padbury

[London]
January 10, 1783

My Dear Sister,

It is not an easy thing for me to refuse anything which *you* desire. As soon as Dr. [Thomas] Coke returns to London (which I suppose will be in two or three weeks) I doubt not but George Whitfield will be ready to take up his cross again. It is certain there is an absolute necessity that something should be done. And it should be done as soon as you possibly can, for fear the roof should fall in.[16]

I hope *you* are gaining ground daily. I love you much and am, my dear Betsy,

Yours most affectionately,

J. Wesley

Address: 'To / Miss Padbury / At Whittlebury / near / Towcester'.
Postmark: '11/IA'.
Source: holograph; Bridwell Library (SMU).[17]

To Joseph Taylor

London
January 16, 1783

Dear Joseph,

I am glad to hear so good an account of Marazion.

You must endeavour to hire a larger room at Truro. We shall not build any more in haste. I often preach abroad in winter as well as summer.

In my *Journals*, in the *[Arminian] Magazine*, in every possible way, I have advised the Methodists to keep to the Church [of England]. They that do this most prosper best in their souls; I have

---

[16] Padbury had likely informed JW of the need for repairs on the Methodist preaching-house in Whittlebury, built in 1763; see JW, *Journal*, June 21, 1763, 21:419 in this edn. Her letter is not known to survive.

[17] Held previously in the WMC Museum, 2002.001.018.

observed it long. If ever the Methodists in general were to leave the Church, I must leave them.

I am, dear Joseph,
    Your affectionate friend and brother,

5
                                                            J. Wesley

Address: 'To / Mr Jos. Taylor / At Mr Batten's Junr[18] / in Penzance / Cornwall'.
Postmark: '16/IA'. *Charge*: '4'.
10
Source: holograph; MARC, MAM JW 5/5.

To John Francis Valton[19]

15
                                                            London
                                                    January 16, 1783
My Dear Brother,
20   Here are two questions: 1) 'Whether I have acted right?' I answer, No. I ought to have resolutely withstood all importunity. 2) 'Whether trustees should place and displace preachers?' (This is the essential question.) I say No again; otherwise intolerable consequences will follow.
25   I am,
        Your affectionate friend and brother,

                                                            J. Wesley

Pray send my love to George Brown, and tell him I have his letter.[20]
30
Address: 'To / Mr Valton / At Birstal / near / Leeds'.
Postmark: '16/IA'.
Endorsements: by Valton, 'Janu 16 1783' and 'Sent 26 Jan to / Mrs(?) Wathen / —W. Gadd / —J. Harrop / Dr. [Thomas] Coke'.
35
Source: holograph; MARC, MAM JW 5/31.

[18] Cf. Joseph Batten in JW to Francis Wolf, Jan. 24, 1782.
[19] As Assistant for the Birstall circuit, Valton was at the focus of debate over the deed for the preaching-house. He had apparently conveyed to JW questions arising from the circular letter sent out in early January.
[20] It is unclear whether Valton was in correspondence with the Irish itinerant George Brown, or if this was someone in Birstall; the letter is not known to survive.

To John Francis Valton

London
January 22, 1783 5

My Dear Brother,

It is right to add as much solemnity as we can to the admission of new members.

I think you may refer the case of the butcher's wife to the leaders. 'Not to sell' would certainly be the more excellent way. But whether 10 she should be expelled upon that account may be matter of doubt.

There must be some particular end designed in every extraordinary work of God. But there are instances wherein it is a considerable time before that end appears. And it may be expedient for us to remain in suspense in order to wean us from our own will and our 15 own wisdom. If there was any particular meaning in that appearance, God will reveal it in due time.

I am,
Your affectionate friend and brother,

[J. Wesley] 20

Address: 'To / Mr. Valton / At the Preaching-house / In Manchester'.
Source: published transcription; Telford, *Letters*, 7:164.

25

To Richard Rodda[21]

30
London
January 23, 1783

Dear Richard,

It is very remarkable that you should have a prospect of doing good at Oxford! And it is certainly a token for good that you should 35 find a magistrate willing to do you justice.

To you who are upon the spot I shall refer that matter whether it be expedient for Roger Westrup, in such a situation of affairs, to preach at High Wycombe?[22] I should doubt it much.

[21] Rodda's letter that drew this reply is not known to survive, leaving the details behind JW's response uncertain.
[22] Westrup may have been courting Hannah Ball; see JW to Ball, Oct. 18, 1783.

As some of our preachers are vehement sticklers for the Birstall trustees, that affair will sleep till the Conference.

I am,

Your affectionate friend and brother,

J. Wesley

Address: 'To / Mr. Rodda / At Mr. Wickens'[23] / In Castle Street / Oxon'.
Postmark: '26/IA'. *Charge*: '3'.
Source: holograph; Bridwell Library (SMU).[24]

To Thomas Tattershall

London
January 23, 1783

Dear Tommy,

I believe you will do well to write your life in as particular a manner as you please.[25] But I do not think you are called to write verses, that is a particular talent.

The *Primitive Physic* will show you how to cure any purging, either by rhubarb and nutmeg, or lemon, sugar, and water. But if you cannot have your health in the Isle, you shall remove to another circuit.[26]

I doubt not you and your fellow labourers exhort all the believers to go on to perfection.[27] And I hope you find more and more who do enter into that rest. I am, dear Tommy,

Your affectionate brother,

[J. Wesley]

Source: published transcription; Byrth, 'Memoir', xxxiii.

---

[23] Joseph Wickens (1753–1814) was a boot and shoemaker on Castle Street in Oxford.

[24] Held previously in the Upper Room Museum, L-166.

[25] JW had likely encouraged him to provide an autobiographical account like those of other preachers being published in *AM*. But no such published account was forthcoming.

[26] Tattershall was currently assigned to the Isle of Man circuit.

[27] See Heb. 6:1.

To William Petty, Earl of Shelburne

City Road [London]
January 25, 1783

My Lord,

Although your Lordship was not pleased to take any notice of my last,[28] yet I take the liberty of troubling you once more; which indeed, I should have done some time ago, but that I knew what an immense weight of business lies upon your Lordship, particularly at this critical season.

I am thoroughly persuaded of your Lordship's humanity, and perhaps your Lordship will judge this a proper occasion of exerting it.

I cannot but beg him who is higher than you to give your Lordship the wisdom that sitteth by his throne! For I earnestly wish your Lordship may prosper in all things, and am, my Lord,

Your Lordship's willing servant,

John Wesley

Endorsement: '25 Jan. 1783 / Revd John Wesley in behalf of John Barnes, in Clerkenwell Prison for an excise debt'. (in separate hand) 'Sent the Petition to Mr. Prose 6th Feb. / J.W.'.
Source: holograph; Drew, Methodist Archives.

To Miss Fuller[29]

[February 1783?]

My Dear Sister,

You did well in giving me a plain and circumstantial account of the manner wherein God has dealt with your soul. Your part is now to stand fast in the glorious liberty wherewith Christ has made you

---

[28] See JW to Petty, Dec. 21, 1782.

[29] This letter is undated and identified as to 'Miss Fuller' in both Benson and Jackson, *Works* (3rd), 12:477. Telford placed it in Feb. 1783, and changed 'Miss' to 'Mrs', on the assumption was the recipient was the 'sister Fuller' / 'Mrs. Fuller' JW visited Jan. 28–29, 1783 (see his diary, 23:438 in this edn.). There is no evidence to confirm (or disprove) this equation, or to identify 'Miss Fuller' with the Elizabeth Fuller (1760–1836) buried at City Road Chapel (see Stevenson, *City Road*, 517).

free. There is no need that you should ever be entangled again in the bondage of pride or anger or desire.[30] God is willing to give always what he grants once. Temptations, indeed, you are to expect. But you may tread them all under your feet. His grace is sufficient
5   for you.[31] And the God of all grace, after you have suffered a while, shall establish, strengthen, and settle you.[32]

    I am, my dear sister,
       Yours affectionately,

J. Wesley

10
Source: published transcription; Benson, *Works*, 16:144–45.

To Zachariah Yewdall

London
February 9, 1783

20 My Dear Brother,
    I am glad you have given another trial to Inishannon.[33] And why not to Kinsale?[34] I am a good deal of your mind. I hope those are only drops before a shower of grace. Over and above the general reasons contained in that tract, a preacher, and above all others a
25   Methodist preacher, has particular reasons for valuing a single life.[35]
    I am glad Andrew Blair and you converse freely together.[36] It will preserve you from many snares. There can be no properer person for a trustee than Andrew Laffan. I have hope that Robert Blake will be more useful than ever.

30   I am,
       Your affectionate friend and brother,

[J. Wesley]

Source: published transcription; Jackson, *Works* (3rd), 13:14–15.

---

[30] See Gal. 5:1.

[31] See 2 Cor. 12:9.

[32] Cf. CW, Hymn for Believers #15, st. 7, *HSP* (1749), 1:219; 'Settle, confirm, and 'stablish me'.

[33] JW's last previous visit to Inishannon was July 15, 1758 (*Journal*, 21:18 in this edn.).

[34] Orig. in Jackson, 'Hinscla'; surely a misreading. JW's last previous visit to Kinsale was June 24, 1762 (*Journal*, 21:370 in this edn.).

[35] The tract was surely JW's *Thoughts on a Single Life* (1765).

[36] Orig. in Jackson, 'C. Blair'; another misreading. JW had arranged for Andrew Blair to join Yewdall in Cork after the death of Richard Boardman; see JW to Yewdall, Nov. 12, 1782.

To John Cricket[37]

London
February 10, 1783

My Dear Brother,   5

Many years ago the society at Barnard Castle, as large as that at Derry, was remarkably dead. When Samuel Meggot (now with God) came to them, he advised them to keep a day of fasting and prayers.[38] A flame broke out and spread through all the circuit.[39] Nor is it extinguished to this day.   10

I advise you to do the same at Derry. On Sunday morning reprove strongly their unfaithfulness and unfruitfulness, and desire all that fear God to humble themselves with fasting on the Friday following. I am much inclined to hope a flame will break out in Londonderry likewise.   15

But you must immediately resume *the form* at least of a Methodist society. I positively forbid you or any preacher to be a [class] leader; rather put the most insignificant person in each class to be the leader of it. And try if you cannot persuade three men, if no more, and three women to meet in band.   20

Hope to the end! You shall see better days! I am,

Yours affectionately,

J. Wesley

The plainer you speak the more good you will do. Derry will bear plain dealing.   25

Name a steward likewise.

Give those books away. Any of us if you desire it will pay brother Thackwray.

I am just as well as I was forty years ago.   30

Address: 'To / Mr Cricket'.[40]
Source: holograph; Wesley's Chapel (London), LDWMM 1994/1997.

---

[37] John Cricket (d. 1806) was admitted 'on trial' as an itinerant in 1780 (see 10:496 in this edn.). Known for his plain manner and clear piety, Cricket continued travelling until a year before his death. See *Minutes* (post-Wesley, 1807), 2:379; and Crookshank, *Ireland*, 345.

[38] Samuel Meggot (c. 1715–64) was from Haxey, Lincolnshire. He began preaching on his own in the area, came to JW's attention, and was considered for becoming a travelling preacher in 1758, but Conference was not yet ready to approve him (see 10:282 in this edn.). Even so, JW encouraged his work as a local preacher in the Dales area in the early 1760s; see JW, *Journal*, May 8, 1742 (19:261–64), and June 12, 1763 (21:416–17).

[39] See Meggot's account, recorded by JW in *Journal*, June 12, 1763, 21:416–17 in this edn.

[40] Apparently part of a packet that included the next letter to Alexander Knox.

To Alexander Knox

London
February 10, 1783

My Dear Alleck,

It seems to me, that your reasons are good. Therefore I consent to your selling the old preaching-house, and building a new one like that at Lisburn. Only it should be a third part larger, for you are to provide for the Sunday's congregation and for a revival of the work of God. Therefore there should be sufficient height for galleries, whether you build them at first or not.

Only remember! You are not to expect any assistance from the English Conference. For we do not now make any collection for building, but only for the expenses of carrying on the work. I believe the exerting yourself herein will be a means of quickening your own soul!

I am, with tender love to all the family, my dear Alleck,
> Yours affectionately,

J. Wesley

Address: 'To / Mr Alexr Knox'.
Source: holograph; Bridwell Library (SMU).[41]

To Ellen Gretton

Deptford
February 16, 1783

My Dear Sister,

If you enter into a new state, the first steps you take will be of the utmost importance.[42] Leave nothing to the morrow, but *begin* exactly as you hope to *go on*. It might be of use for Mr. Christian and you carefully to read over and consider those directions to mar-

---

[41] Held previously in the Upper Room Museum, L-33.
[42] Gretton was preparing to marry William Christian (1756–1834) of Skillington on Feb. 25, 1783.

ried persons which are in the fourth volume of *Sermons*.[43] Whatever family follows those directions will be as a city set upon an hill.[44]

I am glad to hear that regular preaching is already begun at Skillington. We have no time to lose. If a few should be awakened there, I doubt not the work will increase, and perhaps you will have a larger sphere of action than ever you had yet. Meantime be faithful in that which is little!

I am, my dear sister,
    Your affectionate brother,

                                 J. Wesley

Address: 'To / Miss Gretton / At Mr [Robert] Derry's / In Grantham / Lincolnshire'.
Postmark: '18/FE'.
Source: holograph; Drew, Methodist Archives.

To the Rev. J[ames] Bailey[45]

                                London
                    February 23, 1783

My Dear Brother,

The publisher of the *Christian Magazine* (I suppose he is but one, though he pompously styles himself a *society*) has honoured rather than disgraced you.[46] Certainly you are obliged to him. But I apprehend it is your wisest way to take no manner of notice of him. I am,
    Your affectionate brother,

                                 J. Wesley

---

[43] I.e., 'The Duties of Husbands and Wives', extracted by JW from William Whately, *A Bride-bush: or, A Direction for Married Persons* (1619); see Vol. 15 in this edn.

[44] See Matt. 5:14.

[45] This is almost certainly Rev. James Bailey (1753–1816), who was a curate at Otley (Elizabeth Ritchie's parish) in 1778, and named vicar there in 1786 (till his death); he also held the living of perpetual curate at Farnley (1782–1816).

[46] JW was referring to *The New Christian's Magazine* (London: Alexander Hogg, 1782–84), which described itself as 'by a society of clergymen of the diocese of London'. The magazine had just launched in Oct. 1782, and included in its Feb. 1783 issue (1:240–41) a note from 'J. Bailey' and an excerpt from a recent book that he encouraged to be published as he believed it explained the 'locusts' eaten by John the Baptist (Matt. 3:4). It is likely that Bailey had intended this to be published in JW's *Arminian Magazine*, and was chagrined it appeared here instead.

Address: 'To / The Rev Mr J. Bailey'.[47]
Source: holograph; privately held (WWEP Archive holds photocopy).

5

To Thomas Rutherford

London
10
February 23, 1783

Dear Tommy,

I am glad you have wrote to brother [Robert] Blake to go into Ballyconnell circuit. He has wrote me a very proper letter.[48] If you can bring William West to make any concessions, I am willing to try
15
him again.[49]

I believe the books in Dublin were confused enough, for I doubt Joseph did not take much better care of them than he did of the people.[50] If brother [Henry] Moore and his wife should stay awhile in Dublin, I think the two sisters will not quarrel with each other.[51]
20
I scarce know which of them I love best.

Peace be with all your spirits! I am, dear Tommy,
Your affectionate friend and brother,

J. Wesley

25

Address: 'To / Mr Rutherford / At the New Room / in / Dublin'.
Source: holograph; MARC, WCB, D6/3/1/12.

---

[47] The photocopy held by WWEP lacks an address portion; but when the letter was listed in Sotheby's *Catalogue of the … Collection of autograph letters … property of … Samuel Addington … sold by auction… 24th of April, 1876* (p. 53), it was described as addressed to Rev. Mr. J. Bailey.

[48] Cf. JW to Zachariah Yewdall, Dec. 31, 1782 and Feb. 9, 1783. Blake's letter to JW is not known to survive.

[49] William West (c. 1742–1822), a native of Ireland, became a travelling preacher there in 1779, appearing first in the *Minutes* of the 1780 Conference (10:499 in this edn.). Whatever the concern, it was resolved, as he attained full standing at the Conference in Aug. 1783 (10:531) and continued serving until forced by illness to desist in 1817. See *Minutes* (post-Wesley, 1823), 5:381; and *WMM* 1 (1822): 686.

[50] Joseph Pilmore had been Assistant for the Dublin circuit prior to Rutherford.

[51] Moore had been appointed to Londonderry; but when Andrew Blair moved to Cork, he went to Dublin, where he had family business to settle. Moore's wife Anne and Rutherford's wife Isabella were sisters.

To Ambrose Foley

London
February 24, 1783

My Dear Brother,   5

I am glad to hear that sister [Jane] Foley and you are still going on to perfection.[52] On Wednesday, March the 19th, I hope to be at Worcester; and about the 20th at Birmingham. Then we may determine something concerning Quinton!

I am,   10
    Your affectionate brother,

J. Wesley

Address: 'To / Mr Foley / At Quinton, near / Birmingham'.
Postmark: '24/FE'. *Charge*: '4'.
Source: holograph; MARC, MAM JW 3/5.   15

To George Blackall[53]

London   20
February 25, 1783

My Dear Brother,

St. Paul teaches that it is in heaven we are to be joined with 'the spirits of just men made perfect'[54]—in such a sense as we cannot be on earth or even in paradise. In paradise the souls of good men   25 rest from their labours and are with Christ from death to the resurrection. This bears no resemblance at all to the popish purgatory, wherein wicked men are supposed to be tormented in purging fire till they are sufficiently purified to have a place in heaven. But we believe (as did the ancient church) that none suffer after death but   30 those who suffer eternally. We believe that we are to be *here* saved from sin and enabled to love God with all our heart.

I am,
    Your affectionate brother,

J. Wesley   35

Address: 'To George Blackall, Brentford'.
Source: published transcription; *Wesleyan Methodist Magazine* 48 (1825): 248.

---

[52] See Heb. 6:1.

[53] Nothing more is certain; but this may be the 'brother Blackall' with whom JW had tea on Feb. 13, 1783 (see diary, 23:439 in this edn.).

[54] Heb. 12:23.

To Joseph Taylor

London
February 25, 1783

Dear Joseph,

I make no doubt but you will be well able to collect enough in the circuit to enlarge the house at St. Ives. And the sooner you begin, the better. Only see that you have good workmen and a good plan! Remember, light enough and air enough; and do not make a bungling but a neat work.

When I have fixed my plan, I will send you a copy of it. I set out for Bristol on Sunday evening.

I am, dear Joseph,

Your affectionate friend and brother,

J. Wesley

Pray tell Capt. Richard Williams that I have his letter, and will consider it.[55]

Address: 'To / Mr Taylor / At Mr [John] Nance's / In St Ives / Cornwall'.
Postmark: '26/FE'. *Charge*: '4'.
Source: holograph; MARC, MAM JW 5/6.

To William Black Jr.[56]

London
February 26, 1783

My Dear Brother,

I did indeed very strongly expostulate with the Bishop of London concerning his refusing to ordain a pious man, although he had not

[55] Neither this letter nor any response at the time from JW are known to survive.

[56] William Black Jr. (1760–1834), born at Huddersfield, was taken to Nova Scotia by his mother in 1775, following his father who had left in 1774. He was converted in 1779 (see his account published by JW in his *Journal*, Apr. 15, 1782, 23:236–37 in this edn.), and soon after began to exhort and preach locally. In 1786 Black was taken into full connexion in the Methodist Episcopal Church and devoted his life to spreading the gospel, becoming known as 'the Apostle of Methodism to Nova Scotia'. For a fuller account, see Jackson, *EMP*, 5:242–95 (cf. in-letters, June 1, 1788); and Richey, William Black.

learning, while he ordained others that to my knowledge had no piety, and but a moderate share of learning.[57] I incline to think that letter will appear in public some time hence.

Our next Conference is to begin in July, and I have great hopes we shall then be able to send you assistance.[58] One of our preachers informs me he is willing to go to any part of Africa or America. He does not regard danger or toil. Nor indeed does he count his life dear unto himself, so that he may testify the gospel of the grace of God and win sinners to Christ. But I cannot advise any person to go alone. Our Lord sent his disciples two and two.[59] And I do not despair of finding another young man as much devoted to God as he.

The antinomian you mention ought to be guarded against with all possible diligence.[60] Otherwise he will do more hurt in one year than he can do good in twenty. And it is well if he that calls himself Lady Huntingdon's preacher does not do as much hurt as him. Of Calvinism, mysticism, and antinomianism have a care; for they are the bane of true religion, and one or other of them has been the grand hindrance of the work of God wherever it has broke out.

If you come over to England, we will make room for you at Kingswood.

Peace be with all your spirits. I am, my dear brother,

Your affectionate brother,

John Wesley

Address: 'To / Mr Willm. Black Junr / In Halifax / Nova Scotia'.
Postmark: '4/MR'.
Endorsement: 'Revd. Jno Wesley / London 26 Feby 1783'.
Source: holograph; Toronto, Canada, United Church of Canada Archives, 97.002C, 3-19.

[57] See JW to Robert Lowth, Aug. 10, 1780, concerning John Hoskins (29:589–91 in this edn.). The letter was not published during JW's life, but appeared in Whitehead, *Life* (1793), 2:392–94.

[58] The Conference began July 29, 1783, but the *Minutes* include no mention of sending or supporting preachers to regions of North America still connected to Britain. This would wait until 1785.

[59] See Mark 6:7.

[60] While Black's letter to JW is not known to survive, in a subsequent exchange it is clear that the person of concern was Henry Alline (see JW to Black, July 13, 1783).

To Elizabeth (Nangle) Bradburn

London
February 26, 1783

My Dear Betsy,

This morning I have wrote to Mrs. Carr.[61] And I do not despair of its having some effect, especially as I have added that 'I hope to see her in a month or two'. For I believe she would not easily do anything that might make her ashamed to see me. You did well, in dissuading Mr. [Samuel] Bradburn from writing. Let us try all fair means first. Any harshness might afford a pretense for refusing, or at least delaying, the payment.

It has pleased God hitherto to lead Sammy and you in a rough and thorny way. But it is happy, that you have learned to say, 'Not as I will, but as thou wilt.'[62] It is a beautiful saying of Mr. Herbert's:

> Grant, or deny me ease;
> This is but tuning of my breast
> To make the music please![63]

I am, my dear Betsy,
  Yours most affectionately,

J. Wesley

Source: holograph; WHS Ireland Archives.

To William Thompson

Bristol
[March 6] 1783

As we have no preacher to spare, certainly while you are in Edinburgh, settling your affairs and selling your furniture, one of

---

[61] Orig., 'Karr'. Elizabeth (Suthess / Palmer) Carr was Elizabeth (Nangle) Bradburn's widowed step-mother; see the note on JW to Samuel Bradburn, June 4, 1778, 29:423 in this edn. Bradburn had apparently asked JW's help in resolving a dispute over a financial matter.
[62] Matt. 26:39.
[63] George Herbert, 'The Temper', st. 5, as adapted by JW in *HSP* (1739), 54.

the preachers in the Edinburgh circuit must go to your place at Dundee. Let Mr. Saunderson know directly.[64]

Source: secondary holograph; MARC, PLP 94/18/1 (quoted in letter of Joseph Saunderson to Samuel Bardsley).

To John Baxendale[65]

Bristol
March 7, 1783

My Dear Brother,

I had much satisfaction when I was with you last, and hope to spend a night with you again, though I can't yet fix the time. I agree with you it would be well if the chapel were properly settled. You do well to lose no opportunity of enlarging your borders. It is an acceptable time. We are now more especially called to preach the gospel to every creature.[66] And many of the last shall be first.[67] If we live to meet, I shall be glad to converse with that good young woman you speak of.

The happy death of that poor mourner was a token for good. It was intended to encourage you in warning everyone and exhorting [every]one.[68] Even though you do not see any present fruit, in due time you shall reap if you faint not.[69]

Strongly exhort all believers to go on to perfection.[70] I am,

Your affectionate brother,

J. Wesley

Address: 'To / Mr. Baxendale / In Wigan / Lancashire'.
Source: holograph; privately held (WWEP holds photocopy).

[64] Joseph Saunderson (b. 1746), a native of Birstall, was born into a Methodist family there. He was accepted 'on trial' as an itinerant at the 1775 Conference (see 10:440 in this edn.). He served full-time for about ten years and is listed as desisting from travelling in 1784 (10:553). But his name continues to reappear in the *Minutes* as late as 1805, most frequently in Scotland, and often in a supernumerary status. See *WHS* 10 (1915): 94–97.

[65] Little is known for sure about John Baxendale, except that he was active as a local preacher among Methodists in Wigan and beyond, until at least 1790; see John Stott, *Notices of Methodism in Haslingden* (London: Hayman et al., 1898), 38. Baxendale's letter that drew this reply is not known to survive.

[66] See Mark 16:15.
[67] See Matt. 20:16.
[68] See Col. 1:28.
[69] See Gal. 6:9.
[70] See Heb. 6:1.

To John Mason

Bristol
March 7, 1783

My Dear Brother,

I do not know that there was anything amiss in those letters. I hope the ground of complaint is now taken away. I was in the same case with you till the last meetings of the trustees. Five of them then agreed to sign the bonds. Hitherto it has been everybody's business and [no]body's business. I think now it will be done effectually.

Great bodies usually move slowly. Had we five or seven, instead of five-and-twenty trustees, they would not have been so unwieldy.

I hope you go on well in the Isle, and am

Your affectionate friend and brother,

J. Wesley

Address: 'To / Mr Mason / At the Preachinghouse / In Newport / Isle of Wight'.
Postmark: 'Bristol'.
Source: holograph; MARC, MAM JW 4/8.

To Hester Ann Roe

Bristol
March 16, 1783

My Dear Hetty,

I shall not be able to come to Macclesfield quite as soon as usual this year, for the preaching-houses at Hinckley and Nottingham are to be opened, which I take in my way. I expect to be at Nottingham April 1. But how long I shall stay there I cannot yet determine. Thence I shall probably come by Derby to Macclesfield.

It has frequently been in my mind of late that my pilgrimage is nearly at an end, and one of our sisters here told us this morning a particular dream which she had two months ago. She dreamed the time of Conference was come, and that she was in a church expecting me to come in—when she saw a coffin brought in, followed by Dr. [Thomas] Coke and Mr. [John] Fletcher, then by all our preachers, walking two by two. A fortnight ago she dreamed the same dream again. Such a burying I have ordered in my will, absolutely forbidding either hearse or coach.

I intended [here his hand falters[71]] to have written a good deal more, but I am hardly able. For a few days past I have had just such a fever as I had in Ireland a few years ago.[72] But all is well. I am in no pain. But the wheels of life scarcely seem able to turn any longer. Yet I made a shift this morning to preach to a crowded audience, and hope to say something to them this afternoon. I love that word, 'And Ishmael died in the presence of all his brethren.'[73]

I am, in life and death, my dear Hetty,
    Yours affectionately,[74]

                          J. W.

Source: published transcriptions; Benson, *Works*, 16:265–66; (Roe) Rogers, *Extracts*, 240.[75]

To an Unidentified Man

                         Birmingham
                     March 23, 1783

Dear Sir,
If you would have five or ten more, be so kind as to give an hint to
    Yours affectionately,

                       J. Wesley

Source: holograph; Drew, Methodist Archives.

---

[71] This note is added by Roe.

[72] See JW, *Journal*, Mar. 13–23, 1783, 23:264–65 in this edn.; and (for Ireland) JW, *Journal*, June 13–28, 1775, 22:455–57. Benson's transcription moves 'in Ireland' to the end of the sentence.

[73] Cf. Gen. 25:18.

[74] We give the closing as in Roe; Benson has instead: 'Still pray for, my dear Hetty, Yours most affectionately'.

[75] No early source gives the complete letter. The first paragraph is found in Benson, but not Roe's Extract; while the second paragraph is found in Roe, but not Benson. The third paragraph appears in both sources, but with a variant ending (as noted above). Jackson (*Works*, 13:67–68) reproduces Benson; Telford (*Letters*, 7:171–72) combines the two sources, as we do above, but follows Benson for the ending.

To John Francis Valton

Nottingham
April 1, 1783

5 My Dear Brother,

Being more than half recovered from my late illness, I am creeping forward on my way. I purpose staying here till over Sunday. Then I think of moving on toward Dublin.

Your reasons for desiring to spend another year in Birstall circuit seem to me to be of weight. It may be so, if nothing occurs to the contrary between this and the Conference.[76]

I am,

Your affectionate friend and brother,

[J. Wesley]

15

Address: 'To / Mr. Valton / At Birstall / Near Leeds'.
Source: published transcription; Telford, *Letters*, 7:172–73.

20

To the Rev. Charles Wesley

Nottingham
April 4, 1783

25 [[Dear Brother,]]

Yesterday my second disorder left me, and I seem now to be recovering strength.[77] On Monday next I hope to be at Derby; on Tuesday, at Newcastle-under-Lyme; on Wednesday, at Chester; and at Holyhead as soon as God permits. I have no desire to stay above three weeks in Ireland, and hope to be in England again before the end of May.

On the day appointed, March 25, I went from Birmingham to Hilton Park.[78] A little before we reached the park gate Miss Free-

---

[76] Valton was reappointed to Birstall at the 1783 Conference.

[77] See JW, *Journal*, Mar. 6 through Apr. 1, 1783 (23:264–66 in this edn.). He first had a cold that resulted in a deep, tearing cough—which was followed days later by a fever.

[78] Hilton Park (near Wolverhampton, Staffordshire) was an estate currently owned by Sir Philip Gibbes (1731–1815) and his wife Agnes (Osborne) Gibbes (d. 1813). Philip grew up on a sugar plantation in Barbados owned by his father, and inherited it. While his wife and children lived mainly in England by this point, he spent considerable time in Barbados. For more on this family and their relationship to JW, see Clive Norris, 'John Wesley and Enslavement Revisited', *WHS* 64 (2023): 15–23.

man met us in Sir Philip Gibbes's chaise.[79] After staring awhile, she came into my chaise and she was convinced that I was alive.

That afternoon and the next day I gathered strength apace. The place was agreeable, and much more the company. Lady [Agnes] Gibbes put me in mind of one of Queen Elizabeth's dames of honour. Her daughters are exceeding amiable,[80] but sink under Miss Freeman's superior sense, and begin to feel that they are not Christians. She has been of great service to them, and hies[81] at them day and night to show them what is real religion. On Wednesday night they were much struck; the younger sister [Agnes] could not contain herself, but burst out into a passion of tears. Miss Freeman herself seems to be utterly disconcerted, seeking rest, but finding none. If Sally is not hurt by her, she (Sally) will help her much.[82] She now feels her want of help.

I wish King George (like Louis XIV) would be his own Prime Minister.[83] The nation would soon feel the difference. All these things will work together for good.[84] Let us work while the day is![85] I take no thought for the morrow.[86]

Peace be with you all.

[[Adieu.]]

---

[79] Mary Freeman Shepherd (1731–1815) was born to Anthony Freeman (1703–73) and his first wife Ann Fallett (1704–33). She was particularly close to, and received support from, an unmarried uncle named Nathaniel Shepherd (1718–59)—and around 1784 added his surname (she never married). Mary's relationship to her father and the larger Freeman family was strained. A major reason for (or expression of) this strain was her embracing the Roman Catholic faith of her maternal ancestors (the Falletti family in the Piedmont, Italy). It has been suggested that Mary was educated at a convent in Rome. Mary began to appear in Wesley family correspondence in 1783, becoming a close friend of Sarah Wesley Jr. and a key influence in the decision of Charles Wesley's son Samuel to convert to Roman Catholicism. In JW's *Journal* record of this meeting he comments that he had known Mary almost from her childhood (see 23:265 in this edn.). He had corresponded with her from at least 1757; see JW to Ebenezer Blackwell, May 28, 1757, 27:84–85 in this edn.

[80] Philip and Agnes (Osborne) Gibbes had two daughters: Elizabeth (1760–1847), who would marry Charles Abbot in 1796; and Agnes (1761–1843).

[81] See *OED*: 'to use diligence'.

[82] Referring to Sarah Wesley Jr.

[83] Beginning with Robert Walpole, who was 1st Lord of the Treasury (1721–42), it became common to refer to the person in that role as 'Prime Minister'. JW had been unhappy with the responsiveness of William Petty, most recently in that role. This and other offices were in transition in Apr. 1783 with the formation of a new administration, in which William Cavendish-Bentinck (1738–1809), 3rd Duke of Portland was named 1st Lord of the Treasury.

[84] See Rom. 8:28.

[85] See John 9:4.

[86] See Matt. 6:34.

Address: 'To / Revd. Mr. C. Wesley / Marybone / London'.
Postmark: '7/AP'.
Endorsement: by CW, 'B[rother] / April 11. 1783 / meeting Miss Freeman'.
Source: holograph; MARC, MAM JW 5/52.

5

To Alexander Knox

10

Nottingham
April 5, 1783

Dear Alleck,

If it please God to prosper us, Dr. [Thomas] Coke and I shall be at Dublin in ten days. I do not think of staying there above three weeks. Probably Dr. Coke will go through the kingdom. Our Dublin Conference is to begin on Tuesday, May 6th. All the preachers that conveniently can, may be present.

I received from David Harvey, Esq. and Company fifteen guineas, being the amount of an order from Thomas Bateson, Esq. of Londonderry.[87]

Mr. Hadfield doubtless did deliver up the lease; but to whom the lease and assignment were delivered, I know not.[88] In default of these, a bond might be executed when I am [at] Dublin that would secure the purchaser.

I like your plan well. Only I doubt whether you should not have more windows on each side, and all sashes opening downward. And I pray, let there be no tub-pulpit.[89]

I am glad to hear so good an account of John Cricket, and will order Mr. [John] Atlay to pay the ten pounds.

I did not think, Dr. Goodman had been so clear with regard to Christian perfection.[90] My eldest brother [Samuel] used to say that was 'the best book, of its kind, in the English tongue'.

---

[87] David Harvey was a merchant on Laurence Lane in Cheapside, London. Cf. JW to Knox, Sept. 3, 1781, 29:681–82 in this edn.

[88] See JW to Knox, Sept. 20, 1776, 29:285–86 in this edn.

[89] See 'Large' *Minutes* (1770), Q. 68, 10:897 in this edn.: 'Let there be no tub-pulpit, but a square projection, with a long seat behind.'

[90] The reference is almost certainly to John Goodman's, *Winter Evening Conference Between Neighbours: in Three Parts* (orig., 1686; 9th edn., London: Meredith, 1705). See, for example the insistence in Part III, p. 47 that 'the joys of religion come in gradually, and … are always growing higher and higher to a perfect day of glory' which brings 'victory over your passions and corrupt inclinations'. JW assigned this book to his students at Oxford and included an abridgement in his *Christian Library*, 34:9–262 (with this excerpt abridged on pp. 191–92).

Enjoy your present health, and expect the continuance of it. And is not this a token of better things at hand? Peace be with all your spirits! I am, dear Alleck,

Yours most affectionately,

J. Wesley   5

Address: 'To / Mr Alex. Knox / in / Londonderry / +p [i.e., crosspost] Portpatrick'.
Postmarks: 'Nottingham' and 'AP/10'.
Source: holograph; Bridwell Library (SMU).[91]   10

To Elizabeth Gibbes   15

Derby
April 7, 1783   20

I cannot but return my sincere thanks to Lady Gibbes, and to my dear Miss Gibbes and Miss Agnes, for the friendly entertainment I received at Hilton Park, which I shall not easily forget.[92] I have frequently since then reflected with pleasure on those happy moments, and shall rejoice, should it ever be in my power to wait upon   25
you again.

I must beg the favour of you to accept of the *Concise History of England*, which fully clears the character of that much injured woman.[93] And I beg Miss Agnes to accept of *Henry, Earl of Moreland*, which I think will speak to her heart.[94] I have ordered both of   30
them to be put up in one parcel, and directed to *you* at Hilton Park.

How was I delighted to find both my dear Miss Agnes and you (I speak as if I had been long acquainted with you!) resolved in the dawn of life to be as wise and good as if you had lived threescore years. May the God of love confirm every resolution he has given   35

[91] Held previously in the Upper Room Museum, L-34.
[92] I.e., Agnes (Osbourne) Gibbes, Elizabeth Gibbes, and Agnes Gibbes Jr. On these, see JW to CW, Apr. 4, 1783. JW was at their estate Mar. 25–26, 1783 (see *Journal*, 23:265–66 in this edn.).
[93] The 'much injured woman' was Mary Queen of Scots. See JW, *Journal*, Nov. 6, 1769, 22:210 in this edn.; and the opening sections of *Concise History of England*, Vol. 3.
[94] JW's two-volume abridgement *The History of Henry, Earl of Moreland; Bibliography*, No. 414.

you, and bring all your good desires to good effect! This is the earnest wish of, my dear Miss Gibbes,

Your affectionate servant,

John Wesley[95]

In a few days I expect to be in Dublin.

Address: 'To / Miss Gibbes / At Sir Philip Gibbes Bart. / In Hilton Park, near / Wolverhampton'.
Postmark: 'Derby'. *Charge*: '3'.
Source: holograph; National Archives, PRO 30/9/7/15.

To Joseph Saunderson

Derby
April 7, 1783

[quoted in a letter of Saunderson to Samuel Bardsley, April 21, 1783]

Last week I got a letter from Mr. Wesley who was then at Derby, with this interrogation: 'But why does Sammy Bardsley stay so long at Glasgow? Is it no longer than his turn requires?' I am at a loss to understand the following sentence: 'Irregular preachers hinder the work greatly.'

… Mr. Wesley says not one word of his having been ill.

Source: secondary holograph; MARC, PLP 94/18/1.[96]

To Henry Brooke[97]

William Street [Dublin]
April 21, 1783

Dear Harry,

Your letter gave me pleasure, and pain too. It gave me pleasure because it was written in a mild and loving spirit; and it gave me

---

[95] Note the use of his full name in this first letter to her.

[96] JW's holograph to Saunderson is not known to survive.

[97] According to D'Olier, JW had stayed at Brooke's home after arriving in Dublin on Apr. 13, and during a conversation made some observations about 'mystic writers' which Brooke had considered 'harsh and unfounded'. Brooke expressed his objection in a note, to which this is JW's reply.

pain because I found it had pained you, whom I so tenderly love
and esteem. But I shall do it no more. I sincerely thank you for your
kind reproof. It is a precious balm and will, I trust, in the hands
of the Great Physician, be a means of healing my sickness. I am so
sensible of your real friendship herein that I cannot write without   5
tears. The words you mention were too strong. They will no more
fall from my mouth.
  My dear Harry, cease not to pray for
    Your obliged and affectionate brother,

                                                                J. W.   10

Source: published transcription; D'Olier, *Brooke*, 194.

                                                                         15

To Jane (Hilton) Barton

                                                           Dublin
                                                     April 23, 1783
My Dear Sister,   20
  It has pleased God for many years to lead you in a rough and
thorny way. But he knoweth the way wherein you go; and when you
have been tried, you shall come forth as gold.[98] Every proof you
have had of God's care over you is a reason for trusting him with
your children. He will take care of them, whether you are alive or   25
dead; so that you have no need to be careful in this matter. You have
only by prayer and supplication to make your requests known to
God.[99] And whenever he sees it will be best for you, he will deliver
you out of your captivity. In two or three weeks I hope to be in
England again. But it is all one where we are, so we are doing the   30
will of our Lord.
  I am, my dear sister,
    Your affectionate brother,

                                                          [J. Wesley]

                                                                         35

Source: published transcription; Jackson, *Works* (3rd), 12:366–67.

---

[98] See Job 23:10. JW used the same exhortation in his letter to Barton of Dec. 9, 1780.
[99] See Phil. 4:6.

To Alexander Knox

Dublin
April 23, 1783

5 My Dear Alleck,

Above thirty years ago there was a very remarkable revival of religion in Holland. But the good states suppressed it at one stroke, by passing a public edict that no three persons should meet together on a religious account, under a severe penalty. In the present revival it
10 has pleased God to go out of his usual way, by spreading his work, not 'from the least to the greatest', but rather from the greatest to the least. The person to whose house I am invited in Utrecht is the head burgomaster of the city. And those that desire to see me at Haerlem and Amsterdam are some of the chief merchants there. So I hope the
15 spending a few weeks among them may answer a good intention.[100]

You have no business to take thought for the morrow about sickness, or health, or anything else.[101] It is *your* part to make the best of today.[102] What if you took a journey with Mr. [John] Abraham? It would be good both for your soul and body.

20 Dr. [Thomas] Coke will speedily accept of your kind invitation. He quits Dublin as soon as our little Conference is over.[103]

Peace be with all your spirits! I am, dear Alleck,
Yours most affectionately,

J. Wesley

25
Address: 'To / Mr. Alexr Knox, in / Londonderry'.
Source: holograph; Bridwell Library (SMU).[104]

30
To Ellen (Gretton) Christian

Dublin
April 25, 1783

35 My Dear Sister,

In the new sphere of action to which providence has called you, I trust you will find new zeal for God and new vigour in pursuing ev-

---

[100] JW spent the second half of June 1783 in Holland.
[101] See Matt. 6:34.
[102] See John 9:4.
[103] JW's conference with his Irish preachers began on Apr. 29, 1783; see the *Minutes* in 10:967–70 in this edn.
[104] Held previously in the Upper Room Museum, L-35.

ery measure which may tend to the furtherance of his kingdom.[105]
In one of my mother's letters you may observe something resembling your case.[106] She began only with permitting two or three of
her neighbours to come to the family prayers on Sunday evening.
But they increased to an hundred, yea above an hundred and fifty.   5
Go humbly and steadily on, consulting the Assistant in all points,
and pressing on to perfection.[107]

    I am, with love to brother [William] Christian, my dear sister,
        Your affectionate brother,

                                      J. Wesley   10

Source: holograph; MARC, MAM JW 2/30.

                                                 15

To Agnes Gibbes

                                   [Dublin]   20
                              April 25, 1783

    I am much obliged to you, my dear Miss Agnes, for favouring me
with a line, and shall be extremely glad should it ever be in my power to return you thanks in person.[108] I shall not easily forget those   25
happy moments in the evening when we stood together by the fire
in the dining room. The emotion you then showed gave me much
pleasure, and I can hardly now think of it without tears. I believe
it was then, and is now, your desire to be not almost but altogether
Christian;[109] to have that mind which was in Christ,[110] and to walk   30
as Christ also walked.[111] O that the lover of souls may give you your

---

[105] She was now married; see JW to Ellen Gretton, Feb. 16, 1783.

[106] JW was referring to a letter that Susanna (Annesley) Wesley wrote her husband Samuel, dated Feb. 6, 1712, in response to him complaining about a prayer meeting she was holding
at their home which non-family members were attending. JW included an abridgement of this
letter in his *Journal* in an entry on Aug. 1, 1742, after his mother's death; see 19:284–86 in this
edn.

[107] See Heb. 6:1.

[108] None of the letters written to JW by Agnes Gibbes or her sister Elizabeth are known
to survive.

[109] See JW, *The Almost Christian* (1741), 1:131–41 in this edn.

[110] See Phil. 2:5.

[111] See 1 John 2:6.

desire! May make you all like himself! What happiness would this give to, my dear Miss Agnes,

Your ever affectionate servant,

John Wesley

Address: 'To Miss Agnes Gibbes'.[112]
Source: holograph; National Archives, PRO 30/9/7/15.

To Elizabeth Gibbes

Dublin
April 25, 1783

My Dear Miss Gibbes,

The very sight of your name gave me a sensible pleasure. Till I saw it, I was almost in doubt, whether you would think of me any more—considering on the one hand, the fatigue and hurry of travelling; and on the other, the various company and many amusements with which you was likely to be taken up. But it will not be easy for *me* to forget the few agreeable hours I spent at the Park.[113] I little expected to find so much openness and friendliness among strangers. But what gave me still more satisfaction was your willingness to learn what is most worthy of rational creatures, and those that are designed for nobler enjoyments than any of those that perish in the using. You consider yourself, my dear Miss Gibbes, not as a beautiful piece of wax-work but as an intelligent, an immortal spirit, a creature capable of God, intended to know the greatest and best of beings, to love and enjoy him to all eternity! O never let your natural vivacity, company, or the flutter of the world, put this out of your sight! But know yourself, that you may know God, and Jesus Christ whom he hath sent.

According to Miss [Mary] Freeman's desire, I wrote to a friend at Bath concerning her.[114] And I wrote to her about the same time, but

---

[112] This was sent as part of a double letter with the next to her sister Elizabeth.

[113] Their estate of Hilton Park.

[114] This friend was likely Abraham Orchard; see JW's letter to him dated 1783 above. Mary Freeman Shepherd did go to Bath from Hilton Park in Apr. and was staying with or near Sarah Wesley Jr. there; see CW to Sarah Wesley Jr., May 27, 1783 (MARC, DDWes 4/30).

I have not had one line from her since.[115] Probably you can inform me where she is? I am afraid she might be taken ill.

Wishing you and my dear Lady [Agnes] Gibbes every blessing which God has prepared for those that fear him, I remain, my dear Miss Gibbes,

Your very affectionate servant,

John Wesley

I expect to be in Chester in a few days.

Address: 'To / Miss Gibbes / At Lady Gibbes' / In Aberystwith'.
Source: holograph; National Archives, PRO 30/9/7/15.

To [John Watson Jr.][116]

Dublin
April 25, 1783

My Dear Brother,

Yesterday I received yours from Perth.[117] But I do not know how to answer it. If brother McLean has been able to do good at Perth or Dunkeld, it would be worth while to take a room. But truly, I think if the Highlanders will not pay for their own room, they are not worthy of the preaching. To labour and pay for our own labour is not right before God or man.

Are you able to undertake a circuit? You may direct your next to London. I am,

Your affectionate brother,

J. Wesley

Source: holograph; MARC, MAM JW 5/47.

---

[115] Neither of these two letters are known to survive.
[116] The correspondent is the same as JW addressed on Nov. 30, 1782.
[117] This letter is not known to survive.

To the Rev. Charles Wesley

Dublin
April 25, 1783

5 [[Dear Brother,]]
How extremely odd is the affair of Mr. [John] Abraham![118] I scarce
ever remember the like. It really seems to be a providential incident
which fairly acquits us of one that would have been no honour to us.
But how odd also is this affair of Miss [Mary] Freeman! Since I
10 left her at Sir Philip Gibbes's preparing for her journey to Bath, I
have not had so much as one line from her.[119] Yesterday I had a letter
from Miss [Elizabeth] Gibbes and another from her sister [Agnes],
but she is not even mentioned either in one or the other.[120] Do you
know what is become of her? Is she ill? Surely she is not slipped
15 back to Paris!
All is quiet here. God has made our enemies to be at peace with
us. In about ten days I hope to be at Chester.
Peace be with you and yours!
[[Adieu.]]
20
Address: 'To / The Revd Mr C. Wesley / No 1 in Chesterfield Street /
MaryleBoon'.
Endorsement: by CW, 'B[rother] April 25. 1783'.
Source: holograph; MARC, DDWes 3/53.
25

To Joseph Taylor

30   Dublin
April 26, 1783
Dear Joseph,
By all means let James Hall come to the Conference.[121] If he
would put forth all his strength and be exact in every branch of his

---

[118] The details of this incident are unclear, but John Abraham was back in London by
1784, where the last mention JW makes is that he was 'insane' (JW to Alexander Knox, Feb.
7, 1784).
[119] See JW to CW, Apr. 4, 1783.
[120] See JW's replies to both just above.
[121] James Hall, a woollen weaver of Boar Edge, in Bury, Lancashire, was a local preacher
in the society there by 1772. He was admitted 'on trial' as an itinerant in 1776 (see 10:452 in
this edn.) and served over twenty years, before desisting from travel in 1798. He was currently
stationed on the western Cornwall circuit, where Taylor was Assistant.

office, I would appoint him for the Assistant next year. But I should be sorry if the work should decay. Do all you can during this precious season.

I shall have no objection to your being in Nottingham circuit (unless you are in love). But if you go thither, you must take the books into your own hands; though I do not say you will receive many thanks from Matthew Bagshaw.[122] I expect to be in England in about ten days.

I am, dear Joseph,
    Your affectionate friend and brother,

                    J. Wesley

Address: 'To / Mr Jos. Taylor / At the preachinghouse / In Redruth / Cornwall'.
Postmark: 'AP/26'.
Source: holograph; MARC, MAM JW 5/7.

To John Cricket[123]

                    Dublin
                May 2, 1783

My Dear Brother,
We should have been glad to see you at the Conference.[124] But the reasons you give for not coming are good. You was hindered not by choice but by providence. Therefore you would find a blessing where you was. And the more pains you take the more blessings you will find.

I am,
    Your affectionate brother,

                    J. Wesley

Source: holograph; Drew, Methodist Archives.

---

[122] Matthew Bagshaw (d. 1803) was a member of the Methodist society in Nottingham, a local preacher, and the society met at his house until the Hockley chapel was opened in 1783.

[123] The address portion is missing, but the recipient is identified in a note by W. F. Harrison dated Feb. 17, 1825.

[124] The Conference with the Irish preachers, held in Dublin on Apr. 29, 1783.

To Mary Smith[125]

[Dublin]
May 2, 1783

My Dear Sister,

I do not doubt but that fall increased your nervous weakness, which may account for the dullness and heaviness you feel. But this no more proves you to be an ~~heretic~~ hypocrite than it proves you to be a Mahometan. You may be a poor, wavering, feeble-minded creature, hardly holding the little faith which God has given you. But, my soul for yours, you are no hypocrite.

Source: holograph; privately held (extract published in a Sotheby's Catalogue, May 2, 1966, Lot 232).

To the Rev. Charles Wesley

Dublin
May 2, 1783

[[Dear Brother,]]

In three or four days we hope to embark. When we land, you may hear farther. But at a venture you may direct to Chester, and don't forget the verses.[126]

I marvel Miss [Mary] Freeman does not answer my letters. Surely she is not affronted at anything. We parted in much friendship. I think verily you will keep out of debt while I live, if you will give me an hint now and then.[127]

We must positively let Mr. [John] Abraham drop, ⟨...[128]⟩ his relations with him and near him.[129]

---

[125] Lacking the holograph, nothing more specific can be determined about the recipient.

[126] CW may have been sending JW a copy of MS American Loyalists 1783; as he had earlier sent MS Protestant Association for JW's comments.

[127] CW had raised this question in a response to one of JW's letters in Apr. CW's letter is not known to survive.

[128] A small portion is torn away by the wax seal, affecting two lines.

[129] This note is added in longhand at the bottom of the page: 'The clergyman who accompanied me in my first journey to Londonderry. He returned to London, but was quite unmanageable. I saw him there in 1784.' The note could not be by CW, who never went to Londonderry; and it is not in JW's hand. Most likely it was added by Henry Moore, who was assigned to the Londonderry circuit in Aug. 1779, and accompanied there by Abraham (see *Minutes*, 10:488 in this edn.). Moore was one of those who cared for JW's papers after his death. See also Moore's comment on this journey in 'Rev. John Abraham', [Irish] *Christian Advocate*, Aug. 24, 1888, p. 4 [p. 410 for year].

I am ⟨in⟩ hopes ~~he~~ T. M. will satisfy Dr. [Thomas] Coke.
I suppose she loses her annuity if she owns her marriage.
I have not seen Mr. Barnard.[130]
We had an exceeding happy Conference, which concluded this
morning.[131] I wish all our English preachers were of the same   5
spirit with the Irish, among whom is no jarring string. I never saw
such simplicity and teachableness run through a body of preachers before.
Tell me all you know of the good Congress, the [British] loyalists,
and the Colonies.[132]   10
Peace be with you and yours!
    [[Adieu!]]

Address: 'To / The Revd Mr C Wesley / City Road / London'.[133]
Postmarks: 'MY/2' and '8/MA'.   15
Endorsement: by CW, 'B[rother] very brotherly / May 2. 1783'.
Source: holograph; MARC, DDWes 3/54.[134]

                                                                          20

To Alexander Knox

                                                        Dublin   25
                                                    May 3, 1783
My Dear Alleck,
    Since I came to Ireland my health and strength are more fully
restored than they have been for several months. And my journey
will undoubtedly be attended with another good consequence. My   30
friends in England will not be under such dreadful apprehensions
if I should have to take another journey to Ireland. If I do, I shall

---

[130] Thomas Barnard (1727–1806), the oldest son of William and Anne (Stone) Barnard
of Derry; with whom CW was in regular correspondence. Like his father, who was Bishop of
Derry, Thomas pursued clerical life and had been named Bishop of Killaloe and Kilfenora in
1780. Cf. JW to CW, May 12, 1785 on the death of Thomas Barnard's son.
    [131] This was the 1783 Conference for preachers in Ireland, which began Apr. 29; see the
Minutes in 10:967–70 in this edn.
    [132] I.e., events in North America now that the war was over.
    [133] The address is struck out and replaced with: 'No 1 Chesterfield Street / Marybone'.
    [134] On the address leaf CW gives an initial shorthand draft of the first two stanzas of a
hymn that appears in MS Preparation for Death, Hymn 65, pp. 29–30 (see annotations in that
setting).

doubtless see Londonderry; though I do not know, if Sally Knox would be glad to see me.[135]

With regard to Mr. Thomas Abraham, God accepts the will for the deed.[136] Perhaps we are not to meet tell we meet at Londonderry.
5   Your great point is: Believe today! And take no thought for the morrow![137] Peace be with all your spirits! I am,

Your affectionate friend and brother,

J. Wesley

10   *Address*: 'To / Mr. Alex. Knox'.[138]
Source: holograph; Bridwell Library (SMU).[139]

15

To Thomas Tattershall[140]

Dublin
May 3, 1783

20   Dear Tommy,

I thank brother [Jasper] Robinson for his letter, and hope we shall soon be able to supply you with books.[141] At present we have rather too little than too much persecution.[142] We have scarce enough to keep us awake. Send me as particular an account as you can of all
25   that relates to Mary Casement.[143]

---

[135] Alexander's sister Sarah had apparently not written JW lately.

[136] Thomas Abraham was likely one of the 'relations' of John Abraham that JW refers to in his letter to CW on May 2, 1783.

[137] See Matt. 6:34.

[138] This was surely hand-delivered by one of the preachers returning to Londonderry from the Conference just held in Dublin.

[139] Held previously in the Upper Room Museum, L-36.

[140] Tattershall was currently stationed on the Isle of Man circuit, with Jonathan Brown and Jasper Robinson (as Assistant). Neither his letter to JW, nor that of Robinson that was enclosed in it, are known to survive.

[141] Jasper Robinson (1727–97), drawn to the Methodists in 1760, while living in Leeds, was admitted 'on trial' as an itinerant at the 1776 Conference (see 10:452 in this edn.). He served for twenty-one years, right up to his death. See his spiritual autobiography, *AM* 13 (1790): 575–79, 630–36 (and Dec. 1785 in-letters); the account of his death in *MM* 21 (1798): 231–34; and *Minutes* (post-Wesley, 1798), 1:414.

[142] See JW's similar comment in his *Journal*, June 8, 1781, 23:209 in this edn.

[143] Mary Casement, member of a Methodist society on the Isle of Man, had accused clergy in the established Church of being blind. She was called to make public penance, but because of her 'wild enthusiastic effusions' was eventually sent to Peel dungeon. See *Manx Methodist Historical Society Newsletter* 4 (1986): 1–2.

I hope you still find a witness in yourself, not only of your acceptance, but of your salvation from inbred sin and of your loving God with all your heart. And you should constantly and explicitly exhort all believers to aspire after this, and encourage them to expect it *now*.

The advice of brother Robinson herein is good. If you would learn the Manx language, I should commend you. But it is not worth while to learn Greek or Latin. Brother Robinson should send me to London the particulars of that young man's death.

My kind love to Barrow and brother Brown.[144]

I am, dear Tommy,

Your affectionate brother,

J. Wesley

Source: published transcription; *WHS* 6 (1907): 45–46.

To Joseph Benson[145]

Manchester
May 19, 1783

Dear Joseph,

I do not, and never did, consent that any of our preachers should baptize as long as we profess ourselves to be members of the Church of England.[146] Much more may be said for burying the dead. To this I have no objection.

One of the preachers in every circuit usually stays two years— this is generally the Assistant. But when *you* was Assistant at Manchester you quite disappointed me.[147] You was not exact at all. You

---

[144] Jonathan Brown (1750–1825), a native of Stanhope, in Weardale, received assurance of his salvation about 1772. He was admitted 'on trial' as an itinerant preacher in 1778 (see 10:474 in this edn.) and would serve for 38 years. See *Minutes* (post-Wesley, 1826), 6:106. Brown was currently one of three preachers assigned to the Isle of Man.

[145] Telford (*Letters*, 7:178) again cites the now-missing manuscript copy of Benson's *Life* (p. 1248–50) as recording that on Jan. 3, 1783, Benson consented 'with some reluctance' to do what he had never done before, bury someone; and on the same evening 'to baptize a young man, who appeared to be very penitent and to experience a measure of faith in the Lord Jesus'. This led others to request Benson to baptize them, and he wrote to JW for advice on the subject. He also asked that he might remain another year in the Bradford circuit.

[146] A point reiterated in JW to John Valton, Jan. 6, 1784; and JW to William Percival, Mar. 4, 1784.

[147] See Benson's reply to this point in his letter to JW, c. May 22, 1783.

let things go as they *would* go. Therefore you have not been an Assistant since.

I will mend or end Thomas Olivers as a corrector.[148] Next week I hope to be in London; and am, with love to sister [Sarah] Benson,
5   dear Joseph,
        Your affectionate brother,

                                                    J. Wesley

10   *Address*: 'To / Mr Benson / At the Preaching house / In Halifax / Yorkshire'.
     Postmark: 'Manchester'.
     Endorsement: by Benson, 'J Wesley May 83'.
     Source: holograph; Bridwell Library (SMU).

15

To Agnes Gibbes[149]

20
                                                    Manchester
                                                    May 19, 1783

     You point, my dear Miss Agnes, at the very thing which is like-
25   ly to be your greatest hindrance; I mean company, as you are of a
     friendly temper, and unwilling to displease anyone. But this is a
     cross which you must often take up, if you determine to be a Christian. For in many instances your ways will not be like those of other
     young persons. And you will then have need to summon all your
30   resolution, if you will prefer reason before custom. You have now an
     excellent opportunity of confirming yourself, during this season of
     retirement, in every purpose which may be of service to you when
     the hour of temptation returns.[150]
     I do not clearly understand what Miss [Mary] Freeman means by
35   *human attachments*. I do not desire to be less attached to my friends

---

[148] Benson had complained to JW about errors in the text of his extended critique of Martin Madan that began appearing in *AM* 6 (1783): 37ff.; see Benston to JW, c. Feb. 18, 1782. JW proved patient, not finally removing Olivers from his role editing *AM* until 1789; see JW to Thomas Bradshaw, Aug. 15, 1789.

[149] Again neither of the letters of the Gibbes sisters to JW are known to survive.

[150] Lady Agnes (Osborne) Gibbes and her two daughters were spending time in the seaside town of Aberystwyth, Wales.

than I am. I do not desire to love them less. There are few persons
in the world (perhaps not one) to whom I am more attached, particularly after so short an acquaintance, than I am to *you*. And I do
not wish that attachment should be broken off. I trust it never will,
either in this or in a better world. I hope and want to remain both 5
in time and in eternity, my dear Miss Agnes,

    Yours most affectionately,

                J. Wesley[151]

[part of a double letter to her sister Elizabeth, which follows] 10

Source: holograph; National Archives, PRO 30/9/7/15.

15

To Elizabeth Gibbes

                Manchester 20
                May 19, 1783

My Dear Miss Gibbes,
    Your last favour came exactly in time. It could not have found me
at a better place. Three persons have already offered themselves,
one of whom I have made choice of. He is about one and twenty, 25
of no bad appearance, rather genteel, and of a pretty good understanding. His honesty and sobriety are unquestionable. Although
therefore he has not been in service before, yet I am in hopes he
will make a good servant, as he is very willing to learn. The greatest difficulty which I apprehend he will meet with will be from his 30
fellow servants. For he will not be fit for their company—he is too
serious. Of course they will dislike him. They will spare no pains (as
the vulgar saying is) to pick holes in his coat. They will tell things
of him which he never did, and put a wrong construction upon his
words, in order to prejudice you or Lady [Agnes] Gibbes against 35
him. But if he stays a few months, I am persuaded he will not easily
leave you.
    The book you mention I read when I was in Scotland. It is a
very ingenious but a very dangerous one. Lord Kames, the author

---

[151] Note that, after signing his full name in his first two letters to the Gibbes sisters, JW
has now switched to his more familiar signature.

was a confirmed deist, if not atheist.[152] But he was a man of strong understanding. Therefore he was too subtle to speak *openly* against the Bible, though he hated it with a perfect hatred. But he strikes at it obliquely in an hundred places. He slips no opportunity of
5   giving it a side blow. Such as that you mention, which is a home thrust not only at revelation, but at all moral honesty. 'Entire submission to the moral sense' (that is, to conscience) 'would be ill suited to man in his present state, and would prove more hurtful than beneficial.'[153] Well put indeed! Then honesty is not the best
10   policy! What a doctrine for a *judge* to maintain! His other supposition, that a constant consciousness of the presence of God, would make us incapable of transacting temporal business, shows that he is utterly ignorant of the whole affair.

    I am obliged to Lady [Agnes] Gibbes for giving me a little op-
15   portunity of serving her. It gives me pleasure whenever I think of the family. I cannot easily express how sincerely I am, my dear Miss Gibbes,

      Your most affectionate servant,

J. Wesley
20

Address: 'To / Miss Gibbes / At Lady Gibbes / In Aberithwith'.
Postmark: 'Manchester'. *Charge*: '4'.
Source: holograph; National Archives, PRO 30/9/7/15.

25

To Catherine Warren

30
Nottingham
May 26, 1783
My Dear Sister,
    I hope to be at London on Friday. But I will not so long defer the
35   answering yours, which I received an hour ago.[154]

---

[152] Orig., 'Lord Kaim'. Henry Home (1696–1782) was known as Lord Kames. The work in question here is his *Sketches of the History of Man*, 2 vols. (London: Strahan & Cadell, 1774). See JW's comments on reading this in his *Journal*, May 25, 1774, 22:411 in this edn.; and July 6, 1781, 23:214 in this edn.

[153] Kames, *Sketches*, 2:359.

[154] This letter is not known to survive.

I doubt not but Thomas Tenant will do well, if he lives chiefly upon milk and summer fruits.

Sam Hodgson may be with you next year.[155] And so may Mr. [Samuel] Randal, if he is willing. But as to William Moore, I will not station him at Haverford, unless you petition for him. I verily think another man may do as well.

Let honest John Prickard do as much as he can, and *no more*.

I shall probably cross over to Holland in Whitsun-week. But I do not desire to stay there more than two or three weeks. Immediately after the Conference (which is to begin on Tuesday July the twenty-ninth) I hope to set out for Wales. O be zealous! The day is short! And long is the night wherein no man can work![156]

I am, my dear Kitty,

Yours in tender affection,

J. Wesley

Address: 'To / Miss Kitty ⟨…⟩ / Crosspost ⟨…⟩'.[157]
Postmark: 'Nottingham'.
Source: holograph; Bridwell Library (SMU).

To Joseph Taylor

London
June 5, 1783

Dear Joseph,

According to the printed *Minutes*, p. 8, sister [Elizabeth] Rodda is to have her allowance from Cornwall West and sister Day out of the Preachers' Fund.[158] The fault therefore lay first in Joseph Harper, for Cornwall has nothing to do with sister Day this year;

---

[155] Samuel Hodgson (1759–95), a native of Halifax, Yorkshire, became active in the Methodist society in 1775. He underwent an evangelical conversion in 1777 and began to exhort locally. In 1780 he was accepted 'on trial' into the itinerant ministry (see 10:496 in this edn.). He continued to serve until his death, by drowning, while crossing the river Were. See Atmore, *Memorial*, 191–99; and *Minutes* (post-Wesley, 1795), 1:318.

[156] See John 9:4.

[157] Most of the address portion is missing.

[158] JW was referring to the 1782 *Minutes*; see 10:524 in this edn. Grace (Bucknell) Day was the wife of itinerant Simon Day (married May 1769). For her husband, see JW's letter to him of June 1, 1784.

and secondly, in John Atlay, who ought to have sent him and you the *Minutes* immediately after the Conference. Send no more money to sister Day, but to Richard Rodda.

    I am, dear Joseph,

5   Your affectionate friend and brother,

J. Wesley

Address: 'To / Mr Jos. Taylor / At the Preachinghouse / In Redruth / Cornwall'.

10 *Postmark*: '5/IV'. *Charge*: '4'.
Source: holograph; MARC, MAM JW 5/8.

15

To John Francis Valton

London
June 5, 1783

My Dear Brother,

20   What have the Birstall Assistants (even Thomas Taylor himself) been doing these seven years?[159]

    I believe our fast will be productive of many good effects.[160] Many have already found reason to bless God on account of it.

    Sister [Martha] Rogers is a jewel of a woman. She has all the spirit of her husband [James], and desires nothing but to do and 25 suffer the will of God.

    Those trustees are wonderfully injudicious.[161] Are they afraid their sons will be of the same mind as themselves? I would not for all the world leave a preaching-house to my executors. However, do what you judge best.

30   Your affectionate friend and brother,

[J. Wesley]

But your *life*! I want your *life*.[162]

Source: published transcription; Telford, *Letters*, 7:179–80.

[159] Taylor had been Assistant for the Birstall circuit in 1778.

[160] The Methodists were encouraged in the 'Large' *Minutes* to hold a fast every year on the Friday after Midsummer Day (June 27 in 1783); see 10:905 in this edn.

[161] Several of the trustees of the Birstall preaching-house were still resisting JW's call for them to change the deed. Cf. JW's circular letter in early Jan. 1783; and Joseph Charlesworth to JW, Jan. 13, 1784.

[162] Valton had sent JW the first portion of his autobiographical account over a year earlier (see JW to Valton, Jan. 18, 1782). JW was pressing him for the remainder, which came within a couple of months; see Valton to JW, c. Aug. 5, 1783.

To Hannah Ball

near London

June 7, 1783   5

My Dear Sister,

Your mentioning past times puts me in mind of God's remarkable providence in the Oxford circuit. Four young women have been
made the chief support of four societies. One of them quitted her
post at Henley, and both she and the society sank into nothing.[163]   10
The other three by the grace of God stand their ground, and so do
the societies at Wycombe, Watlington, and Witney. And I trust my
dear friends Hannah Ball, Martha Chapman, and Ann Bolton will
never be weary of well doing. I cannot find any fault in them but
that they are not so well acquainted with each other as I would have   15
them to be.

If I possibly can, I will spend a night with you as I go from London to Bristol next month. I was well pleased to hear of Mr. Batting's generosity to our poor friends at Oxford.[164] It seems as if the
time is drawing near for more good to be done there also. We should   20
expect to see still greater things. The right hand of the Lord hath
the pre-eminence![165]

I am, my dear sister,

Your affectionate brother,

J. Wesley   25

Source: published transcription; Ball, *Memoir*, 157–58.

[163] JW's first recorded efforts in Henley-on-Thames, Oxfordshire were in 1763 (see *Journal*, Jan. 19–20, 21:442 in this edn.); his last recorded visit was Oct. 16, 1769 (22:207 in this
edn.). In this light, the fourth young woman was likely Miss Hartly, whom Hannah Ball met in
early 1771 in Wallingford (about 8 miles from Henley), and concerning whom JW commented,
'She departed from us for a season that we might receive her again'; see JW to Ball, Jan. 24,
1771, 28:343 in this edn.

[164] Mr. Batting, of High Wycombe, had been a major contributor to the cost of building
the Methodist preaching-house there, and supervised the work itself; see Ball, *Memoir*, 143. He
had now contributed to renting rooms on New Inn Hall Street, Oxford, for Methodist worship.
JW visited High Wycombe, then preached at the new site in Oxford, on July 14, 1783; see his
Journal, 23:284 in this edn.

[165] See Ps. 118:16 (BCP).

To Agnes Gibbes

London
June 10, 1783

My Dear Miss Agnes,

   The very friendship and good will of sensible and agreeable persons, who have no thought of God or their own souls, may prove a snare by weakening your best desires and damping you in your noblest pursuits. You are an immortal spirit that are lately come forth from the God and Father of spirits, and after you have done his will on earth for a few days or years are to return to your native abode. What pity that any person or thing should ever put this out of your thoughts! I want you al⟨ways⟩[166] to think, and speak and act as one standing on ⟨the brink⟩ of eternity! You and Miss [Elizabeth] Gibbes bring to my mind two young ladies in Ireland (sisters of Lord Mahon) who were some years since about your age, and not unlike you, either in person or disposition.[167] But they are both now in Abraham's bosom. The younger, when very weak, desired but one thing on earth, to see me before she went hence. God gave her what she desired. She rejoiced with joy unspeakable and delivered up her spirit to him. Whenever he calls, I trust you will do the same! O that I might be enabled to help you a little forward in the way! What an unspeakable pleasure would this be to, my dear Miss Agnes,

   Yours most affectionately,

J. Wesley

[included with the letter to her sister which follows]

Source: holograph; National Archives, PRO 30/9/7/15.

---

[166] A small portion is torn away on the right margin, affecting two lines.

[167] By 'Lord Mahon' JW means Ross Mahon (1725–88), whom JW gives this title because in 1762 he married Lady Anne Browne, daughter of the first Earl of Altamont; technically it was their son Ross (1763–1835) who would first bear the title of Baronet. JW's 'Lord Mahon' was the eldest son of Ross Mahon (1696–1767) and Jane (Ussher) Mahon (1694–1768) of Castlegar, whom JW met in May 1749; see JW to CW, May 3–10, 1749 (Vol. 31 in this edn.), and *Journal*, June 19, 1749, 20:281 in this edn. In the letter JW says the Mahons had three daughters. The name is known only of one, Alice, who married John King in 1748 and died in 1769.

To Elizabeth Gibbes

London
June 10, 1783   5

My Dear Miss Gibbes,

When I received your last favour, I was a little concerned lest the young man to whom I had spoken should have delayed his journey, and thereby put you to some inconvenience.[168] But I found, upon reflection, I recollected he could not well leave Manchester before   10
the twenty-third or twenty-fourth of last month. I hope he is now with you, and that though he may be awkward at first, he will mend upon your hands. And I am glad you have not many servants about you at present. He may the more easily learn what you would have him to do.   15

Lord Kames was the author of that very ingenious and very dangerous book.[169] But I do not so much wonder that he should imagine a continual sense of the presence of God would make us incapable of attending to our worldly business, when I find the very same sentiment expressed by a much greater and better man than him,   20
Dr. Blair! It is by this very consideration that fine writer endeavours to account for the present ignorance of man with regard to God and eternity; 'Because if those strong and vivid impressions of God and the other world, which good men are sometimes favoured with, were to remain always, they would be utterly unable to attend to   25
the little affairs of this life.'[170] O no! The very supposition clearly proves that both these great men talk by rote—that they have no experience of the things they talk of. Otherwise they would know, that the stronger and livelier sense anyone has of God and heaven, the fitter he is to do the will of God on earth with the utmost exactness.   30

Do me the justice, my dear Miss Gibbes, to believe your letters are welcome in the highest degree to,

Your most affectionate servant,

J. Wesley

Address: 'To / Miss Gibbes / At Lady Gibbes / in / Aberistwith'.   35
Postmarks: '11/IV' and '12/IV'.
Source: holograph; National Archives, PRO 30/9/7/15.

---

[168] See JW to Gibbes, May 19, 1783.
[169] Ibid. JW again spells 'Kaim'.
[170] This is JW's summary of Hugh Blair's sermon 'On Our Imperfect Knowledge of a Future State', in *Sermons* (London: Strahan & Cadall, 1777), 84–113; see esp. pp. 86–87, 92–94.

To Elizabeth (Buckley) Ferguson[171]

Harwich
June 12, 1783

5 My Dear Sister,

Hitherto God has helped us. As the weather last night was exceeding rough, the captain did not think advisable to sail; for which
I was not sorry. We expect to sail this morning, as it seems the storm
is over. And probably we shall see Helvoetsluys tomorrow. Sally and
10 my other companions are in perfect health, and are all in good spirits, knowing that they are under his protection whom the winds and
the seas obey.[172]

I am, my dear sister,
Your affectionate brother,

15   J. Wesley

Address: 'To / Mrs Ferguson / near the Haberdashers' Almshouse / in
Hoxton / London'.
Source: holograph; privately held (photocopy in MARC, MA 1977/617,
20   Box 1).

To Jane (Hilton) Barton

25

London
July 5, 1783

My Dear Sister,

Last month I made a little journey to Holland, from whence I
30 returned yesterday. There is a blessed work at The Hague, Amsterdam, Utrecht, and many other of the principal cities. And in their
simplicity of spirit and plainness of dress the believers vie with the
old English Methodists. In affection they are not inferior to any. It
was with the utmost difficulty we could break from them.

---

[171] William Ferguson married Elizabeth Buckley (c. 1740–93) in 1760 [this is a correc-
tion to fn. 77 in *Works*, 23:270. Ferguson married Cicely Godbehave after Elizabeth died].
William, who had established a secondary residence at The Hague, invited JW for the visit to
the Netherlands he was just undertaking. JW provides an extended account of this visit to the
Netherlands in his Journal, June 11–July 4, 1783, 23:270–83 in this edn. He was accompanied
on the trip by Robert Carr Brackenbury, John Broadbent, and George Whitfield. Sarah Ferguson (1766–1820; who would marry Abraham Peele in 1785), William and Elizabeth's daughter,
sailed over to the Netherlands with them.

[172] See Matt. 8:23.

I am glad to hear so good an account of my two little maids.[173] I found much love to them when I was at Beverley. Now is the time for them to choose that better part which shall never be taken from them.[174] Now is the time for them to choose whether they will seek happiness in God or in the world. The world never made anyone happy, and it is certain it never will. But God will. He says,

> Love shall from me returns of love obtain;
> And none that seek me early seek in vain.[175]

I am, with love to brother [William] Barton, dear Jenny,
    Your affectionate brother,

J. Wesley

[address portion torn away]
Postmark: '5/IY'.
Endorsement: by Barton, 'No 30 / London / July 5'.
Source: holograph; Drew, Methodist Archives.

To Charles Atmore

London
July 12, 1783

Dear Charles,
    If one to whom I have made half a promise will relinquish his claim, you may be with Jonathan Coussins in Gloucestershire. If not, I see no reason, why you should not be in Yarm circuit.
    I am,
        Your affectionate brother,

J. Wesley

Address: 'To / Mr Atmore / At Capt. Saml. Parker's / In Scarborough'.[176]
Postmark: '12/IY'.
Endorsement: 'Mr. Wesley'.
Source: holograph; MARC, MAM JW 1/5.

---

[173] Hannah and Jane Barton; see JW to Jane (Hilton) Barton, Nov. 6, 1781. JW has last been to Beverley in May 1782.

[174] See Luke 10:42.

[175] James Ward, 'Part of the Eighth Chapter of Proverbs Paraphrased', *ll.* 11–12; as included by JW in *AM* 1 (1778): 428.

[176] Samuel Parker was captain of a British ship that was commissioned to carry wounded soldiers from Philadelphia back to England. While in Philadelphia he met the widow Mary (Evans) Thorne, who was active in the Methodist society there. They married in Feb. 1778 and returned to England, settling near Scarborough.

To William Black Jr.[177]

London
July 13, 1783

My Dear Brother,

It is a rule with me to answer all the letters which I receive. If therefore you have not received an answer to every letter which you have written, it must be either that your letter or my answer has been intercepted.

I do not wonder at all that, after that great and extraordinary work of God, there should be a remarkable decay. So we have found it in almost all places. A swift increase is generally followed by a decrease equally swift. All we can do to prevent it is continually to exhort all who have tasted that the Lord is gracious to remember our Lord's words, 'Watch and pray that ye enter not into temptation.'[178]

Mr. Alline may have wit enough to do hurt; but I fear he will never have wit enough to do good.[179] He is very far from being a man of sound understanding. But he has been dabbling in mystical writers, in matters which are too high for him, far above his comprehension. I dare not waste my time in answering such miserable jargon. I have better work. But I have sent you (with other books) two volumes of Mr. Law's works, which contain all that Mr. Alline would teach if he could.[180] Only it is the gold purged from the dross; whereas he would give you the gold and dross shuffled together. I do not advise you ever to name his name in public (although in private you must warn our brethren), but go on your way exactly as if there were no such person in the world.

The school at Kingswood is exceeding full. Nevertheless there shall be room for *you*. And it is very probable, if you should live to return to Halifax, you may carry one or more preachers with you.[181]

---

[177] This continues a conversation from JW's letter to Black of Feb. 26, 1783. The intervening letters are not known to survive.

[178] Matt. 26:41.

[179] Henry Alline (1748–84) was the 'antinomian' mentioned in JW to Black, Feb. 26, 1783. A native of Rhode Island, he was converted in 1775 in Nova Scotia and became an independent itinerant preacher there, drawing away several of the members of the Methodist society in Amherst in particular. His theology was idiosyncratic and mystical in tone. See J. M. Bumsted, *Henry Alline, 1748–1784* (University of Toronto Press, 1971).

[180] I.e., JW, *An Extract from the Rev. Mr. [William] Law's Later Works*, 2 vols. (1768; *Bibliography*, No. 312).

[181] Circumstances never allowed Black to come to England, to study at Kingswood.

I will order Mr. [John] Atlay to send the books you sent for to our German brethren.[182] I hope you love as brethren, and have a free and open intercourse with each other. I commend you to him who is able to make you perfect, 'stablish, settle you; and am, my dear brethren,

    Your affectionate brother,

John Wesley

Address: '⟨To / Mr Willm. Black Junr / In⟩[183] Halifax / Nova Scotia'.
Endorsement: 'Revd J Wesley / London / 13 July 1783'.
Source: holograph; UCC Maritime Conference, Archives.

To John Evan[184]

Bristol
July 19, 1783

My Dear Brother,

I write just two or three lines because perhaps it may be a comfort to you. I commend you for giving up all that you had. It was acting the part of an honest man. Now you are cast upon the good providence of God—and he will not leave you nor forsake you. I hope to see you after the Conference; and am

    Your affectionate brother,

J. Wesley

Address: 'To / Mr John Evan, in / Cowbridge / +p [i.e., crosspost] Gloucester'.
Postmark: 'Bristol'.
Source: holograph; MARC, MAM JW 2/89.

---

[182] JW had been made aware of the contribution of Philip Embury and Barbara Heck, both of German ancestry, to the creation of a Methodist society in New York in the 1760s; see Thomas Taylor to JW, Apr. 11, 1768. Embury was now dead, but the family of Barbara Heck and other German-speaking Methodists (as British Loyalists) had been driven into Canada by the Revolutionary War. These may be the 'German brethren' to whom JW was referring.

[183] The top portion of the address page is missing.

[184] This may be John Evan (1735–1815), buried in Cowbridge. He had been hosting JW's preachers for at least two years; see JW to William Church, Mar. 12, 1780. Nothing more is known for certain.

To Elizabeth Ritchie

Bristol
July 20, 1783

My Dear Betsy,

5

It seemed a long time since I heard from you.[185] But I believe your not writing was owing to your not knowing how to direct to me while I was abroad. The prayers of many were productive of many

10   blessings, and in particular of the amazing friendship and goodwill which were shown us in every place. We always looked upon the Dutch as an heavy, dull, stoical people. But truly most, nay I may say all, with whom we conversed familiarly were as tender-hearted and as earnestly affectionate as the Irish themselves.

15   Two of our sisters, when we left the Hague, came twelve miles with us on our way.[186] And one of our brethren of Amsterdam came to take leave of us to Utrecht, above thirty miles. There are, indeed, many precious souls in Utrecht full of faith and love, as also at Haarlem, the Hague, and Amsterdam. And one and all (without

20   any human teaching) dress as plainly as you do. I believe, if my life be prolonged, I shall pay them a visit at least every other year. Had I had a little more time, I would have visited our brethren in Friesland and Westphalia likewise, for a glorious work of God is lately broken out in both these provinces.

25   Miss Loten is an Israelite indeed.[187] She is a pattern to all that are round about her. One would scarcely have expected to see the daughter of the head burgomaster dressed on a Sunday in a plain linen gown.[188] She appears to have but one desire, that Christ may reign alone in her heart.

30   I do not remember any storm which travelled so far as that on the 10th.[189] It has been in almost all parts of England, but especially at Witney, near Oxford. The next night they had a far greater, which seemed to cover the whole town for four hours with almost one uninterrupted blaze. And it has made such an impression on high and

35   low, rich and poor, as had not been known in the memory of man.

[185] The previous known surviving letter from Ritchie to JW was Nov. 11, 1782.
[186] Mrs. [Marie Judith (Adams)] Leuliet and her relative; see JW, *Journal*, June 17, 1783, 23:275 in this edn.
[187] See John 1:47. Johanna Carolina Arnodina Loten (1753–1823), whom JW met in Utrecht on June 26, 1783 (see *Journal*, 23:280 in this edn.). Cf. her letters to JW of July 15, 1783; and Feb. 10, 1786.
[188] Her father was Arnout Loten (1719–1801), currently the mayor of Utrecht.
[189] See JW, *Journal*, July 14, 1783, 23:284 in this edn.

I expect a good deal of difficulty at this Conference, and shall stand in need of the prayers of you and your friends.[190] Peace be with all your spirits!

I am,

Yours most affectionately,

J. Wesley

Source: published transcription; Benson, *Works*, 16:251–52.

To George Gidley

Bristol
July 30, 1783

My Dear Brother,

I cannot come into Cornwall myself this year. But I am in hopes one or more of our preachers will make a trial this autumn whether some good may not be done at Bideford.

I am,

Your affectionate brother,

J. Wesley

Address: 'To / Mr Gidley, Supervisor / In Bideford / Devon'.
Postmark: 'Bristol'.
Source: holograph; Oxford, Bodleian Library, MS. Montagu d. 18, ff. 156–57.

To Elizabeth Padbury

Bristol
August 1, 1783

My Dear Betsy,

I am glad to find that you remember me still, and that your love is not grown cold.[191] I love you much, and I trust always shall—as I doubt not you will always deserve it.

---

[190] The two topics most debated were the case of the Birstall preaching-house and the state of Kingswood school. See JW, *Journal*, July 29, 1783, 23:286 in this edn.

[191] Padbury's letter to JW is not known to survive.

I have found several (my own father was one) that could rejoice in the justice as well as mercy of God. But punishing is his strange work; he delights chiefly in showing mercy. I apprehend, when you find those seasons of dryness and heaviness, this is owing either to
5   the agency of the devil, who can easily cloud our mind when God permits, or to the corruptible body pressing down the soul.[192] But believe and conquer all!
    I am, my dear Betsy,
        Yours affectionately,
10   J. Wesley

Address: 'To / Miss Padbury / in / Whittlebury'.
Source: holograph; MARC, MAM JW 4/34.

15

To the Rev. Cornelius Winter[193]

20

                                                             Bristol
                                                    August 1, 1783
Dear Sir,
    I am afraid the editors of that magazine are not of very enlarged
25   sentiments.[194] But they may say or write just what they please. There will be no quarrel between us, for it is the second blow that makes the quarrel. And by the grace of God, I am determined not to strike again.

---

[192] See Wisd. of Sol. 9:15.

[193] Cornelius Winter (1742–1808) was converted under the preaching of George White-field in 1760 and became Whitefield's secretary and understudy as a preacher. He travelled with Whitefield to North America in 1769, and after Whitefield's death in 1770 he returned to England to seek ordination in the Church of England. This being denied, he served for several years as an itinerant lay preacher on his own. Winter was finally ordained in a dissenting tradition in 1777, serving churches in Marlborough and Painswick until his death.

[194] In July 1783 *The New Spiritual Magazine*; or *Evangelical Treasury of Experimental Religion*, began publication. In advertisements it described itself as 'On real scriptural redemption, by Jesus Christ alone, in opposition to the destructive principles of Arminianism, etc. as erroneously maintained by Mr. Wesley etc.' See *Hereford Journal* (July 24, 1783), p. 4; and *Stamford Mercury* (July 31, 1783), p. 1. The periodical lasted only two years, but it may have been the occasion for the appearance in Oct. 1783 of a volume by unnamed editors titled *The Beauties of Methodism*; selected from the *Works of the Rev. John Wesley* (London: J. Fielding, et al., 1783). This compendium of excerpts for JW emphasized his 'Arminian' teachings.

I take kindly your invitation to call upon you at Marlborough. If opportunity serves I shall willingly accept of it. I am, dear sir,
    Your affectionate brother,

J. Wesley

Source: holograph; Drew, Methodist Archives.[195]

To William Roberts[196]

Bristol
August 3, 1783

I have taken your advice, and reunited the Taunton and Tiverton circuits.[197]

At the same time that I wrote to you I wrote to Mr. Jaques at Wallingford, who was barely a member of our society.[198] I wrote to the same effect as I wrote to *you*, and indeed nearly in the same words. He was so far from being offended that he immediately wrote me the most affectionate letter I ever received from him in my life; not only thanking me heartily, but (what I never expected) telling me what his income was and how he laid it out. Why did not Billy Roberts[199] answer me in the same manner? Had he less love than Mr. Jaques? Or more pride? Consider, Billy, consider! You have certainly got out of the way which you and I walked in many years ago!

Address: 'To / Mr Will. Robarts / in / Tiverton'.
Postmark: 'Bristol'.
Endorsement: 'Augst. 3 / 83'.
Source: holograph; Oxford, Lincoln College, Archive, MS/WES/A/2/3.

---

[195] There is no address portion, but the recipient is named in a secondary notation and it fits the content of the letter.

[196] After leaving the matter alone for nearly a year, JW returns here to the tensions between himself and Roberts over the latter's declining a request of financial help from JW; see JW's letters to Roberts of Sept. 12 & 19, 1782; and Roberts's replies of Sept. 16 & 23, 1782.

[197] The Devon circuit had been divided into the Taunton and Tiverton circuits in 1778; they were reunited in 1783.

[198] JW may have been writing to 'brother' Greenaway Jaques Jr., whom he referred to in a letter to Ann Bolton, Sept. 16, 1771; but he died sometime between Aug. and Nov. 1782. This, and the comment about his fringe nature to Methodism, make it more likely JW was writing Greenaway Jaques, the elder, of Wallingford, who died in 1800.

[199] Orig., 'Robarts'; as in address.

To Ann Tindall

Bristol
August 3, 1783

My Dear Sister,

I snatch a moment at this busy time to write a line. I am glad, you get a little forward in temporals, as well as in spirituals[200]. I will subscribe half a crown a week for another year.[201]

Some years [ago] I had the advice of an eminent counsellor in London concerning the deeds of our houses. His judgment was we had no need of any new deeds, but that the remaining trustees must endorse the old deeds in the manner mentioned in the large *Minutes* of the Conference.[202]

I am, dear Nancy,
Yours affectionately,

J. Wesley

Address: 'To / Miss Tindal / in / Scarborough'.
Endorsement: by Tindall, 'Aug 3rd 1783'.
Source: holograph; British Library, Department of Manuscripts, Add. MS. 43695, ff. 72–73.

To William Roberts[203]

Bristol
August 8, 1783

Dear Billy,

Not being well able to write myself, I use George Story's hand.[204] What I wrote to you before was not upon bare suspicion, or from vague information, but I was really frightened by hearing you say

---

[200] Tindall's letter to JW is not known to survive.

[201] For paying off the debt of the preaching-house in Scarborough; see JW to Tindall, Mar. 22, 1782.

[202] See 'Large' *Minutes* (1763), §67, 10:868–70 in this edn.

[203] JW's letter to Roberts of Aug. 3, 1783, drew a pained rejoinder from Roberts dated Aug. 6, 1783.

[204] JW became violently ill on Aug. 5, 1783, suffering for over two weeks; see *Journal*, Aug. 5–23, 1783, 23:286–87 in this edn.

some years ago that you had just been given £3,000 for a little estate.[205] Perhaps your substance is not so great now as then.

Of the things which some officious person said I spoke concerning you I remember nothing, but I suppose they lost nothing in the
telling.

I am, dear Billy,
    Your affectionate brother,

John Wesley

Source: letter by amanuensis; Oxford, Lincoln College, Archive, MS/
WES/A/2/4.[206]

To Ann Bolton

Bristol
August 9, 1783

My Dear Nancy,

If I can I will scrawl a few lines.[207] It seems as if my time of *doing*
draws to an end. Probably I shall be now called to *suffer*. Yesterday
as a little taken of love to my dear friend, I added a codicil to my
will, wherein I bequeathed you an hundred pounds, which I hope
will help you out of part of your trouble.[208] If I live to reach London, you shall have it immediately.[209]

O pray for, my dear Nancy,
    Your weak but ever affectionate,

J. Wesley

Address: 'To / Miss Bolton / In Witney / Oxfordshire'.
Postmark: 'Bristol'.
Endorsement: by Bolton, 'Aug 8 83'.
Source: holograph; privately held (WWEP Archive holds photocopy).

---

[205] Orig., 'been giving'.
[206] As mentioned in the letter, neither the text nor the signature are in JW's hand.
[207] See note on JW to Roberts, Aug. 8, about his current illness.
[208] The text of this specific iteration of JW's will is not known to survive.
[209] Orig., 'If a live'.

To Peter Garforth

Bristol
August 9, 1783

5   My Dear Brother,
I have borrowed the hand of a friend, not being able to write myself. You have great reason to praise God for the late remarkable
instance of his goodness which you mention.[210] It really seems, had
it not been for the mighty power of prayer, the boy would have been
10 blind all his life. The more reason you have entirely to dedicate both
him and yourself to his service. This is manifestly the sign of a gracious dispensation, and I trust it will be answered thereby. Watch
and pray, and you will no more enter into temptation.[211]
I am,
15   Your affectionate brother,

J. Wesley

Address: 'To / Mr Garforth / At Skipton in Craven / Yorkshire'.
Source: holograph; Skipton, North Yorkshire, England, Craven Museum.[212]

20

To Thomas Lee

Bristol
August 15, 1783

25

Joseph Bradford is without delay to desire the assistance of our
friends in London for the [preaching-]house at Nottingham. I hope
all our brethren will exert themselves therein. The importance of
30 the case he will himself explain.

John Wesley

Mr. [John] Atlay will give you my ten pounds.

Address: 'To Mr Tho. Lee'.[213]
35 *Source*: holograph; privately held (WWEP Archive holds digital copy).

---

[210] Garforth's letter to JW is not known to survive.
[211] See Matt. 26:41.
[212] Like that to William Roberts of Aug. 8, this letter is in the hand of George Story;
though in this instance JW has provided the closing signature.
[213] Written at the top of the page; apparently a note carried by Bradford to London after
the 1783 Conference in Bristol. Thomas Lee was stationed in London, and Bradford was the
Assistant for the Leicestershire circuit, near Nottingham.

To Thomas Welch [214]

Bristol
August 15, 1783

Dear Thomas,

You seem to be the man I want. As to salary you will have £30 a year. Board, etc., will be thirty more. But do not come *for money*. 1) Do not come at all unless purely to raise a Christian school. 2) Anybody behaving ill I will turn away immediately. 3) I expect you to be in the school eight hours a day. 4) In all things I expect you should be circumspect. But you will judge better by considering the printed rules.[215] The sooner you come the better.

    I am,

        Your affectionate brother,

J. Wesley

Source: published transcription; *Methodist Magazine* 40 (1817): 324.

To Agnes Gibbes

Bristol
August 16, 1783

I cannot sufficiently thank my dear Miss Agnes for still giving me a place in her remembrance. I have lately seen Miss Freeman at Bath, who is now returned to London, but seems to be quite unhinged, and more than ever out of humour with every person and thing in the world.[216] However I am exceedingly indebted to a kind providence which by her means introduced me to the lovely family at the [Hilton] Park. But an odd thought comes across me. Is

---

[214] Thomas Welch (1760–1813), whose father ran an academy in Nightingale Lane, London, was raised from early childhood in Rugby, Warwickshire, due to the death of both parents. In 1779 Welch was named assistant in a large school at Coventry. There he became acquainted with the Methodist society, and joined it in Sept. 1781. At this same time JW was becoming unhappy with the state of the school at Kingswood (see JW, *Journal*, Sept. 8, 1781, 23:222 in this edn.). Matters came to a head at the 1783 Conference in Bristol, leading to the dismissal of Thomas Simpson as Master (see 1783 *Minutes*, QQ. 15–16, 10:539–40 in this edn.). Cornelius Bayley, the writing instructor, who had recently been ordained, also left the school at that time. This led Welch to write JW, offering to succeed Bayley as writing master, and drew the present reply. See the 'Memoir' of Thomas Welch published in *MM* 40 (1817): 321–31, 481–90.

[215] I.e., *A Short Account of Kingswood School* (1749; Vol. 16 in this edn.).

[216] Referring to Mary Freeman Shepherd.

it not strange to say that I am half afraid to see Sir Philip [Gibbes]? Because I am conscious of my not being able to make good the favourable account you will be apt to give of me.

O may the God of love repay sevenfold all the kindness you have
5   shown to, my dear Miss Agnes,
      Your most affectionate,

John Wesley

10   [included with the letter to her sister which follows]

Source: holograph; National Archives, PRO 30/9/11/2.

15

To Elizabeth Gibbes

Bristol
August 16, 1783
20
If I can hold a pen (which indeed I can hardly do yet[217]) I must write a few lines to my very dear friends at Hilton Park. But you really surprise me! I imagined you would quite have forgotten me long ago.
25   In the late century, Mr. Brooke, a country gentleman in Ireland was sent for by his dying friend, who told him, 'As my wife is dead, I bequeath this infant to you. Train her up as your own.' He did so, and when she was about eighteen, married her.[218] The next year she had twins. The elder, Counsellor Brooke (now just alive[219]) wrote
30   *Henry Earl of Moreland*.[220] One may observe two threads interwoven throughout, the *natural* and the *surprising*. See *nature* in Clement and Arabella, in the death of Matilda, etc., etc. These strokes I admire most of all! I feel them. So do you and my very dear Miss Agnes. The *surprising* I thought (as you likewise do) rose a little too
35   high.

[217] Due to his current illness.
[218] JW seems to be confusing details of Rev. William Brooke (1669–1745) and his wife Lettice (Digby) Brooke, parents of Henry Brooke (1703–83), with Henry himself. Henry was appointed guardian over his twelve-year-old cousin Catherine Meares (1712/13–1773), fell in love with her, and they were married before 1728.
[219] Brooke died Oct. 12, 1783.
[220] JW had made a gift of his two-volume abridgement *The History of Henry, Earl of Moreland* to the Gibbes sisters; see JW to Eliz. Gibbes, Apr. 7, 1783.

Now I must take breath.[221]

I was in doubt before whether the young man had a turn for service.[222] So I am not much disappointed. I believe it be little loss to
him to return to his trade.

If my strength returns, I shall take a journey into Yorkshire short-   5
ly, and possibly wait upon you in a week or two at the Park. My best
respects attend your dear mamma.[223] Living or dying, I shall always
be, my dear Miss Gibbes,
 Your ever affectionate,

               John Wesley   10

Address: 'To / Miss Gibbes / At Sir Philip Gibbes, Bart. / At Hilton Park,
 near Wolverhampton / Staffordshire'.
Postmark: 'Bristol'.
Annotation: 'Mr J. Westley'.   15
Source: holograph; National Archives, PRO 30/9/11/2.

To William Roberts [224]   20

                Bristol
           August 16, 1783
Dear Billy,

The great God fill you with as much of his blessing as your heart   25
can contain! Your letter did me good like a cordial. I am right glad
that you explained yourself.

   Never more come mistrust between us twain.[225]
                    30

Dear Billy, adieu.

Source: holograph; Oxford, Lincoln College, Archive, MS/WES/A/2/5.

[221] I.e., rest for a while, before continuing the letter.
[222] The young man JW had directed to the Gibbes family as a potential servant; see JW
to Eliz. Gibbes, May 19, 1783.
[223] Lady Agnes (Osborne) Gibbes.
[224] Roberts replied to JW's letter of Aug. 3, 1783, explaining matters in a way that resolved
their tensions; unfortunately his letter is not known to survive.
[225] Cf. Shakespeare, *Hamlet*, Act 3, Scene 2, line 213: 'And never come mischance between us twain'.

To Thomas Tattershall

Bristol
August 17, 1783

Dear Tommy,

They need not at all scruple living together until they have certain intimation of his death. The law permits a woman to marry, after her husband has been seven years out of the kingdom. Neither need you scruple meeting her as a member of the society.[226]

Do all you can, in public and in private, to spread the books, and especially the *[Arminian] Magazines*. And every where strongly and explicitly exhort the believers to go on to perfection.[227] I am,

Dear Tommy,

Yours affectionately,

J. Wesley

Address: 'To / Mr Thos. Tattershall / In Coleraine / Ireland'.
Source: published transcription; Byrth, 'Memoir', xxxiii.

To Catherine Warren[228]

Bristol
August 19, 1783

My Dear Sister,

It was never intended that James Perfect should be an Assistant, any more than that he should be a king.[229] The supernumerary, John Prickard will act as Assistant if his journey with me has the effect which I expect. If God permit, we shall set out for Leeds on Monday, and return in about three weeks. Then I shall consign him to

---

[226] Lacking Tattershall's letter to JW, the details under consideration are unclear.

[227] See Heb. 6:1.

[228] While the address portion is missing, the content makes the recipient clear.

[229] James Perfect had just been assigned to the Pembrokeshire circuit, along with William Church and Samuel Hodgson; his name appears first on the list, which typically indicates the Assistant (see 10:533 in this edn.).

you for the rest of the year—provided you will not let him do more
than he can do.[230]

I had much pleased myself with the expectation of spending a
little time with you in Pembrokeshire. But as it pleased God to dispose of me in another manner, all is well. I am content. It is well,
our time is in his hands. He cannot but do what is best. And sick or
well, I shall always be, my dear Kitty,
  Affectionately yours,

               J. Wesley

Source: holograph; Buffalo, New York, Erie County Public Library, Rare
 Book Room, Gluck Manuscript Collection.

To Thomas Welch[231]

              c. August 28, 1783

You use me very ill. I have turned away three masters on your
account. The person who gives you this advice, is wanting either in
common sense or common honesty.

Source: published transcription; *Methodist Magazine* 40 (1817): 324.

---

[230] Repeating an exhortation from his letter to Warren of May 26, 1783. Unfortunately,
Prickard's health did not improve; he was buried on Nov. 3, 1783 in Bathwick, Somerset.
 [231] Welch initially replied to JW's letter of Aug. 15 accepting the position of writing master at Kingswood school. But within a few days a friend raised concern about the impact of
the loss of Welch on the Methodist society in Coventry. This led Welch to reconsider and he
wrote JW again, informing him that he would be staying in Coventry—drawing this response.

To Rachel (Norton) Bayley[232]

Congleton
Saturday, August 30, 1783

5   My Dear Sister,

As I purpose to spend a night at Manchester the week after next, I shall have an opportunity of talking with that young woman myself.[233] So I shall not need any other account.

Mr. McGeary is just such a man as we wanted.[234] I hope he
10   will meet me at Bristol in two or three weeks. I am now gathering strength every day. Probably I shall be at Bristol on this day fortnight.

I am, with love to brother and sister Lewis, my dear Rachel,
    Yours affectionately,

15   J. Wesley

Source: holograph; Philadelphia, Pennsylvania, Historic St. George's United Methodist Church, Archives.

20

To John Atlay

Leeds
September 3, 1783

25   My Dear Brother,

The schoolmasters for Kingswood are fixed, and are expected there every day.[235] Mr. [Thomas] Simpson's sister is the housekeeper, who is come hither in her way to Bristol.[236]

---

[232] While the address portion is missing, the contents enable reliable identification of the recipient. On May 24, 1783 JW had officiated the marriage of Rev. Cornelius Bayley to Rachel Norton; see *Journal*, 23:270 in this edn. Rachel (b. 1762) was the daughter of William and Margaret (Kighley) Norton, Methodists in Manchester; see William's letter to JW, Mar. 31, 1766. Rachel was raised through her mid-teens in Manchester, moving to Derbyshire, where a brother lived, after the death of her parents. Cornelius Bayley was currently helping JW find new staffing at Kingswood School so that he could lay aside his prior role there. He and Rachel would soon settle in Manchester.

[233] The woman was surely being considered for a position at Kingswood School.

[234] Little is known of Thomas McGeary (c. 1760–97) before his current selection by JW to replace Thomas Simpson as headmaster of Kingswood School. Thomas Simpson's sister, Christiana Simpson (d. 1812), joined the staff at Kingswood as housekeeper at the same time (replacing Thomas's wife). In 1786 McGeary married Christiana. McGeary served as headmaster of Kingswood until 1794, when the couple moved to Keynsham.

[235] The new headmaster was Thomas McGeary; see JW to Rachel Bayley, Aug. 30, 1783.

[236] I.e., Christiana Simpson (d. 1812). She would marry Thomas McGeary in 1786.

Let no man or woman go to West Street Chapel without my appointment. It is a matter of deep concern.

The building or not building at Birstall does not depend upon *me*, but the trustees.[237]

John Fenwick is to correct the press chiefly, in the absence of Dr.   5
[Thomas] Coke, and to transcribe tracts for me. And he may receive his little salary (at least) till I return to London.

I never expected the ten pounds to be returned. Take the clock if you can get it.

I am, with love to sister [Sarah] Atlay,   10
    Your affectionate brother,

J. Wesley

Address: 'To / Mr Atlay / City Road / London'.
Postmarks: 'Leeds' and '5/SE'.   15
Endorsement: by Atlay, 'Mr Wesley Sept 5th / 1783'.
Source: holograph; MARC, MA 1992/018.

20

To Sarah Wesley Jr.[238]

Birstall
September 5, 1783   25

My Dear Sally,

You did quite right in spending a ⟨litt⟩le time at Margate.[239] Sea-bathing is a noble ⟨re⟩medy. But if any weakness remains, you ⟨sh⟩ould add another, a laced-stocking either of ⟨li⟩nen or dimity—lacing it on every morning, as ⟨ti⟩ght as you can without giving pain.   30
There ⟨is⟩ little danger, Sally, that I should not approve ⟨of⟩ anything which *you* do.

---

[237] JW met with the trustees of the Birstall preaching-house two days later, trying to persuade them to revise the deed on the house to that used for the City Road Chapel; with the warning that if they did not, then he would stop sending the preachers and build another chapel in Birstall for his connexion. See JW, *Journal*, Sept. 5, 1783, 23:289 in this edn.; and *Minutes* (1782), Q. 22, 10:529 in this edn.

[238] Sarah Wesley Jr. had been in Bristol and Bath in June 1783, meeting Mary Freeman Shepherd there; see Martha (Wesley) Hall to Sally Wesley Jr., June 18, 1783 (MARC, DDWes 7/62). While there she likely stayed with Mrs. Purnell—who then apparently accompanied Sarah to Margate, where they met Mrs. Cheesment.

[239] The left margin of the letter was cropped or torn away a bit, removing 2–3 letters in nearly every line. The missing text has been reconstructed.

I love sister Cheesment much and shall be ⟨al⟩ways glad of an opportunity of seeing her.[240] I am ⟨no⟩w a good deal concerned for her.
She stands upon ⟨sli⟩ppery ground. Be not wanting in any instance
⟨of⟩ friendship to that lovely woman. Particularly ⟨in⟩ speaking your
5   whole mind to her, even on the ⟨mo⟩st delicate subject.

It is your great point now to be continually ⟨se⟩eking for the fullness of the promise: 'I will ⟨cir⟩cumcise thy heart, to love the Lord
thy God ⟨wi⟩th all thy heart and with all thy soul.'[241] How soon may
⟨thi⟩s be fulfilled?

10   I am, with love to Mrs. Purnell, my dear Sally,[242]

Yours affectionately,

J. Wesley

15   *Source*: holograph; Bridwell Library (SMU).[243]

To Robert Hall

20
                                                     Leeds
                                         September 6, 1783

My Dear Brother,

I am not at all well pleased with John Hampson for leaving the
circuit, and hope he will soon be with you again.[244] So undoubtedly
25   will Mr. [William] Myles, if he is not with you already.

Dr. [Thomas] Coke purposes to be with you on Tuesday sennight.

I am,

Your affectionate brother,

30
                                                   J. Wesley

[240] Capt. John Cheesment (1732–83), one of the trustees of City Road Chapel, married
Sarah Grace in Dec. 1780. Capt. Cheesment died in Feb. 1783, with JW performing his burial;
see *Journal*, Feb. 24, 1783, 23:263–64 in this edn. In Oct. 1786 Sarah would marry George
Wolff (1736–1828), one of the executors of JW's last will. See JW's praise of her in his letter to
Sarah Wesley Jr., Sept. 17, 1790.

[241] Cf. Deut. 30:6.

[242] Judith Davis (1731–93) married the widower James Purnell Esq. (1711–72), of Bristol,
in 1763. The couple were supporters of the Methodist society, and after her husband's death
Judith resided in their country home in Almondsbury, just outside Bristol. In Dec. 1786 Judith
(Davis) Purnell would marry John Francis Valton.

[243] Held previously in WMC Museum, 2002.001.019.

[244] The reference is to John Hampson Jr. (1753–1819), son of the itinerant with the same
name. For biographical details see the note on JW to John Fletcher, Apr. 3, 1785.

You may give notice of Dr. Coke's preaching at 7:00 on Tuesday evening.

Address: 'To / Mr Robert Hall, Junr / At Mr Matt. Bagshaw's / in / Nottingham'.

Postmark: 'Leeds'.

Source: holograph; Pitts Library (Emory), John Wesley Papers (MSS 153), 3/29.

To Edward Dromgoole[245]

Bristol
September 17, 1783

My Dear Brother,

The more sensible we are to our own weakness the more strength we shall receive from above. As long as we feel that we are helpless and blind and poor, our strong helper will be always at hand.

I am glad to hear that, notwithstanding all these commotions, he is carrying on his work in America. It is a peculiar blessing that the labourers are connected together, so as to act in concert with each other. And that God has given you all to be of one heart nd one mind that you may 'kindly think and meekly speak the same'.[246] One would have imagined that the 'fell monster war' would have utterly destroyed the work of God.[247] So it has done in all ages and countries. So it did in Scotland a few years ago. But that his work should increase at such a season was never heard of before! It is plain God has wrought a new thing in the earth, showing thereby that nothing is too hard for him.[248]

I had not heard anything concerning Mr. [Devereux] Jarratt for a long season. You send me welcome news concerning him. I am glad

---

[245] Edward Dromgoole (1751–1835) was a native of County Sligo, Ireland. He converted to Methodism in 1770 and immigrated to Maryland later that year. His Methodist convictions were renewed there by the preaching of Robert Strawbridge. Dromgoole soon began preaching himself, and served as a formal itinerant from 1774–86. He then settled in Brunswick County, Virginia as a planter and merchant, while hosting Methodist preachers and remaining active as a local preacher until his death. See *WHS* 26 (1947): 25–28. JW was replying to Dromgoole's letter of May 24, 1783, which provides further biographical information.

[246] Cf. CW, Hymn on Isaiah 11:13, st. 1, *Scripture Hymns* (1762), 1:319.

[247] Nicholas Rowe, *Tamerlane*, I.1.96. For other uses by JW, see Sermon 111, *National Sins and Miseries*, I.4, 3:571 in this edn.; and Sermon 128, 'The Deceitfulness of the Human Heart', II.4, 4:156 in this edn.

[248] See Isa. 43:19 and Jer. 32:27.

to hear that his love is not grown cold. It is well, that you 'agree to disagree' in your opinions concerning public affairs. There is no end of disputing about these matters. Let everyone enjoy his own persuasion. Let us leave God to govern the world, and he will be
5   sure to do all things well.[249] And all will work together for his glory, and for the good of them that love him.[250]

When the government in America is settled, I believe some of our brethren will be ready to come over. I cannot advise them to do it yet. First let us see how providence opens itself. And I am the less
10   in haste, because I am persuaded brother [Francis] Asbury is raised up to preserve order among you, and to do just what I should do myself, if it pleased God to bring me to America. Go on in the name of the Lord and in the power of his might![251]

I am,
15   Your affectionate brother,

J. Wesley

Address: 'To / Mr Edward Drumgoole / In Petersburg / Virginia'.
Source: holograph; University of North Carolina (Chapel Hill) Library,
       Edward Dromgoole Papers, #230.
20

To Jeremiah Brettel[252]

25
Bristol
September 30, 1783

Dear Jerry,

I suppose a preacher is still wanting in the Norwich circuit. If so,
30   let brother Parkin or Ingham remove thither.[253] We will not, cannot, keep a preacher in any circuit merely to preach at two or three places on Sunday.

---

[249] See Mark 7:37.

[250] See Rom. 8:28.

[251] See Eph. 6:10.

[252] Jeremiah Brettel was appointed at the 1783 Conference as the Assistant of the Lynn circuit (adjacent to the Norwich circuit), along with John Ingham and Jonathan Parkin.

[253] John Ingham was admitted 'on trial' as an itinerant at the 1781 Conference (see 10:507 in this edn.); he was expelled from the connexion in 1786 (10:597n). Jonathan Parkin (c. 1758–1817), a native of Sheffield, first appears in the *Minutes* in 1783 (10:533) but apparently began travelling as a preacher the prior year; when he died in 1817 he was credited with 35 years in itinerant ministry. See *Minutes* (post-Wesley, 1818), 4:395.

Put forth all your strength! Do you all you can for God! I am, dear Jerry,

    Your affectionate friend and brother,

                         J. Wesley

Annotation: 'Mr Wesley's Letter / To Lynn'.[254]
Source: holograph; MARC, MAM JW 2/8.

To an Unidentified Woman[255]

                                 Bristol
                     September 30, 1783

My Dear Sister,

    You have reason to be exceeding thankful to God, for he has dealt graciously with you; particularly in giving you a faithful friend [Elizabeth Ritchie], one that can sympathize with you in your trials and advise you on those difficult occasions wherein you cannot depend on your own understanding. Our blessed Lord himself has, by his adorable providence, considerably lessened what might have been your greatest trial, by suffering the affection of your nearest friend to be lessened. Otherwise, I know not how you would have borne his tenderness. It is your wisdom now to recollect wherein you have been most liable to grieve his Holy Spirit, that if any of those temptations should offer themselves again you may be prepared for them. You know not how soon he may touch your nature clean in a more full sense than even before. Only be simple! Be as a little child! Look up, and feel him near!

    I am, my dear sister,

        Your affectionate brother,

                         J. Wesley

Address: 'To / Miss Ritchie / In Otley / Yorkshire'.
Postmarks: 'Bristol' and '2/OC'. *Charge*: '8'.
Source: holograph; Bridwell Library (SMU).

---

[254] In an unknown hand.

[255] While the address portion is to Elizabeth Ritchie, she was not the intended recipient of this specific letter (JW opened contemporary letters to her with 'My Dear Betsy'). This is another instance of a double letter, where the leaf to Ritchie has been removed (before passing it on) and is not known to survive. A narrow strip of the top margin of the remaining leaf, where JW typically gives the name of the second recipient in a double letter, has been cut away. One possible recipient is the Mrs. Horner whom Ritchie mentions in her letter to JW of Jan. 10, 1782.

To Francis Asbury and American Preachers[256]

Bristol
October 3, 1783

5   1. Let all of you be determined to abide by the Methodist doctrine and discipline published in the four volumes of *Sermons* and the *Notes upon the New Testament*, together with the large *Minutes* of the Conference.[257]

    2. Beware of preachers coming from Great Britain or Ireland with-
10 out a full recommendation from me. Three of our travelling preachers here eagerly desired to go to America. But I could not approve of it by any means, because I am not satisfied that they thoroughly like either our discipline or our doctrine. I think they differ from our judgment in one or both. Therefore, if these or any other come with-
15 out my recommendation, take care how you receive them.

    3. Neither should you receive any preachers, however recommended, who will not be subject to the American Conference and cheerfully conform to the Minutes both of the English and American Conferences.[258]

20 4. I do not wish our American brethren to receive any who make any difficulty of receiving Francis Asbury as the General Assistant.

    Undoubtedly the greatest danger to the work of God in America is likely to arise either from preachers coming from Europe, or from such as will arise from among yourselves speaking perverse things,
25 or bringing in among you new doctrines, particularly Calvinism. You should guard against this with all possible care, for it is far easier to keep them out than to thrust them out.

    I commend you all to the grace of God; and am,
        Your affectionate friend and brother,

30   John Wesley

Source: published extract; Lee, *Short History*, 85–86.

[256] The war between Great Britain and the colonies in North America formally concluded with the Treaty of Paris, signed on Sept. 3, 1783. Francis Asbury had been communicating with JW about the challenges facing the Methodist movement in North America. JW's present letter was likely in response to one Asbury wrote around Aug. 25, from New York (which is not known to survive, but see Asbury's reference to it in his letter of Sept. 20, 1783 — the latter letter would not have had time to arrive in England by Oct. 3). Asbury records receiving this letter from JW on Dec. 24, 1783; see Asbury, *Journal*, 1:450. The letter likely included an opening section to Asbury and then this text to read to the preachers.

[257] Echoing language for Methodists preaching-houses in the 'Large' *Minutes* (1763), Q. 67, 10:869–70 in this edn.

[258] Manuscript minutes of Conferences of the Methodist preachers in North America survive from as early as 1773; these appeared in print first in *Minutes of the Methodist Conferences*, annually held in America, from 1773 to 1794 (Philadelphia: Tuckniss, 1794).

To Mrs. Howton[259]

Bristol
October 3, 1783

My Dear Sister, 5

There will never be any trouble about the child, whether anything is paid or not. You need not be apprehensive of any demand upon that account.

Those which I saw at your house were a company of lovely children both in their persons and in their behaviour.[260] Some of them 10 I am in hopes of meeting there again if I should live till spring. The account you gave of that sick maiden is very remarkable; and her spirit must, I trust, influence others.

It is the glory of the people called Methodists that they condemn none for their opinions or modes of worship.[261] They think and let 15 think, and insist upon nothing but faith working by love.

I am, with love to sister Price,

Your affectionate friend and brother,

J. Wesley

Address: 'To / Mrs Howton / At Mrs Price's Boarding School / Worcester 20
/ xpost'.
Postmark: 'Bristol'.
Source: holograph; MARC, MAM JW 3/66.

25

To Hugh Moore[262]

Bristol 30
October 3, 1783

Dear Hugh,

I hope those that follow you in Scotland will do all they can in the new places.[263] It is your part to forget the things behind, and

---

[259] Mrs. Howton may have lived with Mrs. Price, who kept a boarding-school in Worcester: note how JW identifies 'sister Howton's' in his diary as where he was the morning of Mar. 24, 1785 (23:518 in this edn.); while his *Journal* account of the same morning says he 'breakfasted at Mrs. Price's' (23:346 in this edn.).

[260] JW gives a very similar description of the children in Mrs. Price's boarding-school on Mar. 24, 1785 (23:346).

[261] Mrs. Price was a Quaker.

[262] This is the first known surviving letter of JW to Hugh Moore.

[263] Moore had been stationed on the Aberdeen circuit the prior year.

with all possible seriousness and earnestness to redeem the time, and lay yourself out in snatching as many brands as you can out of the fire.[264]

5 Your fellow labourer and you going on hand in hand, will soon put the circuit into a better condition.[265] Only be exact in every part of discipline, and strongly insist upon the old Methodist doctrine, namely salvation from all sin attainable now by faith.

Those commissioners have a large salary for examining all proposals concerning the longitude, therefore they discourage all that 10 attempt to discover it, lest they should lose their salary.[266]

I am, dear Hugh,

Your affectionate brother,

J. Wesley

15 *Source*: published transcription; *WHS* 29 (1954): 114.

20 ## To Richard Rodda

Bristol
October 3, 1783

25 Dear Richard,

If you have received a gift from God, you ought to use it. He may give it to whom he pleases.

John Broadbent exactly observed all our rules.[267] You are bound in conscience to do the same. If any other preachers do not, they 30 are sinners against God, and the people, and their own souls. If reproach follows doing your duty, so much the better. It is the reproach of Christ.

---

[264] See Phil. 3:13, Eph. 5:16, and Jude 1:23.

[265] Moore had been appointed by the 1783 Conference to serve with Thomas Ellis on the Whitehaven circuit.

[266] A means of calculating the exact longitude of ships at sea was a pressing need at the opening of the eighteenth century. In 1714 a Board of Commissioners for the Discovery of the Longitude at Sea was created, and empowered to provide awards, depending on accuracy, to the developer of such a tool. Several small awards had been presented, particularly to John Harrison for his chronometer. But the Board never award a full prize, and was eventually abolished by Parliament in 1828.

[267] John Broadbent had been Assistant over the Staffordshire circuit 1779–81. This circuit included Birmingham and Wednesbury, where Rodda was now Assistant.

I will inquire concerning the clock. Take an exact account of the work of God at Wednesbury.

I am, dear Richard,

Your affectionate friend and brother,

J. Wesley   5

Address: 'To / Mr Rodda / At the Preachinghouse / In Birmingham Wenesbury / Staffordshire / xpost'.

Postmarks: 'Bristol' and 'Birmingham'.

Source: holograph; Pitts Library (Emory), John Wesley Papers (MSS   10
153), 3/30.

15

To Jasper Winscom[268]

London
October 13, 1783   20

Dear Jasper,

You and I have been old friends. We have known one another for many years. Friendship therefore requires me to tell you my thoughts without either disguise or reserve.

Your son, an hopeful young man, fearing God, falls in love with   25
an agreeable, well-bred, sensible woman. After some delays, he takes a wrong step—he marries her without your consent.[269] For this you are angry and forbid him your house; and I cannot blame you.

You may say, 'Well, what would you advise me to do now?' I advise you to forgive him. I advise you to lay aside your anger (it is high   30
time), and to receive him again (occasionally) into your house. For you need forgiveness yourself; and if you do not forgive, you cannot be forgiven.[270]

You will perhaps say, 'Why, I *have* forgiven him. But he shall never come into my house.' And what if God should say the same to   35
you? Then you had better never have been born!

---

[268] JW had been in Winchester on Oct. 10, 1783, when he likely learned of the rift which he addresses in this letter.

[269] Thomas Winscomb (c. 1762–1817), the son of Jasper and Edith (Young) Winscom, married Jane Cave (c. 1760–1813) on May 17, 1783 in Winchester, Hampshire.

[270] See Matt. 6:12.

But beside, what would follow if you should persist in treating your son thus? Probably his patience would be worn out, and he would contract resentment, perhaps bitterness, if not hatred toward you. And if so, what must follow? Why, *your* implacable anger will cause your son's damnation!

'But she has settled her fortune upon herself.'[271] I cannot blame her if she has. Every woman has a right so to do. 'But she will not let him travel with her.' Nay, but he does not desire it, knowing it would be a double expense and inconvenience on many accounts.

Nay, Jasper, take advice. Show yourself a man of sense, a man of piety, and a real friend to

Your affectionate brother,

J. Wesley

Source: holograph; Drew, Methodist Archives.

To An Unidentified Man

London
October 17, 1783

I am glad to hear that you had a safe, though it was a slow, passage to Dublin; and that your master received you not in a civil, but in an affectionate manner. I really hope this is a token that God is turning your captivity. And if you serve him in earnest, he will withhold from you no manner of thing that is good.[272]

I do not well know who your father is. Your mother I remember perfectly well. It seems but as yesterday since I was conversing with Miss Lovelace at Athlone. She had then strong desires to be not only almost but altogether a Christian.[273] If she and your father cast their care on him that careth for them, he will deliver them out of all their trouble.[274]

I am,

Your affectionate brother,

J. Wesley

Source: holograph; Wesley's Chapel (London), LDWMM 1997/6716.

---

[271] The will of Jane (Cave) Winscomb, proved June 1, 1813, mentions that Thomas had entered into an agreement not to inherit her property, so it went to their children.

[272] See Ps. 84:11.

[273] See JW, *The Almost Christian* (1741), 1:131–41 in this edn.

[274] See 1 Pet. 5:7.

To an Unidentified Man

London
October 17, 1783

My Dear Brother, 5

I returned hither an hour or two ago, and am glad to hear that God is still carrying on his own work. But let not that induce you to kill yourself, by doing more than you *can* do. Allow yourself as much rest as nature requires. You must not offer murder for sacrifice.[275] 10

Your point is now to build upon, rather than to awaken; and to attend to the work of sanctification, rather than that of justification. This is the way to prevent *many* instances of backsliding. *Some* we must expect.

I doubt you hit the mark. Probably that is their hope—to delay 15 the matter till I am out of the way. I am,

Your affectionate friend and brother,

J. Wesley

Source: holograph; Sydney, Australia, State Library of New South Wales, 20 Mitchell Library, AM 123/folder 2/ item 15.

25

To Hannah Ball[276]

London
c. October 18, 1783[277]

My Dear Sister, 30

Your wisdom is, as far as is possible, not to think or speak of Mr. [Roger] Westrup at all.[278] You have better things to think of; namely, that God is returning to his people. There is a beginning already. But you should continually expect to see greater things than these.[279]

---

[275] See JW, 'Sermon on the Mount, VII', IV.4, 1:609 in this edn.

[276] While the address portion is missing and no name is used, the holograph was part of the papers of Hannah Ball, and the letter is transcribed in her *Memoir* (pp. 158–59). Ball's letter to JW, which drew this response, is not known to survive.

[277] The letter gives only the month and year; but Oct. 17–18 were the only days when JW was in London long enough to write letters.

[278] See JW to Richard Rodda, Jan. 23, 1783.

[279] See John 1:50.

'Temptations', says Mr. Haliburton, 'and distinct deliverance from temptation, profit us much.'[280] And 'he prepareth for us', as Kempis observes, 'occasions of fighting that we may conquer.'[281]

5   Never scruple to declare explicitly what God has done for your soul. And never be weary of exhorting the believers to 'go on to perfection'.[282] When they are athirst for this in any place, the whole work of God goes on.

I am, my dear sister,
Your affectionate brother,

10   J. Wesley

Source: holograph; MARC, MA 2008/013.

15

To Jane (Hilton) Barton

20   Norwich
                                                    October 26, 1783
My Dear Sister,
Considering how general this disorder was—nay, universal all over the kingdom, it is very remarkable, that in most towns and
25   cities so very few have died.[283] Not one, I believe, in all England that drank largely of lemonade. I think honey and brimstone, as prescribed in the *Primitive Physic* (which I suppose you always have in the house) would have cured your daughter more speedily and more effectually than the doctor did.[284]
30   The deliverance of your little boy was indeed remarkable.[285] And just as easily can the God whom you serve, deliver you out of all

---

[280] Thomas Halyburton, *Memoirs of the Life of the Reverend, Learned, and Pious Mr. Thomas Halyburton* (London: Cruttenden, 1718), 178; using the slightly revised wording of JW in his *Abstract of the Life ... Thomas Haliburton* (1739, *Bibliography*, No. 12), 83. JW used this quote twice previously without indicating the author: JW to Eliz. Briggs, Apr. 14, 1771, 28:370 in this edn.; and JW to Eliz. Ritchie, Nov. 29, 1775, 29:201 in this edn.

[281] *Imitation of Christ*, I.xi.4 (I.ix.4 in JW's abridged version).

[282] Heb. 6:1.

[283] The flu epidemic that reached Great Britain in early summer 1782 carried over into the following year.

[284] See *Primitive Physic*, Ailment #2 (an ague), Receipt #21, 32:126 in this edn.

[285] William and Jane had welcomed a son, John Hilton Barton, bap. Feb. 6, 1783.

your trouble. But his manner and his time are best.[286] First let patience have its perfect work![287]
    I am, with love to brother [William] Barton, dear Jenny,
        Your affectionate brother,

                                J. Wesley

Source: holograph; Bridwell Library (SMU).

To John Ellison[288]

                                   London
                          November 4, 1783
Dear Jack,
    As you desired it, I wrote to Lord North immediately.[289] But I
doubted whether it would avail. Time was when he wanted and was
glad of my assistance; but now he does not want it. So I do not
expect to hear from him any more. It is well, I can do without him.
It is well we have one Friend that will never fail us! Let us trust in
him, and we shall never be confounded.
    I am, your affectionate uncle,

                                J. Wesley

Address: 'To / Mr John Ellison / At the Custom-house in / Bristol'.
Postmark: '4/NO'. *Charge*: '4'.
Source: holograph; Bridwell Library (SMU).

---

[286] Cf. CW, 'Groaning for Redemption', Pt. III, st. 3, *l.* 5, *HSP* (1742), 107.
[287] See James 1:4.
[288] This is the only known surviving letter of JW to his nephew John Ellison (1720–91),
the oldest son of JW's sister Susanna (Wesley) Ellison and her husband Richard.
[289] Lord Frederick North became Home Secretary in Apr. 1783.

To Thomas Longley[290]

London
November 5, 1783

5   My Dear Brother,
     What you mention is an exceeding odd case. I hardly remember
the like. I refer Samuel Edwards wholly to *you*.[291] If you cannot trust
him, he must go home. If you can, you may receive him again as a
fellow labourer—that is, if he is sensible of his fault, of his very
10   uncommon pride and stubbornness and unadvisableness, contrary
both to religion and to reason. But you can't receive him unless he
promises for the time to come to take your advice or reproof, not as
an affront, not as 'trampling him under-foot', but as a favour and
an act of real kindness.
15   I am,
         Your affectionate friend and brother,

                                                  [J. Wesley]

Address: 'To / Mr. Longley / At Mr. M[ichael] Dobinson's / In Derby'.
20   *Source*: published transcription; Telford, *Letters*, 7:194.

To Ann Tindall

London
November 8, 1783

My Dear Sister,
30   I intend to subscribe for two full years, from my first subscription.[292] It may be paid [to] you out of the book-money. But apropos,
a thought strikes me. Would not a greater number of the *[Armin-
ian] Magazines* and of other books be dispersed if the books were
sold in yours, as they are in the other circuits, by the Assistant? Tell
35   me freely and impartially what you think.

---

[290] Thomas Longley (1743–1809), a native of Dewsbury, first appears in the *Minutes* as an
itinerant in 1780 (see 10:498 in this edn.). He served for 26 years, the last three supernumerary;
see *Minutes* (post-Wesley, 1809), 3:69.
     [291] Samuel Edwards had been admitted 'on trial' as an itinerant at the 1783 Conference
and appointed to the Derby circuit, under Longley as Assistant (see 10:531, 534 in this edn.).
Edwards apparently made amends, as he was admitted to full standing at the 1784 Conference
(10:553). But he disappears from the *Minutes* after his appointment to Colne in 1787 (10:626).
     [292] Cf. JW to Tindall, Aug. 3, 1783.

Those you relate are remarkable instances of divine grace, and such as might be had in remembrance.[293]

I am, dear Nancy,
> Your affectionate brother,

J. Wesley 5

Address: 'To / Miss Tindal, in / Scarborough'.
Postmark: '8/NO'.
Endorsement: by Tindall, '8 Nov 1783'.
Source: holograph; British Library, Department of Manuscripts, Add. 10
MS. 43695, ff. 75–76.

15

To Captain Richard Williams[294]

London
November 9, 1783

My Dear Brother, 20

I know the talents which God has lent me, and I dare not bury any of them in the earth. I am a debtor both to the learned and the unlearned. And in the *[Arminian] Magazine* I apply to both—chiefly indeed to the unlearned, because these are the far greater number. And still I keep my original points in view: He died for *all*, to save 25 them from *all sin*.

I think the lines on slavery will do well![295] They are both sensible and poetical.

I am, dear Richard,
> Your affectionate brother,

J. Wesley 30

Address: 'To / Capt. Richd. Williams / In Poldice, near Truro / Cornwall'.
Source: holograph; Redruth, Cornwall, England, Methodist church.

35

[293] Tindall's letter to JW is not known to survive.

[294] Richard Williams sent JW previously both prose and verse items for consideration of publication in *AM*. JW included a few the previous year; see *AM* 5 (1782), 261–65, 378–80, and 581–82. It appears that Williams had protested the JW did not publish some other items he had sent.

[295] JW would decide that these lines did not fit the purpose of *AM* and forward them to a couple of public newspapers; see JW to Williams, Dec. 10, 1783.

To Phoebe (French) Nail [296]

London
November 12, 1783

Dear Sister,

Mr. Wesley desires me to inform you that he has written to Mr. [John] Pritchard on the subject of your letter, and you may expect to hear farther from him soon.[297] He seems highly displeased with Mr. Pritchard for what he has done.

I am,
Yours,

Thomas Tennant

Source: published transcription; Telford, *Letters*, 7:195.

To Mr. Alexander[298]

near London
November 21, 1783

Dear Sir,

It is very certain your day of grace is not passed. If it was, you would be quite easy and unconcerned. It is plain the Lover of souls is still striving with you and drawing you to himself. But you have

---

[296] Phoebe French (b. 1736) married Moses Nail (1744–1814) in Frome, Somerset, in 1768. That same year Moses was drawn into the Methodist society and soon began serving as a local preacher. In Aug. 1783 John Pritchard became Assistant of the Bedford circuit, which included Frome. Pritchard inherited a conflict at Frome over an attempt to replace the society steward. The prior steward would not surrender the office to the person newly named to that role. This led Pritchard on Oct. 29, 1783 to expel both Moses Nail and another local preacher, Robert Dyer (1738–98), who had apparently taken the side of the prior steward, along with Moses' wife Phoebe, even though she had not taken an active role. About 20 members left the society, and Phoebe wrote JW protesting the action (the letter is not known to survive). The Nails eventually reconciled with the Frome society. See Stephen Tuck, *Wesleyan Methodism in Frome* (Frome: S. Tuck, 1837), 51–52.

[297] This letter is not known to survive.

[298] The father's name is uncertain, but James Alexander (d. 1815?) of Harristown, who had served the king in the American war, did not become a Methodist itinerant. By 1798 he was resident at New Ross, Co. Wexford (a schoolmaster at the Ross Academy), and in 1814 at Glanmire, near Cork. During the rebellion of 1798 he became major of New Ross, apparently heading an informal group of loyalists in action against the rebels. For this he was rewarded, he said, with 'an inferior situation under the excise'. Alexander published notes on the rebellion, in Walker's *Hibernian Magazine* (Nov. 1798), and other works.

no time to lose, for 'Now is the accepted time! Now is the day of salvation!'[299] It is therefore your wisdom (without considering what others do, whether clergyman or layman) to attend one thing—that is, to work out your own salvation with fear and trembling.[300] And nothing can be more sure than that if you do this, if it be indeed your one care to 'seek the kingdom of God and his righteousness, all other things shall be added unto you'.[301]

To his protection I commit you and yours; and am, dear sir,
Your affectionate brother,

J. Wesley   10

I write a line to your son:

near London
November 21, 1783   15

Dear James,
Only let your actions correspond with your words, and then they will have weight with all that hear them.

It seems highly probable to me that providence does not intend you should be a tradesman.

I have known a young man that feared God acquire as much learning in one year as children usually do in seven. Possibly you may do the same. If you have a desire to try, and we should live till July, I will give you a year's schooling and board at Kingswood School, and you will then be the better able to judge what it is that God calls you to.

I am,
Yours affectionately,

J. Wesley   30

Address: 'To / Mr Alexander / At Harristown / Near Monasterevan/ Ireland'.
Postmark: '22/NO'.
Source: holograph; MARC, MAM JW 1/1.   35

[299] 2 Cor. 6:2.
[300] See Phil. 2:12.
[301] Cf. Matt. 6:33.

To Walter Churchey

near London
November 21, 1783

5 My Dear Brother,

You have indeed had a sea of troubles. But I have not yet heard anyone say it was your own fault; which I wonder at, because it is the way of the world still (as it was in the days of Job) always to construe misfortune into sin. But you and I know that there is a God in
10 the world, and that he has more to do in it than most men are aware of. So little do they advert to that great truth, 'Even the very hairs of your head are all numbered!'[302]

One thing only I have heard of you, which if it be true, I should not commend. I mean that you have wholly forsaken the poor
15 Methodists,[303] and do not so much as attend the public preaching. One was mentioning this a few days ago, when I was saying something in favour of you, and it stopped my mouth. Nay, supposing it true, I do not know what to say yet. For surely, when affliction presses upon us we need every possible help.
20 Commending you to him that careth for you, I am,

Your affectionate brother,

J. Wesley

My kind love to sister [Mary] Churchey.
25

Address: 'To / Mr Churchey / Near the Hay / Brecon'.
Postmark: '22/NO'.
Endorsement: by Churchey, 'Nov 83 / J. W.'.
Source: holograph; Bridwell Library (SMU).
30

To Dorothy (Furly) Downes
35

near London
November 21, 1783

My Dear Sister,

Through the blessing of God I find no difference at all between
40 the health and strength which are now given me and that which I

---

[302] Matt. 10:30; Luke 12:7.
[303] Churchey inserted in the left margin: 'This was a misrepresentation'.

had forty years ago. Only I had then many pains which I have not now.

You are enabled to give a very clear and standing proof that weakness of nerves cannot prevent joy in the Lord. Your nerves have been remarkably weak, and that for many years, but still your soul can magnify the Lord and your spirit rejoice in God your Saviour![304]

Your affectionate brother,

J. Wesley

Source: published transcription; Benson, *Works*, 16:331.

To Ann Loxdale

near London
November 21, 1783

My Dear Miss Loxdale,

It is probable your letter came to Bristol during the time of my illness, and was then laid so carefully by that it never was found since.[305] I have reason to think some other letters wrote about that time met with the same misfortune. One in particular from a lovely woman at the Hague, which I was exceedingly sorry to lose.[306]

I believe Mr. [Thomas] Walsh's nervous disorders gave rise to many, if not most, of those temptations to which many persons of equal grace but firmer nerves are utter strangers all their lives.[307] As you never yet experienced anything of the kind, so I am persuaded you never will.

Yet I do not wonder at the horrid temptations of Gregory Lopez, because he was in a desert—that is, (so far) out of God's way.

I see much of the goodness and wisdom of God in the particular trial you are now under. As you speak to me without reserve, I will speak to you in the same manner. But summon up all your faith and resignation, or you will not be able to bear it.

---

[304] See Luke 1:46–47.

[305] There is no known surviving correspondence between Loxdale's letter to JW of Apr. 11, 1783 and this letter. JW was referring to his illness in Bristol the first half of Aug. 1783.

[306] If JW was referring to the letter of [Marie Judith (Adams)?] Leuliet, of The Hague, July 16, 1783, the letter was later found (see in-letters file).

[307] In his letter of June 10, 1781, JW commended to Loxdale *The Life and Death of Thomas Walsh* (1763); see 29:655 in this edn.

I cannot doubt at all but some years ago he was earnestly seeking salvation.[308] But I have more and more reasons to believe that he is now far, very far, from it. It was with a doubting conscience I refrained from expelling him the society, because I *heard* he was deeply, uncommonly covetous, and because I knew: 1) that he mortally hated Mr. [James] Rogers, and did him all the ill offices he could; 2) because he equally hated that blessed creature Hetty Roe; and 3) because he is a determined enemy to perfection.

Herein I have given you strongest proof of the sincerity with which I am, my dear Miss Loxdale,

Your affectionate friend and brother,

J. Wesley

Address: 'To / Mrs Hill / In the Mill Lane / Salop'.
Postmark: '22/NO'.
Source: holograph; New York, Pierpont Morgan Library, MA 516.13.

To Elizabeth (Nangle) Bradburn

Sheerness
November 27, 1783

My Dear Betsy,

Although our brethren at Birstall were not so admirable as I could have desired, yet I do not repent me of my journey.[309] I am well pleased that I did *my* part. You are now among a teachable and a loving people.[310] And as you have fewer crosses, I expect you will have better health. Yet crosses of one kind or another you must still expect. Otherwise you must go out of the world. But every cross will be proportioned to your strength, and you will always find his grace is sufficient for you.[311]

When I talked with Mrs. [Elizabeth] Carr about your affair, I did not observe that she resented anything.[312] She spoke of you with much tenderness. But if she does not write, she is certainly a little

---

[308] The man under discussion is one with whom Loxdale was considering marriage; see JW to Loxdale, Dec. 9, 1783. He would eventually withdraw his affection; see JW to Mary (Bosanquet) Fletcher, Apr. 2, 1785.

[309] JW had been in Birstall Sept. 4–5, 1783, preaching and meeting with the trustees; see *Journal*, 23:289 in this edn.

[310] Samuel Bradburn had been moved from the Bradford circuit (which included Birstall) to the Leeds circuit by the 1783 Conference.

[311] See 2 Cor. 12:9.

[312] See JW to Eliz. Bradburn, Feb. 26, 1783.

disgusted. It seems you have nothing to do but to sit still, and in due time God will order all things well.[313]

I am glad you have had a little time with my dear Miss [Elizabeth] Ritchie. There would be no jar between her spirit and yours.

I am, with love to Sammy Bradburn, my dear Betsy,

Yours most affectionately,

J. Wesley

Source: holograph; Drew, Methodist Archives.

To Benjamin Chappell[314]

[Sheerness]
November 27, 1783

My Dear Brother,

It is so long a time since I heard from you that I began to be in doubt whether you had forgotten your old friends, or was safe land-ed in a better world. As I find you are still in the land of the living, I hope you are still making the best of life and labouring by every possible means to make your calling and election sure.[315] Without doubt you have found many trials, and will find many more. But still you know in whom you have trusted, and who is able to deliver you out of all.[316] But what means of grace have you? Have you any church within any reasonable distance? If you have, how often have you divine service? Twice on every Sunday? Have you a clergyman that loves or fears God? Though if he does not, it will not hinder you of the blessing attending the divine ordinances.[317] But if you have no clergyman, see that you constantly meet together, and God will be where two or three are gathered together.[318]

If sister Morse is a lively, zealous, and judicious Christian, she may be of much use among you. But I doubt whether Henry Al-line be not the person concerning whom our brethren in Cumber-land wrote to me, who has wrote and published a book which is

---

[313] See Eph. 1:11.

[314] In Feb. 1774 Chappell married Elizabeth Patterson (1746–1829). That summer they emigrated to North America, ending up at St John's Prince Edward Island (now Prince Edward Island). They became lay leaders of the Methodist society there.

[315] See 2 Pet. 1:10.

[316] See 2 Tim. 1:12 and Dan. 3:17.

[317] Note JW's assumption of the efficacy of sacraments, despite a defect in the minister.

[318] See Matt. 18:20.

full of broad, ranting antinomianism.[319] If it is he, he is a wild, absurd man—wiser in his own eyes than seven men that can render a reason—and has done much mischief among the serious persons there, setting every man's sword against his brother.[320] If it be the same man, have a care of him or he will do more harm among you than ever he can do good. I should think some of our brethren from Cumberland would have zeal and courage enough to come over to you now and then and impart some of their fire to you.

If the case of the island be as you say, why do not the inhabitants send a petition to the Government? It seems this would be a very seasonable time.

It will be a difficult thing to find apprentices who will be willing to take so long a journey to a cold and uncomfortable place.

I am glad to hear so good an account of your wife [Elizabeth]. See that you strengthen each other's hands in God.[321] Beware of lukewarmness. Beware of cleaving to the present world. Let your treasure and your hearts be above![322] I am,

Your affectionate brother,

J. Wesley

Address: 'To / Mr Benj. Chappel / At St John's / Newfoundland'.
Postmark: '2/DE'.
Endorsement: 'No 11'.
Source: holograph; MARC, DDWes 5/28.

To Isaac Twycross[323]

London
November 29, 1783

Dear Isaac,

I love you well, and would be glad to do you any service that is in my power. If I should find any person that has need of a serious curate, I would not fail to recommend you.

I am,

Your affectionate brother,

J. Wesley

[319] See JW to William Black Jr., July 13, 1783.
[320] See Ezek. 38:21.
[321] See 1 Sam. 23:16.
[322] See Matt. 6:21.
[323] Twycross had received ordination in June 1781. He had contacted JW for help in finding a position as curate.

Address: '⟨To⟩ / Revd Mr Twycross / In Dagenham / Essex'.
Postmark: '29/NO'.
Source: holograph; WTS (DC), Archives, Oxham Collection.

5

To Alexander Knox

London   10
December 7, 1783

Dear Alleck,

In the third volume of our *Works* at the 267th and 268th pages, the case is clearly stated and determined.[324] The substance of it is, 'What is that faith whereby we are sanctified?' It is a divine evidence   15
and conviction: 1) that God has promised it in the Holy Scripture; 2) that what God has promised he is able to perform; and 3) that he is able and willing to do it *now*. There needs to be added but one thing more, a divine evidence and conviction, that he *doth* it. In that hour, it is done! God says to the inmost soul, 'According to thy   20
faith, be it unto thee.'[325] Then the soul is pure from every spot of sin. It is clean from all unrighteousness.

Look for it therefore every day, every hour, every moment! Certainly you may look for it *now*, if you believe it is *by faith*. 'But am I to believe I have it *before* I have it?' No; this is nonsense and   25
absurdity. It is a contradiction in terms. 'Which then is first, sanctification or sanctifying faith?' In *order of thinking*, faith is before sanctification. But in *order of time*, neither is before the other. They are simultaneous. In one instant God works and man believes. God *works faith* and man *is sanctified*. *God* enables *man* to believe, and to   30
love him with all his heart. Observe! God works and man believes. The power is God's; the act is man's. 'But if man has no natural power to believe, why is he condemned for not believing?' Because he may believe *if he will*; though not *when he will*. There is therefore *one saving faith*, and one only, of which everyone may be a partaker.   35

I advise you, to read over that sermon. It may considerably clear your apprehension. But God will work *in* those, yea and often *by* those, who have no clear apprehension of his work. We are commanded, to hope and love, as well as to believe. And both hope and

---

[324] In JW, *Works* (1771–74), this is his sermon The Scripture Way of Salvation, III.14–16; i.e., 2:167–68 in this edn.

[325] Matt. 9:29.

love are the work of God in us. But it is man that hopes and loves. Faith, hope, and love are all the *work* and the *gift* of God, but the *act* of man.

What if he should give you them *now*?

5   I am, dear Alleck,

Yours most affectionately,

J. Wesley

10   *Address*: 'To / Mr Alexander Knox / in / Londonderry'.
Postmark: '9/DE'.
Source: holograph; Bridwell Library (SMU).[326]

15

To Ruth Hall [Jr.][327]

London

20   December 9, 1783

Dear Ruth,

It is wise advice, 'if thou wilt ⟨serve⟩[328] the Lord, prepare thyself for temptation'.[329] But we would mention you are placed as much out of the way of temptation, at least a powerful temptation, as any-

25   one can be. You have youth. You have, I suppose, tolerable health. You are your own mistress. You have the conveniences of life. You have friends whom you love, and who tenderly love *you*. Above ⟨all else,⟩ being justified by faith, you have peace with God, and the love of God is shed abroad in your heart.[330] Nay, he has fulfilled his

30   word, by teaching you to love him with *all* your heart and with all your soul.[331]

What then can afflict you? My dear maid, explain this matter to me.[332] I cannot comprehend it. I do not see what crosses you can

---

[326] Held previously in the Upper Room Museum, L-37.

[327] This Ruth Hall, (b. 1759, in Leeds) was the daughter of JW's earlier correspondent Ruth (Crowther) Hall and her husband John Hall.

[328] The typescript includes two blank spaces where there was either a missing piece of the holograph or the transcriber could not decipher it.

[329] Cf. Ecclus. 2:1.

[330] See Rom. 5:1, 5.

[331] See Matt. 22:37.

[332] Orig., 'to you'.

have! If you love me, do as your blessed mother used to do.[333] Speak
to me without reserve. Surely you need not be afraid to trust,
>   Yours affectionately,
>>   J. Wesley

Address: 'To / Miss Ruth Hall / In New Street / York'.
Source: holograph; privately held (Drew, Methodist Archives holds typed
transcription).

To Ann Loxdale[334]

>   London
>   December 9, 1783

My Dear Nancy,

Because I loved you, and because I thought it my duty, I wrote
freely to you on a tender point. But I have done. I do not know that
I shall speak one word more concerning it. The regard which I have
for you will not suffer me to give you any pain which answers no
good purpose. So you may still think him as holy as Thomas Walsh;
I will say nothing against it.

Only beware of one snare of the devil. Do not tack things together which have no real connection with each other—I mean,
your justification or sanctification, and your marriage. God told you
that you was sanctified. I do not say, 'God told you, you should be
married to that man.' Do not jumble these together. If you do, it
may cost you your life!

Profit by the friendly warning of, my dear Nancy,
>   Yours affectionately,
>>   J. Wesley

Address: 'To Miss Loxdale'.[335]
Source: holograph; MARC, MAM JW 3/101.

---

[333] Her mother died in 1778.

[334] Loxdale had apparently replied sharply (in a letter not known to survive) to JW's negative comments on a man with whom she was considering marriage; see JW to Loxdale, Nov.
21, 1783.

[335] Likely part of a double letter.

To Walter Churchey

London
December 10, 1783

My Dear Brother,

For several years it has pleased God to visit you with one affliction after another. And you do not yet see a way to escape, but

> Eternal providence, exceeding thought
> When none appears will make itself a way.[336]

It is well, that you are not of those, who trust the invisible God
no farther than they ⟨can⟩[337] see him. In this sense also, 'Happy are
they that have not seen; and yet have believed.'[338]

I do not wonder that the person you speak of should have used
you unkindly, for you was guilty of the unpardonable sin of poverty. Nonetheless, whatever man do, God has not forgotten you!
Therefore

> Through every threat'ning cloud look up,
> And wait for happy days.[339]

I am,
Your affectionate brother,

J. Wesley

Address: 'To / Mr Churchey / Near the Hay / Brecon'.
Postmark: '10/DE'.
Endorsement: by Churchey, '1783 / De Afflict[ion]e'.
Source: holograph; Dallas, Texas, Harlan Crow Library.[340]

---

[336] Edmund Spenser, *Faerie Queene*, Bk. I, Canto 6, vii.1–2.

[337] A small portion is torn away by the wax seal.

[338] Cf. John 20:29.

[339] Cf. CW, Hymn 5, st. 8, *Hymns for Times of Trouble and Persecution* (1744), 12.

[340] The address portion became separated at some point from the letter; it now resides at
Pitts Library (Emory), John Wesley Papers (MSS 153), 2/32.

To Captain Richard Williams

London
December 10, 1783 5

My Dear Brother,

I have directed your lines to the editor of the *General Post*.[341] But both he and Mr. [William] Pine will insert in their papers only what they believe will promote the sale of them.

You send me an agreeable account of the work of God in Corn- 10
wall and in some places that I do not know.[342] I know nothing of Wheal Rose, nor of the Copperhouse at Hayle.[343] I hope Mr. Edwards will continue in the same state he is now.

I thought the Calvinists were resolved to run away with the society at Kerl[e]y.[344] But the universal Lover of souls is stronger than 15 them! He hath said, 'Hitherto shall you come, and no farther!'[345] The work of God (brother [Francis] Asbury sends me word) goes on both steadily and swiftly in America.[346] I am,

Your affectionate brother,

J. Wesley 20

Address: 'To / Capt. Richd Williams / At Poldice / Near Truro / Cornwall'.
Postmark: '11/DE'. *Charge*: '4'.
Source: holograph; MARC, MAM JW 5/92. 25

---

[341] The piece Williams had written on slavery; see JW to Williams, Nov. 9, 1783.

[342] Williams's letter to JW is not known to survive.

[343] Wheal Rose was a mining town about 3 miles northeast of Redruth. The Copperhouse was a chapel underway (or just completed) in Hayle, in which JW would preach on Aug. 27, 1785; see *Journal*, 23:374–75 in this edn.

[344] I.e., Kerley Downs, about 4 miles west of Truro, Cornwall. JW preached there on Sept. 12, 1768 (see *Journal*, 22:158 in this edn.); and again on Aug. 29, 1785 (see diary, 23:534 in this edn.).

[345] Job 38:11.

[346] This was likely a letter (not known to survive) more recent than that of Sept. 20, 1783.

To an Unidentified Itinerant[347]

London
December 13, 1783

5 My Dear Brother,

No chastening is joyous for the present, but it will bring forth peaceable fruit.[348] The Lord gave, and the Lord hath taken away—that he may give you himself.[349]

We will make room for the little boy at Kingswood. You may send
10 him whenever you have an opportunity.

If you choose it rather, you may change places for two or three months with one of the preachers in any of the neighbouring circuits. I am,

Your affectionate friend and brother,

15   J. Wesley

Source: holograph; MARC, MA 2002/004.

20   ## To Joseph Taylor

London
December 24, 1783

Dear Joseph,

25   Look into the *Minutes* concerning the building of preaching-houses, and see that the directions there laid down be observed.[350] No one can object to your making a collection for the house in your circuit.

I am,

Your affectionate friend and brother,

30   J. Wesley

Address: 'To / Mr Jos. Taylor / At ye Preachinghouse / In Redruth / Cornwall'.

Postmarks: '24/DE' and '25/DE'.

35 *Source*: holograph; MARC, MAM JW 5/9.

---

[347] The address portion is missing. The content of the letter makes clear the recipient was one of JW's itinerant preachers, and suggests the the preacher's wife had died, raising the issue of care for their son. Telford names Matthew Mayer as the recipient, without any documentation. This is very unlikely because Mayer was only a local preacher, never an itinerant, and his wife did not die this year.

[348] See Heb. 12:11.

[349] See Job 1:21.

[350] See 'Large' *Minutes* (1770), Q. 68, 10:896–97 in this edn.

5

To Joseph Thompson

c. 1784[1]   10

Dear Brother,

Whosoever among us undertakes to baptize a child is *ipso facto* excluded from our connexion.

I am,

    Your affectionate brother,

                                   J. Wesley   15

Source: published transcription; *United Methodist Free Church Magazine* 5 (1862): 360.[2]

20

To Isaac Andrews[3]

City Road [London]   25
January 4, 1784

My Dear Brother,

After all I can say, you will not conceive what I mean unless the Holy Spirit open your understanding.   30

---

[1] The letter is not dated in either *UMFCM* or the secondary copies in MARC. Telford (following George Eayrs) absorbed this sentence into JW's letter to Thompson of July 18, 1772 (which appeared immediately above this one on the page of *UMFCM*, though set apart as a distinct letter). It is placed here during a period when the practice of lay preachers performing baptism was under active debate; cf. JW to Joseph Benson, May 19, 1783; JW to John Valton, Jan. 6, 1784; and JW to William Percival, Mar. 4, 1784.

[2] There is a manuscript transcription of this short letter in MARC (MA 1977/485) and a typescript transcription (MA 1977/609). It is unclear whether they are dependent upon the published transcription or independent witnesses to the holograph (whose location is unknown).

[3] On Andrews, see JW's prior letter of Jan. 24, 1776.

Undoubtedly faith is *the work of God*; and yet it is *the duty of man* to believe. And every man may believe *if* he will, though not *when* he will. If he seek faith in the appointed ways, sooner or later the power of the Lord will be present—whereby 1) God works, and by *his* power, 2) man believes.

In order of thinking God's working goes first. But not in order of time. *Believing* is the act of the human mind, strengthened by the power of God. What if you should find it now?

I am

　　Your affectionate brother,

　　　　　　　　　　　　　　　　　　J. Wesley

Address: 'To / Mr. Andrews / Corner of Granby Row / Near James Street / Bethnal Green'.
Postmarks: '6/IA' and 'Paid Penny Post'.
Source: holograph; Bridwell Library (SMU).

To Robert Carr Brackenbury

London
January 4, 1784

Dear Sir,

I rejoice to hear that you have had a safe passage, and that you have preached both in Guernsey and Jersey.[4] It will not, I think, be long before a more commodious preaching-house is procured. But we must not expect many conveniences at first. Hitherto it is the day of small things.[5] From the account you give, I learn that there is a fair prospect. It is a good circumstance that the officers are friendly. And I nothing doubt, many of the people of the island, as well as the soldiers, will be glad to join in the society.

I should imagine the sooner you begin to preach in French, the better. Surely you need not be careful about accuracy. Trust God,

[4] In late 1783 JW received a letter from Jasper Winscom conveying a request from the growing Methodist society on the Isle of Jersey that JW appoint an itinerant preacher specific to that island. This required an itinerant with facility in French. Brackenbury volunteered for the task and sailed for Jersey in Dec. 1783. For two slightly different accounts see Richard D. Moore, *Methodism in the Channel Islands* (London: Epworth Press, 1952), 18–19; and Mary Ann Smith, *Raithby Hall* (London, 1859), 22–24.

[5] See Zech. 4:10.

and speak as well as you can. I wish you many happy years, and am, dear sir,

Your affectionate friend and servant,

J. Wesley

Your brother will send your box speedily, and abundance of letters in it.

Address: 'To / Robert Brackenbury Esq. / At St. Hiliers / Isle of Jersey'.
Postmark: '6/IA'.
Source: holograph; Wesley's Chapel (London), LDWMM 1994/1980.

To John Francis Valton

London
January 6, 1784

My Dear Brother,

I do not suppose Bristol water would have done you much good; but exercise and change of air would. I do not know Dr. Davison.[6] But I have seen (perhaps thrice) more patients than he has done. And I know many that have perished by swallowing large quantities of powdered wood.[7] Beware of this, and you may live and do good.

I shall have no objection to Mr. Taylor if he does not baptize children.[8] But this I dare not suffer. I shall shortly be obliged to drop all the preachers who will not drop this. Christ has sent them not to baptize, but to preach the gospel. I wonder any of them are so unkind as to attempt it, when they know my sentiments. We have heard twice from Dr. [Thomas] Coke. They all go on well.

I am

Your affectionate friend and brother,

J. Wesley

Postmark: '6/IA'.
Endorsement: by Valton, 'Jan 6th 1784'.
Source: holograph; MARC, MAM JW 5/32.

[6] See also JW to Valton, Oct. 13, 1784.
[7] I.e., Peruvian bark.
[8] Thomas Taylor was now serving in Sheffield, but had served previously in Birstall (where Valton was now appointed).

To George Davison[9]

London
January 9, 1784

5 Dear George,
Let the time past suffice. I do not desire that you should be any
longer chained down to one place. I think Mr. Dixon may now employ you in any place which he judges convenient.[10] And I do not
apprehend that any of our brethren would now be offended at it. We
10 have need to work while the day is, for long is the night wherein no
man can work![11]
I am, dear George,
Your affectionate brother,

[J. Wesley]

15

Address: 'To / Mr. George Davison / At Hablington Moor / Near Hexham / Northumberland'.
Source: holograph; privately held (transcription provided to Frank Baker).

20

To Robert Carr Brackenbury

London
January[12] 10, 1784

25
Dear Sir,
While those poor sheep were scattered abroad, without any shepherd and without any connexion with each other, it is no wonder
30 that they were cold and dead. I am glad you have gathered a few of
them together. And surely, if prayer be made concerning it, God
will provide you with a convenient place to meet in.[13] Perhaps an
application to the gentlemen who have hired the ballroom might
not be without success.
35 'Tis pity but you had the *Earnest Appeal [to Men of Reason and
Religion]* to present to the governor, as well as the minister. I trust

---

[9] Davison was apparently a local preacher in the Hexham area.
[10] Thomas Dixon was currently Assistant for the Newcastle circuit, which included Hexham.
[11] See John 9:4.
[12] Misread as 'June' in ms transcription.
[13] The Methodists soon acquired an abandoned Roman Catholic chapel, Notre Dame des Pas, just outside St. Helier, as a meeting place. See Lelièvre, *Méthodisme*, 185.

both you and our newly connected brethren will overcome evil with good.[14] We can easily print the *Rules* here, and send them down with some other books.[15] It is good that everyone should know our whole plan. We do not want any man to go on blindfold. Peace be with your spirit!

I am, dear sir,
Your affectionate friend,

J. Wesley

Address: 'To / Robert Brackenbury Esq. / In St. Hiliers / Isle of Jersey'.
Source: 19th century ms transcription; MARC, MA 1977/609.

To Walter Sellon

London
January 10, 1784

Dear Sir,

I sincerely thank you for your speedy and satisfactory answer.[16] Thomas Maxfield affirms that you either *wrote* such a deed or *signed* it. So fare it well.

On the 28th of last June I finished my eightieth year. When I was young I had weak eyes, trembling hands, and abundance of infirmities. But by the blessing of God I have outlived them all. I have no infirmities now but what I judge to be inseparable from flesh and blood. This hath God wrought.[17] I am afraid you want [i.e., lack] the grand medicine which I use: exercise and change of air. I believe what you say concerning that passage in the *Journal* is true. I can trust *your* memory better than my own.

You used to meet me when I came near you; but you seem of late years to have forgotten

Your old friend and brother,

J. Wesley

---

[14] See Rom. 12:21.

[15] If a French edition of *The Nature, Design, and General Rules of the United Societies* (1743) was published this year, no copies are known to survive.

[16] Neither Sellon's answer, nor JW's initial inquiry, are known to survive; this leaves the deed in question, as well as the passage mentioned in the *Journal*, unclear.

[17] See Ps. 118:23.

Address: 'To / the Revd Mr Sellon / At Ledsham / Near Ferrybridge / Yorkshire'.
Postmark: '10/IA'.
Source: holograph; MARC, MA 1977/712/1/1.

To Thomas Carlill

London
January 12, 1784

Dear Tommy,

It gives me pleasure to have so good an account of all your fellow labourers.[18] Go on in one mind and one spirit, and your labour will not be in vain.[19]

I have received one or two uncommon letters from your wise friend at Louth.[20] It would have been cruelty to the people if you had suffered him to continue leader of a class. Be in earnest to spread the *[Arminian] Magazines.*

I am, dear Tommy,

Your affectionate friend and brother,

[J. Wesley]

Address: 'To / Thomas Carlill / At the Preacher's House / In Great Grimsby / Lincolnshire'.
Source: published transcription; Telford, *Letters*, 7:205.

To Joseph Taylor

London
January 12, 1784

Dear Joseph,

I am sorry that so useful a man as brother [Edmund] Lewty was constrained to leave Worcester. But I am not sorry that the books are delivered into your hands, as I am clearly persuaded a far greater number of them will be disposed of.

---

[18] Carlill was currently Assistant over the Grimsby circuit in Lincolnshire.
[19] See Acts 4:32.
[20] Louth, Lincolnshire; orig., 'Lowth', a mistake.

Take care of the select societies as well as the bands.
I am, dear Joseph,
  Your affectionate friend and brother,

J. Wesley

Address: 'To / Mr Jos. Taylor / At the Preachinghouse / in / Glocester'.
Charge: '5'.
Source: holograph; MARC, MAM JW 5/10.

To Ann Tindall

London
January 14, 1784

My Dear Sister,
  We have found by experience all over England that twice or thrice
as many books were disposed of in every circuit when they were in
the hands of the Assistant as before. But let brother Harrison order
it as he sees best.[21] If he is pleased, so am I.
  Wherever Christian perfection is fully and strongly preached, the
whole work of God prospers. I wonder you did not write and send
me some verses on the death of Betsy Maxfield.[22]
  It is a great thing to say 'Blessed be the name of the Lord', whether he gives or takes away.[23] It is certain he does both for one and the
same end, namely for our profit, that we may be partakers of his holiness. And what is everything in the world, in comparison of this?
  I am, dear Nancy,
    Yours affectionately,

J. Wesley

Address: 'To / Miss Tindall / in / Scarborough'.
Postmark: '15/IA'.
Endorsement: by Tindall, '14 Jan. 1784'.
Source: holograph; British Library, Department of Manuscripts, Add.
  MS. 43695, ff. 78–79.

---

[21] Lancelot Harrison was currently the Assistant over the Scarborough circuit.
[22] Elizabeth (Branford) Maxfield, the wife of Thomas Maxfield, died in 1777; so she is
likely not the 'Betsy' intended.
[23] See Job 1:21.

To Richard Rodda

[London]
January 16, 1784

5 Dear Richard,

One of the most plausible objections to Christian perfection is this: These persons give a clear, scriptural account of their own experience; but by and by their life and conversation do not agree with the account. Is not this a proof that they were deceived? No.
10 It only proves that they did not hold fast what they had attained.[24]

I am glad your son will be a good deal under your own eye, and hope it will be a means of keeping him steadfast.[25]

I am usually in Staffordshire toward the end of March. But I seldom fix my plan till I come to Bristol. I am, dear Richard,

15   Your affectionate friend and brother,

J. Wesley

Address: 'To / Mr. Richd Rodda / At the Preachinghouse / in / Birmingham'.
20 *Postmark*: '16/IA'.
Source: holograph; Melbourne, Queen's College, JW16.

25

To Captain Richard Williams

near London
January 20, 1784

30 My Dear Brother,

You have indeed reason to rejoice over your son.[26] He seems not only to have recovered his ground, but to rise much the higher for his late fall. Surely this God hath wrought.[27]

You likewise find occasion for great thankfulness for the great
35 increase of the work of God in Cornwall. It seems Dr. [Thomas] Coke came into the west in an acceptable time. We have the same accounts from Yorkshire, from Cheshire, and from Lancashire. And if much prayer be made, we shall yet see more fruit.

[24] See Phil. 3:16.
[25] Richard and Elizabeth (Stoplong) Rodda, had a son named Richard, baptized in 1773.
[26] Likely John Williams; see JW to Richard Williams, Oct. 7, 1781, 29:691 in this edn.
[27] See Ps. 118:23.

I am,
> Your affectionate brother,

> > J. Wesley

Address: 'To / Capt. Rich Williams / At Poldice / Near Truro / Cornwall'.   5
Postmark: '22/IA'. *Charge*: '4'.
Source: holograph; Cory Library (South Africa), MS 15724.

10

To Mary (Franklin) Parker

> > > > near London
> > > > January 21, 1784

My Dear Sister,   15
  I have taken time to consider the letter calmly,[28] and now I will speak freely to you concerning it.
  You assign three reasons for discarding the Methodist preachers: one, because several who had left your chapel promised to join you again, on condition that you would suffer the Methodists to preach   20
there no more; a second, that these preached perfection;[29] and a third, that while one of them was preaching several persons were suddenly and violently affected.
  But are these reasons valid? Let us coolly and impartially consider them before God.   25
  1. 'Several who had left you promised to join you again, provided you would suffer the Methodists to preach in your chapel no more.' I cannot but think you ought never to have joined with or received persons of such a spirit. What a narrow popish spirit was this! What vile bigotry! The exact spirit of Calvinism! Such as surely none that   30
is not a Calvinist ought to encourage either by word or deed. Everyone that does, I call the maintainer of *a bad cause*, as bad as bad can be. For whom has God owned in Great Britain, Ireland, and America like them? Whom does he now own like them in Yorkshire, in Cheshire, in Lancashire, in Cornwall? Truly these are the tokens   35
of our mission, the proof that God hath sent us. Threescore thousand persons setting their faces heavenward, and many of them rejoicing in God their Saviour. A specimen of this you yourself saw at Leeds. Come again, and see if the work be not of God. O consider

---

[28] Parker's letter to JW is not known to survive, but its content is reflected in his reply.
[29] See the subsequent letter to JW, apparently from Parker, Feb. 23, 1788.

the weight of that word, 'He that rejecteth you rejecteth me and him that sent me.'[30]

2. ' But they preach *perfection*.' And do not *you*? Who does not that speaks as the oracles of God? Meaning by that scriptural word neither more nor less than 'loving God with all our heart',[31] or having the mind that was in Christ and walking as Christ walked.[32]

3. 'But, while one of them was preaching, several persons fell down, cried out, and were violently affected.' Have you never read my *Journals*? Or Dr. Edwards' *Narrative*?[33] Or Dr. Gillies's *Historical Collections*?[34] Do not you see then that it has pleased the all-wise God for near these fifty years, wherever he has wrought most powerfully, that these outward signs (whether natural or not) should attend the inward work? And who can call him to account for this? Let him do as seemeth him good.[35]

I must therefore still think that neither these nor any other reasons can justify the discarding the messengers of God—and consequently that all who do, or abet this, are maintaining a bad cause.

Yet I am,

Your affectionate friend and brother,

J. Wesley

Address: 'To / Mrs Mary Parker / At Fakenham / Norfolk'.
Postmark: '22/IA'. *Charge*: '4'.
Source: holograph; MARC, MAM JW 4/35.

To Robert Hopkins

London
January 21, 1784

Dear Robert,

The return you are to make for the blessings you have received is to declare them to all mankind and to exhort all believers strongly and

---

[30] Cf. Luke 10:16.

[31] Cf. Mark 12:30.

[32] See Phil. 2:5 and 1 John 2:6.

[33] Jonathan Edwards, *A Faithful Narrative of the Surprising Work of God* (London: C. Whittingham, 1737); published in abridged form by JW in 1744 (*Bibliography*, No. 85).

[34] John Gillies, *Historical Collections Relating to Remarkable Periods of the Success of the Gospel*, 2 vol. (Glasgow: Robert and Andrew Foulis, 1754).

[35] See 1 Sam. 3:18.

explicitly to go on to perfection.[36] You never *need* lose what you now experience, but may increase therein till your spirit returns to God.

You cannot infer that the air of this or that place does not agree with you because you have a fever there.[37] But if there be a necessity, Christopher Peacock will change places with you.[38]

I am, dear Robert,
    Your affectionate brother,

J. Wesley

Sources: transcription by Hopkins, in letter to Adam Clarke (Drew, Methodist Archives); and published transcription, Hopkins, *Life*, 15.[39]

To Thomas Hanson

London
January 28, 1784

Dear Tommy,

I should imagine nothing would be so conducive to the drying of that bad humour as the use of the diet drink (in the *Primitive Physic*) for 'scorbutic sores'.[40] I have known it [to] perform wonders in similar cases.

I am glad you are well rid of that untoward man.

But what you say concerning 'dividing the circuits' is worth considering. I wish you would weigh the matter thoroughly in your mind and (if we live so long) propose it at the Conference. I would second you in good earnest.

I am, dear Tommy,
    Your affectionate friend and brother,

J. Wesley

[36] See Heb. 6:1.

[37] Hopkins was currently stationed on the Whitby circuit.

[38] Christopher Peacock (c. 1752–86) was admitted 'on trial' as an itinerant preacher in 1781 (10:507 in this edn.). He was currently stationed at Yarm, and would die in Dublin in 1786, 'young in years, but old in grace; a pattern of all holiness, full of faith and love and zeal for God' (10:598). See also Hester (Roe) Rogers to JW, Mar. 2, 1786; and James Rogers to JW, c. May 1786.

[39] The first paragraph appears in both sources; the second, only in Hopkins, *Life*.

[40] See Ailment §198, receipt #1; 32:226 in this edn.

Address: 'To / Mr Hanson / At the Preachinghouse / In Huddersfield / Yorkshire'.
Postmark: '29/IA'.
Source: holograph; Drew, Methodist Archives.

5

To Victory Purdy[41]

10
                                                            London
                                                      February 1, 1784
My Dear Brother,
    Your father was one of our first society, which met at Fetter Lane, and one of the first that found peace with God. When it was thought
15 best that I should go to Bristol, we spent a considerable time in prayer, and then cast lots who should accompany me thither. The lot fell upon him; and he was with me day and night till he judged it proper to marry.[42] But I had no curiosity; so that I scarce ever asked him a question concerning his parents, birth, or former way
20 of life. I first saw him when he came to the Foundery[43] and desired to be admitted into the society. He was a man of eminent integrity and simplicity, 'fervent in zeal and warm in charity';[44] both in his spirit and behaviour greatly resembling Joseph Bradford. Be you a follower of him, as he was of Christ![45]
25   I am
        Your affectionate brother,
                                                            J. Wesley

Address: 'To / Mr. Victory Purdy / At the New Room / In Bristol'.
Source: manuscript transcription by Purdy; Bristol Archives, Records of
30   Dr. H. Temple Phillips, 39801/X/1, p. 1.

[41] Victory Purdy (1747–1822) was the son of John Purdy and his second wife, Mary (Highnam / Reynolds) Purdy (d. 1757). John had been a local preacher, and Victory took up this role too in 1771. Victory served briefly in 1773 as an itinerant preacher (see 10:415 in this edn.). He then returned to Bristol (where his father had settled) where he became well known as a local preacher and authored a body of (largely unpublished) religious verse. See Victory Purdy, *Poetical Miscellanies, with a Life of the Untutored Author* (Bristol: John Wansbrough, 1825), i–xxxii. Purdy had written JW, seeking biographical information about his father (the letter is not known to survive).
[42] John Purdy married Elizabeth Reyon (d. 1742) in Bristol on July 23, 1741.
[43] As Victory Purdy notes in a footnote, this was likely a slip by JW, meaning instead 'Fetter Lane'.
[44] Samuel Wesley Jr., 'The Battle of the Sexes', st. 35; included by JW in *MSP* (1744), 3:32.
[45] See 1 Cor. 11:1.

To John Bredin

near London
February 6, 1784

My Dear Brother,   5

I suppose there is not a set of the *[Arminian] Magazines* to be had
in Ireland for love or money. But I believe Mr. Rutherford has both
the *History of England* and that of *Henry Earl of Moreland*.[46] And he
may send you a set of each of these by the first opportunity.

It is not improbable that an issue[47] may be of some service in   10
drawing away that humour from your head. But it is worth considering whether it would not be better to make it under the stave(?)[48]
than in the arm? Perhaps with this help, the diet drink for scorbutic
sores, might have a good affect.[49]

I am glad to hear so good an account of Mr. Thompson,[50] and am,   15
    Your affectionate brother,

J. Wesley

Address: 'To / Mr John Bredin / In Athlone / Ireland'.
Postmarks: '7/FE' and 'FE/17'.   20
Source: holograph; Drew, Methodist Archives.

To Alexander Knox   25

near London
February 7, 1784

Dear Alleck,

A week or two ago a very sensible man wrote me a letter on this   30
very question: if faith is *the gift of God*, how can it be *the duty of man*
to believe? I might have answered, 'The Scripture affirms both the
one and the other. Therefore both are infallibly true. But how to
reconcile them I know not. And I am content to be ignorant, while
I remain in this land of darkness.'   35

---

[46] JW's four-volume set, *A Concise History of England* (1776); and his two-volume
abridgement of The History of Henry, Earl of Moreland (1781).

[47] I.e., a blood-letting.

[48] Perhaps used in sense of bruise or sprain.

[49] See *Primitive Physic*, Ailment §198, receipt #1; 32:226 in this edn.

[50] The referent is unclear, as neither of the current itinerants with this surname (Joseph
and William) were stationed in Ireland at the time; and Bredin's letter to JW is not known to
survive.

But I ventured to go a little farther, and preached twice or thrice on the subject. The substance of what I observed was, faith is a divine conviction, that Christ loved *me* and gave himself for *me*. This is the *work* and the *gift of God*. The power whereby we believe is
5　wholly in the hand of God, and his spirit freely gives it to man. But observe: faith, though it is the gift of God, is the *act of man*. It is not God that believes, but man. God works and man believes. But how then is man accountable for not believing? I defy any Calvinist to answer. But you or I may answer he is therefore accountable for it,
10　because it depends upon himself. He may or may not receive that gift. He can so resist as to prevent God from working. This is the very hinge of the question, and goes a good way toward untying the knot. If some difficulty still remains therein, I think we must leave it to be explained in eternity.
15　　As to the love of praise, I do not doubt but you have much more of it than you want. And I am persuaded the Great Physician shows you the disease on purpose, that he may cure it. But yet, I apprehend you [make] a little mistake. You blame yourself where no blame is. 'To be pleased with the approbation of our fellow creatures' is no
20　part of corrupt nature. It belongs to our pure nature; and to cherish it *in a degree* is a duty, and not a sin.
　　With regard to the house, my simple judgment is this. If your refusal would keep them out of the city, I think you ought at all hazards to refuse them. If it would not, I do not see that you need
25　refuse.[51]
　　John Prickard is gone home, in the full triumph of faith.[52] I know nothing of poor Mr. [John] Abraham but that he is somewhere in London, utterly insane; it is great pity, but he was confined.
　　I compare the bawlers at Westminster to so many flies on the
30　chariot wheels, crying out, 'See! What a dust we make!' But their crests are fallen, since so large a majority in the House of Lords have voted 'the proceedings of the House of Commons to be *illegal and unconstitutional*'.[53]

---

[51] A new preaching-house was being built in Londonderry, and Knox (or the trustees) had been approached about selling it to a buyer who would turn it into a theatre; see JW to Knox, Mar. 18, 1784.

[52] Prickard was buried in Bathwick, Somerset on Nov. 3, 1783.

[53] Charles James Fox, a leading Whig, had been trying to limit the power of the British monarch for two years. Matters came to a head in Dec. 1783 around a bill aimed at setting aside the king's prominence in selecting the governing board of the East India Company. A bill that handily passed the House of Commons was rejected by the House of Lords (under significant pressure from the king). JW's sympathy with the Tory position in this debate is clear.

Peace be with you and yours! I am, my dear Alleck,
    Ever yours,

J. Wesley

Address: 'To / Mr. Alexr Knox / In Londonderry'.
Postmarks: '7/FE' and 'FE/16'.
Source: holograph; Bridwell Library (SMU).[54]

To Samuel Bardsley[55]

London
February 13, 1784

Dear Sammy,

It was a senseless, unreasonable prejudice which two or three persons conceived against James Rogers and laboured to infuse into others, a mere trick of the devil to hinder his being more useful than any Assistant in that circuit had been before. They will never be able to undo the mischief they have done. If brother Garside persists in not hearing him, I will trouble his house no more.

You don't tell me anything of Hetty Roe. I hope you have seen and conversed with Mr. [Edward] Smyth, and that his preaching at Macclesfield had been useful. He is an alarming preacher! Strongly exhort the believers to go on to perfection![56]

I am, with tender love to brother and sister Rogers,[57] dear Sammy,
    Your affectionate brother,

[J. Wesley]

Source: published transcription; Telford, *Letters*, 7:209.

---

[54] Held previously in the Upper Room Museum, L-38.

[55] Bardsley was currently assigned to the Macclesfield circuit, serving under James Rogers as Assistant. Rogers had been there for a year previously and was encountering some resistance.

[56] See Heb. 6:1.

[57] Martha (Knowlden) Rogers, James's wife, died two days later, on Feb. 15; see Rogers to JW, c. Feb. 25, 1784.

To Robert Carr Brackenbury

London
February 13, 1784

5 Dear Sir,

It is undoubtedly our duty to use the most probable means we can
for either preserving or restoring our health. But after all, God does
continually assert his own right of saving both souls and bodies. He
blesses the medicines, and they take place; he withdraws his influ-
10 ence, and they avail nothing.

You will not easily be forgotten by any of this family. I trust we
are all one body united by one Spirit. I doubt not but we have also a
few fellow members in your little islands.[58] May he whom we serve
in the gospel of his Son increase them an hundred-fold! We hear of
15 some increase of the work of God almost in every part of England;
but above all in Cornwall, in Lancashire, Cheshire, and various
parts of Yorkshire.

It pleases God to bless Mr. [John] Valton wherever he turns his
face. But his body sinks under him, and he is still hovering be-
20 tween life and death. Would it not be advisable, if you still continue feeble, to return to England as soon as possible; especially
if you have reason to believe the air of Jersey does not agree with
your constitution?

I commend you to him who is able to heal both your soul and
25 body; and am, dear sir,

Your very affectionate friend and brother,

[J. Wesley]

Source: published transcription; Jackson, *Works* (3rd), 13:5.

30

To John Baxendale

35   London
February 19, 1784

My Dear Brother,

You do well to put me in mind of my promise, for otherwise I
might have forgotten it.[59] It seems at length the time is come for
40 poor Wigan to lift up its head. I shall be glad to give them a sermon

---

[58] Brackenbury was serving on the Isle of Jersey.
[59] Baxendale's letter to JW is not known to survive.

at Wingates myself in my way from Wigan to Bolton.[60] We should mark the places where God is pleased to work eminently, and strive to pour in all the help we can.

You would do well to read over and consider the *Large Minutes* of the Conference. See if you can thoroughly agree with what is there laid down both with regard to doctrine and discipline.[61] If you can, then set your hand to the plough in God's name, and never look back.[62] Begin as soon as you please ordering your affairs, and go on with circumspection. Meantime stir up the gift of God that is in you,[63] and do all the good you can.

I am

Your affectionate brother,

J. Wesley

Address: 'To / Mr John Boxendale / in Wigan / Lancashire'.
Postmark: '20/FE'.
Source: holograph; Beinecke Library (Yale), James Marshall and Marie-Louise Osborn collection.

To John Heald[64]

London
February 23, 1784

My Dear Sir,

I have this morning been with Mr. Wesley, and have laid your letter before him.[65] He is not only willing, but *desires* it be inserted in your deed that, if ever the Conference, or preacher, or preachers appointed by Conference, refuse or neglect to provide a preacher

---

[60] JW preached at Wingates on Apr. 16, 1784, and in the evening at Wigan; see *Journal*, 23:302–03.

[61] Baxendale, already a local preacher, was considering becoming an itinerant. JW would ultimately advise him to remain in his local status; see JW to Baxendale, Apr. 3, 1787.

[62] See Luke 9:62.

[63] See 2 Tim. 1:6.

[64] Little is known of John Heald (d. 1805) beyond his prominence in the Methodist society in Dewsbury; see JW's earlier correspondence with him c. Dec. 15, 1767 (28:113 in this edn.), Jan. 19, 1773 (28:548), and Oct. 18, 1776 (29:292 n).

[65] Atlay is replying (on JW's behalf) to a letter Heald sent, c. Feb. 18, 1784, on behalf of the trustees of the preaching-house in Dewsbury, posing two questions they wanted clarity on before undertaking a financial drive to enlarge the present building. The agreements here are not reflected in JW's later circular letter of Aug. 23, 1789, which addressed controversy with the Dewsbury trustees that recently flared.

for your chapel for three or four Sundays, then the trustees shall
have it in their own power to call one whom they please, and the
power of nomination shall be theirs in future.

5   If any preacher appointed to serve your chapel should be proved
guilty of immorality, the trustees shall have a power to reject him.
And if the Conference does not send another to fill up his place, you
shall have a power to call one to do it.

John Atlay

10   *Source*: published transcription; Thomas Coke, *The State of Dewsbury
House, in Yorkshire* ([London : s.n., 1788]), 6.[66]

15

To Samuel Bradburn[67]

London
20   February 25, 1784
Dear Sammy,
     At present I have but just time to tell you I hope to be at Leeds
on Tuesday, March [9].[68] Your manner of proposing your objection
puts me in mind of your friend Mr. Dodd, your speaker cathedra.[69]
25   But the matter is not half so dear as it appears to you. It is however a point, though considered long ago, worth considering again
and again. But you must stay your stomach till you either see or
hear again from
     Your affectionate brother,
30   [J. Wesley]

Source: published transcription; Telford, *Letters*, 7:211.

[66] Coke states he is transcribing from the holograph; its current location is unknown.
[67] Bradburn's letter to JW is not known to survive. In it he apparently questioned JW's
dietary advice (cf. the regimen in the preface to *Primitive Physic*).
[68] JW ended up going to Scotland first, and did not arrive in Leeds until July 25, just
prior to the start of Conference.
[69] Likely referring to Rev. Dr. William Dodd, who was known as the 'macaroni parson'
due to his worldly style of living.

To Rachel Bailey

Bath
March 3, 1784

My Dear Sister,

I am glad to hear that Mr. Bailey recovers his health and that he is not quite unemployed. The more both he and you are employed for a good Master, the better—seeing it is a sure truth that every man shall receive his own reward according to his own labour.[70] On Monday, April 5 (if nothing unforeseen prevent), I expect to be at Stockport; and Tuesday, [the] 6th, at Manchester.[71]

I am, my dear Rachel,
  Yours affectionately,

J. Wesley

Address: 'To / Mrs Rachel Bailey / In Salford / Manchester / +post [i.e., crosspost]'.
Postmark: 'Bristol'.
Source: holograph; New Room (Bristol), NR2000.14.

To Samuel Bardsley

Bath
March 3, 1784

Dear Sammy,

I am glad Mr. [Edward] Smyth preached at Macclesfield. He is indeed a son of thunder.[72] I believe God employed him to awake several poor sinners at Manchester.

Now Sammy, do all the good you can. Be instant in season and out of season![73] Put forth all your strength!

I am
  Your affectionate brother,

J. Wesley

Address: 'To Mr Bardsley'.[74]
Source: holograph; privately held (WWEP Archive holds digital copy).

---

[70] See 1 Cor. 3:7.
[71] JW actually reached Manchester on Apr. 10.
[72] See Mark 3:17.
[73] See 2 Tim. 4:2.
[74] This torn-off portion is from a double letter; the address page remains: 'To / Mr Rogers / At the Preachinghouse / in Macclesfield / Cheshire / +post'. The portion of the letter to Rogers (which surely dealt with the recent death of his wife) is not known to survive.

To Arthur Keene[75]

Bath
March 3, 1784

5   Dear Arthur,
          It is a true saying,

> There is in love a sweetness ready penned,
> Copy out only that, and save expense.[76]

10   You mean what you speak, and that is enough.
          I am glad the school is begun, and am in great hope that it will be continued.[77] Those that are frequently apt to weary of well-doing might be frequently stirred up; otherwise the love of many, both in England and Ireland, will in process of time wax cold.
15   I am in hopes that Dr. [Thomas] Coke has spoke to my brother [CW] concerning writing a few hymns for the poor widows.[78] But because the Doctor is apt to forget, I have this morning desired Mr. [George] Whitfield to remind him of it. You did well in sending me an account of the widows themselves, living or dead. There is one
20   (if she be yet alive) whom I visited in Cuffe Street several times: Rachael Davis I never recommended before, but I should be glad if she could be admitted when there is a vacancy.
          As yet I do not know any reason why Mr. [Andrew] Blair may not spend the next year at Dublin.[79] I agree with you that a year is
25   generally quite enough for a preacher to spend in one place. When he stays longer, both the people and the preacher usually grow flat and dead together.
          This year, if God prolong my life and health, I am to visit Scotland; otherwise I should have willingly accepted your kind invitation.
30   Peace be with you and yours! I am, dear Arthur,
              Your affectionate brother,

                                                          [J. Wesley]

Source: published transcription; Telford, *Letters*, 7:212.

[75] JW was replying to a letter from Keene that is not known to survive.

[76] George Herbert, 'Jordan', *ll*. 17–18; cf. JW's revision titled 'True Praise', st. 5, *HSP* (1739), 120.

[77] A Free School for forty boys had just been opened, housed in second floor of Whitefriar Street Chapel, with Richard Condy serving as master. See D. A. Levistone Cooney, 'Methodist Schools in Dublin', *Dublin Historical Record* 56.1 (Spr. 2003), 41–52.

[78] JW likely meant for CW to prepare a small collection of hymns that could be sold to raise funds for the Alms House for widows sponsored by the Dublin society. There is no evidence of such a collection being produced.

[79] Blair, currently assigned to the Cork circuit, was moved to Dublin for the coming year.

To Catherine Warren

Bath
March 3, 1784

My Dear Sister,   5
Immediately after the Conference, if God permit, I shall cross
the country to Wales. I hope to reach Carmarthen about the middle
of August; and soon after, Haverfordwest. But probably if we reach
Leeds you will have a more particular account.
I think of Billy Church and his fellow-labourers as you do.[80] What   10
is yet wanting will, I trust be supplied. It is well there is a class of
hearers suited to every class of preachers.
I hope *you* are not weary of well doing, and am, my dear sister,
     Yours very affectionately,
                                             J. Wesley   15

Peace be with all your spirits.

Address: 'To / Miss Kitty Warren / in / Haverford West / +post [i.e.,
     crosspost]'.
Postmark: 'Bristol'.   20
Source: holograph; Des Moines, Iowa, State Historical Society of Iowa,
     Special Collections, Charles Aldrich Autograph Collection.

25

To William Percival[81]

Bristol
March 4, 1784   30

Dear Billy,
I desire Mr. [John] Murlin, if any of our lay preachers talk either in public or private against the Church [of England] or the
clergy, or read the church prayers,[82] or baptize children to require
a promise from them to do it no more. If they will not promise, let   35

---

[80] William Church was currently assigned to the Pembroke circuit, along with Samuel
Hodgson, and under James Perfect as Assistant. All three were moved by Conference in 1784.
Warren's letter raising concern about them is not known to survive.
    [81] William Percival (1744–1803) was admitted 'on trial' as an itinerant in 1773 (see 10:415
in this edn.). He would serve until his death nearly 30 years later; see *Minutes* (post-Wesley,
1803), 2:167. Percival was currently stationed on the Manchester circuit, under John Murlin
as the Assistant.
    [82] I.e., the formal liturgies in the BCP.

them preach no more. And if they break their promise, let them be expelled [from] the society.

From Macclesfield I expect to go to Chester, Monday, April 5; on Wednesday the 7th, to Liverpool; Good Friday, April 9, Warrington; Saturday, 10th, Manchester; Tuesday, 13th, Bolton; Thursday, 15th, Wigan.

I am, dear Billy,

Your affectionate brother,

J. Wesley

Source: holograph; Drew, Methodist Archives.

To Rev. Brian Bury Collins

Bristol
March 11, 1784

Dear Sir,

When I was at Bath last, I found a very uncommon liberty of spirit, both in prayer and preaching, which I supposed to be partly owing to the spirit of the congregation, who appeared more than usually serious. I am therefore a little surprised that you ⟨shoul⟩d[83] find less liberty than you usually do. ⟨If⟩ you have not since then found any change for the better—if you still feel that restraint upon your spirit at Bath—I am of the same judgment with you: it seems to be a divine indication that you are called to other places. Should you think well of taking either a short or a long journey with me? I am to set out on Monday morning for Stroud. I have an easy horse, and whenever you are tired with riding you may come into the chaise. If you like the proposal, come hither either upon Sunday morning or afternoon. If you choose it, you may preach in Temple Church.[84]

---

[83] A small portion is torn away by the wax seal, affecting two lines on this page.

[84] Rev. Joseph Easterbrook (1751–91), the current vicar of Temple Church, regularly opened his pulpit to JW; cf. *Journal*, Sept. 24, 1780 (23:187 in this edn.), Mar. 18, 1781 (23:194), Oct. 6, 1782 (23:256), etc.

I am a little embarrassed with regard to Dr. Witherspoon.[85] It is natural for *you* to be prejudiced in his favour. But he cannot be surprised if most Englishmen are strongly prejudiced on the other side: when they con⟨sider⟩[86] him as the grand instrument of tearing away children from their parents, to which they were united by the 5 most sacred ties. So that I know not with what face I can mention him, or with what probability of success.

Wishing all happiness to you and yours, I am, dear sir,
    Your affectionate friend and brother,
                                John Wesley 10

If you do not come, you will send a line directly.

Address: 'To / The Revd Mr Collins ⟨...[87]⟩'.
Postmark: 'Bristol'.
Source: holograph; Bridwell Library (SMU). 15

To Alexander Knox 20

Tewksbury
March 18, 1784

Dear Alleck,

Your keeping the house will cut off a great occasion of reproach.[88] 25 It cannot be, but many would exclaim loudly, if a preaching-house were turned into a playhouse. It would undoubtedly have the appearance of evil.[89] So all is ordered well. And I doubt not a good providence will find some other way of supplying all your wants.

The twenty days illness which I had in August last, left me much 30 [better] than it found me.[90] All my illnesses tend to improve my health; but none so much as my fever in the north of Ireland.[91] That

---

[85] With the Revolutionary War formally ended, Rev. Dr. John Witherspoon (1723–94), president of the College of New Jersey at Princeton (and a supporter of the Revolution), sailed for England with Joseph Reed in Dec. 1783 in order to raise money for his war-ravaged college. He made contact with Brian Bury Collins in London, and Collins agreed to solicit help in this effort. See *WHS* 9 (1913): 56–57.

[86] The portion torn away by the wax seal affects one line on this side of the sheet.

[87] The remainder of the address portion is missing.

[88] Cf. JW to Knox, Feb. 7, 1784.

[89] See 1 Thess. 5:22.

[90] See JW, *Journal*, Aug. 5–24, 1783, 23:286–87 in this edn.

[91] See JW, *Journal*, June 13–28, 1775, 22:455–57 in this edn.

gave me quite a new constitution, so that since that time I have almost forgot what weariness means. I am never tired either *of* my work, or *in* my work, either in speaking or travelling.[92]

I went to Holland, not expecting to teach, but to learn.[93] But God's thoughts were not as my thoughts. I had scarce landed when I was offered the use of the three English churches in Rotterdam. And the next day I preached in the Episcopal Church (built by the old Duke of Marlborough) morning and afternoon to a lovely congregation. I preached in another English church at Amsterdam, and in a third at Utrecht. And it was near Utrecht that I waited on Burgomaster [Arnout] Loten, at his country seat, when I found one of the most agreeable men and the pleasantest gardens I ever saw. He spoke Latin properly, though not fluently, for want of more practice (as he had discontinued the use of it almost ever since he left the university). His daughter, Miss [Johanna] Loten is an Israelite indeed[94]—full of humble, gently love, zealous of good works,[95] and a pattern to all the women of fortune in the province.

Peace be with all your spirits! I wish my dear Sally Knox may be just like Miss Loten!

Dear Alleck,

[Yours most affectionately,

J. Wesley][96]

Source: holograph; Bridwell Library (SMU).[97]

To Thomas Tattershall

Tewksbury
March 18, 1784

Dear Tommy,

I am afraid poor ____ is fallen low indeed. He does not seem to have any degree of repentance. At first he was much convinced; but I am afraid he is now hardened by the deceitfulness of sin.

[92] See JW to Robert Barry, Feb. 2, 1785, where JW traces this expression back to Rev. Philip Henry.

[93] Referring to his trip of June 11–July 3, 1783, 23:271–83 in this edn.

[94] See John 1:47.

[95] See Titus 2:14.

[96] The bottom of the page, which contained the closing and signature) is missing. We insert a closing used by JW in other letters to Knox.

[97] Held previously in the Upper Room Museum, L-39.

I do not yet know any reason why you may not labour in the Bristol or Huttersfield circuit.[98] Now it has pleased God to prolong your life, see that you use it to the best advantage. In particular, strongly exhort the believers, in every place, to go on to perfection.[99] This is the work which God has peculiarly given you in charge.   5

Dear Tommy,
    Yours affectionately,

                                    J. Wesley

Address: 'To T. Tattershall'.[100]   10
Source: published transcription; Byrth, 'Memoir', xxxiv–v.

          15

To Joseph [Bradford?][101]

                                 Worcester
                        March 21, 1784   20

Dear Joseph,
    All the difficulty is now, what to do with brother Mills,[102] who has had so long a journey for nothing? The best way which I can devise is this: Let him meet me at Macclesfield on Saturday sennight, April 3rd. If I am gone thence, I will leave a letter for him. If   25 he comes a day or two sooner, it will be all one. He may bring this letter with him, and go straight to the preaching house.

    I am, dear Joseph,
        Your affectionate brother,

                                    J. Wesley   30

Source: holograph; Harvard University, Houghton Library, Autograph File, W.

[98] Tattershall, currently stationed in Londonderry, instead was named Assistant of the Waterford circuit the following year.

[99] See Heb. 6:1.

[100] Byrth notes that it appears on missing fly leaf of the letter to Alexander Knox of the same date (i.e., part of a double letter).

[101] While there are other possibilities, like Joseph Benson, Frank Baker judged that this letter was to Joseph Bradford, currently Assistant of the Leicester circuit (but soon to be moved to Macclesfield).

[102] This was likely the itinerant Peter Mill (whose surname was spelled 'Mills' in the *Minutes* in 1783 and 1785), currently stationed in Epworth.

To [Zachariah Yewdall?][103]

Worcester
March 21, 1784

5 My Dear Brother,

My judgment is that you must not have any respect of persons. But whoever will not promise to put away the accursed thing,[104] to refrain from buying *stolen goods* (such are all uncustomed goods), can no longer be a member of our society.[105] And you should every-
10 where scatter the *Word to a Smuggler*.[106]

Let everyone, rich or poor, *show his ticket* or not be admitted at the meeting of the society. You must mend or end that local preacher. Make an example of him, for the good of all.

Let the rail in the new preaching-house go down the middle of
15 the room. We have found this the only effectual way of separating the men from the women. This must be done, whoever is pleased or displeased.[107] Blessed is the man that endureth temptation! When he has been tried, he shall come forth as gold.[108]

I am
20   Your affectionate friend and brother,

J. Wesley

Source: holograph; MARC, MAM JW 6/40.

25

To Ann Bolton[109]

Burslem
30 April 1, 1784

My Dear Nancy,

The recovery of Mr. [Edward] Bolton's health, and much more of his cheerfulness, you should look upon as a token for good, a fresh proof that God is on your side.

---

[103] The address portion is missing. Telford identifies the recipient as Yewdall, though there is nothing in the letter that confirms this.
[104] See Josh. 6:18.
[105] Cf. JW to Joseph Benson, Jan. 11, 1777, 29:315 in this edn.; and JW to Thomas Carlill, May 13, 1777, 29:343 in this edn.
[106] JW, *A Word to a Smuggler* (1767), vol. 15 in this edn.
[107] See note on JW to Sheffield Society, Sept. 4, 1780, 29:592–93 in this edn.
[108] See Job 23:10.
[109] JW was replying to Bolton's letter of Mar. 23, 1784.

It is another blessing that your spirits do not sink, but you are still kept above the billows. It shows indeed how you are called to *trust* God, though without *knowing* which way he will lead you. In due time he will reveal this also, and make it plain before your face. At present it is easier to know what is not to be done than what is. 5
But you are in God's school, and he will teach you one lesson after another, till you have learned all his holy and acceptable will.

'O tarry thou the Lord's leisure. Be strong, and he shall comfort thy heart; and put thou thy trust in the Lord!'[110] I am, my dear Nancy, 10

Yours most affectionately,

J. Wesley

Source: holograph; privately held (WWEP Archive holds photocopy). 15

To Thomas Longley[111]

20

Manchester
April 11, 1784

Dear Tommy,

You have reason to be thankful that the society does not decrease 25
in number. And the members of it will not decrease in grace, if you strongly and explicitly exhort them, to 'go on to perfection'.[112] Especially if you encourage them, both by precept and example, to rise early in the morning. The morning preaching is the glory of the Methodists. Whenever that ceases, the glory is departed from 30
them. I am,

Your affectionate friend and brother,

J. Wesley

Address: 'To / Mr. Longley / At the Preachinghouse / in / Derby'. 35
Postmark: 'Manchester'. *Charge*: '4'.
Source: holograph; Bridwell Library (SMU).

---

[110] Ps. 27:14.
[111] Longley was currently the Assistant for the Derby circuit.
[112] Heb. 6:1.

To an Unidentified Man

Stockport
April 12, 1784

My Dear Brother,

If I had not been absolutely engaged, I should willingly have come forty or fifty miles out of my way to see you. But I shall see you in a better place, where we shall meet to part no more. You have only to wait for the word, 'Come up hither!'[113] Then you shall deliver your soul into the hands of your merciful and faithful Redeemer!

I am

Yours affectionately,

J. Wesley

Source: holograph; privately held (WWEP Archive holds photocopy).

To Hannah Ball[114]

Edinburgh
April 25, 1784

My Dear Sister,

It would not be strange if your love did grow cold. It would only be according to the course of nature. But blessed be God, we know there is a power that controls the course of nature. And the affection which flows from this does not depend upon blood and spirits, and therefore 'never faileth'.[115]

I was afraid there had been some misunderstanding between Mr. Broadbent and you.[116] Let him and you be free and open with each other, and I trust nothing will hurt you.

Whenever the preachers strongly exhort the people to accept of full sanctification, and to accept it now by simple faith, there the

---

[113] Rev. 4:1.

[114] While the address portion is missing and no name is used, the holograph was part of the papers of Hannah Ball, and the letter is transcribed in her *Memoir* (pp. 159–60). Ball's letter to JW, which drew this response, is not known to survive.

[115] 1 Cor. 13:8.

[116] John Broadbent was currently Assistant for the Oxfordshire circuit, which included High Wycombe.

work of God in general will prosper. This is the proper Methodist testimony!

I am, with kind love to Ann [Ball], my dear sister,
Your affectionate brother,

J. Wesley 5

Source: holograph; MARC, MA 2008/013.

10

To Agnes Gibbes

Glasgow 15
April 28, 1784

It is not easy to express, my dear Miss Aggy, how much you oblige me by your free manner of writing.[117] I beg (if you have a real regard for me) that you would always write in this manner. Surely there 20 does not need any reserve (much less disguise) between you and me. No habitation can be *melancholy* to me, where I find so amiable, so dear a friend. Methinks when you either write or speak to me, you need not be afraid to *think aloud*. Need I tell you that you never sent me a letter before which gave so much satisfaction? I should be 25 exceeding glad if I could find an opportunity of waiting upon the good family this summer. But I should be almost afraid to come too often, lest I should hardly know how to leave you. O that you may all have health of body and health of mind! Let this, my dear Miss Aggy, be *your* constant desire, to have the spirit of power, and love 30 and of a sound mind![118] Nay, may you have all the mind that was in Christ Jesus![119]

My dear friend,
Adieu!

35

Address: 'To / Miss Agnes Gibbes / At Sir Philip Gibbes, Bart. / In Hilton Park / Near Wolverhampton / Staffordshire'.
Source: holograph; National Archives, PRO 30/9/11/2.

---

[117] Agnes Gibbes's letter to JW is not known to survive.
[118] See 2 Tim. 1:7.
[119] See Phil. 2:5.

To Elizabeth Gibbes

Glasgow
April 28, 1784

5 My Dear Miss Gibbes,

I return you many thanks for the seeds, which I will order to be planted in my garden at London.[120] And probably we may save some seed by and by, which may be planted in the garden at Kingswood. The coldness of the season makes it difficult to recover from any 10 disorder. Nevertheless, I hope Sir Philip [Gibbes] is better already, and will quite conquer his indisposition without being obliged to have recourse to a physician, who might keep him neither well nor ill till midsummer.

I have not the *Arminian Magazine* here. And I do not know anyone 15 that has. I believe that account is in one of the last year's magazines. The ship was commanded by Capt. Kennedy.[121] If I can procure the magazine at Edinburgh, I will send you a more particular account.

Every time I have the pleasure of being at Hilton Park I find more attachment to it than I did before. Although, to say the truth, it is 20 not the place but the inhabitants that

In lasting bonds my heart have laid.[122]

I love Sir Philip; I love Lady [Agnes] Gibbes. But I confess I have 25 a still greater regard, for those of the family whom I know better. And methinks I know *you* as well as if I had been acquainted with you for many years. I know you fear God and (at least) desire to love him more than all the gilded trifles of the world. You desire to be not almost but altogether a Christian.[123] And not a fashionable but a 30 scriptural Christian! That God may speedily give you the desire of your heart, is the sincere prayer of, my dear Miss Gibbes,

Your affectionate servant,

John Wesley

Address: 'To / Miss Gibbes / At Sir Philip Gibbes', Bart. / In Hilton Park 35 / near Wolverhampton / Staffordshire'.
Postmark: 'AP/29'.
Source: holograph; National Archives, PRO 30/9/7/15.

---

[120] Elizabeth Gibbes's letter to JW, with the seeds, is not known to survive.
[121] 'A Narrative of Capt. Kennedy's Distress and Deliverance', *AM* 4 (1781): 274–75.
[122] John Gambold, 'The Mystery of Life', st. 4, in JW, *HSP* (1739), 8.
[123] See JW, *The Almost Christian* (1741), 1:131–41 in this edn.

To Charles Wesley Jr.

Dundee
May 2 [1784[124]]   5

Dear Charles,

I doubt not but both [Sarah Wesley Jr.] and you are in trouble
because [Samuel] has 'changed his religion'.[125] Nay, he has changed
his *opinions* and *mode of worship*. But that is not *religion*. It is quite
another thing. 'Has he, then', you may ask, 'sustained no loss by the   10
change?' Yes, unspeakable loss; because his new opinion and mode
of worship are so unfavourable to religion that they make it, if not
impossible to one that once knew better, yet extremely difficult.

'What, then, is religion?' It is happiness in God, or in the knowledge and love of God. It is 'faith working by love',[126] producing   15
'righteousness and peace and joy in the Holy Ghost'.[127] In other
words, it is a heart and life devoted to God; or communion with
God the Father and the Son;[128] or the mind which was in Christ
Jesus, enabling us to walk as he walked.[129]

Now, either he has this religion or he has not. If he has, he will   20
not finally perish, notwithstanding the absurd, unscriptural opinions he has embraced and the superstitious and idolatrous modes
of worship. But these are so many shackles which will greatly retard
him in running the race that is set before him.[130]

If he has not this religion, if he has not given God his heart, the   25
case is unspeakably worse. I doubt if he ever will, for his new friends
will continually endeavour to hinder him by putting something else
in its place—by encouraging him to rest in the form, notions, or
externals, without being born again, without having Christ in him,
the hope of glory,[131] without being renewed in the image of him that   30
created him.[132] This is the deadly evil. I have often lamented that
he had not this holiness, without which no man can see the Lord.[133]

---

[124] The letter is dated '1786' in *MM*; a mistake. JW was in Dundee in May 1784.
[125] See the note about Samuel's conversion to the Church of Rome in JW to Samuel
Wesley, Aug. 19, 1784.
[126] Cf. Gal. 5:6.
[127] Rom. 14:17.
[128] See 1 John 1:6.
[129] See Phil. 2:5 and 1 John 2:6.
[130] See Heb. 12:1.
[131] See Col. 1:27.
[132] See Col. 3:10.
[133] See Heb. 12:14.

But though he had it not, yet in his hours of cool reflection he did not hope to go to heaven without it. But now he is or will be taught that, let him only have a right *faith* (that is, such and such notions), and add thereunto such and such *externals*, and he is quite safe. He
5　may indeed roll[134] a few years in purging fire, but he will surely go to heaven at last!

Therefore you and my dear Sarah have great need to weep over him. But have you not also need to weep for yourselves? For have you given God your hearts? Are you holy in heart? Have you the
10　kingdom of God within you?[135] Righteousness and peace and joy in the Holy Ghost?[136] The only true religion under heaven? O cry unto him that is mighty to save for this one thing needful![137] Earnestly and diligently use all the means which God hath put plentifully into your hands! Otherwise I should not at all wonder if God permit you
15　also to be given up to a strong delusion.[138] But whether you were or were not, whether you are Protestant or papist, neither you nor he can ever enter into glory, unless you are now cleansed from all pollution of flesh and spirit, and perfect holiness in the fear of God![139]

I am,
20　　　Your affectionate,

J. Wesley

Source: published transcription; *Methodist Magazine* 24 (1801): 139–40.

25

To James Rogers

30

Aberdeen
May 5, 1784

Dear Jemmy,

All letters to any part of Scotland must go through Edinburgh.
35　Therefore it is sufficient to direct thither till the 15th instant, and then to Newcastle upon Tyne.

---

[134] The holograph may have read 'roil'.
[135] See Luke 17:21.
[136] See Rom. 14:17.
[137] See Zeph. 3:17 and Luke 10:42.
[138] See 2 Thess. 2:11.
[139] See 2 Cor. 7:1.

I objected to nothing in that sermon but a few tart expressions concerning the clergy.[140] When these are altered, I believe it will be of use; and the more of them you can sell, the better.

You have done well in restoring the meetings at 5:00 in the morning. These are the glory of the Methodists. My kind love to Hetty Roe.

I am, dear Jemmy,
>Your affectionate brother and friend,

J. Wesley

Source: published transcription; *Notes and Queries* 21 (1904): 406.

To Vincent De Boudry[141]

near Keith
May 7, 1784

My Dear Brother,

I am always well pleased to hear from you—the rather because you used to be a messenger of good news. I know you have the good of the family at heart, especially of the children. And if it should please God to visit them as he did a few years ago,[142] I am persuaded they would not again be left to themselves. But you will use the utmost diligence to keep the sacred fire alive. Nay, and to blow it into a flame, that many may see the light and glorify your Father which is in heaven.[143] It is he alone who is able to make men of one mind in a house; and while you continue so to be, he will surely bless you.

I am,
>Your affectionate brother,

J. Wesley

Source: secondary transcription; Drew, Methodist Archives.[144]

---

[140] Referring to David Simpson, *The Happiness of Dying in the Lord; with an apology for the Methodists; a sermon preached at Christ-Church, in Macclesfield, on Sunday the 22nd of February, 1784. Occasioned By the Death of Mrs. Martha Rogers, Wife of James Rogers* (London: C. Dilly, 1784).

[141] Vincent De Boudry (d. 1815) was the French master at Kingswood school 1780–87. He married Jane Corham in 1785. After leaving Kingswood he continued to run an academy in Bristol, on Somerset Street. De Boudry was the only master JW retained when he oversaw a major shakeup of Kingswood in 1783 (see 1783 *Minutes*, QQ. 15–16, 10:539–40 in this edn.).

[142] See James Hindmarsh to JW, Apr. 27 and May 18, 1768.

[143] See Matt. 5:16.

[144] The identity of the transcriber is unknown.

To William Black Jr.

Inverness
May 11, 1784

5 My Dear Brother,

I am glad you have given a little assistance to our brethren at Halifax and along the coast.[145] There is no charity under heaven to be compared to this, the bringing light to the poor heathens that are called Christians, but nevertheless still sit in darkness and the
10 shadow of death. I am in great hopes that some of the emigrants from New York are really alive to God.[146] And if so, they will be every way a valuable acquisition to the province where their lot is now cast. This may be one of the gracious designs of God's providence in bringing them from their native country. And if they not only
15 themselves grow in grace and in the knowledge of our Lord Jesus Christ,[147] but are likewise happy instruments in his hand of imparting that knowledge to others, they will have unspeakable reason to praise God, both in time and in eternity.

There is no part of Calvinism or Antinomianism which is not
20 fully answered in some part of our writings, particularly in the *Preservative against Unsettled Notions in Religion.*[148] I have no more to do with answering books. It will be sufficient if you recommend to Mr. [Henry] Alline's friends some of the tracts that are already written.[149] As to himself, I fear he is wiser in his own eyes than seven
25 men that can render a reason. Therefore I have no hope of his being convinced, till death opens his eyes.

The work of God goes on with a steady pace in various parts of England. But still the love of many will wax cold, while many others are continually added to supply their place. In the west of England,
30 in Lancashire, and in Yorkshire God still mightily makes bare his arm.[150] He convinces many, justifies many, and many are perfected in love.

My great advice to those who are united together is: Let brotherly love continue! See that ye fall not out by the way![151] Hold the

---

[145] Black had married Mary Gay, of Cumberland, Nova Scotia, on Feb. 17, 1784, and spent the spring visiting Halifax and towns along the lower coast.

[146] Many Methodists who were British Loyalists moved up into Canada after Britain conceded the independence of its former colonies south of there.

[147] See 2 Pet. 3:18.

[148] See the discussion in 14:298–99 in this edn.

[149] See JW to Black, July 13, 1783; and JW to Benjamin Chappell, Nov. 27, 1783.

[150] See Isa. 52:10.

[151] See Gen. 45:24.

unity of the Spirit in the bond of peace![152] Bear ye one another's
burdens, and so fulfill the law of Christ![153]
    I am
        Your affectionate brother,

                            J. Wesley   5

My brother [CW] is alive and tolerably well.

Address: 'To / Mr Will Black Junr / In Halifax / Nova Scotia'.
Postmarks: 'MY/17' and '21/MY'.
Endorsement: by Black(?); 'Revd Jno Wesley / Inverness 11 May 1784'.   10
Source: holograph; UCC Maritime Conference, Archives.

15

To Mary Clark

                                Newcastle
                            May 31, 1784
My Dear Sister,   20
    Because I love you, I will make free with you. I will send you of
an errand. Go the very first leisure hour you have to Mr. [Jona-
than] Coussins, and tell him from me he has forgot the rule of our
Conference. In case of bankruptcy, the Assistant is to send two or
three brethren to talk with the bankrupt at large, and examine how   25
he came to fail.[154] Till this is done, nothing should be determined.
Now I do not hear that this was done in the case of brother [Wil-
liam] Savage. Then let it be done now. I desire brother [Edmund]
Lewty and [John] Knapp to go and talk with him at large. And then
send me an account (directing to Scarborough) what occasioned   30
this? And in what state his accounts are? Till this is done, he may be
in the society as a private member.
    I thank you for writing, and am, my very dear sister,
        Yours in tender affection,

                            J. Wesley   35

---

[152] See Eph. 4:3.

[153] See Gal. 6:2.

[154] See *Minutes* (1770) Q. 16, 10:388–89 in this edn.; repeated in 'Large' *Minutes* (1770),
Q. 26, 10:884 in this edn.; and revised slightly in 'Large' *Minutes* (1780), 10:914 in this edn.
Cf. Frank Baker, 'John Wesley and Miss Mary Clark of Worcester', *Methodist History* 10.2 (Jan.
1972): 45–51.

Address: 'To / Miss Clark / At Mr [William] Savage's, Glover / Worcester'.
Postmark: 'Newcastle'. *Charge*: '4'.
Source: holograph; Bridwell Library (SMU).[155]

5

To Mary (Edwin) Savage

Newcastle
May 31, 1784

10   My Dear Sister,
     As I have desired brother [Edmund] Lewty and [John] Knapp,
who love you and are capable judges of these things, to talk at large
with Billy Savage, I make no doubt but it will clearly appear the late
event was not his fault but only his misfortune. And undoubtedly
15   it is permitted for good—to wean you from all things here below,
and teach you to say, 'It is the Lord! Let him do what seemeth him
good!'[156]
     I am, my dear sister,
          Your affectionate brother,
20   J. Wesley

Address: 'To S[ister] Savage'.[157]
Source: holograph; Bridwell Library (SMU).[158]

25

To Simon Day[159]

Newcastle
June 1, 1784

30   Dear Simon,
     You shall be in Oxfordshire.[160]
          Adieu.

---

[155] Held previously in the Upper Room Museum, L-228.

[156] 1 Sam. 3:18.

[157] Included as part of a double letter with that to Mary Clark just above.

[158] Held previously in the Upper Room Museum, L-228.

[159] Simon Day (1745–1832) was converted while in a boarding-school at Bristol. Soon after he began to preach in the villages in Somerset. He was admitted 'on trial' as an itinerant in 1766 (10:317), but desisted at next Conference (10:343). In 1779 he returned to the itinerancy, and travelled until infirmity required him to settle in Frome as a supernumerary in 1817. He continued to preach locally for about ten years, until afflicted with paralysis five years before his death. See *Minutes* (post-Wesley, 1832), 7:112.

[160] Day was currently serving the Oxfordshire circuit (see 10:533 in this edn.); JW was informing him that he would be reappointed there for the coming year (see 10:554).

Address: 'To / Mr. Simon Day / At Mr. [Joseph] Wickens' / Shoemaker /
   Near the Castle / Oxon'.
Postmarks: 'Newcastle' and '4/IV'.
Source: holograph; Bridwell Library (SMU).

To John Broadbent

Newcastle
June 2, 1784

My Dear Brother,

I expect to be at Darlington on Saturday the 12th instant, at Scarborough the 19th, at Epworth the 26th.

You do well to preach abroad when occasion serves, and to be exact in discipline. I want a man (and I have been seeking him in vain these ten years) that would be so, in spite of all opposition. I have tried one, and another, and another. But all have proved deceitful upon the weights! I want such an one to be the General Assistant in Scotland. Four of the preachers there are men after my own heart. But none of them has a *head* for that office. I am at my wits' end.

Now dare you *bestride* that kingdom?[161] If God calls you to it, he will give you a body. Pray, and think, and let me know your mind. I am,

Your affectionate friend and brother,

J. Wesley

I have set down brother [Samuel] Hodgson for Oxon.

Address: 'To / Mr. Broadbent / At Mr. [Joseph] Wickens', Shoemaker /
   Near the Castle / Oxon'.
Source: holograph; MARC, MAM JW 2/16.

[161] Broadbent did not take on this role; he was appointed Assistant of the Birstall circuit at the 1784 Conference.

To Alexander Suter

Darlington
June 13, 1784

My Dear Brother,

Your letter gave me not a little satisfaction. I am glad to hear that your spirit revives. I doubt not but it will revive more and more, and the work of the Lord will prosper in your hands.

I have a very friendly letter from Sir Ludovick,[162] and hope you will have an opportunity of calling upon him again; especially if brother [Duncan] M'Allum and you have the resolution to change places regularly, as I proposed.[163] I dearly love the spirit of sister M'Allum.[164] She is a woman after my own heart.

It will be of great and general use, when you have a quantity of little books, partly to sell and partly to give among the poor— chiefly indeed to give. If I live till the Conference, I will take order concerning it. Certainly you shall not want any help that is in the power of

Your affectionate brother,

J. Wesley

Address: 'To / Mr Suter / At the Preachinghouse / in / Inverness'.
Postmark: 'Darlington'. *Charge*: '6'.
Endorsement: by Suter, 'No. 3'.
Source: holograph; privately held (WWEP Archive holds photocopy).

---

[162] Ludovick Grant (d. 1790) became 6th Baronet of Dalvey in 1772. JW visited his estate near Forres, Moray, Scotland June 11, 1764 (21:471 in this edn.), June 7, 1779 (23:134), and most recently May 8–12, 1784 (23:307–09). His letter to JW is not known to survive.

[163] M'Allum was the Assistant for the Aberdeen circuit, on which Suter was serving, which currently serviced Inverness (it would become its own circuit at the 1784 Conference).

[164] Duncan M'Allum married Elizabeth Livingstone (1755–1812) of Inverness on Jan. 14, 1784.

To Zachariah Yewdall

Darlington
June 13, 1784   5

Dear Zachary,

I really think it is a critical case.[165] And as we shall all (if God permit) meet together at the Conference in Leeds, I agree to what you say of referring the full consideration of the matter till that time. Meanwhile I am   10

Your affectionate brother,

J. Wesley

Address: 'To / Mr Zach. Udal / At the Preachinghouse / in / Liverpool'.
Postmark: 'Darlington'. *Charge*: '4'.   15
Source: holograph; Duke, Rubenstein, Frank Baker Collection of Wesleyana, Box WF 1.

20

To [Sophia Theodora (de Beveren) Tydeman][166]

Whitby   25
June 18, 1784

Dear Madam,

I give you many thanks for the favour of your letter.[167] I heard Mr. [William] Ferguson speak of you when I was at Utrecht; indeed the same evening that Mr. Professor Tydeman was so good as to assist   30
me at Miss Loten's.[168] He spoke of you as one that not only feared

[165] Three topics discussed at Conference made it into the 1784 *Minutes*, QQ. 20–22 (10:562–63 in this edn.): 1) how to treat former itinerants who now deny original sin (do not attend their preaching); 2) whether to attend feasts or wakes on Sundays (no; and bear public testimony against them); and 3) whether Methodists can make candles for their own use, without paying duty for them—as required by law (no, it is a species of smuggling). It is unclear which, if any, of these, was the query raised by Yewdall.

[166] While the address portion is missing, the mention of her husband within the letter (and the reference to her in Loten's letter to JW of July 15, 1783) leave little doubt that the recipient was Sophia Theodora (de Beveren) Tydeman (1751–89).

[167] This letter is not known to survive.

[168] Meinard Tydeman (1741–1825), a professor of law at Utrecht, translated for JW when he preached the evening of June 29, 1783 at Johanna Carolina Arnodina Loten's house; see *Journal*, 23:282–83 in this edn.

God, but also believed in the Lord Jesus Christ. So that his account exactly agreed with that which you now give me of yourself. O what cause have you to praise him, who loved you and gave himself for you! And who has given you so many advantages, and so many op-
5   portunities of doing good. A large family gives you many occasions of glorifying God and being useful to others. Indeed it will at the same time afford you many temptations. But he is faithful who has promised you shall not be tempted above that you are able.[169] Surely with every temptation he will make a way to escape, that you may
10   be able to bear it.

     The fear of man is a dangerous temptation, especially when it appears in the shape of prudence. But it cannot stand before the cheerful boldness of faith. Give not place to it; no, not for an hour. Let my dear Miss Loten and you watch over one another, particu-
15   larly in this. Although perhaps she is not quite so much exposed to it as you are. But not only in this, but in many respects, we must fight or we cannot conquer.

     I admired and almost envied, a gentlewoman in London who told my brother's wife [Sarah] some years ago, 'Mrs. Wesley, I have fin-
20   ished my course. I have lived fourscore years. And I bless God for a thousand mercies; and this in particular, that I do not remember ever to have seen anyone sin but I reproved him.' In this, and in every part of Christian holiness may you be a follower of her, as she was of Christ.[170]
25   So prays, my dear madam,

       Your affectionate brother and servant,

                             J. Wesley

30   If you at anytime can(?) favour me with a line, Mr. Ferguson can send it.

Source: holograph; Munich, Germany, Bavarian State Library.

---

[169] See 1 Cor. 10:13.
[170] See 1 Cor. 11:1.

To Joseph Entwisle and David Gordon[171]

Scarborough
June 20, 1784

My Dear Brethren,

Having very little time, I take the opportunity of answering you both together. You have great reason to bless God continually, who has dealt so graciously with you. You have good encouragement to put forth all your strength in publishing the glad tidings of salvation. You are particularly called to declare to believers that the blood of Jesus Christ cleanseth from all sin.[172] Watch and pray that you may be little in your own eyes.[173]

I am, my dear brethren,
    Your affectionate brother,

[J. Wesley]

Source: published transcription; Telford, *Letters*, 7:220.

To Francis Wrigley[174]

Scarborough
June 20, 1784

Dear Francis,

You did right with regard to Capt. Colmer.[175] But you should likewise apply, if it can be done, to all his employers. I think he will soon find he has missed his mark.

---

[171] Joseph Entwisle (1767–1841), a native of Manchester, began preaching locally at the age of 16. On June 3, 1784 he sent JW a brief account of his conversion and experience (see *Memoir*, 20), which lead JW (without his knowledge) to appoint him as an itinerant at the 1784 Conference (see 10:533 in this edn.). Entwisle did not accept this role until 1787 (see 10:623), but then served faithfully (including four years as governor of a theological academy at Hoxton) until age led him to retire. See Joseph Entwisle Jr., *Memoir of the Rev. Joseph Entwisle* (Bristol: for the author, 1848); *Minutes* (post-Wesley), 9:304–05; and Vickers, *Dictionary*, 110.

Entwisle's letter to JW included an enclosure by David Gordon (1757–99), an Irish friend currently in Manchester, with a similar account. Gordon would be admitted 'on trial' as an itinerant in 1786 (see 10:597) and served circuits in Ireland until his death; see *Minutes* (post-Wesley, 1800), 2:44.

[172] See 1 John 1:7.

[173] See 1 Sam. 15:17.

[174] Wrigley had been assigned to the Bradford, Yorkshire circuit at the 1783 Conference, but had apparently been moved to the East Cornwall circuit early, to assist James Thom.

[175] This was most likely a mine captain; possibly Thomas Colmer (1748–1802) of St. Austell.

I advise you to write to Mr. Shipm⟨an(?) and⟩[176] ask whether he did give or offer them ⟨money?⟩ for Ringing(?). I hope it is a slander.

5 Pray inform the minister of St. ⟨…⟩ I have tried that point in Westminster. ⟨…⟩ Whether the Conventicle Act affects the Method⟨ists. ⟩ And if he requires it of me, I will try it again.[177]

If the preaching-places can be su⟨pplied⟩ during his absence, James Thom may come ⟨with⟩ you to the Conference.[178]

I am afraid that kind of rupt⟨ure with⟩ which Mary Hooker la-
10 bours will admit of no natural remedy.

I am, dear Francis,

Your affectionate friend and brother,

J. Wesley

15 *Address*: 'To / Mr. Francis Wrigley / At Mr. Flamank's[179] / In St. Austle / Cornwall'.

Postmarks: 'Scarborough' and '23/IV'.

Source: holograph; Pitts Library (Emory), John Wesley Papers (MSS 153), 3/31.

20

To Ellen (Gretton) Christian[180]

Bridlington[181]
June 21, 1784

25 My Dear Sister,

The summer is already so far spent that I shall have little time to spend in Lincolnshire. I hope to be at Epworth on Saturday, the 26th instant; and after visiting Gainsborough (on Monday the
30 28th) and Owston on Tuesday, at Epworth again on Wednesday, and in the neighbouring towns the rest of the week. On Monday I am

---

[176] About half an inch of the right margin is torn away for the remainder of the letter, affecting a word or two in each line. The likely missing text is provided when possible.

[177] The previous case was in 1760; see Tyerman, *John Wesley*, 2:359.

[178] James Thom had just been admitted 'on trial' as an itinerant at the 1783 Conference (see 10:531 in this edn.); he last appeared with an appointment in 1807.

[179] George Flamank (1751–1831) was an excise officer who financed building a preaching house in St. Austell, Cornwall; and later resided in Plymouth, Devon. See JW's letter to him of June 7, 1789.

[180] The recipient is not named. *WHS* speculates it is to the wife of Rev. Dodwell, but there is no evidence he ever married. It was surely instead to Christian, JW's regular correspondent.

[181] Orig., 'Burlington'; a common pronunciation of the time.

to be at Rotherham. So that I shall not see Mr. Dodwell,[182] unless
I could have the pleasure of seeing him at Epworth. My work is
great, and my time is short. 'I would my every hour redeem.' Why
should any time be spent in vain?
  I am, with kind love to your husband,[183] my dear sister,   5
    Your affectionate brother,

                                                              J. Wesley

Postmark: 'Hull'.
Source: published transcription; *WHS* 17 (1930): 120.
                                                                                10

To Arthur Keene
                                                                                15
                                                              Bridlington[184]
                                                              June 21, 1784

My Dear Brother,
  I agree with you in hoping that brother Blair's labours will be
productive of a blessing to many in Dublin—the rather because   20
he not only preaches but also lives the gospel.[185] And wherever a
man's life confirms his doctrine, God will confirm the word of his
messenger.
  It gives me pleasure to hear that the school succeeds well.[186] It is
an excellent institution. I am very glad that Richard Condy's broth-   25
er has come over to assist him.[187] I hope brother Condy continues
to go out on Sunday noon to the little towns round Dublin. We try
all the little towns round London, and have societies in most of
them. What a shame it is that we should so long have neglected the
little towns round Dublin, and that we have not a society within ten   30
miles of it?

---

[182] Rev. William Dodwell, rector of Welby and North Stoke, a friend of Ellen (Gretton) Christian; see JW to Gretton, Nov. 19, 1781, 29:700 in this edn.

[183] William Christian.

[184] Orig., 'Burlington'; a common pronunciation of the time.

[185] Andrew Blair, who had been stationed in Cork, was moved to Dublin by the Irish Conference, meeting July 6, 1784.

[186] See JW to Keene, Mar. 3, 1784.

[187] Apparently his brother William Jones Condy (1756–1832), who returned to England in 1786 to get married.

During the present state of Mr. Pawson's health he would be of little service at Dublin.[188] You want lively, zealous, active preachers. And to tell you a melancholy truth, few of our elder preachers are of this character. You must look for zeal and activity among the young preachers. I am greatly scandalized at this, that a preacher fifty years old is commonly but half a preacher. I wonder that every preacher does not use Bishop Stratford's prayer: 'Lord, let me not live to be useless.'[189]

A gradual work of grace constantly precedes the instantaneous work both of justification and sanctification. But the work itself (of sanctification as well as justification) is undoubtedly instantaneous. As after a gradual conviction of the guilt and power of sin you was justified in a moment, so after a gradually increasing conviction of inbred sin you will be sanctified in a moment. And who knows how soon? Why not *now*? May the whole blessing of the gospel be on you and sister [Isabella] Keene! I am, dear Arthur,

Your affectionate brother,

J. Wesley

Address: 'To / Mr Arthur Keene / in / Dublin'.
Postmarks: 'Hull' and 'IU/28'.
Endorsement: by Keene, '21 June 1784 / Revd J. Wesley / Burlington'.
Source: holograph; MARC, MAM JW 3/74.

To John Francis Valton

York
June 25, 1784

My Dear Brother,

I just snatch time to write a line. I hope to be at Dawgreen on July 17, at half hour after 6:00; at Birstall on Sunday and on Monday the 19th in the morning.

---

[188] Keene had apparently requested JW to consider sending John Pawson (currently in York) to Dublin.
[189] JW frequently uses this prayer. Here and one other time he attributes it to Nicholas Stratford (1633–1707), who became Bishop of Chester in 1689; see *Journal*, Dec. 8, 1764, 21:496 in this edn. No published source for the prayer has been located.

It will, I believe, be better for you to be at Scarborough, because many there are much alive, and hardly any at Bridlington.[190] John Allen may stay at Birstall another year.

Peace be with you all! I am

Your affectionate friend and brother,

J. Wesley

[added on back fly-leaf]

By talking with brother [Alexander] Mather I am induced to make the following alteration: Friday, July 9, Huddersfield; Saturday, [July] 10, Bradford; Sunday, [July 11], Halifax; Monday, [July] 12, Heptonstall, at 1:00 Todmorden, at 5:00 Padiham; Tuesday and Wednesday, Colne; Thursday [and] Friday, private; Saturday, [July] 17, Keighley; Sunday, [July] 18, Bingley; Monday [and] Tuesday, Otley; Wednesday [and] Thursday, Parkgate; Friday, [July] 23, Bradford; Saturday [July] 24, Dawgreen [in Dewsbury]; Sunday, [July] 25, Birstall; [in] evening, Leeds.[191]

Endorsement: by Valton, 'June 25 1784'.
Source: holograph; Lovely Lane Museum.

To Ann Bolton[192]

Epworth
June 28, 1784

My Dear Nancy,

The strong and tender regard which I have for you makes your letters always welcome. Providence has seen good to try you for many years in the furnace of affliction.[193] But all will work together for your good.[194] You shall lose nothing but your dross. I wonder you do not find one person that knows how to sympathize with you. Surely there must be some such in the society at Witney: although

---

[190] Orig., 'Burlington'; a common pronunciation of the time. Valton was instead made Assistant of the Bradford circuit at the 1784 Conference.

[191] Cf. JW, *Journal*, July 9–25, 1784, 23:321–24 in this edn.

[192] JW was replying to her letter of June 22, 1784.

[193] See Isa. 48:10.

[194] See Rom. 8:28.

you have not yet found them, perhaps for want of praying for this very thing. I advise you to make it a matter of earnest prayer, and certainly God will give you a friend.

5   Accommodableness is only the art of becoming all things to all men without wounding our own conscience.[195] St. Paul enjoins it in those words, 'Please all men for their good unto edification.'[196] Bare rules will hardly teach us to do this. But those that have a single eye may attain it, through the grace of God, by reflection and experience.[197]

10   I am, my dear Nancy,
       Very affectionately yours,

                                                J. Wesley

Address: 'To / Miss Bolton / In Witney / Oxfordshire'.
Source: holograph; Wesley's Chapel (London), LDWMM 1993/1586.
15

To John White[198]

20
                                                [July 1784][199]

John White, whoever is wrong, you are not right.
    I am yours,

                                                John Wesley

25   *Source*: published transcription; *Wesley Banner* 1 (1849): 87.

---

[195] See 1 Cor. 9:21–22. Bolton had mentioned reading an essay on 'accommodableness' in Catherine Talbot, *Essays on Various Subjects*, 2 vols. (London: Charles Rivington, 1772), 1:25ff.
[196] Cf. Rom. 15:2.
[197] See Matt. 6:22.
[198] This letter was transcribed among some manuscript papers that belonged to Adam Clarke. It had the note: 'A class leader in the East Riding, at an early period of Methodism, disagreed with the members of his class. He was determined, however, to make them submit to his measures. To accomplish this purpose he wrote to Mr. Wesley, complaining of their refractiveness, and requesting advice how to proceed. Mr Wesley sent him the following letter [as above]. Poor White was quiet. He saw that he had been acting under the influence of a wrong temper.'
[199] The letter is not dated in *Wesley Banner*. Telford assigned it this date, on the assumption that the recipient was the 'John White' who was upper master of the Sunday school in Bingley that JW visited on July 18, 1784. But Bingley is in West Riding, and the description of White as a 'class leader' in an 'early period of Methodism' argues against this identification. We have retained Telford's date only because no better alternative is evident.

To Alexander Barry[200]

Epworth
July 3, 1784   5

My Dear Brother,

We purpose to consider fully at the Conference the state of our brethren in America, and to send them all the help we can both in Nova Scotia and in other parts.[201] But whoever goes over must voluntarily offer himself for that great work. I not only do not require,   10
but do not so much as advise an⟨y on⟩e[202] to go. His service will do no good there unless it be a free-will offering.

I am glad our preachers at Portsmouth do not coop themselves up in the preaching-houses. The work of God can never make any considerable progress but by field-preaching.   15

We do not now make any yearly collection for the payment of debts. All our public debts would have been paid long before now, had the Methodists been merciful after their power.

I am

Your affectionate brother,   20

J. Wesley

Source: holograph; London, Society of Antiquaries Library, Cely-Trevillian Bequest (MS 444/6), p. 119.

---

[200] While the recipient is not named, it was surely Alexander Barry (c. 1762–1816), a brother of Robert Barry, who was a merchant living in Portsea, Hampshire and active in the Portsmouth society. Cf. Henry Smith, *Wesleyan Methodism in Portsmouth* (London: Kelly, 1894), 37; and next letter to Robert Barry.

[201] Alexander had apparently forwarded to JW an inquiry from his brother Robert. His letter, which also commented on the itinerants in his circuit, is not known to survive.

[202] A small portion was torn away by the wax seal.

To Robert Barry[203]

Epworth
July 3, 1784

My Dear Brother,

I know your brother well, and was at his house the last time I was at Portsmouth, as probably I shall be again in autumn before I return to London.[204] The work of God among the blacks in your neighbourhood is a wonderful instance of the power of God. And the little town they have built is, I suppose, the only town of Negroes which has been built in America—nay, perhaps in any part of the world, except only in Africa. I doubt not but some of them can read. When, therefore, we send a preacher or two to Nova Scotia, we will send some books to be distributed among them; and they never need want books while I live. It will be well to give them all the assistance you can in every possible way.

We purpose to consider fully at the Conference what we can do to help our brethren abroad; not only those that are settled in the southern provinces of America, but those that are in Nova Scotia and Newfoundland. Indeed, it is an invariable rule with me not to require anyone to go over to America; nay, I scruple even to advise them to it. I shall only propose it at the Conference, and then of those that freely offer themselves we shall select such as we believe will most adorn the gospel.

In teaching school you have an opportunity of doing much good, if you consider that you are called of God to teach those you are entrusted with not only to read and write, but to fear and serve God. Indeed, in order to this you will have need of much courage as well as much prudence and patience. And it may be long before you see the fruit of your labour. But in due time you shall reap if you faint not.[205]

---

[203] Robert Barry (c. 1759–1843) was born in Scotland, raised in Portsmouth, Hampshire, and came to North America as an impressed sailor who escaped his ship in New York around 1774. He was a participant in Methodist services at the John Street Chapel and formed a friendship with the Rev. Charles Inglis, the rector of Trinity Church where he was a regular communicant. In 1783 Barry was part of a large group of Loyalists who left New York and ended up in Nova Scotia. Barry settled in Shelburne, where he taught school for a while, then became involved with his brother in a very successful trading practice between Britain and Canada. Barry remained an active Methodist and was a close friend of William Black. [Telford misidentifies the recipient as James Barry.]

[204] See previous letter to Alexander Barry.

[205] See Gal. 6:9.

I wish you would from time to time send an account of the progress of the work of God among you, and of anything remarkable
that occurs, to
>Your affectionate brother,

>>>>[J. Wesley]   5

Address: 'To / Mr. Barry / Shelburne / Nova Scotia'.
Source: published transcription; Telford, *Letters*, 7:225.

10

To Elizabeth Gibbes[206]

15

>>>>Epworth
>>>>July 3, 1784

My Dear Miss Gibbes,
   I am now and shall be for a day or two longer, in the little town
where I first saw the light and which (by a very odd, though com-   20
mon, instinct) I think the pleasantest place in the world. What is
it that so endears our native place to us? Is it this, that it contains
the company which we love best? Surely this is one reason. For this
reason it is that I think the house in Hilton Park so pleasant. Very
possibly I should not think so, if any other family lived there.   25
   I am afraid, it will not be in my power to wait upon you this year,
in my return to London. I shall be obliged to spend the residue of
this month in and near Leeds. And thence to go through Nottingham, Birmingham, and Worcester into Wales, which I have not seen
these two years. I do not expect to reach Bristol till about the end   30
of August. From thence, after taking a large circuit, I am to return
to London.
   There is a great depth of sense in Lord Clarendon's *History* as
well as of piety.[207] We have hardly any history in the English tongue
that is to be compared to it. A little partiality we may expect to find   35
even in this (which is indeed scarce separable from human nature),
but I really think as little as can be found in any writer of that pe-

---

[206] JW was replying to a letter from Elizabeth Gibbes, which is not known to survive.
[207] Edward Hyde, Earl of Clarendon, *The History of the Rebellion and Civil Wars in England* (1641–1660), 2nd edn., 6 vols. (Oxford: Sheldonian Theatre, 1705–06). Cf. JW to Samuel
Furly, Mar. 7, 1758, 27:117 in this edn.; and JW to [Mary Lewis], c. Sept. 1778, 29:436 in this
edn.

riod, wherein men's passions were so exceedingly inflamed on both sides that few could see any thing good but in their own party.

I cannot but commend Mr. Gibbes for choosing to be of some profession.[208] It will employ many hours, which might otherwise hang heavy on his hands. And he may pursue it just as far as he pleases, and as agrees with his other employments. It is likewise proper for a person of some eminence to be well acquainted with the laws of his country. I was agreeably surprised, when Mr. Monckton (whom I had heard mentioned at the Park) took acquaintance with me.[209] And when he told he was canvassing for a seat in Parliament, it readily occurred an honest man may frequently be of service to his country, though he can only say yes or no.

Whether the weather be wet or dry, hot or cold, it is the same thing to me. I am fitted for the work I am called to. And indeed have full as much strength and considerably better health at eighty-one than I had at twenty-one. We have had much rain and much cold in the north of England, but no blights at all. Corn, grass, and all the other productions of the earth smile in an uncommon manner. Surely if we could but trust the governor of the world, he would give us nothing but good!

But my dear Miss Gibbes, consider! You m⟨ust⟩[210] not commend me! For I can scarce help believing everything *you* say.

I almost wondered that I heard nothing either from you, or from my dear Miss Aggy for so long a time![211] There are few persons in England whose letters are so acceptable as yours to, my dear Miss Gibbes,

      Your ever affectionate servant,

                            J. Wesley

My best wishes attend the good family.

Address: 'To / Miss Gibbes / At Sir Philip Gibbes' Bart / In Hilton Park / Near Wolverhampton / Staffordshire'.
Source: holograph; National Archives, PRO 30/9/7/15.

---

[208] It is unclear whether this reference is to Sir Philip Gibbes or to one of his sons.
[209] Edward Monckton (1744–1832), who returned to England in 1778, after sixteen years of civil service in the East India Company, to reside in Somerford Hall, and in 1780 was elected an MP for Staffordshire.
[210] A small piece of the right margin is torn away, affecting one word.
[211] Her sister Agnes Gibbes.

To Arthur Keene

near Leeds
July 23, 1784

My Dear Brother,

It is strange! Two or three weeks ago I was observing, 'I have exactly the same strength and more health at eighty-one than I had at twenty-one.'[212] This hath God wrought.

The Irish preachers have shown both their understanding and their uprightness. I am glad they and you are satisfied with the Declaration, and see Mr. Hampson's wonderful *Appeal* in its true light.[213] Humanly speaking it must do abundance of mischief. But God is over all.

I am in great hopes Mr. Rogers will be useful.[214] He is an Israelite indeed.[215]

I think a cupboard, secured as you intend, will do full as well as an iron chest.

Now Arthur, I will try if you do love me. If you do, serve my friend, poor sister [Isabel] Hyde.[216] Exert yourself to procure employment for her son, who is capable of almost anything. Send me word 'it is done'.

I am, with kind love to sister [Isabella] Keene, dear Arthur,
    Your affectionate friend and brother,

J. Wesley

Address: 'To / Mr. Arthur Keene / Near Dublin'.
Source: holograph; MHS Ireland Archives.

[212] Cf. JW, *Journal*, June 28, 1784 (23:319 in this edn.), where he makes a similar comment on his birthday, though reaching back only to age 42.

[213] The moves JW took in 1783 to insure that deeds of Methodist preaching-houses require preachers to be appointed by Conference heightened concern about how Conference would be constituted after JW's death. In response JW filed in Feb. 1784 a 'Deed of Declaration' that limited 'Conference', for legal purposes, to one hundred preachers—out of nearly two hundred currently active (the text of the Deed can be found in 10:949–56 in this edn.) .This naturally raised questions among those omitted from the 'legal one hundred', especially seasoned travelling preachers. One of these, John Hampson Sr., took the lead in preparing and publishing *An Appeal to the Reverend John and Charles Wesley*, seeking to set aside this change (see in-letters, c. July 1, 1784). At the Conference of Methodist preachers in Ireland, in early July, this issue had been debated and the Deed upheld; see 10:973–74 in this edn. The outcome was the same at the larger Conference in England that took place in late July (although the debate was intense, and was not mentioned in the formal *Minutes*; see 10:546–49 in this edn.).

[214] James Rogers had just been appointed as the Assistant for the Dublin circuit.

[215] See John 1:47.

[216] Orig., 'Hyden'. The son is referred to as 'Robert Hide' in JW to Keene, Feb. 17, 1785. 'Hyde' would be the common Irish spelling of the surname. Cooney, 'Dublin Society', 52, lists Robert Hyde as a member of Keene's class in Dublin (p. 52) and Isabel Hyde (living at a separate address from Robert) as part of a class for women.

To Frances Godfrey[217]

Leeds
July 31, 1784

5   My Dear Sister,

I thank you for giving me so full an account of that extraordinary deliverance.[218] I doubt not but those that were called epileptic fits were owing to a messenger of Satan whom God permitted to buffet you. Therefore all human helps were vain. Nothing but the
10 power of God could deliver you. And if you continue to walk humbly and closely with God, he will continue to bruise Satan under your feet,[219] and will add bodily health to the spirit of an healthful mind. Do all you can for so good a Master! And see that you go on to perfection,[220] till you know all that love of God that passeth
15 knowledge.[221]

I am, my dear sister,
Your affectionate brother,

[J. Wesley]

20 *Address*: 'To Miss Frances Godfrey, of Gainsborough'.
Source: published transcription; Jackson, *Works* (3rd), 13:36.

25 ## To Agnes Gibbes

Leeds
August 1, 1784

30 Forgive me, my dear Miss Agnes, my unjust apprehensions.[222] I began to be apprehensive from your long silence that you had almost forgotten me. But I am well pleased to find you have some regard for me still. I hope nothing will ever be able to deprive you of that amiable

---

[217] We know of JW's letters to Frances Godfrey only through their published transcription by Jackson, who says she was unmarried at the time and lived in Gainsborough. She may be the woman of this name baptized in 1758 in Gainsborough; daughter of Joseph Godfrey (d. 1767) and Susannah (Stead) Godfrey.

[218] Her letter with this account is not known to survive.

[219] See Rom. 16:20.

[220] See Heb. 6:1.

[221] See Eph. 3:19.

[222] Agnes Gibbes was apparently moved to write JW by his comment in a letter to her sister Elizabeth (on July 3, 1784) that he wondered why he had not heard from her for so long.

openness of spirit. But there will ⟨be⟩²²³ great danger if you live a few
years longer ⟨and⟩ come to be more acquainted with the world. For
there is some truth in that melancholy assertion of a very ingenious
man. 'There is in everyone that is young a measure of sincerity and
of disinterested benevolence. But when they come to be hackneyed in 5
the ways of men, they find nothing but guile and selfishness in every
man. Hence the little stock they had of truth and love in a little time
wastes away. And in a few years they learn as much disguised selfishness as those that are round about them.'

Truly if this was a just representation of mankind, I know not 10
who would wish to live thirty years! If we must needs outlive all our
sincerity and all our benevolence! Yet I cannot tell but there is some
truth in this with regard to the men of the world. I know not but it
may be generally true, in respect of those who have no religion; I
mean, ⟨thereby⟩²²⁴ heart religion. No such religion as is ⟨de⟩scribed 15
in Mr. Law's *Serious Call*.²²⁵ I ha⟨ve⟩ seen in a thousand instances
that all *their* professions of truth and friendship are mere grimace.
You cannot depend upon one word that they say. But here, as in
every other instance, religion quite alters the case.

Although that is a sure truth, 'He that fears no God can love no 20
friend,'²²⁶ yet on the other hand, he that truly fears God will continually increase both in sincerity and in benevolence.

I scarce ever remember having so strong a regard for any person
on so short an acquaintance, as I feel f⟨or ...²²⁷⟩ at the Park. I ⟨...⟩
for many year⟨s ...⟩ of seeing you ⟨... I must⟩ visit south Wa⟨les ... 25
⟩ in the end of ⟨...⟩ at Bristol. ⟨...⟩ never forsake ⟨...⟩ be written on
⟨....⟩ Whatever a⟨...⟩ altogether a ⟨Christian ...⟩ more and more
⟨... is the⟩ wish of

Your ⟨affectionate friend and brother⟩,

J. Wesley 30

My best wishes attend all the family.

Postmark: 'Leeds'.
Source: holograph; National Archives, PRO 30/9/11/2.

---

²²³ A portion of the left margin is torn away by the wax seal, affecting two lines.

²²⁴ The portion removed by the wax seal affects three lines on this side of the page.

²²⁵ William Law, *A Serious Call to a Devout and Holy Life* (London: William Innys, 1729);
JW published an abridged version in 1744 (*Bibliography*, No. 86).

²²⁶ Torquato Tasso, *Godfrey of Bulloigne, or the Recovery of Jerusalem*, translated in verse
by Edward Fairfax (London: Hatfield, 1600), Book IV, st. 65.

²²⁷ On the third leaf of this letter a large portion is torn away on the right margin, affecting 12 lines (and the address portion on the other side). About two-thirds of each line (5 to 7
words) is missing.

To Mary Bishop[228]

Haverfordwest
August 18, 1784

5 My Dear Miss Bishop,
    From the time I heard you were rejected by Lady Huntingdon,[229]
I have had a tender regard for you, and a strong hope that, without
regard to the wisdom or spirit or customs of the world, you would
(as those at Publow did once[230])

10
                Square your useful life below
                By reason and by grace.[231]

    Hitherto you have not at all deceived my hope, and I am persuaded
15 you never will.
    In some of the young ones you will undoubtedly find your labour
has not been in vain.[232] What they will be one cannot judge yet;
therefore Solomon's advice is good, 'In the morning sow thy seed,
and in the evening withhold not thy hand; for thou knowest not
20 which shall prosper.'[233]
    It seems God himself has already decided the question concern-
ing dancing. He hath shown his approbation of your conduct by
sending those children to you again. If dancing be not evil in itself,
yet it leads young women to numberless evils. And the hazard of
25 these on the one side seems far to overbalance the little inconveniences on the other. Therefore thus much may certainly be said,
You have chosen the more excellent way.[234]
    I would recommend very few novels to young persons, for fear
they should be too desirous of more. Mr. Brooke wrote one more
30 (besides the *Earl of Moreland*), *The History of the Human Heart*.[235]
I think it is well worth reading; though it is not equal to his former

---

[228] JW was replying to Bishop's letter of Aug. 10, 1784. There had been a three year hiatus
since their last exchange July 17, 1781.

[229] See JW to Mary Bishop, Nov. 5, 1769, 28:252–53 in this edn.

[230] Mrs. Hannah Owen and her daughters; cf. JW to Bishop, May 22, 1781, 29:649 in
this edn.

[231] Cf. CW, 'For a Family of Believers', st. 3, *Family Hymns* (1767), 38.

[232] Bishop had launched a new school in Keynsham in 1781.

[233] Eccles.11:6.

[234] See Luke 10:42.

[235] Henry Brooke, *The Fool of Quality; or, The History of Henry, Earl of Moreland*, 5 vols.
(London: W. Johnston, 1766–70); and *Juliet Grenville; or, the History of the Human Heart*, 3
vols. (Dublin: James Williams, 1774).

production. The want of novels may be supplied by well-chosen histories; such as, *The Concise History of England*, *The Concise History of the Church*, Rollin's *Ancient History*, Hooke's *Roman History* (the only impartial one extant), and a few more.[236] For the elder and more sensible children, Malebranche's *Search after Truth* is an excellent French book.[237] Perhaps you might add Locke's *Essay on the Human Understanding*, with the remarks in the *Arminian Magazine*.[238] I had forgotten that beautiful book *The Travels of Cyrus*, whether in French or English.[239]

On the 28th instant I hope to be at Bristol, and not long after at Keynsham.

I always am, my dear Miss Bishop,
    Your affectionate friend and brother,

J. Wesley

Address: 'To / Miss Bishop / In Keynsham / Somersetshire'.
Endorsement: (by Bishop), '38th'.
Source: holograph; Wesley's Chapel (London), LDWMM 1997/6717.

To Elizabeth Ritchie

Tracwn, Pembrokeshire
August 19, 1784

My Dear Betsy,

I was a little surprised at a letter from sister D[obinson?],[240] in which she seems to approve of all that Mrs. [Sarah] Crosby has

---

[236] JW, *A Concise History of England* (1776); JW, *A Concise Ecclesiastical History* (1781); Charles Rollin, *The Ancient History of the Egyptians, Carthaginians, Assyrians, Babylonians, Medes and Persians, Macedonians and Grecians*, 13 vols. (London: Knapton, 1734–39); and Nathaniel Hooke, *The Roman History; from the Building of Rome to the Ruin of the Commonwealth*, 11 vols. (London: Hawkins, 1766–71).

[237] Nicolas Malebranche, *De la Recherche de la Verité; ou, l'on traitte de la nature de l'esprit de l'homme, & de l'usage qu'il en doit faire pour éviter l'erreur dans les sciences* (Paris: Andre Pralard, 1674).

[238] John Locke, *An Essay concerning Human Understanding* (London: Thomas Bassett, 1689); and 'Remarks upon Mr. Locke's Essay on Human Understanding', serialized from *AM* 5 (1782): 27–30 through *AM* 7 (1784): 314–16.

[239] Andrew Michael Ramsay, *Les Voyages de Cyrus, avec un discours sur la Mythologie*, 2 vols. (Paris: Gabriel-Francois Quillau); *ET: The Travels of Cyrus;* to which is annexed *A Discourse upon the Theology and Mythology of the Ancients*, 2 vols. (London: T. Woodward & J. Peele, 1727).

[240] Rachel Dobinson had hosted Elizabeth Ritchie in her home; see Ritchie to JW, May 20, 1780. She became a close associate of Sarah Crosby.

done; and speaks as if it were just and right and done in obedience to the order of providence! I could not help saying, 'There
is but one advice which I can give her upon the present occasion:
"Remember from whence thou art fallen. Repent, and do thy first
5   works."'[241]

Some years ago I committed a little company of lovely children to
the care of one of our sisters at Haverford[west].[242] I was concerned
yesterday to find she was weary of well-doing and had totally given
up her charge. I hope, my dear Betsy, this will never be your case!
10   You will never leave off your labour of love, though you should not
always (not immediately, at least) see the fruit of your labours. You
may not immediately see Mrs. H[orner] so established in grace as
you desire and hope.[243] But in this, as well as many other instances,
in due time 'you shall reap if you faint not'.[244]

15   I have been often musing upon this, why the generality of Christians, even those that really are such, are less zealous and less active for God When they are middle-aged than they were when they
were young. May we not draw an answer to this question from that
declaration of our Lord (no less than eight times repeated by the
20   evangelists), 'To him that hath', uses what he hath, 'shall be given;
but from him that hath not shall be taken away that he hath'?[245]
A measure of zeal and activity is given to everyone when he finds
peace with God. If he earnestly and diligently uses this talent, it
will surely be increased. But if he ceases (yea, or intermits) to do
25   good, he insensibly loses both the will and the power. So there is
no possible way to retain those talents but to use them to the uttermost. Let this never be the case of my dear friend! Never abate anything of your diligence in doing good. Sometimes indeed the feeble
body sinks under you; but when you do all you can, you do enough.
30   Remember in all your prayers,
        Yours most affectionately,

                                                        J. Wesley

Source: published transcription; Benson, *Works*, 16:253–54.

---

[241] Rev. 2:5.
[242] Catherine Warren; see JW to Warren, Oct. 19, 1779, 29:516 in this edn.
[243] Richie mentions Mrs. Horner in a letter to JW dated Jan. 10, 1782.
[244] Cf. Gal. 6:9.
[245] Cf. Matt. 13:12, 25:29; Mark 4:25; Luke 8:18, 12:48, 19:26; and John 15:2.

To Samuel Wesley (nephew)[246]

Trecwn [Pembrokeshire]
August 19, 1784

Dear Sammy,

As I have had a regard for you ever since you was a little one, I have often thought of writing to you freely. I am persuaded what is spoken in love will be taken in love. And if so, if it does you no good, it will do you no harm.

Many years ago I observed that as it had pleased God to give you a remarkable talent for music, so he had given you a quick apprehension of other things, a capacity for making some progress in learning, and (what is of far greater value) a desire to be a Christian. But meantime I have often been pained for you, fearing you did not set out the right way. I do not mean with regard to this or that set of opinions (Protestant or Romish)—all these I trample underfoot; but with regard to those weightier matters wherein, if they go wrong, either Protestants or papists will perish everlastingly. I feared you was not *born again*; and 'except a man be born again', if we may credit the Son of God, 'he cannot see the kingdom of heaven'.[247] Except he experience that inward change of the earthly, sensual mind for the mind which was in Christ Jesus.[248] You might have throughly understood the scriptural doctrine of the new birth, yea and experienced it long before now, had you used the many opportunities of improvement which God put into your hand while you believed both your father and me to be teachers sent from God. But alas! What are you now? Whether of this church or that, I care not. You may be saved in either, or damned in either. But I fear you are not born again, and 'except you be born again you cannot see the kingdom of God'.[249] You believe the Church of Rome is right. What

[246] This is the first surviving letter of JW to his nephew Samuel, the son of Charles and Sarah (Gwynne) Wesley. It was an unsolicited response to public awareness that Samuel had 'converted' to the Church of Rome. Samuel began attending services in Roman Catholic chapels at foreign embassies in London around fall of 1778, to hear their musical settings of worship. His interaction with Roman Catholic priests and with Mary Freeman Shepherd led Samuel to join the Roman church formally sometime in late 1783. He tried to keep this quiet, so as not to hurt his parents, but reports surfaced of him assisting at a Mass. See Samuel's letter to Mary Freeman Shepherd, Dec. 26, 1783 (in the 'in-letters' collection); Mary Freeman Shepherd's later summary of events to Sarah Wesley Jr. in a letter on Mar. 12, 1794 (MARC, MA 1977/428/1/26a); and Philip Olleson, *Samuel Wesley* (Woodbridge: Boydell, 2003), 12–24.

[247] Cf. John 3:3.

[248] See Phil. 2:5.

[249] John 3:3.

then? If you are not born of God, *you* are of *no church*. Whether Bellamine or Luther be right,[250] you are certainly wrong if you are not born of the Spirit—if you are not renewed in the spirit of your mind in the likeness of him that created you.[251]

5   I doubt you was never deeply convinced of the necessity of this great change. And there is now greater danger than ever that you never will [be convinced], that you will be diverted from the thought of it by a train of new notions, new practices, new modes of worship. All of which put together (not to consider whether they
10 are unscriptural, superstitious, and idolatrous, or no—I would as soon pick *straws* as dispute of this with *you* in your present state of mind); all, I say, put together, do not amount to one grain of true, vital, spiritual religion.

    O Sammy, you are out of your way! You are out of God's way! You
15 have not given him your heart. You have not found (nay, it is well if you have so much as sought) happiness in God! And poor zealots, while you are in this state of mind, would puzzle you about this or the other *church*! O fools and blind! Such guides as these lead men by shoals to the bottomless pit.[252]

20   My dear Sammy, your first point is to repent and believe the gospel.[253] Know yourself a poor, guilty, helpless sinner! Then know Jesus Christ and him crucified![254] Let the Spirit of God bear witness with your spirit that you are a child of God.[255] And let the love of God be shed abroad in your heart by the Holy Ghost, which is
25 given unto you.[256] And then, if you have no better work, I will talk with you of transubstantiation or purgatory.

    Meantime I commend you to him who is able to guide you into all truth;[257] and am, dear Sammy,

        Your affectionate uncle,

30   J. Wesley

Spread this letter before God, not before man!
I expect to be at Bristol next week.

---

[250] Martin Luther (1483–1546), the Protestant reformer; and Robert Bellarmine (1542–1621), the apologist for the Church of Rome.
[251] See Eph. 4:23–24.
[252] See Matt. 15:14.
[253] See Mark 1:15.
[254] See 1 Cor. 2:2.
[255] See Rom. 8:16.
[256] See Rom. 5:5.
[257] See John 16:13.

Address: To / Mr Samuel Wesley / In Chesterfield Street / Marybone / London'.
Endorsement: by Samuel, 'From / The Revd. Mr John Wesley / August 19th, 1784'.
Source: holograph; Wesley's Chapel (London), LDWMM 1997/6598.   5

To Robert Jones Jr.[258]   10

Cardiff
August 27, 1784

Dear Sir,

If you go abroad, I would by no means advise you to go to   15
France. That is no place to save expense; but it is the only place
to make your sons coxcombs and your daughters coquettes. I cannot but think there is no country in Europe which would answer
your design so well as Holland; and no place in Holland so well as
Utrecht.[259] It is within a day's journey of Helvoetsluys, whence you   20
go directly by the packet for England. It is an healthful and a pleasant city, and less expensive than almost any city in France. You may
have more or less company as you please. There are schools for your
children; and if you should choose it, an university for your sons.
And I could recommend you to some valuable acquaintance. I speak   25
freely, because I have your interest at heart. Think of it, and send
your thoughts to, dear sir,

Your affectionate servant,

J. Wesley   30

Address: 'To / Robert Jones Esq.'.[260]
Source: holograph; Cardiff, Wales, Glamorgan Archives, DF/WES.

[258] Although he did not include mention in his published *Journal*, JW apparently met with Robert Jones Jr. when he was in Cardiff on Aug. 26, 1784. The son of Robert and Mary (Forrest) Jones, early supporters of the Wesley brothers in Cardiff, Robert Jr. was sent by his mother to Kingswood School for a time, but proved ill-suited to that setting (see William Spencer to JW, Aug. 9, 1748; 26:320–21 in this edn.; JW to Mary Jones, Nov. 7, 1749, 26:393–94; and JW to Samuel Lloyd, July 3, 1751, 26:467–68). Robert Jr. resumed a more cordial relationship with JW in later years (cf. JW, *Journal*, Aug. 23, 1758, 21:162 in this edn.), which would explain JW learning of his anticipated trip to Europe.
[259] Recall JW's visit to Holland in June 1783.
[260] This note was likely hand-delivered.

To Joseph Taylor

Bristol
August 30, 1784

5   Dear Joseph,
    On no account whatever can I excuse any preacher in the con-
nexion from using his utmost endeavours for the preachers going
to America.[261] What is the furnishing a room or two in comparison
of this? Especially for one who is well able to do it for herself! I
10 wonder she should desire it or indeed accept of it! However, if this
be done, the other must not be left undone.
    I am, dear Joseph,
        Your affectionate friend and brother,

J. Wesley

15 *Address*: 'To / Mr Taylor / At the Preachinghouse / in / Stroud / +post
    [i.e., crosspost]'.
    Postmark: 'Bristol'. *Charge*: '3'.
    Source: holograph; MARC, MAM JW 5/11.

20

To Ann Bolton[262]

Bristol
25   August 31, 1784

My Dear Sister,
    Many years ago Mr. Hall (then strong in faith) believed God
called him to marry my youngest sister.[263] He told her so. She fully
30 believed him, and none could convince one or the other to the contrary. I talked with her about it, but she had 'so often made it matter
of prayer that she could not be deceived'. In a week he dropped her,
courted her elder sister, and as soon as was convenient married her.

---

[261] Thomas Vasey and Richard Whatcoat (along with Thomas Coke) volunteered to go
and assist Methodists in the former British colonies of North America, and were approved for
this task by the 1784 Conference in late July (see 10:557 in this edn.). They were currently raising support for the cost of the voyage. Joseph Taylor was Assistant of the Gloucester circuit; it
is unclear who in this circuit was hesitant about providing some type of assistance.

[262] Bolton appears to have written JW about another twist in her relationship with and
contemplated marriage to John Arundel. Cf. JW to Bolton, May 8, 1780, 29:568 in this edn.;
and JW to Bolton, Feb. 16, 1785.

[263] Referring to Hall's brief courtship of Kezia Wesley, before he opted instead to marry
Martha Wesley. Cf. JW to Westley Hall, Dec. 22, 1747, 26:269–73 in this edn.

The disappointed one then found exactly the same temptations that you do now. But neither did she keep the devil's counsel. She told me all that was in her heart. And the consequence was that by the grace of God she gained a complete victory. So will *you*.

And you will be the better enabled by your own experience to guard all, especially young persons, from laying stress upon anything but the written Word of God. Guard them against reasoning in that dangerous manner: 'If I was deceived in this, then I was deceived in thinking myself justified.' Not at all; although nature, or Satan in the latter case, admirably well mimicked the works of God. By mighty prayer repel all those suggestions, and afterwards your faith will be so much the more strengthened, and you will be more than conqueror through him that loveth you.[264] Whenever you find yourself pressed above measure, you must make another little excursion. While you help others, God will help *you*. This may be one end of this uncommon dispensation. You must not bury your talent in the earth.[265]

Wishing you more and more of that

Lovely, lasting peace of mind,[266]

I am,
    Yours most affectionately,

J. Wesley

Source: published transcription; Benson, *Works*, 16:233–34.

To Christopher Hopper[267]

Bristol
August 31, 1784

My Dear Brother,

It was *your* part to write to me of the behaviour of William Eells, particularly at Warrington, without waiting till I heard of it from so

---

[264] See Rom. 8:37.
[265] See Matt. 25:25.
[266] Thomas Parnell, 'Hymn to Contentment', *l.* 1; in JW, *MSP* (1744), 1:265.
[267] While the address portion is missing, Hopper was Assistant over the Bolton circuit, with Eells serving under his supervision.

many other persons.[268] Seeing I find I cannot overcome him by love,
I am at length constrained to let him drop. Pray inform him he is no
longer in the number of our itinerant preachers. I shall today send
another preacher to supply his place in the Bolton circuit. I have
5   done all I could to save him. But it is in vain, so I must at length
give him up.
     I am
          Your affectionate brother and friend,

                                                       J. Wesley
10

Source: holograph; Bridwell Library (SMU).

15

               For the Rev. Dr. Thomas Coke
                   Testimonial Letter[269]

20   [Bristol]
                                          [September 2, 1784]

     To all to whom these presents shall come, John Wesley, late Fel-
low of Lincoln College in Oxford, Presbyter of the Church of Eng-
25   land, sendeth greeting.
     Whereas many of the people in the southern provinces of North
America who desire to continue under my care and still adhere to
the doctrines and discipline of the Church of England are greatly
distressed for want of ministers to administer the sacraments of
30   baptism and the Lord's Supper according to the usage of the said
Church; and whereas there does not appear to be any other way of
supplying them with ministers:
     Know all men that I, John Wesley, think myself to be providen-
tially called at this time to set apart some persons to the work of

---

[268] William Eells was one of the preachers disgruntled about being left out of 'the legal
hundred' named in the 1784 Deed of Declaration. At the 1784 Conference he sided with John
Hampson, but (unlike Hampson) did not resign from the connexion when the Deed was upheld. JW's resolve, expressed in this letter, led Eells to conform for the time (see JW to Hopper,
Sept. 11, 1784). But he joined John Atlay in leaving the connexion in 1788, due to controversy
over the chapel in Dewsbury; see JW, *Journal*, Aug. 1, 1789, 24:148 in this edn.).

[269] This is the first of the public letters that JW provided for each person whom he formally ordained (or 'set apart') as deacon, elder, or superintendent. For background and more
details see Appendix B.

the ministry in America. And therefore under the protection of Almighty God, and with a single eye to his glory, I have this day set apart as a superintendent, by the imposition of my hands and prayer (being assisted by other ordained ministers[270]), Thomas Coke, Doctor of Civil Law, a Presbyter of the Church of England, and a man whom I judge to be well qualified for that great work. And I do hereby recommend him to all whom it may concern as a fit person to preside over the flock of Christ. In testimony whereof I have hereunto set my hand and seal this second day of September, in the year of our Lord one thousand seven hundred and eighty-four.

John Wesley[271]

Source: holograph; Wesley's Chapel (London), LDWMM 1992/392.[272]

For Thomas Vasey
Testimonial Letter[273]

[Bristol]
[September 2, 1784]

To all to whom these presents shall come, John Wesley, late fellow of Lincoln College in Oxford, Presbyter of the Church of England, sendeth greeting.

Whereas many of the people in the southern provinces of North America who desire to continue under my care and still adhere to the doctrines and discipline of the Church of England are greatly distressed, for want of ministers to administer the sacraments of baptism and the Lord's Supper according to the usage of the said Church; and whereas there does not appear to be any other way of supplying them with ministers:

---

[270] James Creighton; and apparently the newly-ordained elders Thomas Vasey and Richard Whatcoat.

[271] The text of the letter is in the hand of James Creighton; only the signature is by JW.

[272] Facsimile copies reside at MARC, WCB, E4/1/2–3; and Duke, Rubenstein, Frank Baker Collection of Wesleyana, Box WF5.

[273] For background and more details see Appendix B. Thomas Coke and James Creighton joined with JW in the ordination.

Know all men that I, John Wesley, think myself to be providentially called at this time to set apart some persons to the work of the ministry in America. And therefore under the protection of Almighty God, and with a single eye to his glory, I have this day
5   set apart for the said work, as an elder, by the imposition of my hands and prayer (being assisted by two other ordained ministers), Thomas Vasey, a man whom I judge to be well qualified for that great work. And I do hereby recommend him to all whom it may concern as a fit person to feed the flock of Christ, and to adminis-
10   ter baptism and the Lord's Supper according to the usage of the Church of England. In testimony whereof, I have hereunto set my hand and seal this second day of September, in the year of our Lord one thousand seven hundred and eighty-four.

                                                              John Wesley
15

Source: published report; *WHS* 32 (1959): 63.[274]

20

For Richard Whatcoat
Testimonial Letter[275]

                                                              [Bristol]
25   [September 2, 1784]

To all to whom these presents shall come, John Wesley, late fellow of Lincoln College in Oxford, Presbyter of the Church of England, sendeth greeting.
30   Whereas many of the people in the southern provinces of North America who desire to continue under my care and still adhere to the doctrines and discipline of the Church of England are greatly distressed, for want of ministers to administer the sacraments of baptism and the Lord's Supper according to the usage of the said
35   Church; and whereas there does not appear to be any other way of supplying them with ministers:

---

[274] In 1924 the letter was in the possession of Ernest F. Pawson, descendant of Marmaduke Pawson (a brother of John Pawson). Pawson sent a transcription to F. F. Bretherton, showing that it was identical in wording—other than the name—to that of Whatcoat (which follows).

[275] For background and more details see Appendix B. Thomas Coke and James Creighton joined with JW in the ordination.

Know all men that I, John Wesley, think myself to be providentially called at this time to set apart some persons to the work of
the ministry in America. And therefore under the protection of Almighty God, and with a single eye to his glory, I have this day set
apart for the said work, as an elder, by the imposition of my hands   5
and prayer (being assisted by two other ordained ministers), Richard Whatcoat, a man whom I judge to be well qualified for that great
work. And I do hereby recommend him to all whom it may concern
as a fit person to feed the flock of Christ, and to administer baptism
and the Lord's Supper according to the usage of the Church of   10
England. In testimony whereof, I have hereunto set my hand and
seal this second day of September, in the year of our Lord one thousand seven hundred and eighty-four.

John Wesley
                                                                    15

Source: published transcription; Peter P. Sandford, *Memoirs of Mr. Wes-
     ley's Missionaries to America* (New York: Lane and Sandford, 1843),
     363.

                                                                    20

To Ann Tindall

Bristol   25
September 4, 1784
My Dear Sister,
I am glad you had an opportunity of spending so much time with
your sister, whose desires were grown exceeding cold.[276] I hope your
company, especially at so critical a season may be a means of her   30
seeking God more earnestly than she has ever done yet.[277]
Your vicar is a bold man. I know not that anyone for these forty
years before has ventured to preach such a sermon before my face.
It had one awkward effect. I could not insist on our people's going
to Church, as I designed to do.[278]   35

---

[276] Jane Tindall (1760–1800) married John Thornton (1754–1832) in 1781. Both Jane and
John were later active at City Road Chapel and are buried there; see Stevenson, *City Road*, 361.
     [277] Jane (Tindall) Thornton was currently living in Bradford and gave birth about this
time to a son William, baptized Oct. 24, 1784.
     [278] Rev. John Kirk (1753–1827), a native of Scarborough, was named vicar there in late
1782. See JW's reflections on the sermon that Kirk preached on June 20, 1784 (with JW in the
audience) in *Journal*, 23:317 in this edn.

I take Mr. King to be a man much devoted to God, and expect you will see a good work this year.[279]

It is well you have settled the house.[280] It can now be no longer objected, 'We do not know what the word *Conference* means.' And every impartial person may see how much more desirable it is that any preaching-house should be at the disposal of an hundred, than of six or seven trustees.

I am, my dear sister,
    Your affectionate brother,

J. Wesley

Address: 'To / Miss Tindall / in / Scarborough'.
Postmarks: 'Bristol' and '6/SE'.
Endorsement: by Tindall, '4th Sept 1784'.
Source: holograph; British Library, Department of Manuscripts, Add. MS. 43695, ff. 81–82.

To William Pitt (the Younger)[281]

Bath
September 6, 1784

Sir,

Your former goodness shown to one of my relations, Mr. Thomas Ellison,[282] emboldens me to take the liberty of recommending to your notice an old friend, Lieutenant [Thomas] Webb. On my mentioning formerly some of his services and losses to Lord [Frederick]

[279] John King (1752–1822), a native of Guisborough, Yorkshire, was converted in his late teens and began to serve as a local preacher. He was admitted 'on trial' as an itinerant in 1783 (see 10:531 in this edn.), and had been appointed by the 1784 Conference to the Scarborough circuit (10:556). King retired in 1811 and spent his last years in Sevenoaks. See *Minutes* (post-Wesley, 1823), 5:382–83; and a 'Memoir' in *WMM* 47 (1824): 1–8.

[280] I.e., that the preaching-house in Scarborough had adopted the 'model deed'; see 'Large' *Minutes* (1763), §67, 10:868–70 in this edn. Cf. JW to Tindall, Feb. 1, 1782.

[281] William Pitt the younger (1759–1806) became Prime Minister in Dec. 1783. He inherited a disastrous economic situation (due in large part to several preceding years at war). The British national debt stood at £250 million, while the annual revenue from taxes was only £12.5 million from taxes. Pitt adopted several strategies over the coming years to reduce spending and raise income.

[282] If 'Thomas' is correct, this would be Thomas Farr Ellison (b. 1764) of Bristol, the son of JW's nephew John Ellison (1720–91). It is possible JW misspoke here, meaning to refer to his nephew John instead. In neither case is it clear what 'goodness' was shone.

North, his lordship was pleased to order him £100 a year. But as it has since been reduced, it is hardly a maintenance for himself and his family. If you would be so good as to remember him in this or any other way, I should esteem it a particular favour.

Will you excuse me, sir, for going out of my province by hinting a few things which have been long upon my mind? If those hints do not deserve any further notice, they may be forgiven and forgotten. 5

New taxes must undoubtedly be imposed; but may not more money be produced by the old ones? For instance:

1. When the land tax is four shillings in the pound, I know some towns which pay regularly seven or five pence.[283] Nay, I know one town where they pay one penny in the pound. Is there no help for this? 10

2. As to window tax: I know a gentleman who has near an hundred windows in his house; he told me he paid for twenty.[284] 15

3. The same gentleman told me, 'We have above an hundred *man-servants* in this town, but not above ten are paid for.'[285]

4. I firmly believe that in Cornwall alone the king is defrauded of half a million yearly in customs. What does this amount to in all Great Britain? Surely not so little as five millions. Is there no way of extirpating those smuggling villains, notwithstanding their Honourable or Right Honourable abettors? 20

5. Servants of distillers inform me that their masters do not pay for a fortieth part of what they distil. And this duty last year (if I am rightly informed) amounted only to £20,000. But have not the spirits distilled this year cost 20,000 lives of his Majesty's liege subjects? Is it not then the blood of these men, vilely bartered for £20,000? (Not to say anything of the enormous wickedness which has been occasioned thereby! And not to suppose that these poor wretches have any souls!) But to consider money alone, is the king a gainer or an immense loser by the distillery? To say nothing of many millions of quarters of corn destroyed, which if exported would have added more than £20,000 to the revenue. Be it considered that 'dead men pay no taxes'; so that by the death of 20,000 persons yearly (and this computation is far under the mark) the revenue loses far more than it gains.[286] 25 30 35

---

[283] A land-value tax had been in place in Great Britain since 1693.

[284] A window tax was instituted in England in 1696. It sought to impose a tax relative to the means of the taxpayer by taxing homes progressively for the more windows they possessed.

[285] Lord North introduced a man-servant tax in 1777 to help finance the American wars.

[286] This paragraph echoes JW's 1772 *Thoughts on the Present Scarcity of Provisions*, I.3 (vol. 15 in this edn.).

But I may urge another consideration to you. You are a *man*. You have not lost human feelings. You do not love to drink human blood. You are a son of Lord Chatham.[287] Nay, if I mistake not, you are a Christian. Dare you then sustain a sinking nation? Is the God
5   whom you serve able to deliver from ten thousand enemies? I believe he is. Nay, and *you* believe it. O may you fear nothing but displeasing him!

May I add a word on another head? How would your benevolent heart rejoice if a stop could be put to that scandal of the English
10 nation: suicide! The present laws against it avail nothing; for every such *murderer* is brought in *non compos*.[288] If he was poor, the jurors forswear themselves from pity. If he was rich, they hope to be well paid for it. So no ignominy pursues either the living or the dead, and self-murder increases daily. But what [may] help? I conceive
15 this horrid crime might be totally prevented, and that without doing the least hurt to either the living or the dead. Do you not remember, sir, how the rage for self-murder among the Spartan matrons was stopped at once? By ordering that the body of every woman that killed herself should be dragged naked through the streets of the
20 city.[289] Would it not have the same effect in England if an Act of Parliament were passed repealing all other acts and appointing that every self-murderer should be hanged in chains?[290]

Suppose your influence could prevent suicide by this means, and distilling by making it felony, you would do more service to your
25 country than any Prime Minister has done these hundred years. Your name would be precious to all true Englishmen as long as England continued a nation. And, what is infinitely more, a greater Monarch than King George would say to you, 'Well done, good and faithful servant.'[291]
30 I earnestly commit you to his care, and am, sir,

Your willing servant,

John Wesley

Source: secondary transcription; MARC, MA 1977/609.[292]

---

[287] William Pitt (1708–88), 1st Earl of Chatham.

[288] I.e., '*non compos mentis*'; mentally incompetent or insane.

[289] Cf. Plutarch, *Moralia: Bravery of Women*, #11, 'The Women of Miletus'.

[290] JW repeated this suggestion in his public letter on suicide, dated Apr. 8, 1790, Vol. 31 in this edn.

[291] Matt. 25:23.

[292] While not in JW's hand, he may have had an amanuensis make a copy for his records. MARC also holds a subsequent transcription by Eliza Tooth (MA 1977/502, p. 37).

To Sarah Wesley Jr.

Bristol
September 8, 1784

Dear Sally,   5

You do well to let me know when there is anything wherein it is
my power to serve you.[293] But I find you are not much acquainted
with poor folks. You must make a little money go a great way among
them unless you had a thousand a year. In common I myself give
but sixpence or a shilling to one person. (Nay, and a nobleman gen-   10
erally does no more.) The case must be very peculiar; otherwise I
do not rise so high as half a crown. Else my stock would soon be
exhausted.

'Why is that agreeable young woman', one asks me, 'so pale and
sickly?' Why, she eats trash; and while she does this, she can't have   15
health. Is it not your case? Do *you* eat trash: novels, romances, and
the like?[294] How can you then expect spiritual health? And I doubt
you eat (that is read) too much.

I am, dear Sally,

Yours very affectionately,   20

J. Wesley

Endorsement: 'Sepr. 8. 1784'.[295]
Source: holograph; MARC, DDWes 5/15.

25

To Dorothea (Garret / King) Johnson[296]

Bristol   30
September 9, 1784

My Dear Sister,

I sincerely congratulate my good old friend John Johnson and
you on your happy union. I am clearly persuaded that it is of God,

---

[293] Sarah had been in Bristol with her father CW in early Sept. Thus her inquiry to JW
may have been verbal, rather than in a letter (not known to survive).

[294] Cf. the list of recommended books to study JW sent exactly three years earlier; JW to
Sarah Wesley Jr., Sept. 8, 1781, 29:684–85 in this edn.

[295] There is also part of a poem in French transcribed on the verso.

[296] Dorothea (Garret) King married the retired itinerant John Johnson on Aug. 31 in
Dublin. She and JW had been correspondents since the early 1760s, and he published excerpts
from several of her letters in *AM*. Yet this is the first letter from JW to Dorothea which is
known to survive (cf. the postscript on JW to [Thomas Garret?], Sept. 28, 1767, 28:99.

and cannot doubt but it was his will and gracious providence which pointed out to you both the time and the persons. May you be a lasting blessing to each other!

But one thing has been much upon my mind. Both brother Johnson and you love the work of God, and would not easily be induced to take any step that would hinder it. But if so, I advise you by no means to think of leaving Dublin.[297] In the city, indeed, he cannot have health. But you may have an healthy abode in the skirts of it. Pray give my kind love to my dear sister Freeman.[298] Peace be with your spirits!

> I am, my dear sister,
>   Your invariable friend,
>
>   [J. Wesley]

Source: published transcription; Telford, *Letters*, 7:237.

To 'Our Brethren in America'[299]

Bristol
September 10, 1784

1. By a very uncommon train of providences many of the provinces of North America are totally disjoined from their mother country and erected into independent states. The English Government has no authority over them, either civil or ecclesiastical, any more than over the states of Holland. A civil authority is exercised over them, partly by the Congress, partly by the provincial Assemblies. But no one either exercises or claims any ecclesiastical authority at all.[300] In this peculiar situation some thousands of the inhabitants of these states desire my advice; and in compliance with their desire I have drawn up a little sketch.

---

[297] John Johnson had retired to Lisburn in northern Ireland, where Dorothea joined him. See JW's letters to the couple on Sept. 26, 1784.

[298] Jane Esther (Lee) Freeman, the widow of James Freeman.

[299] This letter, in which JW defends the moves he had taken to provide for his followers in North America, was published as a two-sided flyer, so that Coke, Vasey, and Whatcoat could carry copies when they departed from King's Road, Bristol, on Sept. 18, 1784. The letter reveals that JW had been preparing for this transition for several months—particularly in preparing the *Sunday Service*.

[300] Actually, specific ecclesial bodies retained establishment for several years in some states, particularly in the upper-northeast.

2. Lord King's *Account of the Primitive Church* convinced me many years ago that bishops and presbyters are the same order, and consequently have the same right to ordain.[301] For many years I have been importuned from time to time to exercise this right by ordaining part of our travelling preachers. But I have still refused, not only for peace' sake, but because I was determined as little as possible to violate the established order of the national Church to which I belonged.

3. But the case is widely different between England and North America. Here there are bishops who have a legal jurisdiction. In America there are none, neither any parish ministers.[302] So that for some hundred miles together there is none either to baptize or to administer the Lord's Supper. Here therefore my scruples are at an end—and I conceive myself at full liberty, as I violate no order and invade no man's right by appointing and sending labourers into the harvest.[303]

4. I have accordingly appointed Dr. [Thomas] Coke and Mr. Francis Asbury to be joint *Superintendents* over our brethren in North America; as also Richard Whatcoat and Thomas Vasey to act as *elders* among them, by baptizing and administering the Lord's Supper. And I have prepared a liturgy little differing from that of the Church of England[304] (I think, the best constituted national Church in the world), which I advise all the travelling preachers to use on the Lord's Day in all the congregations; reading the Litany only on Wednesdays and Fridays, and praying extempore on all other days. I also advise the elders to administer the Supper of the Lord on every Lord's Day.

5. If anyone will point out a more rational and scriptural way of feeding and guiding those poor sheep in the wilderness, I will glad-

---

[301] Peter King (1699–1734) served as Lord High Chancellor of Great Britain, 1725–33. JW is referring to King's *An Enquiry into the Constitution, Discipline, Unity, and Worship of the Primitive Church* (London: Robinson, 1691); cf. JW, *Journal*, Jan. 20, 1746, 20:112 in this edn. But note as well that in his letter making this point to CW, June 8, 1780 (29:574 in this edn.), JW cites Edward Stillingfleet, *Irenicum, A Weapon Salve for the Church's Wounds* (London, 1660).

[302] JW overstates the case. A number of Church of England elders serving as parish clergy remained in the former colonies and were trying to create a national episcopal Church in continuity with the Church of England. They had selected Samuel Seabury as their first bishop, but he was still seeking formal consecration back in Britain.

[303] See Matt. 9:38.

[304] *The Sunday Service of the Methodists in North America, with Other Occasional Services* (London: [Strahan], 1784); *Bibliography*, No. 433 (vol. 8 in this edn.).

ly embrace it. At present I cannot see any better method than that I have taken.

   6. It has, indeed, been proposed to desire the English bishops to ordain part of our preachers for America. But to this I object:
5 1) I desired the Bishop of London to ordain only one, but could not prevail.[305] 2) If they consented, we know the slowness of their proceedings; but the matter admits of no delay. 3) If they would ordain them *now*, they would likewise expect to govern them; and how grievously would this entangle us! 4) As our American breth-
10 ren are now totally disentangled both from the state and from the English hierarchy, we dare not entangle them again either with the one or the other. They are now at full liberty simply to follow the Scriptures and the primitive church. And we judge it best that they should stand fast in that liberty wherewith God has so strangely
15 made them free.[306]

                                                          John Wesley

Source: published broadsheet; *Bibliography*, no. 435.[307]

20

To Christopher Hopper[308]

25   Bristol
                                               September 11, 1784

My Dear Brother,
   The information I received was not from ___[309] but from the
30 body of leaders at Warrington and at Liverpool. But if the things which they mention were antecedent to the Conference, they may die and be forgotten. If brother [William] Eells behaves well *now*, I shall think no more of *past* things.

---

[305] See JW to Robert Lowth, Aug. 10, 1780, 29:589–91 in this edn.

[306] See Gal. 5:1.

[307] Copies of the broadsheet survive at Austin, Texas, Archives of the Episcopal Church, White Mss. Vol. 3, #110; MARC, MA 1977/502; and Pitts Library (Emory), John Wesley Papers (MSS 153), 4/28. The letter was also inserted at the front of the *Sunday Service* (1784); and published in the *Minutes* of the 1785 Conference—see *AM* 8 (1785): 602–04; and 10:586–88 in this edn.

[308] Hopper had replied (in a letter not known to survive) to JW's letter of Aug. 31, 1784 pertaining to Eells.

[309] The name has been crossed out to the point of being illegible (likely by a later hand).

O exhort the believers to go on to perfection![310] Perhaps you have been sometimes a little wanting in this. I am, dear Christopher,
Your affectionate friend and brother,

J. Wesley

Source: holograph; WTS (DC), Archives, Oxham Collection.

To [Jonathan Hern][311]

Bristol
September 11, 1784

My Dear Brother,
I am afraid, John Acutt is weary of the cross, and does not design to be a travelling preacher any longer.[312] He is now quietly and comfortably lodged at home, and I doubt will not be dislodged easily.
I gave the 'Scripture test',[313] together with other papers, to Thomas Olivers long ago, with order to insert it in the *[Arminian] Magazine* as soon as there should be room. I know [not] what has so long delayed the publication of it, and shall make enquiry.

September 12
I have been talking this afternoon with your son. He seems to be in a good spirit. I have great hopes he will live to be a comfort to you. I am,
Your affectionate brother,

J. Wesley

Postmark: 'Bristol'.
Source: holograph; Bridwell Library (SMU).[314]

---

[310] See Heb. 6:1.

[311] Hern had sent items to JW before to include in *AM*; such as 'An Account of the Life and Death of Thomas Slater', *Arminian Magazine* 8 (1785): 197–99 (sent as a letter to JW on Oct. 14, 1783), and his son Jonathan had just been admitted to Kingswood School (see 10:561 in this edn.).

[312] Orig., 'Accutt'. John Acutt (1756–1820) was admitted 'on trial' in 1778 (see 10:474 in this edn.). He was assigned to the western Cornwall circuit at the 1784 Conference (10:555), and included among those leaving the itinerancy in the 1785 *Minutes* (10:565). Acutt settled in Bethnal Green and pastored an independent congregation; see the 'Elegy' written on his death in *Evangelical Magazine and Missionary Chronicle* 28 (1820); 378.

[313] Nothing of this title appeared in *AM*.

[314] Held previously in the WMC Museum, 2002.001.020.

To John Francis Valton

Bristol
September 13, 1784

⁵ My Dear Brother,

My last letters from Bolton gave me reason to hope that William Eells is greatly changed, and has for some time past given no offence, but quietly and carefully attended his circuit.[315] Dr. [Thomas] Coke, on receipt of this information, wrote immediately ¹⁰ to Macclesfield that brother Butterfield might be sent forward, as we have great need of other preachers in the west.[316]

You must sacredly abstain from holding watch-nights and from continuing any service above an hour at a time. It is not so much preaching and praying, as preaching or *praying long*, that hurts ¹⁵ you.[317]

Strongly advise Mr. Crosse not to continue that wretched curate or lecturer at Bradford.[318] Mr. Webster, a pious and learned man near Derby, wrote me just now to offer me his service. I could not receive [him], because my little salary would not keep a married ²⁰ man. I wish Mr. Crosse would take him. It might be good for both of them.

I am

Your affectionate friend and brother,

J. Wesley

²⁵

The Assistant here has given Dr. Coke the money.[319] They expect to sail tomorrow.

Postmarks: 'Bristol' and '??/SE'.
³⁰ *Endorsement*: 'Septr 13 1784'.
Source: holograph; MARC, DDWes 5/41.

---

[315] See JW to Christopher Hopper, Sept. 11, 1784. Hopper was Assistant of the Bolton circuit.

[316] William Butterfield (1755–94) was born near Halifax, and had just begun to itinerate (cf. 10:567 in this edn.). He died during his eleventh year of appointment. See *Minutes* (post-Wesley, 1795), 1:317.

[317] Valton was struggling with some health issues. He had spent much of Aug. 1784 in Hartlepool, for the sea water; but also preached some in the area. See Jackson, *EMP*, 6:112–13.

[318] John Crosse (the former student at St. Edmund Hall; see JW to Cradock Glascott, May 13, 1764, 27:366 in this edn.) had been appointed vicar of St. Peter's church in Bradford on Aug. 20, 1784. The identity of the curate is uncertain.

[319] Samuel Bradburn was Assistant for the Bristol circuit. The money was for Coke, Vasey, and Whatcoat, who sailed Sept. 18 for North America.

To John Johnson[320]

Bristol
September 26, 1784

My Dear Brother,

There may be a deeper design of divine providence in sister [Dorothea] Johnson's removal to Lisburn than at first appeared. Probably God is about to revive his work *there*; and being freed from the encumbrance of worldly business, she may be more at leisure to attend it. The more she exerts herself therein the more she will increase both in spiritual and bodily strength. See that you do not cramp but give her full scope for the exertion of all the talents which God hath given her.

Pray tell sister [Henrietta] Gayer I send her such a sister as she never had before.

I am
    Your affectionate brother,

[J. Wesley]

Source: published transcription; Telford, *Letters*, 7:241.

To Dorothea (Garret / King) Johnson

Bristol
September 26, 1784

My Dear Sister,

How wise are all the ways of God! Just before his providence called you to leave Dublin, he sent sister Rogers thither in the same spirit of faith and love, to step into your place and prevent that scattering of the little flock which might otherwise have ensued.[321] And if he sees it best, after you have finished the work he is preparing for you to do in Lisburn, you will see Dublin again. Meanwhile redeem

[320] Johnson, the itinerant preacher who located in Lisburn, married Dorothea (Garret) King on Aug. 31. See JW's letter to Dorothea, Sept. 9, 1784; and his double letter that follows.

[321] James Rogers had just been appointed Assistant for the Dublin circuit. His first wife, Martha (Knowlden) Rogers, had died Feb. 15, 1784 with James and her friend Hester Ann Roe at her side. On Aug. 19, 1784, before setting out for Ireland, James and Hester were married. So the providential replacement for Dorothea was Hester Ann (Roe) Rogers.

the time,[322] catch the golden moments as they fly, and continue to love and pray for, my dear sister,
    Your affectionate brother,

J. Wesley

Source: published transcription; Telford, *Letters*, 7:241.

To Alexander Knox

Bristol
September 26, 1784

Dear Alleck,

Yours of the seventh instant found me out yesterday.[323] You may direct your next to London. I am not afraid of your writing too often. I answer, in few or more words, as I have time.

So much may be said on both sides that I do not care to determine the question.[324] I stand neuter; let the majority of the society do as they judge best. It is certain, very heavy encumbrances attend your keeping the present house. If you do sell it, take care none of the money be wasted, but every shilling of it reserved for the building of a new one. But I know not what house you could take for a pattern. The most tolerable one I know in the north of Ireland is that at Lisburn.

I am glad to hear that your preachers have formed a circuit about Londonderry, and have hopes that the work of God will now prosper. May it prosper in all your hearts! This is the constant prayer of, my dear Alleck,
    Yours most affectionately,

J. Wesley

Address: 'To / Mr. Alexander Knox / In Londonderry'.
Postmarks: 'Bristol' and 'OC/3'.
Source: holograph; Bridwell Library (SMU).[325]

[322] See Eph. 5:16.
[323] This letter is not known to survive.
[324] About selling their current preaching-house to finance building another; see JW to Knox, Feb. 7, 1784 and Mar. 18, 1784.
[325] Held previously in the Upper Room Museum, L-40.

To Agnes Gibbes

Bristol
October 2, 1784   5

See my dear Miss Aggy how tastes differ![326] Why noise and hurry are the delight of the gay world! It is their very element, the thing that saves them from thinking. And they find by experience that

10

> Pleasures on levity's smooth surface flow;
> Thought brings the weight that sinks the soul to woe.[327]

Take care my dear Miss Aggy! You are in harm's way. You have a natural propensity to thinking. Nay, you are apt to think deeply; 15
not to be content with a cursory view of things. If you give way to this, if you go on to weigh everything calmly and deliberately, are you aware what the consequences will be? You will infallibly be a Christian! Not a fashionable one—there is no great harm in that. But such a Christian as is described in the Bible, or in Mr. [Wil- 20
liam] Law's *Serious Call*. You will have that mind in you which was in Christ; and you will walk as Christ walked![328] And what a fall will this be! You will no longer be the admiration of the 'male lillies of our land' (as Dr. Young styles them with great propriety).[329] Nay, some of them will, it is very probable, shake their heads and say, 25
'Alas! She is quite out of her senses!' And what have you to counter-balance this loss? Let wise Dr. Pope (no enthusiast) tell you.

> Th' eternal sunshine of the spotless mind,
> Each prayer accepted, and each wish resigned? [...]   30
> Desires composed, affections ever even;
> Tears that delight, and sighs that waft to heaven?[330]

And will you then be any considerable loser upon the whole? Nay, will not your gain be far greater than your loss? Instead of the fa- 35

---

[326] Gibbes has replied to JW's letter of Aug. 1, 1784. While her reply is not known to survive, it carries on the conversation started there.

[327] Matthew Prior, *Solomon*, ii.767–68.

[328] See Phil. 2:5 and 1 John 2:6.

[329] See Young, *Night Thoughts*, *Night Two*, ll. 234–35; included by JW in *MSP* (1744), 2:250.

[330] Alexander Pope, *Eloisa to Abelard*, ll. 209–10, 213–14.

vour of a few poor, worthless men, you shall have the favour and the peace of God! O may his love flow in your heart as a river! May it be in you as 'a fountain of water, springing up into everlasting life'.[331]

5 I am inclined to think your ill health is wisely and mercifully permitted for this very end, to make you altogether a Christian;[332] to lessen your taste for things which (though not evil in themselves, yet) would hinder your aspiring after better things, and attach you too much to those silly pleasures which perish in the using.

Miss Freeman I believe is still in London, and seems to have no 10 thought of leaving.[333]

I do not remember when it was that I saw Mrs. Hambleton. One of the most sensible as well as the most pious women that I know in Scarborough is Miss [Ann] Tindall. If you was to converse with her, it would not be lost labour. She is as open as you are. Her word 15 is the picture of her thought. So let yours be always! As I am persuaded it is now, in all you say or write to, my dear Miss Aggy,

Yours in tender affection,

J. Wesley

20 Tomorrow I set out for London.

I did not know her name, but I imagine that was the sensible and agreeable lady whom I met with at Dunbar.[334]

Address: 'To / Miss Agnes Gibbes / At Scarborough'.
25 *Postmark*: '4/OC'.
Source: holograph; National Archives, PRO 30/9/11/2.

30 # To Alexander Suter

Bristol
October 3, 1784

My Dear Brother,
35 Others consider the state of one or two circuits only. But I see and consider the state of the whole kingdom, and consequently can more easily judge in what circuit each preacher is likely to

---

[331] See John 4:14.
[332] See JW, *The Almost Christian* (1741), 1:131–41 in this edn.
[333] Mary Freeman Shepherd; see JW to CW, Apr. 4, 1783.
[334] JW was returning to Gibbes's mention of him meeting a 'Mrs. Hambleton'. He is likely thinking in this case of the wife of James Hamilton of Dubar.

be useful. And I doubt not you will be useful in Dundee circuit, provided you 1) strive to strike out into new places (and you know we may preach anywhere in Scotland without any danger of riots), and 2) constantly visit *all the society* in course from house to house. To do this exactly will be a cross. But it will be worth your while to bear it. 5

The house at Arbroath should be settled as near the Conference plan as possible. The way of doing this in Scotland you may learn either from Mr. Smith in Aberdeen or Mr. Grant in Edinburgh.[335]

If Joseph Saunderson, brother Bartholomew, and you act in 10 concert, as was agreed when I was in Dundee, much good will be done—especially if you take care, in spite of flesh and blood, to keep up the morning meetings.[336]

Mr. [Richard] Watkinson at Edinburgh has now the charge of the books in Scotland, and will provide you with any that you want. He 15 is the General Assistant for Scotland this year.

You should send me a full and particular account of that poor man at Inverness. I am to set out for London tomorrow. I hope Dr. [Thomas] Coke and his companions are now near half-way over the Atlantic. Although I dreamed last night (indeed at two o'clock this 20 morning) that he came to me with a calm and placid countenance, but exceeding pale and his hair all wet.

I am
    Your affectionate friend and brother,

J. Wesley 25

Address: 'To / Mr Suter / At the Preachinghouse / in / Dundee'.
Postmarks: 'Bristol' and '4/OC'.
Endorsement: by Suter, 'No. 4'.
Source: holograph; MARC, MAM JW 4/74. 30

---

[335] William Smith (c. 1722–93) was a lawyer in Aberdeen who was supportive of the Methodists; see Batty, *Scotland*, 20–21; and William Smith to JW, Dec. 22, 1767. The second person is likely Sir Ludovick Grant, who had a residence in Edinburgh for his parliamentary duties.

[336] Thomas Bartholomew (1759–1819), a native of Keighley, Yorkshire, was converted and serving as a local preacher by 1780. He was admitted 'on trial' as an itinerant in 1782 (see 10:519 in this edn.). His knowledge of biblical languages aided his preaching. He travelled nearly 38 years, dying under appointment. See *Minutes* (post-Wesley, 1820), 5:96–97.

To Richard Rodda

London
October 13, 1784

5 My Dear Brother,
   I have no objection to your having a third preacher in the circuit.[337] But what to say of John Oliver I know not. He has been greatly to blame. But who can tell whether he be inwardly changed or not?[338]

10 Your proposal of building a new preaching-house I like well, provided it can be done without bringing any burden upon the Conference. Complaint is made to me that the preaching is taken from Stourshead. If so, I am sorry for it. Peace be with you and yours!
   I am

15   Your affectionate friend and brother,

[J. Wesley]

Address: 'To / Mr. Rodda / At the Preaching-house / In Birmingham'.
Source: published transcription; Telford, *Letters*, 7:242–43.

20

To John Francis Valton

London
25   October 13, 1784

My Dear Brother,
   Dr. Davison's advice was good.[339] I desire you would not offer to preach within these four weeks. I was suspended for near four
30 months.[340] But good is the will of the Lord! I suppose nettle tea is the best bracer in the world; and next that, elixir of vitriol (ten drops in a glass of water at 10:00 or 11:00 in the morning).
   I am inclined to think that temptation is purely preternatural.[341] I was strongly assaulted by it toward the close of my fever, when
35 I could hardly set a foot to the ground. Many years ago I told you

---

[337] Rodda was currently Assistant for the Birmingham circuit, assisted only by Thomas Warrick.

[338] Oliver's last listing with an appointment was in the 1782 *Minutes* (10:521 in this edn.). Cf. JW to Christopher Hopper, Oct. 25, 1780, 29:601 in this edn.

[339] See JW to Valton, Sept. 13, 1784. Valton's health challenges had continued, and he had been advised to cease preaching and retire for a time from public activities.

[340] See JW, *Journal*, Nov. 24, 1753 through Mar. 26, 1754, 20:482–85.

[341] Apparently the temptation to get married.

the case of Mr. Colley, who was just in *your* case. He married and died.[342] And do we not know:

> All the promises are sure
> To persevering prayer?[343]

I am
    Ever yours,

J. Wesley

Address: 'To / Mr Valton / In Bradforth / Yorkshire'.
Endorsement: by Valton, 'Octr 13 1784'.
Source: holograph; Bridwell Library (SMU).

To William Black Jr.

London
October 15, 1784

My Dear Brother,

A letter of yours some time ago gave me hopes of meeting you in England, as you seemed desirous of spending some time here in order to improve yourself in learning.[344] But as you have now entered into a different state, I do not expect we shall meet in this world.[345] But you have a large field of action where you are without wandering into Europe. Your present parish is wide enough, namely, Nova Scotia and Newfoundland.

I do not advise you to go any further. In the other provinces there are abundance of preachers.[346] They can spare four preachers to you, better than you can spare one to them. If I am rightly informed, they have already sent you one or two. And they may afford you one or two more, if it please God to give a prosperous passage to Dr. [Thomas] Coke and his fellow labourers.[347] Does there not

---

[342] See JW to Valton, Sept. 18, 1773, 28:599 in this edn.

[343] CW, Hymn on Luke 18:1, st. 4, *HSP* (1749), 2:39.

[344] Cf. JW to Black, Feb. 26, 1783 and July 13, 1783.

[345] Referring to Black getting married in Feb.; cf. JW to Black, May 11, 1784.

[346] I.e., the now-independent provinces that would form the United States of America.

[347] Following the arrival of Coke, Thomas Vasey, and Richard Whatcoat, there was a gathering of Methodist preachers in Baltimore in late Dec. 1784, where ordinations took place and The Methodist Episcopal Church was founded. One of their initial acts was to appoint Freeborn Garrettson and James Cromwell to assist in the northern provinces that remained aligned with Britain.

want a closer and more direct connexion between you of the north and the societies under Francis Asbury? Is it not more advisable that you should have a constant correspondence with each other and act by united counsels? Perhaps it is for want of this that so 5   many have drawn back.

I want a more particular account of the societies in Nova Scotia and Newfoundland. And I wish you would give me a full account of the manner wherein God hath dealt with you from the beginning.

I am not at all glad of Mr. Scurr's intention to remove from 10   Nova Scotia to the south. That is going from a place where he is much wanted to a place where he is not wanted.[348] I think if he got £10,000 thereby, it would be but a poor bargain; that is, upon the supposition which you and I make, that *souls* are of more value than *gold*. Peace be with all your spirits!
15   I am

Your affectionate brother,

John Wesley

Source: published transcription; Richey, *William Black*, 126–27.

20

To Sarah Baker[349]

25   near Norwich
October 27, 1784

My Dear Sally,

You send me an agreeable account of the work of God in Monmouth.[350] If there are only two more in the society that have (like 30   you) a real love for perishing souls, and will go on with you, hand in hand, visiting the sick and the well, that blessed work will undoubtedly go forward and you will see the fruit of your labours.

This will not and cannot be hindered long by the noise made by the beasts of the people. A person of Mr. Gwinnett's rank and

---

[348] Thomas Scurr (1739–91) and his wife Elizabeth (Appleton) Scurr immigrated from Yorkshire in England to Nova Scotia in 1774. Scurr hosted Methodist services in his home and may have served as a local preacher. He was in the process of selling his farm and moving to Princess Anne, Virginia. Cf. Richey, *William Black*, pp. 48, 128.

[349] Sarah Baker (b. 1755) was the daughter of Thomas Baker (1732–87) and Jane (Hughes) Baker (1733–1813) of Monmouth. JW may have met her during his recent visit to Monmouth. They corresponded for a couple of years, until she married the widower Isaac Skinner of Cowbridge, Glamorgan, and moved there; cf. JW, *Journal*, Aug. 15, 1788, 24:105 in this edn.

[350] This letter is not known to survive.

influence is quite an overmatch for unseemly petty rioters;[351] even
if they are encouraged underhand (as probably they are) by some
wretched gentleman, so called by the courtesy of England.

Throughout England, Wales, and Ireland each of our travelling
preachers has three pounds a quarter.

I am, my dear Sally,

    Yours affectionately,

                          J. Wesley

My best wishes to Mr. and Mrs. Gwinnett (I forget his Christian
name),[352] and Miss Fortune.[353]

Address: 'To / Miss Baker / At Gwinnett, Esq. / in / Monmouth'.
Postmarks: '29/OC' and 'Yarmouth'.
Source: holograph; Toronto, Canada, United Church of Canada Archives,
    97.002C, 3-23.

To Hannah Ball[354]

                              near Norwich
                         October 27, 1784

My Dear Sister,

Simon Day sincerely fears God. Therefore I do not think him
incurable. And the way I advise you to take is this. Tell Mr. [Samuel]
Hodgson I desire him to carry to brother Day the *Plain Account of
Christian Perfection*, and beg him to read it entirely over. Afterwards
let him desire his thoughts upon it, and answer his objections. It
will be an hour or two well bestowed. I am in hopes it will have
good effect.

---

[351] William Catchmayd (1747–93) had assumed the surname Gwinnett in Aug. 1782, on inheriting the Shurdington estate from the widow of George Gwinnett; see J. A. Bradney, *A History of Monmouthshire* (London, 1904–32), 2 (pt. 2): 215–17. William, a Justice of the Peace, protected JW against opposers during a visit to Monmouth in 1781 (see *Journal*, May 14, 1781, 23:203–04 in this edn.), and again on his most recent visit (ibid., Aug. 9, 1784, 23:326).

[352] William Catchmayd married Betty Collins (d. 1812) in 1778 in Bristol.

[353] Theodosia Fortune (1735–1803), a native of Monmouth who never married, was supportive of Methodist work there since at least 1770; see Alexander Mather to JW, c. Dec. 1779, §39.

[354] Ball had written JW (in a letter not known to survive) with concerns about Simon Day, the junior itinerant on the Oxfordshire circuit, serving under Samuel Hodgson as Assistant.

Some time since, I wrote and desired he would not go any more to the Dissenting meeting—seeing if the preachers go there, the people undoubtedly will. It is *your* part and Nancy's[355] to go straight forward, whoever praises or blames.

5   I am, dear sister,

Your affectionate brother,

J. Wesley

10   *Address*: 'To / Miss Ball / in / High Wycombe'.
Postmarks: '29/OC' and 'Yarmouth'. *Charge*: '8'.
Source: holograph; Bridwell Library (SMU).[356]

15

To Dorothea (Garret / King) Johnson[357]

Norwich
October 27, 1784

20   My Dear Sister,

I am now in great hopes that the work of God in Dublin will not much suffer by your removal, seeing he just at the time prepared sister [Hester Ann] Rogers, who is both able and willing to tread in your steps.

25   You are now happily delivered from worldly cares; but it is to that end that your soul may be vacant for thoughts and cares of a nobler kind, how you may promote the work of God upon earth. Your calling is not only to do good, but to do *all* the good which you possibly can. I doubt not but you will be of use to my friend sister [Henri-

30   etta] Gayer in particular. She has much zeal, and 'let knowledge *guide*, not *cool* its fires'.

I hope brother (John) Johnson or you will send me an account of what occurs in Lisburn.

I am, my dear sister,

35   Your ever affectionate brother,

[J. Wesley]

Source: published transcription; Telford, *Letters*, 7:245.

[355] Hannah's sister Ann Ball.

[356] Held previously in WMC Museum, 2002.001.021.

[357] This letter echoes that of JW to Mrs. Johnson, Sept. 26, 1784. JW may have feared the earlier letter had gone astray.

To Francis Asbury[358]

Norwich
October 31, 1784

My Dear Brother,

Some weeks before you receive this, I hope you will see Dr. [Thomas] Coke (with his associates[359]) and find him a man after your own heart—seeking neither profit, pleasure, nor honour; but simply to save the souls for whom Christ has died and to promote his kingdom upon earth.

You are aware of the danger on either hand. And I scarce know which is the greater? One or the other, so far as it ⟨takes⟩[360] place will overturn Methodism from the ⟨fo⟩undation; either our travelling preachers turning independents and gathering congregations each for himself, or procuring ordination in a *regular way* and accepting parochial cures.[361] If you can find means of guarding against both evils the work of God will prosper more than ever.

I suppose the Doctor and you have now considered at large what method will be most effectual to fix the work on such a stable foundation as will not easily be overturned. If that good man, Mr. Ogden, could be prevailed on to join with you heart and hand, it might be of admirable service to the cause of God, and such a threefold [cord] would not soon be broken.[362] But herein you must proceed with the utmost caution. Go on slowly, step by step, lest you should put it into the power of any one to hurt you. Let not him that believeth make haste![363] I know not but he will do you most good at a little distance. You will soon be able to judge whether this would not also be the case, with regard to Mr. [Devereux] Jarr⟨at.⟩ Admit none into the *closest union* with you, but those whose heart is *altogether* as your heart.[364]

5

10

15

20

25

30

---

[358] JW was replying to a letter from Asbury that is not known to survive.

[359] Thomas Vasey and Richard Whatcoat, both now ordained.

[360] A small portion is missing, affecting two lines on each side.

[361] Note that JW's concern is not just to provide access to sacraments, but to preserve an itinerant ministry.

[362] Rev. Uzel Ogden (1744–1822), born in New Jersey, had graduated Princeton and received ordination by the bishop of London in 1773. He currently served as a missionary priest for the Church of England in Sussex County, New Jersey, and preached occasionally in Trinity church, Newark. He was supportive of Asbury and the Methodists; indeed Asbury had been in his home as recently as Aug. 24, 1784 (see Asbury, *Journal*, 1:467). Ogden would join the newly organized Protestant Episcopal Church, and even be nominated (but not approved) as a bishop.

[363] See Isa. 28:16.

[364] See 2 Kings 10:15.

When you have once settled your plan with respect to the provinces, you will easily form a regular connexion with our society in Antigua on the one hand, and with those in Nova Scotia and Newfoundland on the other.

5   John Helton's is a very harmless performance.[365] It will soon die and be forgotten. I don't believe Anthony Benezet ever recommended it.

I shall be glad to see the papers which you speak of. Probably they have a place in the *[Arminian] Magazine*.

10   Those who hoped for a division among the Methodists here are totally disappointed.

As to your having a bishop from England in every province, it will be long enough before that plan is brought into execution. Meanwhile use the means you have—only with much circumspection

15   and much prayer!

I am,

Your affectionate friend and brother,

J. Wesley

20   *Address*: 'To / Mr Francis Asbury / At Mr [Samuel] Spraggs / in / New York'.

Postmarks: '1/DE' and 'Post paid'.

Source: holograph; Bridwell Library (SMU).

---

[365] Referring to Helton's *Reasons for Quitting the Methodist Society; Being a Defense of Barclay's Apology* (London: J. Fry, 1778; see in-letters file, May 28, 1778). The pamphlet had a 3rd edn. in 1784, which was the last. Asbury was likely worried that it would persuade some of his fellow Methodists to join the Quakers.

To John Stonehouse[366]

Norwich
October 31, 1784

My Dear Brother,   5
I had some doubt concerning another person; but I have none at
all concerning Dr. Bayley.[367] I believe his eye is single,[368] and that he
has no other view than that of promoting the glory of God. If therefore the steward and trustees, upon mature consideration, judge it
expedient to invite Dr. Bayley to officiate every Sunday in the new   10
chapel, I have no objection. It seems to me it might be productive
of much good.
  I am
    Your very affectionate brother,

J. Wesley   15

The other person is the Rev. Edward Smyth.[369]

Address: 'To Mr Stonehouse / Manchester'.
Source: holograph; Manchester, Rylands, English Ms 844.
                                                                       20

To Martha Chapman
                                                                       25
near London
November 3, 1784

My Dear Sister,
  I was a little disappointed at your not seeing me at Wallingford, as
you used to do, before I went away.[370] But I took it for granted there   30

---

[366] John Stonehouse was a hat-maker, with an office on Oldham Street, and a leading lay
Methodist in Manchester. Stonehouse had contacted JW, on behalf of a few 'Church Methodists' at the Oldham Street chapel about having prayerbook service on Sundays in the chapel,
and were seeking an ordained person to lead the service. Their effort was defeated by John Pawson, the current Assistant in Manchester, and other lay leaders. See Henry D. Rack, 'The Providential Moment: Church Building, Methodism, and Evangelical Entryism in Manchester,
1788–1825', *Transactions of the Historic Society of Lancashire and Cheshire* 141 (1991): 235–60.

[367] Orig., 'Bailey'. The former writing instructor at Kingswood had been ordained in 1780
and served (part-time) as curate to John Fletcher and Richard Conyers. In 1783 he wed Rachel
Norton (JW performed the marriage) and left Kingswood. The couple settled in Manchester.

[368] See Matt. 6:22.

[369] See in this regard, JW to Richard Rodda, c. Jan. 1791.

[370] JW preached at Wallingford on Oct. 18, 1784, and left the next morning.

was some circumstance which I did not know. So I did not blame you, as I am not ready to condemn those I love.

I am glad you do not let go your confidence or lose the witness of your sanctification.[371] Take care that you lose not any of the things that you have gained, but that you receive a full reward. Surely it is a most uncomfortable thing to lose any part of what God hath wrought in us. I wonder how any that have lost the pure love of God can find any rest in their souls till they have regained it.

It was well for you that God did not suffer you to find rest in any creature. He had better things in store for you. One more degree of his love makes you large amends, even in the present world, for every other loss.

I am, dear Patty,
	Your affectionate brother,

					J. Wesley

Address: 'To / Miss Chapman / At Watlington / near Tetsworth / Oxford-shire'.
Postmark: '4/NO'. *Charge*: '4'.
Endorsement: by Chapman, '13th 1784 / the last'.
Source: holograph; MARC, MAM JW 2/29.

To John Mason

near London
November 3, 1784

My Dear Brother,

You judge right. If the people were more alive to God, they would be more liberal. There is money enough, and particularly in Somersetshire. But they are straitened in their own bowels.[372] When I complied with the desire of many and divided the circuit into two, we were not a jot better.[373] You have one thing to point at, the revival and increase of the work of God. Get as many as possible to meet in band. Be exact in every part of discipline, and give no ticket to any that does not meet his class weekly.

---

[371] See Heb. 10:35.
[372] See 2 Cor. 6:12.
[373] The Plymouth circuit first appears as separate from the Devonshire circuit in the 1783 *Minutes*; see 10:533 in this edn.

I am
    Your affectionate friend and brother,

[J. Wesley]

Source: published transcription; Jackson, *Works* (3rd), 12:438.

To Sarah Crosby

London
November 7, 1784

My Dear Sister,

To those who know the world, hardly anything that is wrong or foolish in it appears strange. Otherwise we should have thought it strange that so good a woman should take such a step.[374] One would not have expected her to marry at all—at least, none but an eminent Christian. I am more and more inclined to think that we have been a little mistaken in this matter, that there are none living so established in grace but that they may possibly fall.

The case of Hetty Rogers (notwithstanding the misrepresentation of her wretched cousin) was widely different.[375] I know more of it (beginning, middle, and ending) than most people in England.[376] And I am clear that, first to last, she acted in all good conscience toward God and man. As things stood, it was not a sin for her to marry, but a duty; and to marry when she did. And never was any one woman so owned of God in Dublin as she has been already.

Thomas Brisco, I am persuaded, will do some good.[377] But his wife [Ann] will do much more if you encourage her and strengthen her hands.

I am glad Nancy Tripp keeps easy. That is almost as much as one can expect. I think she has tried the quicksilver and aqua sulphurata.[378]

---

[374] Likely referring either to Ann Bolton (who was considering marriage again to John Arundel; see JW to Bolton, Feb. 16, 1785), or Ann Loxdale (see JW to Mrs. Mary Fletcher, Apr. 2, 1785).

[375] It is not clear which Roe cousin had spread rumours about Hester marrying James Rogers just six months after Rogers lost his first wife (and a close friend of Hester).

[376] Orig., 'that most'; a mistake.

[377] Brisco had been appointed by the 1784 Conference to the Leeds circuit.

[378] A recommended treatment for asthma, cholic, and 'the whites' in *Primitive Physic*.

Peace be with all your spirits! I am, my dear sister,
Your affectionate brother,

J. Wesley

Endorsement: by Crosby (?), 'Mr Wesley's Letter'.
Source: holograph; Bridwell Library (SMU).[379]

To John Francis Valton[380]

London
November 13, 1784

My Dear Brother,

Before I read your letter my first thought was, 'He will not recover till spring.' But a second immediately followed, 'Yes, at or before Candlemas [i.e., Feb. 2].' And I trust so it will be. But in the meantime you ought undoubtedly to follow the directions of your physician. Only I wish you to add daily riding and the daily use of decoction of nettles, which is a nobler restorative than all the quinquina in Peru—though in many cases that is an excellent medicine.[381]

I was confined from the 28th of November till the end of February.[382] The Hot Well water completed the cure.

You are now God's prisoner, and are learning that deep lesson, 'Be content to do nothing.' That God may teach you this and all things is the prayer of

Your affectionate friend and brother,

J. Wesley

Endorsement: by Valton, 'Nov. 13, 1784'.
Source: holograph; MARC, MAM JW 5/33.

---

[379] Held previously in the Upper Room Museum, L-190. There are several marks to elide text in the holograph. These were likely made by Telford, who omits all these instances.

[380] While there is no address portion, this letter elaborates on JW to Valton, Oct. 13, 1784, and bear's Valton's typical endorsement.

[381] Quinquina was a wine infused with 'Peruvian bark'.

[382] In 1753; cf. JW to Valton, Oct. 13.

To Thomas Tattershall

London
November 27, 1784

Dear Tommy, 5

The main point is to get money. If you can procure this in Ireland, well. But you must not depend upon England! We make no collections yearly for buildings; neither have done for many years. Therefore take care you do not attempt more than you can perform.

Look into the large *Minutes* of the Conference, and you will find 10 sufficient directions as to the form of preaching houses.[383] That at Kilkenny is tolerable; that at Limerick is beautiful.

I have no leisure to seek after Mr. Boulton.[384] Neither do I concern myself with such matters. His agent is sufficient. I have other things to do. I am, 15

Dear Tommy,

Your affectionate friend and brother,

[J. Wesley]

Source: published transcription; Byrth, 'Memoir', xxxv.

20

To [John Francis Valton][385]

25

London
December 4, 1784

My Dear Brother,

It seems to be that nothing under heaven is so likely to restore your health as the Bristol waters. It struck me as soon as ever you 30 named them. I think you should not lose a day. If it be possible, be at Bristol before Christmas, before the severe weather sets in. I pray God to give you health of soul and of body, and am,

Your affectionate friend and brother,

J. Wesley 35

Source: holograph; Drew, Methodist Archives.

---

[383] See 'Large' *Minutes* (1770), §68, 10:896–97 in this edn.

[384] Lacking Tattershall's letter to JW, it is impossible to tell whether the reference is to Matthew Boulton (1728–1809), the engineer; cf. JW, *Journal*, Mar. 22, 1774, 22:400 in this edn.

[385] While there is no address portion or endorsement, this letter almost certainly continues JW's advice to Valton; cf. the earlier letters of Oct. 13 and Nov. 14.

To Jonathan Hern[386]

London
December 11, 1784

Dear Jonathan,

I am heartily glad that our brethren have come to that noble resolution of enlarging the chapel, and also that by removing those pews they will make more room for the poor. I am persuaded this will be greatly for the advancement of the work of God.

But when they are about it, let it be done throughly, in such a manner as will be a credit to them.

I am, with love to sister Hern,[387]

Your affectionate friend and brother,

J. Wesley

I hope to see you in spring, if I live.

Address: 'To / Mr. Hern / At the Preaching-house / in / Liverpool'.
Source: holograph; Wesley's Chapel (London), LDWMM 1997/6752.

To Ann Tindall

London
December 11, 1784

My Dear Sister,

I am in great hopes your sister's late illness will be a lasting advantage to her.[388] And so may her present weakness, which will continue no longer than she has need of it.

I think a subscription and collection ought to have been made among our friends, both in the town and country, for repairing the roof of the [preaching-]house. Surely the money subscribed for the original debt should have been reserved for that use alone. I am not

---

[386] Hern's letter, to which JW was replying, is not known to survive.
[387] Hern's wife was named Rachel (maiden name possibly Stead; c. 1748–1827). According to a letter from Hern to Elizabeth Bennis, he and Rachel were married in 1764 (see Bennis, *Christian Correspondence*, 182).
[388] Jane (Tindall) Thornton; see JW to Tindall, Sept. 4, 1784.

willing to subscribe any further unless the money produced by this subscription be sacredly reserved for the payment of the debt and not applied to any other purpose whatsoever. On this condition I will subscribe as before, another year.[389]

I am, dear Nancy,

Your affectionate brother,

J. Wesley

But have you done writing verses?
The subscription may be paid out of the book money.

Address: 'To / Miss Tindall / in / Scarborough'.
Postmark: '11/DE'. *Charge*: '6'.
Endorsement: by Tindall, '11 Dec 1784'.
Source: holograph; British Library, Department of Manuscripts, Add. MS. 43695, ff. 84–85.

To Samuel Bradburn

December 17, 1784

I have letters from Dr. [Thomas] Coke, dated at New York.[390] I am with kind love to Betsy,[391] dear Sammy,

Your affectionate friend and brother,

J. Wesley

Source: holograph; Wesley's Chapel (London), LDWMM 1997/6777 (a fragment).

---

[389] See JW to Tindall, Aug. 3, 1783.
[390] No letters of this time from Coke are known to survive.
[391] Elizabeth (Nangle) Bradburn, his wife.

To Robert Blake[392]

London
December 24, 1784

5   Dear Robert,
    You have reason to praise God, who has once more lifted up your head above the enemies of your soul. You never need be overcome again by the sin which did so easily beset you. Watch and pray, and you will no more enter into temptation.
10   You may show this to Mr. Myles, and he will give you a guinea on my account.[393]
        I am
            Your affectionate brother,
                                    [J. Wesley]

15

Source: published transcription; Telford, *Letters*, 7:249.

20

To Hugh Bold, Esq.

London
December 24, 1784

25 Sir,
    The Reverend Mr. Wesley desires me to ask you, who is agent for the Reverend Dr. [Thomas] Coke? Or if you can give any information in a matter that nearly concerns the Doctor?
    It is this: when the Dr. sailed for America he desired that such
30 and such demands upon him might be answered; and that for that purpose I should receive 200 pounds from Wales, 100 of which I would get before Christmas. Now I have heard nothing from Wales. Nor do I know who to apply to.
    Your speedy answer will oblige Mr. Wesley, together with, sir,
35   Your humble servant,
                            H[enry] Moore

You will be pleased to direct for me at the New Chapel, City Road, London.

---

[392] Blake had struggled in the itinerancy; see JW to Zacariah Yewdall, Dec. 31, 1782. His last appointment had been in 1783 at Athlone (see 10:535 in this edn.). He was listed as having desisted from travelling by the 1784 Conference (10:553).

[393] William Myles was the Assistant for the Leicester circuit.

Address: 'To / Hugh Bold Esq. / Brecknock'.
Postmarks: '24/DE' and '25/DE'. *Charge*: '6'.
Endorsement: '24 Decr 1784 / Letter from Mr Moore'.
Source: holograph; Wesley's Chapel (London), LDWMM 2000/7962/7.

5

To Ann Bolton

London   10
December 24, 1784

My Dear Nancy,

You have seldom had hatred, but you have often had coolness,
returned for your goodwill. And your tenderness for your bosom
friends made this a close trial to you. But I am not conscious that   15
this was ever the case between you and me. I loved you much the
first time that you was with me at the Foundery.[394] And so I have
done ever since, without any intermission at all. You have therefore one friend (if no more) that has never deceived your hope, or
proved to you as the staff of a broken reed.[395] And, I trust, never   20
will. Use me, my Nancy, on all occasions, as the friend whom God
has provided for you. Perhaps as one 'that cleaveth closer to you
than a brother'.[396] And surely nothing but death shall part us.

I hardly think it possible for any of us to do too much for our parents, especially if they are under any trial or affliction. While my   25
mother lived, I often thought, 'I have known many persons wish that
they had done more for their parents while they had them. But I was
resolved, to have nothing of that kind to reproach myself with by
and by.' All that you do or suffer for them, God will repay sevenfold
into your own bosom.[397] And in due time he will make a way for you   30
to feed his lambs also. Meanwhile you shall sink deeper and deeper
into humble, gentle, patient love. And do not forget, my dear Nancy,

    Yours most affectionately,

J. Wesley

Address: 'To / Miss Bolton / In Witney / Oxfordshire'.   35
Postmark: '27/DE'. *Charge*: '4'.
Endorsement: by Bolton, 'Dec 24 1784'.
Source: holograph; Godalming, Surrey, Charterhouse School, Archive 0134.

[394] See JW to Bolton, Apr. 7, 1768, 28:142–43 in this edn.
[395] See Isa. 36:6.
[396] Cf. Prov. 18:24.
[397] Cf. Ps. 79:12.

To Jeremiah Brettel

London
December 24, 1784

5 Dear Jerry,
  If I live till the Conference, I shall have no objection to your begging in the Newcastle and Sunderland circuits.[398] But let them not build a scarecrow of an house like most of those in the north. Copy after that at Newcastle or Yarm, which is one of the prettiest in
10 England. Look at the *Minutes* of the Conference with regard to the building of preaching-houses, and follow those advices.[399]
  I am, dear Jerry,
      Your affectionate friend and brother,

J. Wesley

15

Address: 'To / Mr. Brettell / At the Orphan-House / Newcastle upon Tyne'.
Postmark: '24/DE'.
Source: holograph; MARC, MAM JW 2/9.
20

To Thomas Taylor[400]

25   London
                                                      December 24, 1784
Dear Tommy,
  In fifty years I have not met with six mothers who did not suffer their children to cry aloud—no, nor seriously endeavoured it. So
30 that I see no manner of need to caution them against that extreme.
  To speak without reserve, I believe John Valton to be a better Assistant than either you or me. I believe he has more of the Spirit of God resting upon him, and is more deeply devoted to God than almost any man or woman I know. And I do not think myself a jot
35 better than him because I was born forty years before him. But I earnestly desire he would go to Bristol, and that you would sup-

---

[398] It was judged at the 1783 Conference that there were presently too may places trying to build preaching-houses, and that for the future no one was to be permitted 'to beg for any house except in the circuit where it stands'; see 10:541 in this edn.
[399] See 'Large' *Minutes* (1770), §68, 10:896–97 in this edn.
[400] Thomas Taylor was currently stationed on the Bradford circuit, under John Valton as the Assistant. Taylor appears to have registered a concern about Valton to JW.

ply his place as Assistant. I am of opinion this is the only possible means of restoring his strength.

I am, with kind love to sister [Ann] Taylor, dear Tommy,
    Yours affectionately,

J. Wesley

I corrected the last part of the new hymnbook this morning.[401]

Source: holograph; MARC, MA 1992/035.

To Ann Tindall[402]

London
December 30, 1784

My Dear Sister,

It was expressly determined in the Conference that 'none should make any collection out of their own circuit'.[403] I cannot make a precedent of breaking this rule. I do not therefore see that you can do any more than set your subscription on foot for another year, and take care not to apply the money to any other purpose.

I am, dear Nancy,
    Your affectionate brother,

J. Wesley

Address: 'To / Miss Tindal / in / Scarborough'.
Postmark: '30/DE'. Charge: '6'.
Endorsement: '30 Dec 1784'.
Source: holograph; British Library, Department of Manuscripts, Add. MS. 43695, ff. 87–88.

[401] *A Pocket Hymn Book; Bibliography*, No. 438; published in Feb. 1785.

[402] Tindall had replied to JW's letter of Dec. 11, drawing this response. Her letter to JW is not known to survive.

[403] *Minutes* (1783), Q. 23, 10:541 in this edn.

To a Member of the Methodist Society in Bath[1]

[c. 1785]

My Dear Betsy,

I write you a few lines because I think you stand in need of comfort; and I would give you all in my power, as I know you would me on a like occasion. I will tell you how to do it then. Look kindly on them that have wronged you most. Speak civilly, yea affectionately, to them. They cannot stand it long:

> Love melts the hardness that in rocks is bred;
> A flint will break upon a feather-bed.[2]

I have set my heart upon your being a happy woman and overcoming all your enemies by love. And then I shall be more than ever, my dear Betsy,

Your affectionate brother,

John Wesley

Source: published transcription; *Wesleyan Methodist Magazine* 48 (1825): 675.

---

[1] The transcription does not name the recipient or date the letter. Telford assumed it was to Elizabeth (Nangle) Bradburn (apparently because JW addresses her as 'Betsy') and dated the letter at the very end of Dec. 1785 (since she died in Feb. 1786). It is extremely unlikely that this was the recipient, as Bradburn was never a member of the society in Bath. An alternative name has not emerged, and we left the letter in 1785 since there was no means of being more exact.

[2] Cf. John Cleveland, 'Antiplatonick', st. 2, *Poems* (London: s.n., 1651), 73: 'Love melts the rigor which the rocks have bred, / Flint will break upon a feather-bed'. JW included an adaptation close to the above in his MS Poetry Miscellany, p. 70.

To Rebecca (Yeoman) Gair

London
January 5, 1785

My Dear Sister,   5

You did well to write.[3] Although I have not much time, yet I am
always well pleased to hear from a friend. If outward losses be a
means of stirring you up to gain more inward holiness, you will
never have need to repent of that loss but rather to praise God for
it. How soon will the moment of life be gone! It is enough if we se-   10
cure an happy eternity. Let brother [Robert] Gair and you earnestly
seek to be wholly devoted to God; and all things else will be added
to you.

I am, dear Becky,
Your affectionate brother,   15
[J. Wesley]

Source: published transcription; Jackson, *Works* (3rd), 12:494.

20

To Patrick Henry Maty[4]

City Road [London]   25
January 11, 1785

1. A day or two ago this *Review* fell into my hands, which contains a letter from the Rev. Mr. [Samuel] Badcock.[5] I have not the
pleasure of knowing this gentleman, but I esteem him for his useful   30

---

[3] Gair's letter is not known to survive.

[4] Paul Henry Maty (1745–87) was the editor of *A New Review; with Literary Curiosities, and Literary Intelligence*. JW first came across Samuel Badcock's letter-essay on the Wesley family in its slightly abridged form in *New Review* 6 (Dec. 1784): 460–69. JW's reply is framed to address Maty as editor. When Maty failed to publish the reply, JW did so in *AM*.

[5] Rev. Samuel Badcock (1747–88) pastored a Dissenting congregation in Barnstaple, Devonshire from 1769–77. While there he came into possession of manuscripts related to Samuel Wesley Jr. through Samuel's daughter, Philadelphia (Wesley) Earle; see Badcock to JW, Apr. 22, 1780. Raised with evangelical leanings, Badcock was drawn by Joseph Priestly into more liberal views, which led to dismissal from his congregation. He returned to his hometown of South Moulton and supported himself in part by publishing ventures. This included an account of the Wesley family dated Dec. 5, 1782 [see in-letters file], which he published in *Bibliotheca Topographica Britannica* 20 (1784): xli–xlviii. An abridged form and/or excerpts were republished in several settings.

and ingenious publications. And I think it my duty to inform both him and the public better, of some points wherein they have been misinformed.

2. He says, 'Mr. Samuel Wesley, of Epworth, in Lincolnshire, *was
5   sent* to the university.'[6] This is not accurate. He was educated for some years at a Dissenting academy, from which he then privately retired, and entered himself at Exeter College in Oxford. 'His heroic poem, *The Life of Christ*, excited the ridicule of the wits.'[7] His own account of it was, 'the cuts are good; the notes pretty good,
10 the verses so so'. 'At a very advanced age he published a Latin work on the book of Job, which was never held in any estimation by the learned.'[8] I doubt that. It certainly contains immense learning; but of a kind which I do not admire.

3. 'He married a woman of extraordinary abilities, the daughter
15 of Dr. Samuel Annesley." (Dr. Annesley and the then Earl of Anglesey were brother's sons.[9]) 'Samuel, his eldest son, was a noted Jacobite.' Nay, he was no more a Jacobite than he was a Turk. And what amends can Mr. Badcock, or Mr. Maty make, for publishing this egregious falsehood? 'Many of his political satires remain un-
20 published, on account of their treasonable tendency.' Here is a double mistake: for 1) he never published anything political, whether satirical or not; 2) he never wrote anything of a treasonable tendency—he sacredly avoided it.[10] 'In his rage of Jacobitism, he poured out the very dregs of it on royalty itself.' No, never. He never wrote,
25 much less published, one line against the king. I speak it from per-

---

[6] Page numbers for JW's quotations from the abridgement published in *A New Review* can be found in the notes of 9:522–26 in this edn. This abridgement followed the text of Badcock's original closely, eliding mainly Badcock's footnotes and quotations from the poem 'Religious Discourse'. All of the material quoted appears in Badcock's original as well.

[7] Samuel Wesley Sr., *The Life of our Blessed Lord & Saviour, Jesus Christ* (London: Harper and Motte, 1693).

[8] Samuel Wesley Sr., *Dissertationes in Librum Jobi* (London: William Bowyer, 1736).

[9] While this connection was handed down by Susanna, and is repeated by JW in his letter to Thomas Maunsell, Nov. 16, 1773 (28:617 in this edn.), it is not well substantiated in records; see Betty I. Young, 'Sources for the Annesley Family', *WHS* 45 (1985): 47–57.

[10] Note the carefulness of JW's claims. He was surely aware of the two bound volumes of Samuel Wesley Jr.'s manuscript poems that Sarah Wesley Jr. would eventually donate to the British Library (Manuscript Collections, Add. 42051 and 42052). There are many satirical political pieces in these volumes, particularly aimed at Robert Walpole, but Samuel Jr. did not publish these at the time; cf. Samuel Wesley, *Poems on Several Occasions* (London: Simpkin, Marshall, 1862), 610ff. Samuel Jr.'s commitment to monarchy is clear in this collection. But this did not rule out favouring one living monarch (James) against another (George). Badcock quotes a poem he claims is by Samuel, titled 'Regency', to prove this latter type of 'treason' in his reply to JW (May 10, 1785). Unfortunately this poem is not in the volumes at the British Library, nor known to survive in manuscript (to allow verifying authorship).

sonal knowledge, having often heard him say, 'If it reflects on the king, it is none of mine.' His constant practice may be learnt from those lines, in *The Battle of the Sexes*,

> Forgive the voice that useful fiction sings 5
> Not impious tales of deities impure;
> Not faults of breathless queens, or living kings,
> In open treason, or in veil obscure.[11]

'Time however changed the satirist against Sir Robert, into an 10 humble suppliant.' Nay, I do not believe he ever wrote a line to Sir Robert, either in verse or prose.[12]

4. 'Mrs. [Susanna] Wesley lived long enough to deplore the extravagance of her two sons, John and Charles; considering them as "under strong delusions, to believe a lie".'[13] By vile misrepresenta- 15 tions she was deceived for a time. But she no sooner heard them speak for themselves than she was thoroughly convinced they were in no delusion, but spoke 'the words of truth and soberness'.[14] She afterward lived *with me* several years, and died rejoicing and praising God. 20

5. I was born in June 1703, and was between six and seven years old when I was left alone in my father's house, being then all in flames, till I was taken out of the nursery window by a man strangely standing on the shoulders of another. Those words in the picture, 'Is not this a brand plucked out of the burning?'[15] chiefly allude to 25 this.

6. 'He had early a very strong impression of his designation to some extraordinary work.' Indeed not I. I never said so. I never thought so. I am guiltless in this matter. The strongest impression I had till I was three or four and twenty, was, 30

Inter sylvas Academi quaerere verum;[16]

---

[11] SW Jr., 'The Battle of the Sexes', st. 50, *Poems* (1743), p. 40; included by JW in *MSP* (1744), 3:38.

[12] The reference is to the Whig politician, Sir Robert Walpole (1676–1745). While Samuel Wesley Jr. wrote satirical private poems about him, there is no evidence that Samuel *ever* wrote to Walpole (in keeping with JW's focussed claim).

[13] Cf. 2 Thess. 2:11.

[14] Acts 26:25.

[15] Badcock had referred to a print made by George Vertue in 1745, drawing upon a picture of John Michael Williams, that bore this inscription.

[16] Horace, *Epistles*, II.ii.45; 'to search for truth in the groves of learning'.

and afterwards (while I was my father's curate), to save my own
soul and those that heard me.[17] When I returned to Oxford, it was
my full resolve to live and die there; the reasons for which I gave
in a long letter to my father, since printed in one of my *Journals*.[18]
5   In this purpose I continued till Dr. [John] Burton, one of the
Trustees for Georgia, pressed me to go over with General [James]
Oglethorpe (who is still alive, and well knows the whole transac-
tion), in order to preach to the Indians. With great difficulty I was
prevailed upon to go, and spend upwards of two years abroad. At
10 my return, I was more than ever determined to lay my bones at
Oxford. But I was insensibly led, without any previous plan or
design, to preach first in many of the churches in London, then in
more public places; afterwards in Bristol, Kingswood, Newcastle,
and throughout Great Britain and Ireland. Therefore all that Mr.
15 Badcock adds of the incidents that 'gave an additional force' to an
impression that never existed, is very ingenious; yet is in truth a
castle in the air.

7. It is true that for awhile I admired the mystic writers. But I
dropped them even before I went to Georgia—long before I knew
20 or suspected anything as justification by faith. Therefore all that
follows of my 'making my system of divinity more commodious
for general use', and of 'employing myself to search for some common bond whereby the most dissonant sects might have a center of
union'; having no foundation to stand upon, falls to the ground at
25 once. I had quite other work while I was at Oxford, being fully engaged, partly with my pupils, and partly with my little offices, being
Greek lecturer and moderator of both the classes.

8. 'His dexterity in debate has been so long known, that it is almost become proverbial.' It has been my first care for many years to
30 see that my cause was good; and never, either in jest or earnest, to
defend the wrong side of a question. And shame on me if I cannot
defend the right after so much practice, and having been so early
accustomed to separate truth from falsehood, how artfully soever
they were twisted together.

35 9. If the poem on 'Religious Discourse'[19] 'delineates the disposition and character of the author', it does not delineate mine—for I

---

[17] See 1 Tim. 4:16.
[18] JW to Samuel Wesley Sr., Dec. 10, 1734, 25:397–410 in this edn.; cf. *Journal*, Mar. 28, 1739, 19:39–45 in this edn.
[19] A poem quoted at some length by Badcock. JW published a much revised form of the poem (without naming an author) in *HSP* (1739), 58–63; and *MSP* (1744), 3:200–05.

was not the author, but Mr. John Gambold.[20] What becomes then of that good natured remark? 'The wonder is not that John Wesley should have shown an inclination to insult the memory of a sober divine, but that Samuel Wesley should have been disposed to show lenity to a Whig of the Revolution.' Mistake upon mistake! 1) Those marginal notes were not wrote by Samuel but Charles Wesley; he told me so this very day. 2) Both my father and all his sons have always praised God for the happy Revolution.[21] — I let Bishop [William] Warburton alone.[22] He is gone to rest; I well hope, in Abraham's bosom.

10. 'Mr. Wesley had very important end in view.' What end, but to save sinners? What other end could I possibly have in view? Or can have at this day? 'Deep projects of a subtle mind.' Nay, I am not subtle, but the veriest fool under the sun, if I have any earthly project at all now! For what do I want which this world can give? And, after the labour of fourscore years,

> No foot of land do I possess,
> No cottage in the wilderness,
>   A poor, wayfaring man
> I dwell awhile in tents below,
> Or gladly wander to and fro,
>   Till I my Canaan gain.[23]

John Wesley

Source: published transcription; *Arminian Magazine* 8 (1785): 151–54.[24]

---

[20] Cf. *The Works of the late Rev. John Gambold* (Bath: S. Hazard, 1789), 251–56. JW had access to this poem in manuscript form in the 1730s from his friend Gambold. Badcock apparently quoted from a manuscript copy of Gambold's original poem in JW's hand, which JW had sent his brother Samuel.

[21] I.e., when William and Mary displaced James from the British throne in 1688.

[22] Badcock had quoted one of Warburton's sharp criticisms of JW.

[23] Cf. CW, 'The Pilgrim', st. 6, *Redemption Hymns* (1747), 67.

[24] Shortly after the letter appeared in *AM*, one of JW's supporters sent it to *Gentleman's Magazine* 55 (1785), 246–47.

To Agnes Gibbes[25]

London
January 14, 1785

5

It is not for *me*, my dear Miss Agnes, to expect any long continuance here.

My race of glory's run, and race of shame,
10   And I shall shortly be with those that rest.[26]

But I cannot believe that the going hence will make any change
in the regard I feel for my dear friend. No! I rather think (as a good
man knows) that 'our union hereafter will be more intimate and
15 perfect, than it can be here'[27]—where our spirits are kept asunder
by these clogs of flesh and blood. And how grievously, in every respect, do these corruptible bodies press down the soul![28] Especially
during the time of sickness or weakness, as you have largely experienced. There is no doubt but a dry, clear air would be great service
20 to you. Especially if exercise were added to air, without which you
can hardly have either health or strength. But what exercise are you
capable of using during your present weakness; especially in such a
season as this, when you can hardly step out of doors but in a carriage? There is one and only one exercise (except walking gently,
25 a quarter of an hour at a time, in the house) which you might use
to what degree you pleased, and without the least fatigue. I mean
that which was invented by the late Bishop [George] Berkeley; and
which kept him alive many years: a chamber horse. I mean that sort
of it (sold by the upholsterers) which is in the form of an armed
30 chair rising upon springs, whereon you might, if you pleased, soon
put yourself into a sweat.[29]

It is a great paradox, and yet an undoubted truth, that God is the
center of spirits, and that no created spirit is on earth happy, but in
the knowledge and love of him.[30] While we are pursuing this, 'He

---

[25] Gibbes's letter informing JW of her illness, and wishing him long life, is not known
to survive.

[26] Cf. John Milton, Samson *Agonistes, ll.* 597–98.

[27] Jean Baptiste de Saint Juré, *The Holy Life of Monsieur de Renty* (London: John Crooke,
1657), 338; retained in JW's *Extract* (1741), Ch. 10, §10, p. 64.

[28] See Wisd. of Sol. 9:15.

[29] JW owned such a piece of furniture, see JW to Sarah Wesley Jr., Aug. 18, 1790.

[30] A form of JW's frequent allusion to Augustine, *Confessions,* I.1: 'Thou hast made us
for thyself, and restless is our heart till it comes to rest in thee.' See note 77, 1:148 in this edn.

giveth us all things richly to enjoy.'[31] Not that we may acquiesce in these *instead of him*, but that they may lead us to him. I believe he is jealous over you, lest you should forget that kind advice, 'My child give me thy heart!'[32]

That you and all the dear family may be thoroughly willing to do this is the earnest wish of, my very dear Miss Agnes,

Yours most affectionately,

John Wesley

Address: 'To / Miss Agnes Gibbes / At Sir Philip Gibbes, Bart / at Hilton Park, near / Wolverhampton'.
Postmark: '14/IA'.
Source: holograph; National Archives, PRO 30/9/11/2.

To the Rev. Peard Dickinson[33]

London
January 15, 1785

My Dear Brother,

I think the best model that ever was for the language of a Christian preacher is the First Epistle of St. John.

I know no tolerable commentator on the Old Testament. What is valuable in Poole and Henry you have in the *Notes*.[34]

Dodwell's *Letters* may be very useful; so may Dr. Doddridge's *Lectures*.[35]

---

[31] 1 Tim. 6:17.

[32] Cf. Prov. 23:26.

[33] Peard Dickinson (1758–1802) was born at Topsham and educated at Taunton School. While apprenticing under a jeweler in Bristol whose wife was Methodist, Dickinson converted and joined the local society. With the encouragement of JW and help from a widowed relative, he enrolled at St. Edmund Hall, Oxford in 1779, receiving his BA in 1783 and MA in 1785. He was ordained deacon in 1783 and was currently serving as curate to Rev. Vincent Perronet in Shoreham. Unsuccessful in succeeding Perronet later this year, Dickinson would serve other curacies until 1786, when JW recruited him to assist at City Road Chapel. This is JW's first surviving letter to Dickinson, responding to a letter from Dickinson (not known to survive) seeking advice about future study.

[34] Matthew Henry, *An Exposition of the Old Testament in Four Volumes* (1706); and Matthew Poole, *Annotations upon the Holy Bible* (1683–85); two of the main sources JW drew upon for comments in his own *OT Notes*.

[35] Henry Dodwell, *Two Letters of Advice: I. For the Susception of Holy Orders, II. For Studies Theological* (Dublin: Benjamin Tooke, 1672); and Philip Doddridge, *A Course of Lectures on the Principle Subjects of Pneumatology, Ethics, and Divinity* (London: J. Buckland, 1763).

Leland's *View* is excellent in its kind; so is Grotious.[36] That *Theory of Religion* I do not know.[37]

Hammond's *Catechism*, Wake, and Clark I think scarce worth reading.[38] Everything of Worthington is good.[39] Erasmus' cate-
5 chism I do not know; neither Stevenson.[40]

[Edward] Welchman's, [Charles] Wheatly's, and Archbishop [Edward] Synge's tracts are the best in their kind. Howe's *Living Temple*, Jones, *Clemens Romanus*, and Patrick's *Advice* are excellent.[41] That *Attempt to Explain* I doubt is a weak attempt.[42]

10 [George] Herbert, [Marco Girolamo] Vida, [George] Buchanan, and [Samuel] Johnson are excellent [poets] in their several kinds.

Austin's *Meditations* (not his) are devout.[43] The *Exercitium Pietatis* I have not seen.[44] The *Gentleman Instructed* is a well-wrote book.[45] [Ezekiel] Hopkins is a strong and a pious writer.

---

[36] John Leland, *A View of the Principal Deistical Writers that have appeared in England in the last and present Century*, 4 vols. (London: Benjamin Dod, 1754–57); and Hugo Grotius, *The Truth of the Christian Religion* (London: Knapton, 1711).

[37] Dickinson had likely asked JW about another work in apologetics: John Orr, *The Theory of Religion* in its absolute internal state, in three parts: *I. Of the Nature and End of Religion* …. *II. Of the Evidences of Natural and Revealed Religion* …; *III. Of the Excellence and Importance of True Religion* (London: Millar, 1762).

[38] Henry Hammond, *A Practical Catechism* (London: Richard Royston, 1645); William Wake, *The Principles of the Christian Religion Explained; Being a Commentary on the Church Catechism* (London: Richard Sare, 1699); and Samuel Clarke, *An Exposition of the Church-Catechism* (London: John & Paul Knapton, 1729).

[39] John Worthington, *A Form of Sound Words; or, A Scripture-Catechism* (London: Meredith, 1673).

[40] Desiderius Erasmus, *A Plain and Practical Exposition of the Creed and Decalogue* (orig. 1533); and William Stevenson, *The Whole Faith and Duty of a Christian* (London: Holland and Hartwell, 1717).

[41] John Howe, *The Living Temple; or, A Designed Improvement of that Notion that a Good Man is the Temple of God* (London: R. Clavel, 1702); the *Epistles of Clement of Rome*; and Simon Patrick, *Advice to a Friend* (London: R. Royston, 1673) are clear. Given the genre, 'Jones' likely refers to JW's friend Thomas Jones of Southwark, *The Religious Remembrancer: …On the great subjects of real and practical religion* (London: [s.n.,] 1756).

[42] Possibly referring to William Robertson, *An Attempt to explain the Words Reason, Substance, Person, Creeds* … (London: W. Johnston, 1766).

[43] I.e., *Pious Breathings: Being the Meditations of St. Augustine, His Treatise of the Love of God, Soliloquies, and Manual. To which are added Select Contemplations for St. Anselm and St. Bernard* (London: Knapton et al., 1701).

[44] Johann Gerhard, *Exercitium Pietatis Quotidianum Quadripartitum* (Jena: Steinmannus, 1613); ET: *Gerards Prayers; or, A Daily Exercise of Piety, divided into four parts* (London: Jackson, 1625).

[45] William Darrell, *A Gentleman Instructed in the Conduct of a Virtuous and Happy Life* (London: Evets, 1704).

I do not know Küster or the *Ellipses Graecae*.[46] Ockley's Introduction is counted good.[47] Clerc's works are middling.[48] The *Antiquitates Hebraicae* I have not seen.[49] Seneca's *Tragedies* and Ovid's *Metamorphosis* are worth reading once. So are Valleius Paterculus, and the *Excerpta ex Ovidio, Virgilio, Horatio, Juvenali, Persio*.[50] Their *whole* works are not worth reading. Neither are Seneca's. Terence is worth studying; it is the finest Latin in the world. That tract of Erasmus I have not read. [Decimius Magnus] Ausonius is little worth. Epictutus' and More's *Enchiridion* are excellent books.[51] Tully's *Offices* deserve an attentive reading.[52] I have not seen the *Polymetis*, Upton's *Delectus*, or the *Scriptores Graeci*.[53] Sallust writes Latin next to Terence. Duncan, Watts, and Sanderson are the best next Aldrich.[54] Aristotle is an admirable writer. Callinus is not a bad one. Scapula's *Lexicon* is not to be compared to Hederic's.[55] Schlinler's I know not.[56] Nor Schickard.[57] All [Johannes] Leusden's publications are good. He was an excellent scholar.

But you need not half these books. A few well digested are better than ten thousand. It would be worth your while to consider the 'Course of Female Study', in the *Arminian Magazine*.[58]

Peace be with all your spirits! I am,

[46] Ludolph Küster (1670–1716), a Greek linguist; and Lambert Bos, *Ellipses Graecae* (Franeker: Strickius, 1702).

[47] Simon Ockley, *Introductio ad linguas orientales* (Cambridge: John Owen, 1706).

[48] Given the context, likely referring to the various editions of Latin and Greek authors produced by Jean Le Clerc (1657–1736).

[49] Apparently Conrad Iken, *Antiquitates Hebraicae* (Bremen: H. Jaeger, 1732).

[50] Velleius Paterculus, *Historiae romanae;* and JW's abridged collection, *Excerpta ex Ovidio, Virgilio, Horatio, Juvenali, Persio, et Martiali* (1749, *Bibliography*, No. 174).

[51] Epictetus (55–135), *Enchiridion;* and Henry More, *Enchiridion ethicum* (London: J. Flesher, 1668).

[52] I.e., Marcus Tullius Cicero, *De Officiis.*

[53] Joseph Spence, *Polymetis: or, An Enquiry concerning the Agreement between the Works of the Roman Poets, and the Remains of the Ancient Artists* (London: Dodsley, 1747); James Upton, *Poikilē historia; sive, Novus historiarum fabellarumque delectus* (London: Samuel Smith, 1701); and John Hudson, *Geographiae Veteris Scriptores Graeci Minores* (Oxford: Sheldonian, 1698).

[54] William Duncan, *The Elements of Logic* (London: R. Dodsley, 1748); Robert Sanderson, *Logicae Artis Compendium* (Oxford: Davis, 1664); Henry Aldrich, *Artis Logicae Compendium* (Oxford: Sheldonian Theatre, 1691).

[55] Comparing Johann Scapula, *Lexico Graeco Latinum* (Basel: Hervagiana, 1580); to Benjamin Hederich, *Lexicon manuale Graecum* (London: H. Knaplock, 1739).

[56] JW's spelling is a bit unclear; the likely work is: Valentin Schindler, *Lexicon pentaglotton, Hebraicum, Chaldaicum, Syriacum, Talmudico-Rabbinicum, [et] Arabicum* (London: William Jones, 1635).

[57] Wilhelm Schickard, *Horologium Ebraeum sive consilium* (London: Robert Scott, 1675).

[58] I.e., JW's letter, c. Sept. 1778, to Miss L. [Mary Lewis?], 29:434–38 in this edn. It was published with the title JW gives above in *AM* 3 (1780): 602–04.

Your affectionate brother,

J. Wesley

Address: 'To / The Revd Mr. Dickenson / To be left at Mrs. George's[59] / In Sevenoaks'.
Postmark: '15/IA.
Endorsement: by Dickinson, 'Rev. J. W. / Jan 15 85'.
Source: holograph; Bridwell Library (SMU).

To John Johnson

London
January 26, 1785

My Dear Brother,

It is plain the time is come for God to lift up the light of his countenance upon poor Lisburn.[60] This is the answer of many prayers offered up by good sister Gardner and many others.[61] His providence brought both you and sister [Dorothea] Johnson thither in good time. She was more wanted now in Lisburn than even in Dublin, as Hetty Rogers was enabled in a great measure to supply her place there. You will prevail upon more and more to meet in band, and more and more backsliders will be healed. I expect you will in a little time have a select society also.

If my life and health are continued, I hope to cross the sea about the beginning of April. But how many blessings may you receive before that time!

I am
Your affectionate friend and brother,

[J. Wesley]

Source: published transcription; Telford, *Letters*, 7:253.

[59] Mrs. Amy George (d. 1798; maiden name unknown) was the widow of William George (d. c. 1753). She ran a grocery in Sevenoaks and often hosted Methodist preachers there. See *MM* 41 (1818): 561–68; and *WHS* 34 (1964): 89.

[60] See Num. 6:26.

[61] Possibly Catherine (Skerrett) Gardner (1724–91), mother of Mary Gardner (1764–1821) who became the second wife of William Black (1746–1835) in 1782.

To Dorothea (Garret / King) Johnson

London
January 26, 1785

My Dear Sister,

I nothing doubt but the death of that young man will be a means
of life to many souls.[62] How admirably was it timed! Just when
brother [John] Johnson and you were returning to Lisburn, here
was a divine preparation for your coming and work ready prepared
for you. I hope my poor dear Harriet will run away from us no
more. She was unspeakably happy when she was young; but she
may be happier now than ever she was. I am in hopes you now will
have full employment. But you need not confine yourself altogether
to Lisburn. You are a debtor also to our sisters in the neighbouring
societies. Go on and prosper!

I am, my dear sister,
Your affectionate brother,

[J. Wesley]

Source: published transcription; Telford, *Letters*, 7:253–54.

To Jane (Lee) Freeman

London
February 1, 1785

My Dear Sister,

So strange things come to pass![63] I did not expect to hear of Mr.
Smyth's 'living in lodgings'.[64]

I do not remember the person who is so kind as to offer me a
lodging; and I know no reason why I should not accept of it, if I live
to see Dublin again.[65]

---

[62] JW enlarged upon this situation in his *Journal* on June 11, 1785, when he visited Lisburn (see 23:367 in this edn.). The young man was the only child of John Wilson and his wife, who had been pillars of the society in Lisburn for many years but had left it. Their son was killed by a fall from his horse, and the parents were inconsolable. When Dorothea arrived in Lisburn after her recent marriage to John Johnson, she took the couple into her care and helped them find consolation—whereupon they rejoined the society. Dorothea had apparently sent JW a summary of these events in a letter (not known to survive).

[63] Freeman's letter with this news is not known to survive.

[64] Rev. Edward Smyth had returned to Dublin after the death of his wife Agnes in 1783.

[65] Arthur Keene likely made the earlier offer, which he reiterated; see JW to Keene, Feb. 17, 1785.

It gives me pleasure to hear that the work of God flourishes among you. I did not doubt but it would when he sent that earnest couple to Dublin.[66] He will send a blessing with them wherever they go. And that you and yours may partake of it more and more is

5 the wish of, my dear sister,

Yours affectionately,

J. Wesley

10 *Address*: 'To / Mrs Jane Freeman / to be left at the New Room / in / Dublin'.
Postmark: 'FE/3'.
Source: holograph; privately held (WWEP Archive holds photocopy).

15

To Robert Barry

[London]
20 February 2, 1785

My Dear Brother,

Between ten and eleven years ago I had a violent fever, which brought me to the gates of death.[67] I had no discernible pulse, and seemed to be just upon the wing, when I was suddenly seized with a

25 violent vomiting. My pulse then began to beat again; and from that hour I have had, as it were, a new body with such health as I never had before.

Mr. Henry said, 'I bless God that I am never tired *of* my work, yet I am often tired *in* my work.'[68] By the blessing of God I can

30 say more, I am never tired *in* my work. From the beginning of the day, or the week, or the year, to the end I do not know what weariness means. I am never weary of writing, or preaching, or travelling, but am just as fresh at the end as at the beginning. This hath God wrought![69] Thus it is with me today, and I take no thought for the

35 morrow.[70]

---

[66] James and Hester Ann (Roe) Rogers.

[67] See JW, *Journal*, June 13–28, 1775, 22:455–57 in this edn.

[68] JW's adaption of Matthew Henry, *An Account of the Life and Death of the Rev. Philip Henry* (London: Parkhurst & Lawrence, 1698), 174; 'he scarce thought the Lord's Day well-spent if he was not weary in body at night—wearied with his work, but not weary of it, as he used to distinguish'. JW retained in his abridgement in the *Christian Library*, 50:117.

[69] See Ps. 118:23.

[70] See Matt. 6:34.

I am in hopes Dr. [Thomas] Coke will come to you, with brother [William] Black, and bring a preacher that may spend some time among you. The passage from New York to Shelbourne is far shorter than the passage from England—so that it is probable, for the time to come, you will be supplied with preachers from thence, and the more exactly you observe the old Methodist discipline, the more your souls will prosper.

If your brother [Alexander] comes over merely to get money, he will get little grace by the change. That is by no means a sufficient reason for giving up his Christian friends, and so many spiritual advantages. Many have left their country from this poor motive. Is it any wonder their souls did not prosper? Their eye was not single; how then should the body be full of light?[71] I advise you, by all lawful means, to keep favour with your clergymen. If they can do little good, they can do much harm to the work of God. They can lay more hindrances in your way than you are sensible of. If it be possible, as much as lieth in you, live peaceably with all men;[72] but with the clergy in particular. If you can do it without violating your conscience, make and keep them your friends. At least, if it can be avoided, make them not your enemies. I commend you all to him who is able to lead into all holiness, and am, my dear brother,

Your affectionate brother,

J. Wesley

Address: 'To Mr. Robert Barry, Shelburne, Nova Scotia'.
Source: published transcription; *Christian Witness* 18 (1861): 79–80.

To Samuel Bardsley

London
February 12, 1785

Dear Brother,

Mr. Wesley desires me to inform you that he is glad to find that you go on so well in your circuit, and hopes that the work of the Lord will prosper more and more.[73] Mr. Wesley cannot say anything positive respecting his coming into your circuit, but does intend to

---

[71] See Matt. 6:22.
[72] See Rom. 12:18.
[73] Bardsley was currently stationed in Nottingham; see 10:555 in this edn.

contrive to pay you a visit; though his usual way, you know, is but once in two years. I suppose you will know in time before he comes. Peace be with your spirit!

I am

5   Yours affectionately,

T. Tennant

Source: holograph; Duke, Rubenstein, Frank Baker Collection of Wesley-
10   ana, Box WF 1.

To Adam Clarke[74]

15

London
February 12, 1785

Dear Adam,

20   I do not remember ever to have seen that letter from Norwich, else I should certainly have answered it.

If you build at St. Austell,[75] take care that you do not make the house too small. And pray let those directions be observed which are given in the large *Minutes* of the Conference.[76]

25   It gives me pleasure to hear that the work of the Lord so prospers in your hands. It will do so as long as you do not shun to declare the whole counsel of God.[77] There is one part of it which seems to be almost forgotten by the Methodists throughout the three king-doms—that is, the Christian duty of fasting. And yet our Lord an-
30   nexes a peculiar promise even to secret fasting: 'The Father that seeth in secret, he shall reward thee openly.'[78] You might begin to recommend this by reading to every society the sermon concerning fasting.[79] The blessing would soon follow.

I am, dear Adam,

35   Yours affectionately,

J. Wesley

[74] This is JW's first known surviving letter to Adam Clarke.
[75] JW spells 'Austle'; here and in address portion.
[76] 'Large' *Minutes* (1770), §68, 10:896–97 in this edn.
[77] See Acts 20:27.
[78] Matt. 6:18.
[79] I.e., 'Upon our Lord's Sermon on the Mount, VII', 1:592–611 in this edn.

Address: 'To / Mr Adam Clarke / At Mr [George] Flamank's / In St.
Austell / Cornwall'.
Postmark: '12/FE'.
Endorsement: by Clarke, 'Recd Feb. 17. 1785'.
Source: holograph; MARC, WCB, D6/1/68.

To Robert Carr Brackenbury

London
February 15, 1785

Dear Sir,

Your having the opportunity of giving them a few discourses in
Dover, and then travelling with so pious and friendly a person as
Mr. [James] Ireland, I could not but look upon as clear instances
of a gracious providence.[80] I cannot doubt but the mild air which
you now breathe, will greatly tend to the re-establishment of your
health. And so will the suspension of your public labours, till you
are better able to bear them. You was reduced, before you left England, almost to the condition of Mr. [John] Valton—who (as I am
informed by his last letter[81]) is absolutely forbidden by his physician
to speak in public at all. But it is well, if that prohibition does not
come too late, if his health can ever be re-established.

With regard to perfecting yourself in the French language, it is
certain this may be done more speedily and effectually in a family where French, than in one where English, is constantly spoken.
And undoubtedly you may learn the purity of the language far better in Languedoc than in Normandy.

It is clear that you are not called at present to any public labour.
But should not you be so much the more diligent in private? To redeem the time? To buy up every opportunity?[82] Should not you be
instant 'in season and out of season'?[83] That is, to *make* the opportunities which you cannot *find*? Surely the all-wise and all-merciful
Saviour of men, did not send you into France for nothing! Oh no!

---

[80] James Ireland, a sugar and wine merchant made regular trips to France. John Fletcher
had accompanied him before and Brackenbury did so in the fall of 1784.
[81] This letter, which JW replied to this same day, is not known to survive.
[82] See Eph. 5:16 (*NT Notes*).
[83] 2 Tim. 4:2.

You are at least to pluck one brand (perhaps several) out of the burning.[84]

'Two or three years in Jersey?'[85] I had almost said God forbid! Has he no more work from you to do in England? I have no objection to your staying there two or three months, so that you may be present at the Conference in London. May the God whom you serve in all things direct your paths![86] So prays, dear sir,

> Your affectionate friend and servant,

> J. Wesley

Address: 'A / Monsieur / Monsr Brackenbury / Chez Monsr Ferrier Junr / A Ganges / en Languedoc'.

Postmark: '16/FE'.

Source: holograph; Wesley's Chapel (London), LDWMM 1994/1981.

To John Francis Valton

> London
> February 15, 1785

My Dear Brother,

I am entirely of Dr. Davison's opinion that nothing but the spring and cold bathing, with an entire cessation from speaking in public, can possibly restore you.[87] I desire therefore you would not, on any solicitation whatever, speak in public at all. If you are censured for this, bear it as your cross. You are herein not to please man but God.

I myself was silent from November till March, or I should not have been alive now.[88] I am,

> Your affectionate friend and brother,

> J. Wesley

Postmark: '16/FE'.

Endorsement: by Valton, 'Feb 15th 1785'.

Source: holograph; MARC, MAM JW 5/34.

---

[84] See Zech. 3:2.
[85] Brackenbury had been stationed to the Channel Islands at the 1784 Conference; he would serve there until 1790.
[86] See Prov. 3:6.
[87] Cf. JW to Valton, Oct. 13, 1784.
[88] In 1753; cf. ibid.

To Captain Richard Williams[89]

London
February 15, 1785

My Dear Brother, 5

I am exceeding glad at your going to Plymouth Dock.[90] I am persuaded that God has sent you. And I should not wonder if you find a greater blessing upon your labours than ever you found before. I pray, stay there as long as you can. And send a particular account of what occurs there to, dear Richard, 10

Your affectionate brother,

J. Wesley

Source: holograph; Huntington Library, Manuscripts, HM 57051.

15

To Ann Bolton

20

near London
February 16, 1785

My Dear Nancy,

Your last a little surprised me. Shall I speak freely? I have always done so to *you*. 25

Some years since an agreeable man courted you. But though you liked his person and his temper, yet you refused him 'because he was not religious'.[91] And now a scruple comes into your mind: 'Whether you did well in refusing him?' And 'whether you ought not to accept him now?' 30

To the former question I answer: If the Bible be true, you undoubtedly did well in obeying his word, in not being *unequally yoked*, in offering a costly sacrifice to God.[92] If so, it is easy to answer second. After God has once and again delivered you from the snare, though almost against your will, and by very severe means, 35

---

[89] While the address portion is missing, the identity of the recipient is confirmed by JW to Mary Clarke, Feb. 16, 1785. William's time in Plymouth Dock was brief.

[90] JW had received word that William Moore, one of two preachers in the Plymouth circuit, had renounced the Methodists and was setting up an independent church there; see JW, *Journal*, Feb. 25, 1786, 23:343 in this edn.

[91] See JW to Bolton, Dec. 12, 1773 (28:624 in this edn.); Jan. 20, 1774 (29:8); Feb. 17, 1774 (29:18); and May 8, 1780 (29:568).

[92] See 2 Cor. 6:14.

can you once think of entangling yourself again? Is Mr. [John] Arundel more religious now than before? Nay, less if possible. He has now neither the power of religion nor the form. You can't there-fore have anything to do with him, without violating a plain com-5 mand of God. O start from every thought of the kind!

It seems to have been a kind providence withheld your going to Stroud while this temptation was upon you—which I thought bodily pain, with other heavy pressures, had not only suspended but utterly annihilated.

10 If a woman of piety, one deeply experienced in religion, and deeply engaged in the work of God, should take such a step as this, probably she would do more harm at one stroke than she had done good in her life! And shall Nancy Bolton lay such a stumbling block in the way of the weak?[93] Yea, and the strong? Better that she were 15 taken to Abraham's bosom.

See, my dear Nancy, how freely I speak, because I am,
Your truly affectionate friend and brother,

J. Wesley

20 From many heavy pressures you are already delivered. And doubtless God will deliver you out of all. You have been honoured to save from ruin your father, mother, brother! And to save many precious souls from death. And shall you *now* faint? God forbid! Awake! Praise God! Woman, remember the faith!

25 *Address*: 'To / Miss Bolton / In Witney / Oxfordshire'.
Postmarks: '16/FE' and '17/FE'. *Charge*: '4'.
Endorsement: by Bolton, 'Feb 16 –85'.
Source: holograph; privately held (WWEP Archive holds photocopy).

30

To Mary Clark

35
near London
February 16 [1785]
My Dear Sister,
Although I suppose you already know what is determined, yet I 40 send you a few lines because I love you.

---

[93] See 1 Cor. 8:9.

I have desired Mr. [John] Mason, who is in the Devonshire circuit, to step down to the Dock as soon as he can.[94] And in the meantime God has sent thither out of Cornwall a son of thunder, Captain
Richard Williams.[95] I hardly know such another man in England,
for a business of this kind.

> [...] God and his son except
> Created thing naught values he nor fears.[96]

I wish *you* a portion of his Spirit, and am, my dear sister,
>   Yours affectionately,
>>   J. Wesley

Address: 'To / Miss Clarke / Near St Johns / in / Worcester'.
Postmark: '16/FE'. *Charge*: '3'.
Source: holograph; Bridwell Library (SMU).[97]

To Arthur Keene

>   London
>   February 17, 1785

My Dear Brother,
    I thank you for the pains you have taken on behalf of poor Robert
Hyde,[98] and am sincerely glad you have at length succeeded. Now,
if he continue honest and industrious, he will not want either employment or food. Want either of the one or the other must have
exposed him to a thousand temptations.
    When several disapproved of my sending Mr. [James] Rogers and
his wife [Hester] to Dublin, supposing them unequal to the task,
I was determined to overrule, believing myself to be a competent
judge both of their gifts and grace. And the event has answered my
expectations. I am not disappointed of my hope.[99] And I am persuaded neither they nor you will ever be weary of well-doing.

---

[94] Mason was going to replace William Moore, who had abruptly left the Methodist connexion; see JW, *Journal*, Feb. 25, 1785, 23:343 in this edn.
[95] See JW to Williams, Feb. 15, 1785.
[96] Cf. Milton, *Paradise Lost*, ii.678–79.
[97] Previously held in WMC Museum, 2002.001.035.
[98] Orig., 'Hide'; cf. note on JW to Keene, July 23, 1784.
[99] See Rom. 5:5.

You have great reason to bless God for the good state of your temporal affairs also. And indeed I have always observed, whenever the work of God goes on, he withholds no manner of thing that is good.[100]

5   It was impossible to keep the present schoolmaster unless his spirit had been entirely changed.[101] He is ostensively insane. But I am afraid another is recommended to you that is likely to prove no better. I have known him from a child, and give you fair warning. Take care what you do. If you are wise, secure Mr. Fox at any

10   price. That man is sterling gold.[102] But you will have no blessing from God and no praise from wise men if you take that vile sordid measure (especially at *this time*!) of so reducing the salary. You *must* give £40 a year at the least.

As soon after the 10th of April as I can I purpose (God willing) to

15   embark for Dublin. I should be glad to accept of your kind invitation. But it is a great way to go, particularly at night. Otherwise I should be more at home with you than anywhere else.[103]

I commend you and yours to the divine protection; and am, dear Arthur,

20   Your affectionate friend and brother,

J. Wesley

I abhor the thought of our master's keeping an evening school. It would swallow up the time he ought to have for his own improve-

25   ment. Give him enough to live comfortably upon, without this drudgery.

Feb. 20. Pray tell Mr. Rogers I hope to see him before the middle of April and to visit the classes. I am glad he has written to Mr. Fox; but I have told you my mind about the salary.

30   *Address*: 'To / Mr Arthur Keen / Miltown Road / near / Dublin'.
Postmarks: '21/FE' and 'FE/25'.
Endorsement: by Keene, '17th Feby 1785 / Revd Jno Wesley / London / concerning Condy, etc.'.
Source: holograph; MARC, MAM JW 3/75.

35

[100] See Ps. 84:11.

[101] See JW to Keene, Mar. 3, 1784; Richard Condy was the initial master of the school.

[102] Patrick Fox (c. 1753–1830), of a Liverpool Catholic family, was converted in his early twenties and became a member of the Liverpool Methodist society. In 1781 JW appointed him a class leader there. With JW's encouragement he moved to became master of the school in Dublin, and served for 8 years. Fox remained in Ireland, prominent in the Dublin society and beyond. See *WMM* 10 (1831): 68; and Cooney, 'Methodist Schools', 42.

[103] JW stayed at the preachers' house; see *Journal*, Apr. 11, 1785, 23:348 in this edn.

To Ann Tindall

Dorking
February 18, 1785   5

My Dear Sister,

It is a general rule, established in the Conference, that 'none should beg for preaching houses out of their own circuit'.[104] And I do not often give consent to the violation of any of our established rules. The proper method of reducing the debt is that which you   10 have already adopted. Procure as many yearly subscribers as you can; only assure them that the money raised thereby shall be applied to no other purpose whatsoever but paying the debt that is upon the house.

As you have already peace and love among you, I expect you will   15 soon have an increase; especially if meetings for prayer be constantly held, and duly attended.

I am, my dear Nancy,
Your affectionate brother,

J. Wesley   20

Address: 'To / Miss Tindall / in / Scarborough'.
Postmarks: '21/FE' and '22/FE'.
Endorsement: by Tindall, '18 Feb. 1785'.
Source: holograph; British Library, Department of Manuscripts, Add.   25
  MS. 43695, ff. 90–91.

30

To John Broadbent

London
February 23, 1785   35

My Dear Brother,

Take care you do not *scream* again, unless you would murder yourself outright.

It is very probable we *must* take in some married preachers if we live to see another Conference. The week after next I set [out] for   40

---

[104] See *Minutes* (1783), Q. 23, 10:541 in this edn.

Bristol. From thence (after stopping there a few days) I must make the best of my way to Ireland.

Concerning dividing the circuit, I may answer you and our brother together.[105] I like the proposal well, especially as it would give our preachers a little more walking. But I very rarely divide circuits unless at a Conference, because I am willing to hear what can be said on both sides.

I am

Your affectionate friend and brother,

J. Wesley

Address: 'To / Mr Broadbent / At the Preachinghouse / In Birstall, near / Leeds'.

Source: holograph; privately held (WWEP Archive holds a lithograph).

To John Baxendale

London
February 25, 1785

My Dear Brother,

You send me an agreeable account of the work of God in and near Wigan.[106] Indeed, his work will flourish in every place where full sanctification is clearly and strongly preached. This year I only call on a few societies on my way. My business is with the societies in Ireland. I hope to call at Manchester on Saturday, April 2; at Bolton, the 4th; Wigan, Tuesday, the 5th. Perhaps I might preach at Wingate on my way thither.

I am

Your affectionate brother,

[J. Wesley]

Source: published transcription; Jackson, *Works* (3rd), 13:35–36.

---

[105] Broadbent was currently Assistant for the Birstall circuit, with three other preachers. 'Our brother' was likely Robert Roberts, one of these three. At the 1785 Conference a circuit for Dewsbury was split off from the Birstall circuit, and Roberts was named Assistant for Dewsbury. See 10:571 in this edn.

[106] This letter is not known to survive.

To Ann Bolton

London
February 25, 1785

My Dear Nancy,

In your former letter you spoke as if you was afraid to speak. In your last you speak just as *I* would speak to *you*.[107] I have tenderly loved you for many years—indeed ever since I was acquainted with you. Although I have sometimes been a little pained at your reserve, and have thought you had almost forgotten me.

You have not yet thoroughly learnt to apply that exhortation, 'Despise not thou the chastening of the Lord, nor faint when thou art rebuked of him.'[108] You are apt to *faint*. You will not give God time to work his own work, in his own way. Woman, remember the faith! Help is at hand. I will give you five and twenty pounds. I do not say, 'I will *lend* you.' For you are my friend. Therefore you might command much more than this, suppose I had it by me. In the meantime, accept this as a little token of the sincere affection with which I am, my dear Nancy,

Ever yours,

J. Wesley

Address: 'To / Miss Bolton / In Witney / Oxfordshire'.
Postmark: '28/FE'. *Charge*: '4'.
Endorsement: by Bolton, 'Feb 25 –85'.
Source: holograph; privately held (WWEP Archive holds photocopy).

To Jonathan Coussins

London
February 25, 1785

My Dear Brother,

The Lord *will* work; and who shall hinder him? Only let us against hope believe in hope.[109] And walk in all his appointed ways, whether

---

[107] Neither of the letters from Bolton are known to survive. The first drew JW's letter of Feb. 16, 1785; the second was in response to that letter from JW.
[108] Heb. 12:5.
[109] See Rom. 4:18.

we see present fruit or not.[110] Now encourage all believers to meet
in band and to observe the band rules exactly.[111] In one thing Dr.
Hunt and his people shame us;[112] I mean in fasting, which we have
well-nigh forgotten! Let us begin again!

5   I am, with love to sister [Penelope] Coussins,
            Your affectionate friend and brother,

                                                            J. Wesley

10   *Address*: 'To / Mr. Coussens / At the Preachinghouse / in / Norwich'.
      Postmark: '26/FE'. *Charge*: '5'.
      Source: holograph; MARC, MAM JW 2/64.

15

To John Stretton[113]

                                                            London
20   February 25, 1785
My Dear Brother,
      You did well in breaking through that needless diffidence; if you
had wrote sooner, you would have heard from me sooner.[114] Although I have not been at Limerick for some years, yet I remem-
25   ber your father and mother well. They truly feared God when

---

[110] See Eph. 2:10.
[111] See 9:77–79 of this edn.
[112] John Hunt (c. 1738–1824), of Norwich, was a surgeon by trade and ornithologist by
avocation. He was also a spiritual 'seeker', aligning himself at various times with Presbyterians,
Independents, Baptists, and others; but most at home among the Methodists in later years.
Hunt lived on Ber Street, and his garden included a summer house. In 1781 he licensed this
house with the bishop for religious worship, and called it Ebenezer chapel. JW preached there
in 1781 and 1783. Hunt and his wife Susanna eventually retired to Gissing in south Norfolk
(see *Norfolk Chronicle*, July 3, 1824).
[113] John Stretton (1744–1817), a native of Limerick, moved to Waterford to engage in
trade with Newfoundland. While there he was converted to Methodism by Eliza Bennis. In
1770 he immigrated to Newfoundland, briefly in Carbonear, but by 1771 in Harbour Grace.
Stretton became a central figure in continuing the Methodist presence Laurence Coughlan had
birthed in that setting. He also wrote Bennis frequently, reporting on the state of Methodism
there. See Crookshank, *Ireland*, 169; Bennis, *Correspondence*, 199–256; and Alexander Suther-
land, *Methodism in Canada* (London: Kelly, 1903), 103–11.
[114] Stretton had written to JW in the fall of 1784, asking him to send a preacher to Harbour Grace; see Bennis, *Correspondence*, 243.

I conversed with them. Be a follower of them, as they were of Christ.[115]

The last time I saw Mr. [Lawrence] Coughlan he was ill in body but in a blessed state of mind.[116] He was utterly broken in pieces, full of tears and contrition for his past unfaithfulness. Not long after I went out of town, God removed him to a better place.

If that deadly enemy of true religion, popery, is breaking in upon you, there is indeed no time to be lost; for it is far easier to prevent the plague than to stop it. Last autumn Dr. [Thomas] Coke sailed from England, and is now visiting the flock in the midland provinces of America, and settling them on the New Testament plan—to which they all willingly and joyfully conform, being all united, as by one Spirit, so in one body.[117] I trust they will no more want [i.e., lack] such pastors as are after God's own heart. After he has gone through those parts he intends, if God permit, to see the brethren in Nova Scotia, probably attended with one or two able preachers who will be willing to abide there.

A day or two ago I wrote and desired him, before he returns to England, to call upon our brethren also in Newfoundland, and perhaps leave a preacher there likewise.[118] About food and raiment we take no thought. Our heavenly Father knoweth that we, need these things, and he will provide.[119] Only let us be faithful and diligent in feeding his flock. Your preacher will be ordained.

Go on in the name of the Lord and in the power of his might! You shall want no assistance that is in the power of

Your affectionate friend and brother,

John Wesley

Address: 'To / Mr John Stretton / In Harbour Grace / Newfoundland'.
Source: holograph; Drew, Methodist Archives.

---

[115] See 1 Cor. 11:1.

[116] Coughlan's support of Methodist spirituality and values led to conflicts with some local merchants. They in turn urged the governor and the SPG to discipline him. Tiring of the conflict, Coughlan returned to England in 1773, where he served in Lady Huntingdon's connexion until his death in early 1784.

[117] See 1 Cor. 12:13.

[118] This letter is not known to survive.

[119] See Matt. 6:25–26.

To Zechariah Yewdall

London
February 25, 1785

My Dear Brother,

I am glad to hear that the work of God goes on at Sheerness, and that there is such a noble spirit among the people with regard to building.[120] But as we are yet early in the year, I do not advise you to begin till two hundred pounds are subscribed. Try first what you can do in Kent and at Norwich, after keeping a day of fasting and prayer.

I am
Your affectionate friend and brother,

[J. Wesley]

Source: published transcription; Jackson, *Works* (3rd), 13:15.

To the Methodist Preachers and People[121]

Plymouth Dock
March 3, 1785

1. In June 1744 I desired my brother and a few other clergymen to meet me in London, to consider how we should proceed to save our own souls and those that heard us.[122] After some time, I invited the lay preachers that were in the house to meet with us. We conferred

---

[120] Sheerness was one of the places endorsed for building a preaching-house in the 1785 *Minutes*; 10:585 in this edn.

[121] The debate which flared before the 1784 Conference, sparked by the Deed of Declaration, and fuelled by the *Appeal* of John Hampson Sr. and others to have it overturned, did not end with the decision of both the Irish Conference and the British Conference to uphold the Deed (see the note on JW to Arthur Keene, July 23, 1784). While some backers of the *Appeal* withdrew from the connexion after the 1784 Conference, questions continued to ripple among itinerants, local preachers, and general members of Methodist societies. See particularly the letter of John Hampson Jr. to JW, Jan. 25, 1785; and the later petition by James Oddie and others, June 14, 1785. This public letter was intended to quiet that concern but did not appear in print until Aug.

[122] See 1 Tim. 4:16.

together for several days, and were much comforted and strengthened thereby.[123]

2. The next year I not only invited most of the travelling preachers, but several others, to confer with me in Bristol. And from that time, for some years, though I *invited* only a part of the travelling preachers, yet I *permitted* any that desired it to be present, not apprehending any ill consequences therefrom.

3. But two ill consequences soon appeared: one, that the expense was too great to be borne; the other, that many of our people were scattered while they were left without a shepherd. I therefore determined 1) that for the time to come, none should be present but those whom I invited; and 2) that I would only invite a select number out of every circuit.

4. This I did for many years, and all that time the term 'Conference' meant not so much the conversation we had together as the persons that conferred; namely, those whom I invited to confer with me from time to time. So that all this time it depended on me alone, not only what persons should constitute the Conference, but whether there should be any Conference at all. This lay wholly in my own breast; neither the preachers nor the people having any part or lot in the matter.

5. Some years after, it was agreed that after the decease of my brother and me, the preachers should be stationed by the Conference.[124] But ere long a question arose, What does that term mean? Who are the Conference? It appeared difficult to define the term. And the year before last all our brethren who were met at Bristol desired me to fix the determinate meaning of the word.[125]

6. Hitherto, it had meant (not *the whole body of travelling preachers*, it never bore that meaning at all; but) *those persons whom I invited yearly to confer with me*. But to this there was a palpable objection: such a Conference would have no being after my death. And what other definition of it to give, I knew not. At least I knew none that would stand good in law. I consulted a skilful and hon-

---

[123] This first Conference ran June 25–30, 1746; for the Minutes see 10:123–46 in this edn.

[124] See the paper that JW read at Conference on Aug. 4, 1769, esp. 10:377–78 in this edn. The plan was then placed in the 'Large' *Minutes* (1770ff.) as Q. 78, 10:903–04 in this edn.

[125] The question had become urgent because of JW's efforts to enforce the Model Deed on all Methodist preaching-houses. Trustees wanted to know who would be in charge of sending preachers once JW had died. The specific request to develop a legal definition of 'Conference' is not recorded in the published 1783 *Minutes*.

est attorney;[126] and he consulted an eminent counsellor,[127] who answered, 'There is no way of doing this but by naming a determinate number of persons. The Deed which names these must be enrolled in Chancery. Then it will stand good in law.'

5   7. My first thought was to name a very few, suppose ten or twelve persons. Count [Nicholas] Zinzendorf named only six who were to preside over the community after his decease. But on second thoughts, I believed there would be more safety in a greater number of counsellors, and therefore named a hundred—as many as I
10   judged could meet without too great an expense, and without leaving any circuit naked of preachers while the Conference met.

       8. In naming these preachers, as I had no adviser, so I had no respect of persons. But I simply set down those that, according to the best of my judgment, were most proper. But I am not infal-
15   lible. I might mistake, and think better of some of them than they deserved. However, I did my best. And if I did wrong, it was not the error of my will, but of my judgment.

       9. This was the rise, and this is the nature, of that famous Deed of Declaration, that vile, wicked Deed, concerning which you have
20   heard such an outcry! And now, can anyone tell me how to mend it, or how it could have been made better? 'O yes. You might have inserted two hundred, as well as one hundred, preachers.' No; for then the expense of meeting would have been double, and all the circuits would have been without preachers. 'But you might have
25   named other preachers instead of these.' True, if I had thought as well of them as they did of themselves. But I did not, therefore I could do no otherwise than I did, without sinning against God and my own conscience.[128]

       10. 'But what need was there for any Deed at all?' There was the
30   utmost need of it. Without some authentic Deed fixing the meaning of the term, the moment I died the Conference had been nothing. Therefore any of the proprietors of the land on which our preaching-houses were built might have seized them for their own use, and there would have been none to hinder them—for the Confer-
35 · ence would have been nobody, a mere empty name.

---

[126] This was surely the lawyer who filed the Deed of Declaration, William Clulow (1757–1822). He was the son of Elizabeth (Whitaker) Clulow (1731–93), one of the first Methodist converts in Macclesfield and a pillar of the society there, and her husband John Clulow (1734–90). William attended Kingswood School and then trained as a lawyer in London.

[127] John Maddocks Esq. (1727–94) of Lincoln's Inn, a barrister whom JW had consulted in 1782 about the Birstall preaching-house deed; see Tyerman, *John Wesley*, 3:381.

[128] See 1 Cor. 8:12.

11. You see then, in all the pains I have taken about this absolutely necessary Deed, I have been labouring not for myself (I have no interest therein) but for the whole body of Methodists, in order to fix them upon such a foundation as is likely to stand as long as the sun and moon endure. That is, if they continue to walk by faith, and to show forth their faith by their works. Otherwise, I pray God to root out the memorial of them from the earth.

John Wesley

Source: published transcription; *Arminian Magazine* 8 (1785): 267–69.[129]

To Richard Rodda

Bristol
March 11, 1785

My Dear Brother,

I hope to be with you on Good Friday [March 25], between one and two o'clock. Then you dispose of me as you see best till Easter Monday in the afternoon; but that day I am to dine with Sir Philip Gibbes at Hilton Park.

The Assistant has need in most places to have a strict eye to the leaders. But they are *nothing* in the Methodist constitution, but single men who are employed by the Assistant as long and as far as he pleases.[130]

The account of good Sarah Wood is remarkable.[131]

I am, dear Richard,

Your affectionate friend and brother,

J. Wesley

---

[129] Titled 'Thoughts upon some late Occurrences'.

[130] This suggests that there was a type of 'leader' in early Methodism distinct from band-leaders and class-leaders (sort of an assistant to the Assistant); as JW says, no such type of 'leader' is required by or described in the *Minutes*.

[131] Sarah Wood (d. 1785) was one of the early converts to Methodism in Wednesbury, Staffordshire. JW preached 'a kind of funeral sermon' for her at Wednesbury on Mar. 28, 1785; see *Journal*, 32:347 in this edn. The letter from Rodda giving an account of her death is not known to survive.

Address: 'To / Mr. Rodda / In Moore Street / Birmingham / +post [i.e., crosspost]'.

Postmark: 'Bath'. *Charge*: '5'.

Source: holograph; MARC, MAM JW 4/57.

To Alexander Knox

Bristol
March 19, 1785

Dear Alleck,

If his colleague is *now free* from actual sin, then Mr. [Jonathan] Brown is in the right.[132] If he is not *now* clear from it, then Mr. [James] Rogers is in the right.

The good providence of God has been very conspicuous for some years in favour of Ireland. The Volunteers have been the occasion of much good; particularly in suppressing lawless violence.[133] I wonder they do not prevent the Whiteboys from lifting up their head again.[134]

On Monday I am to set out from hence. But I do not expect to reach Holyhead before the tenth or eleventh of next month. About the end of it, you will probably see me at your house. If Sally has forgot me, you must tell her who I am.[135] If I am brought safe to Dublin, you may expect to hear from me again.

As it has pleased God to give you a clear, undeniable answer to prayer, you have good reasons to trust him for the time to come. Look up! Help while yet you ask is given![136] Peace be with all your spirits!

I am, dear Alleck,
Yours most affectionately,

J. Wesley

---

[132] The 'colleague' was George Dice, who had begun itinerating in 1780 (see 10:496 in this edn.) and was currently stationed at Londonderry under Jonathan Brown as Assistant (10:557). Dice would be dismissed from the connexion for cause in 1786 (see 10:597, n. 178; and 10:978).

[133] On the Irish Volunteers, see the note on JW to James Creighton, May 8, 1780, 29:570 in this edn.

[134] The Whiteboys (Irish: *na Buachaillí Bána*) were an Irish agrarian organisation that arose in the early 1760s to defend tenant-farmer land-rights for subsistence farming, often by violence. Their name derives from the white frock members wore in their nighttime raids.

[135] Referring to Knox's sister Sarah.

[136] See CW, 'Psalm 121', st. 1, l. 1, *CPH* (1743), 86.

Address: 'To / Mr Alexander Knox / in / Londonderry'.
Postmarks: 'Bristol' and 'MR/28'.
Source: holograph; Bridwell Library (SMU).[137]

5

To Barnabas Thomas[138]

Birmingham   10
March 25, 1785

Dear Barnabas,

I have neither inclination nor leisure to draw the saw of controversy. But I will tell you my mind in a few words.

I am now as firmly attached to the Church of England as I ever 15
was since you knew me. But meantime I know myself to be as real
a Christian bishop as the Archbishop of Canterbury. Yet I was always resolved, and am so still, never to act as such except in case
of necessity. Such a case does not (perhaps never will) exist in England.[139] In America it did exist. This I made known to the Bishop of 20
London and desired his help. But he peremptorily refused it.[140] All
the other bishops were of the same mind—the rather because (they
said) they had nothing to do with America. Then I saw my way
clear, and was fully convinced what it was my duty to do.

As to the persons amongst those who offered themselves, I chose 25
those whom I judged most worthy, and I positively refuse to be
judged herein by any man's conscience but my own.

I am, dear Barnabas,
    Your affectionate brother,

J. Wesley   30

Source: secondary transcription; MARC, MA 1977/609.[141]

[137] Held previously in the Upper Room Museum, L-41.

[138] Thomas was assigned to the Gloucester circuit, and likely raised his concerns when
JW was there on Mar. 22, rather than in a letter. Thomas clearly pressed JW on why he had
ordained only two lay-preachers in Sept. 1784, and only for service in America—to which JW
repeats the justifications in his Sept. 10, 1784 letter to 'Our Brethren in America'.

[139] In Aug. 1788 JW would decide that it was necessary to ordain as well at least a few lay
preachers to serve in England, beginning with Alexander Mather (see Appendix B in this vol.).

[140] See JW to Robert Lowth, Aug. 10, 1780, 29:589–91 in this edn.

[141] MARC also holds a copy of this letter in a notebook of Eliza Tooth (MA 1977/502, p.
32), which she describes as taken from a secondary copy.

To Ann Bolton[142]

Wednesbury
March 28, 1785

My Dear Nancy,

In everything that concerns your happiness I am nearly concerned. I have been so for many years, and my affection to you remains unalterable. But perhaps I should not have loved you so well if you had not seen affliction. Many times I have found that reflection true that 'pity melts the mind to love'.[143]

You are in danger of falling into both of the extremes: of 'making light' of, as well as fainting under his chastening. This you do whenever you look at any circumstance without seeing the hand of God in it—without seeing at the same instant '*this* unkindness, *this* reproach, *this* returning evil for good; as well as *this* faintness, *this* weariness, *this* pain; is the cup which my Father hath given me'. And shall I not drink it? Why does he give it me? Only for my profit, that I 'may be a partaker of his holiness'.[144]

I have often found an aptness both in myself and others to connect events that have no real relation to each other. So one says, 'I am as sure this is the will of God as that I am justified.' Another says, 'God as surely spake *this* to my heart as ever he spoke to me at all.' This is an exceeding dangerous way of thinking or speaking. We know not what it may lead us to. It may sap the very foundation of our religion. It may insensibly draw us into deism or atheism. My dear Nancy, my sister, my friend, beware of this! The grace of God is sufficient for you![145] And whatever clouds may interpose between, his banner over you is love.[146] Look to yourself that you lose not the things that you have gained, but that you may receive a full reward.[147]

I cannot imagine why you should not tell *me* all your troubles, of whatever kind they are. You have known me for many years. And have I ever deceived you yet? Have I refused to do you any good that was in my power? Then hide nothing from your friend!

My dear Nancy,
     Adieu!

---

[142] This letter continues the current interchange of JW with Bolton; Bolton has replied to JW's letter of Feb. 25, 1785 (her letter is not known to survive).

[143] John Dryden, 'Alexander's Feast', *l.* 78.

[144] Heb. 12:10.

[145] See 2 Cor. 12:9.

[146] See Song of Sol. 2:4.

[147] See 2 John 1:8.

Address: 'To / Miss Bolton / In Witney / Oxfordshire / +post [i.e., cross-post]'.
Postmark: 'Wolverhampton'. *Charge*: '4'.
Endorsement: by Bolton, 'Mar 28 –85'.
Source: holograph; MARC, MAM JW 1/96.   5

To Mary (Bosanquet) Fletcher   10

Manchester
April 2, 1785
My Dear Sister,
I have nothing to do with Yorkshire this year. After a swift journey   15
through Bolton, Wigan, and Liverpool, I must hasten by Chester to
Holyhead, in order to take the first packet for Dublin. The spring is
already so far spent that I shall have much ado to go through all the
provinces of Ireland before the end of June.
It is well if that inconstant man has ⟨not⟩[148] destroyed poor Miss   20
[Ann] Loxdale body and soul.[149] I am af⟨raid⟩ he had long since
stole her heart from God. And she had so long persuaded others
that their union was the will of God, that it is well if the disappoint-
ment does not quite unsettle her, and make her turn back to the
world.[150] I wish you would write a letter to her on this head. Who   25
knows but you may save a soul alive.
The account of Michael Onions is very remarkable and may be of
use to the public.[151]
I am, my dear sister,
Yours most affectionately,
J. Wesley   30

Address: To / The Revd Mr Fletcher / In Madeley, near Shiffnal / Salop'.
Postmark: 'Manchester'. *Charge*: '5'.
Source: holograph; Wesley's Chapel (London), LDWMM 1992/408.   35

[148] A small portion is torn away by the wax seal, affecting two lines.
[149] The man who had been courting her; see JW to Loxdale, Nov. 21, 1783, and Dec. 9, 1783.
[150] JW's fear was averted; see JW to Loxdale, Oct. 8, 1785.
[151] JW published this account, which Mary sent in a letter dated Mar. 22, 1785, in *AM* 8 (1785): 522–25.

To Sarah Crosby

Manchester
April 3, 1785

My Dear Sister,

So that good man has left fifteen thousand pounds behind him![152] He would have been a much wiser man, if he had given away ten thousand of it, before he went to give an account to God. A blot is no blot till it is hit.[153] But this scandalizes *me* more than ten bankruptcies!

All our people should be gently but earnestly guarded against having itching ears. I believe Thomas Rutherford will be a very proper person to spend another year in Leeds circuit.[154]

I am glad that you have full employment for the little strength you have, and likewise that you assist poor sister [Ann] Brisco.[155] She used to have a peculiar love for children, and an uncommon talent in building them up into Christians. I hope the preachers do not suffer her to bury her talent in the earth!

I hope to be in Dublin seven or eight days hence, and in England again (if I live) in little above three months. Peace be with all your spirits!

I am, my dear sister,

Yours very affectionately,

J. Wesley

Address: 'To / Mrs Crosby'.
Source: holograph; Drew, Methodist Archives.

To the Rev. John Fletcher

Manchester
April 3, 1785

Dear Sir,

Our Dublin Conference is appointed to begin the first Tuesday in July; our London Conference, the last Tuesday in that month. I

---

[152] The identity of this man is unclear; it is possible but unlikely (since Crosby was in Leeds) that it was the man who lived in Darlington, about whom JW commented similarly in his *Journal*, June 10, 1786, 23:397 in this edn.

[153] An English proverb, rephrased in Nathan Bailey, *Dictionarium Britannicum* (London: T. Cox, 1736) as 'a fault is no fault, till it be found out'.

[154] Rutherford, currently stationed on the Leeds circuit, was returned for another year.

[155] Thomas Brisco was also currently stationed on the Leeds circuit.

am afraid there will be very little time to spare between the one and the other.

I have very little hopes of doing any good to either deists or Socinians. But it is worth all our labour to prevent their doing mischief—at least, more than they have done already. For this reason I look upon everything with a jealous eye which prevents your answering Dr. Priestley.[156] He is certainly one of the most dangerous enemies of Christianity that is now in the world. And I verily think *you* are the man whom God has prepared to abate his confidence. Dr. Horsley has good matter; but he is an heavy writer, and perhaps sometimes a little too severe.[157] I believe you will be enabled to speak home, and yet to keep your temper.

I really hope the Sunday schools will be productive of great good to the nation. They spread wider and wider, and are likely to reach every part of the kingdom.

It seems to be a great happiness, not a misfortune, that those turbulent men have taken themselves away.[158] John Hampson Jr. is going to the university.[159] He may be an useful clergyman.

I hope, if we live, you will not fail to be present at the Conference in London.[160] Do not you stay at home too much?

---

[156] For JW's concern about Joseph Priestley, see the note on his letter to Ann Tindall, Feb. 24, 1779, 29:482 in this edn. This concern had been increased by Priestley's *History of the Corruptions of Christianity*, 2 vols. (Birmingham: J. Johnson, 1782). Fletcher had been at work on a response to Priestley for over a year; see JW, *Journal*, Mar. 27, 1784, 23:299 in this edn. He would die before this work came to press, but Joseph Benson and JW joined in bringing it into print in 1788; see JW to Benson, Mar. 10, 1787.

[157] Samuel Horsley (1733–1806), *Letters from the Archdeacon of St. Albans, in reply to Dr. Priestley* (London: James Robson, 1784).

[158] The 'turbulent men' were supporters of John Hampson's *Appeal* debated at the 1784 Conference.

[159] John Hampson Jr. (1753–1819), son of the itinerant with the same name, was educated at Kingswood School and admitted 'on trial' as an itinerant in 1777 (see 10:464 in this edn.). He served circuits in England, Ireland, and Scotland. By the 1783 Conference both John Jr. and his father were growing uncomfortable with the leadership style of JW and Thomas Coke; see John Hampson [Jr.], *Memoirs of the Late Rev. John Wesley* (Sunderland: Graham, 1791), 3:206–07. This was heightened when JW filed the Deed of Declaration in Feb. 1784, leading John Sr. to lead in framing the *Appeal* for its overthrow (see in-letters, c. July 1, 1784). The *Appeal* was rejected at the 1784 Conference, and both Hampsons soon withdrew from the connexion. John Jr. matriculated in July 1785 at St. Edmund Hall, Oxford; receiving his BA in 1791, and MA in 1792. He was ordained and served Church of England parishes in Bradford and Sunderland.

[160] Fletcher was prevented from attending the 1785 Conference in July by illness; and he died on Aug. 14, 1785. See Mary (Bosanquet) Fletcher's letter to JW, describing her husband's last days, dated Aug. 18, 1785.

Wishing you both to be more and more happy and useful, I am, dear sir,

Ever yours,

J. Wesley

5   *Address*:[161]
Source: holograph; MARC, MAM JW 2/96.

To [Mary (Walsh / Leadbetter) Gilbert][162]

Manchester
April 3, 1785

My Dear Sister,

15   Mr. Baxter has promised once or twice to send me a particular account of the society in Antigua.[163]

Some thousand of them in North America likewise have heard the joyful sound. [...]

20   *Source*: holograph; privately held (extract published in Sotheby's *Catalogue*, Mar. 5, 1935, lot 451).

To the Methodist Conference[164]

Chester
April 7, 1785

My Dear Brethren,

Some of our travelling preachers have expressed a fear that af-
30   ter my decease you would exclude them either from preaching in

[161] This was surely sent as part of a double-letter with that to Mary (Bosanquet) Fletcher dated the day before; the address portion survives on her letter.

[162] The recipient is not named, but Mary had recently returned to Antigua after the death of her husband and was in correspondence with JW (see her letter of Feb. 7, 1784).

[163] John Baxter (1739–1805), immigrated to Antigua as a government shipwright in 1768. Having experience as a local preacher, he soon became the leader of the society formed by Nathaniel Gilbert at St. Johns. Baxter was appointed an 'elder' at the Christmas Conference that formed The Methodist Episcopal Church in Baltimore in 1784, and ordained the following year by Thomas Coke. He spent the remainder of his life in ministry in Antigua. See Vickers, *Dictionary*, 22–23; and Baxter's letters to JW of Apr. 16, 1778, June 10, 1779, and June 10, 1782.

[164] Like the public letter of Mar. 3, 1785, this letter was elicited by the continuing unrest among some preachers (particularly those left out of the 'legal hundred') about the Deed of Declaration. In this case the letter was not immediately made public, but entrusted to Joseph Bradford to be opened and read at the Conference after JW's death.

connexion with you or from some other privileges which they now enjoy. I know no other way to prevent any such inconvenience than to leave these my last words with you.

'I beseech you by the mercies of God that you never avail your-selves of the Deed of Declaration to assume any superiority over your brethren, but let all things go on among those itinerants who choose to remain together exactly in the same manner as when I was with you, so far as circumstances will permit.

'In particular, I beseech you, if you ever loved me and if you now love God and your brethren, to have no respect of persons in stationing the preachers, in choosing children for Kingswood School, in disposing of the Yearly Contribution and the Preach-ers' Fund or any other public money. But do all things with a single eye, as I have done from the beginning.[165] Go on thus, do-ing all things without prejudice or partiality, and God will be with you even to the end.'

Source: published transcription; *Minutes* (1791), [p. 4].[166]

To Joseph Taylor

Liverpool
April 7, 1785

Dear Joseph,

I do not see that I can in conscience employ brother [Barnabas] Thomas as a travelling preacher.[167] Do not you know what I have often said? I would not employ an apostle as such, if he could not preach in the morning. And this he cannot do. Neither is he able, if he was willing, regularly to keep a circuit. Be faithful to God and the people, and your own soul! And keep an active, zealous man,

---

[165] See Matt. 6:21.

[166] 10:740–42 in this edn.

[167] Taylor was currently the Assistant for the Gloucester circuit, in which Thomas was stationed. Despite the concerns expressed here (and in JW to Thomas, Mar. 25, 1785), Thomas continued under appointment through 1788.

Mr. McGeary, while you have him.[168] Else there is want of a preacher in the Canterbury circuit.

I thank you for the account of brother Tregellas;[169] and am, dear Joseph,

Your affectionate friend and brother,

J. Wesley

Source: holograph; MARC, MAM JW 5/12.

To Roger Crane[170]

Conway
April 9, 1785

Dear Roger,

What you observe is true. The new places ought not to be neglected. Therefore it is not expedient to remove William Bramwell yet.[171] So I have sent to Derbyshire, and hope Nathanael Ward will speedily remove to Chester to assist Mr. [Duncan] Wright.

Meantime take care that *you* be not weary of well-doing. In due time you shall reap if you faint not.[172] I am, dear Roger,

Your affectionate brother,

J. Wesley

[168] John McGeary, an Irishman who emigrated to America, served as a Methodist itinerant there 1782–84. The fall of 1784 he travelled to England, where he met JW on Oct. 30 (*Journal*, 23:332–33 in this edn.). JW seems to have sent him to assist Joseph Taylor in Gloucester. By fall 1785 McGeary was back in North America, now Newfoundland, assisting John Stretton. This became a formal appointment by the British Conference in 1786 (see 10:605 in this edn.). McGeary struggled in this appointment (with a brief return to England) through 1791. In 1792 he again returned to England and was given an appointment in Collumpton, but desisted from itinerant ministry the following year.

[169] Taylor had sent JW an account of the death of John Tregellas, of St. Agnes, Cornwall in a letter dated Apr. 2, 1788; JW published it in *AM* 9 (1786): 249–52.

[170] Roger Crane (1758–1836), an ironmonger, was drawn to Methodism in 1777, served as a class leader and local preacher, and gave leadership to the society in Preston between the visits of the itinerants. See *WMM* 62 (1839), 532; and John Taylor, *Apostles of Fylde Methodism* (London: T. Woolmer, 1885), 18–25.

[171] William Bramwell (1759–1818) encountered Methodists in Preston, where he was apprenticed to a currier, and joined the society in 1779. He was converted under a sermon by JW the following year and soon joined Roger Preston as a local preacher. JW had apparently mentioned having him become an itinerant, drawing Crane's concern that Bramwell had recently opened a new preaching spot in the area. JW left him there for the time. Bramwell would be admitted as an itinerant in 1786 (see 10:596 in this edn.), and continued to serve, with one brief interruption, until his death. See Taylor, *Apostles*, 26–37; and *Minutes* (post-Wesley, 1819), 5:5.

[172] See Gal. 6:9.

Address: 'To / Mr Roger Crane, Ironmonger / In Preston / Lancashire'.
Postmark: 'Conway'.
Source: holograph; MARC, MAM JW 2/65.

To George Gibbon

Holyhead
April 9, 1785

Dear George,

What you said was exactly right. The work of God is undoubtedly instantaneous, with regard to sanctification as well as justification. And it is no objection at all that the work is gradual also. Whatever others do, it is *your* duty strongly and explicitly to exhort the believers to go on to perfection.[173] And encourage them to expect perfect love by simple faith; and consequently, to expect it *now*. This is the preaching which God always has blessed, and which he always will bless to those that are upright of heart.

With God's leave we shall set sail tonight.[174] I am, dear George,
Your affectionate brother,

J. Wesley

Address: 'To / Mr Gibbon / At the Preachinghouse / in / Sheffield'.
Source: holograph; Toronto, Canada, United Church of Canada Archives, 97.002C, 3-24.

To the Rev. Charles Wesley[175]

Dublin
April 11, 1785

[[Dear Brother,]]

I just write a line to let you know that we came to Holyhead on Saturday afternoon, and went onboard about ten at night. But we had a dead calm till between ten and eleven in the morning, at

---

[173] See Heb. 6:1.
[174] For Dublin.
[175] This is JW's first surviving letter to CW since the ordinations JW performed on Sept. 1–2, 1784 in Bristol (an event of which CW was not aware, even though he was in Bristol at the time). CW was stunned by the act.

which time I began the public service. After sermon I prayed that God would give us a moderate wind, with a safe, easy, and speedy passage. While I was speaking, the wind sprung up and carried us at an average five miles an hour; so that we sailed from Holywell Bay to Dublin Bay in exactly twelve hours. The sea meantime was as smooth as a looking-glass, so that no creature in the ship was sick a moment. Does not God hear the prayer?

All is quiet here. Love to all.

[[Adieu!]]

Address: 'To / The Revd Mr C. Wesley / City Road[176] / London'.
Postmarks: 'Ireland', 'AP/11', '15/AP', and 'Penney Post Paid'.
Endorsements: by CW, 'B[rother] Apr. 11 1785' and 'April 11, 1785 / B.'s smooth passage'.
Source: holograph; MARC, DDWes 3/55.

To the Rev. Charles Wesley[177]

Athlone
April 23, 1785[178]

[[Dear Brother,]]

Certainly you have heard from me, for I sent you one, and intended to send you two journals.[179] Only George Whitfield made a blunder and directed the second to Henry Moore.[180]

Several months since, I wrote to Dr. [Thomas] Coke concerning the extract he had taken from your journal. I will write to him again.

---

[176] 'City Road' was struck out; replaced with 'in Chesterfield Street / Marybone'. This explains the Penny Post stamp.

[177] CW seems to have written JW, asking why he was not getting reports on JW's time in Ireland. He also inquired about an extract Thomas Coke made, either surreptitiously or with CW's approval, from CW's Manuscript Journal; if it was with CW's approval, it was surely to publish it as another source of revenue for his family. This extract was not published and is not known to survive.

[178] Orig., 'June 23'. CW gives the correct month in his endorsement. JW was in Dublin on June 23, but had been in Athlone on Apr. 23.

[179] I.e., journal letters, or daily accounts of his current preaching tour. Unless JW considered the brief letter of Apr. 11 one of these, neither of the two are known to survive.

[180] Whitfield was accompanying JW on his preaching tour; Moore was keeping watch over matters in London.

But he must *bring* it, not *send* it by post. My letters today cost me eighteen shillings.

I promise you not to publish your picture in the *[Arminian] Magazine* before midsummer 1786.[181] I think that is long enough to look forward.

Mr. Barnard is dead.[182]

I know nothing of M[iss] Fr[eeman].[183]

Ireland is full as quiet as England, and our societies were never so much alive as they are now.

I cannot believe *that* history.[184]

If Sally is ill, why does she not go into the country? Peace be with all your spirits!

[[Adieu!]]

Endorsement: by CW, 'B[rother] Apr. 23. 1785 / ~~elusive~~ promise ambi / guous'.

Source: holograph; MARC, DDWes 3/59.

To Thomas Carlill

Cork
May 6, 1785

Dear Tommy,

I desire you and no other preacher out of the Gainsborough circuit to come to the Conference. I will pay the two guineas to Robert Armstrong.[185] You may take brother [William] Fish[186] in the place of

---

[181] There had likely been plans to print CW's portrait in *AM* earlier, which he delayed after the Sept. 1784 ordinations; the delay would grow longer (see JW to CW, May 12).

[182] In his letter of May 12, JW clarifies that this is the *son* of Thomas Barnard.

[183] I.e., Mary Freeman Shepherd.

[184] CW had likely related to JW an account he received in a letter from Robert Windsor on Apr. 15, 1785, contending that Robert's recently deceased wife Mary (Walmsley) Windsor was a relative of the Robert Glover listed among martyrs during the reign of Queen Mary.

[185] I.e., JW would pay a debt to the Irish itinerant Robert Armstrong, since he was there.

[186] William Fish (d. 1843) would be admitted 'on trial' at the 1785 Conference (10:568 in this edn.). He served in England until persuaded by Thomas Coke to go to Jamaica in 1792. Fish returned to England in 1805, due to health, and continued to itinerate until 1816. He then settled in Guernsey, where he continued active on the local level until his death in 1843. See *Minutes* (post-Wesley, 1848), 10:5–6.

Samuel Botts.[187] Simon Kilham must in no wise be removed from Epworth.[188] Encourage James Christie to read, and his gifts will increase.

5　We cannot allow a baker to remain in our society if he *sells bread* on the Lord's Day. But if he only *bakes pies*, as they call it, we do not exclude him—although we are convinced that to abstain even from this is the more excellent way.[189]

I am, dear Tommy,
　　　Your affectionate friend and brother,

10　　　　　　　　　　　　　　　　　　　　　　　　J. Wesley

Source: published transcription; *Arminian Magazine (Bible Christian)* 6 (1827): 286.

15

To Alexander Knox

20　　　　　　　　　　　　　　　　　　　　　　　　　Cork
　　　　　　　　　　　　　　　　　　　　　　　　May 6, 1785
My Dear Alleck,

I hope to be at Sligo, on Saturday the twenty first instant; on Monday the 23rd at Ballyconnell; on Wednesday, 25th at Kilmore; 25　Thursday, 26, Clones; Saturday, 28th, Armagh; Monday, [30th], Charlemont; Wednesday, June 1, Derry; Saturday, 4th, Coleraine. So I allow *you* a day longer than to any other place. Indeed I am so straitened for time, that I can hardly spend so much of it anywhere as I could do a few years ago. My work increases continually, so that 30　I am obliged to shorten my stay almost at every place.

If I live to return to London, I will consider what you say concerning printing the text of the New Testament alone.[190] I see no

---

[187] Samuel Botts (1759–1812) was admitted as an itinerant 'on trial' in 1782 (10:520). He was currently stationed in Gainsborough, where Carlill was the Assistant (and would be reappointed there by the 1785 Conference). Botts served until about six months before his death; see *Minutes* (post-Wesley, 1812), 5:267–68.

[188] Simon Kilham Sr. (1729–1802) and his wife Elizabeth (Ingham) Kilham (1728–85) were active members of the Methodist society in Epworth. Simon may have been thinking of leaving Epworth after the recent death of his wife. Alternatively, JW may have been referring to their son Simon Kilham Jr. (1758–1836), who had done some local preaching.

[189] See 1 Cor. 12:31.

[190] JW did take up Knox's suggestion, publishing in 1790 *The New Testament, with an Analysis; Bibliography*, No. 455.

objection to it at present but that it would require a good deal of time—because I must critically review the whole, and again compare it with the original.

    Peace with you all! I am, dear Alleck,
        Yours most affectionately, 5

                                    J. Wesley

Source: holograph; Bridwell Library (SMU).[191]

10

To Agnes Gibbes[192]

                                 [Cork] 15
                          c. May 9, 1785

My Dear Miss Aggy,
    Of all the voyages which I have had to this kingdom, I never had such an one as the last. Indeed it was a dead calm when we went into the ship at Holyhead. But the gentlemen on board desiring me 20 to give them a sermon, while I was praying that 'God would give us an easy and speedy passage', a steady wind sprung up, which brought us from Holyhead Bay to Dublin Bay in just twelve hours. The sea in the meantime was all the way like a looking-glass, so that no one was sick in the ship. 25
    I have now gone through about a third part of the kingdom, and find most of my friends just such as I wish. And I do not envy

        The brute philosopher, that ne'er has proved
        The joy of loving or of being loved.[193] 30

Many of them, it may be, showed the more affection now because they had not seen me for seven years, and hardly expected to see me again till we should meet in a better world. I can never look upon *you* without a tender regard, though I hope to see you again, prob- 35 ably in a few months. But I know not how I should look, or how I should feel, if I thought it the last time I should see you till I saw you in that happy abode, where sorrow and parting are no more.

---

[191] Held previously in the Upper Room Museum, L-42.

[192] JW was responding to a letter from Gibbes that is not known to survive.

[193] Nicholas Rowe, *The Ambitious Step-Mother* (London: Peter Buck, 1701), Prologue, ll. 8–9. JW also quotes in his sermon 'The Important Question', III.3, 3:189 in this edn.

If by *agitations* that author means *affections*, I scorn the art of concealing them. I will cherish no affections but such as are rational; and these will bear the light. Let my love and joy, whenever I am at the Park,[194] be shown by my eyes, my tongue, and my whole behaviour. Nay, if I grieved or feared, either with or for my friend, I should not desire to hide it. Perhaps a Frenchman might, for they generally love dissembling. But we English love openness.

Bare philosophy could never yet conquer, much less extirpate, even irregular passions. But true religion can:

> Soft peace she brings wherever she arrives
> She builds our quiet, as she forms our lives.
> Lays the rough paths of peevish nature even,
> And opens in each breast a little heaven.[195]

This, my dear friend (may I not say?) I wish *you* fully to experience. May you be filled with humble, gentle, patient love, which is glory upon earth begun.

When I went to the university, my father told me, 'I give you one advice, with respect to your health. Fail not, on any account whatever, to walk an hour every day.'[196] I did so (whenever it was fair, in the open air) for fourteen years together. I wish my dear Miss Aggy had resolution to follow the same advice. I believe you would in a few weeks, or perhaps days, find the advantage of it. That you may be easy and happy, in soul and in body, in time and in eternity, is the sincere desire of, my dear Miss Aggy,

Yours most affectionately,

John Wesley

The same I cannot wish for the whole family.

Address: 'To / Miss Agnes Gibbes / At Sir Philip Gibbes's Bart. / Near Wolverhampton / Staffordshire'.
Postmarks: 'Ireland', 'Cork', 'MY/10'.
Source: holograph; National Archives, PRO 30/9/11/2.

---

[194] Hilton Park, the Gibbes family estate.
[195] Matthew Prior, 'Charity', *ll.* 23–26; republished by JW in *MSP* (1744), 88.
[196] Advice JW repeated to others; see JW to John Bredin, June 19, 1780, 29:578 in this edn.

To Jasper Winscom

Cork
May 9, 1785   5

Dear Jasper,

You are in the right: that ground would be too small.[197] Either have a proper place or none at all.

If you have any magistrate that is determined to do justice, he will soon make those rioters afraid to move a finger; and those that   10
support them will soon be weary of the expense.[198] They further will likewise quietly make an end of your valorous women, for they may send women rioters to jail as well as men. The law makes no distinction. But if you have no resolute magistrate, you have another way. Let any man that was struck order a King's Bench   15
writ against him that struck him, and arrest him immediately. And he may refuse insufficient bail. This will soon make them weary of their bad work.

But you must take particular care not to make it up with the rioters till they have made good all the damage which has been done   20
by any person whatever from the beginning, and given sufficient security for their future good behaviour. Unless you do that, you do nothing at all.

Prosecute them not on the Toleration Act, which allows only £20 damage, but on the Riot Act, which brings their riches in question.   25

I am, dear Jasper,

Your affectionate brother,

J. Wesley

Source: manuscript transcriptions (19th century), MARC, MA 1977/485,   30
p. 322; and Duke, Rubenstein, Frank Baker Collection of Wesleyana, VOLS 7, Letter book 10, p. 28.

---

[197] Winscom was seeking an appropriate site for a preaching house in Winchester.

[198] There had been opposition to Methodist services at Sutton Scotney, between Winchester and Whitchurch. The Methodists applied to a justice for redress, and the opposers had been reprimanded and ordered to pay the costs. The rioting grew worse, and the Methodists had to appeal to the Justices again.

To the Rev. Charles Wesley[199]

Cork
May 12, 1785

[[Dear Brother,]]

Twice I have wrote to Dr. [Thomas] Coke concerning the journal.[200] I suppose one, if not two, of his letters have miscarried. I will not sentence him till he answers for himself.

All I can say, and all I will say, is I do not intend ever to publish your picture in the *[Arminian] Magazine*.[201]

At Dublin I was informed Mr. Barnard, the present Bishop's son, is dead.[202] In the north I may learn more.

I speak of myself, as of other men, with a single eye. I am glad you have been at Newgate.[203]

All we have heard in England of danger from Ireland is pure invention. We have been humbugged by the Patriots.[204] There is no more danger from Ireland than from the Isle of Man.

If Sally wants the sinews of war,[205] give me an hint. John Atlay has not complained to me of poverty for above this month,

I am fully persuaded that the measure of peace which enables me to go on cheerfully in my work and to employ all my time and strength therein is not from Satan, nor from nature, but from God.

To save ten pence postage I will write a few lines to Patty in your letter.[206] Peace be with you all!

[[Adieu.]]

Endorsement: by CW, 'B[rother] May 12. 1785 / promising *Never* to publish my / picture in his Magazine.

Source: holograph; MARC, DDWes 3/56.

---

[199] JW was replying to CW's letter of c. Apr. 30, 1785.

[200] Cf. JW to CW, Apr. 23, 1785.

[201] True to his word, no portrait of CW appeared in *AM* until after JW's death (in the May 1792 issue).

[202] This would be William Barnard (b. 1757), the eldest child of Bishop Thomas and Anne (Browne) Barnard.

[203] CW was regularly visiting those at Newgate prison in London that were condemned to death; see his *Prayers for Condemned Malefactors* (London: Paramore, 1785); and MS Malefactors.

[204] See the note on JW to James Creighton, May 8, 1780, 29:570 in this edn.

[205] *OED*: 'i.e., money'.

[206] The address portion is missing, likely where the lines to Martha (Wesley) Hall were added; these lines to Martha are not known to survive.

To the Rev. Charles Wesley

Killyman,[207] near Armagh
June 2, 1785   5

[[Dear Brother,]]

So the good man will know pain no more![208] But I suppose he died without disclosing that his son Vincent charged him not to reveal till he came to die![209] If it had been of any consequence to the cause of God, he *could not* have died without disclosing it.   10

Pray talk with, as well as inquire concerning, the clergyman you mention.[210] Many times you see further into men than I do.

I suppose you have before now received my journal, as well as preceding letter.[211] Probably the first ship that sails after the 6th of July will bring me to Holyhead. I hope to see Dr. [Thomas] Coke in   15
London before the end of it.

About once a quarter I hear from Mr. [John] and Mrs. [Mary] Fletcher. I grudge his sitting still; but who can help it? I love ease as well as he does, but I dare not take it while I believe there is another world.   20

The Patriots here are nobody.[212] They are quite scattered, and have no design, bad or good. All is still in Ireland—only the work of God flourishes, spreading and deepening on every side.

Peace be with all your spirits!

[[Adieu!]]   25

Address: 'To / The Revd Mr C. Wesley /...'.[213]
Postmarks: 'JU/6', 'Ireland', and '11/IU'.
Endorsement: by CW, 'B[rother] June 2. 1785'.
Source: holograph; MARC, DDWes 3/57.   30

---

[207] Orig., 'Killaman'.

[208] JW was replying to a letter of CW (not known to survive), informing him that Rev. Vincent Perronet died on May 9, 1785. CW performed Perronet's funeral on Sunday, May 15.

[209] Little is known of Vincent Perronet Jr. (1727–46).

[210] Lacking CW's letter, the identity of this clergyman is uncertain. He had possibly said something to JW about Rev. Peard Dickinson, curate to Vincent Perronet, with whom JW was already familiar (see JW to Dickinson, Jan. 15).

[211] No journal letter, or regular letter, from JW to CW between May 12 and June 2 is known to survive.

[212] See JW to CW, May 12, 1785.

[213] The remainder of the address is missing.

To Alexander Knox[214]

Coleraine
June 8, 1785

5   Dear Alleck,

I have sent you Dr. Horneck, which I have done with. He appears to have been an exceeding good man. And he is a lively and affectionate writer, but a dealer in many words.[215] But Mr. Firmin's *Life* I have not done with. I purpose taking a large extract from it
10 (letting his opinions alone) and inserting it in the *Arminian Magazine*.[216] He was not a Socinian, but a Sabellian. So was Count Zindendorf; as he clearly declared in those words, '*nullum deum agnosco praeter crucifixum*'.[217]

Having now deeply considered your case, I send you my maturest
15 thoughts; which I beg Mrs. Knox and you impartially to consider in the presence of God. But beware you do not fix your judgment before you hear the cause. Otherwise I shall lose my labour, and you may lose your life, if not your soul.

You say: 'The reason why I do not go out is this, I am afraid of
20 falling in the street. And I do not attend the Church or the preaching-house, for fear I should fall down there and disturb the congregation.'

This is the clear state of the case. The question is then: Is this reason sufficient, or is it not?

25 I am fully persuaded it is not. For first, you are by no means sure that you shall fall down in the Church or in the congregation. You have great reason to hope you shall not. Although I should not wonder if your fits were now both more frequent and more severe than they are.

30 But secondly, Does not common sense teach us *Ex malis minimum*?[218] Now I insist upon it that your falling in the street or

---

[214] JW was in Londonderry June 3–5, 1785, where he surely met with Knox. This letter is a followup on their time together.

[215] JW was already familiar with Dr. Anthony Horneck (1641–97), having included an abridgement of his *Happy Ascetick* in the *Christian Library*, 28:267–29:140. Knox likely shared with JW Horneck's *Several Sermons upon the Fifth of St. Matthew … being part of Christ's Sermon on the Mount* (London: Aylmer, 1698), which was prefixed with a life of Horneck.

[216] Stephen Nye, *The Life of Mr. Thomas Firmin, late Citizen of London* (London: A. Baldwin, 1698). JW serialized his extract over eight months in *AM* 9 (1786): 253–56ff.

[217] 'I know no God beyond the crucified one.' No published source for this quotation has been located, but Zinzendorf (and other Lutherans) spoke in such terms without embracing Sabellianism.

[218] 'Of evils, choose the lesser'.

the congregation once every month is a less evil than the shutting
yourself up. So that were it pronounced by a voice from heaven,
'Either shut thyself up, or endure this shame once a month, or even
once a week. Take thy choice', it would be wisest to choose the latter—for it is incomparably the less evil of the two.   5

It is indisputably plain to every impartial person that, by thus
cooping yourself up, you *hurt your body*. By want of air and exercise
you weaken it continually. I wonder you have not fits every day. And
you *hurt your soul* by neglecting the ordinances of God, which you
have no authority to do unless you was sick in bed.   10

My dear Alleck, let there be no delay! Break through! At all hazards, break through! Go out this very day and trust God! If your
mother hinders you, she kills you with kindness. And I am not sure
that it will not cost her the life of another child,[219] though God tries
milder methods first. I say again, Go out today, and every day. It   15
will help both your body and your soul, as well as remove a great
burden from the mind of

Yours in tender affection,

J. Wesley
20

Address: 'To / Mr. Knox'.
Source: holograph; Bridwell Library (SMU).[220]

25

To Francis Wrigley

Lisburn
June 11, 1785   30

My Dear Brother,

I am glad you are so far recovered. Do as much as you [can] and
no more.

You that are upon the spot are the best judges concerning William Ellis.[221] I refer it wholly to you whether he should preach or no   35
till I come into Cornwall myself.

---

[219] Alexander had one sister who died young (name unknown).

[220] Held previously in the Upper Room Museum, L-43.

[221] William Ellis was last stationed in eastern Cornwall in 1772 (10:407 in this edn.).
He desisted travelling the following year (10:416), but was apparently still serving as a local
preacher.

You cannot suffer any one to preach, either at St. Austell[222] or elsewhere, that is tainted with Calvinism or antinomianism. It is far easier to prevent the plague than to cure it.

I am

5   Your affectionate friend and brother,

J. Wesley

Address: 'To / Mr Wrigley / At Mr [George] Flamank's / In St Austle / Cornwall'.

10   *Postmarks*: 'JW/15' and 'Ireland'.

Source: holograph; MARC, MAM JW 6/37.

15

To the Rev. Charles Wesley[223]

Dublin

20   June 19, 1785

[[Dear Brother,]]

I came hither (as I proposed when I set out) yesterday. This week I am to meet the classes. Next week we have our little Conference. The week following I hope to cross the Channel. The work of God, almost in every part of the kingdom, is in a prosperous state. Here
25   is a set of excellent young preachers. Nine in ten of them are much devoted to God. I think, number for number, they exceed their fellow labourers in England. These in Dublin particularly are burning and shining lights.[224]

I am glad you have paid them one more visit at Shoreham. What
30   the poor people will do now I know not.[225] But the Great Shepherd knows, and will order all things well.[226] But what becomes of Betsy Briggs?[227]

---

[222] Orig., 'St. Austle'; as in address.

[223] The letter of CW, to which JW replies, is not known to survive.

[224] James Rogers and Andrew Blair. See John 5:35.

[225] Referring both to the congregation Rev. Vincent Perronet had pastored, and the society in the area.

[226] See Eph. 1:11.

[227] Elizabeth Briggs had been living with her grandfather, helping care for him. She remained there a while, then moved to London. In Apr. 1788 she would marry Rev. Peard Dickinson, who was Perronet's last curate.

Would not her shortest way be to marry him?[228] But I doubt he hangs back.

The letter from Rome is curious enough.[229] Fine words! And you know the Italians are famous for sincerity.

I should be sorry indeed if Sammy Tooth were a sufferer. But surely he knows his own business.

Many here know and love you well. My love to all.

[[Adieu!]]

Address: 'To / The Revd Mr C. Wesley / City Road / London'.
Postmarks: 'JU/20' and '27/IU'.
Endorsement: by CW, 'B[rother] June 19 1785'.
Source: holograph; MARC, DDWes 3/58.

To Zachariah Yewdall

near Dublin
June 22, 1785

Dear Zachary,

Let him not be afraid. I will take care that not one word of that affair shall be mentioned at the Conference. Let him come up thither in the name of God, and it will be a blessing to him.

Let [Henry] Foster likewise come that he may have the advice of Dr. [John] Whitehead.[230] I shall have no objection, unless some particular objection arise, to your going to Sunderland. I think you will

---

[228] JW makes this a new paragraph, rendering it unclear whether he is referring to Briggs or (more likely) another woman CW had mentioned.

[229] In the fall of 1784 CW's son Samuel completed a musical setting of mass (*Missa de spiritu sancto*), had it lavishly bound, and attached a plate dedicating it to Pope Pius VI. He sent it to Rome through the agency of Bishop James Talbot. The mass was performed for Pius, who returned a letter to Bishop Talbot on May 4, 1785, expressing the pleasure it had given him. This letter (or a copy of it) came into the possession of Mary Freeman Shepherd, who prodded Samuel to share it with his father. See Olleson, *Samuel Wesley*, 30.

[230] Orig., 'Let C. Foster ...'; but JW certainly meant Henry Foster, who was serving near Yewdall. Foster would go on disability leave in 1786, and die in Apr. 1787 (see 10:624 in this edn.).

do well to bring brother Adamson with you to the Conference.[231] You will both be acceptable to, dear Zachary,

Your affectionate brother,

J. Wesley

Source: published transcription; Jackson, *Works* (3rd), 13:15.

To the Rev. Freeborn Garrettson[232]

Dublin
June 26, 1785

My Dear Brother,

Dr. [Thomas] Coke gives some account of you in one of his journals; so that, although I have not seen you, I am not a stranger to your character. By all means send me, when you have opportunity, a more particular account of your experiences and travels. It is in no wise improbable that God may find out a way for you to visit England. And it might be a means of your receiving more strength, as well as more light. It is a very desirable thing that the children of God should communicate their experience to each other. And it is generally most profitable when they can do it face to face. Till providence opens a way for you to see Europe, do all you can for a good Master in America.

I am glad brother Cromwell[233] and you have undertaken that labour of love, the visiting Nova Scotia, and doubt not but you act in full concert with the little handful who were almost alone till you

---

[231] William Adamson first appears in the *Minutes*, on trial as an itinerant in 1783 (see 10:533 in this edn.). He was currently teamed with Henry Foster on the Sussex circuit. He was granted full status in 1785 (10:567) but desisted from travelling the next year (10:598).

[232] This is JW's first surviving letter to Freeborn Garrettson (1752–1827). He is replying to Garrettson's letter of Apr. 20, 1785, which had finally caught up with JW. Garrettson was born in the colony of Maryland, and drawn to Methodist ways through the preaching of Robert Strawbridge. He began itinerating in 1775, was admitted into the American Conference in 1776, and ordained at the Christmas Conference in 1784 (first appearing in the British *Minutes* as serving in that location in 1785; see 10:567 in this edn.). After ordination he served first in Canada and then particularly in New England. See *DEB*, 428–29.

[233] James Oliver Cromwell (c.1760–1826) had been admitted to the Conference of American itinerants in 1780, and ordained at the 1784 Christmas Conference. He sailed with Garrettson from New York to Nova Scotia in Feb. 1785, but poor health required him to return two years later.

came. It will be the wisest way, to make all those that desire to join together thoroughly acquainted with the whole Methodist plan, and to accustom them from the very beginning to the accurate observance of all our rules. Let none of them rest in being half Christians. Whatever they do, let them do it with their might.[234] And it will be well, as soon as any of them find peace with God, to exhort them to go on to perfection.[235] The more strongly and explicitly you press all believers to aspire after full sanctification as attainable now by simple faith, the more the whole work of God will prosper.

I do not expect any great matters from that bishop.[236] I doubt his eye is not single.[237] And if it be not, he will do little good either to you or anyone else. It may be a comfort to you that you have no need of him. You want nothing which he can give.

It is a noble proposal of Mr. Marchington's, but I doubt it will not take place.[238] You do not know the state of the English Methodists. They do not roll in money, like many of the American Methodists. It is with the utmost difficulty that we can raise five or six hundred pounds a year to supply our own contingent expenses. So that it is utterly impracticable to raise five hundred pounds among them to build houses in America. It is true they might do much. But it is a sad observation: they that have most money have usually least grace.

The peace of God be with all your spirits! I am

Your affectionate friend and brother,

J. Wesley

Address: 'To / Mr. Garrettson / At Mr. Philip Marchington's, Merchant / In Halifax[239] / Nova Scotia'.

Source: holograph; Wesleyan University Library.

[234] See Eccles. 9:10.

[235] See Heb. 6:1.

[236] JW was likely referring to Samuel Seabury (1729–96), who had been elected by the Church of England elders remaining in the former American colonies as their bishop and been consecrated by the bishop of the Scottish Episcopal Church in Nov. 1784.

[237] See Matt. 6:22–23.

[238] Philip Marchington (1736–1808) was a merchant and prominent Methodist in Nova Scotia.

[239] 'Halifax' is crossed out and replaced with 'Shelburne', in another hand.

To Elizabeth Ritchie

Dublin
June 26, 1785

My Dear Betsy,

Our Lord has indeed poured out abundance of blessings almost in every part of this kingdom. I have now gone through every province and visited all the chief societies, and I have found far the greater part of them increasing both in number and strength. Many are convinced of sin, many justified, and not a few perfected in love. One means of which is that several of our young preachers, of whom we made little account, appear to be (contrary to all expectation) men full of faith and of the Holy Ghost.[240] And they are pushing out to the right hand and the left, and wherever they go God prospers their labour. I know not whether Thomas Walsh will not revive in two, if not three, of them.

Many years ago I was saying, 'I cannot imagine how Mr. Whitefield can keep his soul alive, as he is not now going through honour and dishonour, evil report and good report,[241] having nothing but honour and good report attending him wherever he goes.'[242] It is now my own case. I am just in the condition now that he was then in. I am become, I know not how, an honourable man. The scandal of the cross is ceased; and all the kingdom, rich and poor, papists and Protestants, behave with courtesy—nay, and seeming goodwill! It seems as if I had wellnigh finished my course, and our Lord was giving me an honourable discharge.

My dear Betsy, have you not something to do in Dublin? If so, the sooner you visit our friends the better.[243] Peace be with your spirit! Adieu!

J. Wesley

Source: published transcription; Benson, *Works*, 16:254.

---

[240] Cf. JW to CW, June 19, 1785.
[241] See 2 Cor. 6:8.
[242] Cf. JW to Penelope Newman, Nov. 1, 1778.
[243] I.e., James and Hester Ann (Roe) Rogers.

Circular to Preachers Attending Conference

[London, via Henry Moore]
c. July 1, 1785

'A little before conference at London 1785 there were circular letters wrote by Mr. Wesley's order and executed by Henry Moore and sent to the preachers who were to constitute the then Conference, informing them "After this time, no preacher will be permitted to be present at any Conference, only those whom Mr. Wesley writes for by name."'

Source: published description; Moorhouse, *Defence*, 63.

To Samuel Purvis Jr.²⁴⁴

Dublin
July 7, 1785

I am glad to hear that the labours of Mr. [William] Warrener among you have not been without success.²⁴⁵ If the pure word of God be spoken in simplicity, it is seldom without fruit. Wherever there is a little company who are not ashamed to join together, the fruit generally remains. So that I do not now doubt but even at Belford the work of God will continue and increase. It seems not improbable that Mr. Warrener may be useful a little longer in your circuit.

Be all in earnest. I am
Yours affectionately,

J. Wesley

Address: 'To / Mr Saml Purvis Junr / In Belford / Northumberland / +post Portpatrick'.
Source: holograph; privately held (WWEP Archive holds digital copy).

---

²⁴⁴ Samuel Purvis Jr. (c. 1761–1835) was the son of Samuel and Mary (Arkle) Purvis of Belford, and active in the Methodist society there. He would later marry and settle as a grocer and tallow chandler in Alnwick. See his obituary in *WMM* 14 (1835), 635. Purvis's letter encouraging the continuance of Warrener in his circuit is not known to survive.

²⁴⁵ For Warrener, see his ordination 'letter', Aug. 1, 1786.

To Ann Bolton

Dublin
July 8, 1785

My Dear Nancy,

It is undoubtedly expedient for you to have a friend in whom you can fully confide, that may be always near you or at a small distance, and ready to be consulted on all occasions. The time was when you took *me* to be your friend. And (to speak freely) I have loved you with no common affection. I 'have loved you'; nay, I do still. My heart warms to you while I am writing. But I am generally at too great a distance, so that you cannot converse with me when you would. I am glad, therefore, that a good providence has given you one whom you can more easily see and correspond with. You may certainly trust her in every instance; and she has both understanding, piety and experience. She may therefore perform those offices of friendship which I should rejoice to perform, were I near you. But wherever you can, give me the pleasure of seeing you. You know, while I have an house, you will always be welcome to it.

I desire brother [Simon] Day to meet me in London on the 26th instant.[246]

I do not know how you can have more preaching by the travelling preachers unless you had more preachers; which indeed might easily be, if your monied men did not love their money more than they do their souls.

I hope neither marriage nor business makes Neddy less zealous for God or less active in his work.[247]

Peace be with all your spirits! I am, my dear Nancy,
Ever yours,

J. Wesley

Address: 'To / Miss Bolton / In Witney / Oxfordshire'.
Postmarks: 'JY/8', 'Ireland', and '13/IY'.
Endorsement: by Bolton, 'July 8 85'.
Source: holograph; Wesley's Chapel (London), LDWMM 1997/6591.

---

[246] I.e., for the Conference that began that day.
[247] Edward Bolton Jr. had married Hannah Sheppard on Sept. 7, 1784.

To Thomas Wride[248]

Dublin
July 8, 1785   5

Dear Tommy,

I wonder at nothing in poor Nicholas [Manners]. But I wonder much at James Kershaw. Unless our preachers had already left their preaching-house, surely he would not have let it to any others!

I love John Fenwick well, but I know he was a faulty man then 10 once or twice. However, if there be no fresh matter of complaint, what is past shall go for nothing.

I desire you to come to the Conference. A Conference while I live is 'The preachers whom I *invite* to confer with me'.[249]

Many years ago one informed me at London, 'The stewards have 15 discovered they are not *your* stewards, but the *people's*; and are to direct, not *be directed* by, you.' The next Sunday I let them drop, and named seven other stewards.

No contentious persons shall for the future meet in any Conference.[250] They may *dispute* elsewhere if they please. 20

I am, dear Tommy,
    Yours affectionately,

               J. Wesley

I never said a word of publishing that account.[251]   25

Address: 'To / Mr Wride / at Mrs [Etheldred] Hutton's / In Epworth, near Thorne / Yorkshire'.
Postmark: 'JY / 8'.
Endorsements: by Wride, 'No. 25. / July 8th 1785' and 'Came to hand / ye 30 17th of July / 1785'.
Source: holograph; MARC, MAM JW 6/27.

---

[248] JW was replying to Wride's letters of May 30 and June 23, 1785. In the first Wride drew attention to some recent publications of Nicholas Manners, mentioned James Kershaw had rented out a chapel the Methodists had been using to Lady Huntingdon, conveyed some concerns about John Fenwick, and wondered if he was supposed to attend Conference since he had not been included among the 'one hundred' in the Deed of Declaration.

[249] See JW's public letter of Mar. 3, 1785.

[250] In his letter of June 23, Wride sent JW a copy of the petition drawn up by James Oddie (June 14, 1785) being circulated among stewards and other lay leaders in circuits, related again to the Deed of Declaration.

[251] An account of purported appearances of ghosts at Leverton; see Wride to JW, c. June 1785.

To Alexander Knox

Dublin
July 10, 1785

Dear Alleck,

The letters will do exceeding well.[252] You are a very tolerable translator, and use will make perfectness. The more you translate, the more accurate you will be. Melanchton was a truly great man. None of the German Reformers was equal to him.

What I advise you to is this: every fair day walk to, if not round, the churchyard. When you are a little hardened by this, you may venture at a convenient opportunity (suppose on a Sunday morning) to attend the public worship. Till you do, I cannot say you are in God's way; and therefore I am not sure you will find his blessing.[253]

You may wait till February.[254] But you must think of less than forty by twenty-two or twent-four. Contract with a builder before you lay the stone—no after-claps! If it comes to two hundred and twenty pounds, fear not! God will provide. Observe! No roof ought to rise above one third of the breadth of any building. If it does, the builder wants either skill or honesty.

Peace be with all your spirits! We are to sail tonight.

My dear Alleck,

Adieu!

Address: 'To / Mr Alexr Knox, in / Londonderry'.
Postmark: 'JY/12'.
Source: holograph; Bridwell Library (SMU).[255]

---

[252] Knox had translated from the Latin at least four letters found in *Epistolarum D. Erasmi roterodami Libri XXI, et, P. Melanchtoni libri IV* (London: Flesher and Young, 1642). JW published at least excerpts of these translations in the Oct. issue of *AM* 8 (1785): 537–40.

[253] Cf. JW to Knox, June 8, 1785.

[254] To start building the new preaching-house in Londonderry.

[255] Held previously in the Upper Room Museum, L-44.

To Arthur Keene

London
July 16, 1785   5

Dear Arthur,

I forgot to show you a letter from Mr. Beardmore[256] which I received when I was in Dublin, wherein he says, 'I wrote a letter in January 1783 to Mr. [James] Deaves, to whose son-in-law, Mr. Featherstone, I sent power to recover a debt of upwards of £119   10 from Mr. Neill, now of Ballinasloe, who is well able to pay it.' Has Mr. Featherstone received that power? And what has he done in consequence thereof? I wish you would ask him and send me word directly, that Mr. Beardmore may know how to proceed.

And pray send me word how my poor Amelia does?[257] I have been   15 much troubled concerning her. She appeared so much affected on Sunday evening when I took my leave, that I was afraid lest it should bring back her fever.

Sister Blair bore her journey admirably well.[258] She is most comfortably situated at Chester. And all our sisters cleave to her as if   20 they had known her seven years, just as they would to my Bella Keene if they had her among them.[259] Don't think you have all the love in Ireland. We have a little in England too. For God is here!

To him I tenderly commend you and yours, and am, dear Arthur,
Ever yours,   25
J. Wesley

Address: 'To / Mr. Arthur Keene, in / Dublin'.
Postmarks: '16/IY' and 'JY/20'. *Charge*: '6'.
Endorsements: by Keene, '16 July 1785 / Revd. J: Wesley / London' and   30
'Answered / 23d July 1785'.
Source: holograph; MHS Ireland Archives.

---

[256] Joseph Beardmore (c. 1745–1829) had married Mary Owen (c. 1750–1809), formerly of Publow, in 1776. The couple were close friends of JW. Joseph helped fund building of City Road Chapel and was a trustee there. See Stevenson, *City Road*, 384–85.

[257] This was most likely Amelia Singleton, who was the leader of two classes in Dublin in 1788. See Cooney, 'Dublin Society', 45; and follow-up in JW to Keene, July 31, 1785.

[258] The Irish itinerant Andrew Blair was being moved from Dublin to Birmingham this Conference; this would be his wife Mary.

[259] Isabella (Martin) Keene, Arthur's wife.

To Lancelot Harrison

London
July 16, 1785

5 My Dear Brother,
I came hither last night.
If you are holier by your marriage (as I trust you will [be]) then
you will be happier.[260] I reserve Leeds, Birstall, and Bradford circuits for invalids, such as brother [John] Shaw, [John] Valton, etc.
10 Colne and Keighley are bespoke, but hardly any that lie north of
these.
If brother [Thomas] Longley is able to travel slowly, it will do
him much good with regard to his health.[261] If he is not able, Thomas Wride may come in his place.
15 I am, with love to sister [Elizabeth] Harrison,
Your affectionate brother,

J. Wesley

Address: 'To / Mr Harrison / At Mrs [Etheldred] Hutton's / In Epworth,
20   near Thorne / Yorkshire'.
Postmark: '16/IY'.
Source: holograph; St. Andrews, Scotland, University Library, ms 30120.

25

To Alexander Suter

London
30   July 16, 1785
My Dear Brother,
I told you in Scotland that you might come to the Conference,
but it is no great matter. Mr. [Richard] Watkinson does not come;
but Mr. Inglis and Robert Johnson are come in his place.[262] Ac-

---

[260] Harrison's first wife, Susannah (Moody) Harrison, died in early 1783. Harrison had married Elizabeth Robinson in Apr. 1785 in Haxey, Lincolnshire.

[261] To come to Conference.

[262] Andrew Inglis (fl. 1780–90) was admitted as an itinerant in 1780 (see 10:496 in this edn.), after serving four years in Scotland he was moved to England, where he continued serving until he was listed as desisting from travelling in the 1793 *Minutes*. Robert Johnson (c. 1762–1829) was converted under the ministry of Robert Carr Brackenbury, became an itinerant in 1783 (see 10:534), served for 42 years, and spent his last years in Hull. See *Minutes* (post-Wesley, 1829), 6:451.

cording to their own desire, I will station both brothers [Duncan] M'Allum and Johnson in the Dundee circuit.

It is pity that brother [Joseph] Saunderson should be buried alive in one town.[263] God has qualified him for more extensive usefulness. Since this time twelvemonth what has he done in comparison of what he might have done? Perhaps slipped out for a month once or twice! Oh why does he not rather choose to 'receive a full reward'![264]

But why do you quarrel with poor Agnes Ramsay? Is there no living at Dundee without quarrelling? O follow peace with all men, and holiness![265] I am

Your affectionate friend and brother,

J. Wesley

Address: 'To / Mr Suter / At the Preachinghouse / in / Dundee'.
Postmarks: '16/IY' and 'JY/20'.
Endorsement: by Suter, 'Nr. 5'.
Source: holograph; St. Simon's Island, Georgia, South Georgia Conference Commission on Archives and History.

To Ellen (Gretton) Christian

London
July 17, 1785

My Dear Sister,

I sailed from Dublin Bay on Monday morning, came into Holyhead Bay about noon, and on Friday in the afternoon (stopping only a few hours at Chester) was brought safe to London. After the Conference (at which I should be glad to see Mr. [John] Pugh or Mr. [William] Dodwell, or both[266]) I shall with God's help visit the west of England.

The gravel may be easily prevented by eating a small crust of bread the size of a walnut every morning, fasting. But your nervous disorders will not be removed without constant exercise. If you can have no other, you should daily ride a wooden horse, which is only

---

[263] Saunderson had been stationed on the Dundee circuit in 1783, but desisted from travelling the following year.

[264] 2 John 1:8.

[265] See Heb. 12:14.

[266] Cf. JW to Thomas Davenport, Aug. 14, 1782.

a double plank nine or ten feet long, properly placed upon two tres-
sels. This has removed many distempers and saved abundance of
lives.[267] I should advise you likewise to use nettle tea (six or eight
leaves) instead of foreign tea for a month, and probably you will see
a great change.

No person will hereafter be present at any Conference but whom
I invite by name to come and confer with me. So we will have no
more contention there.[268]

I am, with love to brother Christian, my dear sister,

Your affectionate brother,

J. Wesley

Our Conference begins on Tuesday the 26th instant; but the first
two days only travelling preachers are present.

Postmark: '18/IY'. *Charge*: '6'.[269]
Source: holograph; MARC, MAM JW 2/31.

To Elizabeth Gibbes

London
July 17, 1785

It would have grieved me, if I had thought my dear Miss Gibbes
had quite forgotten me.[270] For I do not place *you* in the rank of acquaintance only: I rejoice to call you my friend.

While I am in Ireland, a letter directed to Dublin finds me in
whatever part of the kingdom I am. I set sail from Dublin Bay on
Monday morning, and came into Holyhead Bay in the afternoon.
We reached Chester on Wednesday, took coach the same evening, and came hither on Friday. I thought of you when we passed
through Stafford, and should not have failed to call at the Park, had
I been in my own carriage. But the approach of our yearly Conference laid me under a necessity of being in town as soon as possible.
It gives me pleasure to hear that my dear Miss Agnes [Gibbes] has

---

[267] See note on JW to Samuel Bradburn, Apr. 7, 1781, 29:639 in this edn.
[268] Like there had been at the 1784 Conference.
[269] Remainder of address portion missing.
[270] JW's last apparent letter from Eliz. Gibbes had been in June 1784. Her current letter
is not known to survive.

the courage to rise early and to use exercise. If she persists herein, it will do her more good, than all the medicines in the dispensary.

I was agreeably surprised as I travelled through all the provinces of Ireland, the northern in particular, at finding out what was the principal cause of the alarm which has spread through both the kingdoms. For three or four years a few bold, lively persons—but of no note (some of them very low mechanics) and therefore wisely concealing their names—have filled the public papers with inflammatory letters and paragraphs (personating men of great importance), which our English news-writers have eagerly retailed. But in reality Ireland is full as quiet as England, and the Irish Volunteers as harmless as the English Life Guards.[271] In the Irish Parliament a few mock patriots still snarl at everything, till they gain their point, places, or pensions.

The other day, a gentlewoman came into the stagecoach, near Stafford, who hearing Hilton Park mentioned, after speaking very respectfully of you, said, 'I hear the affair of Miss Gibbes and Sir ___ ___ is over.' Although no more was said upon the subject, this led me to a train of reflections. I could not but wish that a person whom I valued so much might never fall into the hands of one that did not abound either in sense or religion, merely because he had a large estate. Will money bring happiness? Is content to be purchased, even by thousands of gold or silver? Prior's words sound prettily.

> The joys of wedlock with the cares we mix:
> Tis best repenting in a coach and six.[272]

But I cannot wish that either you or your dear sister should ever make the experiment. I am persuaded you will act, in this and in all things, in such a manner as you will never repent of. I feel myself nearly concerned in the happiness of all the amiable family. And should rejoice in any opportunity of showing my deep regard for every branch of it.

I am, my dear Miss Gibbes,
    Your ever affectionate servant,

J. W.

[271] For the Volunteers, see note on JW to John Bredin, Feb. 20, 1782. The Life Guards were the most senior regiment of the British cavalry.

[272] JW's memory has failed him; cf. lines 17–18 of Samuel Garth's Epilogue to Joseph Addison's *Cato: A Tragedy* (London: Tonson, 1713), [p. 63]: 'The woes of wedlock with the joys we mix / Tis best repenting in a coach and six'. A 'coach and six' is a coach pulled by six horses — a symbol of status.

Address: 'To / Miss Gibbes / At Hilton Park / Near Wolverhampton / Staffordshire'.
Postmark: '18/IY'. *Charge*: '5'.
Source: holograph; National Archives, PRO 30/9/7/15.

To Ann Tindall

London
July 17, 1785

My Dear Sister,

There is something remarkable in this. The greatest blessing does not always attend them we call the greatest preachers but generally them that are most devoted to God, though their talents are not extraordinary. I believe all your preachers this year were devoted men, therefore the work of God prospered in their hand.[273]

I hope Tommy Brown's troubles are now over, and that all things will work together for his good.[274] As he has a regard for *you*, your speaking freely to him from time to time may be a means of strengthening him.

If the subscribers are not weary, you will work yourselves out of debt.[275]

I am glad to hear that Mr. Coulson has at length ventured to join the society.[276] I doubt not but his soul will now prosper.

Be zealous for God, my dear Nancy! And still be a comfort to,

Your affectionate brother,

J. Wesley

Address: 'To / Miss Tindall / in /Scarborough'.
Postmarks: '18/IY' and '19/IY'.
Endorsement: by Tindall, '17 July 1785'.
Source: holograph; British Library, Department of Manuscripts, Add. MS. 43695, ff. 93–94.

[273] The preachers assigned to the Scarborough circuit by the 1784 Conference were William Simpson, Charles Bond, and John King. On Simpson, see JW's letter to him of Sept. 6, 1786. Charles Bond became an itinerant in 1783 (see 10:531 in this edn.). He was laid aside in 1789 (10:677), but reinstated in 1790 (10:715). Bond desisted from travelling in 1793.

[274] See Rom. 8:28.

[275] On their preaching-house.

[276] This is apparently William Coulson (b. c., 1744), who would marry Mary Dickson in 1789; see JW to Tindall, Aug. 1, 1789.

To Robert Carr Brackenbury

London
July 23, 1785   5

Dear Sir,

Yours of June the 15th I received this morning, that of July the 10th a day or two since.[277]

It seems the Protestants in France are full as far from true religion as the Romanists.[278] Or rather farther; for some of the latter have even   10
lately wrote some truly spiritual books—the Jansenists in particular, some of whose writings breathe a truly Christian spirit.[279]

You have surely done well, in taking a [preaching-]house. It will give you more influence. And although I should have been glad to see you here at this important season, yet I could not have wished   15
you to leave the poor people in so critical a situation.

In great haste,
I am, dear sir,
    Your affectionate friend and brother,

J. Wesley   20

On Monday Aug. 8, and Thursday the 11th, I expect to be at Portsmouth. On Friday 12th, at Winchester.

Address: 'To / Robert Brackenbury Esq. / At St. Helier's / Isle of Jersey'.
Postmark: '23/IY'. *Charge*: '4'.   25
Source: holograph; Wesley's Chapel (London), LDWMM 1994/1982.

---

[277] Neither of these letters are known to survive.

[278] Brackenbury had recently visited France for a few months.

[279] JW particularly admired the prominent Jansenist, Jean Duvergier de Hauranne, Abbé de Saint-Cyran (1581–1643)—translating selections from his *Instructions chrestiennes* as '*Christian Instructions*' in *Sermons on Several Occasions*, Vol. 4 (1760), 269–324; later incorporated in 'Christian Reflections', in *Works* (Pine), 24:172–232; and in a further reduced form in *Farther Thoughts on Christian Perfection*, II, 13:123–31 in this edn. JW also published an abridgement of an English translation of *Pensees sur la Religion by Blaise Pascal* (1623–62) in his *Christian Library*, 23:3–233.

To Catherine Warren

London
July 25, 1785

5 My Dear Sister,

I don't know how much I am in arrears to you on account of the debt.[280] But let me know, and your demand shall be answered. And I am willing to subscribe another year. It is well, you met with that annuity. That is a sure way of paying debts.

10 I believe Joshua Keighley will be at least as useful to you the second year as he was the first.[281] He is a workman that needs not to be ashamed, as his doctrine and his life agree together.[282] But I hear a preacher of another kind has promised to pay you a visit: I mean William Moore.[283] But I am in hopes he will not be able to unsettle

15 many. Indeed he would spare no pains, and would assert anything, true or false. But in spite of all the efforts of men or devils, the counsel of the Lord, that shall stand.[284]

I hope you are not weary of well-doing, but that you still continue to feed the lambs. May the Great Shepherd still feed you with his

20 love! So prays, my dear Kitty,

Yours very affectionately,

J. Wesley

Address: 'To / Miss Warren / in / Haverford West'.
25 *Postmark*: '26/IY'.
Source: holograph; Harrisburg, Illinois, First United Methodist Church.

---

[280] JW had apparently been subscribing to help pay off the debt on the preaching-house in Haverfordwest, as he had that in Scarborough; see JW to Ann Tindall, Dec. 11, 1784.

[281] Joshua Keighley (1761–88), a native of Halifax, Yorkshire, became an itinerant in 1780 (see 10:496 in this edn.). He was the Assistant for the Pembrokeshire circuit in 1784 and returned there the following year. In 1786 JW ordained Keighley for service in Scotland, where he died two years later, just before a planned marriage (see 10:645).

[282] See 2 Tim. 2:15.

[283] Moore had left the Methodist connexion and was trying to raise his own congregation; see JW, *Journal*, Feb. 25, 1785, 23:343 in this edn.

[284] See Prov. 19:21.

To Sarah Baker[285]

London
July 30, 1785

My Dear Sister,

Mr. [William] Sanders earnestly entreated that he might not return to Wales. But when I insisted upon it, he consented. And his fellow labourer is full as sensible as himself, and as much devoted to God. Totally different from that noisy, boisterous, self-conceited wretch, who has now no more place amongst us.[286] Although we have expelled him out of our connexion; not for vanity and self-sufficiency (shocking as it was) but for repeated acts of immodesty, such as I could not name to a woman.

Now go on in the Lord, and in every power of his might![287] Be zealous, be active for God! Feed the lambs! Put forth all your strength! Yet a little while and the Great Shepherd will give you a full reward![288] I am, my dear Sally,

Yours affectionately,

J. Wesley

Source: holograph; MARC, MAM JW 1/9.

To Thomas Hanson

London
July 30, 1785

Dear Tommy,

You seem to be surprised that anyone should blame you, when you are not blameworthy![289] Did you never hear of such a thing before? Marvel not at the matter. Go on, through evil report and good report.[290] Be

---

[285] While the address portion is missing, Saunders had been assigned to the Glamorgan circuit, near Monmouth, where Sarah Baker resided.

[286] I.e., William Moore; see JW to Catherine Warren, July 25, 1785.

[287] See Eph. 6:10.

[288] See 1 Pet. 5:4.

[289] Hanson's situation likely related to why he was absent from Conference in 1785, and placed on disability in following years.

[290] See 2 Cor. 6:8.

Patient in bearing ill, and doing well[291]

The more you suffer now, the more you will rejoice hereafter.
I am, dear Tommy,
Yours affectionately,

J. Wesley

Address: 'To / Mr. Tho. Hanson'.
Source: holograph; Wesley's Chapel (London), LDWMM 1994/1951.

To Arthur Keene

London
July 31, 1785

My Dear Arthur,
Yours of the 23rd instant gave me great satisfaction.[292] I am glad
that Mr. Featherstone has wrote to Mr. [Joseph] Beardmore,[293] who
will easily concur in his judgment that it is very imprudent to sue
a man for what he is not able to pay. I suppose it was some ill-
minded man who informed Mr. Beardmore that Mr. Neill was in
so flourishing circumstances—which was not likely to be the case
while he was only a common clerk to a person in business. And it
showed great honesty and generosity in Mr. Featherstone to give so
impartial advice.
I hope he is diligently engaged in the little affair you entrusted
him with in respect of sister Jaques's legacy. If that be pressed in
earnest, it may turn out well; otherwise it will drop into nothing.
I must charge you with another little business. At the Conference it was judged proper that the married preacher should live in
our preaching-house at Athlone. But our brother William Rayner
writes me word 'He has convinced brother [Matthias] Joyce that it
cannot be.' Be so kind as to write a line to brother Joyce and inquire
how this matter stands; and desire him to tell brother Rayner at the
same time that I thank him for his letter.[294]

---

[291] SW Jr., 'The Battle of the Sexes', st. 25, *Poems* (1743), p. 34; reprinted by JW in *MSP*
(1744), 3:32.
[292] The letter is not known to survive.
[293] See JW to Keene, July 16, 1785.
[294] This letter is not known to survive.

You give me pleasure by talking of my dear Isabella.[295] I love to see her, and I love to hear of her. I love likewise to hear of her twin soul, my precious Amelia.[296] I was afraid she would grieve too much when I went away, especially as she did not shed a tear, I mean while I was in the room. I rejoice so much the more to hear that our blessed Lord undertook her cause and sent her help in time of need. It would give me pain indeed, if one that is as my own soul should receive hurt from me. O may we always meet for the better and not for the worse. May we always 'love one another with a pure heart fervently'.[297]

I hope both she, and you, and my Isabella will not forget to pray for, dear Arthur,

Yours most affectionately,

J. Wesley

Amelia does well in spending a little time in the country. Nothing will restore her like air and exercise.

When is Mrs. [Theodosia] Blachford to come hither?

I had forgot to mention that if that excellent woman, sister Cox, desired when there is room to be admitted to the widows' house, I think no one is more worthy.

[on outside] I opened this to insert the postscript.

Address: 'To / Mr Arthur Keene / in / Dublin'.
Postmarks: '1/AU' and 'AU/5'.
Endorsement: by Keene, '31 July 1785 / Revd. J: Wesley / London'.
Source: holograph; MARC, MAM JW 3/76.

To John Ogylvie[298]

London
August 7, 1785

My Dear Brother,

As long as you are yourself earnestly aspiring after a full deliverance from all sin, and a renewal in the whole image of God,[299]

[295] Arthur's wife.
[296] Amelia Singleton; see JW to Keene, July 16, 1785.
[297] 1 Pet. 1:22.
[298] John Ogylvie (d. 1839) was admitted 'on trial' as an itinerant in 1782 (see 10:519 in this edn.) and had been stationed to the Isle of Man at the most recent Conference. He would travel nearly forty years, settling in 1821. See *Minutes* (post-Wesley, 1841), 8:420.
[299] See Col. 3:10

God will prosper you in your labour, especially if you constantly and strongly exhort all believers to expect full sanctification now by simple faith. And never be weary of well-doing; in due time you shall reap if you faint not![300]

5   I am
           Your affectionate brother,

                                                              [J. Wesley]

Source: published transcription; Jackson, *Works* (3rd), 12:511.

10

To the Rev. Charles Wesley[301]

15   Plymouth[302]
                                                         August 19, 1785
Dear Brother,
      I will tell you my thoughts with all simplicity, and wait for bet-
ter information. If you agree with me, well; if not, we can (as Mr.
20   [George] Whitefield used to say) agree to disagree.
      For these forty years I have been in doubt concerning that ques-
tion, 'What obedience is due to "heathenish priests and mitred
infidels"?'[303] I have from time to time proposed my doubts to the
most pious and sensible clergymen I knew. But they gave me no
25   satisfaction. Rather, they seemed to be puzzled as well as me.
      Obedience I always paid to the bishops in obedience to the laws of
the land.[304] But I cannot see that I am under any obligation to obey
them further than those laws require.
      It is in obedience to these laws that I have never exercised in Eng-
30   land the power which I believe God has given me. I firmly believe I
am a scriptural ἐπίσκοπος, as much as any man in England or in Europe.[305] (For the *uninterrupted succession* I know to be a fable, which
no man ever did or can prove.) But this does in no wise interfere
with my remaining in the Church of England; from which I have

----

[300] See Gal. 6:9.

[301] JW was replying to CW's letter of Aug. 14, 1785, who reminded JW of the tract *Reasons against a Separation from the Church of England* (1758) and urged him to read it again—for JW's act of ordaining lay preachers for the Methodists in North America was sure to lead to a separation.

[302] *AM* reads 'Plymouth Dock'.

[303] Quoting CW, *Elegy on Robert Jones* (Bristol: Farley, 1742), l. 388, p. 19.

[304] In *AM* this sentence begins: 'Some obedience …'.

[305] Cf. JW, *Journal*, Jan. 20, 1746, 20:112 in this edn.

no more desire to separate than I had fifty years ago. I still attend all the ordinances of the Church at all opportunities; and I constantly and earnestly desire all that are connected with me so to do. When Mr. [Edward] Smyth pressed us to 'separate from the Church', he meant, 'Go to Church no more.' And this was what I meant twenty-seven years ago when I persuaded our brethren 'not to separate from the Church'.

But here another question occurs: 'What is the Church of England?' It is not all the people of England. Papists and Dissenters are no part thereof. It is not all the people of England except papists and Dissenters. Then we should have a glorious Church indeed! No; according to our twentieth Article, a particular church is 'a congregation of faithful people' (*coetus credentium* are the words in our Latin edition) 'among whom the word of God is preached and the sacraments duly administered'. Here is a true logical definition, containing both the essence and the properties of a church. What then, according to this definition, is the Church of England? Does it mean 'all the believers in England (except the papists and Dissenters) who have the word of God and the sacraments duly administered among them'? I fear this does not come up to your idea of the Church of England. Well, what more do you include in that phrase? 'Why, all the believers that adhere to the doctrine and discipline established by the Convocation under Queen Elizabeth.' Nay, that discipline is well-nigh vanished away. And the doctrine both you and I adhere to.

All those reasons against a separation from the Church in this sense I subscribe to still. What then are you frighted at? I no more separate from it now than I did in the year 1758. I submit still (though sometimes with a doubting conscience) to 'mitred infidels'. I do indeed vary from them in some points of doctrine, and in some points of discipline (by preaching abroad, for instance, by praying extempore, and by forming societies). But not an hair's breadth further than I believe to be meet, right, and my bounden duty. I walk still by the same rule I have done for between forty and fifty years. I do nothing rashly. It is not likely I should. The high-day of my blood is over. If you will go on hand in hand with me, do. But do not hinder me if you will not help. Perhaps, if you had kept close to me, I might have done better. However, with or without help, I creep on. And as I have been hitherto, so I trust I shall always be,

Your affectionate friend and brother,

J. Wesley

A phrase that occurs above needs explication. I do not mean I never will ordain any *while I am in England*, but not to use the power they receive while they are in England.[306]

5 *Source*: manuscript transcription by CW; MARC, MA 1977/157, JW V.III, pp. 24–26.[307]

10

To Thomas Tattershall

St. Austell[308]
August 22, 1785

15 Dear Tommy,

After the circuit had been under the care of two such wonderful preachers, it is no wonder it should be in a miserable condition.[309] So much the more have you need to stir up the gift of God that is in you.[310] Put forth all your strength! And you will soon see matters

20 wear quite a different face.

Nathanael Ward sent word to London that he did not intend to act as a travelling preacher any longer. Indeed he could not with any degree of honesty, for he does not preach or believe the Methodist doctrine. He not only does not believe perfection, but has directly

25 preached against it.

I do not know whether the account of Ramsey is in the *[Arminian] Magazine* or no.[311]

You must not go out of the circuit yet. I am, dear Tommy,

Your affectionate friend and brother,

30

[J. Wesley]

[306] This postscript does not appear in *AM*. JW quietly set aside this commitment in 1788, after CW's death; see Appendix B.

[307] We present the text as CW transcribed it—assuming it is the closest to JW's original letter. JW published the letter subsequently in *AM* 9 (1786): 50–51; we annotate the few changes of content in the published form.

[308] Orig., 'St. Austle'.

[309] JW was speaking ironically of John Brettel and Nathanael Ward, who had served the Derby circuit the previous year.

[310] See 2 Tim. 1:6.

[311] Tattershall was inquiring about an account of the life and execution of Thomas Ramsey in Nov. 20, 1784, which he sent JW in a letter c. June 1785. It would appear in *AM* 9 (Sept. 1786): 485–90.

Address: 'To / Mr. Tho. Tattershall / At the Preaching House / In Derby'.
Source: published transcription; Byrth, 'Memoir', xxxv–vi.

5

To Christopher Hopper[312]

Redruth
August 27, 1785   10

My Dear Brother,
    The utmost that can be done at present is to permit him to preach as a local preacher.[313] For I will not run my head against all the Conference, by reversing what they have determined. I cannot, with either decency or prudence, go any further yet. If his behaviour is unblameable in this lower station, by-and-by he may rise higher.   15
    I am
        Your affectionate friend and brother,

J. Wesley   20

Endorsement: 'Pri[vate]'.[314]
Source: holograph; Bridwell Library (SMU).[315]

25

To Agnes Gibbes

Camelford   30
August 30, 1785

It was with great satisfaction that I received my dear Miss Agnes' letter yesterday, at my return from the Land's End.[316] The people

---

[312] The holograph does not name the recipient; but Jackson includes this in a series of letters to Hopper (Jackson, *Works*, 12:303).

[313] The referent is likely John Fenwick. Fenwick was a long-time associate of Hopper, who was expelled by the 1785 Conference (see 10:569 in this edn.), but would be given an appointment again the following year (10:600). Cf. JW to Thomas Wride, July 8, 1785.

[314] This is written on the outside, with a seal; the note was clearly included in another letter or packet.

[315] Held previously in the Upper Room Museum, L-54.

[316] This letter is not known to survive.

of this county much resemble those of Ireland, being earnestly affectionate to their friends. Those of them in particular whose minds are at once softened and strengthened by religion. I never saw so much of this among the Irish as in my late journey through the
5 kingdom. Surely people of so fine a temper are scarce to be found in any other part of Europe! But they have not, in general, the English steadiness. They easily receive and as easily lose an impression. And yet I have found many who are unvariable in their friendship, and have been so, even from their childhood.

10 And if I mistake not, this is the temper of my dear Miss Agnes. I believe all your affections are naturally strong—but yet not very variable, not apt to change, without some particular reason. This is a great blessing, steadiness of temper. For which, and for a thousand other blessings, you have reason to be thankful to him, who is
15 daily helping you, and pouring his benefits upon you.

I am glad you have the resolution to use that domestic exercise, when you cannot so well go abroad.[317] But it should be used constantly, once if not twice a day; otherwise it will have little effect. And I am still in doubt whether your health will be confirmed un-
20 less another thing also be added. Unless you thoroughly follow that kind direction, 'My child, give me thy heart!'[318] You have frequently a desire to do this; but 'something or other' comes between. Then your thoughts are *dissipated* and that good desire insensibly dies away. *Dissipation* therefore, whether at London, at Bath or else-
25 where, I take to be your grand hindrance.[319] Anything which you knew to be evil, you could not admit of. But this which seems to be so harmless (though it is really nothing better than practical atheism) steals upon you unawares! If you can avoid this, in the hurry and bustle of the gay world, you must have more than human
30 power. Especially in places of public resort. But the God whom you serve is able to deliver you.[320]

On Saturday next, September 2,[321] I expect to be at Bristol. But I am afraid you will not be at Bath before I set out for London, which will be on Monday, October 3rd. As soon as you are there, you will
35 be so good as to let me know.

---

[317] Walk an hour every day; cf. JW to Gibbes, c. May 9, 1785.
[318] Cf. Prov. 23:26.
[319] Cf. JW's sermon 'On Dissipation', 3:116–25 in this edn. He published the sermon in *AM* 7 (1784), 7–13, 66–70.
[320] See Dan. 3:17.
[321] Orig., '3'; a mistake.

I thought you had had the *Moral and Sacred Poems*, which were published many years ago. But I conjecture you have not, from your not knowing where to find those lines. They are part of Mr. Prior's paraphrase of the thirteenth chapter of the first of Corinthians.[322] That you may enjoy every part of that holiness which is there so beautifully described, is the earnest wish of, my dear Miss Agnes,
Yours in tender affection,

John Wesley

My mind was so full of you, that I had quite forgot Mr. Gibbons. He is the more dangerous, because he is *decent*.

Address: 'To / Miss Agnes Gibbes / At Hilton Park / Near Wolverhampton / Staffordshire / xp [i.e., crosspost] Glo'ster'.
Postmark: 'Camelford'. *Charge*: '6'.
Source: holograph; National Archives, PRO, 30/9/11/2.

To the Methodist Preachers and Societies[323]

Camelford
August 30, 1785

Of Separation from the Church

1. Ever since I returned from America, it has been warmly affirmed, 'You separate from the Church.' I would consider how far, and in what sense, this assertion is true.
2. Whether you mean by that term the building so called, or the congregation, it is plain I do not separate from either; for wherever I am, I go to the Church [of England], and join with the congregation.

[322] JW had quoted Matthew Prior, 'Charity', *ll.* 23–26 [republished in *MSP* (1744), 88] in his letter to Gibbes, c. May 9, 1785.

[323] JW's decision to ordain three of his preachers to serve in Scotland on Aug. 1–2, at the closing of the 1785 Conference, offered new opportunity for his critics to charge him with separating from the Church of England. This included critics within Methodism like CW; see JW's letter to him of Aug. 19, above. This public letter distills JW's response to such charges, though there is no evidence he circulated it at the time. Over the coming months it became clear that the second ordination served to intensify calls from those of his preachers and followers who *wanted* him to separate the movement from the Church. This became a focus of debate at the 1786 Conference, and JW appended this letter to the published *Minutes* of that Conference.

3. Yet it is true that I have in some respects varied, though not from the doctrines, yet from the discipline of the Church of England—although not willingly, but by constraint. For instance, above forty years ago I began 'preaching in the fields', and that for two reasons: first, I was not suffered to preach in the churches; secondly, no parish church in London or Westminster could contain the congregation.

4. About the same time several persons who were desirous to save their souls prayed me to meet them apart from the great congregation. These little companies ('societies' they were called) gradually spread through the three kingdoms. And in many places they built houses in which they met, and wherein I and my brethren preached—for a few young men, one after another, desired to serve me as 'sons in the gospel'.[324]

5. Some time after, Mr. De Leznot, a clergyman, desired me to 'officiate at his chapel' in Wapping.[325] There I read prayers, and preached, and administered the Lord's Supper to a part of the society. The rest communicated either at St. Paul's [cathedral] or at their several parish churches. Meantime, I endeavoured to watch over all their souls, as one that 'was to give an account',[326] and to assign to each of my fellow-labourers the part wherein I judged he might be most useful.

6. When these were multiplied I gave them an invitation to meet me together in my house at London, that we might consider in what manner we could most effectually 'save our own souls', and 'them that heard us'.[327] This we called a Conference (meaning thereby the persons, not the conversation, they had). At first I desired all the preachers to meet me, but afterwards only a select number.

7. Some years after, we were strongly importuned by our brethren in America, to 'come over and help them'.[328] Several preachers willingly offered themselves for the service; and several went from time to time. God blessed their labours in an uncommon manner. Many sinners were converted to God, and many societies formed under the same Rules as were observed in England; insomuch that at present the American societies contain more than eighteen thousand members.

---

[324] Cf. 1 Tim. 1:2.

[325] J. L. De Leznot (the spelling in his signature) sent a letter inviting JW to this role on July 10, 1741, which JW initiated on Aug. 2 of that year (see *Journal*, 19:208 in this edn.).

[326] Rom. 14:12.

[327] Cf. 1 Tim. 4:16.

[328] Cf. Acts 16:9.

8. But since the late Revolution in North America, these have been in great distress. The clergy having no sustenance, either from England or from the American States, have been obliged almost universally to leave the country, and seek their food elsewhere. Hence those who had been members of the Church [of England] 5 had none either to administer the Lord's Supper, or to baptize their children. They applied to England over and over. But it was to no purpose. Judging this to be a case of real necessity, I took a step which for peace and quietness I had refrained from taking for many years: I exercised that power which I am fully persuaded the Great 10 Shepherd and Bishop of the Church has given me.[329] I appointed three of our labourers to go and help them, by not only preaching the Word of God, but likewise administering the Lord's Supper and baptizing their children, throughout that vast tract of land, a thousand miles long and some hundreds broad. 15

[9.] These are the steps which, not of choice but of necessity, I have slowly and deliberately taken.[330] If anyone is pleased to call this 'separating from the Church', he may. But the law of England does not call it so. Nor can anyone properly be said so to do, unless out of conscience he refuses to join in the service and partake of the sacra- 20 ments administered therein.

John Wesley

Source: published transcription; *Minutes* (1786), 19–21.[331]

25

To Mary (Bosanquet) Fletcher[332]

c. September 1785 30

My dear Sister,

I do not remember you ever disobliged me in anything. On the contrary you have for these many years done everything in your power to

---

[329] See JW to 'Our Brethren in America', Sept. 10, 1784.

[330] Notice that JW quietly passes over his more recent ordination of preachers to serve in Scotland!

[331] See 10:615–16 in this edn. In addition to the separate pamphlet of the *Minutes*, the letter was included in an extract of the *Minutes* published in *AM* 9 (Dec. 1786): 675–77.

[332] Mary comments in her journal after JW's death, 'When I was very low after my dear husband's death, among the many gloomy thoughts which came to my mind, one was that I had not so profited by Mr. Wesley's excellent advice as I might have done, and I wrote to him, expressing that sentiment; to which he gave me the following answer.'

oblige me. Indeed I saw it my duty so to do, and must acknowledge my many and great obligations to that great and good man.

Source: published transcription; Moore, *Mary Fletcher*, 383.

To Robert Costerdine[333]

Bristol
September 4, 1785

Dear Robert,

All I can say at present is, if matters be as you represent, the thing shall be set right at the next Conference, and the £12 paid you.

But our friends at Wednesbury are afraid lest you should inflame the old quarrel. O beware of this! Meddle not with Francis White-head. Live peaceably with all men![334]

I am, dear Robert,

Your affectionate brother,

J. Wesley

Source: holograph; MARC, MAM JW 2/63.

To John Francis Valton

Bristol
September 5, 1785

My Dear Brother,

Neither sister [Ann] Brisco nor her husband ever made application to me for money.[335] Now and then I have given her a guinea; but, I think, never more at a time. We could not regularly give her any more for her child;[336] but I would have given her five pounds at a word speaking. Now she must take some trouble to get it.

Our preachers (I mean many of them) are inexcusably apt to judge and undervalue each other. Henry Foster is a weak man, but by no

---

[333] While the address portion is missing, it was surely Robert Costerdine, an itinerant on the Birmingham circuit, which included Wednesbury.

[334] See Rom. 12:18.

[335] Thomas Brisco was currently stationed on the Thirsk circuit.

[336] This is likely for their youngest daughter, Mary Ann, who would be given £6 out of the Kingswood Collection in 1789; see 10:700 in this edn.

means a weak preacher. This was never objected to him before in any circuit where I have followed him. He is a sound, judicious man and one of deep piety.

I am thinking the shortest way is, if anyone will give sister Brisco five guineas, I will repay it. 5

Consider, a person that was very happy in God is now less happy than he was. Then he thinks, 'I should be happier if I was married.'[337] Is not this feeling

> Love's all-sufficient sea to raise 10
> With drops of creature happiness?[338]

I am
Your affectionate friend and brother,

J. Wesley 15

Address: 'To / Mr Valton / At Captain Robinson's[339] / In Bridlington Key / Yorkshire'.
Postmarks: 'Bristol' and '7/SE'. *Charge*: '8'.
Endorsements: by Valton, 'Sept. 5th 1785' and 'Not received / till 13 Sept.'. 20
Source: holograph; Wesleyan University Library.

To Thomas Wride[340] 25

Bristol
September 5, 1785

Dear Tommy,

When you do what you can, you do enough. I trust you will now 30
use every possible means of redeeming the time.[341] I wish you would never neglect sleeping early and rising early. Beware of anything

---

[337] Valton had recently been advised by John Fletcher to get married. See Jackson, *EMP*, 6:116–17. Cf. JW to Valton, Sept. 13, 1785.

[338] CW, 'In Desertion or Temptation', st. 11, *HSP* (1739), 149. Valton added a comment on this paragraph: 'Blessed by my God that this is a mistake of my ever dear and truly venerable father!'

[339] William Robinson (1728–1819) had been captain of one of the ships in his father's fleet before marrying and settling, first in North Shields, and in 1769 in Bridlington. See *WMM* 49 (1826): 290.

[340] JW was replying to Wride's letter of Aug. 28, 1785, informing JW of how illness had delayed him reaching his new circuit.

[341] See Eph. 5:16.

like lightness or trifling. Wherever you are, be obliging and be serious. Disappoint those who wait for your halting.

I am, with love to sister [Jane] Wride, dear Tommy,
Your affectionate friend and brother,

J. Wesley

Address: 'To / Mr. Wride / At the Preachinghouse / in / Norwich'.
Postmarks: 'Bristol' and '7/SE'.
Endorsement: by Wride, 'No. 26. Sepr. 5th 1785'.
Source: holograph; MARC, MAM JW 6/28.

To Mary Cooke[342]

Bradford[-on-Avon]
September 10, 1785

My Dear Sister,
While I had the pleasure of sitting by you I quite forgot when I intended before we set out: Considering the bent of your mind, I cannot doubt but you have many copies of verses by you. Probably you have some (beside those on Mrs. Turner) made upon affecting subjects.[343] Will you favour me with two or three of them? Do, if you have any desire to oblige, my dear friend,
Yours affectionately,

J. Wesley

Address: 'To / Miss Cook / at / Trowbridge'.
no postmarks (hand delivered).
Endorsement: by Cooke, 'Nothing 1st'.
Source: holograph; MARC, WCB, D6/1/326.

---

[342] Mary Cooke (1760–1836) was the eldest daughter of John Cooke (d. 1792), a clothier in Trowbridge, Wiltshire, and his second wife Mary Pitney (1742–1809). Although her immediate family remained staunch members of the Church of England, they were supportive of Methodist preachers, including Adam Clarke who was stationed in nearby Bradford in 1782. JW met Mary Cooke on Sept. 8, 1785 when he preached in Trowbridge, and she travelled to hear him preach in Bradford the next day. The following morning JW wrote this letter interested in her poetry. This initiated a correspondence that continued after Cooke married Adam Clarke in 1788. See Mary Ann Cooke Smith, *Mrs. Adam Clarke* (London: Partridge and Oakey, 1851).

[343] Joanna (Cooke) Turner (1732–84), Mary's aunt, was a prominent figure in the Methodist society at Trowbridge. Mary's poem on her death was dated Dec. 27, 1784. JW eventually persuaded Mary to allow its publication; see 'On the Death of Mrs. Turner' By Miss C., *AM* 13 (1790): 223–24.

To Michael Moorhouse[344]

[Bath]
September 10, 1785

'… those words which the Rev. Mr. Wesley wrote in a letter to me dated September 10, 1785: "Finding fault with others is not the way to recommend yourself."'

Source: published excerpt; Moorhouse, *Defence*, 96.

To Mary (Mitchell) Warrick[345]

Bath
September 10, 1785[346]

My Dear Sister,

I know not what to do or what to say. This untoward man so perplexes me! It is not *my* business to find houses for the preachers' wives. I do not take it upon me. I did not *order* him to come to Burslem. I only *permitted* what I could not help.[347]

I must leave our brethren to compromise these matters among themselves. They are too hard for me. A preacher is wanted in Gloucester circuit. One of them may go thither.

I am, with love to brother [Thomas] Warrick, my dear sister,
    Your affectionate brother,

J. Wesley

---

[344] Michael Moorhouse became increasingly disgruntled about actions by JW and some of the other preachers that he believed were unfair to him. As early as the 1780 Conference he expressed his concern in a long letter to JW (not known to survive); see Moorhouse, *Defence*, 26. His dissatisfaction grew when he was excluded from the 'legal hundred' by the Deed of Declaration adopted in 1784. This sparked the letter described above, which surely went on to rehearse all of the wrongs that Moorhouse perceived he had suffered (cf. the rambling 128 pages of his *Defence*).

[345] Thomas Warrick married Mary Mitchell in 1772 in Duffield, Derbyshire. Thomas was currently the Assistant for the Burslem circuit.

[346] A secondary transcription (MARC, WCB, D6/3/1/19) misread JW's '5' as a '9'. This was Telford's source for placing it under that date; see *Letters*, 8:168.

[347] The secondary transcription has the annotation: 'To Mrs. Warrick concerning Michael Moorhouse'. Moorhouse was assigned to serve the Devonshire circuit by the 1785 Conference (see 10:570 in this edn.). But he reminded JW a few weeks later that being near the sea air made him ill, and requested to be moved to Burslem, and that a house be provided there for his wife. According to Moorhouse, JW agreed to this request at first, but later changed his mind; see Moorhouse, *Defence*, 69–71. Cf. JW's letter to Moorhouse of this same date.

Address: 'To / Mrs Warrick / at the Preachinghouse / In Burslem / near /
    Newcastle under Line [sic] / xp [i.e., crosspost] Glo'ster'.
Postmark: 'Bath'. *Charge*: '5'.
Source: holograph; privately held (WWEP Archive holds photocopy).

5

To John Francis Valton

10

Bristol
September 13, 1785

My Dear Brother,

  It is plain the time for your preaching is not yet come. You must
delay a little or disable yourself altogether. If we live till spring, and
I take you with [me] five or six hundred miles, that I believe will set
you up.

  I have appointed to go to Almondsbury[348] a week or two hence,
and then it is probable, she will ask my advice.[349] I apprehend, she
will find it difficult to re⟨conc⟩ile[350] the leaving the little society, to
her feelings or to her conscience. And herein one is hardly capable
of judging for another. The determination must ultimately rest in
her own bosom. It should be a matter of much prayer. I am,

  Your affectionate friend and brother,

J. Wesley

Address: 'To / Mr. John Valton / At Bridlington Key / Yorkshire'.[351]
Postmarks: '14/SE' and '15/SE'.
Endorsement: by Valton, 'Sept. 13 1785'.
Source: holograph; Melbourne, Queen's College, JW17.

---

[348] Orig., 'Amesbury'.

[349] Valton had convalesced at the home in Almondsbury of the widow Judith (Davis) Purnell in Dec. 1779. He had informed JW that she was one with whom he was considering marriage. Cf. JW to Valton, Oct. 8, 1785.

[350] A small portion is torn away by the wax seal.

[351] The address has been struck through and changed to 'The Methodist Chapel / York'.

To the Rev. Charles Wesley[352]

near Bristol
September 13, 1785

[[Dear Brother,]]   5

I see no use of you and me disputing together, for neither of us is likely to convince the other. You say I separate from the Church; I say I do not. Then let it stand.

Your verse is a sad truth.[353] I see fifty miles more of England than you do, and I find few exceptions to it.[354]   10

I believe Dr. [Thomas] Coke is as free from ambition as from covetousness. He has *done* nothing *rashly* that I know. But he has *spoken rashly*, which he retracted the moment I spoke to him of it.[355] To publish as his *present thoughts* what he had before retracted was not fair play.[356] He is now such a right hand to me as Thomas Walsh   15 was. If you will not or cannot help me yourself, do not hinder those that can and will.

I must and will save as many souls as I can while I live without being careful about what may *possibly be* when I die.

[[Adieu]]   20

I pray do not confound the intellects of the people in London. You may thereby a little weaken my hands, but you will greatly weaken your own.

                                                                                     25

Address: 'To / The Revd Mr C. Wesley / City Road / London'.[357]
Postmarks: 'Bristol', '16/SE', and 'Penny Post Paid'. *Charge*: '5'.
Endorsement: by CW, 'Sept. 13. 1785 / B[rother]'.
Source: holograph; MARC, DDWes 3/60.

---

[352] JW was replying to CW's letter of Sept. 8, 1785.

[353] The line about 'heathenish priests and mitred infidels' cited in JW to CW, Aug. 19, 1785.

[354] Sic; but JW likely meant 'fifty times'.

[355] In Thomas Coke, *The Substance of a Sermon, preached at Baltimore, in the state of Maryland, before the General Conference of the Methodist Episcopal Church, on the 27th of December, 1784, at the ordination of the Rev. Francis Asbury, to the Office of a Superintendent* (London: W. Paramore, 1785); to which CW drew attention in his letter.

[356] Referring to: A Methodist of the Church of England, *Strictures on 'The Substance of a Sermon preached at Baltimore in the state of Maryland, Before the general conference of the Methodist Episcopal Church, On the 27th of December 1784: At the Ordination of the Rev. Francis Asbury, to the Office of Superintendent'. By Thomas Coke, L.L.D. Superintendent of the said Church* (London: G. Herdsfield, [1785]). Some attribute this work to CW, and JW may be suggesting the same.

[357] The address is crossed out and replaced with 'Great Chesterfield Street / Marybone'.

To Jasper Winscom

Bristol
September 13, 1785

5   Dear Jasper,
     I think I can serve you as far as an hundred pounds will go.[358] If
you can pay me in a year, you may; if not, I shall not quarrel with
you about it. I want no interest. You may draw upon John Atlay for
it, to whom I shall write this morning.
10   I am, dear Jasper,
         Your affectionate brother,

J. Wesley

15   *Address*: 'To / Mr Jasper Winscom / in / Winton'.
     Source: holograph; Pitts Library (Emory), John Wesley Papers (MSS
     153), 3/41.

20

To Mary Bosanquet Fletcher

Bristol
September 16, 1785

25   My Dear Sister,
     I wanted much to hear from you, being desirous to know whether
you have thought where you should settle, if God should please to
prolong your life.[359] I should love to be as near you as I could; and
on that account should be glad if you chose Bristol or London. I
30   expect to be in town on Monday fortnight, October the 1st.
     Mr. [James] Ireland has printed a thousand or two of your *Letter*,
with some little variations, I think for the worse![360]
     Peace be with your spirit! I am, my dear sister,
         Ever yours,

35   J. Wesley

[358] Winscom was trying to build a preaching-house in Winchester; see JW to Winscom,
May 9, 1785. JW would preach at the opening of this new location on Nov. 24, 1785; see *Journal*, 23:381 in this edn.

[359] The letter from Fletcher, mentioning her questions over whether to remain in Madeley after the death of her husband, is not known to survive. But see her subsequent diary
entries, leading to her resolve to stay, in Moore, *Mary Fletcher*, 179–85.

[360] Mary Fletcher, *A Letter to the Rev. Mr. Wesley on the Death of the Rev. Mr. Fletcher,
Vicar of Madeley in Shropshire* (Madeley: J. Edmunds, 1785).

I am glad the people desire to join us. I shall reprint your letter
when I come to London.[361]

Address: 'To / Mrs. Fletcher / At Madeley, near Shifnal / Salop'.
Postmark: 'Bristol'. *Charge*: '5'.
Endorsement: 'Sepr. 15th 1785'.
Source: holograph; MARC, DDWes 5/63.

To Alexander Suter

Bristol
September 16, 1785

My Dear Brother,

I doubt, we can do sister [Agnes] Ramsay little good, till she is of
another spirit.[362]

If any one had said a word about it at the Conference, your plea
would have been allowed. But possibly it is not too late now, for we
are not yet run aground.

To *you* I may speak in confidence.[363] He is a good man, and a
remarkably sensible man. But he is in no wise fit for an Assistant.
I have made trial of him in time past. Read over the duty of an Assistant in the *Minutes*; and then do your best.[364]

I wrote before that the thirty pounds legacy is good for nothing.
Give the executor or heir good words, and take whatever he will
give you. I shall soon be returning to London.

If the work of God prospers, you will want nothing. Whoever will
return in a loving spirit, let them return. I am,

Your affectionate friend and brother,

J. Wesley

[361] Instead, JW included several extracts from the letter in his sermon *On the Death of John Fletcher* (1785), 3:609–29 in this edn.

[362] See JW to Suter, July 16, 1785.

[363] Suter was assigned by the 1785 Conference as the Assistant for the Whitehaven circuit, with Joseph Thompson serving under him. While his letter to JW is not known to survive, he had clearly asked for these roles to be reversed, pleading his inexperience. In keeping with JW's comments, Thompson was given the Assistant role on the Hull circuit in 1782, but never again.

[364] See *Minutes* (1749), Qq. 7–10, 10:233–34 in this edn.; and 'Large' *Minutes* (1753ff.), §63, 10:865–66.

Address: 'To / Mr Suter / At the Preachinghouse / In White⟨haven⟩'.[365]
Postmark: '⟨1⟩7/SE'.
Endorsement: by Suter, 'Nr. 6'.
Source: holograph; Bridwell Library (SMU).[366]

To Thomas Wride[367]

Kingswood
September 16, 1785

Dear Tommy,

Your next will, I suppose, find me in London, where I hope to be in about a fortnight. We know not what stops our northern schoolmaster, and expect to see him every day.[368] As soon as he comes, Mr. Jones will make the best of his way to Norwich.[369] I leave it wholly to *you* whether and how far you should accept of Dr. [John] Hunt's offer.[370] With regard to Mr. Proud and your capital singer, you acted exactly right; but I expect you will hear of it at both ears.[371]

Those doggerel verses must not remain in the chapel.[372] I wish Lake Houlton would spend two or three weeks with you.[373] He is not eloquent, but he is useful.

---

[365] A portion of the address side is torn away.

[366] Held previously in WMC Museum, 2002.001.022.

[367] Replying to Wride's letter of Sept. 7–10, 1785.

[368] I.e., Thomas McGeary, who arrived later this year. See JW to Rachel (Norton) Bayley, Aug. 30, 1783.

[369] Thomas Jones (fl. 1785–90) had been admitted 'on trial' at the 1785 Conference, and assigned to serve with Wride in Norwich (see 10:568–69 in this edn.). Jones apparently was not able to take that assignment, as he was admitted 'on trial' again in 1786 (10:596). He may have spent the intervening time at Kingswood school. Jones last appeared with an appointment in the 1792 *Minutes*.

[370] Hunt had offered to supply preaching in some of the outlying parts of the circuit since Wride was lacking a helper. Wride feared Hunt would proselytize the people.

[371] Joseph Proud (1745–1826), son of Rev. John Proud, General Baptist pastor in Wisbech, Cambridgeshire, had been pastor of a General Baptist church in Fleet, Lincolnshire. His introduction of singing into the worship service there led to tension, and he was currently in Norwich. He asked Wride for permission to preach in the Methodist chapel and Wride refused.

The songleader (likely James Hey) had adopted a practice of singing more songs, and different songs, from those considered typical among Methodists, and Wride had tried to halt this practice.

[372] The verses Susanna (Cooke) Turner had carved on a monument placed in the Methodist chapel honouring her recently departed husband, Robert Turner (1735–84).

[373] Lake Houlton (c. 1739–1816) was a prominent member of City Road society in London (now buried there), who served as a lay exhorter. See Stevenson, *City Road*, 329.

You do well in insisting on every person showing his ticket. I wonder Jonathan Coussins did not.[374] It is of importance to mind the select society. That, I apprehend, he never neglected. If the leaders and the bands are closely attended to, they will do well; otherwise not.

I am, with love to sister [Jane] Wride, dear Tommy,
Your affectionate friend and brother,

J. Wesley

Endorsement: by Wride, 'No. 27 / Sepr. 16th 1785'.
Source: holograph; MARC, MAM JW 6/29.

To Richard Locke

Bristol
September 19, 1785
My Dear Brother,
The matter of Shepton Mallet is at an end.[375] But I should have been glad to see you on other accounts. I wanted to know what was become of you? Now you in some measure inform me. Pity but you had informed me before. Then much evil might have been either prevented or remedied. Instead of hiding everything, you ought to have hid nothing from me. But tell me all or nothing. I will never bring *your name* into question, if you tell me who those four blessed preachers are.[376] It is good for them that I should know them.

Any service that is in my power you may expect from
Your affectionate brother,

J. Wesley

Address: 'To / Mr Lock'.[377]
Endorsement: by Locke, 'From Mr. Wesley / 19 Sep. 1785'.
Source: holograph; MARC, MAM JW 3/96.

---

[374] Coussins had been the Assistant at Norwich the previous year.

[375] Locke's letter to JW is not known to survive, leaving the matter at Shepton Mallet unclear.

[376] These preachers were surely a topic of conversation when JW visited Locke in Burnham on Sept. 28; see JW, Diary, 23:537 in this edn.

[377] Apparently hand-delivered.

To Richard Rodda

Bristol
September 23, 1785

My Dear Brother,

I hope the poor people in Thirsk circuit will now take courage. They made heavy complaints for want of preachers.

It is no wonder the flock at Madeley require some pains before they are brought into order. Mr. [John] Fletcher had no conception of discipline. But by and by they will request all our labour.

I think Dr. [Thomas] Coke will do well to call at Madeley. In what manner could the circuit be divided?

I don't know what to say to sister Barry.[378] I am not made of money, and have many dependent upon me. I do not like the girls staying at home, in hopes of getting an husband. However you may let her have two or three guineas. I am

Your affectionate friend and brother,

J. Wesley

Address: 'To / Mr Rodda / At the Octogon in / Chester / +post [i.e., crosspost]'.
Postmark: 'Bristol'.
Source: holograph; MARC, MAM JW 4/58.

To Mary Cooke[379]

Bristol
September 24, 1785

My Dear Sister,

It is highly probable my letter to you was intercepted by some person of the same name, who having opened it (likely by a mistake) was afterwards ashamed to send it you. However, as you have now favoured me better information, I hope there will be no such mistake for the time to come. But I beg, when you write to me hereafter, do not write as to a stranger but a friend. Be not afraid me because

---

[378] The widow of James Barry was named Sarah (maiden name unknown). She had received £24 from Conference in 1784, and was allotted £20 in 1785.

[379] JW was replying to Cooke's letter of Sept. 23, which informed him she had not received his reply to her earlier letter of Sept. 15, 1785. He repeats in this letter what had been in that which was lost.

I have lived so much longer than you. I assume nothing upon that account, but wish to stand upon even ground with you and to converse without either disguise or reserve.

I love you all three, and not a little, especially since your sisters spoke so freely to me.[380] Yet I do not say in the same degree. There   5
is a mildness and sweetness in your spirit, such as I wish to find in one that is more to me than a common friend. Not that I impute this to nature. Whatever is truly amiable is not of nature, but from a higher principle. Cultivate this, my dear friend, to the uttermost. Still learn of him who was meek and lowly in heart.[381] O what a   10
blessing it is to be little, and mean, and vile in our own eyes!

You are an amiable woman, it is true. But still you are a sinner, born to die! You are an immortal spirit come forth from God and speedily returning to him. You know well that one thing, and one only, is needful[382] for you upon earth, to ensure a better portion, to recover   15
the favour and image of God.[383] The former by his grace you have recovered; you have tasted of the love of God. See that you cast it not away. See that you hold fast the beginning of your confidence steadfast unto the end![384] And how soon may you be made a partaker of sanctification! And not only by a slow and insensible growth in grace,   20
but by the power of the Highest overshadowing you in a moment, in the twinkling of an eye, so as utterly to abolish sin and to renew you in his whole image![385] If you are simple of heart, if you are willing to receive the heavenly gift, as a little child, without reasoning, why may you not receive it now? He is nigh that sanctifieth![386] He is with you.   25
He is knocking at the door of your heart![387]

> Come in, my Lord, come in,
> And seize her for thine own.[388]

---

[380] Two of Mary's sisters, Frances Cooke (1767–1823) and Anne Cooke (1771–1820), were also active in the Methodist society in Trowbridge. Both married London Methodists and are buried at City Road chapel. Frances married James Pond (d. 1854) in 1790; and Anne married Joseph Butterworth (1770–1826) in 1791.

[381] See Matt. 11:29.

[382] See Col. 3:10.

[383] See JW's early sermon on Luke 10:42, 'The One Thing Needful', 4:352–59 in this edn.

[384] See Heb. 3:14.

[385] See Col. 3:10

[386] See Heb. 2:11.

[387] See Rev. 3:20.

[388] JW combines and adapts here individual lines from two CW hymns. Cf. CW, 'Waiting for Christ the Prophet', st. 5, *l.* 8, *HSP* (1742), 208; and CW, 'A Prayer Against the Power of Sin', st. 1, l. 4, *HSP* (1740), 79.

This is the wish of, my dear friend,
Yours in tender affection,

J. W.

5 I pray be not so brief in your next.

Address: 'To / Miss Cook / In Duke Street, Trowbridge / Wilts'.
Endorsement: by Cooke, 'Not much 2[n]d'.
Source: holograph; MARC, WCB, D6/1/328.

10

To Simon Day

Bristol
15   September 24, 1785

My Dear Brother,

I expect to see James Toomer next week, and I am in hopes he will
be induced to keep his promise.[389] But if he loves his money more
than his conscience, we shall find another way.

20   I am

Your affectionate brother,

J. Wesley

Address: 'To / Mr Simon Day / At Mr Blunt's, near / Frome'.[390]
25 *Postmark*: 'Bristol'.
Source: holograph; WTS (DC), Archives, Oxham Collection.

30
To Robert Carr Brackenbury

Bristol
September 26, 1785

Dear Sir,
35   It is well that the Lord sitteth above the water-floods and re-
maineth a king for ever.[391] It is no wonder that Satan should fight
for his own kingdom when such inroads are made upon it. But

---

[389] James Toomer (1736–1806), a druggist, lived in Brent Knoll, Somerset, between
Burnham (which JW visited on Sept. 28) and Midsomer Norton (where he was on Sept. 30).
[390] Robert Blunt (1745–1821) was a clothier in Frome, and supporter of the Methodists.
[391] See Ps. 29:9 (BCP).

Beyond his chain he cannot go;
Our Jesus shall stir up his power
And soon avenge us of our foe.[392]

After we have observed a day of fasting and prayer, I have   5
known the most violent commotions quelled at once. But doubtless all probable means are to be used. One in particular it might
be worth while to attempt, namely, to soften the spirit of that angry magistrate. God has the hearts of all men in his hand; and if
the heart of this warrior was once turned, then those that have   10
hitherto been encouraged by him would vanish away like smoke. It
is not improbable your answer to that scurrilous libel may be one
means of abating his prejudice. If it is not published yet, it would
be easy to find friends in London who are perfect masters of the
French language.[393]   15
The varnish used by the cabinet-makers seldom fails to cure the
piles in a day or two.[394] I mean the blind piles, so called; but the
bleeding ones are not so easily removed.
I almost wonder that you have not yet a fair opening into the Isle
of Guernsey. An invitation from a pious man, who is able and will-   20
ing to entertain you, I judge to be a providential call.
In the Isle of Man the work of God continues to flourish in an
extraordinary manner. I do not know that there are above thirteen
or fourteen [hundred] adults in the whole island. And there [are] already upwards of two and twenty hundred members in our societies.   25
I commend you to him who is able to preserve you both in soul
and body,[395] and am, dear sir,
Your affectionate friend and brother,

J. Wesley
30
Address: 'To / Robert Brackenbury Esq. / In St Helliers / Isle of Jersey'.
Postmark: 'Bristol'. *Charge*: '5'.
Source: holograph; Wesley's Chapel (London), LDWMM 1994/1983.

---

[392] CW, Hymn on Isaiah 18:16, Pt. IV, st. 3, *HSP* (1742), 275.
[393] The title of the angry pamphlet published against the Methodists has not been determined; see JW to Brackenbury, Jan. 16, 1786.
[394] I.e., haemorrhoids.
[395] See 1 Thess. 5:23.

To Richard Rodda

Bristol
September 29, 1785

5   My Dear Brother,
    Today we have sent that bad boy, Isaac Barry, to his mother.[396]
But she has no food to spare. Therefore give her six guineas, in the
manner you see best.
    Dear Richard,
10   Adieu!

Address: 'To / Mr Rodda / At the Octogon in / Chester / +post [i.e.,
    crosspost]'.
Source: holograph; MARC, MAM JW 4/59.

15

To the Rev. Francis Asbury

Bristol
20   September 30, 1785
My Dear Brother,
    It gives me pleasure to hear that God prospers your labours
even in the barren soil of South Carolina.[397] Near fifty years ago I
25 preached in the church at Charlestown and in a few other places,
and deep attention sat on every face. But I am afraid few received
any lasting impressions.
    At the next Conference it will be worth your while to consider
deeply whether any preacher should stay in one place three years to-
30 gether. I startle at this. It is a vehement alteration in the Methodist
discipline. We have no such custom in England, Scotland, or Ireland.
    We s⟨…⟩ the Assistant who ⟨…⟩ second) to stay more than ⟨….⟩[398]
I myself may perhaps have as much variety of matter as many of
our preachers. Yet, I am well assured, were I to preach three years
35 together in one place, both the people and myself would grow as
dead as stones. Indeed, this is quite contrary to the whole economy

---

[396] Isaac Barry (1775–92), the son of the (now deceased) itinerant James Barry and his
wife Sarah, had been admitted to Kingswood School in 1783 (see 10:539 in this edn.). His
return home deepened his mother's financial stress; see JW to Rodda, Sept. 23, 1785.

[397] Asbury's letter to JW with this report is not known to survive.

[398] A portion of the lower right corner of the page is missing, affecting 3–4 words each in
three lines. It was missing already when a transcription was published in John Emory, *A Defence
of 'Our Fathers'* (New York: Mason & Lane, 1838), 121–22.

of Methodism—God has always wrought among us by a constant change of preachers.

Newly awakened people should, if it were possible, be plentifully supplied with books. Hereby the awakening is both continued and increased. In two or three days I expect to be in London. I will then 5 talk with Mr. [John] Atlay on this head.

Be all in earnest for God.

I am

Your affectionate friend and brother,

J. Wesley 10

Source: holograph; privately held (WWEP Archive holds photocopy).

15

To Elizabeth Ritchie

[Bristol]
c. September 30, 1785

20
It was remarkable that God should remove in so short a space, two such burning and shining lights as Mr. [Vincent] Perronet and Mr. [John] Fletcher.[399] But, as a good man observes, when we say, 'this is the will of God,' all is concluded.[400] We can then only lay our mouths in the dust, and say, 'We cannot choose. Thou canst not err.'[401] 25

Source: published transcription; Bulmer, *Mortimer*, 315 [quoted by Ritchie in a letter to Miss Salmon, Oct. 5, 1785].

30

To Mary (Bosanquet) Fletcher

Bristol
October 2, 1785 35
My Dear Sister,

There is much of divine providence in this, that the people are permitted to choose their own curate! I believe Mr. Horne to be a sound Methodist, and think he will serve them well if he can pro-

---

[399] See John 5:25. Perronet died on May 9, 1785; Fletcher on Aug. 14.
[400] Monsieur de Renty; see JW to Ann Bolton, Dec. 2, 1781, 29:704 in this edn.
[401] Cf. CW, 'Waiting for Christ', st. 4, *l.* 4, *HSP* (1740), 40.

cure ordination.[402] If he cannot, Mr. [Peard] Dickinson may do near as well, a very pious and sensible young man, who has for two or three years served good Mr. [Vincent] Perronet at Shoreham, but expects to be turned away by the new vicar.

5   Surely your thought of spending much of your time in London is agreeable to the will of God.[403] I never throughly approved of your going so far from it, although much good was drawn out of it. I hope to be there tomorrow. Should not you now consider me as your *first* human friend? I think none has a more sincere regard for 10 you than, my dear sister,

Yours most affectionately,

J. Wesley

Address: 'To / Mrs Fletcher / At Madeley near Shifnal / Salop / +post 15   [i.e., crosspost]'.
Postmark: 'Bristol'.
Endorsement: by Fletcher, 'Octr 2d 1785'.
Source: holograph; Huntington Library, Manuscripts, HM 57052.

20

To Thomas Hanson

London
25   October 8, 1785

Dear Tommy,

Your name was not inserted in the *Minutes* of the Conference because our brethren judged you was not able to supply a circuit, by reason of bodily disorder. Nevertheless your name might have been 30 set down as that of John Brettel is, though he cannot labour at present.[404] I suppose you can and do preach a little. And you are learning a great lesson, namely to say, 'Not as I will, but as thou wilt.'[405] I am,

---

[402] Melville Horne (c. 1761–1841) was the son of an Antiguan barrister and planter, and the nephew of Nathaniel Gilbert. Now in England, he would be accepted 'on trial' as an itinerant preacher in 1784. In 1786, with JW's recommendation, he was ordained in the Church of England and appointed a curate at Madeley. Horne would go on to serve as vicar of Olney from 1796 to 1799, then to succeed David Simpson at Christ Church, Macclesfield. He remained supportive of Methodism until about 1809. See *DEB*, 572–73.

[403] Within days Mary would learn from Roger Kynaston, who owned the rectory in Madeley, that she could stay and rent it for as long as she lived; which she did. See Moore, *Mary Fletcher*, 181.

[404] Brettel was listed as 'supernumerary' on the Birmingham circuit.

[405] Matt. 26:39.

Dear Tommy,
    Your affectionate brother,

J. Wesley

Tell Dr. [Thomas] Coke (who will be with you soon) if you have not received your little stipend.[406]

Address: 'To / Mr Tho. Hanson / At Horbury, near Wakefield / Yorkshire'.
Postmark: '8/OC'. *Charge*: '6'.
Source: holograph; Wesley's Chapel (London), LDWMM 1994/1952.

To Ann Loxdale

London
October 8, 1785

My Dear Miss Loxdale,

    Not once but many times I have been making all the inquiries I could concerning you. The rather as I was afraid you might suffer loss by the severe trials you had met with.[407] I should not have wondered if you had contracted a degree of suspicion towards all who professed either friendship or religion. I rather wonder how you have escaped. But, indeed, as long as you can say from your heart, 'Lord, not as I will, but as thou wilt',[408] no weapon formed against you shall prosper.

    You unquestionably did enjoy a measure of his pure and perfect love. And as you received it at first by naked faith, just so you may receive it again.[409] And who knows how soon? May you not say,

> If thou canst so greatly bow,
> Friend of sinners, why not *now*?[410]

[406] Hanson would be officially set aside by the 1786 Conference, and given a stipend that year of £12. See 10:597, 613 in this edn.
[407] The end of a troubled courtship; see JW to Mary (Bosanquet) Fletcher, Mar. 28, 1785.
[408] Cf. Matt. 26:39.
[409] See note on JW to Francis Wolf, Oct. 25, 1776, 29:295 in this edn.
[410] CW, Hymn on Ps. 101:2, st. 1, *Scripture Hymns* (1762), 1:270.

You send me comfortable news concerning Mrs. Eden.[411] And
certainly this gracious visitation is designed for a blessing not only
to her, but likewise to her poor husband. You should lose no opportunity of speaking a word to him whenever providence throws him
5   in your way. Let not a voluntary humility hinder you. God can bless
a few and ordinary words. Nay, and let it not hinder you from praying with, as well as for, your friends. I advise you, my dear Nancy, to
begin without delay. Why not this very day? Make haste, my friend,
to do whatever may be for the good of your own or any other soul.
10   I thank you for writing freely to me. If I had you now by the hand,
I would tell you, you can never write or speak too freely to, my dear
Miss Loxdale,

    Yours most affectionately,

                           J. Wesley

15

Source: holograph; Wesley's Chapel (London), LDWMM 1994/1958.

20   ## To John Francis Valton

                            London
                   October 8, 1785

My Dear Brother,

25   I cannot advise you to marry anyone upon *those conditions*.[412] But
surely either Yorkshire or Oxfordshire might supply a person that
would receive you upon your own conditions, and that would be a
blessing to you and to many.[413] If you continue instant in prayer, I
nothing doubt but such a person might be found.[414] But take care in
the meantime, that you do not take upon yourself more work than
30   you are able to do.

I am much inclined to think Henry Foster might yet live, if he
would ride daily and take no sustenance at all but bread and buttermilk (a spoonful at a time at first) churned every day.

[411] Ann's older sister Mary Loxdale (1754–85) married Thomas Eden Jr. in 1778. Thomas
was now ordained and serving as a curate in Bedstone, Shropshire. Mary would die Nov. 26,
1785, leaving Thomas with their only child, William Henry Loxdale Eden (1782–1868), who
became a Wesleyan Methodist minister.

[412] Judith (Davis) Purnell had declined travelling with Valton, insisting he locate, in order
to marry her. Acceding to JW, Valton did not take that option immediately. The following year
he did desist from travelling, and married Purnell on Dec. 20, 1786.

[413] Some of the women in these shires that JW might have in mind would be Anne Bolton,
Elizabeth Ritchie, and Ann Tindall.

[414] See Rom. 12:12.

I am,
>Your affectionate friend and brother,

>>>J. Wesley

Address: 'To / Mr John Valton / In Bradforth / Yorkshire'.
Postmark: '10/OC'.
Endorsement: by Valton, 'Octr 8 1785'.
Source: holograph; MARC, MAM JW 5/35.

To Thomas Wride[415]

>>London
>>October 8, 1785

Dear Tommy,

On Monday sennight, the 17th instant, I hope to be at Norwich (coming by the mail-coach), on Tuesday at Yarmouth, on Wednesday and Thursday at Lowestoft, preaching everywhere at half-hour past 6:00 in the evening. On Friday noon at Beecham (or where you please), in the evening at Loddon, and on Saturday evening at Norwich.

The verses must be effaced some way before I come down.[416] Be as exact in discipline as you please. Lake Houlton was on the road, but one met him and told him he was not wanted. I always lodge in our own houses. I think those sermons may stop bottles.[417]

I am, with love to sister [Jane] Wride, dear Tommy,
>Your affectionate friend and brother,

>>>J. Wesley

Address: 'To / Mr Wride / At the Preachinghouse / in / Norwich'.
Postmark: '8/OC'. *Charge*: '5'.
Endorsements: by Wride, 'No. 28' and 'Octr. 8th, 1785'.
Source: holograph; MARC, MAM JW 6/30.

---

[415] Replying to Wride's letter of Oct. 3, 1785.

[416] On the memorial to Robert Turner; see JW to Wride, Sept. 16, 1785.

[417] Wride had received some copies of Thomas Coke, *The Substance of a Sermon,… at the ordination of the Rev. Francis Asbury, to the Office of a Superintendent* (London: W. Paramore, 1785). He was hesitant to circulate because it seemed to endorse separation from the Church of England. JW's response was likely meant in the sense 'use them as corks', rather than circulate them. Cf. JW to CW, Sept. 13, 1785.

To Charles Atmore

London
October 15, 1785

5 Dear Charles,

If God gives you and your fellow labourers union of spirit, he will surely bless you together.[418]

When you build at Blackburn, do not build a scarecrow of an house.[419] But take either Keighley or Colne House for your pattern.
10 Observe in this and in all things the large *Minutes* of the Conference. If I live till spring, I shall probably spend more time there than I have done hitherto. As long as you feel your own weakness and helplessness, you will find help from above.

I am, dear Charles,
15   Your affectionate friend and brother,

J. Wesley

Address: 'To / Mr Atmore / At the Preachinghouse / In Coln / Lancashire'.
Postmarks: '17/OC', 'Yarm', and 'Wetherby'.
20 *Source*: holograph; Huntington Library, Manuscripts, HM 57053.

To Mary (Bosanquet) Fletcher[420]

25   Norwich
October 22, 1785

My Dear Sister,

This morning I received and read over your papers. You have done justice to the character of that excellent man, as far as you
30 could be expected to do in so small room. I do not observe any sentence that need be left out, and very few words that need to be omitted or altered. Only I omit a very little, which I had inserted before I received yours in that part of my sermon which I had transcribed. I hope to procure some more materials in order to the writing of
35 his *Life*.

---

[418] Atmore was the Assistant for the Colne circuit.

[419] Cf. JW to John Francis Valton, Mar. 24, 1782.

[420] JW put the finishing touches on his sermon *On the Death of John Fletcher* (3:609–29 in this edn.) on Oct. 23–24; see his diary, 23:540 in this edn. He delivered the sermon in London on Nov. 6. As he worked on this he decided to write several persons requesting further accounts of John Fletcher, which he incorporated into *A Short Account of the Life and Death of the Rev. John Fletcher* (London: Paramore, 1786).

May the Lord bless you, and keep you! I am, my dear sister,
  Yours in tender affection,

                                                  J. Wesley

Address: 'To / Mrs Fletcher / At Madeley, near Shiffnal / Salop'.   5
Postmarks: 'Norwich' and '24/OC'.
Endorsement: by Fletcher, 'Octr 22d 1785'.
Source: holograph; MARC, DDWes 5/64.

                                                                           10

To Joseph Benson

                                                  London   15
                                          October 30, 1785
Dear Joseph,
  You have given me a clear and satisfactory account of Mr. Fletcher's behaviour at Trevecca, and of the reason of his leaving it—the
same in effect, but far more full than that which he gave me him-   20
self.[421] I hope to glean up many more circumstances of his life from
a few of his surviving friends, particularly Mr. [James] Ireland, if
he is as willing as he is able to inform me.[422] Your caution as to
the manner of writing is very proper.[423] For no one should write or
speak of him in any other spirit than he wrote and spoke.   25
  I am, dear Joseph,
    Your affectionate friend and brother,

                                                  J. Wesley

Address: 'To / Mr Benson / At the Preachinghouse / in / Sheffield'.   30
Postmark: '31/OC'.
Source: holograph; Bridwell Library (SMU).

---

[421] See Benson to JW, Oct. 15, 1785.
[422] See the letters which JW received (all c. Nov. 1785) from Sarah Crosby, Mary (Thornton) Greenwood, Jane Thornton, Mr. Vaughan, and Samuel Webb.
[423] See Benson to JW, c. Oct. 25, 1785.

To Mary Cooke[424]

London
October 30, 1785

5

My Dear Miss Cook[e] leans to the right-hand error. It is safer to
think too little than too much of yourself. I blame no one for not believing he is in the favour of God till he is in a manner constrained
10   to believe it. But, laying all circumstances together, I can make no
doubt of your having a measure of faith.

Many years ago when one was describing the glorious privilege
of a believer, I cried out, 'If this be so, I have no faith.' He replied,
'*Habes fidere, sed exiguam*: "You have faith, but it is weak."'[425] The
15   very same thing I say to you, my dear friend. You have faith, but it
is only as a grain of mustard seed.[426] Hold fast what you have, and
ask for what you want. There is an inconceivable variety in the operations of the Holy Spirit on the souls of men, more especially as
to the manner of justification.[427] Many find him rushing upon them
20   like a torrent, while they experience

The o'erwhelming power of saving grace.[428]

This has been the experience of many—perhaps of more in this
25   late visitation than in any other age since the times of the apostles.
But in others he works in a very different way:

He deigns his influence to infuse,
Sweet, refreshing, as the silent dews.[429]

30

It has pleased him to work the latter way in you from the beginning.
And it is not improbable he will continue (as he has begun) to work
in a gentle and almost insensible manner. Let him take his own way.
He is wiser than *you*. He will do all things well.[430] Do not reason
35   against him; but let the prayer of your heart be,

[424] JW was replying to her letter of Oct. 25, 1785.
[425] August Gottlieb Spangenberg; see JW to J. Benson, Oct. 11, 1771, 28:425 in this edn.
[426] See Matt. 17:20.
[427] Telford misread as 'irreconcilable variability in …' (*Letters*, 7:298).
[428] CW, Hymn on Luke 14:7, st. 10, *HSP* (1749), 1:260.
[429] Samuel Wesley Jr., *A Paraphrase of the Song of the Three Children*, st. 16, (London: E.
Say, 1728); included by JW in MSP (1744), 2:116.
[430] See Mark 7:37.

Mould as thou wilt the passive clay![431]

I commit you and your dear sisters [Anne and Frances] to his
tender care; and am, my dear friend,
     Most affectionately yours,   5
                                                                                               J.W.

Address: 'To / Miss Cook / At Mrs Cook's[432] / Trowbridge / Wilts'.
Charge: '5'.
Endorsement: by Cooke, 'very good 3[r]d'.
Source: holograph; MARC, WCB, D6/1/330.   10

To William Roberts[433]   15

London
November 8, 1785

Dear Billy,
     Yesterday I read your tract, which I thoroughly approve of. But I   20
dare not depend on my own single judgment. I will desire someone
that has more judgment to read and consider it, and then send you
word what I think is best to be done. But I apprehend that debt will
never be paid, because the numerous villains who gain by its continuance will never consent to the abolishing of it.[434]   25
     I should apprehend your best way would be to sell the estate
which you purchased some years ago. What if you sold it for only
half the value? It seems this would be better than to remain in such
perplexities.
     I am, dear Billy,   30
          Your affectionate brother,
                                                                                            J. Wesley

Source: holograph; Oxford, Lincoln College, Archive, MS/WES/A/2/6.

---

[431] CW, 'An Act of Devotion', st. 4, *HSP* (1749), 1:207.
[432] Mary's mother, Mary (Pitney) Cooke (1742–1809).
[433] While there is no address portion, the letter is among a set of letters to William Roberts.
[434] Likely the debt of £1800, owed by Benjamin Dickinson to Roberts, which was re-
deemed in Mar. 1787; see Devon Archives and Local Studies Service, 213 M/T/171.

To Thomas Wride[435]

London
November 8, 1785

Dear Tommy,

I suppose James Byron is now in the circuit, as he set out from Thirsk on the 3rd instant.[436] He is [an] amiable young man, at present full of faith and love. If possible guard him from those that will be inclined to love him too well. Then he will be as useful a fellow labourer as you can desire. And set him a pattern in all things.

I am, dear Tommy,
Your affectionate friend and brother,

J. Wesley

Source: published transcription; *Christian Miscellany* 3 (1848): 86.

To Zachariah Yewdall

London
November 11, 1785

My Dear Brother,

I hope sister Yewdall and you will be a blessing to each other.[437] I think it a pity to remove you from Kent. Otherwise Oxford circuit is nearer to London than Canterbury circuit; for High Wycombe is nearer to it than Chatham. I cannot visit all the places I want to visit in Kent in one journey. I purpose (God willing) to begin my first journey on the 28th instant. Shall I visit Margate or Sheerness first?

I am, dear Zachary,
Your affectionate brother,

[J. Wesley]

Source: published transcription; Jackson, *Works* (3rd), 13:15–16.

[435] Replying to Wride's letter of Nov. 5, 1785.

[436] James M'Kee Byron (1760–1827), an Irishman, was just beginning to consider the itinerant ministry when JW sent him to Norwich. He would be admitted 'on trial' at the 1786 Conference (see 10:596 in this edn.), and serve faithfully until retiring in 1823. See *WMM* 52 (1829): 577–91.

[437] On Sept. 9, 1785, Yewdall married the widow Agnes (Hunt) Mackarall (c. 1740–1819) in London. Since she already had children, Yewdall apparently requested to be moved nearer to London.

To Thomas Tattershall

London
November 13, 1785

Dear Tommy,

I heard all the complaints in Norfolk, face to face, and trust that they will go on well.[438]

The affair of Derby [preaching-]house should be mentioned at the Conference; that is the proper time.

You must immediately drop any preacher that gives any countenance to Nathanael Ward.[439]

While I live I will bear the most public testimony I can to the reality of witchcraft.[440] Your denial of this springs originally from the deists, and simple Christians lick their spittle. I heartily set them at open defiance. I know of no extracts from novels, but I publish several excellent extracts from the *Spectator*.[441] And I am certainly a better judge of what is fit to be published than those little critics. But let them pass over what they do not like.

There never was so useful a plan devised as that of the Methodists.

But what is this? James Deaves[442] says that you received £10 and a guinea towards building an house at Waterford and carried it away.

I am, dear Tommy,

Your affectionate friend and brother,

J. Wesley

Source: published transcription; John Lowther Murphy, *An Essay Towards a Science of Consciousness* (London: Simpkin, Marshall and Co., 1838), 167–68.[443]

---

[438] The complaints were mainly in Norwich, which JW visited Oct. 15–23, 1785. See the letters of Thomas Wride to JW at this time for background.

[439] See JW to Tattershall, Aug. 22, 1785.

[440] This paragraph replies to criticisms of *AM* that Tattershall made (or passed on) to JW. The first decried extracts JW republished from various sources describing instances of witchcraft in *AM* 6 (1783), monthly installment from Feb. through Dec.; and starting with the Jan. issue of *AM* 8 (1785).

[441] The first of JW's extracts from Joseph Addison & Richard Steele, *The Spectator* (London: Sharpe & Hailes, 1711–14), appeared in *AM* 7 (1784), 663–67.

[442] Orig., 'Drew'; surely a misreading. Deaves lived in Waterford, where Tattershall had been stationed the previous year.

[443] Murphy says the holograph was shown at a Pottery Mechanics' Institution exhibition; its current location is unknown.

To John Bredin

London
5   November 16, 1785
My Dear Brother,
I hope James Rogers will exert himself in behalf of sisters [Mary] Penington and [Margaret] Teare, who should send me a particular account of the fire.[444] I will give them ten pounds, and I am in hopes
10   of procuring a little more in London. And I advise Molly Penington to write to Miss [Jane] March. I trust God will open her heart. It will be *my* part to replace her books.
You must not expect much health on this side the grave. It is enough that his grace is sufficient for you.[445]
15   In the *Minutes* of the Conference, as well as in the *Magazine* there is a clear account of all that concerns the late ordination.[446] It is a wonder the High Churchmen are so silent.[447] Surely the bridle of God is in their mouth.
Whatever you judge would be proper for the *Magazine*, send. You
20   can comprise much in a sheet. I am
Your affectionate brother,

J. Wesley

Address: 'To / Mr John Bredin / In Athlone / Ireland'.
25   *Postmarks*: '17/NO' and 'NO/21'.
Source: holograph; Drew, Methodist Archives.

[444] The room in Athlone shared by Mary (Teare) Penington and her sister Margaret had suffered a fire, damaging her library in particular.

[445] See 2 Cor. 12:9.

[446] JW's letter to 'Our Brethren in America', Sept. 10, 1784, was printed at the end of the 1785 *Minutes* (see 10:586–88 in this edn.); and in *AM* 8 (1785): 602–04.

[447] JW was receiving more personal criticism from CW and other 'Church Methodists' than this comment suggests.

To Matthew Stewart[448]

London
November 16, 1785

My Dear Brother,

It is very probable the desire you have of going to America comes from God. If it is, you may very possibly (if you are a single man) go over with Dr. [Thomas] Coke at the late end of next summer.[449]

I am

Your affectionate brother,

J. Wesley

Address: 'To Matthew Stewart'.[450]
Source: holograph; Drew, Methodist Archives.

To Thomas Wride[451]

London
November 17, 1785

Dear Tommy,

Deal plainly yet tenderly with James Byron, and he will be a very useful labourer. But none can be a Methodist preacher unless he is both able and willing to preach in the morning, which is the most healthy exercise in the world.[452]

I desire that none of our preachers would sing oftener than twice at one service. We need nothing to fill up our time.

In every place where there is a sufficient number of believers, do all you can to prevail upon them to meet in band. Be mild, be serious, and you will conquer all things.

---

[448] Matthew Stewart (1762–1827), an Irish native, enlisted in his late teens in the Light Dragoons. Converted through the influence of a fellow soldier active in Methodism, he had met JW briefly in Apr. 1785 in Athlone. In the summer of 1786 Stewart agreed to take Richard Condy's place as a missionary in the western portion of County Donegal. He was well received and in 1788 was formally admitted 'on trial' as an itinerant (see 10:645 in this edn.). Stewart served various appointments in Ireland until health issues led to a full retirement in 1817. See *Irish Evangelist* 5 (1862), 234; and *Minutes* (post-Wesley, 1827), 6:222.

[449] Stewart was already married, with three children, so he did not go. Cf. JW to Stewart, c. July 10, 1787.

[450] This was a double letter with that to John Bredin, appearing on the flyleaf with the header to Stewart.

[451] Replying to Wride's letter of Nov. 14, 1785.

[452] Wride had mentioned that John M'Kersey was resisting preaching in the morning.

I am, dear Tommy,
    Your affectionate friend and brother,

J. Wesley

Endorsement: by Wride, 'No. 30. / Novr. 17th, 1785'.
Source: holograph; MARC, MAM JW 6/31.

To Robert Carr Brackenbury

London
November 24, 1785

Dear Sir,
    God will hearken to the prayer that goeth not out of feigned lips,[453] especially when fasting is joined therewith. And, provided our brethren continue instant in prayer, the beasts of the people will not again lift up their head.[454] The work of God still increases in Ireland, and in several parts of this kingdom. I commend you and all our brethren to him who is able to preserve you from all evil and build you up in love;[455] and am, dear sir,
        Your affectionate friend and brother,

[J. Wesley]

Source: published transcription; Jackson, *Works* (3rd), 13:7.

To William Black Jr.

London
November 26, 1785

My Dear Brother,
    It is indeed matter of joy that our Lord is still carrying on his work throughout Great Britain and Ireland. In the time of Dr. Jonathan Edwards there were several gracious showers in New England. But there were large intermissions between one and another; whereas with us there has been no intermission at all for seven-and-forty

---

[453] See Ps. 17:1.
[454] See JW to Brackenbury, Sept. 26, 1785.
[455] Cf. Jude 1:24.

years, but the work of God has been continually increasing. The same thing I am in hopes you will now see in America likewise.

See that you expect it, and that you seek it in his appointed ways—namely, with fasting and unintermitted prayer. And take care that you be not at all discouraged, though you should not always have an immediate answer. You know

His manner and his time is best.[456]

Therefore pray always![457] Pray and faint not.[458] I commend you all to our Great Shepherd; and am,
    Your affectionate brother,

                       J. Wesley

Address: 'To / Mr [Philip] Marchington / and W[illiam] B[lack] / In Halifax / Nova Scotia'.
Endorsement: by Black(?), 'Revd. J. Wesley / London 26 Nov. 1785'.
Source: holograph; UCC Maritime Conference, Archives.

To Frances (Mortimer / Wren) Pawson[459]

                    London
          November 26, 1785

My Dear Sister,

I thank you for the clear and circumstantial account you have given me of the manner wherein God wrought upon your soul. As he wrought the work both of justification and sanctification so distinctly, you have the less temptation to cast away your confidence. But you cannot keep it unless you are zealous of good works.[460] Be fruitful therefore in every good work,[461] and God shall see very soon his whole image.

---

[456] Cf. CW, 'Groaning for Redemption', Pt. III, st. 3, *l.* 5, *HSP* (1742), 107.
[457] See 1 Thess. 5:17.
[458] See Luke 18:1.
[459] John Pawson lost his first wife, Grace (Davis) Pawson, in 1783. On Aug. 11, 1785 he married the widow Frances (Mortimer) Wren (1736–1809) in York. She had sent JW an account of her Christian experience (not known to survive) as a way of introducing herself.
[460] See Titus 2:14.
[461] See Col. 1:10.

I am
    Yours affectionately,

                             J. Wesley

Address: 'To / The Revd[462] Mr. Pawson / At the Preachinghouse / in / Edinburgh'.
Endorsement: by Frances Pawson, 'Mr. Westley's Letter to me / Novr. 26. 1785'.
Source: holograph; MARC, MAM JW 4/36.

To Ann Tindall[463]

                               London
                    November 26, 1785

My Dear Sister,

I thank you for your verses on Mr. Fletcher.[464] The others which you mention I hope to receive shortly.

I am glad to hear that the work of God prospers in your neighbourhood. Whether it will be promoted or hindered by Mr. ___ settling among you, I cannot tell. He is not a Methodist, but keep him steady if you can.

I think the Doctor must be in a dream or out of his senses to talk of the Methodists separating from the Church![465] Stay till I am in a better place. It will hardly be while I live.

    I am, dear Nancy,
        Yours affectionately,

                             J. Wesley

Address: 'To / Miss Tindall / in / Scarborough'.
Postmark: '26/NO'.
Endorsement: by Tindall, 'Nov. 26. 1785'.
Source: holograph; British Library, Department of Manuscripts, Add. MS. 43695, ff. 96–97.

[462] Note use of 'Revd'; JW ordained Pawson for service in Scotland in early Aug.

[463] Tindall's letter conveying the information that drew this reply is not known to survive.

[464] 'Reflections, occasioned by hearing of the death of the late Rev. Mr. Fletcher, Vicar of Madeley in Shropshire, who departed this life August 14, 1785, in the 56th year of his age' (17 stanzas; see British Library, Add. MS. 43695, ff. 103–08.

[465] Upon his initial return from establishing The Methodist Episcopal Church in America (July 1785ff.), Thomas Coke 'was as ardent a Dissenter as he had formerly been a Churchman', encouraging the British Methodists to sever their remaining ties to the established Church; see John Vickers, *Thomas Coke: Apostle of Methodism* (London: Epworth, 1969), 100–13.

To George Snowden[466]

London
c. December 1, 1785

5

[…] [I] had nothing to do with Dr. [Patrick] Watson. The people upon the spot must be the best judges of what was proper; only [I] would advise [you] to have nothing to do with *banky ground*, but to get *level ground*, and *freehold if possible*.[467]

10

[J. Wesley]

Source: published excerpt; Coates, *New Portrait*, 3.

15

To John Francis Valton

London
December 2, 1785   20

My Dear Brother,

Indeed I did not think of her, though I know few so holy women in England.[468] But I doubt whether she would marry at all. If she was so minded, I would not hinder.

Be content to do as much as you can without wearying yourself.   25
You must not attempt to do more unless you would do a pleasure to the enemy of God and man.

Satan (with his angel's face) may humble you, but he cannot materially hinder the work of God. In spite of all hindrances that do or

---

[466] The lease on the first preaching-house in North Shields expired in late 1783. Shortly after this Dr. Patrick Watson (d. 1827) a surgeon in North Shields offered to sell to the Methodist society (of which he was not a member) a piece of property he owned. It was judged by most to be an inappropriate site because it was small and on a bank running down to the river. In Sept. 1785 Watson brought the offer again (having recruited John Reed, a member of the society as his agent), and claimed he had written JW about it and received an answer that the new preaching-house should be built '*on his ground and nowhere else*'. George Snowden was the Assistant of the Newcastle circuit at the time and found himself caught between those supporting purchase of Watson's land and those opposed. After a couple of further contentious meetings Snowden wrote JW describing the situation and received this letter in reply. For the continuing story, see the extended (and one-sided) account in Coates, *New Portrait*.

[467] The quotation is given from the perspective of the recipients ('he' and 'us'). We have rendered in first person from JW.

[468] Cf. JW to Valton, Oct. 8, 1785. Valton likely raised the possibility of marrying Sarah Crosby, another resident of Yorkshire.

may occur, form bands everywhere. Meantime it is impossible but offences will come. But still go calmly on your way. Richard Stocks was not a knave, but a fool. He wanted prudence, not honesty.

I am,

Your affectionate friend and brother,

J. Wesley

Address: 'To / Mr John Valton / in Bradforth / Yorkshire'.
Postmark: '3/DE'.
Endorsement: by Valton: 'Decr 2nd 1785'.
Source: holograph; privately held (WWEP Archive holds digital copy).

To Walter Churchey

London
December 6, 1785

My Dear Brother,

If affliction drives you nearer to God, it will prove an unspeakable blessing. You are welcome to send your children to Kingswood, and to pay for them when and as it is convenient for you.

I am, with love to sister [Mary] Churchey,

Your affectionate brother,

J. Wesley

Address: 'To / Mr Walter Churchey / Near the Hay / Brecon'.
Postmark: '6/DE'.
Endorsement: by Churchey, '11 Decr 1785 J: W:'.
Source: holograph; MARC, MAM JW 2/41.

To William Roberts

London
December 6, 1785

Dear Billy,

I am glad it was in my power to give you some little assistance, and should have rejoiced if I had been able to do more.[469] Mr. [John] Atlay will answer your demands. Your tract is the most sensible I

---

[469] JW apparently loaned Roberts £70 (or part of that); see Roberts to JW, Nov. 28, 1786.

have seen on the subject. But all the booksellers here say it will never sell, so I will deliver it to whom you please. Wishing all happiness to sister Roberts and you,[470] I am, dear Billy,
Your affectionate friend and brother,

J. Wesley 5

Source: holograph; Oxford, Lincoln College, Archive, MS/WES/A/2/7.

10

To Alexander Knox[471]

London
December 8, 1785

Dear Alleck, 15
I do not believe that any fistula is incurable, even without any incision at all. I suppose the late king was near seventy when he told his physicians, 'I will not be cut. Either cure me without cutting or I will die.' They did then effect a perfect cure, without any cutting at all. 20
And several years since a young man came to me, at the return from one of my journeys, and told me, he had used Sir Kenelm Digby's remedy, set down in the *Primitive Physic*, and that it had perfectly cured his fistula in six weeks time.[472] When I mentioned this to Dr. Crommelin (whom I would trust, beyond any other physician in Ireland[473]) he told me, 'Sir, I have myself cured several fistulas by the same medicine. Only I prescribe but half the quantity.' 25
Some years since, I was walking with Mr. Charles of Rosmead[474] (who I suppose has tiled more houses than most men in the county)

---

[470] William Roberts married Elizabeth Lock (1729–88) in Tiverton, Devon in 1748.

[471] Sometime after this extended letter, JW became aware of the tract Knox had recently published: *Free Thoughts Concerning a Separation of the People called Methodists from the Church of England* (see c. Dec. 1785 in in-letters file). This tract was critical of JW ordaining lay-preachers. The strain it imposed on JW's relationship is Knox is evident in that, after writing Knox four times in 1785, there are no known letters in 1786 (Knox carefully preserved his letters from JW), and only scattered perfunctory letters thereafter.

[472] See the receipt for a fistula that included powdered copperas (Digby made this popular as 'the powder of sympathy'); *Primitive Physic*, Ailment #112, remedy 4, 32:183–84 in this edn.

[473] Alexander Crommelin (d. 1785), a Huguenot surgeon, who apprenticed at Lisburn and studied in Edinburgh. David Agnew, *Protestant Exiles from France* (London: Reeves and Turner, 1871), 2:132.

[474] Joseph Charles was usually described as from Drumcree (about 4 miles from Rosmead). He was converted by JW's preaching in 1749, and served as a local preacher in later years. See JW, *Journal*, May 7, 1749, 20:271 in this edn.; and July 17, 1756, 21:69.

when looking on the roof of an house nearly built he said, 'The men who roofed that house wanted either skill or honesty. For no roof need rise above one third of the breadth.' This rule I observe in all my houses. And yet they all turn the rain perfectly well. If therefore
5   your builders can't roof an house in the same manner, so as to turn the rain, it is plain they have not the skill either of Joseph Charles or of the English builders.

'Mr. D. is resolved to leave Derry early in the next summer',[475] suppose five months hence. But who has assured him he shall live
10 five months? Has he renewed the lease of his life with God? I think if Mrs. D. and he should live till Lady Day,[476] it will be soon enough in all reason to consider that question.

Some of St. Cyprian's letters are worth translating. I read Mr. Bonnell's *Life* above fifty years ago, and thought it *good* but not *very*
15 *good*.[477] Perhaps I may like it better now.

Probably this winter I shall begin printing the New Testament.[478]

I am persuaded Mr. Hanway is a pious man. And he is an ingenious writer.[479] I never saw the tract you mention, but will read it if it comes my way.

20   I incline to think your late illness will prevent your fits, by driving the humour the other way. Peace be with all your spirits! I am, dear Alleck,

Ever yours,

J. Wesley

25

Address: 'To / Mr Alexr. Knox, in / Londonderry'.
Postmarks: '9/DE' and 'DE/13'.
Source: holograph; Bridwell Library (SMU).[480]

---

[475] JW was quoting from Knox's letter, which is not known to survive.

[476] Mar. 25.

[477] William Hamilton, *The Exemplary Life and Character of James Bonnell, Esq. 3rd edn.* (London: Downing, 1707). JW records reading this in late Oct. 1730 in his Oxford diary.

[478] See JW to Knox, May 6, 1785.

[479] The one work of Jonas Hanway (1712–86) that JW recorded reading was *An Historical Account of the British Trade over the Caspian Sea ...*, 4 vols. (London: Dodsley, 1753). Cf. JW, *Journal*, Dec. 13–19, 1756, 21:83 in this edn.

[480] Held previously in the Upper Room Museum, L-45.

To Jane (Cave) Winscom[b]

near London
December 10, 1785   5

Dear Mrs. Winscom[b],

When Mr. [Jasper] Winscom went up into the chamber with me, he told me with tears in his eyes that although he had no enmity to you, yet he did not dare to invite you to his house, because he was afraid it might be an encouragement to his other children to act as their brother had done.[481] And who can convince him that this is a needless fear? I am not able to do it. But as long as this remains I do not see how he can act otherwise than he does. I know no way you have to take but this: behave as obligingly to him as you can, never speaking against him, for whatever you say will come round to him again. Then you will gain him by little and little.

I am, dear Jenny,
    Yours affectionately,

[J. Wesley]
20

Address: 'To / Mrs. Jane Winscom / At Mr. Tiller's / In Winton'.
Source: published transcription; Telford, *Letters*, 7:303.

25

To the Rev. Thomas Hanby[482]

London   30
December 13, 1785

My Dear Brother,

If you should have any fair, mild Sundays, I would commend you for preaching abroad in the afternoon. When it is rainy or cold, you must be content to make as much room within as you can. You must not quite forget poor Perth and Dunkeld. Good may be done there also.   35

---

[481] Jasper Winscom was distressed when his eldest son Thomas married Jane Cave in 1783, without getting his father's approval; see JW to Jasper Winscom, Oct. 13, 1783. Perhaps due to this alienation Thomas and Jane change the spelling of their surname to 'Winscomb'.

[482] JW ordained Hanby for service in Scotland in early Aug. 1785.

I greatly approve of the little alteration you have made in the manner of administering the Lord's Supper.[483] It is certainly more solemn and more suitable to the Scripture-account of the original institution. It is highly probable that our blessed Lord delivered a
5   portion of the consecrated bread to each of his disciples. And (as you well observed, and as we may judge from our own feelings) they could not but desire everyone to receive it from his own hands. I therefore much commend our brethren, either at Arbroath or Dundee, who chose to conform to what we may reasonably suppose
10   to be that most scriptural.

Let those be bitter that will. But see that you never return evil for evil or railing for railing. Grace and peace be with all our spirits! I am,
      Your affectionate friend and brother,
15   J. Wesley

Address: 'To / The Revd Mr Hanby / at / Dundee'.
Postmark: '13/DE'.
Source: holograph; Oxford, Lincoln College, Archive, MS/WES/A/6/3.

20

To Mary Cooke

25   London
                                                      December 14, 1785

I love to see the handwriting of my dear Miss Cooke even before I open the letter. The thinking of you gives me very sensible pleasure
30   ever since you spoke so freely to me. There is a remedy for the evil of which you complain—unprofitable reasonings—and I do not know whether there is any other. It is the peace of God. This will not only keep your *heart*, your affections and passions, as a garrison keeps a city; but your *mind* likewise, all the workings and all the
35   wanderings of your imagination. And this is promised: 'Ask, and it shall be given you. Seek, and you shall find.'[484]

                  Though it seem to tarry long,
                  True and faithful is his word.[485]

---

[483] Hanby's letter describing this alteration in more detail is not known to survive.
[484] Matt. 7:7.
[485] CW, 'Waiting for the Promise', st. 2, *HSP* (1742), 237.

A small measure of it you have frequently found, which may encourage you to look for the fulness. But if you were to give scope to your reasonings, there would be no end. The farther you went the more you would be entangled; so true it is that, to our weak apprehension,

> The ways of heaven are dark and intricate,
> Puzzled with mazes, and perplexed with error.[486]

But that peace will silence all our hard thoughts of God, and give us in patience to possess our souls.[487] I believe, at the time that any first receive the peace of God, a degree of holy boldness is connected with it. And that all persons when they are newly justified are called to bear witness to the truth. Those who use the grace which is then freely given to them of God will not only have the continuance of it, but a large increase. For 'unto him that hath' (that is, uses what he hath), 'shall be given, and he shall have more abundantly.'[488] We shall grow in boldness the more, the more we use it. And it is by the same method, added to prayer, that we are to recover anything we have lost. Do what in you lies, and he will do the rest.

My best service attends Mr. L[ocke], who I hope will be holier and happier by means of his late union.[489] He certainly will if Mrs. L[ocke] and he provoke one another to love and to good works.[490] I do not despair of having the pleasure to wait on them at the Devizes. My best wishes wait likewise on Miss Shrapnell.[491] I hope you two are one. Indeed, I am, my dear Miss Cooke,[492]

Yours in tender affection,

J. Wesley

Source: published transcription; Benson, *Works*, 16:299–300.

[486] Joseph Addison, *Cato*, I.i.47–48.
[487] See Luke 21:19.
[488] Cf. Matt. 13:12, 25:29.
[489] Thomas Locke (1743–98) married Margaret Coles Bennett (d. 1814) on Nov. 9, 1785 in Trowbridge; Mary Cooke signed as a witness. Thomas was an attorney and the new couple resided in Devizes.
[490] See Heb. 10:24.
[491] Likely Mary Shrapnell (1767–1823), a cousin, who would marry Thomas Naish (1768–1828) in Nov. 1787.
[492] A fragment of the holograph, containing the last four sentences and closing, survives at MARC, WCB, D6/1/98b.

To John M'Kersey and James Byron[493]

London
December 14, 1785

If you do not choose to obey me, you need not. I will let you go when you please and send other preachers in your place. If you do choose to stay with me, never sing more than twice, once before and once after sermon.

I have given Mr. [Thomas] Wride directions concerning the singers. Pray assist him in seeing these directions observed. You are young; I am in pain for you. Follow *his* advice. He is older and wiser than you. You would do well to meet the children and the select society, though it be a cross. I will thank you if you will do all you can to strengthen Mr. Wride's hands. Beware of strengthening any party against him. Let you three be one. Nothing will give greater satisfaction than this to
Your affectionate brother,

J. Wesley

Address: 'To J. Muckersey & Byron'.[494]
Source: published transcription; *WHS* 1 (1898): 143–44.[495]

To Thomas Wride[496]

London
December 14, 1785

Dear Tommy,

Have patience with the young men, and they will mend upon your hands.[497] But remember, soft and fair goes far! For twenty years and upwards we had good morning congregations at Norwich. But they might begin at 6:00 till Lady Day.[498] I desire brother [James] Byron to try what he can do. Better days will come.

[493] This note is part of JW's reply to Thomas Wride's letter of Dec. 9, 1785. John M'Kersey (d. 1800) was admitted on trial as a travelling preacher in 1784 (see 10:553 in this edn.) and assigned to Norwich the following year. Health issues required him to cease travelling after 1792. See Atmore, *Memorial*, 236–37; and *Minutes* (post-Wesley, 1800), 2:43.

[494] The original note was surely written on the flyleaf of JW to Wride that follows.

[495] The published transcription is from Thomas Wride's copy of JW's letter.

[496] Replying to Wride's letter of Dec. 9, 1785.

[497] M'Kersey and Byron; see previous letter.

[498] Mar. 25.

I pray let that doggerel hymn be no more sung in our chapel.[499] If they do not soon come to their senses at Norwich, I will remove you to Colchester.

I am, dear Tommy,

Your affectionate friend and brother,

J. Wesley

Be mild! Be serious!

Address: 'To / Mr Wride / at the Preachinghouse / in / Norwich'.
Postmark: '14/DE'. *Charge*: '5'.
Endorsements: by Wride, 'Recd. it Decbr / 24 –85' and 'No. 31'.
Source: holograph; MARC, MAM JW 6/32.

To John Gardner[500]

Highbury Place
December 21, 1785

My Dear Brother,

I like the design and rules of your little society, and hope you will do good to many.[501] I will subscribe three-pence per week, and will give you a guinea on advance, if you call on me Saturday morning.

I am,

Your affected brother,

J. Wesley

Address: 'To John Gardner'.
Source: published transcription; *Grain of Mustard Seed* (c. 1815).[502]

---

[499] Likely referring to 'Hark how the gospel trumpet sounds, ...', a hymn in Spence's *Pocket Hymn Book* (1783) that JW omitted in his *Pocket Hymn Book* (1785). See Wride's comment on this being a favourite in Norwich in his letter to JW of Sept. 7–10, 1785.

[500] JW was replying to a letter from Gardner, c. Dec. 1785. John Gardner (d. 1807) served in the British army during the Revolutionary War and settled in London after his discharge. He was soon concerned with relief of the poor around his home in Long Acre, near Covent Garden. Gardner later became a doctor, and had a career filled with scientific discoveries and charitable works. See Stephenson, *City Road*, 328–29; and *WMM* 139 (1916), 29.

[501] The initial Strangers' Friend Society in London (in which Gardner took a lead role). See Thomas Marriott, 'Strangers Friend Societies', *WMM* 1 (1845): 661–68; and Tim Macquiban, 'British Methodism and the Poor, 1785–1840', University of Birmingham Ph.D. thesis, 2000.

[502] A printed single-leaf flyer; copy held at MARC, MA 1977/609.

To the Editor of the 'Gentleman's Magazine'

City Road [London]
December 24, 1785

5   Mr. Urban,
   If you will insert the following in your magazine, you will oblige
      Your humble servant,

John Wesley

10   This morning a friend sent me the *Gentleman's Magazine* for last
May, wherein I find another letter concerning my eldest brother.[503]
I am obliged to Mr. Badcock for the candid manner wherein he
writes, and wish to follow his pattern in considering the reasons
which he urges in defense of what he wrote before.[504]

15   1. Mr. Badcock says: 'His brother cannot be ignorant that he always bore the character of Jacobite, a title to which I really believe
he had no dislike.' Most of those who gave him this title did not
distinguish between a Jacobite and a Tory—whereby I mean 'one
that believes God, not the people, to be the origin of all civil power'.

20   In this sense he was a Tory; so was my father; so am I. But I am no
more a Jacobite than I am a Turk; neither was my brother. I have
heard him over and over disclaim that character.

   2. 'But his own daughter affirmed it.' Very likely she might, and
doubtless she thought him such. Nor is this any wonder, consider-

25   ing how young she was when her father died.[505] Especially if she did
not know the difference between a Tory and a Jacobite; which may
likewise have been the case with Mr. Badcock's friends, if not with
Mr. Badcock himself.

   3. Mr. Wesley says, 'He never published anything political.'

30   This is strictly true. 'He never wrote, much less published, *one line*
against the king.' He never *published one*. But I believe he did write
those verses entitled 'The Regency', and therein, 'by obliquely exposing the regents, exposed the king himself'.[506]

   In this my brother and I differed in our judgments. I thought

35   exposing the king's Ministers was one way of exposing the king

---

[503] Samuel Badcock's letter, dated May 10, 1785, published in *Gentleman's Magazine* 55 (1785): 363–66.

[504] Badcock was replying to JW's letter to Patrick Henry Maty, Jan. 11, 1785.

[505] Philadelphia Wesley was born in Dec. 1728; her father, Samuel Wesley Jr., died in Nov. 1739.

[506] Badcock transcribed several lines of this poem in his May 10 letter, along with the characterization that JW quotes. The manuscript of the poem Badcock transcribes is not known to survive.

himself. My brother thought otherwise; and therefore without scruple exposed Sir Robert Walpole and all other evil Ministers. Of his writing to Sir Robert I never heard before, and cannot easily believe it now.

4. From the moment that my mother heard my brother and me answer for ourselves, she was ashamed of having paid any regard to the vile misrepresentations which had been made to her after our return from Georgia. She then fully approved both our principles and practice, and soon after removed to my house, and gladly attended all our ministrations till her spirit returned to God.

John Wesley

Source: published transcription; *Gentleman's Magazine* (1785), 932.

To Thomas Tattershall

London
December 29, 1785

Dear Tommy,

Write your letter on the same paper with your plan, and you save half the postage. I am glad the debt of the circuit is paid. This is a token for good.

You must immediately either convince or remove these disputatious leaders. If need be, let the preacher lead the class. But lend any of them *The Plain Account of the People called Methodists*.[507]

The *Christian Library* is not now to be had at any price. It is quite out of print. But any books which are in print you may have, as well without money as with. The *Appeals*, the four volumes of *Sermons*, and the *Notes on the New Testament*, every one of our preachers should be thoroughly acquainted with.[508] I am,

Dear Tommy,

Your affectionate friend and brother,

J. Wesley

---

[507] See 9:252–80 in this edn.

[508] The four existing volumes of *Sermons* and *NT Notes* are of obvious importance, named in the 'Model Deed'; see 'Large' *Minutes* (1763), §67, 10:869–70 in this edn. For other instances where JW adds the *Appeal to Men of Reason and Religion* and the *Farther Appeal to Men of Reason and Religion* to this list see JW to Philothea Briggs, May 2, 1771, 28:376 in this edn.; and JW to Arthur Keen, Apr. 20, 1787.

Address: 'To / Mr Tattershall / At the Preachinghouse / In Derby'.
Source: published transcription; Byrth, 'Memoir', xxxvi.

5

To the Rev. Joseph Taylor[509]

London
10   December 29, 1785

Dear Joseph,

I advise you:

1. Till March do not preach more than twice a day.
2. Nver preach above three-quarters of an hour.
15   3. Never strain your voice.
4. For a month (at least) drink no tea. I commend you if you take to it no more. The wind is not an original disease, but a symptom of nervous weakness.
5. Warm lemonade cures any complaint in the bowels.
20   6. If you have a bathing-vessel, put a gallon of boiling water into the cold water. Then you might bathe thrice a week.

And send me word next month how you are. I am, dear Joseph,

Your affectionate friend and brother,

J. Wesley

25 *Address*: 'To / The Revd Mr Joseph Taylor / In / Aberdeen'.
Postmarks: '29/DE' and 'JA/2'.
Source: holograph; Drew, Methodist Archives.

30

To Jasper Winscom[510]

London
35   December 29, 1785

Dear Jasper,

I am not at all surprised at any of these things. And I am glad that you keep your temper. Indeed I should expect much more from *you*

---

[509] JW had ordained Taylor for service in Scotland in early Aug. 1785.
[510] This letter reflects the continuing estrangement between Jasper Winscom, his oldest son Thomas, and his daughter-in-law; see JW to Jane (Cave) Winscomb, Dec. 10, 1785.

than from those who have not the same experience. Be not overcome of evil, but overcome evil with good![511]

And whenever it shall appear, that her spirit is softened, that she is mild and gentle, then I advise you to invite her to your house.

I am, dear Jasper,

    Your affectionate brother,

J. Wesley

Address: 'To / Mr Jasper Winscom / In Winton'.
Source: holograph; privately held (WWEP Archive holds photocopy).

To Mary (Bosanquet) Fletcher

London
December 31, 1785

My Dear Sister,

I thank you for the papers.[512] It was not needful that you should copy them over again, as they are very legibly written and I am well acquainted with your hand. I love to see it. Indeed, I love everything that belongs to *you*, as I have done ever since I knew you.

A few more materials I have procured from Mr. Vaughan,[513] and some more from Joseph Benson.[514] I am willing to glean up all I can before I begin putting them together. But how am I to direct to Mr. [James] Ireland ? Or would *your* writing a line be of more weight to induce him to give me what assistance he can by the first opportunity?

I thank you for mentioning that mistake in the sermon.[515] I doubt not but you and Mr. Ireland may set me right in many other particulars wherein I have hitherto been mistaken. But it would be pity to stay till next year.

---

[511] See Rom. 12:21.

[512] See JW to Mary (Bosanquet) Fletcher, Oct. 22, 1785.

[513] See Vaughn to JW, c. Dec. 25, 1785. Vaughan was described by JW in his published *Life of Fletcher* as 'a pious domestic' of Thomas Hill (formerly Harwood; 1693–1782) of Tern Hall, near Atcham, Shropshire. Fletcher was tutor to Hill's two sons from 1752–60.

[514] See Benson to JW, c. Dec. 20, 1785.

[515] Mary informed JW of the inaccuracy of a quote attributed to Susanna (Noel) Hill in JW's sermon *On the Death of John Fletcher*, III.2 (3:615 in this edn.). Cf. Elizabeth Ritchie to JW, Oct. 25, 1786.

Was it in London he met with the honest Jew? That is a very remarkable circumstance. Do you know any particulars of his ill usage at the custom-house? Where was this custom-house?[516]

Tenderly commending you to him who will make all things work
5 together for your good,[517] I am, my dear sister,

Your ever affectionate brother,

J. Wesley

Address: 'To / Mrs Fletcher / At Madeley, near Shifnal / Salop'.
10 *Postmark*: '31/DE'. Charge: '5'.
Source: holograph; MARC, MAM JW 2/97.

---

[516] For Fletcher's account of ill-treatment by customs officials when he first arrived in London, and the help he received from an honest Jew, see Tyerman, *Fletcher*, p. 10.
[517] See Rom. 8:28.

1786

5

James Oliver Cromwell

near London
January 2, 1786

My Dear Brother,
  Health you shall have if health be best.[1] But then you must use the means. [1)] First, never scream! Never strain your voice. 2) Never preach too long—never a⟨bove⟩[2] an hour. 3) Drink largely when need is of ⟨warm⟩ lemonade. It cures all bilious complaints whether they are attended with purging or not.
  Let both of you take pains to confirm brother [William] Black, and to heal any hurt which he may have received. To establish such a preacher as he has been will reward all your labour.
  The more exact your discipline is in every place the more the work of God will prosper in your hands. The soul and body make a man. The Spirit and discipline make a Christian.[3]
  My kind love to brother Black. I am,
    Your affectionate friend and brother,

J. Wesley

Address: 'To Mr Cromwell'.[4]
Source: secondary transcription; privately held (WWEP Archive holds digital image).

---

[1] Cf. CW, Hymn on Isaiah 40:31, st. 7, *HSP* (1742), 226.
[2] A small portion is torn away, affecting two lines.
[3] See note on JW to William Church, Oct. 13, 1778, 29:447 in this edn.
[4] This appears as a header. At the bottom is transcribed the address: 'To / Mr Freeborn Garrettson / In Halifax / Nova Scotia'. Thus this was a double-letter with Cromwell's portion on the fly-leaf of the address portion. The half of the letter to Garrettson is not known to survive.

419

To the Rev. William Roots[5]

London
January 2, 1786

5 Dear Sir,

I am glad you are connected with so good a man as Dr. [James]
Stonhouse, and that you do not want employment.[6] But I am not at
all of your mind that you will be useless therein, although you do
not immediately see the fruit of your labour.

10 I *could* send you a clergyman directly, but I won't—because he is
a *dead* man. But I have another in my eye whom I will send to immediately to know if he is willing to accept the offer.[7]

If I can get time in going to or returning from Bristol, I will call
upon you at Cheverell. Peace be with both your spirits! I am

15   Your affectionate friend and brother,

J. Wesley

Address: 'To / The Revd Mr Roots / At Great Cheveral / Near the Devizes / Wilts'.

20 *Postmark*: '2/IA'. *Charge*: '5'.

Endorsement: by Roots, 'From the Righteous man of God. Janr. 5th, 1787
[sic]'.

Source: holograph; MARC, MAM JW 4/60.

25

To Sarah (James) Wyndowe[8]

London
30   January 7, 1786

My Dear Sally,

From the time that I first took acquaintance with you at Earl's
bridge,[9] I have still retained the same regard for you. Therefore I
am always well pleased with hearing from you; especially when you

---

[5] For Roots, see the note on JW to Samuel Bradburn, Mar. 16, 1776, 29:235 in this edn.
He had now been ordained and was serving as curate at Cheverell Magna and Little Cheverell.

[6] For Stonhouse, see the note on JW to Rev. Thomas Stedman, Sept. 1, 1774, 29:70 in
this edn. Stedman had served previously as Stonhouse's curate in Cheverell.

[7] Likely Rev. Peard Dickinson.

[8] Sarah James (1753–1826) grew up in the Earl's Meads neighbourhood of east Bristol;
see JW's prior letters to her of Aug. 28, 1772 (28:513–14 in this edn.) and Nov. 29, 1774 (29:94).
Sarah married Henry Wyndowe, a clothier in Ryeford, Aug. 5, 1783 in Bristol.

[9] A bridge crossing to Earl's Meads in Bristol.

inform me that, you are still pursuing the best things. And you will not pursue them in vain, if you still resolutely continue to spend some time in private every day. It is true, you cannot fix any determinate measure of time because of numberless avocations. And it is likewise true, that you will often find yourself so dead and cold 5 that it will seem to be mere labour lost. Not; it is not. It is the way wherein he that raises the dead has appointed to meet you. And we know not how soon he may meet you, and say, 'Woman! I say unto thee, arise!'[10] Then the fear of [death?] which has so long triumphed over you, shall be put under your feet. Look up, my friend![11] Expect 10 that he who loves you will soon come and will not tarry![12]

To his care I commit you, and am, my dear Sally,

Yours most affectionately,

J. Wesley

15

Address: 'Mrs Wyndowe / Byeford[13] near Stroud / Gloucest[ershir]e'.[14]
Source: holograph; MARC, MA 2008/016.

20

To Joshua Keighley

London
January 8, 1786

My Dear Brother,   25

Poor James seems to have lost all conscience.[15] You may speak of him in the congregation, provided you do not name his name. But I think he will soon have spent his fire. Go you calmly and steadily on your way.

Brother [William] Hoskins is a good man, and not a bad preach- 30
er.[16] He may change with brother [William] Warrener for a month or two.

I am, dear Joshua,

---

[10] Cf. Mark 2:11.
[11] See Luke 21:28.
[12] See Heb. 10:37.
[13] I.e., Ryeford.
[14] The address is an annotation at the bottom of the letter; not in JW's hand.
[15] This is likely the itinerant James Perfect, who had been removed from the connexion for cause at the 1785 Conference (see 10:569 in this edn.). He had been the Assistant of the Pembroke circuit in 1784, before being replaced in that role by Keighley.
[16] William Hoskins had been admitted 'on trial' as an itinerant preacher at the 1782 Conference (see 10:519 in this edn.). He desisted travelling in 1789 (10:677).

Your affectionate friend and brother,

J. Wesley

Address: 'To / Mr Kighley / At the Preachinghouse / in / Carmarthen'.
Postmark: '⟨8⟩/IA'.
Source: holograph; privately held (WWEP Archive holds photocopy).

To Mary (Bosanquet) Fletcher

London
January 13, 1786

My Dear Sister,

When I receive letters from other persons, I let them lie perhaps a week or two before I answer them. But it is otherwise when I hear from *you*—I then think much of losing a day, for fear I should give a moment's pain to one of the most faithful friends I have in the world.

The circumstance you add respecting the behaviour of those custom house officers is very well worth relating.[17] Oh what pity that it was not *then* made known to their superiors, that those inhospitable wretches might have been prevented from misusing other strangers!

I think your advice is exactly right. With the materials I have already, or can procure in England, I will write and publish as soon as I conveniently can.[18]

I am, my very dear sister,

Your ever affectionate brother,

J. Wesley

Address: 'To / Mrs Fletcher / At Madeley, near Shifnal / Salop'.
Postmark: '16/IA'.
Endorsement: by Fletcher, 'Jany. 13th 1786'.
Source: holograph; MARC, DDWes 5/65.

[17] See JW to Fletcher, Dec. 31, 1785.
[18] Referring to *A Short Account of the Life and Death of the Rev. John Fletcher* (1786; *Bibliography*, No. 442).

To Francis Wrigley

London
January 13, 1786

My Dear Brother,

If brother [William] Green will give up the places you mention without delay, there needs no more to be said about them. If he does not, write me the names of the places and I will send an express order. I apprehend this will be sufficient to put a full end to the altercation.[19]

I have sent your order to Mr. [John] Atlay. You have done nobly with regard to the *[Arminian] Magazines.* I wish fifty of our Assistants were of the same spirit with you, both in this and in other respects.

I am,
    Your affectionate friend and brother,

J. Wesley

Address: 'To / Mr Francis Wrigley / In Redruth / Cornwall'.
Postmark: '16/IA'. *Charge*: '6'.
Source: holograph; Drew, Methodist Archives.

To Samuel Bradburn[20]

London
January 14, 1786

Dear Sammy,

It is well we know, that trouble springeth not out of the dust.[21] But that the Lord reigneth.[22] But still, even when we can say, 'It is the Lord', tis hard to add, 'let him do what seemeth him good'.[23]

---

[19] The prior division of Cornwall into an eastern and western circuit had been changed at the 1785 Conference, adding a circuit at St. Austell and locating the other two in Redruth and St. Ives. Wrigley was Assistant for the Redruth circuit; William Green was Assistant for the neighbouring St. Ives circuit. The altercation was about which circuit served some societies.

[20] The address portion is missing and the identification of Bradburn is in a secondary hand; but this is surely correct, as his wife Elizabeth (Nangle) Bradburn was ill, and would die on Feb. 11, 1786. See Bradburn to JW, Feb. 12, 1786.

[21] See Job 5:6.

[22] See Ps. 96:10.

[23] 1 Sam. 3:18.

I remember formerly, when I read those words in the church at Savannah, 'Son of man, behold I take from thee the desire of thine eyes with a stroke', I was pierced through as with a sword, and could not utter a word more.[24] But our comfort is, he that made the heart, can heal the heart! Your help stands in him alone! He will command all these things to work together for good.[25] To his tender care I commend you, and am, dear Sammy,

Your affectionate friend and brother,

J. Wesley

Source: holograph; Drew, Methodist Archives.

To Samuel Mitchell

London
January 14, 1786

Dear Sammy,

George Dice desired to be heard face to face with his accusers. I ordered it should be done. But are all the people out of their senses? Why does not either he or someone else send me an account of the issue?[26]

You say, 'The strength of my colleague and me is almost exhausted.'[27] What wonder, if you continue the service four hours! A mere trick of the devil, to make you murder yourselves. Keep sacredly to the Methodist rule: conclude the service *in an hour*.[28] Then your strength will not be exhausted. And then you will have leisure to write down from time to time all the remarkable particulars of the work of God.

I am, dear Sammy,
Your affectionate brother,

J. Wesley

---

[24] Ezek. 24:16. JW was referring to his surrender of Sophia Hopkey; see JW, Manuscript Journal, Feb. 5, 1737, 18:469–70 in this edn.

[25] See Rom. 8:28.

[26] George Dice was expelled, for adultery, at the 1786 Conference; see 10:597 in this edn.

[27] Mitchell's letter to JW is not known to survive.

[28] At this point this was an unwritten rule. It appears first in the 1786 *Minutes*, as part of an address of JW (see 10:618 in this edn.); and was added to the Irish *Minutes* in 1787 (10:988).

Address: 'To / Mr Sam. Mitchell / At Mcguire's Bridge / Near Lisnaskea / Ireland'.
Source: holograph; WHS Ireland Archives.

To Robert Carr Brackenbury

London
January 18, 1786

Dear Sir,

We have great reason to praise God for giving you so open a door in Guernsey. This was indeed more than could have been expected, as undoubtedly the father of lies had taken care to send that virulent pamphlet before you.[29] If John Ville continues alive to God, I make no question but he will be useful there.[30]

I am in great hopes that the labours of Dr. [Thomas] Coke (though his time is short) will be attended with a blessing.[31] As long as we insist on the marrow of religion, Christ reigning in the heart, he will certainly prosper our labours.

To his care I commit you; and am, dear sir,
Your affectionate friend and brother,

J. Wesley

Address: 'R. C. Brackenbury Esqr. / St. Helyar's / Isle of Jersey'.[32]
Postmark: '17/IA'.
Endorsement: 'Forw[arde]d by y[ou]r H[um]ble Serv[an]t / T. Dunn / 5d.'.
Source: holograph; MARC, MAM JW 1/107.

[29] See JW to Brackenbury, Sept. 26, 1785.
[30] Jean De Quêteville (1761–1843), a native of the Isle of Jersey, would be formally admitted as a travelling preacher at the 1786 Conference. He became the French-speaking patriarch of Methodism in the Channel Islands, translating many Methodist writings into French, and for thirty-four years editing the *Magazin Methodiste*. See Henri de Jersey, *Vie de Rev. Jean de Queteville* (London: J. Mason, 1847); and *WHS* 53 (2001): 42–45.
[31] On the back of JW's letter was one by Thomas Coke to Brackenbury, informing him that Coke would soon be sailing to visit the Channel Islands.
[32] The address is in the hand of Thomas Coke.

To Ann Loxdale

near London
January 26, 1786

My Dear Miss Loxdale,

I thank you for the remarkable and comfortable account, of Mrs. [Mary] Eden's death.[33] Is not this a time that may be much improved to the advantage of Tommy Eden? If he loved her, his heart will be softened at such a season, and made susceptible of the best impressions. And probably, as he loves and esteems *you*, you will most effectually fix these upon him.

In order to recover that blissful knowledge of God which you once enjoyed, I think what you want is to converse with those who are deeply alive to God. This would be a means of stirring up the gift of God which is in you,[34] of increasing your hunger and thirst after righteousness,[35] and enlivening your expectations of receiving all the promises of being fully renewed in the image of him that created you.[36] Mrs. [Mary] Fletcher is one of this sort.

But I fear you will find few others of the same spirit.

I hope to be at Broadmarston on Friday, March 17; at Birmingham, Saturday, [March] 18; and at Madeley, Friday the 24th. Possibly you might meet me there. This would give a particular pleasure to, my dear Miss Loxdale,

Yours affectionately,

J. Wesley

Address: 'To / Miss Loxdale / At Ilmington / Near Shipston upon Stour / Warwickshire'.
Postmark: '26/IA'.
Source: holograph; MARC, WCB, D5/33/2.

---

[33] This account is not known to survive; cf. JW to Loxdale, Oct. 8, 1785.
[34] See 2 Tim. 1:6.
[35] See Matt. 5:6.
[36] See Col. 3:10.

To Adam Clarke[37]

London
February 3, 1786   5

My Dear Brother,

You do well in insisting upon full and present salvation, whether men will hear or forbear; as also in preaching abroad (when the weather permits) and recommending fasting, both by precept and example. But you need not wonder that all these are opposed, not 10 only by formalists but by half Methodists.

You should not forget French or anything you have learned. I do not know whether I have read the book you speak of.[38] You may send your translation at your leisure.

Be all in earnest, and you shall see greater things than these. I am, 15 my dear Adam,

     Your affectionate brother,

J. Wesley

Address: 'To / Mr Adam Clark / At Mr [Robert] Walters' in / Plymouth   20
   Dock'.
Postmark: '3/FE'. *Charge*: '6'.
Endorsement: by Clarke, 'Recd bona Ave / Feb 5. 1786 / Ans[were]d the
   9[th]'.
Source: holograph; MARC, WCB, D6/1/72.   25

To Mary Cooke[39]   30

London
February 12, 1786

35
I do not usually visit any of the smaller societies in the spring. My time will not permit. Accordingly I had designed, after spending a

---

[37] JW was replying immediately to Adam Clarke's letter of Jan. 30, 1786.

[38] Clarke mentioned reading and translating an extract from Jean Siffrein Maury, *Principes d'éloquence pour la chaire et le barreau, où l'on trouve des discours* (Paris: Lamy, 1782).

[39] Replying to her letter of Jan. 24, 1786. This is an example of letting a letter lie 'a week or two' before answering—see JW to Mrs. Fletcher, Jan. 13, 1786.

day or two at Bath (about the first of March) to go on straight to
Bristol. But it is hard for me to deny you anything. I do not know
that I can. If it is possible I will contrive to visit you at Trowbridge,
and when we meet, I pray let there be no reserve between us. ...[40]

Source: secondary extract; Bridwell Library (SMU); Mary Cooke Letter-
book.[41]

To Ann Tindall

London
February 20, 1786

Dear Nancy,

That a good work may not be hindered, I will continue to do
more than I ever did for any other—to subscribe a third year toward
paying the debt of Scarborough [preaching-]house.[42]

The verses are too long to be inserted in one magazine. If they are
inserted, it must be in two.[43]

O be all in earnest! Life is short! I am, dear Nancy,
    Yours affectionately,

J. Wesley

Address: 'To / Miss Tindall / in / Scarborough'.
Postmark: '21/FE'. *Charge*: '6'.
Endorsement: by Tindall, 'Feb. 20. 1786'.
Source: holograph; British Library, Department of Manuscripts, Add.
MS. 43695, f. 99.

---

[40] JW also advised Cooke to read his sermon 'The Wilderness State' (2:205–21 in this
edn.) in this letter; see Cooke to JW, Feb. 20, 1786.

[41] Cooke included an extract in her 'Answer to Eliza [Peacock]'s 22nd and 23rd letters'.

[42] See JW to Tindall, Dec. 11, 1784.

[43] Her verses on the death of John Fletcher; see JW to Tindall, Nov. 26, 1785. These
verses were not inserted in *AM*.

To Ann Bolton

London
February 21, 1786 5

My Dear Nancy,

Though I am now uncommonly encumbered with various business, I must steal time to write two or three lines. I love you, because you are doing the will of God. And I love you the more, because you are suffering it. How easily could our Lord prevent or remove all these trials, if he saw it was best for you? *How* it is best for you thus to suffer, you know not now. But you shall know hereafter.

I make little doubt but as Mr. Bolton now understands that affair, he will make an alteration in his will.[44] But be that as it may, you will not be in want, at least as long as I live. I look upon you as one of my nearest and dearest friends. You have been and are exceeding pleasant to me. Never let there be any shyness between you and, my dear Nancy,

Yours most affectionately,

J. Wesley 20

Address: 'To / Miss Bolton / In Witney / Oxfordshire'.
Postmark: '21/FE'. *Charge*: '4'.
Endorsement: by Bolton, 'Feb 21 –86'.
Source: holograph; privately held (WWEP Archive holds photocopy). 25

To Adam Clarke 30

London
February 21, 1786

My Dear Brother, 35

I like the extract from Mr. Bridaine's sermon well.[45] Probably it may have a place in the *[Arminian] Magazine*.

---

[44] Edward Bolton Sr. (1718–91), Ann's father.
[45] See JW to Clarke, Feb. 3, 1786. On Feb. 9 Clarke sent JW a translation from the introduction to the book by Jean Siffrein Maury about Jacques Bridaine (1701–67), a Roman Catholic preacher in Paris. This appeared as 'Account of a French Preacher', *AM* 14 (1791): 565–68. Clarke's letter to JW is not known to survive.

It is well you have broken into Ston[e]house.[46] Now enlarge your borders while I am with you. Probably you will have rougher weather when I am gone.

You may come to the Conference.

5   You and your fellow labourers should spend some time in consulting together how you may enlarge your borders. This mild weather is almost as good as summer. I preached abroad last Monday. Oh let us snatch every means of redeeming the time![47] Eternity is at hand![48]

10   I am, dear Adam,
         Your affectionate brother,

                                                              J. Wesley

In a few days I shall set out for Bristol.

15
Address: 'To / Mr Adam Clark / At Mr. [Robert] Walters' in / Plymouth
    Dock'.
Postmark: '21/FE'. *Charge*: '6'.
Endorsement: 'Recd Bona Ave / Feby. 23d 1786'.
20 *Source*: holograph; MARC, MAM JW 2/49.

To Thomas Dobson[49]

25
                                                         [London]
                                              February 21, 1786

My Dear Brother,

If you do not choose to act as steward for our school any longer,
30 give the money which remains in your hands to George Whitfield, who will take the labour upon himself. If you do choose it, pay sister Metsham(?) her week's salary,

    I am
        Your affectionate brother,

35   J. Wesley

[46] A neighbourhood in Plymouth.
[47] See Eph. 5:16.
[48] See Rev. 1:3.
[49] Thomas Dobson (fl. 1780s) was a pipe and bucket maker, who lived at 427 Oxford Street, near Seven Dials. He continued to serve as the steward for the charity school run at West Street Chapel at least through 1789. See Dodson to JW, Feb. 20, 1788; and JW to Thomas Coke, Sept. 5, 1789.

Address: 'To / Mr Dobson'.
Endorsement: 'Rev Mr Wesley to T D'.
Source: holograph; MARC, MAM JW 2/85.

5

To John Ogylvie

London
February 21, 1786   10

My Dear Brother,

You see God orders all things well.[50] You have reason to thank
him both for your sickness and your recovery. But whether sick or
in health, if you keep in his way you are to prepare your soul for
temptations. For how shall we conquer if we do not fight? Go on,   15
then, as a good soldier of Jesus Christ.[51] Fight the good fight of
faith, and lay hold on eternal life![52] Salvation is nigh![53] Seek, desire
nothing else!

    I am,

        Your affectionate brother,   20

                     [J. Wesley]

Source: published transcription; Jackson, *Works* (3rd), 12:511–12.

25

To Thomas Taylor[54]

London   30
February 21, 1786

Dear Tommy,

    Mr. [Martin] Madan was the person who informed me that add-
ing new stamps is sufficient. Probably other lawyers would deny
this. Why? To make work for themselves.   35

---

[50] See Eph. 1:11.
[51] See 2 Tim. 2:3.
[52] See 1 Tim. 6:12.
[53] See Luke 21:28.
[54] While the address portion is missing, this letter is almost certainly to Taylor; cf. the
continuation in the letter of Feb. 24, 1786 below.

'Why can't these gentlemen' (said wise Bishop Gibson) 'leave the Church? Then they could do no more harm!'[55] Read 'no more good'. I believe so. I believe if we had then ⟨left the⟩[56] Church, we should not have done a tenth part ⟨of the⟩ good which we have
5   done. But I do not ⟨argue⟩ upon this head. I go calmly and quietly on my way, doing what I conceive to be the will of God.

I *do* not, will not concern myself with what will be done when I am dead. I take no thought about that. If I did, I should probably shut myself up at Kingswood or Newcastle, and leave you all to
10   yourselves. I am, dear Tommy,

Your affectionate friend and brother,

J. Wesley

15   *Postmark*: '21/FE'.
Source: holograph; MARC, MA 1992/035.

20   To Peter Walker[57]

London
February 21, 1786

Dear Peter,
25   Our Lord saw it good to humble you first, and then in due time to lift up your head.[58] But the increase of his work which you have hitherto seen you may look upon as only the promise of a shower. If you and your fellow labourers are zealous for God, you will see greater things than these. Only exhort all that have believed to go
30   on to perfection,[59] and everywhere insist upon both justification and full sanctification as receivable *now* by simple faith.

I am, dear Peter,
Your affectionate brother,

J. Wesley

[55] For Edmund Gibson's criticisms of Methodism, and JW's reply, see 11:327–51 in this edn.

[56] A small portion is torn away by the wax seal, affecting three lines.

[57] Peter Walker was admitted 'on trial' as an itinerant at the 1785 Conference (see 10:568 in this edn.) and was stationed at St. Ives. He was assigned to the Tiverton circuit in 1786, but apparently left mid-year and never appears again in the *Minutes*; see JW to [George Gidley], Mar. 10, 1787.

[58] See 1 Pet. 5:6.

[59] See Heb. 6:1.

Address: 'To / Mr Peter Walker / At the Preaching House / In St. Ives / Cornwall'.
Postmark: '21/FE'.
Source: holograph; Bridwell Library (SMU).

To Mary (Ratcliffe) Middleton[60]

London
February 21, 1786

My Dear Sister,

If it please God to continue my health and strength, I hope to be at Yarm about the 10th of May, and the next day at Darlington. But I shall be obliged to make the best of my way from thence via [the] north of Scotland. I have now so many places to visit that the summer hardly gives me time for my work.

How differently does it please him who orders all things well to dispose the lot of his children![61] I am called to work; you are called to suffer. And if both these paths lead to the same parish,[62] it is enough. Only let us take heed that we lose not the things which we have gained, but that we insure a full reward.[63]

To be under the same roof with *you*, whether in a palace or a cottage, will be a pleasure to, my dear sister,

Yours affectionately,

[J. Wesley]

Source: published transcription; Telford, *Letters*, 7:317.

---

[60] John Middleton (1724–95), who developed a weaving mill business in Guisborough, Yorkshire, was drawn into Methodism there. In July 1763 he married Mary Ratcliffe of Bingley. They moved to Hartlepool, Co. Durham, where they were pillars of the Methodist society. See John's biography in *WMM* 33 (1810): 209–17.
[61] See Eph. 1:11.
[62] Telford's transcription of this word seems doubtful.
[63] See 2 John 1:8.

To Emma Moon

London
February 22, 1786

5 My Dear Sister,

I expect (if it pleases God to continue my health and strength) to be at York from the 4th to the 8th; of May. On Monday the 8th I shall probably be at Thirsk, and the next day (Tuesday) at Potto and Hutton.

10 My business is continually increasing, so that I am obliged to hasten along. It is a satisfaction to me to think of our meeting once more on earth, for I sincerely love you; and am glad you have not forgotten, my dear sister,

Your affectionate brother,

15 J. Wesley

Address: 'To / Mrs. Emma Moon / At Potto / Near Yarm / Yorkshire'.
Postmark: '23/FE'.
Source: holograph; MARC, MAM JW 4/19.

20

To Mary Cooke[64]

25 London
February 23, 1786

By your manner of writing you make me even more desirous of seeing my dear friend than I was before. I hope to have that pleasure 30 next week. On Tuesday evening I expect to be at Bath (probably I shall preach about six o'clock); and on Wednesday noon, at Trowbridge. And remember what I told you before! You are not to have a jot of reserve about you.

I have frequently observed the passage to which you refer in the 35 third chapter to the Romans; and I have always thought there is no manner of difference between *by* faith and *through* faith.[65] So that I still believe the meaning is: It is one God *who will show mercy* to both, and by the very same means.

---

[64] Cooke had replied to JW's letter of Feb. 12, 1786 on Feb. 20; drawing this reply in turn.
[65] Cooke had inquired about Rom. 3:30.

I shall be glad if it should be in my power to do any service to Miss Martins.[66]

If it was convenient for you to be at Bath on Tuesday, I could take you with me to Trowbridge on Wednesday.

Peace be with all your spirits.

Adieu!

Address: 'To / Miss Cook / In Duke street, Trowbridge / Wilts'.
Endorsement: by Cooke, 'very little 6th'.
Source: holograph; MARC, WCB, D6/1/332.

To Elizabeth Ritchie

London
February 24, 1786

My Dear Betsy,

It is doubtless the will of our Lord we should be guided by our reason so far as it can go. But in many cases it gives us very little light; and in others, none at all. In all cases it cannot guide us right but in subordination to the unction of the Holy One.[67] So that in all our ways we are to acknowledge him, and he will direct our paths.[68]

I do not remember to have heard or read anything like my own experience. Almost ever since I can remember I have been led in a peculiar way. I go on in an even line, being very little raised at one time or depressed at another. Count Zinzendorf observes there are three different ways wherein it pleases God to lead his people: some are guided almost in every instance by apposite texts of *Scripture*, others see a clear and plain *reason* for everything they are to do, and yet others are led not so much by Scripture or reason as by particular *impressions*.[69] I am very rarely led by impressions, but generally by reason and by Scripture. I *see* abundantly more than I *feel*. I want to feel more love and zeal for God.

[66] Cooke had asked JW to help two sisters, surnamed Martin, one of whom had been a member of the society in Trowbridge. The sisters had recently moved to Shepton Mallet, where they were starting a school.

[67] See 1 John 2:20.

[68] See Prov. 3:6.

[69] See Nikolaus von Zinzendorf, *Sixteen Discourses on the Redemption of Man by the Death of Christ* (London: James Hutton, 1740), 164; or JW's *Extract of Count Zinzendorf's Discourses … * (1744, *Bibliography*, No. 90), 62.

My very dear friend, adieu!

                                                    J. Wesley

Source: published transcription; Benson, *Works*, 16:255.

To Thomas Taylor[70]

                                                    London
                                          February 24, 1786

Dear Tommy,
    I believe, if we had *then* left the Church, we should not have done
a tenth of the good which we have done. But I do not trouble myself
on this head. I go calmly and quietly on my way, doing what I conceive to be the will of God. I do not, will not concern myself with
what will be when I am dead. I take no thought about that. If I did, I
should probably hide myself either at Kingswood or Newcastle and
leave you all to yourselves. I remain,
        Your affectionate friend and brother,

                                                    J. Wesley

Source: published transcription; *United Methodist Free Church Magazine*
    5 (1862): 360.

To the Rev. Freeborn Garrettson

                                                    London
                                          February 25, 1786

My Dear Brother,
    In the states,[71] you know, the Dissenters do not at all object to
our corrected Common Prayer Book. But I do not confine myself.
I constantly add extemporary prayer both to the morning and evening service. I will communicate what you say concerning 'adapting

---

    [70] Taylor apparently replied immediately to JW's letter of Feb. 21, 1786, drawing this
elaboration.
    [71] JW first wrote 'provinces', then struck it through and inserted 'states'.

the prayer books to the northern provinces' to Dr. [Thomas] Coke and we will consider what can be done.[72]

If you are in the way to the kingdom, you must not expect to travel in it long without meeting a cross. ⟨Many of them will thr… your way. And many … himself as a Christian ….⟩[73]

It is a doubt with me, whether it will be possible for us to send over any preacher before the Conference. For whoever comes must come of his own free choice. I dare not so much as *advise* anyone to go. It must be of his own motion.

Be little in your own eyes, and God will exalt you.[74] You should not delay sending your journal to,

Your affectionate friend and brother,

J. Wesley

Source: holograph; Drew, Methodist Archives.[75]

To William Sagar

Bristol
February 25, 1786

My Dear Brother,

I expect to be at Manchester on Wednesday, April 5; at Chester, Monday, 10th; at Liverpool, Wednesday, 12th; at Warrington, Saturday, 15th; at Preston, Monday, 17th; at Blackburn, Tuesday, 18th; Wednesday, 19th, at Padiham at 9:00, Burnley [at] 12:00, Colne [at] 6:00—so as to lodge with you on Thursday, 20th. I am to be in the evening at Keighley. I am obliged to make haste.

Concerning building and other matters, I hope we shall have time to talk when we meet. I am

Your affectionate brother,

J. Wesley

---

[72] Garrettson's letter with this suggestion for Canada is not known to survive. Thomas Coke added a letter on the back of JW's, giving advice and saying, 'I shall also, God willing, bring with me one or two hundred copies of our abridged Liturgy suited to the British Dominions. It is now in the press.' Two forms of the altered *Sunday Service of the Methodists* were published in London in 1786; one with the title ending 'in the United States of America', the other ending 'in His Majesty's Dominions'. In the second the prayers for the president were replaced with prayers for King George. For more detailed comparison, see vol. 8 in this edn.

[73] Text on three lines has been scored through heavily, rendering some unreadable. It is in a different ink, so likely not by JW.

[74] See 1 Sam. 15:17.

[75] See note on JW to Stretton, Feb. 26, 1786.

If you know how to mend my plan, send me word to Manchester.

Address: 'To / Mr Sagar / At Southfield / Near Coln / Lancashire'.
Postmark: '27/FE'. *Charge*: '6'.
5   *Source*: holograph; Bridwell Library (SMU).

To James Oliver Cromwell
10

London
February 26, 1786

My Dear Brother,
    One reason why it pleases God frequently to remove some of the
15 most eminent labourers in his vineyard is to show that he has no
need of man, seeing the help which is done upon the earth, he doth
it himself.[76] And yet the Holy Ghost does not fix any censure on
those devout men who, when they carried Stephen to his burial,
'made great lamentation over him'.[77] I wish Mr. [Joseph] Pilmore
20 may do much good.[78] But I am afraid he will rather do hurt. For he
does not believe anything of Christian perfection. And I think he
does believe final perseverance.
    You may set down that Negro for a very wretch. Such another liar
I have scarce ever known. I fear he has not one grain of religion, and
25 that his conscience is seared as with a hot iron. It is well you are ap-
prised of his coming, that you may guard our brethren against him.
His talents are very small, but his assurance is very great.
    I now almost give up the thought of seeing America any more.
Our borders are now enlarged, including not only Great Britain
30 and America, but the Isle of Man, the Isle of Wight, with Jersey
and Guernsey.
    I am, dear James,
        Your affectionate brother,

                                                    J. Wesley
35
I visit Holland too.

[76] See Ps. 74:12 (BCP).
[77] Acts 8:2.
[78] Pilmore had volunteered to go over to North America in 1769 as a preacher for the
Methodists there. He returned to England in 1776, as fighting broke out in the colonies, and
was appointed in Great Britain. But in 1785 he withdrew from the Methodist connexion, returned to North America, was ordained by Bishop Seabury, and became a leading evangelical
in the Protestant Episcopal Church.

Address: 'To / Mr James Ol. Cromwell / In Shelburne / Nova Scotia'.[79]
Source: published transcription; *Christian Advocate and Journal* 20 (June 24, 1846): 183.

To John Stretton

London
February 26, 1786

My Dear Brother,

It pleases God that my health and strength are just the same now that they were forty years ago. But there is a difference in one point: I was then frequently weary, my body sunk under my work; whereas now, from one week or month to another, I do not know what weariness means.

By removing such instruments as Arthur Thomey[80] and Mr. [John] Fletcher, our Lord puts us in mind of what we are ever prone to forget, that the help which is done upon earth he doeth it himself,[81] and that he has no need of man. The pillars fall, yet the building stands. Why? The hand of the Most High supports it.

'If an angel' (says one) 'could be sent down from heaven, and were to dwell in a body threescore [years], and in that time converted but one immortal soul, it would be worth all his labour.' But you have now seen more than one sinner converted to God. Probably the number now is not small of those who are translated into the kingdom of God's dear Son.

Go on, my brother! Be your present success more or less, be not weary! In due time you shall reap if you faint not![82] I am

Your affectionate brother,

J. Wesley

---

[79] See note on JW to Stretton, Feb. 26, 1786.

[80] Arthur Thomey, an Irish trader who emigrated to Newfoundland in 1771, was converted by Laurence Coughlan and became a local preacher, assisting Stretton. But in Nov. 1784, during a trip to Portugal, Thomey died unexpectedly. See Stretton's letter to Eliza Bennis, June 29, 1785, Bennis, *Correspondence*, 243.

[81] See Ps. 74:12 (BCP).

[82] See Gal. 6:9.

Address: 'To / Mr Stretton / Harbor Grace / Newfoundland'.[83]
Source: holograph; Bridwell Library (SMU).[84]

To the Rev. Peard Dickinson

[Bristol]
March 1786

[In the month of March 1786 I gave him an account of my own state, of the situation of the people, and of the manner in which the Lord was leading me on.] In a few days I received an answer, full of encouragement, and which breathed a spirit of endearing and paternal kindness. This letter concluded with these remarkable words, 'My dear brother, I think you should come *nearer* to your affectionate brother, John Wesley'.[85]

Source: secondary summary; Joseph Benson, *Memoirs of the Life of the Rev. Peard Dickinson* (London: Conference Office, 1803), 52.

To Charles Atmore

Bristol
March 3, 1786

Dear Charles,

Mr. [William] Sagar, I doubt not, has shown you before this what places I propose visiting in the Colne circuit.[86] If you think it best that any alteration should be made, you may send me word in time. I expect to be at Birmingham on Saturday, the 25th instant, and

---

[83] Added at the bottom left corner: 'To the care of / Mr. Henderson / at No. 50 Broad / street, Bristol'. The letter was likely sent over in a packet, along with those to Garrettson and Cromwell.

[84] Thomas Coke added a letter on the back.

[85] A further interchange of letters led to JW meeting with Dickinson in Newark-on-Trent on June 24, 1786; at which time JW invited Dickinson to become his assistant in London for the chapels where sacraments were offered. See Benson, *Memoirs*, 52–55.

[86] See JW to Sagar, Feb. 25, 1786.

ten days after at Manchester. I will administer the Lord's Supper wherever you see good.

O be zealous, especially in enforcing Christian perfection. I am, dear Charles,

Your affectionate friend and brother,   5

J. Wesley

Address: 'To / Mr Atmore / At the Preachinghouse / In Coln / Lanca-
shire'.
Postmark: 'Bristol'.   10
Endorsement: by Atmore, 'From Mr Wesley'.
Source: holograph; Pitts Library (Emory), John Wesley Papers (MSS 153), 3/32.

15

To the Rev. Joseph Taylor[87]

20
Kingswood
March 3, 1786

My Dear Brother,

If you will, take care never to preach too long or too loud, whatever liberty you may find. There is a very thing which hardly fails   25
to strengthen your stomach in a short time. Buy a little carduus at
the apothecary's. Chew a leaf of it every morning, fasting, and swallow your spittle.[88] I think in a week or two you will find a surprising
effect of it.

I am pleased to observe that there is some increase in your cir-   30
cuit, and doubt not that there will be more. Indeed wherever the
doctrine of perfection is insisted on, God will surely both convince,
convert, and sanctify.

If I can go no farther, I hope at last to visit Aberdeen and New-
borough. But I would fain step over to Lady Banff's,[89] unless I meet   35
her in Edinburgh.

---

[87] While the address portion is missing, the letter is surely to Joseph Taylor, Assistant for the Aberdeen circuit.

[88] Cf. *Primitive Physic*, Ailment #223, remedy 2, 32:234 in this edn.

[89] Jean Nisbet (1723–90) was the widow of Alexander Ogilvie (1727–71), 7th Lord Banff. JW had her at her Forglen estate on May 6, 1784; see *Journal*, 23:306–07 in this edn. He would return on May 24, 1790, just months before her death; *Journal*, 24:176.

I am, dear Joseph,
Your affectionate friend and brother,

J. Wesley

Source: holograph; Huntington Library, Manuscripts, HM 57057.

To Samuel Bardsley

Bristol
March 4, 1786

Dear Sammy,

I am glad to hear that God has been pleased to enlarge his work in Scarborough, where I hope to be (on my return from Scotland) about the 14th of June. How the circuits may be more advantageously [divided] is proper to be considered at the Conference.[90]

The alteration which has been made in America and Scotland has nothing to do with our kingdom.[91] I believe I shall not separate from the Church of England till my soul separates from my body.

The life of Mr. John Fox[e] is really remarkable.[92] I do not know but it may be worth while to republish it.

If Mr. [John] Fletcher had travelled like you or me, I believe he would have lived these twenty years.

I am, dear Sammy,
Your affectionate brother,

[J. Wesley]

Address: 'To / Mr. Bardsley / At Capt. [William] Robinson's / In Bridlington Quay / Yorkshire'.
Source: published transcription; Telford, *Letters*, 7:321.

---

[90] A new circuit was established by the 1786 Conference in Pocklington, drawing parts from the Hull, Scarborough and York circuits.

[91] I.e., JW's decision to ordain preachers as elders for North America and Scotland.

[92] A biographical account of John Foxe (1516–87), written by his son, was prefaced to Foxe's *Acts and Monuments*. JW included it in his *Christian Library*, 2:211–34; followed by extended extracts from *Acts and Monuments*. He never republished it separately.

To Hannah Bowmer(?)[93]

Bristol
March 4, 1786

My Dear Sister,

I write freely to you, because I love you. While you are providentially called to this confinement, it will be sanctified to you, and will prove a greater blessing than it would prove if you had more liberty. In this case, private exercises will supply the want of public. So that you will see our Lord does all things for your profit, that you may be a partaker of his holiness.[94]

You have only one thing to do, leaving the first principles of the doctrine of Christ, go on to perfection.[95] Expect continually the end of your faith, the full salvation of your soul. You know, whenever it is given, it is to be received only by naked faith.[96] Therefore who knows but you may receive it *now*? The Lord is nigh at hand, my dear Hannah.[97] Trust him and praise him!

I am

Yours affectionately,

J. Wesley

Address: 'To / Miss Hannah Bowmer / to the care / of Mrs Moore'.
Source: holograph; Drew, Methodist Archives.

---

[93] Telford read the final letter as 'n', and assumed it was the Hannah Bowman JW wrote on Mar. 14, 1789. But that letter was to Hannah (Turpin) Bowman, long married. She had a daughter named Hannah Bowman (1776–1817), but JW's letter does not sound like it is directed to a ten-year old. No convincing alternative identification has been found.

[94] See Heb. 12:10.

[95] See Heb. 6:1.

[96] See note on JW to Francis Wolf, Oct. 25, 1776.

[97] See Luke 21:31.

To John Stretton

London
March 9, 1786

My Dear Brother,

The opposition of Mr. Balfour was only intended to exercise your trust in God.[98] And the issue of it is an additional proof that our Lord has all power in heaven and earth. I believe, before you have lived a year longer, you will [have] all the advantages which your brethren in the southern provinces have.[99]

The more proof you have of him, the more you will be convinced that John McGeary is a workman that needeth not to be ashamed.[100] His one care is to follow Christ:

> To trace his example
> The world to disdain,
> And constantly trample
> On pleasure and pain.[101]

I am,
Your affectionate brother,

J. Wesley

Address: 'To / Mr. John Stretton / In Harbour Grace'.
Source: holograph; WHS Library.

---

[98] Rev. James Balfour (1731–1809, another SPG priest) replaced Laurence Coughlan at Harbour Grace in Oct. 1774. Balfour was critical of Methodists and (with backing of the current governor of Newfoundland, Richard Edwards) in the early 1780s enjoined anyone for leading worship in religious buildings, including the Methodist chapels at Carbonear and Blackhead, who lacked his specific sanction. With a change of governor (to John Campbell, 1782–85) this was appealed and the freedom of Methodists to worship was restored on Oct. 8, 1785.

[99] I.e., the Methodist Episcopal Church in the emerging United States.

[100] See 2 Tim. 2:15. John McGeary had returned to Newfoundland to assist Stretton in fall 1785; it was not working out well; see John Stretton to Elizabeth (Patten) Bennis, Nov. 15, 1785, Bennis, *Christian Correspondence*, 246.

[101] Cf. CW, 'Hymns for Christian Friends, #17', st. 3, *HSP* (1749), 2:284.

To the Rev. Dr. Thomas Coke[102]

Bristol
March 12, 1786 5

Dear Sir,

I greatly approve of your proposal for raising a subscription in order to send missionaries to the Highlands of Scotland, the Islands of Guernsey and Jersey, the Leeward Islands, Quebec, Nova Scotia, and Newfoundland. It is not easy to conceive the extreme want 10 there is in all those places of men that will not count their lives dear unto themselves, so they may testify the gospel of the grace of God.

I am, dear sir,
Your affectionate brother,

John Wesley 15

Source: published transcription; Coke, *Address*, preface.

20

To Robert Carr Brackenbury

Stroud 25
March 14, 1786

Dear Sir,

Miss [Elizabeth] Morgan, now at Bristol, will be much obliged to you if you will be so kind as to speak to a gentleman in Guernsey (perhaps you know something of him, Mr. C. Guiller Jr.[103]), who 30 brought a large box of books for her from France. They are directed to James Ireland, Esq., Bristol. She would be obliged to him if he would send them thither.

---

[102] Thomas Coke had a keen interest in foreign missions, but had recently replied to an inquiry from a director of the East India Company that Methodists had all they could handle at the moment; see Coke to [Charles Grant], Jan. 25, 1786, *AM* 15 (1792): 331–33. Instead he sought to rally support for the Methodist missionary efforts already underway in An Address to the Pious and Benevolent; proposing an annual subscription for the support of missionaries (London: s.n., 1786). JW provided this prefatory letter.

[103] JW's spelling of the last name is a bit unclear. He likely meant Clement Guillaume Jr. (1754–97), of St. Helliers, who was a member of the Methodist society there and contributed to building a chapel; see Lelièvre, *Méthodisme*, 320 n. 1.

Dr. [Thomas] Coke gives us a very pleasing account of the work
of God in Jersey and Guernsey. It is plain, your labour there has
not been in vain. And I am in hopes Guernsey will overtake Jersey.
I am now moving toward Scotland. Perhaps after the Conference, if
5 I live, I may pay one more visit to Holland.
   I am, dear sir,
        Your affectionate friend and brother,

                                                         J. Wesley

10 *Address*: 'To / Robert Brackenbury Esq. / In St Helliers / Isle of Jersey'.
    Source: holograph; Wesley's Chapel (London), LDWMM 1994/1984.

15

To Thomas Tattershall[104]

                                                       Birmingham
20   March 20, 1786
   Dear Tommy,
   I expect to be at Macclesfield April 1st; Manchester, Wednes-
day, 4th; Warrington, Saturday, 15th; Halifax, Monday, 24th; York,
Thursday, May 4th; Newcastle, Friday, 12th; at Newcastle again,
25 June 3rd; at Nottingham, Saturday, July 8th. Then I am to visit
Derby, Hinckley, and Birmingham. I allow two nights for Derby.
Dispose of them in the manner you think best. But I am apt to
imagine it would be most advisable to preach at Belper about noon.
   But is it not best to take Derby in my way from Sheffield to Not-
30 tingham?
   I am, dear Tommy,
        Your affectionate friend and brother,

                                                         J. Wesley

35 Blessed is the man that endureth temptation.[105]

    Source: published transcription; John Lyth, *Glimpses of Methodism in York*
       (York: W. Sessions, 1885), 149.

---

[104] Tattershall was the Assistant for the Derby circuit.
[105] See James 1:12.

To Thomas Cooper[106]

Newcastle-Under-Lyme
March 31, 1786   5

Dear Tommy,

I am glad to hear that sister Cooper begins to recover her health; probably the spring will complete her cure.

It does not appear to me that it will be practicable for you to go into a circuit before the Conference. Wherever you are, the greater   10 plainness of speech you use, the greater blessing you will find.

My best wishes attend sisters Parminter and Cooper.[107] I am, dear Tommy,

     Your affectionate brother,

J. Wesley   15

Address: 'To / Mr Cooper / At Mistley Thorn / Near Manningtree / Essex'.
Postmark: 'Newcastle under Lyme'. *Charge*: '5'.
Source: holograph; MARC, MA 1977/101 (MAM JW 2/57a).   20

To an Unidentified Man   25

Macclesfield
April 3, 1786

My Dear Brother,   30

All I can do at present is this: Ashton[-under Lyme], Rochdale, and Oldham. I must visit Ashton on Friday noon (coming from Manchester and returning thither). I purpose (God willing) to preach at Rochdale.

---

[106] Thomas Cooper (c. 1760–1832) was admitted 'on trial' as an itinerant in 1781 (see 10:507 in this edn.). While assigned to the Colchester circuit 1784–85, he met Ann Parminter (1759–88) in Mistley, Essex. He desisted travelling at the 1785 Conference (10:569), and the couple were married in Nov. 1785. Cooper's mother-in-law built a chapel for him in neighbouring Manningtree; and he formed a society in Harwich. But Cooper was not content so situated, and was reinstated in the connexion in 1787 (10:623). He continued travelling until health issues led to his retirement in 1821. See *Minutes* (post-Wesley, 1833), 7:225; and Cooper's autobiography in *WMM* 14 (1835): 1–14, 81–92.

[107] Ann (Parminter) Cooper's mother was Mary Parminter (maiden name unknown).

I am, my dear brother,
    Your affectionate brother,

J. Wesley

Source: holograph; privately held (transcription provided to Frank Baker).

To the Rev. Charles Wesley

Manchester
April 6, 1786

[[Dear Brother,]]

I am glad you are again able to officiate at the chapels.[108] Let us 'manage wisely the last stake'.[109]

For some years John Davies was a mere mule; he would neither lead nor drive. But it is enough that he finished his course well.[110] And we are sure Nancy Shorland did so.[111]

Sammy Bradburn thought of going further with me. But the frost and snow drove him back. I believe the loss of his wife will be one of the greatest blessings which he has ever met with in his life.[112]

Mrs. [Mary] Fletcher will not be in haste to remove from Madeley, though her light is there almost hid under a bushel.[113] Mr. [James] Ireland will give me no help with regard to writing Mr. Fletcher's *Life*, 'because he intends to publish it himself'![114] Let

---

[108] Replying to a letter from CW that is not known to survive.

[109] Final line of Abraham Cowley's poem 'Age'.

[110] John Davies (c. 1738–86) had been a Methodist for at least 16 years, and joined with George Cussons in founding the Naval and Military Bible Society in 1780. He died on Feb. 27, 1786. A brief account of his life survives among the papers of CW (MARC, MA 1977/501/49). JW spelled 'Davis'.

[111] For Ann Shorland, see JW to Sarah Wesley Jr., Nov. 15, 1780, 29:606 in this edn. JW visited her on Feb. 21, 1786; see *Journal*, 23:385 in this edn. She died on Feb. 25, and was buried at City Road Chapel on Mar. 2. JW again spells the surname 'Sharland'.

[112] Elizabeth (Nangle) Bradburn died on Feb. 11, 1786; see Samuel Bradburn to JW, Feb. 12, 1786. While JW thought Bradburn would flourish as again a single man, he had already met Sophia Cooke on Mar. 15 in Gloucester, and by the 21st had proposed marriage. See Bradburn to JW, June 3, 1786; and Bradburn, *Memoirs*, 103–05.

[113] See Matt 5:15.

[114] Ireland's anticipated publication never appeared.

him do it, and I will *follow him*. Where is your elegy?[115] You may say
(as my father in his verses on Mr. Nelson),

> Let friendship's sacred name excuse
> The last effort of an expiring muse.[116]

Can you or I ever have such another subject?

Melville Horne hopes to be ordained on Trinity Sunday.

Indeed, I love the Church as sincerely as ever I did; and I tell our
societies everywhere, 'The Methodists will not leave the Church, at
least while I live.'

I doubt I shall not half agree with our friends in Scotland.[117] But I
shall know more, and you will hear more, when I see them.

While I live, Dr. [Thomas] Coke and I shall go through Ireland
by turns. He will have work enough this year with gentle Edward
Smyth.[118] I doubt Edward 'needs a bridle'. But who can put the bit
into his mouth?

I am not sorry your concerts are come to an end.[119] Remember your dream concerning Sammy! 'The damsel is not dead, but
sleepeth!'[120]

Mr. Pennant's I know.[121] And Dr. Johnson's I know.[122] But I know
nothing of Mr. Boswell's *Tour to the Hebrides*.[123] I should imagine it
was worth reading.

Peace be with all your spirits!

[[Adieu!]]

[115] JW was hoping to append an elegy by CW to his *Short Account … of Fletcher,* but CW never completed one; cf. JW to Mary Fletcher, Dec. 9, 1786.

[116] Cf. Samuel Wesley Sr., 'On Mr. Nelson', in Robert Nelson, *The Practice of True Devotion*, 3rd edn. (London: Joseph Downing, 1716), xiii–xx (last stanza, p. xx).

[117] CW had likely heard that the preachers JW ordained for Scotland were celebrating the Lord's Supper according to the ritual of the Church of Scotland, rather than the BCP. See Batty, *Scotland*, 30–31.

[118] Smyth would be installed at Bethesda Chapel in Dublin (an evangelical chapel built by his brother William) on June 25, 1786.

[119] The concerts given in CW's home by his two sons took a short break after Apr. 6, 1786; they were held again on Apr. 20 and May 4.

[120] Mark 5:39.

[121] Thomas Pennant, *A Tour in Scotland and Voyage to the Hebrides, 1772,* 2 vols. (London: Benjamin White, 1776).

[122] Samuel Johnson, *Journey to the Western Islands of Scotland* (London: Strahan et al., 1775).

[123] James Boswell, *The Journal of a Tour to the Hebrides, with Samuel Johnson* (London: Charles Dilly, 1785). JW later included excerpts from this work in *AM* 10 (1787): 646, 652; and *AM* 13 (1790): 533–37, 586–90, 653–57.

Address: 'To / The Revd Mr C. Wesley / City Road / London'.
Postmarks: '10/AP' and 'Manchester'.
Endorsement: by CW, 'April 6. 1786 / B[rother]'.
Source: holograph; MARC, DDWes 3/61.

To Hannah Ball

Liverpool
April 13, 1786

My Dear Sister,

I am glad to hear that your society prospers, and that the work of God continues to increase in the town. It always will if prayer meetings are kept up (without interfering with the classes and bands). These have been and still are attended with a blessing in every part of England. And sister [Penelope] Coussins, joining heart and hand with you, may greatly forward the work of God.[124] See that there never be any shyness or coldness between you. Still provoke one another to love and to good works.[125]

But I am sorry that you do not love me. You did once, or I am much mistaken. But if you did so still, you would not barely tell me, and that in general terms only, that you had been in distress—but you would have enlarged upon it and told me all the particulars.[126] What! Do you think I do not care for you? That my love to my dear friend is grown cold? Nay; surely I am as much interested in your happiness now as I was ten years ago. Therefore use as a friend, my dear sister,

Yours as ever,

J. Wesley

My kind love to Nancy.[127]

Address: 'To / Miss Hannah Ball / In High Wycombe / Bucks'.
Postmark: 'Liverpool'. *Charge*: '6'.
Endorsement: '13th April 1786'.
Source: holograph; MARC, MAM JW 1/19.

---

[124] Jonathan Coussins was now Assistant of the Oxfordshire circuit.

[125] See Heb. 10:34.

[126] This was a period which Ball described as 'a long and great conflict with the powers of darkness'; see Ball, *Memoir*, 166.

[127] Her sister Ann Ball.

To Lancelot Harrison

Blackburn
April 17, 1786

My Dear Brother,

When I return out of Scotland, I shall be able to fix my journey through Lincolnshire, of which you will have notice time enough. You may be at the Conference. I would be glad if you would take as particular an account as you possibly can of the disturbances at brother Wilson's house from the beginning till now.[128] When these accounts are sufficiently attested, they may be of great use.

I expect to be at York from May the 4th to the 8th. I am
Your affectionate friend and brother,

J. Wesley

Address: 'To / Mr. Lanct. Harrison / At Mr. Robert Green's / In Louth / Lincolnshire'.
Postmark: 'Blackburn'.
Source: holograph; Drew, Methodist Archives.

To the Rev. Charles Wesley[129]

Keighley
April 18, 1786

[[Dear Brother,]]

My fever lasted hardly three days, and then went away in a violent fit of the cramp.[130] So did a fever I had a year ago.

Eight or ten preachers, it is probable (but I have not met with one yet) will say something about leaving the Church before the Conference ends.[131] It is not unlikely many will be driven out of it where there are Calvinist ministers. The last time I was at Scarborough I

---

[128] The 'disturbances' were likely assumed to be spirits or ghosts—something which JW was very ready to publish in *AM*, but no account specific to this family has been found.

[129] Replying to a letter from CW that is not known to survive.

[130] JW fell ill shortly after reaching Manchester on Friday, April 7; by Monday he was back to his full regular schedule (see JW, Diary, 23:556 in this edn.).

[131] According to JW, the 1786 Conference 'weighed what was said about separating from the Church. But we all determined to continue therein, without one dissenting voice. And I doubt not but this determination will stand, at least till I am removed to a better world.' JW, *Journal*, July 27, 1786, 23:410–11 in this edn.

earnestly exhorted our people to go to church, and I went myself.
But the wretched minister preached such a sermon that I could not
in conscience advise them to hear him any more.[132]

5   *They* will ordain no one without my full and free consent. It is
not true that they *have done* it already. As to the Scots, I have no
hopes of winning them by fair means.[133] If I see Scotland again, I
shall fight with a flail. The work of God goes on gloriously in many
places, and most of the preachers are much devoted to God.

Peace be with you and yours!

10   [[Adieu.]]

Address: 'To / The Revd Mr C. Wesley / City Road / London'.[134]
Postmarks: '25/AP' and 'Penney Post Paid'.
Endorsement: by CW, 'B[rother] April 18 1786'.
15   *Source*: holograph; MARC, DDWes 3/62.

To the Rev. Dr. Thomas Coke[135]

20

c. April 25, 1786

About twenty years ago, I talked with Mr ___ largely on joining
with the Moravians, which I had long desired. I asked him, on what
25   terms they will unite with us? He said, on one condition alone, you
must be *implicit*. Implicitly believe and implicitly obey! Then said I,
we must remain as we are.[136]

Source: secondary transcription; quoted by Coke in a May 8 letter to Ben-
30   jamin La Trobe (Herrnhut, Germany, Unitätsarchiv der Evangelischen Brüder-Unität, R.13.A.43.a).

---

[132] See JW, *Journal*, June 20, 1784, 23:317 in this edn.; and JW to Ann Tindall, Sept. 4,
1784.

[133] See the note on JW to CW, Apr. 6, 1786.

[134] 'City Road' is struck out; replaced with 'Great Chesterfield St. / Marybone'. This
explains the Penney Post marking.

[135] Of his own accord, Coke approached Benjamin La Trobe in late Dec. 1785, trying
to encourage a union between the Moravians and Methodists. He met several times with La
Trobe over the next months, and around Apr. 20, 1786, finally mentioned the venture briefly in
a letter to JW on other subjects (which is not known to survive). For an overview of this venture, which proved unfruitful, see William George Addison, *The Renewed Church of the United
Brethren, 1722–1930* (London: SPCK, 1932), 194–224. For JW's letter, see p. 219.

[136] JW was referring to his exchange with Frances Okeley in 1758; see JW to Okeley, Oct.
4, 1758, 27:135–37 in this edn.

To Samuel Newham[137]

Dewsbury
April 28, 1786

My Dear Brother,   5
I am of the same mind with you. I believe it will be of use for Billy
Palmer to spend another year in Lynn circuit.[138]
Be all in earnest! Leaving the first principles of the gospel of
Christ, go on to perfection![139] Peace be with all your spirits! I am,
Your affectionate brother,   10
J. Wesley

Endorsement: by William Palmer, 'From the Rev. John / Wesley to Samuel
New / ham of Lynn, on my / staying a 2nd year in / Lynn circuit. /
Dewsbury Aprl. 28 1786'.   15
Source: holograph; privately held (WWEP Archive holds photocopy).

To Thomas Carlill[140]   20

near Birstall
April 30, 1786

Dear Tommy,
1. Where will you get five hundred pounds?   25
2. I like the Gainsborough proposal well.
3. We are not a little obliged to Mrs. [Dorothy] Fisher; but advise
her that she may not build a scarecrow house. Epworth house is the
prettiest I remember in Lincolnshire.
If I live till June I hope to see both Gainsborough and Epworth.   30
I am, dear Tommy,
Your affectionate friend and brother,
J. Wesley

---

[137] Samuel Newham (1749–1816), an active Methodist in King's Lynn, would later serve
as architect and builder of a Methodist chapel opened there in 1813. See Henry J. Hillen, *History of the Borough of King's Lynn* (Norwich: East of England, 1907), 549.

[138] William Palmer (c. 1756–1819) was admitted 'on trial' as an itinerant at the 1784 Conference (see 10:553 in this edn.) and assigned to the Norwich circuit. He was made Assistant for
the Lynn circuit at the 1785 Conference (10:569) and returned there by the 1786 Conference
(10:538). Palmer continued as an itinerant until 1817, when he suffered a stroke—dying two
years later. See *Minutes* (post-Wesley, 1820), 5:95.

[139] See Heb. 6:1.

[140] The letter to which JW was replying is not known to survive.

Address: 'To / Mr Carlill / Gainsborough'.
Endorsement: by Carlill, 'J. Wesley / 1789'.
Source: holograph; MARC, MAM JW 2/24.

5

To the Rev. Charles Wesley[141]

10
Leeds
May 3, 1786

[[Dear Brother,]]

If there be a man in England who understands Mrs. Horton['s] case, it is Dr. Wilson.[142] I advise John Horton to find him out if he
15 be above ground.

I do not know that anyone opens your letters. They come to me with the seal unbroken.

As you observe, one may leave *a* church (which I would advise in some cases) without leaving *the* Church. Here we may remain in
20 spite of all wicked or Calvinistical ministers.[143]

Commonly when I am in London, I am so taken up that I cannot often spare time to go three miles backward and forward. That was the πρῶτον ψεῦδος,[144] the getting you an house so far from me, as well as far from both the chapels.

25 I cannot help it if people have no *docity*.[145] Seven guineas Patty has had from me within this month, besides ten or eleven which she has worried me to give Nancy Jarvis this winter.[146]

It is a bad dog that is not worth whistling for. In the times I have been at Bedford, Mr. Barham never owned me, much less invited

---

[141] Replying to a letter from CW that is not known to survive.

[142] Mary Durbin (1752–86), the oldest daughter of Henry Durbin of Bristol, married John Horton of London on Sept. 21, 1780 (JW officiated; see his *Journal* entry for the day). Andrew Wilson, M.D. (1718–92) was now living and practising in London. Mary died on May 4, 1786, before this letter reached CW. A close friend of Henry Durbin, CW wrote a plaintive elegy for Mary; see MS Death of Mary Horton.

[143] See JW to CW, Apr. 18, 1786.

[144] 'The first false step.'

[145] *OED*, 'energy' or 'gumption'.

[146] Referring to his sister Martha (Wesley) Hall, and his great-niece Ann (Lambert) Jarvis. JW spell 'Jervas'.

me to his house.[147] I do not know him if I meet him. Perhaps he
loves me, at a distance.
  Peace be with you and yours!
    [[Adieu.]]

  Pray tell brother [John] Horton and [Richard] Kemp I have had
two letters from Mrs. Holmes (Mr. Holmes's widow) informing me
that John Price has been for some time quite sober and very diligent
in attending the school.[148] In consequence of which she pleads hard
for payment of his salary.
  My route is: Monday, [May] 8, Thirsk; Wednesday, 10, Barnard
Castle; Saturday, 13, and Wednesday, 17, Edinburgh and Wednesday, 31; Tuesday, 23, Aberdeen.

Address: 'To / The Revd Mr C. Wesley / City Road / London'.
Postmarks: 'Leeds' and '6/MA'. *Charge*: '6'.
Endorsement: by CW, 'B[rother]. May 3 / 1786'.
Source: holograph; MARC, DDWes 3/63.

To David Leslie, 6th Earl of Leven[149]

Richmond
May 9, 1786
My Lord,
  If it be convenient, I purpose to wait upon your Lordship at Melville House about 2:00 in the afternoon on Friday on the 22nd instant.[150] Wishing all happiness to your Lordship and all your good
family, I am, my Lord,

[147] Joseph Foster Barham (1729–89) was a prominent Moravian in Bedford, the widowed
husband of Dorothea (Vaughan) Barham, a Welsh family of JW's acquaintance. CW was in
current conversation with Benjamin La Trobe (as a counterbalance to Thomas Coke) about
fostering closer connections between Methodists and Moravians, and had apparently urged
JW to seek out Barham while in Bedford. See the note on JW to Thomas Coke, c. Apr. 25, 1786.
  [148] These letters are not known to survive.
  [149] David Leslie, 6th Earl of Leven (1722–1802) was currently the High Commissioner to
the General Assembly of the Church of Scotland, which was surely one of the reasons that JW
hoped to see him. But JW's contact with this family was likely through his wife, Wilhelmina
Nesbit (c. 1724–98), the sister of Jean Nesbit (Lady Banff). See JW to Joseph Taylor, Mar. 3,
1786.
  [150] JW's schedule changed a bit. JW reached Melville House (about a mile east of Col-
lessie) on May 19, 1786. He met the Countess Wilhelmina, along with her daughters and sons-
in-law; but Lord Leven was in Edinburgh. See JW, *Journal*, 23:312 in this edn.

Your Lordship's obedient servant,

John Wesley

Source: holograph; MARC, MAM JW 3/88.

5

To Ann (Bignell) Brisco[151]

Richmond
10   May 10, 1786

Dear Sister,

The work of God is, I am afraid, much hindered in Thirsk by the misunderstanding between Mr. Oastler and Mr. Taylor.[152] If it be possible, an end should be put to this. They should in any wise meet 15   and compromise matters. That things should stand as they are is a scandal to religion.

I have known *you* for many years. You love to do good. Forward this reconciliation, and you will oblige many, as well as, my dear sister,

20   Yours affectionately,

J. Wesley

Source: holograph; MARC, MAM JW 2/14.

25

To James Copeland[153]

Glasgow
May 14, 1786

30 My Dear Brother,

There is no reasonable doubt you had at the time you mention a real blessing from God. I make no question but he did then give

[151] Ann's husband Thomas was one of the preachers assigned to the Thirsk circuit. JW had preached in Thirsk on May 8, 1786, at which time he became aware of the issue addressed.

[152] The first person is almost certainly Robert Oastler (1749–1820), a cloth merchant, who was one of three men with that surname listed on the current deed for the preaching house in Thirsk. His uncle Samson Oastler had died in Feb. 1786; leaving only John Oastler as the other possibility. Robert Oastler had taken an active role, along with James Oddie, in a petition to qualify the Deed of Declaration the previous year (see Oastler to Oddie, June 4 and June 24, 1785 in in-letters). The second person may be William Taylor, a bridle cutter, who was a trustee of the preaching-house in 1766, but left the Methodist society in 1771. See John Ward, *Methodism in the Thirsk Circuit* (Thirsk: David Peat, 1860), 14–15.

[153] James Copeland (1750–1815) settled in Lisbellaw about 1778. He hosted JW at his home there on May 29, 1787. See Crookshank, *Ireland*, 432; and *WHS* 6 (1907), 46n.

you a taste of his pardoning love. But you was not then thoroughly convinced of inbred sin, of the sin of your nature. God is now convincing you of this, in order to give you a clean heart. And Satan strives hereby to drive you to despair. But regard him not. Look unto Jesus![154] Dare to believe! On Christ lay hold![155] Wrestle with Christ in mighty prayer. Yea,

> A sigh will reach his heart! A look
> Will bring him down from heaven.[156]

He is at hand![157]
 I am
  Your affectionate brother,

J. Wesley

Endorsement: 'Written to Late / Mr James Copeland / Lisbellaw'.
Source: holograph; Wesley's Chapel (London), LDWMM 1998/7127.

To the Rev. Dr. Thomas Coke[158]

Edinburgh
May 17, 1786

I see no possible objection to Mr. La Trobe's proposal so far as you have gone yet.[159] The steps you mention may certainly be taken without any manner of danger, and this is all that can be done at present. I am exceeding willing to have a private conference with Mr. La Trobe; but it is certain that nothing that passes therein should be spoken out of it, inasmuch as the premature mention of

---

[154] See Heb. 12:2.

[155] See Phil. 3:12.

[156] Cf. CW, 'After a Relapse into Sin', st. 7, *HSP* (1742), 141.

[157] See Phil. 4:5.

[158] Replying to Coke's letter of May 6, 1786, in which Coke informed JW of discussions he had been holding with Benjamin La Trobe about greater cooperation, or even union, between Methodists and Moravians. Cf. the note on JW to Coke, c. Apr. 25, 1786.

[159] Rev. Benjamin La Trobe (1727–86) was born in Dublin, of Huguenot ancestry, and raised a Baptist. He was converted to the evangelical revival by John Cennick (now a Moravian) in 1746. Over the next year La Trobe played a role in transforming the initial Methodist work at Skinner's Alley, Dublin, into a Moravian society. La Trobe moved to England and became a leading figure in the Moravian community there, but one who continued to seek a union of Methodists and Moravians. See *DEB*, 663–64.

anything might frustrate our whole design. Undoubtedly nothing is more desirable than a cordial union among the children of God. I am not conscious of having neglected any step which had a tendency to this. And I am as ready now as ever I was to do anything
5   that is in my power to promote it.

Source: secondary transcription; copied by Coke in a June 7 letter to Benjamin La Trobe (Herrnhut, Germany, Unitätsarchiv der Evangelischen Brüder-Unität, R.13.A.43.a).[160]

10

To the Rev. Charles Wesley[161]

near Edinburgh
May 18, 1786
15
Dear Brother,

So sister [Mary] Horton is in peace! This may be a blessed visitation for Mr. [John] Horton.[162] Perhaps it will prove in the event one of the greatest blessings which he ever received in his life. I hope
20   you have wrote to Mr. Durbin.[163] Alas, what do riches avail him!

Certainly providence *permitted* injudicious men to thrust you three miles from me, who should rather have been always at my elbow.[164]

I doubt whether there be not an anachronism in the case of John
25   Price; whether they do not *now* impute to him what was done long ago.[165]

My journal[-letter] should have been sent several days since, but Joseph Bradford trusted another person to transcribe it. This society flourishes much.
30   I hope to be here again on the 31st instant.

Peace be with you all!

[[Adieu.]]

Endorsement: by CW, 'B[rother] May 18. 1786'.
Source: holograph; MARC, DDWes 3/64.
35

[160] Cf. Addison, *Renewed Church*, 221–22.
[161] CW's letter, to which JW was replying, is not known to survive.
[162] See JW to CW, May 3, 1786.
[163] Henry Durbin (1718–99), father of Mary (Durbin) Horton, was an apothecary in Bristol. Henry and his wife Hester (Thrilby) Durbin were early members in the Wesleyan work in Bristol, with Henry serving as a trustee of the New Room chapel. They were also close friends with CW and his wife Sarah.
[164] At his house on Great Chesterfield Street; see JW to CW, May 3, 1786.
[165] See ibid.

To John King

My Dear Brother,

I could easily contrive one of these two things: either that you should be stationed near home, or that Adam Clarke and you should be in the same circuit.[166] But I do not know how I can contrive both. He and you do well to 'redeem the time',[167] to improve every hour. Life is short, and a long eternity is at hand. I am,

Your affectionate brother,

[J. Wesley]

Source: published transcription; *Memorials of the Rev. William Toase* (London: Wesleyan Conference Office, 1874), 189.

To Lancelot Harrison

My Dear Brother,

I hope to be at Epworth on Wednesday, the 21st instant; at Grimsby on Thursday, the 22nd; at Horncastle on Friday, 23rd; and at Gainsborough on Saturday, the 24th. You will take care that timely notice be given at every place.

Strongly and explicitly exhort all the believers to go on to perfection.[168] Then their soul will live.

I am, with love to sister [Elizabeth] Harrison,

Your affectionate friend and brother,

J. Wesley

Address: 'To / Mr Lancelot Harrison / At Great Grimsby / Lincolnshire'.
Postmark: 'Newcastle'.
Source: holograph; Bridwell Library (SMU).[169]

---

[166] King and Clarke were currently both assigned to the Plymouth circuit. They were separated the following year.

[167] Cf. Eph. 5:16.

[168] See Heb. 6:1.

[169] Held previously in the WMC Museum, 2002.001.023.

To Catherine Warren[170]

Sunderland
June 8, 1786

My Dear Sister,

I am glad our brethren are aware of that bold bad man, who has bid adieu both to conscience and shame.[171] Their wisdom is now, not to think of him or talk of him at all. I am afraid he would turn Calvinist, Turk, or anything for food and idleness.

Mr. [John] Valton has not been able to preach in two years so much as he used to do in eight or ten months. Every year I have many applications for the continuance of profitable preachers more than two years in a circuit. I have had several such within these two or three months, as well as the continence of two preachers in the same circuit. But I dare not comply. I advise Mr. Cole to instruct the next preachers thoroughly in the nature of the case, and to encourage them to persist in the whole Methodist discipline.[172]

I hope you are not weary of well-doing, and that you will never bury your talent in the earth.[173] Your labour has not been in vain, and in due time you will reap if you faint not.[174] It is always a pleasure to me to see you, and I love to converse with you. But sometimes it has been a concern to me that I could see you so seldom. There is something in your spirit that is exceedingly agreeable to me. I find in you sprightliness and sweetness joined together. May you be filled, my dear Kitty, with the whole fruit of the Spirit![175] This is the constant wish of

Yours most affectionately,

J. Wesley

Source: holograph; Drew, Methodist Archives.

---

[170] While the address portion is missing, the content makes the recipient clear.

[171] William Moore, see JW to Warren, July 25, 1785.

[172] Joseph Cole (c. 1748–1826) was admitted 'on trial' as an itinerant in 1780 (10:496). He remained under assignment for 35 years, dying on June 8, 1826; see *Minutes* (post-Wesley, 1826), 6:108–09. Cole was currently posted in the Pembroke circuit, and remained as Assistant for the circuit the following year.

[173] See Matt. 25:25.

[174] See Gal. 6:9.

[175] See Gal. 5:22.

To Henry Brooke

Whitby
June 14, 1786

Dear Henry,

I will give you an answer to your heart's content.[176]

In the year 1729 four young gentlemen joined together at Oxford, all zealous members of the Church of England, and all determined to be Bible Christians. In six years they increased to sixteen, and were exactly of the same mind still. In 1738 only two of these were left together; but a few more joined them, who continually increased till some hundreds were joined together. But they still constantly attended the Church—only if any Dissenter desired to unite with them, they had no objection to his attending that worship to which he had been accustomed.

But in 1740 Dr. [Edmund] Gibson, then Bishop of London, said, 'Cannot Messrs. Wesleys leave the Church? Then they could do no more harm.' This we well understood. It meant, 'They could do no more good; for not one in ten of their present hearers would hear them.'[177] But whether they would or no, we would not leave it. Our conscience would not permit.

In 1743 the Rules of our society were published; one of which was, 'to attend the Church and sacrament'.[178] This all our members (except Dissenters) were required to do, or they could not remain with us.

In 1744, at our first Conference, we considered ourselves (Methodist preachers) as extraordinary messengers whom God had raised up to provoke to jealousy the ordinary messengers, the clergy; to preach the gospel to the poor, and to call all men of every denomination to worship him in spirit and in truth.[179]

But it did not once come into our mind to separate from the Church or form ourselves into a distinct party. And herein was a new phenomenon in the earth, a thing never seen before, a body of men highly favoured of God, who yet chose to abide in their own religious community and not to separate themselves, from this very motive, that they might be servants of all.

---

[176] Replying to Brooke's letter of c. June 4, 1786. This reply is more extensive than JW's reflections of Aug. 30, 1785 (which had not yet been published). Like those reflections, JW ignores here the ordinations for Scotland, which had spurred Brooke to write!

[177] See JW to Thomas Taylor, Feb. 21, 1786, with note.

[178] Cf., *General Rules*, §6, 9:72–73 in this edn.; and 'Directions given to the Band Societies', III.1, 9:79.

[179] See John 4:24.

But it was not easy to keep to this resolution. For those among us who had been Dissenters were frequently urging those words, 'Come out from among them, and be ye separate.'[180] And many of the clergy strengthened their hands, either by their railing and ly-
5 ing accusations or by their wicked lives or false doctrines—whereby many were hardened in sin, and many who began to run well returned as a dog to his vomit.[181]

These objections were so frequently and strongly urged that in the year 1755 it was fully considered in the Leeds Conference 'whether
10 we should separate from the Church or no'.[182] After weighing the whole matter calmly, we determined upon the negative. Mr. [Benjamin] Ingham, being present, commended our determination in very strong terms—concluding whenever the Methodists leave the Church [of England], God will leave them.

15 To prevent it, we all agreed: 1) to exhort all our people constantly to attend the Church and sacrament; and 2) still to preach on Sundays, morning and evening, not in the church hours.[183] Indeed by taking the contrary steps, by exhorting our people not to go to Church, or (which came to the same thing) by appointing to preach
20 in the church hours, we should separate from it at once.

Last year the case of our brethren in North America was considered, wholly cut off both from the English Church and State. In so peculiar a case I believed it my duty to take an extraordinary step in order to send them all the help I could.[184] And I bless God it has had an admirable effect.
25
'But why', say some, 'should not you take the same step here?' Because it is not the same case. They separate from nobody. They had no Church, alas! No king! We have both.

'Well, but weigh their reasons. Should we go to Church to hear ourselves abused, by railing; yea, and lying accusations?' What said
30 that blessed man Philip Henry, when his friend said (after hearing such a sermon), 'I hope, sir, you will not go to Church any more?' 'Indeed, I will go in the afternoon; if the minister does not know his duty, I bless God I know mine.'[185]

[180] 2 Cor. 6:17.

[181] See Prov. 26:11; 2 Pet. 2:22.

[182] Orig., 'in 1758', a faulty remembrance. See the document JW prepared in advance for this meeting; 9:567–80 in this edn.

[183] The brief 'Minutes' of the 1755 Conference do not include this resolution; see 10:270–71 in this edn.

[184] See JW to our 'American Brethren', Sept. 10, 1784.

[185] Cf. Matthew Henry, *An Account of the Life and Death of the Rev. Philip Henry* (London: Parkhurst & Lawrence, 1698), 160; retained by JW in his abridgement in the Christian Library, 50:106.

We are members of the Church of England. We are no particular sect or party. We are friends to all. We quarrel with none for their opinions or mode of worship. We love those of the Church wherein we were brought up, but we impose them upon none. In some unessential circumstances we vary a little from the usual modes of worship, and we have several little prudential helps peculiar to ourselves. But still we do not, will not, dare not separate from the Church till we see other reasons than we have seen yet. Till then I say with St. Austin (only taking the word 'heretic' in the scriptural sense, which has nothing to do with opinions), '*Errare possum, haereticus esse nolo.*'[186]

I am, dear Harry,
Yours very affectionately,

John Wesley

Source: secondary manuscript transcription; MARC, MA 1977/489, pp. 26–28.

To Jasper Winscom

Epworth
June 17, 1786

Dear Jasper,
I am afraid your attorney at the Assizes was greatly wanting, either in skill or honesty. Otherwise why did he not move the court for costs of suit.[187] These ought to be borne by those that are cast in any trial. As to commencing another prosecution, I know not what to say. I can neither advise one way nor the other.

I am
Your affectionate brother,

J. Wesley

Source: manuscript transcriptions (19th century), MARC, MA 1977/485, p. 322; and Duke, Rubenstein, Frank Baker Collection of Wesleyana, VOLS 7, Letter book 10, p. 29.

---

[186] 'I may err, but I will not be a heretic.' The exact quote does not appear in Augustine's writings, but JW would have known it from Izaak Walton, *The Life of Richard Hooker* (London: Richard Marriott, 1670), 83, where Hooker attributes the quote to St. Austin (it may be Hooker's gloss on Augustine's De Trinitate, I.3.5). JW's brief abridgement of Walton's *Life of Hooker* in *Christian Library* (27:92–110) omits a large section that includes the quote.
[187] Likely relating to the matter discussed in JW to Winscom, May 9, 1785.

To Samuel Bradburn[188]

Crowle
June 20, 1786

5 Dear Sammy,

As soon as I saw you and Sophy Cooke together at Gloucester it came into my mind at once, 'There is a wife for Bradburn' (though I did not tell anybody). I was therefore nothing surprised the other day when I received hers and your letters, and I am inclined to think

10 London will be the best place both for you and her. It will be safer for you to *visit* Gloucester now and then, than it would be to reside there.[189] As to your children, two of them may be kept abroad, as they are now.[190] And I imagine that, as our family is not very large, Sophy would very well supply the place of an housekeeper. But this

15 should be a time of much prayer to you both.

I am, dear Sammy,

Your affectionate friend and brother,

[J. Wesley]

Source: published transcription; Telford, *Letters*, 7:334.

20

To Sophia Cooke[191]

25   Crowle
June 20, 1786

Surely, my dear Sophy, you never can have need to use any ceremony with me! You know I love you. Therefore you may think

30 aloud, and tell me all that is in your heart. As soon as ever I saw Mr. [Samuel] Bradburn and you together, I believed you would be more nearly united. His former wife [Elizabeth] never wanted [i.e., lacked] anything; neither need any of our preachers' wives. They

---

[188] Replying to Bradburn's letter of June 3, 1786, which informed JW of Bradburn's desire to marry Sophia Cooke; on Cooke, see next letter.

[189] Since Sophia's uncle was an alderman in Gloucester, both JW and Bradburn worried Bradburn would be drawn from his focus on ministry there.

[190] Samuel was currently stationed in Bristol; his two older children were likely kept at Kingswood.

[191] Sophia Cooke (c. 1759–1834) was the daughter of John and Elizabeth (Weaver) Cooke, of Gloucester. She had written JW separately from Samuel Bradburn, seeking his advice about their potential marriage. Her letter to JW is not known to survive. The couple were wed on Aug. 10, 1786 and moved to London, where Samuel was stationed.

neither want nor abound. They have all things needful for life and godliness.

But I am not a *fair* judge. I am partial. I long so much to have you under my own roof that I cannot divest myself of prejudice in the matter. I can only say, 'Give yourself to prayer; and then act, in   5
the name and in the fear of God, as you are fully persuaded in your own mind.'

I am, my dear Sophy,
    Yours affectionately,

                                      J. Wesley   10

Address: 'To / Miss Sophia Cooke / at Thomas Weaver's Esq[192] / In King
    Street / Glocester'.
Source: holograph; MARC, MAM JW 2/57.

                                                  15

To Adam Clarke[193]

                                          Sheffield
                                    July 2, 1786   20
Dear Adam,

I really know not what to say. Many desire that you should be in Bradford circuit next year. And I imagined it was your own desire, which therefore I intended to comply with. But if you think you could do more good in another place you may be in another.   25

I commend you for staying in the Dock during the Conference.[194] Brother [John] King may either come or stay with you, as you shall agree. Be much in prayer, and God will direct you right.

I am, dear Adam,
    Yours affectionately,   30

                                        J. Wesley

Address: 'To / Mr Adam Clark / At the Preachinghouse / in / Plymouth
    Dock'.
Postmark: 'Sheffield'.   35
Source: holograph; Bridwell Library (SMU).

[192] Thomas Weaver (d. 1805), Sophia Cooke's uncle, was a pinmaker and since 1779 had been an alderman for the city of Gloucester.

[193] Replying to Clarke's letter of June 19, 1786, wherein he echoed John King's earlier letter that the two of them would like to serve together again the following year.

[194] While JW had invited Clarke to Conference, Clarke demurred because it would leave the circuit shorthanded at a time when William Moore and others were trying to draw away Methodists.

To Thomas Rankin

Sheffield
July 2, 1786

5 Dear Tommy,

I hope to be in Birmingham on Tuesday, the eleventh instant, and to take the mail coach on Wednesday evening. So (if God permit) I shall be in London on Thursday morning. I shall very willingly hide myself at your house on Friday and Saturday. The rather because I 10 can then confer with Henry Moore and you on many heads without interruption.[195] I am glad to get my brother to the Conference on any terms, although he can ill be spared from London.[196] I do not know but our friend may hold out till Michaelmas, as afflicted as he is for the loss of his dear Betsy, before he takes a second.[197] I hope 15 to be in Bristol five or six days before the Conference. What if you and I and Moore, and his wife [Anne] took the whole mail coach for the 18th or 19th instant?

Peace be with all your spirits. I am, dear Tommy,
Your affectionate brother,

20 J. Wesley

Address: 'To / Mr. Rankin / In North Green / Moorfields / London'.
Source: published transcription; *Wesley's Chapel Magazine* 8.29 (March 1938): 16.

25

To Francis Wrigley[198]

30 Nottingham
July 7, 1786

My Dear Brother,

You are to stay in Redruth circuit another year. I think Charles Bond need not come to the Conference.

35

[195] The topics surely included the push of some preachers to declare separation from the Church of England and JW's intent to ordain five more preachers to serve in Scotland and North America.

[196] CW did attend the 1786 Conference; it was his last.

[197] JW was referring to the pending marriage of Samuel Bradburn and Sophia Cooke (see his letters to each on June 20, 1786). They were wed on Aug. 10, rather than waiting till Michaelmas (Sept. 29).

[198] Wrigley was currently Assistant over the Redruth circuit, with Charles Bond assigned under him.

You should not have paid for Michael Moorhouse's letters, but redirected them to him.[199]

I expect immediately after the Conference to go and take leave of my friends in Holland.[200] There is a considerable increase of the work of God this year almost in every part of the kingdom. Indeed, we have good encouragement to put forth all our strength. I am
    Your affectionate friend and brother,

J. Wesley

Address: 'To / Mr Wrigley / At the Preachinghouse / In Truro / Cornwall'.
Postmarks: 'Nottingham' and '8/IY'.
Source: holograph; Bridwell Library (SMU).

To an Unidentified Methodist Layman

London
July 15, 1786

My Dear Brother,
    For fear I should have less leisure when I come to Bristol, I write a few lines now. I shall be glad to see you and our brothers at the Conference the week after next. On the Wednesday or Thursday in that week we shall have finished our temporal business.[201]
    I am
        Your affectionate brother,

[J. Wesley]

Source: published transcription; Telford, *Letters*, 7:336.

---

[199] JW is referring to the circular letter that Moorhouse sent out to every itinerant c. June 10, 1786 (see in-letters file for a description). This action led the 1786 Conference to expel Moorhouse 'for malice and obstinacy'; see 10:597n in this edn.

[200] JW spent the last three weeks of Aug. 1786 in Holland.

[201] One of the main topics of the 1786 Conference was the renewed efforts by some to separate from the Church of England. Given the importance of the issue, after dealing in closed session the first two days with matters of the character of the preachers, JW records: 'On Thursday in the afternoon we permitted any of the society to be present and weighed what might be said about separating from the Church.' See *Journal*, July 27, 1786, 23:410 in this edn.

To Sarah [M'Kim][202]

Bristol
July 21, 1786

5   My Dear Sister,
    You do well to write. I am well pleased to hear you do not let go
the blessing which God has given you. See that you hold fast the
beginning of your confidence steadfast unto the end![203] And you
know, there are still greater blessings behind! There is no end of his
10 goodness.
    If any of our brethren in Sligo will give you a guinea, he may re-
ceive it again of Mr. [James] Rogers in Dublin.
    I am, dear Sally,
        Yours affectionately,
15   J. Wesley

Source: holograph; MARC, WCB, D5/38.

20

To Catherine Warren

Bristol
July 21, 1786[204]

25 My Dear Sister,
    Every day's experience confirms the truth of that observation that

    Love, like death, makes all distinctions void.[205]

30 If I was sitting by you just now and taking hold of your hand, I
should feel we were one, neither of us higher or lower than the
other. I have loved you ever since I knew you; and the longer, the
better. How dearly shall we love one another when we come into
our own country?

---

[202] The address portion is missing, but this is almost certainly Sarah M'Kim, the 'old dis-
ciple' Matthew Lanktree visited in Sligo in 1796–97, who 'had letters from several preachers,
one of them from Mr. Wesley'. See Lanktree, *A Biographical Narrative of Matthew Lanktree*
(Belfast: James Wilson, 1836), 56.

[203] See Heb. 3:14.

[204] While the date is written clearly, one wonders if JW meant instead July 31. The ordinations assumed in this letter took place on July 28–29 (see Appendix B).

[205] Matthew Prior, *Solomon*, ii.242.

Mr. [Joshua] Keighley is waiting for a ship.[206] So is Mr. [William] Warrener and two or three more of our preachers, who are minded to go over to America by the first opportunity.[207] For anything I see, we shall send over no more after these. America is now nearly able to provide for itself. Next month I shall probably take leave of my 5 friends in Holland, till we meet in a better world.

I promised to let Mr. [Charles] Atmore labour for one year among his own relations.

A year longer I will continue my little subscription.[208] Then I hope your burden will be removed. 10

I ever am, my dear Kitty,

Yours most affectionately,

J. Wesley

Address: 'To / Miss Warren / in / Haverford West'. 15
Postmark: 'Bristol'.
Source: holograph; New York, Pierpont Morgan Library, MA 7306.

20

To Edward Jackson[209]

Bristol
July 22, 1786
25
My Dear Brother,

It is quite proper for those that live in the [preaching-]house to have the management of the sale of books, which is of more importance as to the … assuring the work of God than one can easily imagine. Both your fellow labourers are not only stout active men, 30 but also are alive to God and will go on with you hand in hand.[210] I advise you to read over carefully the large *Minutes* of the Conference, and to observe them in *every part*.

---

[206] JW ordained Keighley for service in Scotland during the 1786 Conference.

[207] In addition to Warrener (to serve in the West Indies), JW ordained John Clarke and William Hammet (for Newfoundland) during the 1786 Conference.

[208] For the debt on the preaching-house; see JW to Warren, July 25, 1785.

[209] Jackson had been stationed on the Colne circuit in 1785, serving under Charles Atmore as Assistant. With Atmore now going to Scotland, Jackson was being named Assistant of the circuit for 1786, and had raised some questions to JW about this.

[210] The preachers assigned to assist Jackson on the Colne circuit for 1786 were Samuel Bardsley and James Ridall.

Then the work of the Lord will surely prosper in your hands. I am, dear Neddy,

Your affectionate friend and brother,

J. Wesley

Address: 'To / Mr Jackson / At the Preaching House / In Coln / Lanca-shire'.

Source: published transcription; *WHS* 20 (1935): 63.

To the Methodist Preachers and Societies[211]

Bristol
July 22, 1786

After Dr. [Thomas] Coke's return from America, many of our friends begged I would consider the case of Scotland, where we had been labouring so many years and had seen so little fruit of our labours. Multitudes indeed have set out well, but they were soon turned out of the way—chiefly by their ministers either disputing against the truth or refusing to admit them to the Lord's Supper; yea, or to baptize their children, unless they would promise to have no fellowship with the Methodists. Many who did so soon lost all they had gained, and became more the children of hell than before.[212] To prevent this, I at length consented to take the same step with regard to Scotland which I had done with regard to America. But this is not a separation from the Church at all. Not from the Church of Scotland, for we were never connected therewith, any further than we are now; not from the Church of England, for this is not concerned in the steps which are taken in Scotland.[213] What-

---

[211] While JW ignored his most recent ordination of preachers for Scotland in his earlier reply to the charge that his act of ordaining amounted to a separation from the Church of England (see the public letter of Aug. 30, 1785 above), this second instance served to intensify calls from many of his preachers and followers to *separate* from the Church. It also drew renewed warnings from Church-Methodists like Henry Brooke (see his letter of July 4, 1786) and CW (see his letter to JW of July 27, 1786). JW prepared this response just prior to the 1786 Conference, where the possibility of separation was a focus of debate—but rejected. He then appended it to the Minutes of that Conference as a public letter.

[212] See Matt. 23:15.

[213] JW was ignoring the small non-established episcopal Church of Scotland at this point.

ever then is done either in America or Scotland is no separation from the Church of England. I have no thought of this. I have many objections against it. It is a totally different case.

'But for all this, is it not possible there may be such a separation after you are dead?' Undoubtedly it is. But what I said at our first Conference, above forty years ago, I say still: 'I dare not omit doing what good I can while I live, for fear of evils that may follow when I am dead.'[214]

John Wesley

Source: published transcription; *Minutes* (1786), 21–22.[215]

To James Gildart [via Lawrence Frost][216]

Bristol
July 29, 1786

Sir,

Some preachers in connexion with me have thought it their duty to call sinners to repentance even in the open air. If they have violated any law thereby, let them suffer the penalty of that law. But if not, whoever molests them on that account will be called to answer it in his majesty's court of King's Bench. I have had a suit already in that court with a magistrate (Heap), and if I am forced to it, am ready to commence another.[217]

I am, sir,
> Your obedient servant,

John Wesley

Source: published transcription; Tyerman, *John Wesley*, 3:486.

---

[214] Cf. 'Minutes', June 27, 1744, Q. 12, 10:136 in this edn.

[215] See 10:616–17 in this edn. In addition to the separate pamphlet of the *Minutes*, the letter was included in an extract of the *Minutes* published in *AM* 9 (Dec. 1786): 677–78.

[216] James Gildart (1750–1811) was the current mayor of Liverpool. Lawrence Frost (1743–1826) was a leader of the Methodist society in Liverpool—see JW's subsequent letter of Oct. 23, 1789; and Thomas P. Bunting, *The Life of Jabez Bunting* (London: Longman et al., 1859), 1:85n. At the 1786 Conference JW learned that one of his preachers had been interrupted while preaching in a public setting. He sent this letter to Frost, to deliver to the mayor.

[217] The state of records is such that we have not been able to locate this case.

To Richard Terry

Bristol
July 30, 1786

5 My Dear Brother,

We entirely disapprove of such a d⟨ivision⟩[218] of the Hull circuit as has b⟨een⟩ sent to us.[219] We totally reject the thought ⟨of a⟩ preacher staying a fortnight together in ⟨one⟩ place. There is no precedent of this in ⟨all⟩ England, nor shall be as long as I live. ⟨I⟩

10 have desired those of our brethren who ⟨are⟩ acquainted with this and the neighbouring ⟨circuits⟩ to draw up a Methodist plan. They have ⟨done⟩ so, and I like it well.[220] None of our preachers must ⟨be⟩ still while I live.

I am, my dear brother,

15   Your affectionate brother,

J. Wesley

Address: 'To / Mr. Terry / in / Hull'.
Postmarks: 'Bristol' and '2/AU'. *Charge*: '8'.
20 *Source*: holograph; New York, Pierpont Morgan Library, MA 516.14.

25 # To the Methodist Preachers and Societies[221]

Bristol
August 1, 1786

30 Perhaps there is one part of what I wrote some time since which requires a little further explanation. In what cases do we allow of service in church hours? I answer:

---

[218] A strip along the right margin (on a fold-seam) is missing. It affects about one word in each line. The missing text is fairly obvious.

[219] The plan for the division of the Hull circuit, which Richard Terry sent to be considered at the 1786 Conference, is not known to survive. Cf. JW to Samuel Bardsley, Mar. 4, 1786.

[220] Written on two sides of the leaf (in another hand) is a list of preaching locations in the circuit, with days of the week that preachers shall be present. The preachers move daily. Cf. Telford, *Letters*, 7:337n.

[221] At the 1786 Conference Thomas Coke argued during a public session that Methodist services ought to be held in church hours in large towns because nearly all the awakened clergy were Calvinists. On hearing this CW shouted 'No.'—reportedly the only word he spoke at this Conference (see John Pawson manuscript report in MARC, MA 1977/486, p. 61). This drew forth from JW an open letter, dated the last day of Conference, and appended to its *Minutes*.

1. When the minister is a notoriously wicked man.

2. When he preaches Arian or any equally pernicious doctrine.

3. When there are not churches in the town sufficient to contain half the people; and

4. When there is no Church [of England] at all within two or three miles. And we advise everyone who preaches in the church hours to read the Psalms and Lessons with part of the Church prayers; because we apprehend this will endear the Church service to our brethren, who probably would be prejudiced against it if they heard none but extemporary prayer.

John Wesley

Source: published transcription; *Minutes* (1786), 22–23.[222]

For Charles Atmore
Testimonial Letter[223]

[Bristol]
[August 1, 1786]

To all to whom these presents shall come, John Wesley, M.A., late fellow of Lincoln College in Oxford, sendeth greeting.

Whereas it has been represented to me that many of the people called Methodists under my care in north Britain [i.e., Scotland] stand in need at present of proper persons to administer the sacraments of baptism and the Lord's Supper among them, I therefore do make known unto all men that I did on the twenty-ninth day of July last solemnly set apart for the office of an elder in the church of God, by the imposition of my hands and prayer (being assisted herein by other ordained ministers), and with a single eye to the glory of God, Charles Atmore, whom I judge to be a proper person to administer the sacraments of baptism and the Lord's Supper.

[222] See 10:617–18 in this edn. In addition to the separate pamphlet of the *Minutes*, the letter was included in an extract of the Minutes published in *AM* 9 (Dec. 1786): 677–78. A set of advices for preachers appears after this letter in *Minutes*, but was not included in the extract in *AM*, so it is not included here.

[223] This is one of only two known testimonial letters for the five persons that JW ordained first deacon, then elder, on July 28–29, 1786, during Conference, of which there is surviving record of the text (the other is that for William Warrener below). For background and more details see Appendix B.

And I do recommend him as such to all whom it may concern. In testimony whereof I have hereunto set my hand and seal the first day of August, in the year of our Lord one thousand seven hundred and eighty-six.

5
John Wesley

Source: secondary manuscript transcriptions; MARC, MA 1977/478 and
MA 1977/502/3/2.

10

To Josiah Dornford[224]

15
Bristol
August 1, 1786

Dear Sir,
   Go on in the name of God and in the power of his might![225] If
20 he sees, and when he sees best, he will put more talents into your hands. In the meantime, it is your wisdom to make the full use of those which you have! Only taking care not to trust in yourself, but in him that raiseth the dead.[226]
   I am
25   Your affectionate brother,
J. Wesley

Address: 'To / Josiah Dornford Esq / In Philpot Lane'.
Endorsement: by Dornford, 'The Revd. Mr Wesley / Aug 11th 1786'.
30 *Source*: holograph; University of Sydney (Australia), Rare Books and Special Collections Library, Wesley College Collection.

[224] Josiah Dornford (1734–1810) was a wine merchant and justice of the peace for the county of Kent. He was born at Deptford, and after his conversion joined the local Methodist society. When he married Eleanor Leyton in Dec. 1759, William Romaine performed the ceremony and JW gave the bride away; see JW, *Journal*, Dec. 14, 1759, 21:236 in this edn. Eleanor died in 1790 and was buried by JW in Bunhill Fields. When Josiah died he was buried in the same grave.
[225] See Eph. 6:10.
[226] See 2 Cor. 1:9.

For William Warrener[227]
Testimonial Letter

[Bristol]
[August 1, 1786]   5

To all to whom these presents shall come, John Wesley, M.A., late
Fellow of Lincoln College, Oxford, sendeth greeting.

Whereas it hath been represented to me that many of the people
called Methodists under my care in America stand in need at pres-   10
ent of proper persons to administer the ordinances of baptism and
the Lord's Supper among them, I therefore do hereby make known
unto all men that I did on the twenty-ninth day of July last solemnly set apart for the office of an elder in the church of God,
by the imposition of my hands and prayer (being assisted herein   15
by other ordained ministers), and with a single eye to the glory of
God, William Warrener, whom I judge to be a proper person to
administer the sacraments of baptism and the Lord's Supper. In
testimony whereof I have hereunto put my hand and seal the first
day of August, in the year of our Lord one thousand seven hundred   20
and eighty-six.

John Wesley

Source: holograph; Methodist Missionary Society Archives (School of
Oriental and African Studies, London University), 2015/046/F3.

25

To Elizabeth Davenport[228]

London   30
August 2, 1786

Dear Betsy,

It is true that our blessed Lord continually liveth to make intercession for us.[229] And yet it is equally true that he does not forbid

35

---

[227] William Warrener (c. 1750–1825) was admitted 'on trial' as an itinerant in 1779; see
10:484 in this edn. After serving seven years in Britain, JW ordained him for service in the West
Indies, ministering to enslaved Africans. Warrener returned to England in 1797, and retired
from the itinerancy in 1818. He settled in Leeds, where he remained active at a local level until
near his death on Nov. 27, 1825. See *Minutes* (post-Wesley, 1826), 6:108.

[228] Elizabeth Davenport was apparently the daughter of JW's correspondent Rev. Thomas Davenport, vicar of Radcliffe on Trent, and his wife Margaret (Lancelot) Davenport. No
baptismal record has been located to confirm this.

[229] See Heb. 7:25.

but encourage us to pray for one another.[230] This is one of the chief means that he has appointed for increasing our love to each other. And this love almost necessarily leads us to prayer, which is the very breath of love. I felt much love for *you* when I saw you last, together with great concern ⟨for⟩[231] you, as you are just entering on the stage of life, and walking on the slippery paths of youth! O what numberless dangers will surround you! And what need have you of continual watchfulness and prayer? At *your* age, how can you escape inordinate affection, but by the mighty power of God? To arm you against this, and all foolish and hurtful desires, I advise you carefully to read Mr. Law's *Serious Call to a Devout Life*.[232] If you have it not, let me know, and I will send it [to] you, with any other books which you desire.

And you shall never want anything which is in the power of, my dear Betsy,

Yours affectionately,

J. Wesley

The more freely you write, the better.

Address: 'To / Miss Eliz. Davenport / In Radcliffe upon Trent / near / Nottingham'.
Postmark: '27/SE'.[233] *Charge*: '5'.
Source: holograph; Huntington Library, Manuscripts, HM 57054.

To Ann Bolton

London
August 7, 1786

My Dear Nancy,

Never let it come into your mind that you write too often.[234] The oftener you write, the more I love you. I think we did not come through Witney in our way from Birmingham. We came by Enstone and Woodstock to Oxford, and so on to London. If I had

---

[230] See James 5:16.
[231] A small portion is torn away by the wax seal.
[232] William Law, *A Serious Call to a Holy Life* (JW's abridged version, 1744, Bibliography, No. 86.).
[233] JW apparently forgot to mail the letter before he left for his trip to Holland.
[234] Bolton's letter to JW is not known to survive.

been at Witney, I should scarce have missed seeing so dear a friend. Tomorrow we expect to set out for Holland. I do not purpose to contract any new acquaintances, but to spend a few days, if it please God, with those I know already, and whom I do not look to see again in this world. 5

If you love me do not fail to let me know if there be anything else wherein I can serve you. Look over the catalogue of our books and see if there are any others which you like to have. Herein you give me a singular pleasure. I would not have you want anything which I can supply. 10

I commend you for rising early in the morning. This is one excellent means of health. The more entirely you dedicate yourself to our good Master, the more his work will prosper in your hands. But should you not encourage Neddy Bolton likewise, to stir up the gift of God that is in him?[235] I suppose his worldly troubles are now 15 subsided, and that he is in a fair way, to owe no man anything.[236]

Peace be with all your spirits! My dear Nancy,
Adieu!

Address: 'To / Miss Bolton / In Witney / Oxfordshire'. 20
Postmark: '8/AU'. *Charge*: '4'.
Endorsement: by Bolton, 'Aug. 7 –86'.
Source: holograph; privately held (WWEP Archive holds photocopy).

25

To Elizabeth (Perronet) Briggs[237]

London
[August 7, 1786][238] 30

My Dear Betsy,

You may do me a considerable piece of service by informing me of all you know concerning Mr. [John] Fletcher, chiefly when he

---

[235] See 2 Tim. 1:6; referring to her brother Edward Bolton Jr.

[236] See Rom. 13:8.

[237] Despite the address line, the content of this letter makes clear that JW was addressing Elizabeth (Perronet) Briggs (1728–1807). A daughter of Vincent and Charity (Goodhew) Perronet, Elizabeth married William Briggs on Jan. 28, 1749. CW presided at the wedding. She was buried at City Road Chapel on May 2, 1807. See Margaret Batty, *Vincent Perronet, 1693–1785: 'The Archbishop of the Methodists'* (WMHS Publications, 2002).

[238] The note is undated, but it fits well with Telford's suggestion of Aug. 7, 1786, as JW was soliciting other input on Fletcher at this time.

was abroad. Perhaps you can give me light from some letters or papers of your brother William's, as I suppose all his papers are in your hands.[239] Perhaps you may have some valuable letters which he (Mr. Fletcher) wrote to your good father [Vincent].

5   I think both for my sake and for Mr. Fletcher's sake you will give all the help you can herein to, my dear Betsy,

      Yours affectionately,

          J. Wesley

10   *Address*: 'To / Miss Briggs'.[240]
Source: holograph; MARC, MAM JW 2/12.

15

To Mary Bosanquet Fletcher

            London
20   August 7, 1786

My Dear Sister,

    Several of the fragments may be of use. I purpose to insert them in the *[Arminian] Magazine*.[241] Some of the letters I think to insert in the *Life*.[242]

25   As to dates, you can probably help me:
  1. In what year did Mr. Fletcher come to England?
  2. In what year did he go to Tern?
  3. In what year [did he go] to Madeley?
  4. In what year did he travel with me?
30   5. [In what year did he] go to Newington?
  6. [In what year did he] go to Switzerland?

---

[239] William Perronet (1729–81), Elizabeth's brother, and trained as a physician in Bristol, and served as an army surgeon during the Seven Years War (1756–63). He then settled at Stoke Newington in civilian medical practice. Here he cared for John Fletcher. Fletcher in turn nurtured William's conversion, and a deep friendship ensued. In 1779 William accompanied Fletcher on an extended trip to Switzerland—where William fell sick and died in Dec. 1781. See Batty, *Perronet*, 89–100; and *WHS* 22 (1940): 187–88.

[240] JW was writing Mrs. Briggs by means of her daughter Elizabeth Briggs Jr.; see JW to Briggs, Oct. 15, 1786.

[241] While a few Fletcher letters appeared in *AM* between the date of this exchange and JW's death, none of the numerous fragmentary writings Fletcher left behind appear then.

[242] JW worked on his *Short Account ... of Fletcher* during his trip to Holland, dating the Preface, 'Amsterdam, September 12, 1786' (even though he had returned to England on Sept. 4).

7. [In what year did he] return to England?
8. In what month and year did he marry?
[9.] In what year did he go to Trevecca?
[10. In what year did he] return from it?[243]
Tomorrow we are to set out for Holland. I hope to return before   5
the end of this month; and am, my dear sister,
    Your affectionate brother,

                                                        J. Wesley

Source: holograph; MARC, MA 1983/027 (Mather scrapbook).   10

To Samuel Bradburn[244]   15

                                                        Harwich
                                                 August 8, 1786
Dear Sammy,
    I beg there may be no preaching at Deptford in church hours   20
before my return.[245] What need of any innovation there? The case
does not fall under any of those four that were allowed at the Conference.[246]
    And pray give an hint to Benjamin Rhodes. I do not take it kindly
that he should run his head against *me*. I fear he has underhand   25
abetted the malcontents there. If he loves *me*, he should bid them
'know when they are well'.
    We expect to sail in a few hours.[247]
    I am, with kind love to Sophy, dear Sammy,
        Your affectionate friend and brother,   30

                                                        J. Wesley

Source: holograph; privately held (WWEP Archive holds photocopy).

---

[243] Some notes starting to answer these questions appear on the backside, in another hand.
[244] While the address portion is missing, the content makes clear the recipient.
[245] A contingent of the Deptford society were pushing strongly for their Sunday service to be held at the time of regular worship in the Church of England. They had apparently induced Benjamin Rhodes to do so. See JW's follow-up meeting in Deptford on Oct. 24, 1786, *Journal*, 23:422 in this edn.
[246] See JW's open letter to the Methodist societies and preachers, Aug. 1, 1786.
[247] For Holland.

To the Rev. Dr. Thomas Coke[248]

London
September 6, 1786

5   Dear Sir,
    I desire that you would appoint a General Conference of all our
preachers in the United States, to meet at Baltimore on May the
1st, 1787. And that Mr. Richard Whatcoat may be appointed Superintendent with Mr. Francis Asbury.

10

Source: published transcription; John Emory, *A Defense of 'Our Fathers'*
(New York: N. Bangs & J. Emory, 1827), 74.

15

To Mary (Bosanquet) Fletcher

London
September 6, 1786

20   My Very Dear Sister and Friend,
    Excuse me if I write just as I *feel*. I have not of a long season
felt so tender an affection for you as I have done in reading your
last.[249] I love you much for the care you have taken of my dear
Miss [Elizabeth] Ritchie.[250] If she is worse, send me word to Bris-
25   tol, where I hope to be on Monday. I would travel day and night
to see her before she is called hence. But as God has already heard
the prayer, I trust he will permit her to stay a little longer with us.
If the vomiting returns, apply half a slit onion warmed, to the pit
of her stomach.[251]
30   The children of travelling preachers only are sent to Kingswood
school. David Evans has had uncommon help.[252] I gave him five-
and-twenty pounds at once.

---

[248] The first of these directives from JW was honoured by the preachers of the Methodist Episcopal Church. But they refused to acknowledge Whatcoat as Superintendent—partly
because they believed this office should be by their election, rather than JW's appointment; and
partly because they feared that JW would then recall Asbury to England. See JW to Richard
Whatcoat, c. July 1787.

[249] This letter is not known to survive.

[250] Ritchie had travelled to Dublin earlier this year, to visit James and Hester Ann (Roe)
Rogers. On her return she stopped by Madeley, where she suffered a serious bout of ill health,
but recovered. See Bulmer, *Mortimer*, 107–08.

[251] See *Primitive Physic*, Ailment #276, remedy 1, 32:253 in this edn.

[252] Evans had last served as an itinerant in 1783.

Peace be with your spirit! I am, my dear sister,
    Yours most affectionately,

                                                                 J. Wesley

Tuesday afternoon   5
I have just received your last,[253] and am glad to hear that my dear
sister Ritchie is not worse.
    My dear friend, Adieu.

Address: 'To / Mrs Fletcher / At Madeley, near Shifnal / Salop'.
Postmarks: '6/SE' and 'Shrewsbury'.[254] *Charge*: '5'.   10
Source: holograph; MARC, MA 1983/027 (Mather scrapbook).

                                                                          15

To William Simpson[255]

                                                                 London
                                                      September 6, 1786
Dear Billy,   20
    I am ashamed that Thirsk circuit should be in debt! It is a sign
Andrew Inglis is not Billy Simpson.[256] I shall wonder if that debt
remains a twelvemonth.
    I desire you would exert yourself in this matter. Speak to as many
of our friends as you can. Explain the thing to them and beg them   25
for God's sake, and for my sake, to assist to the uttermost of their
power. I will give five pounds to set them forwards. Afterwards begin a weekly subscription, for every member of the society. Go on
in faith, and God prosper the work of your hands upon you.
    I am, with kind love to your wife,[257] dear Billy,   30
    Your affectionate friend and brother,

                                                                 J. Wesley

[253] This letter is not known to survive.

[254] The letter was misdirected to Shrewsbury, then delivered correctly.

[255] William Simpson (d. 1804) was admitted 'on trial' as an itinerant at the 1779 Conference; see 10:484 in this edn. Simpson continued as an itinerant for 22 years, settling in Leeds
when he could travel no longer. See *Minutes* (post-Wesley, 1804), 2:221.

[256] This comparison is puzzling, and likely reflects a slip on JW's part. Simpson had just
been appointed Assistant for the Thirsk circuit, but Andrew Inglis had not held that role at any
preceding time (it was Philip Hardcastle in 1785).

[257] William Simpson married Anne Crosby of Ellerton by Bubwith, Yorkshire, on July
6, 1783.

Address: 'To / Mr Simpson / At the Preachinghouse / In Thirsk / York-shire'.
Source: holograph; Drew University, Methodist Library, Archives.

5

To Mary Cooke[258]

10

Bath
September 9, 1786

It gives me much satisfaction, my dear friend, to observe you are
happier than when you wrote last.[259] I do not doubt but you have at
some times a rich foretaste of the state which your soul pants after.
And even

These wandering gleams of light
And gentle ardours from above
Have made you sit, like seraph bright,
Some moments on a throne of love.[260]

But you know you are not to rest here. This is but a drop out
of the ocean. Only this has been known again and again, that one
of those happy moments has been the prelude of pure love. It has
opened into the full liberty of the children of God. Who knows but
this may be your happy experience? But the next time your soul is
so caught up, he that loves you may touch your nature clean, and so
take you into the holiest, that

You may never leave the skies,
Never stoop to earth again?[261]

I am now intent upon my own work, finishing the *Life* of Mr.
[John] Fletcher. This requires all the time I have to spare. So that,
as far as it is possible, I must for two or three months shut myself
up. Two weeks I give to Bristol; after that time I return to London.

---

[258] Replying to Cooke's letter of Aug. 30, 1786; and he had seen her this very day in Bath (see Cooke to JW, Oct. 24, 1786).
[259] See Cooke to JW, June 23, 1786.
[260] Cf. John Gambold, 'The Mystery of Life', st. 5, *HSP* (1739), 8.
[261] No source has been located for these two lines.

I cannot, therefore, have the happiness of seeing Trowbridge this autumn. But might I not see *you* or your sisters [Anne and Frances] at Bristol? If I am invisible to others, I would not be so to *you*. You may always command everything that is in the power of,
   My very dear friend, 5
      Yours in life and in death,
                            J. Wesley

Source: published transcription; Benson, *Works*, 16:300–301.

10

To Robert Barry

Bristol 15
September 15, 1786
My Dear Brother,
I fear Marrant has not a grain of religion left.[262] If pains be taken with those whom he drew away, I trust they will be recovered.
One of the holiest men in the last age was Mr. Philip Henry. 20 Though he was deprived of his living, he went every Sunday to the parish church with all his family. But one Sunday morning the minister preached a violent sermon against the nonconformists. 'Now sir,' said his friend 'I hope you have enough of it, you will not go to church any more.' 'Indeed sir,' said he 'I will, with God's 25 leave I will go in the afternoon. If the minister does not know *his* duty I bless God that I know *mine*.'[263] A hundred good sermons I have heard at Church and five hundred bad ones. But it never came to my mind that I should leave the Church because the minister preached a bad sermon. Pious Herbert says 30

[262] Orig., 'Morant.' Drew's copy includes this annotation by Robert Barry: 'Morant was a black preacher said to have been sent out by the pious Lady Huntingdon …. He effected a great division of our society of coloured people in Birch Town, which consisted of about 200 members, the most of whom went with Mr. Clarkson to Sierra Leone.' The preacher in question was John Marrant (1755–91). Born a freeman in New York city, his family had moved to Charleston, SC. After the death of his father the family moved further south to Georgia, then Florida (occasioned by the outbreak of the Revolutionary War and Marrant's loyalist stance). After the war Marrant resettled in England and became involved with Lady Huntingdon's connexion. He was ordained, and with LH's blessing went to Nova Scotia as a missionary in 1785, starting a Methodist congregation in Birch Town. Tensions grew rapidly between Marrant and the Wesleyan Methodist already in the area, partly concerning continued participation in worship in Church of England chapels. This led Marrant to resettle in Boston within a couple of years, then return to England in 1790.
[263] Cf. Matthew Henry, *An Account of … Philip Henry*, 160.

> The worst say something good: if all want sense,
> God takes a text and preacheth patience.[264]

5   'What do you do sir', said I to a popish gentleman in this town, 'when there is no mass?' He answered, 'Sir I go to the church every Sunday. I know it is the duty of every man to worship God in public, therefore when I cannot hear such services as I would, I use such as I have.' Go thou and do likewise.[265] I advise you by all means to go to Church next Sunday and so on. You may tell Mr. Walter *I*
10   advised you so to do.[266]

You began with him at the wrong end. I never begin with talking of dress, or innocent diversions; these are the last things men are convinced of. We see the evil of these things, but many good men do not. My father and mother feared God greatly; nay, and loved
15   him too—and yet they saw no evil in either cards or dancing to their lives end. Neither did I myself, till some years after I was admitted into holy orders. Deal mildly and tenderly with Mr. Walter, and you may do him much good. I love him for his gentleness toward you. I wish you had Mr. Law's *Serious Call* to lend him.[267] I think I must
20   desire his acceptance of two or three tracts. You have been a little too hasty with him.

Peace be with your spirits! I am,
Your affectionate brother,

J. Wesley

25   *Address*: 'To / Mr Robert Barry / Shelburne / Nova Scotia'.
Source: secondary manuscript transcriptions; Drew, Methodist Archives; and UCC Maritime Conference, Archives.[268]

---

[264] George Herbert, 'The Church Porch', [st. 68], in *The Temple* (1633); retained by JW in Select Parts of Mr. Herbert's Sacred Poems (1773), 10.

[265] See Luke 10:37.

[266] Orig., 'Walters'. Rev. Dr. William Walter (1737–1800), a native of Massachusetts, was ordained in the Church of England and served Trinity Church in Boston until his loyalist stance required him to flee to Nova Scotia with his family in 1776. While his family remained there, Walter returned with General Howe and the British fleet to New York, and when the fleet was driven out travelled with them to England. By Aug. 1783 he was in Shelburne, Nova Scotia, supported by the SPG as a missionary priest. In 1791 he returned to Boston, where he was appointed rector of Christ Church, which office he held until his death.

[267] William Law, *A Serious Call to a Holy Life* (JW's abridged version, 1744, *Bibliography*, No. 86.).

[268] The copy at Drew is a bit more complete. That in the UCC archives includes a note that the original was given to John A[lexander] Barry, Esq. (1792–1872), Robert Barry's son.

To Thomas Longley[269]

Bristol
September 15, 1786

Dear Longley, 5

Grimsby circuit undoubtedly ⟨is able⟩ to assist you. You will do well to as⟨k for the⟩ help of all the persons of substance. Your overseers at Horncastle ⟨....⟩ They know well enough there is no danger. However you may show them your certificate. I am

Your affectionate friend and brother, 10

J. Wesley

15

[The Certificate]

Bristol
September 15, 1786

20

This is to certify [to] whom it may concern that Mr. Thomas Longley is a preacher in connexion with me. And that I will be answerable for any expense which he or his family may bring upon any parish in England.

John Wesley 25

Source: holographs; privately held (WWEP Archive holds a transcription).

30

To Walter Churchey

Bristol
September 20, 1786

My Dear Brother, 35

At length Jenny has broke through, and given me the satisfaction of exchanging a few words with her.[270] You send us strange news that the lions of Wales are become lambs! I really think a spirit of

[269] Longley had been moved after two years as Assistant at Epworth, to become Assistant of the newly established circuit at Horncastle, created by splitting the Grimsby circuit.

[270] Jane Churchey (1770–1842), the oldest child of Walter and Mary (Bevan) Churchey. The letters exchanged are not known to survive.

humanity and benevolence is gone forth upon the earth, perhaps intimating that the time is drawing near when men shall not know war any more.[271] Mr. [Francis] Wrigley has been detained here by a sore face ever since the Conference; but is now also on the mending hand, though he is not yet able to go abroad.[272] I am glad to hear that Dr. Powell, of Brecon, continues in the good way. He seems to be of a frank, open temper, and to be skilful in his profession. I am rather gaining than losing ground as to my health.

I think Mr. Cowper has done as much as is possible to be done with his lamentable story. I can only wish he had a better subject.[273] Peace be with you and yours!

I am

Your affectionate brother,

J. Wesley

I set out for London on Monday.

Source: published transcription; Jackson, *Works* (3rd), 12:423.

To Elizabeth (Perronet) Briggs[274]

Bristol
September 24, 1786

My Dear Betsy,

I thank you for the letters which you sent, and shall be glad to see those which you mention.

There is no doubt but Shoreham is the place which God at present points out for your residence. And it is well that you have such

---

[271] See Isa. 2:4.

[272] Wrigley may have promised to visit Churchey before returning to serve a second year as Assistant at Redruth.

[273] Referring to William Cowper, *The Task. A Poem in Six Books* (London: Johnson, 1785), which was a biting criticism of the slave trade and those who think they need slaves.

[274] In response to JW's letter of Aug. 7, Briggs sent JW a packet of materials about John Fletcher. Her accompanying letter is not known to survive.

an assistant there as honest Sampson Staniforth.[275] Great care should be taken to preserve a perfect good understanding between him and the travelling preachers.

I know not who in Shoreham is able to give me a night's lodging now.

Tomorrow I expect to set out for London.

I am, my dear Betsy,

    Yours affectionately,

                                  J. Wesley

Source: holograph; MARC, MAM JW 2/13.

To Thomas McGeary[276]

                                      London
                    September 25, 1786

Tommy, Tommy! You put me in mind of my father. Once and again he has laid his hand upon my breast and said, 'Down, proud heart!' I did not like it then. But I knew afterwards, it was wholesome for me.

But how it is that you thus kick and wince at censure?[277] Did you never read the Rules of our society? O Tommy, you are a poor Methodist! Had I been of your mind, I should have turned back long ago. I perceive your spirit has been hurt. The foot of pride has come against you.[278] But God is able to heal you.

I am,

    Your affectionate brother,

                                    J. Wesley

[275] Sampson Staniforth (1720–99) was born in Sheffield, joined the army about 1739, and was converted while on a campaign in Europe about 1744. Back in England briefly on leave, he came under JW's preaching in 1745. Staniforth returned to England in Feb. 1748, took his leave of the army and settled in Greenwich, working as a master baker and supporting the Methodist cause, including financing the construction of a preaching house. Over the years he also served as a local preacher, particularly in Deptford and Rotherhithe. He had recently retired from his business and moved (for a few years) to Shoreham, at the request of Rev. Vincent Perronet. See Staniforth to JW, c. Dec. 1782; and Jackson, *EMP*, 4:149.

[276] On McGeary, see JW to Rachel (Norton) Bayley, Aug. 30, 1783.

[277] McGeary's letter of complaint is not known to survive.

[278] See Ps. 36:11.

Address: 'To / Mr McGeary / At Kingswood School / near / Bristol'.
Postmark: '26/SE'. *Charge*: '5'.
Source: holograph; Bath, Kingswood School, Wesley Centre Archives.

To William Roberts[279]

Bristol
September 25, 1786

My Dear Brother,

I doubt not but you could say in the hour of trial, 'The Lord gave, and the Lord hath taken away: blessed be the name of the Lord!'[280]

Still, I really think you are not in your place. You are called to better things than standing behind a counter.[281] Your spirit, your understanding, your gifts of various kinds, point out to you a more excellent way! O when will you break loose, and join heart and hand with, dear Billy,

Your affectionate brother,

J. Wesley

I set out for London this afternoon.

Source: holograph; Oxford, Lincoln College, Archive, MS/WES/A/2/8.

To the Rev. Freeborn Garrettson[282]

London
September 30, 1786

My Dear Brother,

I trust before this comes to hand Dr. [Thomas] Coke and you will have met and refreshed each other's bowels in the Lord.[283] I

---

[279] While there is no address portion, this is one in a set of letters to Roberts. Roberts had informed JW that he was in danger of losing his business (his initial letter does not survive, but see Roberts to JW, Nov. 28, 1786).

[280] Job 1:21.

[281] Roberts had become a grocer after he left the itinerant ministry.

[282] Replying to Garrettson's letter of Apr. 25, 1786, in which he requested help in getting several books, and wondered if some funding could come from Britain toward building a chapel in Shelburne.

[283] See Philem. 1:7, 20.

could exceedingly ill spare him from England, as I have no clergy-man capable of supplying his lack of service. But I was convinced he was wanted in America even more than he was in Europe. For it is impossible but offences will come, and of yourselves will men arise speaking perverse things and striving to draw away disciples after them.[284] It is a wonderful blessing that they are restrained so long, till the poor people are a little grounded in the truth. You have need to watch over them with your might—you few that have set your hand to the plough.[285] And continually pray to the Lord of the harvest, that he would send forth more labourers into his harvest.[286]

It is far better to send your journals as they are than not to send them at all.

I am afraid it is too late in the season to send books this year. But I hope Dr. Coke has brought many with him to serve you for the present. I was far off from London when he set sail.

Most of those in England who have riches love money, even the Methodists—at least, those who are called so. The poor are the Christians. I am quite out of conceit with almost all that have this world's goods. Let us take care to lay up treasures in heaven![287]

Peace be with your spirit! I am,

    Your affectionate friend and brother,

                           J. Wesley

Source: holograph; Wesleyan University Library.

To the *Leeds Intelligencer*[288]

                          London
                 October 6, 1786

Sir,

    If A. B. desires an answer, let him tell his name to me or the public, and he shall hear farther from

                         John Wesley

---

[284] Garrettson had mentioned challenges to his work by a small group of followers of Henry Alline, and the work of Rev. John Marrant in Birch Town.

[285] See Luke 9:62.

[286] See Matt. 9:38.

[287] See Matt. 6:20.

[288] 'A. B.' had published a rebuttal, dated Sept. 14, 1786, to what the writer took to be a negative portrayal of the Moravian community in Fulneck in the most recent published extract of JW's *Journal* (Apr. 17–18, 1780, 23:165 in this edn.).

Source: published transcription; *Leeds Intelligencer* (Oct. 17, 1786), p. 4, and *Leeds Mercury* (Oct. 17, 1786), p. 3.

5

To George Merryweather

London
October 9, 1786

10 Dear George,

Do not wish to have a grain less of sensibility than you have. I love you the better for it. And so does he that is greater than all!

That family I know and love well. We will help them all we can. I have no access to Mr. Thornton—the Calvinists take care to keep
15 him to themselves.[289] But if you will give them five pounds from me, John Atlay will answer your draft here.

I am, with best wishes to all the family, dear George,
Your affectionate brother,

J. Wesley

20

Address: 'To / Mr G. Merryweather / In Yarm / Yorkshire'.
Postmark: '9/OC'.
Source: holograph; Garrett-Evangelical, Methodist Manuscripts Collection.

25

To John Francis Valton[290]

30
London
October 9, 1786

My Dear Brother,

I know not but I mentioned to you before that *James Timbrell* of Bath *hates John Fowler as he hates the devil* and has for several years
35 been constantly labouring to prejudice both preachers and people, against him and his wife.[291] Therefore I desire of you three things:

---

[289] Merryweather apparently encouraged JW to approach the philanthropist John Thornton (1720–90), of Clapham and London, for financial support.

[290] Valton had been appointed Assistant for the Bristol circuit at the 1786 Conference, though in a supernumerary capacity to lower his preaching load. It is unclear whether the extensive underlining in this letter is by JW, or by Valton when reading it.

[291] See JW to Francis Wrigley, Apr. 4, 1782.

1) that you will go to his house either *seldom* or *not at all*; 2) that you will *talk largely* with *him* and *sister Fowler*, and give them opportunity of speaking for themselves; 3) that if the *travelling preachers*, as was agreed, fill up the Monday evenings, *he* may preach at *some other time*, whoever is offended. For God has owned *his* preaching more than that of most local preachers in England.

One thing more. Unless Mrs. Pitt asks sister Fowler's pardon, I *require* you to *expel her [from] the society*.[292]

I am

Your affectionate friend and brother,

J. Wesley

Address: 'To / Mr Valton / At the New Room / Bristol'.
Postmark: '11/OC'.
Endorsement: by Valton, 'Octr. 9th 1786'.
Source: holograph; MARC, MAM JW 5/36.

To Ann Bolton

Lynn
October 12, 1786

My Dear Nancy,

About three weeks I stayed in Holland before, and about the same time now.[293] That being sufficient for visiting my little set of acquaintances at Rotterdam, Haarlam, Amsterdam, and Ultrecht and for declaring the plain gospel in each place to as many as could understand me.

I was in hopes that the chief of your pressures had been removed some time ago; as Neddy Bolton seemed at last to have a fair prospect of extracting himself from his difficulties. How do his affairs stand now? Can he a little more than 'wind his bottom(?) round the year'? Does he every year pay off a little debt, and has he a probability of getting quite clear?

I almost wonder that Mr. Peck should remove from a large and well-situated shop in such a city as Oxford, to a little country

---

[292] Mrs. Pitt had revealed to others something Mrs. Fowler said in a band meeting (which was supposed to remain confidential to the band); see JW to Valton, Oct. 29, 1786.

[293] I.e., his visits in 1783 and 1786.

town.[294] What advantage would he propose to himself from such a change? Does he propose entering into some other way of ⟨work⟩?[295] I suppose, he was in easy circumstances. I shall be glad to call upon them and to preach at Eynsham whenever I come that way. But
5   when that will be, I cannot tell for the writing of Mr. Fletcher's *Life* so engrosses my time that I do not know I shall have leisure to take any journey before Christmas.

It is well you know in whom you have believed, and that he has all power as well as all love.[296] To his tender care I commit you and
10 am, my dear Nancy,

Your ever affectionate,

J. Wesley

Address: 'To / Miss Bolton / In Witney / Oxfordshire'.
Postmark: '14/OC'. *Charge*: '4'.
15 *Endorsement*: by Bolton, 'Oct 12 –86'.
Source: holograph; privately held (WWEP Archive holds photocopy).

20   To Elizabeth (Perronet) Briggs[297]

London
October 15, 1786

My Dear Betsy,
25   I thank you for the extracts and the use of the letters, several of which will do very well.

It is true many of your friends are gone before you into Abraham's bosom. But you have a competent number left. And indeed no Methodist can be quite alone. And besides, our best friend has
30 told us, 'Lo! I am ever with you!'[298]

I am, my dear Betsy,

Yours most affectionately,

J. Wesley

---

[294] John Peck had a drapery and textiles shop in Oxford, 1780–84. In Mar. 1784 he married Delia Wickens (d. 1786), the mother (out of wedlock) of William Upcott (1779–1845). This may explain their move to Eynsham, just east of Witney. See the account of Delia's death later this year, in a letter of William Shepherd to JW, Dec. 18, 1786.

[295] A word inserted at the bottom is cut off in the photocopy at Duke.

[296] See 1 Tim. 1:12.

[297] This is a follow-up of JW's letter to Briggs, Sept. 24, 1786.

[298] Cf. Matt. 28:20.

Sarah Crosby³⁰⁰

[Wrestlingworth]
October 18, 1786

My Dear Sister,

At present I have no remains of any illness but am far healthier than I was forty years ago.

Your account will do admirably well, and needs very few wants to be altered. But it has met with a misfortune. Half a page was thrown into the fire, before I had transcribed it. I have transcribed as far the wedding day. The last words I wrote were 'can truly say …', so there is wanting to 'Adam who had purchased his bride …'. So about half is wanting, which I hope you can supply either from a final copy, or from your memory.³⁰¹ Send it, if you can, within ten or twelve days to, dear Sally,

Your affectionate brother,

J. Wesley

Source: holograph; Pitts Library (Emory), John Wesley Collection (MSS 153), 3/33.

To Thomas Carlill

London
October 21, 1786

Dear Tommy,

I apprehend those deeds cannot be altered without the consent of all the trustees.³⁰² But do not say one word about enrolling them. They will probably let the time slip, and then they will be null and void. So new ones may be drawn without any lawyer at all.

---

²⁹⁹ JW again writes the mother via the daughter; cf. JW to Briggs, Aug. 7, 1786.
³⁰⁰ While the address portion is missing, JW was responding to a long letter that Sarah Crosby sent him c. Oct. 1, 1786.
³⁰¹ Crosby did supply the missing text; cf. JW to Crosby, Oct. 28, 1786, and the section for Monday, Nov. 12, [1781] as printed by JW of her letter c. Oct. 1, 1786.
³⁰² Carlill was currently the Assistant for the Derby circuit.

I am, dear Tommy,
    Your affectionate friend and brother,

                                                    J. Wesley

5   Now procure all the subscribers you can for Mr. Fletcher's *Life*.[303]

Address: 'To / Mr Carlill / At the Preachinghouse / in / Derby'.
Charge: '5'.
Endorsement: by Carlill, 'Revd. Jno. Wesley / Octr. 21. 1786'.
10 *Source*: holograph; MARC, MAM JW 2/25.

To the Rev. Peter Lièvre[304]

15

                                                    London
                                            October 25, 1786

20   Last night I had a long conversation with a few sensible men
    concerning going to church.[305] I asked them what objection they
    had to the hearing of Mr. L[ièvre]. They answered, '*They could not
    hear him*. He generally spoke so low that they lost a good part of
    what he said. And that what they *could* hear was spoken in a dead,
    cold, languid manner, as if he did not *feel* anything which he spoke.'
25 This would naturally disgust them the more, because Dr. C[onyers]
    leaned to the other extreme.[306]
        I doubt there is some ground for their objection. But I should
    think you might easily remove it.
        I asked again, 'Have you any objection to anything in his behav-
30 iour?' They answered, 'One thing we cannot approve of, his being
    ashamed of the Methodists. His never recommending or defending
    them at all, we think, is a full proof of this. For everyone knows his

---

[303] No printed copy of the Proposal for subscriptions (*Bibliography*, No. 822) is known
to survive.

[304] Peter Lièvre (1746–1819) was a great-nephew of JW; the grandson of his sister Susanna (Wesley) Ellison and Richard Ellison, by their daughter Susanna (Ellison) Lièvre and
Elie Lièvre. He was ordained in June 1776 and serving currently as a curate at Deptford St.
Paul, Kent, and Master of the Free Grammar School in Lutterworth, Leicestershire. In 1803
he would become vicar of Arnesby, Leicestershire.

[305] JW was in Deptford on Oct. 24, 1786; see *Journal*, 23:422 in this edn.

[306] Rev. Dr. Richard Conyers (1725–86), an evangelical, but aligned with the Calvinist
wing of the movement, was rector of Deptford St. Paul from 1775 to his death.

near relation and his many obligations to *you*.[307] They know how you have loved and cherished him from a child.' They might have added, 'You owe your whole education to him; and therefore, in effect, your ordination, your curacy, your school; yea, and your wife. None of which you would in all likelihood have had, had it not been for him.'[308]

I would add a word upon this head myself. I do not think you act wisely. Not one of your genteel friends can be depended on. They are mere summer flies. Whereas, had you condescended to make the *Methodists* your friends, they would have clave to you, one and all. And they are already no inconsiderable body of people. Besides that they are increasing more and more.

Suffer me now to speak a word between *you* and *me*. Is not the reason of your preaching so languidly and coldly that you do not *feel* what you say? And why not? Because your soul is not alive to God! Do you know that your sins are forgiven? I fear not. Can you say, 'I *know* that *my* Redeemer liveth'?[309] I doubt, if you did know it once, whether you know it now! Have you fellowship with the Father and the Son?[310] Alas, it is well if you know what it means! And are you content to have your portion *in this world*?[311] Do you favour only earthly things? Then I do not wonder that you are shy to the Methodists; for they are not *to your taste*! O think and pray today! For I do not promise you that you shall live another year! I now give you a full proof that I am

Your truly affectionate,

John Wesley

Source: published transcription; *Methodist Magazine* 22 (1799): 601–02.

---

[307] See Lièvre's earlier appreciative letter to JW of July 29, 1778.

[308] Peter's father died when he was only a year old, and his subsequent step-father by the time he was ten. JW then helped care for Peter and his mother. This included sending Peter (at JW's expense) to Kingswood school. Peter was ordained based on this education, being admitted to Cambridge as a 'ten year man' only in 1778. He married Mary Sturges (c. 1760–1826) in 1783.

[309] Job 19:25.

[310] See 1 John 1:3.

[311] See Ps. 17:14.

To Jasper Winscom

London
October 27, 1786

My Dear Brother,

The sooner the affair is settled the better. I desire, therefore, that Mr. Ashman will receive what is in Mr. Smith's hands.[312] You say you can borrow as much more than Mr. Gifford's ten pounds as will make up the hundred.[313] As soon as this is paid the house may be transferred to five or more trustees on the Conference plan. I forbid engaging any attorney. You have the form of conveyance in the *Minutes*, which anyone may transcribe.[314]

I am
　　Your affectionate brother,

J. Wesley

Address: 'To / Mr Jasper Winscom / in / Winton'.
Postmark: '28/OC'. *Charge*: '4'.
Endorsement: by Winscom, 'J Wesley / Oct 26 1786'.
Source: holograph; Bridwell Library (SMU).

To Sarah Crosby

London
October 28, 1786

My Dear Sister,

You have sent me exactly the part I wanted, which (together with the rest) I have now transcribed for the press.[315]

I am glad to hear that my dear Miss [Elizabeth] Ritchie is recovered. I was afraid she was stealing away from us. If all your

---

[312] William Ashman (1734–1818), a native of Holcombe, was converted in his mid-teens and admitted 'on trial' as an itinerant in 1765 (see 10:303 in this edn.). He was currently Assistant of the Sarum circuit, which included Winchester. He continued to serve as an itinerant until health issues led him to desist in 1798, and return to his home town. See Jackson, *EMP*, 5:296–311 (also in 1790 in-letters) and *Minutes* (post-Wesley, 1818), 4:396.

[313] The £100 JW had advanced toward building the chapel in Winchester; see JW to Winscom, Sept. 13, 1785.

[314] See the 'Large' *Minutes* (1763), §67, 10:868–70 in this edn.

[315] Cf. JW to Crosby, Oct. 18, 1786.

preachers speak with one voice, and exhort the believers to go on to perfection,[316] there will be an increase of the whole work of God.

Peace be with your spirits! I am, dear Sally,

Your affectionate brother,

J. Wesley 5

Address: [not in JW's hand], 'To Mrs Crosby'.
Source: holograph; Drew, Methodist Archives.

10

To John Francis Valton

London 15
October 29, 1786

My Dear Brother,

Striking a woman in the street, and crying amain, 'Strumpet, strumpet!' was enough to enrage a women, even to madness. It had not been strange if, instead of scolding, she had shot her husband 20 or herself. I wonder she can sustain life.

Do not cast water upon a drowning man; and take care of receiving anything upon Joseph Brundrell's testimony.

Speaking is not the thing, but revealing what is spoken *in band*, had it been true. Unless sister Pitt be convinced of *this sin*, I will 25 expel her [from] the society the first time I come to Bath.[317] I must do justice if the sky falls. I am the last resort. A word to the wise!

I am sure Michael Griffith is *good enough* for the place, if he is not too good.[318] I hope Mr. Jones is set out for Brecon.[319] See that Michael have fair play. 30

John Atlay knows nothing about the hundred pounds; neither do I. I am afraid it is a castle in the air.

I am glad to hear you have so fair a prospect in the circuit. You will find all things work together for good. I am

Your affectionate friend and brother, 35

[J. Wesley]

[316] See Heb. 6:1.
[317] See JW to Valton, Oct. 9, 1786.
[318] Griffith was likely being considered as a Master at Kingswood school, see JW to Valton, Dec. 22, 1786.
[319] Thomas Jones, who had not been able to join Thomas Wride at Norwich the previous year (perhaps spending it helping at Kingswood), had been readmitted 'on trial' as an itinerant and assigned to the Brecon circuit.

Address: 'To / Mr Valton / New Room / Bristol'.
Source: published transcription; Telford, *Letters*, 7:347.[320]

5

To Thomas Wride[321]

London
10   October 29, 1786

Dear Tommy,

I am entirely of your mind. If any man (to waive everything else)
can make me sleep without touching me, he may call the matter
what he pleases. I know it is not magnetism, but magic.[322]

15   Mr. Mears did not tell me (that I know) anything about letters
one, two, three.[323] Women told me at Chatham. 'We called on Mrs.
[Jane] Wride and offered her any service in our power. But she was
so sullen and surly, we had not the heart to go again.'

But is it true, Tommy, that you have an estate left you? I fear it is
20   not so large as the Duke of Bedford's! I should be glad to bring you
all to a good agreement. If I knew how.

I am, dear Tommy,
                    Your affectionate friend and brother,
                    J. Wesley
25

Endorsement: by Wride, 'No. 32 / Octor. 29th. 1786'.
Source: holograph; MARC, MAM JW 6/33.

---

[320] An abridged form of the letter appeared in *WMM* 48 (1825): 824; reproduced from
there in Jackson, *Works* (3rd), 12:474.

[321] Replying to Wride's letter of Oct. 27, 1786.

[322] Wride had drawn JW's attention to an English exponent of Franz Mesmer's 'animal
magnetism'.

[323] William Mears (1758–1814) was a Methodist local preacher in Rochester / Chatham,
Kent.

To Henry Moore[324]

London
November 4, 1786

My Dear Brother,

I am glad you spoke freely to Mr. [Brian Bury] Collins. He is a good man, but not very advisable. If he should declare open war in England, he will do little or no harm. Mr. Smyth will not be fond of him if he preaches at Plunket Street.[325] There will not soon be a coalition between Arminianism and Calvinism. This we found even in Holland.

If brother [James] Rogers and you keep to the Church still, a few I doubt not will follow your example. We made just allowance enough for leaving the Church at the last Conference.[326]

At all hazards let there be a free and open correspondence between Jemmy Rogers and you. I hope your sister Becky is gaining ground, and that Nancy is not losing any.[327]

I have an affectionate letter from Mrs. Slacke at Annadale.[328] To save expense I send a few lines which you will forward to her.[329]

I hope your lawsuit is almost or quite at an end. I am, with kind love to Nancy, dear Henry,

Yours affectionately,

J. Wesley

Address: 'To / Mr Moore / At the New Room / in / Dublin'.
Postmark: '4/NO'.
Source: holograph; Pitts Library (Emory), John Wesley Papers (MSS 153), 3/34.

---

[324] Moore had been moved from Bristol, to assist James Rogers in Dublin, at the last Conference.

[325] Edward Smyth was now the chaplain of Bethesda Chapel on Granby Row, in Dublin. Collins had filled the pulpit for Smyth recently (see Elizabeth Ritchie to JW, June 2, 1786) and was now apparently considering taking charge of the old Presbyterian meeting house on Plunket Street in Dublin, that Lady Huntingdon reopened as a chapel in her connexion in 1773.

[326] See JW's public letter to the Methodist Preachers and Societies, Aug. 1, 1786.

[327] Rebecca Moore, Henry's sister, was a class leader in Dublin; see Cooney, 'Dublin Society', 44, 52. 'Nancy' is Moore's wife, Anne (Young) Moore.

[328] Angel Anna (Slacke) Slacke (1750–96), the only daughter of William Slacke of Portarlington, married her cousin William Slacke of Kiltubbrid, who built their home in a vale they called Annadale. She was converted to Methodism during a visit to Dublin in 1780 and then introduced it to her family. They hosted JW at their home more than once. Anna was active in her society, visiting the poor, tending the sick, etc. See Crookshank, *Irish Women*, 180–90.

[329] Neither the letter from Slacke, nor the portion of JW's double letter directed to her are known to survive.

To 'A. B.' Alias 'C. D.'[330]

[London]
November 4, 1786

I advise you to know when you are well. For if you constraint me to speak (if you *will* tear open a sore that is almost healed), I shall say more than you will like.

John Wesley

Source: published transcriptions; *Leeds Intelligencer* (Nov. 21, 1786), p. 3, and *Leeds Mercury* (Nov. 21, 1786), p. 3.

To the Epworth Circuit

London
November 5, 1785

My Dear Brethren,

You did not well understand the case of John Fenwick. Though I set down the name of James Watson before his;[331] yet I told him [i.e., Fenwick], 'You are to act as Assistant and to change the stewards in every place.' This James deeply resented, and set himself to blacken him in every place and to prejudice the people against him—in which he has been but too successful. The fault of John Fenwick was the doing the *right* thing in the *wrong* manner. And I know not but, when he was hunted like an hare, he might be harried to say something that was not strictly true. But what then? In every circuit where he has been, he has been one of the most useful Assistants in England. I *can* remove him. But I have no preacher to send in his place. Therefore I would advise you *for a time* to make the best of him. But I desire those stewards may stand whom I appointed.

[330] JW replying to the public letter of 'C. D.' to the editor of the *Leeds Intelligencer*, dated Oct. 17, 1786. While 'C. D.' may be another pseudonym simply following in order from 'A. B.', JW seems to assume that it is his old friend Charles Delamotte.

[331] In the list of preachers assigned to Epworth by the 1786 Conference, Watson's name comes first—which typically means he is the one to serve as Assistant. See 10:600 in this edn.

I am, my dear brethren,
    Your affectionate brother,

                 John Wesley[332]

Till that man who shut the preaching door owns his fault, I desire   5
none of our preachers will preach at Crowle. I dare not submit in
such a case.

Address: 'To / Mr Simon Kilham / In Epworth, near Thorne / Yorkshire'.
Postmark: '6/NO'.   10
Source: holograph; WHS Library.

    15

To Richard Rodda

                    London
             November 11, 1786   20
My Dear Brother,
    You have done well in discharging the debt of the society.
    Let John Sellers produce the letter wherein I promised to pay the
expense of his lawsuit. I do not remember anything of it. And it is
certain, I will never pay a shilling of it out of my own pocket. I think   25
what you said to him was exactly right. The yearly collection, you
know, is never to be anticipated, but produced at the Conference.
    If the book you speak of is excellent, I would insert it in the *[Ar-
minian] Magazine*. And then it would go all over the kingdom.
    Peace be with you and yours! I am,   30
    Your affectionate friend and brother,

                     J. Wesley

Address: 'To / Mr Richd. Rodda / At the Preaching House / Chester'.[333]
Postmark: '11/NO'. *Charge*: '6'.   35
Source: holograph; Drew, Methodist Archives.

---

[332] Note the use of JW's full signature in this stern letter.
[333] The address is not in JW's hand; likely John Broadbent.

To William Simpson[334]

near London
November 11, 1786

Dear Billy,

Busy as I am, I snatch time to write a few lines, as I judge you had rather see my handwriting than John Broadbent's.[335]

You must in any wise write a few loving lines to brother [Andrew] Inglis, and tell him I desired you so to do. It may enduce him to be a little more careful for the time to come.

The Sunday preaching may continue at Jervas for the present. I suppose the society at Jervas is as large as that at Northallerton, and this is a point which is much to be considered.

You must needs expel out of the society at Knaresborough those that *will be* contentious.

I am, with love to Nancy, dear Billy,

Your affectionate friend and brother,

J. Wesley

Source: holograph; University of York, Borthwick Institute for Archives, MR/Y/CEN 93.

To the Rev. Joseph Taylor

near London
November 11, 1786

My Dear Brother,

I am not afraid of your doing too little, but of your doing too much—either by preaching oftener than your strength will yet bear or by speaking too long or too loud. Our preachers have as great need of temperance in preaching as in eating or drinking; otherwise our grand enemy will carry his point, and soon disable us from preaching at all.

---

[334] Simpson was now the Assistant for the Thirsk circuit. Andrew Inglis continued serving at Newcastle, where he had been Simpson's colleague the previous year.

[335] Broadbent was currently serving as JW's assistant; see 10:598 in this edn.

I hope my dear friends Mr. [William] Smith and his wife continue in the good way; and that you still earnestly exhort all the believers to go on to perfection.[336]

I am, dear Joseph,

Your affectionate friend and brother,   5

[J. Wesley]

I have nearly finished Mr. [John] Fletcher's *Life*; now let brother [Richard] Watkinson and you exert yourselves and procure as many subscribers as you can.   10

Source: published transcription; Telford, *Letters*, 7:351.

15

To Ann Bolton

London   20
November 12, 1786

My Dear Nancy,

Some time since, when Neddy Bolton got rid of his heavy load, when he threw that oppressive farm off of his shoulders, I was in hopes the trouble what you so kindly took upon you for his sake was   25
at an end. But I find you do not see land yet. If one trouble goes, another comes in its place. One wave sinks, but it seems it is only to make way for the rising of another. It is well we know that God governs the world, and that he does all things well![337] It is true. *How* this or that situation is best for us we cannot see now, but we shall   30
see hereafter.

Some crosses every child of man must have. But how variously are they dealt unto us? Yours are in a great measure of an outward nature, but in the mean time you have tolerable health and strength. Miss [Elizabeth] Ritchie has no temporal crosses but she is almost   35
continually tottering over the grave. Well, after all, it is wisest to hold fast that word,

I cannot choose; thou canst not err.[338]

[336] See Heb. 6:1.
[337] See Mark 7:37.
[338] CW, 'Waiting for Christ', st. 4, *l*. 4, *HSP* (1740), 40.

It will be well to balance the inconveniences of your present state with those you are to expect in the other. What is it that is most grievous in your present state? Is there anything that particularly burdens you now? Our acquaintance is not of yesterday. You know how long I have sincerely and tenderly loved you. And surely you may say anything to, my dear Nancy,

Yours most affectionately,

J. Wesley

Address: 'To / Miss Bolton / In Witney / Oxforshire'.
Postmark: '13/NO'. *Charge*: '4'.
Endorsement: by Bolton, 'Novr 12th –86'.
Source: holograph; privately held (WWEP Archive holds photocopy).

To Jasper Winscom

London
November 12, 1786

Dear Jasper,

I am glad to hear so good an account of the work of God in Witney. If the Lord will work, who shall hinder?[339] This should encourage you to still greater zeal and activity. The death of that miserable backslider was a signal instance of divine providence, and very probably might excite some others to flee from the wrath to come.

I am, dear Jasper,

Your affectionate brother,

[J. Wesley]

Source: published transcription; Jackson, *Works* (3rd), 12:510.

To Thomas Warrick

near London
November 16, 1786

Dear Tommy,

Whoever is pleased or displeased (as some will certainly be), it is your duty to remove every leader whom you judge to be unprofit-

---

[339] See Isa. 43:13.

able to the people, or indeed less profitable than another that lives at a convenient distance. Some will likewise be displeased if you diligently exhort the believers to go on to perfection.[340] But you need only secure one point, to please God.

I am, with love to sister [Mary] Warrick, dear Tommy,

Your affectionate friend and brother,

J. Wesley

Address: 'To / Mr Warrick / At the Preachinghouse / in Burslem / Staffordshire'.
Postmark: '16/NO'.
Endorsement: by Warrick(?), 'J Wesley Nov. 16 1786'.
Source: holograph; MARC, WCB, D6/3/1/13.

To John Hollis

City Road [London]
November 17, 1786

Sir,

Several years since, Mr. Hollis came to me at the Foundery and said, 'Sir, I have a little house in Porridge Pot Alley, Old Street, and I wish you would recommend two or three poor people to live in it!' I recommended three, and took care that they should not want the necessaries of life. Your father desired me 'If any of them died, to put another in her place', which I accordingly did. But certainly whenever you require it, they must go to the workhouse or find other lodgings, for the house is yours, not mine.

Wishing you all happiness, I am, sir,

Your humble servant,

John Wesley

Probably you may have been a little mistaken in one point. I did not much lessen your father's substance. I believe all that he gave me for the poor (for myself he gave me nothing) in our long acquaintance did not amount to twelve pounds.

Address: 'To / John Hollis Esq / At No. 48 / Great Ormond Street'.
Source: holograph; Bridwell Library (SMU).

[340] See Heb. 6:1.

To William Simpson[341]

London
November 23, 1786

Dear Billy,

You have taken in this intricate affair the very best method that could be taken. When you have to do with those stubborn spirits, it is absolutely necessary either to mend them or to end them;[342] and ten persons of a quiet temper are better than thirty contentious ones.[343] Undoubtedly some of the eloquent men will be sending me heavy complaints. It is well therefore that you spoke first.

I am, dear Billy,
    Your affectionate friend and brother,

J. Wesley

Address: 'To / Mr Simpson / At the Preachinghouse / In Thirsk / York-shire'.
Source: holograph; Wesley's Chapel (London), LDWMM 1997/6726.

To Francis Wrigley[344]

London
November 26, 1786

My Dear Brother,

Now is the very time wherein you should earnestly exhort the believers to go on to perfection.[345] Those of them that hunger and thirst after righteousness will keep their ground.[346] The others will lose what God has wrought.

---

[341] Neither of Simpson's recent letters to JW are known to survive; so we have no insight into the nature of the contention.

[342] See the note on JW to Thomas Taylor, Oct. 30, 1775, 29:188 in this edn.

[343] The contentious persons were at Knaresborough; see JW to Simpson, Nov. 11, 1786.

[344] Wrigley had written JW an account of revival currents in Cornwall on Nov. 1, 1786. The other items mentioned by JW are likely responding to a subsequent letter that is not known to survive.

[345] See Heb. 6:1.

[346] See Matt. 5:6.

You may certainly give a note to the serious inn-keeper till you can do more.

I look upon that very common custom to be neither better nor worse than murder. I would no more take a pillow from under the head of a dying person than I would put a pillow upon his mouth.

I am

Your affectionate friend and brother,

J. Wesley

Address: 'To / Mr Francis Wrigley / In Redruth / Cornwall'.
Postmark: '29/NO'. *Charge*: '6'.
Source: holograph; MARC, MAM JW 6/38.

To an Unidentified Correspondent[347]

Norwich
November 28, 1786

I am glad to hear that God has inclined the heart of that good man Mr. [George] Merryweather towards you, and shall be always ready to assist in any way that can be proposed, for enabling you to procure a competent maintenance. But it is no great matter that I can do for any one person. I have so many to care for. If I had about twenty thousand pounds a year, I should want as much more for my poor neighbours. At present I can only commend them to God.

My love attend all the family. I am

Yours affectionately,

J. Wesley

Source: published transcription; *Christian Advocate and Journal* 25 (Jan. 24, 1850): 13.

[347] The recipient is likely the person needing aid that is mentioned in JW to George Merryweather, Oct. 6, 1786.

To the Rev. Freeborn Garrettson[348]

Lowestoft
November 30, 1786

My Dear Brother,

You have great reason to be thankful to God that he lets you see the fruit of your labours. Wherever any are awakened you do well to join them together immediately. But I do not advise you to go on too fast. It is not expedient to break up more ground than you can keep, to preach at any more places than your brethren or you can constantly attend. To preach once in a place and no more, very seldom does any good. It only alarms the devil and his children, and makes them more upon their guard against a first assault.

Wherever there is any Church service, I do not approve of having our service at the same hour—because I love the Church of England, and would assist, not oppose, it all I can.

How do the inhabitants of Shelburne, Halifax, and other parts of the province go on as to temporal things? Have they trade? Have they sufficiency of food and the other necessaries of life? And do they increase or decrease in numbers? It seems there is a scarcity of one thing, of good ink: for yours is so pale that many of your words are not legible.

As I take it for granted that you have had several conversations with Dr. [Thomas] Coke, I doubt not but you have proposed all your difficulties to him, and received full satisfaction concerning them.[349] Commending you to him that is able to guide and strengthen you in all things,

I am

Your affectionate friend and brother,

J. Wesley

Probably we shall send a little help for your building, if we live till the Conference. Observe the rules for building laid down in the *Minutes*.

I see nothing of your journal yet. I am afraid of another American revolt! I know not how to get the enclosed safe to Dr. Coke; prob-

---

[348] Replying to Garrettson's letter of Sept. 25, 1786.

[349] Actually, Thomas Coke's ship to North America was driven south by the weather and he ended up in the West Indies instead of Halifax, as originally planned; see Coke to JW, Jan. 2–5, 1787.

ably you know. On second thoughts I think it best not to write to
⟨…⟩ till I ⟨…⟩.[350]

Address: 'To / The Revd Mr Freeborn Garrettson / In Halifax / Nova
    Scotia'.   5
Source: holograph; Wesleyan University Library.

To Samuel Bradburn[351]   10

[London]
December 1786
Dear S[ammy,]   15
    You know I love you. Ever since I knew you I have neglected no
way of showing it that was in my power. And you know how I esteem
you for your zeal and activity, for your love of discipline, and for
your gifts which God has given you, particularly quickness of apprehension, and readiness of utterance, especially in prayer.   20
    Therefore I am jealous over you, lest you should lose any of the
things you have gained, and not receive a full reward.[352] And the
more so because I fear you are wanting in other respects. And who
will venture to tell you so? You will scarce know how to bear it from
me unless you lift up your heart to God. If you do this, I may ven-   25
ture to tell you what I fear without any further preface.
    I fear you think of yourself more highly than you ought to
think.[353] Do not you think too highly of your own understanding?
Of your gifts? Particularly in preaching, as if you were the very best
preacher in the connexion? Of your own importance, as if the work   30
of God here or there depended wholly or mainly on you? And of
your popularity, which I have found, to my surprise, far less, even
in London, than I expected?
    May not this be much owing to your want of brotherly love? With
what measure you mete, men will measure to you again. I fear there   35

---

[350] A portion of the last line is torn away and missing.
[351] Whitehead does not name the recipient, but Joseph Sutcliffe says it was sent to Samuel
Bradburn, who had been appointed to London in July, but struggling. See Sutcliffe's manuscript 'History of Methodism' (MARC, MA 1977/514, Vol. III), pp. 1124–25; and Bradburn,
Memoirs, 105–06.
[352] See 2 John 1:8.
[353] See Rom. 12:3.

is something unloving in your spirit, something not only of rough-
ness, but of harshness, yea of sourness! Are you not likewise extremely open to prejudice, and not easy to be cured of it? So that
whenever you are prejudiced you commence bitter, implacable, un-
5   merciful? If so, that people are prejudiced against you is both the
natural and the judicial consequence.

I am afraid lest your want of love to your neighbours should
spring from your want of love to God, from want of thankfulness. I
have sometimes heard you speak in a manner that made me tremble;
10   indeed, in terms that not only a weak *Christian* but even a serious
deist would scruple to use.

I fear you greatly want evenness of temper. Are you not generally
too high, or too low? Are not all your passions too lively? Your anger
in particular? Is it not too soon raised? And is it not too impetuous,
15   causing you to be violent, boisterous, bearing down all before you?

Now lift up your heart to God, or you will be angry at *me*. But I
must go a little further. I fear you are greatly wanting in the government of your tongue. You are not exact in relating facts. I have
observed it myself. You are apt to amplify, to enlarge a little beyond
20   the truth. You cannot imagine, if others observe this, how it will affect your reputation.

But I fear you are more wanting in another respect—that you give
a loose to your tongue when you are angry; that your language then
is not only sharp but coarse and ill-bred. If this be so, the people
25   will not bear it. They will not take it either from *you* or *me*. ...

Source: published transcription; Whitehead, *Life*, 2:439–41.

30

To William Palmer[354]

Norwich
December 3, 1786

35   Dear Billy,

I am glad to hear that the work of God still goes on well at [King's]
Lynn. It will go on more and more if you encourage all the believers to meet in band, and then exhort them to go on to perfection.[355]

---

[354] The address portion is missing, but William Palmer was currently serving as the Assistant for the [King's] Lynn circuit. There is also a note on the back of the letter, in an unknown
hand, identifying him as the recipient.
[355] See Heb. 6:1.

On Tuesday I am to set out for London. What you do, do with your might. And remember in your prayers, dear Billy,
> Your affectionate friend and brother,

J. Wesley

Source: holograph; Garrett-Evangelical, Methodist Manuscripts Collection.

To Mary Bosanquet Fletcher

London
December 9, 1786

My Dear Sister,

The book is now finished; I have the last proof now before me.[356] Two of the three accounts you give, I have at large. I only wait a few days, to see if my brother will write his elegy.[357]

I am clearly satisfied that you will do well to spend a considerable part of your time at Madeley. But I can by no means advise you to spend all your time there. I think you are a debtor to several other places also, particularly to London and Yorkshire. Nay, and if we live I should rejoice if you and I can contrive to be in those places at the same time—for I feel a great union of spirit with you. I cannot easily tell you how much I am, my very dear sister,
> Yours invariably,

J. Wesley

Address: 'To / Mrs Fletcher / At Madeley, near Shifnal / Salop'.
Postmark: '9/DE'. *Charge*: '5'.
Endorsement: by Fletcher, 'Decr 9th 1786'.
Source: holograph; MARC, DDWes 5/66.

---

[356] JW, *A Short Account of the Life and Death of the Rev. John Fletcher* (1786).
[357] Cf. JW to CW, Apr. 6, 1786; the elegy never came.

To William Roberts[358]

London
December 9, 1786

My Dear Brother,

In all probability you would now have been a wealthy man; and if so, your money would have paved your way to hell. God saw this, and prevented it. It is certainly the best way now to make a fair surrender. Place that money either in mine or any other name; it is little matter which.

Undoubtedly this is the best, if not the only way for the salvation of your soul. But it is plain. God seeth not as man seeth.[359] He judges by far other measures. Oh that you had continued an itinerant! Never man was better qualified for it.

I commend you to him who can make all things work together for good,[360] and am, dear Billy,

Your affectionate brother,

J. Wesley

Source: holograph; Oxford, Lincoln College, Archive, MS/WES/A/2/10.

To [John Eggleston][361]

London
December 10, 1786

My Dear Brother,

Although I can ill spare any time in the last month I am to spend here, yet I will (if God permit) spare you a few days. I hope to be

[358] Replying to Roberts's letter of Nov. 28, 1786, in which Roberts informed JW that he was declaring bankruptcy for his business.

[359] See 1 Sam. 16:7.

[360] See Rom. 8:28.

[361] There is no address portion. When a transcription was published in *WHS* 23 (1941): 51, it was said to be addressed to Frederick Eggleston of Newark. This seems unlikely. The letter came down through Rev. John Eggleston (1813–79), a Wesleyan minister who served as a missionary in Australasia. Rev. Eggleston's father was Frederick Eggleston (1785–1872). The letter was most likely to his grandfather, John Eggleston (1737–1813), one of the early members of the Methodist society in Newark, Nottinghamshire.

at Newark on the 12th or 13th of February, coming by the mail coach, and to open the room at noon.[362] For you will have company enough.

Peace be with all your spirits! I am,
Your affectionate brother,

J. Wesley

Source: holograph; Melbourne, Queen's College, JW18.

To Mary Cooke[363]

London
December 12, 1786

My Dear Sister and Friend,

Once or twice I have been a little out of order this autumn, but it was only for a day or two at a time. In general my health has been better for these last ten years than it ever was for ten years together since I was born. Ever since that good fever which I had in the north of Ireland,[364] I have had, as it were, a new constitution. All my pains and aches have forsaken me, and I am a stranger even to weariness of any kind. This is the Lord's doing, and it may well be marvellous in all our eyes.[365]

You oblige me much (and so your very dear sisters[366]) by being so solicitous about my health. I take it as a mark of your sincere affection. Meantime I wonder at you! I am almost ashamed that you should love me so well. It is plain how little you know me.

I am glad to find that the hunger and thirst after righteousness which God has given you does not abate. His promise cannot fail. You shall be filled, yea satisfied therewith.[367] But when you express

---

[362] JW ended up arriving at Newark on Sat., Feb. 10, 1787, but was not able to preach in the new preaching-house (Guildhall Street Chapel) until 9:00 am the next morning. See *Journal*, 24:3 in this edn.

[363] Replying to Cooke's letter of Dec. 4, 1786.

[364] In June 1775.

[365] See Ps. 118:23.

[366] Anne Cooke and Frances Cooke.

[367] See Matt. 5:6.

it, not many will understand you, except Mrs. Ballard[368] and our
dear Betsy Johnson.[369] However, do not fail to encourage all the believers round about you to press on to this mark.[370] Some will gladly
receive the word of exhortation. And surely a few witnesses will be
5   raised up. I cannot tell you how much I am
         Yours,

                                                        J. W.

10   *Address*: 'To / Miss Cook / In Duke Street / Trowbridge / Wilts'.
     Endorsement: by Cooke, 'good'.
     Source: holograph; MARC, WCB, D6/1/334.

15

To Ann Bolton

                                                   near London
20   December 15, 1786
My Dear Nancy,
     There can be no possible reason to doubt concerning the hap-
piness of that child. He did fear God, and according to his circumstances work righteousness.[371] This is the essence of religion,
25   according to St. Peter. His soul, therefore, was 'darkly safe with
God',[372] although he was only under the Jewish dispensation.[373]
     When the Son of Man shall come in his glory and assign every
man his own reward,[374] that reward will undoubtedly be proportioned: first, to our inward holiness, our likeness to God; secondly,
30   to our works; and thirdly, to our sufferings. Therefore for whatever
you suffer in time, you will be an unspeakable gainer in eternity.
Many of your sufferings, perhaps the greatest part, are now past.

---

[368] JW had visited a Mrs. Ballard in Bradford-on-Avon several times over the years. She
is possibly the Betty Ballard buried on Aug. 31, 1788; cf. JW *Journal*, Sept. 12, 1788, 23:109
in this edn.

[369] Elizabeth Johnson, of Bristol.

[370] See Phil. 3:14.

[371] See Acts 10:35.

[372] See CW, 'On the Death of Mrs. Ann Wigginton', Pt. I, st. 5, *Funeral Hymns* (1759), 32.

[373] John Fletcher used the term 'Jewish dispensation' in his 'Essay on Truth' to refer to
those who are obedient to the law, but have not yet received the witness of the Spirit. See JW to
Alexander Knox, Aug. 29, 1777, 29:365 in this edn.

[374] See Matt. 16:27.

But the joy is to come! Look up! My dear friend, look up! And see the crown before you![375] A little longer, and you shall drink of the rivers of pleasure that flow at God's right hand for evermore.[376]

My dear Nancy,

Adieu!   5

Address: 'To / Miss Bolton / In Witney / Oxfordshire'.
Postmark: '15/DE'. *Charge*: '4'.
Endorsement: by Bolton, 'Dec 15 –86'.
Source: holograph; MARC, MAM JW 1/97.   10

To Samuel Mitchell[377]   15

London
December 17, 1786

My Dear Brother,

You have great reason to praise God for his marvellous works,   20
and to take care that you do not grieve his Holy Spirit by taking
any glory to yourself. But I see a danger which you are not aware of.
Many in England have thought they attained to something higher
than loving God with all their hearts.[378] But this all came to nothing.
It is a snare of the devil.   25

I wish you could ask Dr. [Alexander] Crommelin's advice what
kind of truss you should wear.

Write to Mr. [James] Rogers concerning a fourth preacher.

I am, dear Sammy,

Yours affectionately,   30

J. Wesley

Address: 'To / Mr Saml. Mitchell / Near Iniskillen / Ireland'.
Postmarks: '17/DE' and 'DE/25'.   35
Source: holograph; MARC, MAM JW 4/17.

[375] See 2 Tim. 4:8.
[376] See Ps. 36:8.
[377] Mitchell was currently the Assistant for the Enniskillen circuit, with two itinerants assisting him.
[378] See the note on JW to Hester Ann Roe, Apr. 10, 1781, 29:640–41 in this edn.

To William Shepherd[379]

London
December 20, 1786

5   My Dear Brother,
    You did exceeding well in sending us so circumstantial an account
of our dear sister Peck's death.[380] We can only say, 'The Lord gave,
and the Lord hath taken away.'[381] He knows what is best for all his
children. This is a loud call to all that knew her as a burning and
10 a shining light![382] To you of Oxford in particular. Stir up the gift
of God that is in you![383] Provoke one another to love and to good
works![384] Who can tell which of you will be called next? O be ready!
Let him find you watching![385]
    I am, my dear brethren,
15   Your affectionate brother,

J. Wesley

Source: holograph; MARC, MAM JW 4/64.

20

To John Francis Valton[386]

London
[December 20, 1786]

My Dear Brother,
25 When I was quite worn down, it pleased God to make *my* marriage a means of restoring my health and strength. I trust yours will

---

[379] While there is no address portion, JW was replying to Shepherd's letter of Dec. 18,
1786. William Shepherd (1760–1836) lived in Banbury and was active in the Oxford society,
including as a local preacher; see *WMM* 8 (1852), 785. His younger brother, Rev. Richard
Herne Shepherd (1775–1850), once assisted JW with the sacrament in Bath; see JW, *Journal*,
Sept. 14, 1788, 24:109 in this edn.

[380] Delia (Wilkens) Peck, of Oxford and Eynsham; see JW to Ann Bolton, Oct. 12, 1786.

[381] Job 1:21.

[382] See John 5:35.

[383] See 2 Tim. 1:6.

[384] See Heb. 10:24.

[385] See Luke 12:37.

[386] Previous published transcriptions of this letter are problematic. The first was in
WMM 48 (1825): 824, which gives an abridged version of the material presented in this present letter, mixed with a paragraph that appears in a facsimile of a distinct letter that is dated
Dec. 22 (see below). Jackson, *Works* (3rd), 12:474, duplicates *WMM*. Telford had access to a
more complete text of the initial portion (and we follow Telford here), but adds at the end the
distinct letter of Dec. with paragraphs inverted. It seems unlikely JW sent two letters the same
day. We are proposing that this portion was sent Dec. 20, 1786; on the day that Valton married
Judith (Davis) Purnell in Bristol.

have the same effect upon you, though not by natural but divine efficacy. But this cannot be, unless you intermit preaching. I therefore positively require you, for a month from the date of this, not to preach more than twice in a week. And if you preach less, I will not blame you. 5

But you should at all hazards ride an hour every day, only wrapping yourself up very close. Take care not to lodge in too close a room and not to draw your curtains. For medicine I should chiefly recommend stewed prunes, and either beef tea or a small cup of *fresh churned* buttermilk four times a day. Let my dear friend sister 10 Valton take note of this.

As we are just entering upon the affairs of the poor at London, I want to know what has been done at Bristol. A particular account of the steps which have been taken there may both animate and instruct our friends here. 15

That grace and peace may be multiplied upon you both is the prayer of

Your affectionate friend and brother,

[J. Wesley]
20
I will speak to Dr. [John] Whitehead.

Address: 'To / Mr. Valton / At the Preaching-room / In Bristol'.
Source: published transcription; Telford, *Letters*, 7:360–61.

25

To Zachariah Yewdall

London 30
December 20, 1786

My Dear Brother,

You do well to tell me where you are and what you are doing.[387] Do not you know that several envy you, because, they say you are one of my favourites? I am glad to hear that you find some fruit 35 again even at poor Musselburgh. I expect more from the new than the old hearers, most of whom are as salt that has lost its savour.[388] Possibly some good may be done at Dalkeith too. But you will have

---

[387] Yewdall had been stationed on the Berwick circuit by the 1786 Conference. John Pawson was Assistant on the neighbouring Edinburgh circuit.
[388] See Matt. 5:13.

need of patience. I do not despair even of Preston Pans if you can procure a tolerable place.

It is a great point gained if Mr. Collis is diligent in attending his lectures. If he has likewise resolution to refrain from gay company, there is reason to hope that he will be a valuable man.

You cannot have a better adviser than Mr. [John] Pawson. Take care to husband your time. Peace be with you and yours!

I am

Your affectionate brother,

[J. Wesley]

Source: published transcription; Jackson, *Works* (3rd), 13:16.

To James Hall

London
December 22, 1786

This is to certify whom it may concern that I give my full and free consent to the sale of our old preaching-house in Bury, Lancashire. Witness so my hand,

John Wesley

Address: 'To / Mr James Hall / At Mr James Ninds[389] / In Tewkbury/ Worcestershire'.
Source: holograph; Bury, Lancashire, England, Bury Methodist Circuit.

To John Francis Valton

London
December 22, 1786

My Dear Brother,

We have great reason to rejoice at the prosperity of the work of God in Bristol. And I hope *you* have also reason to rejoice for your

---

[389] After the death of his first wife, Sarah (Ward) Nind, in 1783, James Nind resettled in Tewkesbury, Gloucestershire and married Meliora Prior (1760–1833).

union with an Israelite indeed.[390] Pray do as much as you can, and don't attempt to do more, or you will very soon do nothing.

It is amazing that we cannot find in the three kingdoms a fit master for Kingswood school! Talk largely with Michael Griffith. Then pray with him and for him, and God will give him gifts.[391]

Peace be with your spirits!

Adieu!

Source: facsimile of holograph; *WHS* 25 (1945), cover page and p. 1.[392]

To an Unidentified Recipient

London
December 23, 1786

It would give me pleasure to do you service at any time. But at present I am afraid it is not in my power. It is not the Lords of the Treasury, but the Commissioners of the Customs, that dispose of all the places of the Custom House officers. But I have not the least interest with any of them. I do not know them so much as by name. And I have no money at all beforehand, but live from hand to mouth.

I am, with love to all the family,

Yours affectionately,

J. Wesley

Source: holograph; WTS (DC), Archives, Oxham Collection.

---

[390] See John 1:47; referring to Valton's new wife (see letter of Dec. 20, 1786 above).

[391] See JW to Valton, Oct. 29, 1786.

[392] At the time the facsimile was published the holograph was part of the collection of the Mitchell Library, Sydney, Australia; it cannot now be located.

5

To Theophilus Lessey[1]

10

[London]
c. January 1787

My Dear Brother,
    There is no one point in all the Bible concerning which I have
said more or written more for almost these fifty years than faith. I
15 can say no more than I have said. To believe the being and attributes
of God is the faith of an heathen. To believe the Old Testament and
trust in him that was to come was the faith of a Jew.[2] To believe
Christ gave himself for *me* is the faith of a Christian. This faith he
did give to *you*, and I hope does still. Hold it fast without any philo-
20 sophical refinement. When we urge any to *believe*, we mean, 'Accept
that faith which God is now ready to give.' Indeed, believing is the
act of man, but it is the *gift* of God. For no one ever did believe unless God gave him the power. Take it simply without reasoning, and
hold it fast.
25   I am
      Your affectionate brother,
      J. Wesley

30

Source: published transcription; *Wesleyan Methodist Magazine* 45 (1822):
    419.

<hr>

[1] Theophilus Lessey (1757–1821) lived for several years with his grandfather, Rev.
Theophilus Lessey (1700–74), rector of West Bagborough, Somerset, where he was apprenticed to a coach-builder. Converted to Methodism during a visit to his mother in Bristol, Lessey
married Philadelphia Coussins in 1778, and served for several years as a local preacher. In 1786
he entered the itinerant ministry, a role he filled for 34 years. See 10:596 in this edn.; *Minutes*
(post-Wesley, 1822), 5:294; and *WMM* 45 (1822), 345–51, 417–23, 485–91, 553–60. Lessey
had written JW during his first appointment about the nature of faith, and received this reply.
   [2] JW's distinction between the faith of a heathen and that of a Jew is more recent than he
suggests here; cf. Sermon 1, *Salvation by Faith*, I.1–3, 1:115–16 in this edn.; to Sermon 106,
'On Faith', I, 3:493–98 in this edn.

To Adam Clarke³

near London
January 3, 1787   5

Dear Adam,

You see, none that trust in him are confounded.⁴ When God is for us, who can be against us?⁵ Discipline is the great want in Guernsey; without which the work of God cannot prosper. You did well to set upon it without delay, and to be as exact as possible. It is a true   10
saying, 'The soul and the body make the man, and the spirit and discipline make a Christian.'⁶

We heard of a remarkable awakening in some part of the island. I hope those who were then awakened are not all fallen asleep again. Preaching in the morning is one excellent means of keeping their   15
souls awake.

If you desire to have any health, you must never pass one day without walking at least an hour. And take care not to speak too loud or too long. Never exceed an hour at a time. Grace be with all your spirits!   20

I am, dear Adam,
Yours affectionately,

J. Wesley

Address: 'To / Mr Adam Clark / At Capt. [George] Walker's⁷ in /   25
Guernsey'.
Postmark: '3/IA'.
Endorsement: by Clarke, 'R[e]c[eive]d Jany. 7, 1787'.
Source: holograph; MARC, WCB, D6/1/78.

30

³ JW was replying to Clarke's letter of Dec. 20, 1786, describing progress in his ministry in Guernsey.
⁴ See Ecclus. 2:10; 1 Pet. 2:6.
⁵ See Rom. 8:21.
⁶ See note on JW to William Church, Oct. 13, 1778, 29:447 in this edn.
⁷ Capt. George Walker was a member of the English class of the Methodist society in Guernsey. See Clarke to JW, Dec. 20, 1786; Lelièvre, *Méthodisme*, 215; and *WMM* 16 (1870), 237.

To Ann Dupuy Taylor[8]

London
January 12, 1787

My Dear Nancy,

I do not at all blame you for your bashfulness; yet I commend you for overcoming it. From the time I talked with you first, I felt a great concern for you. And though you have such parents to assist you as few young persons have, yet considering the dangers to which youth is exposed, you may possibly want still more help. And if you can speak freely to me, then (not otherwise) I may be helpful to you. This you will need, particularly if you come into any trials. But hitherto

> Secluded from the world, and all its care,
> Hast thou to joy or grief, to hope or fear?[9]

Yet still you must watch and pray, or you will enter into temptation.[10] Did you ever enjoy a sense of the love of God?[11] Did you ever know him as a God of pardoning love? If you did, in what manner did you first receive that knowledge? You may write as simply and as artlessly to me as you please. For I am no critic. And besides, I love you too well to criticize upon anything that you say. Therefore you may write without any reserve to, my dear Nancy,

Yours affectionately,

J. Wesley

Address: 'To / Miss Nancy Taylor / at the Preachinghouse / near / Leeds'.
Source: holograph; MARC, MA 1992/035.

---

[8] Ann Dupuy Taylor (c. 1771–1847) was the daughter of the itinerant Thomas Taylor and his wife Ann (Dupuy) Taylor. Her father was currently the Assistant in Leeds.

[9] Matthew Prior, *Solomon*, ii.386–87.

[10] See Matt. 26:41.

[11] Orig., 'the love of love'; almost certainly a slip on JW's part.

To William Holmes[12]

London
January 13, 1787 5

Dear Billy,

You do well to exclude all disorderly walkers. We shall be far better without them than with them.[13]

I am afraid the loss of Sally Baker will not easily be supplied at Monmouth,[14] unless her sister[15] or one of Mr. John's daughters 10 would rise up and take her place.

Build nowhere, till you find a very convenient situation. And this should be a matter of solemn prayer. I am glad to hear my dear sister Skinner has not quite forgotten me. My kind love to her and sister Lewis. See that brother Baldwin and you strengthen each other's 15 hand in God![16]

I am, dear Billy,[17]

Address: 'To / Mr Will Holmes / At the Preachinghouse / In Cardiff /
   South Wales'. 20
Postmark: '13/IA'. *Charge*: '6'.
Source: holograph; Bridwell Library (SMU).[18]

---

[12] William Holmes (d. 1833), a native of Devonshire, became a member of a Methodist society in 1767. He served as a local preacher, until appointed by JW to serve as an itinerant in the western Cornwall circuit in 1783 (see 10:593 in this edn.). He would continue to itinerate for 32 years, until retiring in High Wycombe in 1815. Holmes was currently appointed as Assistant of the Glamorgan circuit. See *Minutes* (post-Wesley, 1834), 7:340.

[13] Orig., 'that with them'; a slip by JW.

[14] Sarah Baker of Monmouth had now married Isaac Skinner of Cowbridge, Glamorgan and moved there. See JW to Baker, Oct. 27, 1784.

[15] Thomas and Jane (Hughes) Baker, of Monmouth, had a second daughter, Elizabeth (1762–1843), who did not marry until 1792.

[16] George Baldwin (d. 1810) had been admitted 'on trial' as an itinerant at the 1786 Conference and assigned to serve with Holmes on the Glamorgan circuit. He continued to serve for 24 years, until dying during the 1810 Conference. See *Minutes* (post-Wesley, 1811), 3:194.

[17] The final closing and signature are missing.

[18] Held previously in WMC Museum, 2002.001.024.

To Joseph Algar

London
January 15, 1787

Dear Joseph,

Poor Lakenheath revived! That is good news indeed! I have no objection to the sending Thomas Cooper into Birmingham circuit immediately, if I can but find a single man capable of assisting you in Colchester circuit. Tommy Cooper has fairly recovered his credit, and I trust will be more useful than ever he was in his life.[19]

I am, dear Joseph,

Your affectionate friend and brother,

J. Wesley

Is there any young man in your circuit whom you could recommend for a writing-master at Kingswood School?

Postmark: '17/IA'.
Source: holograph; Drew, Methodist Archives.

To Richard Rodda

London
January 17, 1787

My Dear Brother,

I am glad you have taken in hand that blessed work of setting up Sunday schools in Chester.[20] It seems to me that these will be one great means of reviving religion throughout the nation. I wonder Satan has not yet sent out some able champion against them.

---

[19] See the note on JW to Cooper, Mar. 31, 1786.

[20] Sunday School may have been offered by Methodists in Chester as early as 1782, but Rodda brought greater focus to this effort when he was appointed Assistant for the circuit in 1786. See Bretherton, *Chester*, 225–33.

It is a good thing to stop Mr. Salmon, but it would be a far greater to reclaim him.[21] And why should we suppose it to be impossible? Who knows the power of mighty prayer?

As I must take Plymouth Dock in my way to Bristol, I must make as swift a journey as I can from Bristol to Dublin. So I shall [have] little time to halt by the way.

I am

    Your affectionate friend and brother,

                J. Wesley

Address: 'To / Mr. Rodda / At the Octagon / In Chester'.
Source: published transcription; *Wesleyan Methodist Magazine* 69 (1846): 562–63.

To an Unidentified Recipient[22]

                London
           January 17, 1787

Sir,

I return you my sincere thanks for your generous benefaction. In spring, if I live, I shall be in Dublin myself, and I shall then try what can be done for poor Mr. Bull.[23] I really believe our Lord is striving by this severe method to make him not almost but altogether a Christian.[24]

Wishing you every gospel blessing, I remain, sir,

    Your obliged and obedient servant,

                John Wesley

Source: holograph; Duke, Rubenstein, Wesley Family Papers, Box WF 1.

[21] Orig., 'Salmons'. Joseph Wittingham Salmon (1747–1826), who lived in Nantwich, Cheshire, part of Rodda's circuit, had corresponded with JW (see his letter of July 2, 1777) and JW had visited him on Apr. 6, 1779 (see *Journal*, 23:123 in this edn.). In recent years Salmon had drifted toward the mysticism of Madame Guyon and others. This had led Rodda to prevent his preaching in Methodist settings.

[22] On the back of the letter is an annotation (not in JW's hand) that lists 13 shillings tied to the name of 'Revd. Mr. Bull' and 15 shillings tied to 'Mr. Bull Junr.'. It is unclear whether this note has anything to do with the benefaction mentioned in JW's letter.

[23] This is apparently the John Bull of Dublin, mentioned in JW to John Whitehead, Feb. 21, 1767, 28:66 in this edn.; and JW to Henry Brooke, Sept. 6, 1779, 29:506 in this edn.

[24] See JW, *The Almost Christian* (1741), 1:131–41 in this edn.

To Andrew Inglis[25]

London
January 20, 1787

5   Dear Andrew,

Are you afraid lest James Wood's coming to [North] Shields will tear the society in pieces? In the name of wonder, why then do you not prevent it while it is in your power? I have said I will not require you to do this, but I advise you immediately to take that house into
10   your own hands.[26] You may do it so as to bring no burden upon us, and I see nothing that hinders you but a *silly sense of honour*.

I am, dear Andrew,
    Yours,

[J. Wesley]

15
Source: published transcription; Coates, *New Portrait*, 12.

20   ## To John Mason[27]

London
January 24, 1787

My Dear Brother,

25   I do not wonder that the work of God should flourish at Trow-bridge, where a few of our sisters are a pattern to the whole town. But it is exceeding strange that any considerable good should be

---

[25] This letter picks up the story of replacing the first preaching-house in North Shields, on which the lease expired in late 1783; see JW to George Snowden, c. Dec. 1, 1785. A sharp split had developed between those who supported building on the land on the river bank offered for sale by Patrick Watson, and those (led by Edward Coates) who rejected this site and had found an alternative site on level ground further from the river at Millbourn Place. JW's interaction with the two groups was inconsistent (at best). And his itinerants in the area exacerbated the situation. Those stationed in Newcastle (with Andrew Inglis now Assistant) backed Coates's party, with the intention of incorporating the new house into their circuit; while the itinerants stationed in Sunderland (where James Wood was Assistant) backed the other party, with the intention of bringing the preaching-house on the river bank into their circuit.

[26] That is, JW wanted Inglis and the Newcastle circuit to take responsibility for *both* of the new preaching-houses being constructed in North Shields—something the party led by Edward Coates stoutly resisted, as they did not think there was need for two houses so close together.

[27] Mason was currently Assistant for the Bradford-on-Avon circuit, which included the four localities mentioned.

done at poor, dead, quarrelsome Frome![28] We can only say, 'The wind bloweth where it listeth!'[29] Now avail yourself of the opportunity! It is equally strange that there should be such peace at Stalbridge.

At Ditcheat I doubt not but you will overcome evil with good.   5
I am
    Your affectionate friend and brother,

                                          J. Wesley

Address: 'To / Mr Mason / At the Preachinghouse / in the Devizes /   10
    Wilts'.
Postmark: '24/IA'. *Charge*: '5'.
Source: holograph; Lovely Lane Museum.

                                                  15

To the Rev. Dr. William White[30]

                                City Road [London]
                                January 24, 1787   20
Reverend Sir,
I am just now favoured with a line from you, which I answer immediately.[31] I am sorry that I am engaged to set out for Dorking early tomorrow morning. I would have waited on you myself on Saturday or on Monday, but that it is the time appointed for exam-   25
ining our society, which finds me full employment from morning to night. If you stay a week or two longer in town, to have an hour's conversation with you will be a great pleasure to, reverend sir,
    Your obedient brother and servant,

                                        John Wesley   30

---

[28] See JW to Phoebe (French) Nail, Nov. 12, 1783, on the split that took place in Frome.

[29] John 3:8.

[30] William White (1748–1836), a native of Philadelphia, served as a Church of England priest in Pennsylvania prior to the Revolutionary War and was one of the leaders in organizing the Protestant Episcopal Church in the United States after the war. He was currently in London to be consecrated a bishop for the new church, which took place Feb. 4, 1787 at Lambeth Palace.

[31] White wrote on the back side of JW's holograph: 'I wished to have held a conversation with Mr. Wesley concerning his recent system respecting America, and had conveyed to him a letter of introduction from Mr. [Joseph] Pilmore with that design. But I considered this letter as a civil evasion, and being hurried with business preparatory to my departure did not expend any effort.' Pilmore (and Coke for a time) was hopeful that the Methodist Episcopal Church could be united to the Protestant Episcopal Church.

Address: 'To / The Revd Dr White / At Mr Steele's / In Derby Street
Parliament Street / Westminster.
Postmark: 'Penny Post Paid'.
Source: holograph; Austin, Texas, Archives of the Episcopal Church,
White Mss. Vol. 2, VII. 366.

To William Carne[32]

London
January 26, 1787

My Dear Brother,

Fifty by thirty-two or thirty-four I suppose will do. I think Busveal house is of the best form I have seen in Cornwall.[33] I beg you
will employ no lawyer to settle it when built, but transcribe the
Conference form verbatim, and observe the little rules laid down
in the *Minutes*.[34] You may consider whether the preachers' house
should not be two rooms of a floor and three stories high? It seems
a good thought to add a penny a week, which will ruin nobody. Certainly you ought to keep the writings in your hands, giving a bond
to settle the house on trustees when the debt is paid.

I hope to be at the Dock on Wednesday, March 3, but I doubt I
shall not get a mile farther.

I am

Your affectionate brother,

J. Wesley

St. Austle is in the list of 'houses to be built' in the *Minutes* of
1786.

Address: 'Mr. William Carne / In Penzance / Cornwall'.
Source: holograph; privately held (Bridwell Library [SMU] holds transcription).

[32] Carne's letter to JW is not known to survive. As steward of the east Cornwall circuit, he
had apparently sought advice about the preaching-house in St. Austell, which was approved to
be built at the 1786 Conference; see 10:614 in this edn.

[33] Orig., 'Bisweal house'. Busveal was a mining settlement about 1 mile east of Redruth,
the location of Gwinnap Pit. JW was apparently referring to the house in which the preachers
for the circuit stayed, since there was no preaching-house here at the time.

[34] See 'Large' *Minutes* (1763), §67, 10:868–70 in this edn.; and 'Large' *Minutes* (1770),
§68, 10:896–97 in this edn.

To Edward Coates[35]

London
January 31, 1787 5

Dear Sir,

Mr. [John] Wesley begs me to inform you that he has but one end in all things, he wishes to do all he can for the good of mankind, as it stands connected with the will of God. If in any thing he mistakes the means, in order to effect the thing he so much wishes, it is be- 10 cause of the smallness of his judgment and not the badness of his intention. I am therefore to say he now thinks it his duty to take the Dr. [Patrick Watson]'s house into one of the circuits, if he (the Dr.) agrees to the conditions contained in Mr. [Thomas] Rankin's let- ter.[36] If Mr. [Andrew] Inglis can take it into the Newcastle circuit, 15 Mr. Wesley thinks it will be the best; if not, Mr. [James] Wood can take the house into his circuit.[37] Only Mr. Wesley thinks it would not be proper to open the house before the matter in contest is over betwixt the Earl and the Dr.[38]

I wish my letter was more pleasing to all of you. I can now only 20 recommend you to God, and that you may be directed by him in all things, is the prayer of

Yours,

John Broadbent[39]

---

[35] Edward Coates (fl. 1780s), an upholsterer in Newcastle upon Tyne, had been a trustee of the first preaching-house in North Shields. When the lease on this house expired in late 1783, he opposed from the beginning the option of building on the river-bank lot offered for sale by Patrick Watson (see JW to George Snowden, Dec. 1, 1785). Coates led the group that purchased and started building a preaching-house on the alternative site of Millbourn Place. Coates believed there was need for only one preaching-house in the area, and pressed JW to disavow any interest in the house on the river bank (see Coates to JW, Jan. 24, 1787). JW's ulti- mate response was to say that he would accept which ever house (or both!) that was offered to the Conference *at no cost* (i.e., without reimbursing the expense for the land or construction). This stance eventually led Coates's party (with the encouragement of John Atlay) to refuse settling their house on the Conference plan. In 1789 the Millbourn preaching-house went independent, and Edward Coates aligned with the Methodist New Connexion. See Charles Federer, 'Wesley and the North Shields Chapel Case', *WHS* 4 (1904): 223–31; and Coates, *New Portrait*.

[36] This is apparently a mental slip on JW's part. The letter to Patrick Watson on Aug. 12, 1786, laying out the conditions for the Conference accepting the preaching-house built on Watson's land was written by Thomas Coke. See Coates, *New Portrait*, 8–9.

[37] See the note on JW to Andrew Inglis, Jan. 20, 1787.

[38] A question had arisen about whether some of the land that Watson added to his offered lot on the river bank was his, or belonged instead to the Earl of Carlisle.

[39] Broadbent was the itinerant currently travelling with JW as his assistant.

Address: 'To / Mr. Edward Coates / North Shields'.
Source: published transcription; Coates, *New Portrait*, 14.

5

To Ann (Foard) Thornton[40]

London
February 4, 1787

10 My Dear Sister,

I think Mr. [John] Hutchinson was a man of strong understanding, but greatly obscured by uncommon pride and sourness of temper. He was the twin soul of Dr. [Richard] Bentley.[41] Many of his remarks I exceedingly approve of. That upon the sin of Uzzah is

15 highly probable.[42] His writings are far more agreeable to my taste than those of Dr. Hunter, an exceeding pretty writer, who seems to propose Dr. Blair for his pattern.[43] Both the one and the other are quite too elegant for me. Give me plain, strong Dr. Horne.[44]

Your letters (as well as your conversation) are always agreeable to,

20 my dear sister,

Your affectionate friend and brother,

J. Wesley

25 My best wishes attend Mr. Thornton and all your family.[45]

---

[40] Ann Foard had been a regular correspondent with JW for several years before her marriage. JW had previously cautioned her against Hutchinson's rejection of the traditional vowel points in reading Hebrew; see JW to Foard, Feb. 4, 1769, 28:200–01 in this edn.

[41] See the comment on Bentley, and the broader reservations about Hutchinson, in JW to William Digby, c. July 1787.

[42] Uzzah was struck dead by God for 'taking hold' of the Ark of the Covenant (see 2 Sam. 6:3–8, 1 Chr. 13:7–11). Hutchinson argued that the sin was not in touching the Ark, but in attempting to retain possession of the Ark for him and his family; see John Hutchinson, *Philosophical and Theological Works* (London: J. Hodges, 1748–49), 6:151–55.

[43] JW read Henry Hunter's *Sacred Biography; or, the History of the Patriarchs from Adam to Abraham* (London: J. Murray, 1784) on Jan. 5–6, 1787; see his *Journal* (24:2 in this edn.) and diary (24:196 in this edn.). Thornton apparently asked for JW's opinion on Hunter. JW's comparison is to Hugh Blair, *Sermons* (London: Strahan & Cadall, 1777); cf. JW, *Journal*, May 10, 1779, 23:130–31 in this edn.

[44] JW was apparently referring to George Horne's *Commentary on the Book of Psalms* (Oxford: Clarendon, 1776); cf. the comment on reading it in JW, *Journal*, Mar. 28–31, 1783, 23:266 in this edn.

[45] Ann Foard married John Thornton (1740–1804), an undertaker in Southwark, on July 7, 1772.

Address: 'To / Mrs Thornton / At No 86 in / Blackman Street'.
Source: holograph; Pitts Library (Emory), John Wesley Papers (MSS 153), 3/35.

5

To George Gidley

near London
February 9, 1787   10

My Dear Brother,

I hope to be at Exeter on the 27th instant and the next day at Plymouth. But I have no intention to go any further than the Dock, having no time to spare before I set out for Ireland. On the Monday following I propose to return to Exeter, and on Tuesday (by the   15 coach) to Bath.

I apprehend it requires a far greater interest than mine to procure a collector's place for anyone.[46] But I will inquire. I am

Your affectionate brother,

J. Wesley   20

Address: 'To / Mr Gidley / Supervisor / In Bideford / Devonshire'.
Postmark: '9/FE'.
Source: holograph; Drew, Methodist Archives.

25

To Jonathan Edmondson[47]

Newark   30
February 10, 1787

Dear Jonathan,

Keep in the very same path you are now.[48] Hear nothing of the disputes on the one side or the other. But earnestly exhort those on

---

[46] Gidley was a supervisor of collection of excise taxes. It is not clear whether he was seeking a new placement, or asking for JW's assistance in getting someone else appointed.

[47] Jonathan Edmondson (1767–1842), raised a Methodist in Keighley was accepted 'on trial' as an itinerant at the 1786 Conference (see 10:596 in this edn.). He would serve for half a century, including as President of Conference. See his autobiography in *WMM* 6 (1850): 1–16, 115–23; and *Minutes* (post-Wesley, 1842), 9:311–12.

[48] Edmondson wrote JW about a conflict between the two other itinerants assigned with him to the Epworth circuit (James Watson and John Fenwick), stating his intention not to side with either party, and asking for JW's advice; cf. *WMM* 6 (1850), 5.

both to follow after peace and holiness, without which they cannot see the Lord.[49]

I am

Your affectionate brother,

J. Wesley

Address: 'To / Mr Jon. Edmondson'.
Source: holograph; Huntington Library, Manuscripts, HM 57055.

To the Rev. Thomas Cursham[50]

Hinckley
February 14, 1787

Dear Sir,

I visit my friends here in my return to London.

I think the reasons you allege are quite sufficient for not accepting Mr. Root's curacy,[51] but waiting till the good providence of God opens some other door. It seems highly probable that you will be enabled to raise a good school at Sutton[-in-]Ashfield. Certainly there is no impropriety in making the trial. Wherever you are, I advise you to hang out no false colours, but go on in simplicity and godly sincerity.[52] If I can assist you in anything, it will be a real pleasure to, dear sir,

Your affectionate friend and brother,

J. Wesley

My best wishes attend your wife.[53]

Address: 'To / The Revd Mr Cursham / To the care of Mr [Thomas] Carlill / In Derby'.
Source: holograph; MARC, MAM JW 2/73.

---

[49] See Heb. 12:14.

[50] Thomas Cursham (1750–1805), was currently curate at Ashover, Derbyshire, and operating a boarding school in Sutton-in-Ashfield, Notts., nearby; cf. JW to Cursham, July 12, 1788. Cursham would be named vicar of Annesley, Notts., in 1794.

[51] Rev. William Roots had added a curacy at Edington to his appointments and was likely seeking someone to fill it for him.

[52] See 2 Cor. 1:12.

[53] Cursham married Ann Leeson (1761–1843), of Skegby, Notts., in 1784.

To the Rev. Joseph Taylor

Hinckley
February 14, 1787   5

Dear Joseph,

Constant exercise will be full as necessary for the establishment of your health as even temperance in speaking.[54] On Sunday morning the whole service may continue an hour and an half. At any other time, morning and evening, our service should not exceed an hour.   10

I cannot at all approve of that dull way of spinning out many sermons from the same text, unless your text be the thirteenth [chapter] of the first Epistle to the Corinthians or the Sermon on the Mount. It is this chiefly which occasions so many sermons in Scotland without any application. A sermon should rather be all application. This is the better extreme.   15

It seemed to be the design and endeavour of Mr. Henry to say all that could be said on every subject.[55] But he will never be imitated herein by any who take either our Lord or his apostles for their pattern.   20

I expect to be at Bristol from March the 8th to the 19th, at Birmingham on the 24th, at Manchester April the 2nd, and at Dublin as soon after as possible.

Put forth all the strength you have, and you shall have more. I am, dear Joseph,   25

Your affectionate friend and brother,

J. Wesley

Address: 'To / Revd Mr Joseph Taylor / in / Aberdeen'.
Postmark: 'FE/18'. *Charge*: '5'.   30
Source: holograph; Vancouver (British Columbia) School of Theology, H. R. MacMillan Library, Rare Book Room.

---

[54] Cf. JW to Taylor, Nov. 11, 1786.
[55] Apparently referring to Matthew Henry's 4 vol. *Exposition of the Old Testament*.

To Thomas McGeary

London
February 15, 1787

Dear Tommy,

It is a wonderful strange thing that in all the three kingdoms we cannot find such a schoolmaster as we want![56] I have sent to every part of England, and to every Assistant I wrote to; but none can give me any information. We are expecting every day to hear from one and another. But still we hear nothing. There is only one point more, that *I* should be weary and say, 'Let it go as it will. I will trouble myself about it no more.' Then there is an end of Kingswood School, and the labour of near forty years is lost! But I trust that will not be the case yet, for God heareth the prayers!

I am, with love to sister McGeary,[57] dear Tommy,
Your affectionate brother,

J. Wesley

Address: 'To / Mr McGeary / At Kingswood School / near / Bristol'.
Postmark: '15/FE'. *Charge*: '5'.
Source: holograph; Bath, Kingswood School, Wesley Centre Archives.

To Abraham Andrews

Deptford
February 16, 1787

My Dear Brother,

'It is good to *conceal* the secrets of a king, but to *declare* the lovingkindness of the Lord.'[58] I am afraid you have indulged silence and retirement *too* much. If you retire from Hertford, you must not retire from all the world. 'Man was not born in shades to lie',[59] but to

---

[56] Cf. JW to John Francis Valton, Dec. 22, 1786; and JW to Joseph Algar, Jan. 15, 1787.
[57] McGeary married Christiana Simpson (d. 1812) in 1786.
[58] See Tob. 12:7.
[59] [Anne Winchilsea,] 'Alcidor', st. 11, in John Dryden (ed.), *Miscellany Poems* (4th edn., London: Jacob Tonson, 1716), 6:53–54. JW copied in his MS Poetry Miscellany, 134–35; and published in *AM* 1 (1778): 479–81. For other uses, see JW, *Journal*, July 27, 1775, 22:459 in this edn.; and JW, *Journal*, Sept. 11, 1789, 24:155 in this edn.

assist and be assisted by his fellow creatures. Wherever you choose to reside, you should see that it is a place where you may either *find* fellow-travellers to heaven or *make* them. It will be easiest if you fix upon some place where there is a little society already. The liveliest I have lately seen in the south of England is at Mitcham. 5 About thirty plain, simple people are there joined together, and are all athirst for salvation.

I commend you to him in whom you have believed,[60] and am,
Your affectionate brother,
J. Wesley 10

Address: 'To / Mr Abr. Andrews'.
Source: holograph; privately held (WWEP Archive holds photocopy).

15

To Robert Carr Brackenbury

20
Deptford
February 16, 1787
Dear Sir,
There is something very remarkable in the experience of that blessed man, Thomas Basker. If I can get a little time, I will make 25 a large extract from it for the *Arminian Magazine*.[61] But the experience of our sister is far more remarkable, and equal to almost any that I have seen; which I am the more surprised at, because she is of so short standing—being a mere novice in comparison of Miss [Elizabeth] Johnson, Miss [Elizabeth] Ritchie, and a few 30 others whose experience most nearly resembles hers.[62] I know not but I should write a few lines to her, only I suppose she does not understand English.[63]

---

[60] See 2 Tim. 1:12.

[61] It appeared after JW's death: 'The Experience of Thomas Basker, of Ashby near Spilsby, in Lincolnshire', *AM* 15 (1782): 638–43 (see in-letters, c. Feb. 10, 1787).

[62] The 'sister' is Jeanne Le Gros Bisson; for details see JW's letter to her of Aug. 4, 1787. JW moved quickly to publish 'The Experience of J. B. of St. Hellier's in the Isle of Jersey' in *AM* 11 (1788): 71–73, 127–30, 182–84, 235–37, 295–97 (see in-letters, c. Feb. 10, 1787).

[63] Brackenbury likely urged Jeanne to write after receiving this letter; see her letter to JW of July 11, 1787.

I hear you enforce my advice to Adam Clarke 'not to speak too long or too loud'.[64] He must be reminded of this again and again. Otherwise his usefulness, if not his life, will soon be at an end.

Whoever reads our *Journals*, or the account of the work of God
5   near Everton,[65] may observe that there always were in the beginning of any work, divine dreams and visions. That these may be abused is certain; but still the rule obtains, '*Tolletur abusus, maneat usus*'.[66] Bodily convulsions also have constantly accompanied the dawn of a general work of God. The nature of these likewise I have explained
10 again and again, to the satisfaction of all sincere enquirers. Those of another character never were, and never will be satisfied. The despisers will 'wonder and perish'.[67] But you have need to take great care, to settle the heads of the preachers right, that *they* may not hurt either themselves or others. Nay, that they may not grieve the
15 Holy Spirit of God, by denying or undervaluing his work.

The marrying such a person as you mention would probably be a blessing to our brother [Jean] De Quêteville.[68] I do not doubt but he will take your advice concerning immoderate or improper self-denial. For every reasonable Christian knows that we must not offer
20 murder for sacrifice.[69] We must not weaken, or any way injure our body, for the good of our soul.

Dr. Coke's intended subscription, I am afraid, has produced little or nothing.[70] I never received or saw one guinea on that account. Whatever he received, I suppose he carried with him. It is well if he
25 did not carry it to the bottom of the sea; for we have heard nothing either from him or of him, since he left England![71]

Any person's losing a degree of what God had given, does by no means prove it was not given at all. She *was* undoubtedly saved from sin, whether it has since re-entered or not. Let her now stand
30 fast in the grace of God.[72]

---

[64] See JW to Clarke, Jan. 3, 1787.

[65] See JW, *Journal*, May 30, 1759, 21:195–200 in this edn.

[66] 'Let the abuse be removed, let the use remain.'

[67] Acts 13:41.

[68] Jean De Quêteville would marry Susanne de Jersey (1768–1843) on Apr. 30, 1788 in Castel, Isle of Guernsey.

[69] See JW, 'Sermon on the Mount, VII', IV.4, 1:609 in this edn.

[70] Coke, *An Address to the Pious and Benevolent*; proposing an annual subscription for the support of missionaries (London: s.n., 1786); see JW's prefatory letter, Mar. 12, 1786.

[71] Coke had embarked at Gravesend for Nova Scotia on Sept. 24, 1785. Bad weather delayed the voyage and eventually drove his ship to Antigua. See Coke's account in a letter to JW, dated Jan. 2–5, 1787, which eventually reached JW.

[72] See 1 Pet. 5:12.

Had not you better expend those two guineas toward supplying the wants of the preachers? To which our brethren here will doubtless add what is needful.[73]

I think our sister may preach in private houses.

I expect to be in Bristol, March 8–19; in Dublin, about the middle of April. I see nothing amiss in the tract, only that you seem to lay too great stress upon *sufferings*.[74] They are not essential either to the being or even the *degree* of holiness. St. John was full as holy as Paul, though without an hundredth part of his sufferings.

My dear sir,
Adieu!

Address: 'To / Robert Brackenbury Esq / In St Helier's / Isle of Jersey'.
Source: holograph; Wesley's Chapel (London), LDWMM 1994/1985.

To John King[75]

near London
February 16, 1787

I generally write to all that desire it, though not often in many words. What I have to say may be confined in a narrow compass. It requires a great degree of watchfulness to retain the perfect love of God. And one great means of retaining it is frankly to declare what God has given you, and earnestly to exhort all the believers you meet with to follow after full salvation.[76]

Source: published transcription; *Wesleyan Methodist Magazine* 47 (1824): 3.

---

[73] Orig., 'what what is needful'.

[74] Brackenbury had shared with JW a draft of a tract he would publish the following year: *An Estimate of Human Life: being an humble attempt to vindicate the ways of God to man* (London: Wilson and Spence, 1788). Cf. his emphasis on suffering as integral to salvation on pp. 28, 32–33, 65.

[75] This is the British itinerant, currently assigned to the Bradford-on-Avon circuit.

[76] See Heb. 6:1.

To William Percival[77]

London
February 17, 1787

Dear Billy,

You cannot be too watchful against evil speaking, or too zealous for the poor Church of England. I commend sister Percival for having her child baptized there, and for returning public thanks.[78] By all means go to Church as often as you can, and exhort all Methodists so to do. They that are enemies to the Church are enemies to *me*. I am a friend to it, and ever was. By our reading prayers we prevent our people's contracting an hatred for forms of prayer, which would naturally be the case if we always prayed extempore.

I am, with love to sister Percival, dear Billy,
Your affectionate brother,

J. Wesley

Address: '⟨…⟩l / ⟨…⟩se / ⟨…⟩upon Tyne'.[79]
Postmark: '17/FE'. *Charge*: '6'.
Source: holograph; MARC, MAM JW 4/38.

To John Johnson

London
February 19, 1787

My Dear Brother,

It gives me pleasure to hear that the work of God continues to prosper in Lisburn. I hope to be in Dublin about the middle of April, and I shall then be able to determine whether to move north or southward first.

We have at present such peace with all round about us, (which is strangest of all) with the clergy, that if possible we should avoid

---

[77] Percival was currently the third itinerant stationed on the Newcastle circuit.

[78] William Percival married Elizabeth Greenwood on Jan. 31, 1786, while stationed in Liverpool. Their first child, William, born Dec. 7, 1786, was baptized in Newcastle on Jan. 25, 1787.

[79] Most of the address portion is missing.

taking any step which would be likely to anger them. One would wish to avoid this, if possible, both for *their* sakes and for the sake of the work; which, if their minds were inflamed, they might exceedingly hinder, as we know from past experience. Now it is certain nothing would anger them more than the appointing *our* preaching   5
in church hours, as this would imply a formal separation from the Church, which I believe to be both inexpedient and unlawful.

I am, with kind love to sister [Dorothea] Johnson,
    Your affectionate friend and brother,

                                J. Wesley   10

Address: 'To / Mr John Johnson / In Lisburn / Ireland'.
Source: published transcription; *WHS* 10 (1916): 153.

                                                 15

To the Rev. Joshua Keighley[80]

                                                 20
                                       London
                            February 19, 1787

My Dear Brother,

It seems the people in the north of Scotland are of a different mind from those in the south. In the south they flocked together   25
in great numbers at first when the preachers began to officiate in church hours. But after a while they began to fall off till they were at last the usual number. But in the north, you say, few would hear you at first; but afterwards the number increased. Before the time of the Conference we shall be able to judge which is more for the   30
glory of God and the increase of his work in North Britain, the new or the old plan.[81] Hitherto I am not able to determine, but a year's experience will give us more light.

I do not think that a man of so slender abilities as Alexander Ross is likely to gather societies anywhere. Whether he is qualified   35

---

[80] JW had ordained Keighley for service in Scotland in July 1786.

[81] The 'old plan' prohibited holding Methodist services during the hours for Sunday worship in the established Church in England, Wales, and Ireland (10:00–12:00); see *Minutes* (1766), Q. 28, 10:326 in this edn. JW apparently condoned the move of the ordained preachers he sent to Scotland to begin holding services in late 1786 (with the Lord's Supper, but following the Scottish rite) during regular church hours. See Batty, *Scotland*, 32–33. This practice was not reversed at the next Conference.

to be a travelling preacher or not will be finally determined at the Conference.[82]

If you make it matter of prayer, God will surely provide a better place for his service. When you have found and secured a well-situated piece of ground, then we may talk further of this.

The main point is: Let the people be alive to God, and they shall want nothing. I am, dear Joshua,

Your affectionate friend and brother,

J. Wesley

I shall be at [Stroud[83]] March 19; by the middle of April I hope to be in Dublin.

Address: 'To / the Revd Mr Keighley / In Elgin / Scotland'.
Postmark: '20/FE'.
Source: holograph; Bridwell Library (SMU).

To William Black Jr.

London
February 20, 1787

My Dear Brother,

After various unfortunate hindrances and delays, Dr. Coke embarked on board a small brig in the middle of October, and was by furious winds twice beat back into the harbour. They set sail a third time, with a crazy, shattered vessel, on the 18th of October.[84] We have not heard anything either from him or of him since. I hope you have heard of him in America.

You have great reason to be thankful to God for the progress of his work in Nova Scotia. This is far from being the case in Newfoundland, where poor John McGeary appears to be utterly discouraged,[85] not only through want of success, but through want of the conveniences, yea necessaries of life. Truly, if I could have suspected that those who made fair promises would have suffered

---

[82] No one of this name was admitted during JW's life.
[83] JW omitted the town name in the holograph.
[84] Coke's letter to JW, dated Jan. 2–5, 1787, had still not reached him.
[85] See the note on JW to John Stretton, Mar. 9, 1786.

a preacher to want bread, I should have sent him into other parts, where he would have wanted nothing.

I hear very different accounts here of the state of your provinces. Is there plenty or scarcity in Nova Scotia and New England? How does it fare with Halifax and Shelburne in particular? Do the build- 5 ings and the people increase or decrease? Public accounts I cannot at all depend upon. But upon *your* word I can depend.

Peace be with all your spirits! I am, dear Billy,
    Your affectionate friend and brother,

                                     J. Wesley 10

Source: holograph; privately held (transcription held by McGill University Library, Rare Books and Special Collections).

15

To William Thompson(?)[86]

                                        London 20
                            February 21, 1787
Dear ___,

Deal tenderly with [Billy Eells?], and I think he will be more use-ful than ever he was. On Monday, March 19, I expect to set out from Bristol; March 24 I am to be in Birmingham, and April 2 at 25 Manchester. Modern laziness has jumbled together the two distinct offices of preaching and administering the sacraments.[87] But, be that as it may, I will rather lose twenty societies than separate from the Church.

    I am, dear ___, 30
        Your affectionate friend and brother,

                                     J. Wesley

Source: published transcription; *British Magazine* 6 (Sept. 1834), p. 297.

35

[86] The transcription given here was sent to the *British Magazine* in 1834, omitting all names. William Thompson is the likely recipient, as he was the Assistant of the Manchester circuit. William Eells, who had sided initially with John Hampson and others in rejecting the Deed of Declaration, was back under appointment and serving with Thompson.

[87] See JW's sermon 'Prophets and Priests', completed in 1789, 4:72–84 in this edn.

To the Rev. Brian Bury Collins[88]

City Road [London]
February 22, 1787

5 Dear Sir,

I do not remember the receiving any letter from you which I did not answer.[89] But I cannot affirm this. I cannot charge my memory with things at so great a distance.

Certainly, if we do part, we shall part in love. I feel nothing but 10 love towards *you*. And I am persuaded that you are not otherwise inclined toward

Your affectionate friend and brother,

John Wesley

15 I shall always be glad to see you.[90]

Source: holograph; Bridwell Library (SMU).

20

To William Holmes

London
February 23, 1787

25 My Dear Brother,

I have wrote a line to one of the Commissioners of the Excise, and must leave the event to God.[91]

I am glad to hear that you see some fruit of your labour. You will reap, if you faint not.[92] I am

30 Your affectionate friend and brother,

J. Wesley

---

[88] JW had become uncomfortable with Collins's frequent ministry in evangelical Calvinist circles, rejecting the suggestion that a coalition could again be formed; see JW to Henry Moore, Nov. 4, 1786. From this point Collins focussed his ministry more among the Calvinists.

[89] JW's most recent surviving letter to Collins had been Mar. 11, 1784. No evidence survives of letters from Collins since then.

[90] JW may have visited Collins in his London home this very evening; see JW, Diary, 24:201 in this edn.

[91] JW was likely arguing that his preachers ought to be exempted from the 10 shillings per annum tax on riding horses (but not draft or 'work' horses) that had been imposed by the Duties on Horses Act of 1784 (24 Geo III c 31). Cf. JW to Joseph Benson, Mar. 9–10, 1784.

[92] See Gal. 6:9.

Address: 'To / Mr Will Holmes / At the Preaching house / In Bridge End
/ Glamorganshire'.
Postmark: '23/FE'. *Charge*: '6'.
Source: holograph; MARC, MAM JW 3/50.

To Adam Clarke[93]

Plymouth Dock
March 3, 1787

Dear Adam,

After staying a few days in Bristol, I am engaged to visit the intermediate societies between Stroud and Chester. I must then hasten
to Dublin, or I shall not have time to go through the four provinces
of Ireland. I shall not, therefore, have a day to spare before the Conference. Possibly after the Conference I may be able to steal two or
three weeks. And if so, I shall slip away to Southampton, in order
to spend two or three days at Guernsey, and as many in Jersey. This
will we do, if God permit.

I am glad you are minded to make a trial at Alderney. If God send
you, he will make a way for you. The hearts of all men are in his
hands. To his care I commend you; and I am, dear Adam,

Your affectionate brother,

J. Wesley

Address: 'To / Mr Adam Clark / in Guernsey / By way of Southampton'.
Source: holograph; MARC, WCB, D6/1/80b.[94]

To Arthur Keene

Plymouth Dock
March 3, 1787

Dear Arthur,

All that is past is forgotten, on one condition, that you supply the
defect for the time to come.[95]

---

[93] JW was replying to Clarke's letter of Feb. 23, 1787, inviting him to visit the Channel
Islands. JW spent most of the second half of Aug. there.

[94] William Myles added a note of his own to Clarke with JW's letter.

[95] Keene's letter to JW is not known to survive, leaving the nature of the 'defect' unclear.

If you required me 'not to come to your house' you would lay me under a difficulty, and I should not easily be persuaded to comply with your requisition. But when you require the contrary I feel no repugnance in my mind to agree to your proposal—were it only
5   for the sake of seeing your lovely children, my dear little maid in particular.[96]

If it please God to bring me safe to Dublin, we shall then consider what other parts of the kingdom I should go to. I shall undoubtedly, if my health continues, visit Cork and Londonderry, and as many
10 more of the capital places as (all things considered) shall be judged expedient.

The parting with those we dearly love is a noble exercise of resignation. I doubt not but it has been and will be greatly sanctified both to sister [Isabella] Keene and you.
15 On Monday I am to set out for Bath and Bristol. I then purpose visiting the intermediate societies; hoping to be at Manchester on Tuesday, April 2, and then at Holyhead as soon as possible. Peace be with all your spirits! I am, dear Arthur,

Your affectionate friend and brother,
20   J. Wesley

Address: 'To / Mr Arthur Keene / in / Dublin'.
Postmarks: 'Plymouth Dock' and 'MR/8'.
Endorsement: by Keene, '3d March 1787 / Revd. J. Wesley / Plymouth-
25   dock'.
Source: holograph; MARC, MAM JW 3/77.

30

To Ann Dupuy Taylor

[Bath]
35   [March 7, 1787]
Dear Nancy,

I felt a particular concern for you ever since you was a little one; and more particularly from that time when I had some conversation

---

[96] Arthur and Isabella (Martin) Keene had two surviving children: Mary Ann (1777–1846) and Martin (1780–1846). Mary Ann apparently served as JW's 'maid' during his last visit. JW stayed at their home again on Apr. 7–15, 1787; cf. JW to Keene, Apr. 21, 1787.

with you at York.[97] I observed even then that you had a real desire to love and serve God. And I am in hopes that desire will never decay, but rather grow stronger and stronger. Your great temptation will be, especially while you are young, to seek happiness in some creature. It is well if you are not entangled already—if you do not already begin to think 'O how happy I should be if I were to spend my life with this or that person!' Vain thought! Happiness is not in man. No, nor in any creature under heaven.

> Search the whole creation round,
> Can it out of God be found?[98]

No. When you begin to know God as *your* God, then and not before, you begin to be happy. But much more when you love him. And as you increase in loving faith, your happiness will increase in the same proportion. Steer steady to this point. Keep the issues of your heart! By Almighty grace keep yourself from idols! To converse freely with one or two sensible friends, who are deeply devoted to God, will be an unspeakable help on your way. And private prayer you must never omit. Next [to] the Bible, the books you might profit by would be Mr. [William] Law's *Works* and some of the *Sermons*.[99]

I am now going to Bristol.[100] I hope to be at Birmingham on the 24th instant, and at Macclesfield on the 30th. O be in earnest, my dear Nancy! And whenever you have a mind, write to

Yours affectionately,

J. Wesley

Address: 'To / Miss Nancy Taylor / At the Preachinghouse / in / Sheffield'.
Charge: '5'.
Source: holograph; MARC, MAM JW 5/15.

---

[97] See JW to Taylor, Jan. 12, 1787; her father Thomas was stationed in York 1780–81.
[98] CW, Hymn on John 6:67ff., st. 7, *HSP* (1749), 1:208.
[99] I.e., JW's *Sermons on Several Occasions*.
[100] JW arrived in Bristol on Mar. 8, 1787.

To Joseph Benson

Kingswood

March 9[–10], 1787

Dear Joseph,

I advise you to pay the tax if it be again demanded; which perhaps is due in law, though not in equity.[101] And I advise all our other preachers to pay, if it be demanded of them.

Certainly you have great need of a larger preaching-house at Hull. I hope you will observe the advices given in the Large *Minutes*, which are the result of long experience.[102] I shall be glad when you are able to preach out of doors. Field-preaching has done the most execution.

You are no novice among the Methodists. You have frequently seen at the time of Conference how much every shilling of the money brought in was wanted. Therefore you cannot omit the [yearly] Collection on any account. But you will consider which is the most proper time to make it.

Peace with you and yours! I am, dear Joseph,

Your affectionate friend and brother,

J. Wesley

Bristol

March 10, 1787

I have just been talking with Mrs. [Mary] Fletcher about Mr. [John] Fletcher's *Letters* to Dr. Priestley.[103] She was very desirous that I should correct and publish them. But Mr. [James] Ireland was very violently averse, having chose it should be done by Mr. Townsend,[104] who is full as capable of doing it as John Fenwick.[105] Mrs. Fletcher and I saw no way of splitting the difference but to

---

[101] Like referring to a tax of his riding horse; see JW to William Holmes, Feb. 23, 1787.

[102] 'Large' *Minutes* (1770), §68, 10:896–97 in this edn.

[103] John Fletcher began a response to Joseph Priestley's *History of the Corruptions of Christianity*, 2 vols. (Birmingham: J. Johnson, 1782) shortly after it was published (see JW, Journal, Mar. 27, 1784, 23:299 in this edn.; and JW to Fletcher, Apr. 3, 1785).

[104] Rev. Joseph Townsend, an earlier acquaintance of Fletcher and JW, who was now aligned with Lady Huntingdon and the Calvinists; see JW to Townsend, Aug. 1–3, 1767, 28:88–91 in this edn.

[105] I.e., not at all.

beg of Joseph Benson to do it. You are quite equal to the task, being in every respect a match for this all-assuming man.[106]

From the Conference you may ride up to Madeley and receive with the papers any further information that may be necessary. I think you cannot be employed in anything that will be more to the glory of God![107]

Address: 'To / Mr Benson / At the Preachinghouse / in / Hull'.
Postmarks: 'Bristol' and 'March 10'.
Endorsement: by Benson, 'J Wesley March 10 87'.
Source: holograph; Bridwell Library (SMU).

To [George Gidley][108]

Bristol
March 10, 1787

My Dear Brother,

I advise you never to mention the reading prayers any more, either at Exeter or Collumpton. Wherever the people make an objection, let the matter drop.

I have found a preacher for you; a man much devoted to God, who will be with you in a few days.[109] I am

Your affectionate friend and brother,

J. Wesley

---

[106] JW knew that Benson was already working on a rebuttal of Priestley's earlier works. See Benson, *Remarks on Dr. Priestley's System of Materialism, Mechanism, and Necessity, in a series of letters to the Reverend Mr. Wesley* (Hull: George Prince, 1788); and *A Scriptural Essay Towards a Proof of an Immortal Spirit in Man, being a Continuation of Remarks on Dr. Priestley's System ...* (Hull: George Prince, 1788).

[107] Benson was not able to go to Madeley after Conference, but had Mary (Bosanquet) Fletcher send him Fletcher's papers. He finished revising the first portion of these in late 1788, published as John Fletcher, *A Rational Vindication of the Catholic Faith; being the first part of a Vindication of Christ's Divinity [contra] Priestley* (Hull: G. Prince, [1788]). The remainder appeared as Fletcher, *Socinianism Unscriptural ... being the second part of a Vindication of [Christ's] Divinity* (Birmingham: E. Jones, 1791).

[108] While there is no address portion or first name given, this was almost certainly to George Gidley, a key lay leader of the society in Exeter.

[109] Peter Walker, who was assigned to the Tiverton circuit by the 1786 Conference seems to have left mid-year, and never appears again in the *Minutes*. The preacher being sent was surely George Button, who is listed as the Assistant for the circuit in the 1787 *Minutes*.

Pray tell Hugh Saunderson he must not say one word of what passed at Exeter. Otherwise nothing can be done.[110]

Source: holograph; MARC, MAM JW 6/51.

To Samuel Bradburn[111]

Bristol
March 13, 1787

Dear Sammy,

Pray let two or three thousand of Dr. Coke's journal be printed immediately and dispersed everywhere.[112]

Who appointed the Sunday school to be kept in our Preaching-house at Deptford? Who had a right so to do? I hear the children fill it with vermin. If so, they must meet there no more.

Write me the name of two men fit to be stewards and I will send word, 'Let there be stewards the ensuing year.'

I am, with love to sister [Sophia] Bradburn,

Ever yours,

J. Wesley

Address: 'To / Mr Bradburn / At the New Chappel / City Road / London'.
Postmarks: 'Bristol' and 'March 15'.
Source: holograph; Drew, Methodist Archives.

---

[110] It is unclear whether this relates to the fracture in the Methodist society in Exeter which Saunderson helped foster (see JW, *Journal*, Aug. 15, 1782, 23:249 in this edn.) or a more recent matter.

[111] Bradburn was now in London, to assist with running operations there. This letter opens in the hand of John Broadbent, giving JW's journal account of Feb. 25 through Mar. 5, 1787 (as it appears in the published *Journal*, 24:5–7 in this edn.). We give here only the letter in JW's hand that follows this account.

[112] Coke's letter of Jan. 2–5, 1787 had reached JW and was soon published as *An Extract of the Rev. Dr. Coke's Journal from Gravesend to Antigua, in a Letter to the Rev. J. Wesley* (London: Paramore, 1787).

To Ann Bolton

Bristol
March 15, 1787   5

My Dear Nancy,

On Monday, March 19, I hope to be at Stroud; and on Tuesday noon, at Cirencester. But from thence I must hasten away by Gloucester and Birmingham to Chester, in order to embark for Ireland. Very probably after the Conference (at Manchester) I may   10
contrive to call at Witney. To see you or converse with you has always been a pleasure to me, ever since I knew you first, and especially since I knew you to be a child of affliction—as 'pity melts the mind to love'.[113] Indeed, which has pleased God to lead you for many years on a rough and thorny path. But he knoweth the way   15
wherein you walk, and when you have been tried, you shall come forth as gold.[114]

When you was at Finstock I was sometimes afraid that you was confined to too narrow a field of action. But your sphere is now enlarged. And you have full exercise for every talent which God has   20
entrusted you with. Now, my dear Nancy, use all the gifts which God has entrusted you with.

It seems to me that you are particularly called to explain the nature of perfection to all those that meet with you, and to exhort all those that have believed, to press forward toward the mark.[115] In   25
this respect you may be of use to the preachers themselves, most of whom are, I believe, prejudiced in your favour. The way to retain that measure of pure love which God has vouchsafed to *you*, is continually to encourage others to aspire after the same blessing.

May the peace and love of God be continually in your heart! So   30
prays, my dear Nancy,

Yours most affectionately,

J. Wesley

Source: holograph; privately held (WWEP Archive holds a transcription   35
by Cynthia Aalders).

---

[113] John Dryden, 'Alexander's Feast', *l.* 78.
[114] See Job 23:10.
[115] See Phil. 3:14.

To John Francis Valton

Birmingham
March 24, 1787

5   My Dear Brother,
     Mr. Heath (that is to be the President of Cokesbury College) must
go by London to Bristol.[116] His wife, with her two lovely daughters,
may come directly to Bristol from hence. Be so kind as to inquire
of Tommy Roberts what ships are likely to sail soon for New York
10   or Baltimore.[117] Ships convey passengers far cheaper from Bristol
than from London, but a bargain must be made with the captain.
Pray make everything as easy for them as you can. I have not seen a
more amiable family. Be so kind as to write to Mr. [Andrew] Blair
here when you have agreed for their passage.[118]
15   I am, with love to sister [Judith] Valton,
     Your affectionate friend and brother,

[J. Wesley]

Address: 'To / Mr. Valton / At the New Room / In Bristol'.
20   *Source*: published transcription; Telford, *Letters*, 7:376.

To Samuel Bardsley[119]

25

Birmingham
March 25, 1787

Dear Sammy,
     You send me good news concerning the progress of the work of
30   God in Colne circuit. I should think brother [Edward] Jackson or
[William] Sagar might set the heads of the people at Bacup right.
Brother Jackson should advise brother Ridall not to please the devil
by preaching himself to death.[120]

---

[116] For details on Heath and his family, see JW's letter to him of May 18, 1787.

[117] This would not be the itinerant of that name admitted at the 1786 Conference, as he was stationed in Ireland. It was likely the Thomas Roberts who appears in a register of the society in Bristol, 1770–86.

[118] Blair was currently the Assistant for the Birmingham circuit.

[119] While the holograph lacks an address page, Samuel Bardsley was one of the preachers assigned to the Colne circuit. His letter to JW is not known to survive.

[120] Jackson was Assistant for the Colne circuit. James Ridall (d. 1822), assigned to serve under him, had been admitted 'on trial' as an itinerant in 1785 (see 10:568 in this edn.). Ridall would serve for 30 years; retiring in 1815; see *Minutes* (post-Wesley, 1823), 5:382.

I still think when the Methodists leave the Church of England, God will leave them. Every year more and more of the clergy are convinced of the truth and grow well-affected towards us. It would be contrary to all common sense, as well as to good conscience, to make a separation now.

I am, dear Sammy,

Your affectionate brother,

J. Wesley

Source: holograph; British Library, Department of Manuscripts, Add. MS. 27457, f. 6.

To Adam Clarke[121]

Birmingham
March 26, 1787

Dear Adam,

You have reason to praise God for giving you such favour in the eyes of the poor people of Alderney. And I am in hopes our brother [Jean] De Quêteville will meet with a blessing in watering the seed which is already sown. But I observe in the map the name of another island, not very far from Alderney. Are there none that understand English in the Isle of Sark? If there are, I cannot tell whether you are not a debtor to those poor souls also.

If confinement hurts you, do not submit to it. Spread yourself abroad through all the four islands. But I doubt *speaking loud* hurts you more, if not *speaking long* too. Beware of this for conscience' sake. Do not offer murder for sacrifice![122] But, before it be too late, take the advice of, dear Adam,

Your affectionate brother,

J. Wesley

Address: 'To / Mr Adam Clarke / At Mr [George] Walker's / In St Peters / Isle of Guernsey'.
Postmarks: 'Birmingham' and 'March 27'. *Charge*: '8'.
Endorsement: by Clarke, 'Recd April 2d 87'.
Source: holograph; MARC, MA 1994/022/9.

---

[121] JW was replying to Clarke's letter of Mar. 16, 1787.
[122] See JW, 'Sermon on the Mount, VII', IV.4, 1:609 in this edn.

To Mary Cooke[123]

Macclesfield
March 31, 1787

5 Now you give me a proof, my dear Miss Cooke, that you have not forgotten me. But considering that I am usually obliged to write in haste, I often doubt whether my correspondence is worth having.

When the witness and the fruit of the Spirit meet together, there
10 can be no stronger proof that we are of God. But still you may relapse into painful doubts if you do not steadily watch against evil reasonings. And were you to substitute the deductions of reason for the witness of the Spirit, you never would be established. That all trials are for good you cannot always *see* (at least for the present),
15 but you may always *believe*.

You have doubtless reason to be thankful when you feel love in your heart. Nay indeed, thankfulness, gratitude, and love for benefits received are almost if not quite the same. Accordingly in this world (whatever be the case in the next), we love *him because* he
20 hath first loved *us*.[124] This love is undoubtedly the spring of all both inward and outward obedience. But we delight to do what he has commanded for that very reason, because he has *commanded* it. So,

Obedience is our pure delight,
25 To do the pleasure of our Lord.[125]

I was a good deal refreshed with the company of you and your dear sisters when we last met.[126] The more so because I trust you are all going forward in the good way.
30 Peace be multiplied unto you! My dear friend,
Adieu!

Address: 'To / Miss Cook / In Duke Street, Trowbridge / Wilts / xp [i.e., crosspost] Glo'ster'.
35 *Postmark*: 'Macclesfield'.
Endorsement: by Cooke, 'Good – 15th'.
Source: holograph; MARC, WCB, D6/1/336.

[123] JW was replying to Cooke's letter of Mar. 24, 1787.
[124] See 1 John 4:19.
[125] Cf. CW, 'Psalm 1', st. 2, *CPH* (1743), 1.
[126] JW met Mary and her sisters Anne and Francis in Bath on Mar. 7, 1787.

To the Rev. Thomas Hanby

Macclesfield
March 31, 1787

Dear Tommy,

It is impossible for anyone that has been used to much exercise, to leave it off without prejudice to his health. Therefore as long as you stay in Scotland, you should take care, every day you do not ride, to walk or dig two or three hours. If you do not, you will surely suffer for it, for nothing can supply the want of exercise.

It seems there is sufficient reasons for your coming to the Conference at Manchester. When we meet there, we shall [have] opportunity to consider what further steps are to be taken. I am, dear Tommy,

Your affectionate friend and brother,

J. Wesley

Address: 'To / The Revd Mr Hanby / At the Preachinghouse / in Dundee / North post'.

*Postmark*s: 'Macclesfield' and 'AP/4'. *Charge*: '7'.

Source: holograph; Boston, Massachusetts, Public Library, MS E.9.4, 67–69.

To John Baxendale

Manchester
April 3, 1787

My Dear Brother,

I have thoroughly considered your case. And considering two things; first, the peculiar love of the people towards you, and secondly, your usefulness to many of them; I judge that providence clearly calls you to remain at Wigan.[127]

I am

Your affectionate brother,

J. Wesley

---

[127] Baxendale, a local preacher, was debating whether to became an itinerant; cf. JW's prior letters to him of Mar. 7, 1783 and Feb. 19, 1784.

Address: 'To / Mr Baxendale / in / Wigan'.
Annotation: by JW, 'Pri[vate]'.
Source: holograph; Bridwell Library (SMU).

5

To Arthur Keene

Athlone
10   April 20, 1787

Dear Arthur,

We came hither this morning, and find a pleasing prospect.

I really think, as Mr. Handy does, that when there is a vacancy, to admit sister Finlay into the Widows' House will be a deed of
15   mercy.[128]

All sister [Mary] Penington's riches (in this world) were her books; but the fire swept them all away.[129] She has not one left. I desire brother [James] Rogers to send her by the first opportunity: the large hymn-book;[130] *[Explanatory] Notes on the New Testament*,
20   quarto; the *Appeals*, bound;[131] the four volumes of *Sermons*; *Life of Mr. [John] Fletcher*, of *David Brainerd*, and of *Madame Guyon*;[132] *Night Thoughts, Milton*.[133]

I remember, with much love, sister [Isabella] Keene with my dear Mary Ann and her brother [Martin].[134] Peace be with all your spirits!
25   I am, dear Arthur,

Ever yours,

J. Wesley

Address: 'To / Arthur Keen Esq / Dublin'.
30   *Postmarks*: 'Athlone' and 'AP/25'.[135]
Source: holograph; MHS Ireland Archives.

[128] Samuel Wesley Handy (1751–1829) was the son of JW's old friends Samuel and Ruth (Bertrand) Handy. The son inherited the manor his parents had in Coolalough (3 miles west of Killbeggan). JW visited there on Apr. 18, 1787, at which time Handy presented him with a note supporting Sarah Finlay, widow of Archibald Finlay (see in-letters). JW's letter to Keene is on the reverse side of Handy's note.

[129] See JW to John Bredin, Nov. 16, 1785.

[130] I.e., the 1780 *Collection of Hymns for ... Methodists*.

[131] The *Earnest Appeal ... and Farther Appeal ...* [Pts. I–III] bound together.

[132] *Bibliography*, Nos. 442, 310, 363.

[133] JW's extracts; *Bibliography*, Nos. 323, 253.

[134] JW had stayed in the Keene home Apr. 7–15, 1787, while visiting Dublin; see *Journal*, 24:15–16 in this edn.

[135] The second postmark is the date the letter arrived in Dublin.

To John King[136]

Athlone
April 21, 1787

My Dear Brother,   5

Adam Clarke is doubtless an extraordinary young man and capable of doing much good. Therefore Satan will shorten his course if possible. And this is very likely to be done by his still preaching too loud, or too long, which is a sure way of cutting his own throat.[137] Whenever you write, you should warn him of this. It may be he will   10 take advice before it is too late. He may have work enough to do if he adds the Isle of Alderney to those of Guernsey and Jersey. If you have a desire to go and labour with him you may after the Conference. By that time I expect they will have both work and food for another labourer.   15

With what is past, or what is to come, we have little to do. *Now* is the day of salvation.[138] The *great salvation* is at hand, if you will receive it as the free gift of God.[139] What you have already attained hold fast by whatever name you call it.[140] And whatever you want he is ready to give. Reason not about it, but believe. His word is, 'Open   20 thy mouth wide, and I will fill it.'[141]

There is a wonderful work of God in several parts of this kingdom, and it increases more and more.

I am

Your affectionate brother,   25

J. Wesley

Address: 'To / Mr John King / At the Preachinghouse / In Bradford / Wilts'.

Postmarks: 'Athlone', 'Ireland', and 'Bristol'.   30

Source: holograph; MARC, MAM JW 3/81.[142]

[136] John King and Adam Clarke had served together on the Plymouth circuit 1785–86, and had encouraged JW to keep them together the following year; see JW to King, June 1, 1776. Clarke had clearly shared with King some of his frustrations in his current appointment, which he also shared with JW.

[137] See JW to Clarke, Mar. 26, 1787.

[138] See 2 Cor. 6:2.

[139] See Heb. 2:3.

[140] See Phil. 3:16.

[141] Ps. 81:10.

[142] Two pages of this holograph are filled with a letter of Adam Clarke to John King, dated May 15, 1787, apologizing for opening the letter while back in England briefly from his assignment to the Channel Islands, and informing King of Clarke's intention to marry Mary Cooke. Clarke informs King his health is better and dissuades King from joining Clarke in the islands.

To James Rogers

Athlone
April 21, 1787

Dear Jimmy,

I thank you for yours.[143] You did well to write; though in one sense there was no need of it, for there is no great danger of my being angry either at Hetty or you.[144]

My eyes are as well as ever. But I see nothing of Dr. Coke's *Journal*.[145] I wish I had taken you with me. Peace be with your spirits!

Dear Jimmy, adieu!

Address: 'To Mr. Rogers'.[146]
Source: holograph; privately held (WWEP Archive holds photocopy).

To Alexander Knox

Aughrim
April 23, 1787

Dear Alleck,

You are best able to answer for yourself. In the letter now before me I read:

I must be free to say to you that in my dealings with Church-people and Methodists, I have met with better treatment from the former. I could show you copies of some letters that passed between Mr. Alexander Knox and myself, on the subject of the house at Bishop Gate, which I had set to him just after you left Derry.[147] To bind the bargain, Mrs. Knox offered me a guinea—which I declined taking, as I thought hers and her son's word sufficient. Mrs.

---

[143] This letter is not known to survive.
[144] I.e., James or his wife Hester Ann (Roe) Rogers.
[145] See JW to Samuel Bradburn, Mar. 13, 1787.
[146] JW added this note the following morning to the letter he drafted Apr. 20 to Arthur Keene (see above).
[147] Apparently referring to JW's visit to Londonderry in early June 1785.

Babington, who is not a Methodist, to whom I set the house afterward, behaved as a Christian and a gentlewoman.[148]

I can say nothing to this till you answer for yourself. I do not suppose he states the matter fairly, but I must let the matter rest, till I
hear from you.
    Peace be with all your spirits! I am, dear Alleck,
        Yours most affectionately,

                           J. Wesley

Address: 'To / Mr. Alexander Knox / In Londonderry'.
Postmarks: 'Ballinasloe' and 'AP/27'.
Source: holograph; Bridwell Library (SMU).[149]

To Arthur Keene

                           Waterford
                         May 2, 1787
My Dear Arthur,
    Although Miss [Jane] Acton is to acquit you of your promise
in favour of sister [Hannah] Timmins,[150] yet I can in no wise avail
myself of her condescension—were it only on this account, that
sister Timmins is considerably older than sister [Sarah] Finlay. It
is reasonable therefore that sister Finlay should wait for another
vacancy.[151]
    Pray inform brother [James] Rogers that I have considered the
letters of John Price and brother [Samuel] Mitchell, and have al-

---

[148] The letter was by a Mr. Dawson; see JW to Knox, May 16, 1787.

[149] Held previously in the Upper Room Museum, L-46.

[150] Jane Acton (c. 1745–94) was the youngest daughter of William Acton Esq. (1711–79), of West Aston, and his wife Jane (Parsons) Acton. She had become a Methodist and active in the Dublin society. Jane never married, adopted an ascetic lifestyle, and devoted her significant financial resources to religious and charitable objects. See Cooney, 'Dublin Society', 49; and A. Stewart & G. Revington, *Memoir of ... Rev. Adam Averell* (Dublin: Methodist Book Room, 1848), 33–34. Hannah Timmins, of the Widow's Home, is listed as a member of a class led by Arthur Keene in 1788 (see Cooney, 'Dublin Society', 52). She is likely the wife of the Mr. Timmins mentioned in JW, *Journal*, July 26, 1762, 21:376–77 in this edn.

[151] Cf. JW to Arthur Keene, Apr. 20, 1787.

tered my plan according to their advice.[152] And appointed to preach:
Monday, [May] 28, at 6:00, Ranghan(?).[153] Tuesday, 29, noon,
Aghalun;[154] 6:00, Lisbellaw. Wednesday, 30, Sidaire.[155] Thursday,
31, noon, Omagh; at 6:00, Kirlish Lodge. Saturday, noon, New-
townstewart; 6:00, Londonderry. I wish he would certify Samuel
Mitchell and John Price of this.

Sisters Cookman, Moore, and [Jane] Acton are in perfect health,
much the better for their journey.[156] We all remember you and yours
with much love. The work of God goes on well in Waterford; here
is a wise, steady people.

Wishing you and yours every blessing, I remain, dear Arthur,
      Ever yours,

                                                        J. Wesley

Address: 'To / Arthur Keene Esq / near / Dublin'.
Postmark: 'MY/4'. *Charge*: '5'.
Endorsement: by Keene, '2 May 1787 / Revd. J. Wesley / Waterford'.
Source: holograph; MHS Ireland Archives.[157]

To the Rev. Peard Dickinson

                                                        Cork
                                                   May 6, 1787
Dear Sir,

I am now come to my second *station* in Ireland; for here we expect
to stay seven days, only with a digression of two out of the seven
to Bandon and to Kinsale. I know not that I shall spend two whole
days in any other place before I return to Dublin.

I am glad you are fairly discharged from Oxford; although there is
a little seed left there still. When we were there, we profited much by

[152] Price and Mitchell were Assistants of the Omagh and Enniskillen circuits. Their letters are not known to survive.

[153] JW's writing is a bit unclear, and there is no evidence in his *Journal* or diary that he
left Clones on May 28.

[154] Orig., 'Aughalun'. Now known as Brookeborough.

[155] Orig., 'Sydare'.

[156] These three Methodist women from Dublin met JW at Newtownbarry and travelled
with him to Waterford and Clonmel; see JW, *Journal*, Apr. 30, 1787, 24:21 in this edn. Elizabeth Cookman is one of the Methodists in Dublin who signs the formal letter to JW on Mar.
29, 1789. Crookshank (*Ireland*, 428) assumes sister Moore is Anne (Young) Moore, the wife of
Henry Moore; but she may be instead Rebecca Moore (Henry's sister).

[157] John Broadbent added a letter to the Keenes on a blank side of JW's holograph.

watching continually against 'the lust of *finishing*'—to mortify which we frequently broke off writing in the middle of a sentence, if not in the middle of a word, especially the moment we heard the chapel bell ring or a knock at our door. If nature reclaimed, we remembered the word of the heathen: *Ejicienda est hac mollities animi.*[158]   5

I am glad there is so good an understanding among the preachers; a great deal depends upon it. But I hope you do not forget gentle Thomas Olivers. May not you venture to give him an hint that your *Hints* were incorrectly printed?[159] If he says, 'They were wrote so I could hardly read them', you can tell him, 'I hope to write the next   10 better.'

Have you seen poor Mr. [Levi] Heath? He is extremely ill-used. At Dr. [Thomas] Coke's ins[is]tance he has given up both his school and curacy. And now the Doctor leaves him and his wife and his lovely children either to sink or swim, having made no manner   15 of provision for the payment of the money which he had articled to give him.[160] But he shall not sink. Neither he nor his shall want anything while I have either money or credit. If he comes to London, I wish you would take acquaintance with him and speak comfortably to him. He is a man of sense and of an excellent spirit; besides that   20 he has a considerable share of learning.

Miss [Elizabeth] Briggs spending so much of her time at Shoreham answers an excellent design. It in a great measure supplies the want both of Miss Perronet and of her father.[161] I remember her with sincere affection.   25

I am, dear sir,
　　Your affectionate friend and brother,

J. Wesley

Address: 'To / the Revd Mr Dickenson / In the City Road, Moorfields /   30 London'.
Postmarks: 'Cork', 'MY/8', and 'May/12/87'.[162]
Endorsement: by Dickinson, 'Mr Wesley / May 6 1787'.
Source: holograph; MARC, MAM JW 2/82.

---

[158] Cf. Terence, *The Eunuch*, II.i.222, '*eicienda hercle haec est mollities animi*'; 'I must banish this softness of heart' (Loeb).

[159] The publication in question has not been located.

[160] See JW to Heath, May 18, 1787.

[161] Damaris Perronet, a leading force in the Methodist society in Shoreham, died in 1782. Her father, Rev. Vincent Perronet, died in 1785.

[162] London had adopted a new postmark: the month and year were in an outer circle, with the day in the middle.

To Hannah Ball

Cork
May 9, 1787

My Dear Sister,

I am not willing you should quite forget me, and am therefore always well pleased to hear from you.[163]

It is certain those men who have occasioned public scandal are not proper to preach or pray in public.[164] It is well that little contest is now over—so let it die and be forgotten.

I doubt not there is and always will be a good understanding between Mr. [Joseph] Harper and you. It has frequently been one of the contrivances of Satan to create suspicion or coldness between you and the preachers. Let none of you be any longer ignorant of his devices. Labour all you can to strengthen their hands in God.[165]

It is well for our society at High Wycombe that Mr. [John] Murlin is settled among them. He is a wise, zealous man, and may be of use to you in many respects, if not as a poet.[166]

I am, my dear sister,

Yours very affectionately,

J. Wesley

Address: 'To Miss Hannah Ball'.[167]
Source: holograph; Duke, Rubenstein, Frank Baker Collection of Wesleyana, Box WF 1.

To Alexander Knox

Limerick
May 16, 1787

My Dear Alleck,

Yours of the 4th instant I received an hour ago.[168]

---

[163] Ball's letter to JW is not known to survive.

[164] The reference is almost certainly to John Robotham, who had been admitted 'on trial' as an itinerant in 1785 (see 10:568 in this edn.). He was currently stationed on the Oxfordshire circuit, and disappears from the *Minutes* thereafter. He likely proved problematic in his first appointment as well (to the Gloucester circuit); see JW to Mary Clark, July 26, 1789.

[165] See 1 Sam. 23:16.

[166] Murlin had just retired from the itinerant ministry. He published a set of *Hymns* in 1781, which JW largely dismissed; see JW to Joseph Benson, Apr. 3, 1781, 29:638 in this edn.

[167] This header at the top of the page, and the lack of an address page, indicate that this was likely a double letter—with the main portion (not known to survive) addressed to Joseph Harper, the Assistant of the Oxfordshire circuit, concerning the 'little contest'.

[168] This letter, in reply to JW's of Apr. 23, 1787, is not known to survive.

What Mr. Dawson wrote concerning you (as well as what he wrote concerning others) made no great impression upon me. I easily perceived he was too angry at a letter I had sent him, to judge very clearly of anything.[169] You do well to send me a circumstantial account of the affair. If anymore be said, I shall now know how to answer. 5

On Saturday, June 2, I hope to see you and my dear Mrs. Knox. As to George and Sally, perhaps they have forgot me.[170] But *you* will not easily forget, dear Alleck,

Yours affectionately,

J. Wesley 10

Address: 'To / Mr Alexr Knox / in / Londonderry'.
Postmarks: 'Limerick' and 'MY/18'.
Source: holograph; Bridwell Library (SMU).[171]

15

To the Rev. Levi Heath[172]

Limerick
May 18, 1787 20

Dear Sir,

I trust you have long since received my last, the purport of which was that 'neither you nor your family shall want anything so long as I have either money or credit'.[173]

---

[169] JW's letter to Dawson is not known to survive.
[170] Referring to Alexander's mother and his two siblings.
[171] Held previously in the Upper Room Museum, L-47.
[172] Rev. Levi Heath (c. 1748–1806) was baptised in 1748 in Ledbury, Herefordshire. By 1779 Heath had gained appropriate education to be elected Low Master of the Free Grammar School of Kidderminster, though he does not appear to have attended Cambridge, Dublin, or Oxford. Heath was ordained in 1783, taking on in addition to his teaching role the office of curate at Highley, Shropshire. By early 1787 Heath had come to the attention of JW and Thomas Coke. The latter persuaded Heath to resign his current living and immigrate to Maryland in order to take charge of Cokesbury College, which would open in Dec. 1787. Coke proved slow to provide the financial support needed both for the move and for maintaining Heath in his new position (See JW to Peard Dickinson, May 16, 1787). This led to the present letter. Continuing weak financial support and differences with Coke led Heath to resign his position at Cokesbury in Oct. 1788. The last years of his life were devoted to serving as rector of several Episcopal parishes in New England. See JW, *Journal*, Mar. 23, 1787 (24:11 in this edn.); CCED; and Frank Baker, 'John Wesley and Cokesbury College's First President', *Methodist History* 11.2 (1973): 54–59.
[173] Levi Heath married Rachel Donne in 1768 in Overbury, Worcestershire. They had two daughters: Maria (b. 1769) and Anna (b. 1771). JW's letter in this regard is not known to survive. JW's commitment to Heath remained steady; he left a bequest of £60 to Heath in his final will (see vol. 15 in this edn.).

But I am sadly embarrassed for the present by not hearing from Dr. [Thomas] Coke. I had, indeed, a short letter from him last month, written in March from Charlestown in Carolina.[174] But as he had not then seen Mr. [Francis] Asbury, he could give me no
5   material intelligence. It fails out awkwardly that I am at so great a distance from you, otherwise I should easily have removed your painful apprehensions, which must naturally arise from your being left in so strange an uncertainty.

I am just setting out for the west of Ireland. But I could not go
10 into my chaise till I had again done what is in my power to ease your mind and to testify my invariable affection, both to you, and to dear Mrs. Heath and my beloved children.[175] You now trust in God farther than you can see him. This is well pleasing to him.

15   Far, far beyond thy thought,
                His counsel shall appear,
            When fully he the work hath wrought
                That caused thy needless fear.[176]

20 To his care I commit you; and am, dear sir,
        Ever yours,

                                                J. Wesley

Source: holograph; Boston University School of Theology, Library, Archi-
        val Collections, New England Conference Commission on Archives
25   and History.

To the Rev. Joshua Keighley

30
                                                Castlebar
                                                May 20, 1787

My Dear Brother,

I am quite undetermined whether I shall ever ordain again.[177] At
35 the Conference this must be thoroughly discussed. I know not but I have already gone too far.

---

[174] This letter is not known to survive.

[175] JW typically would speak of 'your' children; but his letters to the Heaths consistently used the possessive 'my'; showing his affection for the children. See esp. JW to Levi Heath, June 26, 1789.

[176] Cf. Paul Gerhardt, 'Trust in Providence', st. 14, *HSP* (1739), 143 (trans. by JW from German).

[177] JW did ordain again; see Appendix B of this volume.

Certainly we can afford to give six pounds to New Mills, so much I will engage for.

It would be a pity to leave any circuit in Scotland without preachers. A loss might be incurred which would not soon be repaired. Therefore if brother [Thomas] Bartholomew can be tolerably contented to stay longer, well.[178] But if he has set his [heart] upon coming to the Conference, let him come.

I think either Edinburgh or Glasgow would afford a comfortable residence both to you and your spouse elect.[179]

I am, dear Joshua,

Your affectionate friend and brother,

J. Wesley

Letters to the north of Ireland should be directed to Portpatrick.

Address: 'To / The Revd Mr Keighley / in / Inverness / +p [i.e., cross-post] Portpatrick'.
Postmarks: 'Castlebar', 'Ireland' and 'MY/29'.
Source: holograph; MARC, DDWes 5/48.

To Adam Clarke[180]

Clones
May 27, 1787

Dear Adam,

If our friends had been wise, they would not have suffered you to return to Guernsey till your health was re-established. In all probability this is throwing away your life. While this hangs in suspense it is certain you have no business at all to think of marriage.[181] I am sorry anything should hinder Mr. [Robert] Brackenbury from coming to the Conference. I depended upon seeing him, and doubt whether you will be able to come in his stead.

I am, dear Adam,

Your affectionate friend and brother,

J. Wesley

---

[178] Bartholomew was assisting Joshua Keighley in the Inverness circuit.
[179] Keighley died before the intended wedding took place (see 10:645 in this edn.).
[180] JW was replying to Clarke's letter of May 13, 1787.
[181] Clarke was considering marriage to Mary Cooke; they would be wed Apr. 17, 1788.

Address: 'To / Mr Adam Clarke / At St Peter's / Isle of Guernsey'.
Postmarks: 'Ireland' and 'MY/30'.
Endorsement: by Clarke, 'Recd June 6. 1787'.
Source: holograph; MARC, WCB, D6/1/84.

5

To Hugh Moore[182]

10
Lisbellaw
May 30, 1787

My Dear Brother,

I used often to be afraid for Mr. [George] Whitefield that he had
not reproach enough. Honour will destroy any man living, unless
15 it be balanced with a proportionable degree of dishonour. I have
wrote a few lines to Mr. Caulfield; he truly fears God.[183]

Probably I shall preach in the new house at Armagh. Fight on and
conquer. I am, dear Hugh,

Your affectionate friend and brother,

20
J. Wesley

Source: holograph; Boston University School of Theology, Library, Archival Collections, New England Conference Commission on Archives
and History.

25

To Zachariah Yewdall

30
Lisbellaw
May 30, 1787

My Dear Brother,

I am glad to hear that you have a society at Dalkeith.[184] But I am
not pleased that the Edinburgh preacher has not preached there
35 once a week. I desire he would constantly do it for the time to come,

---

[182] The address portion is missing, but Hugh Moore was currently Assistant for the Charlemont circuit, which included Armagh.

[183] Rev. Charles Caufield (c. 1739–1817), had been rector of Killyman, about 3 miles from
Charlemont, since 1775. He was sympathetic to Methodism, and allowed JW to preach at his
house on June 2, 1785 (see *Journal*, 23:363 in this edn.) and June 14, 1789 (24:143). JW's note
to Caufield is not known to survive.

[184] Yewdall was presently assigned to the Berwick circuit, which included Dalkeith and
Edinburgh.

without asking leave of the leaders. Those have no business to direct the preachers. It is no part of their office. I am glad to hear so good an account of Mr. Collis;[185] and hope he will be a comfort to his mother. I will consider what you say concerning your being at Glasgow.

I am,

Your affectionate brother,

[J. Wesley]

Source: published transcription; Jackson, *Works* (3rd), 13:16.

To Benjamin Chappell

Londonderry
June 4, 1787

My Dear Brother,

A day or two ago I met with your letter, which came to me later by way of London and Dublin, and I am much pleased to hear that sister [Elizabeth] Chappell and you do (in some sense) live comfortable.[186] But you do not give me any account of the manner wherever you are. Do you live as Christians or as heathens? Have you any such thing as public worship? Have you ten or twenty companions that either love or fear God? Have you any meeting with them, or do you ever put them in mind that there is another world? When we were together at Inverness you were a bold witness for God.[187] I hope you have not lost that honest boldness, although you must have many temptations so to do. Do you live in a town or in a lone house? Have you any Indians with you or near you? Do you make any difference between the Lord's Day and other days? How do you spend the Lord's Day? And how do you employ yourselves on other days? If you receive this letter in time, send me a particular answer, and then show me that my dear Betty and you have not forgotten

Your affectionate brother,

J. Wesley

Source: holograph; Garrett-Evangelical, Methodist Manuscripts Collection.

[185] See JW to Yewdall, Dec. 20, 1786.

[186] This letter is not known to survive.

[187] Chappell and his brother assisted JW on a preaching mission at Inverness in early 1770; see *Journal*, Apr. 26, 1770, 22:226 in this edn.

To the Rev. Peard Dickinson[188]

Londonderry
June 5, 1787

5   Dear Sir,

The Irish posts are not the quickest in the world, though I have known one travel full two miles in an hour. And they are not the most certain. Letters fail here more frequently than they do in England.

10   Mr. [Levi] Heath has need of abundance of faith and patience. He is in a very unpleasing situation. As Dr. Coke (who did not use to be sparing of his letters) keeps us entirely in the dark with regard to what is doing in America, I know not how to take one step forward. But of this I am determined on: Mr. Heath shall not want as long

15   as I have either money or credit.[189] He is a truly pious and a very amiable man; his wife and children are cast in the same mould. I am glad you all showed him, while he was in London, the respect which he well deserves.

As the work of God increases in so many parts both of England

20   and Ireland, it would be strange if there were no increase of it in London, especially while all the preachers are of one mind and speak the same thing.[190] Only do not forget strongly and explicitly to urge the believers to 'go on to perfection'.[191] When this is constantly and earnestly done, the word is always clothed with power.

25   Truly I deserve no thanks for loving and esteeming Betsy Briggs, for I cannot help it. And I shall be in danger of quarrelling with you if you ever love her less than you do now.[192] Peace be with all your spirits! I am

Your affectionate friend and brother,

30   J. Wesley

Source: secondary manuscript transcription; MARC, MA 1977/502, p. 48.

---

[188] This letter reiterates points in JW to Dickinson, May 6, 1787.
[189] See JW to Heath, May 18, 1787.
[190] See Acts 4:32.
[191] Heb. 6:1.
[192] Dickinson had clearly revealed to JW his budding relationship with Elizabeth Briggs; they would marry Apr. 30, 1788.

To the Rev. Levi Heath

Lisburn
June 10, 1787

Dear Sir,

Yours of the 3rd instant I received a quarter of an hour ago.[193]

I have been afraid of explaining myself, for fear of grieving you. But I think I ought to delay it no longer—only promising that you need not be concerned, for the love I feel to you and your dear family is a stronger bond than any that could be wrote on parchment.

I have no more to do with Cokesbury College than with the College of Douay.[194] And I fear Dr. [Thomas] Coke has not; for I doubt Francis Asbury has shaken us all off.[195] Therefore you cannot stir till you hear from him.

I never promised him, or any in America, to advance a shilling. But some of them *took it for granted* I would advance £50. Dr. Coke, not I, engaged for the rest. I never engaged for anything. But that makes no difference. I love you. I love your wife. I love my dear children.[196] Therefore my heart is engaged to you for all that I have. Even an heathen teaches me,

Vilis amicorum est annona, bonis ubi quid deest.[197]

You see I have desired brother [John] Knapp of Worcester to let you have whatever money you please.[198] And I have wrote to Mr. [John] Atlay to answer his draughts.

I love to see the very names of your young ones, but I cannot tell you with what tenderness I am,

Yours and theirs,

J. Wesley

Address: 'To / the Rev. Mr. Heath / At Mr. Knapp's / Glover, Lowesmoor / Worcester'.[199]

Postmarks: 'Ireland' and 'JU/12'.

Source: holograph; Lovely Lane Museum.

---

[193] This letter is not known to survive.

[194] The Roman Catholic school in Douai, France, which trained priests for England.

[195] See the note on JW to Whatcoat, c. June 1787.

[196] See the note on JW to Heath, May 18, 1787.

[197] Horace, *Epistles*, I.xii.24: 'The market-price of friends is low, when good men are in need'.

[198] See next letter.

[199] JW first listed Heath's address as 'In Kidderminster'; this was then struck out and replaced as given.

To John Knapp

Lisburn
June 10, 1787

My Dear Brother,

I have a favour to desire of you, to give Mr. [Levi] Heath whatever money he wants, be it twenty or thirty pounds, or more. I have wrote to Mr. [John] Atlay to answer your draught for whatever you advance. I am,

Your affectionate brother,

J. Wesley

Address: 'To Mr. Knapp At Worcester'.
Source: double letter; on back of previous to Heath.

To the Rev. Dr. Henry Leslie[200]

Charlemont
June 16, 1787

Reverend and Dear Sir,

I have obligations to you on many accounts from the time I first saw you; particularly for the kind concern you showed when I was ill at Tandragee.[201] These have increased upon me every time I have since had the pleasure of waiting upon you. Permit me, sir, to speak without reserve. Esteem was added to my affectionate regard when I saw the uncommon pains you took of the flock committed to your care; as also when I observed your remarkably serious manner wherein you read prayers in your family.

---

[200] Henry Leslie (1719–1803), whose father Peter was clergy in the Church of Ireland, graduated from Trinity College, Dublin (BA, 1738; MA, 1742; BD 1749; and LLD). He married Catherine Meredyth (b. 1733) in 1753; and served as rector of the Ballymore parish church in Tandragee from 1757 to his death.

[201] JW first met Rev. Leslie on June 13, 1773, when he was invited after church to the rectory for dinner (see *Journal*, 22:375–76 in this edn. When JW became ill in mid-June 1775, during a preaching tour of Ireland, he spent at least one night at the Leslie home (see *Journal*, July 17, 1775, 22:456). Other visits include June 24–25, 1778 (23:97); June 13–14, 1785 (23:368); and most recently, June 13–14, 1787 (24:36–37).

Many years have passed since that time, many more than I am
now likely to see under the sun. But before I go hence I would fain
give you one instance of my sincere regard—the rather because I
can scarce expect to see you again till we meet in a better world.[202]
But it is difficult for me to do it, as I feel myself inferior to you   5
in so many respects. Yet permit me to ask a strange question: 'Is
your soul as much alive to God as it was once?' Have you not suffered loss from your relations or acquaintance, that are sensible and
agreeable men but not encumbered with religion? Some of them,
perhaps, as free from the very form as from the power of it![203] O sir,   10
if you *lose* any of *the things which you have wrought*, who can make
you amends for that loss?[204] If you do *not receive a full reward*, what
equivalent can you gain? I was pained even at your hospitable table,
in the midst of those I loved so well, as we did not *begin* and *close* the
meal in the same manner you did ten years ago! You was then, con-   15
trary to almost universal custom, unfashionably serious in asking a
blessing and returning thanks. I know many would blame you for it.
But surely your Lord said, 'Servant of God, well done.'[205]

Wishing you and your lovely family every blessing, I am, dear and
reverend sir,   20

Your obliged and affectionate brother and servant,

J. W.

Source: JW's copy for records; MARC, MAM JW 3/87.

25

To the Rev. ____ [206]

30

Armagh
June 18, 1787

Dear Sir,

You ask, 'Why do not the clergy, whether in England or Ireland,   35
avail themselves of the Methodist preachers?' You say you 'wonder

[202] JW would see the Leslie family one more time, on June 11–12, 1789; see *Journal*,
24:142–43 in this edn.

[203] See 2 Tim. 3:5.

[204] See 2 John 1:8.

[205] Cf. Matt. 25:23.

[206] The one raising the question may have been Rev. Dr. Henry Leslie.

they do not thankfully accept of their assistance, who desire no pay
for their service, in repressing error and wickedness of every kind
and propagating truth and religion?' You inquire, 'Upon what rational principles can this be accounted for?'

5   To give a complete answer to this question would require a whole
treatise. I have not leisure for this; but I will give as full an answer
as my time will permit.

Only, before I answer, I must observe that many both of the English and Irish clergy are entirely out of the question. They are not
10   only learned but truly religious men, and as such are an honour to
their profession. I speak only of those that are of a different character, be they many or few. Let them wear the cap whom it fits. That
is no concern of mine.

This premised, I think it easy to be accounted for even upon hea-
15   then principles. Horace observed long ago,

> *oderunt hilarem tristes, tristemque jocosi, [...;]*
> *vinosi porrecta negantem pocula.*[207]

20   Accordingly, grave and solemn men (though too few are guilty of
this fault) dislike many of the Methodist preachers for having nothing of *that* gravity or solemnity about them.

Jocose clergymen, on the other hand, cannot but dislike those
who are steadily serious. And those that love to take a cheerful glass
25   are not fond of such as are strictly temperate. You need go no farther than this consideration to have a clear answer to the question,
'Why do many of the clergy refuse to receive any assistance from
the Methodist preachers?'

But this may be more fully accounted for upon Christian prin-
30   ciples. What says our Lord to the first preachers of the gospel, and
in them to all their successors? 'If the world hate you, ye know that
it hated me before it hated you. If ye were of the world, the world
would love its own. But because ye are not of the world, therefore
the world hateth you. [...] These things will they do unto you, be-
35   cause they know not him that sent me.'[208]

Does not this give us sufficient reason to expect that, if we are
'not of the world', all 'the world', all who 'know not God', whether
clergy or laity, will be so far from accepting our assistance that they

---

[207] Horace, *Epistles*, I.xviii.89–92 (using potores instead of vinosi): 'The grave hate the
gay, the jocose the grave. Winebibbers hate the man who declines the proffered cups' (Loeb).
[208] John 15:18–21.

will sincerely hate us and openly or privately persecute us, so far as God permits? We have therefore reason to wonder, not that they do not desire any union or coalition with us, but that they bear with, yea, and on many occasions treat us with courtesy and civility. This is a peculiar instance of the providence of God, causing in some measure the scandal of the cross to cease.

'But do not many clergymen who are not pious men acknowledge that the Methodists do good and encourage them to persevere therein?' They do, but observe how far they would have them go. They wish them to repress outward sin—to reclaim the people from cursing, and swearing, and drunkenness, and Sabbath-breaking (unless the squire gains by it). They are well pleased that their parishioners grow more diligent and honest and are constant attendants on the church and sacrament. Nay, they are glad that they are brought to practice both justice and mercy: in a word, to be 'moral men'.

But the truth is, the Methodists know and teach that all this is nothing before God. That whoever goes thus far and no further is 'building upon the sand'.[209] That he who would worship God to any purpose must worship him 'in spirit and in truth'.[210] That true religion is 'righteousness and peace and joy in the Holy Ghost',[211] even giving God our heart, the seeking and finding happiness in him. Here then they divide from the Methodists, whom they judge to be going too far. They would have their parishioners 'moral men'— that is, in plain terms, honest heathens. But they would not have them *pious* men, men devoted to God, *Bible Christians*. If therefore the Methodist preachers would stop here, would preach outward religion and no more, many clergymen would not only encourage them therein but likewise cordially join them. But when they persuade men *not* to be *almost but altogether Christians*;[212] to maintain a constant 'fellowship with the Father and his Son Jesus Christ',[213] to be *transformed* into that 'image of God wherein they were created',[214] and thenceforth to live that 'life which is hid with Christ in God',[215]

---

[209] Cf. Matt. 7:26.

[210] John 4:24.

[211] Rom. 14:17.

[212] See JW, *The Almost Christian* (1741), 1:131–41 in this edn.

[213] 1 John 1:3.

[214] Cf. 2 Cor. 3:18.

[215] Col. 3:3.

let them not expect that any will give them the right hand of fellowship but those God hath 'chosen out of the world'.[216]

I am

Yours, etc.,

J. W.

Source: published transcription; *Arminian Magazine* 11 (1788): 264–66.

To Samuel Bradburn

Dublin
June 27, 1787

Dear Sammy,

Dr. [Thomas] Coke informs me that he gave Mr. [Levi] Heath
fifty guineas before he left England, and you will be accountable for
what remains due to him.[217] So that makes it easy.

Dr. [John] Whitehead is a valuable acquisition.[218] I wish we could
gain twenty more like him.

I have journal enough ready for transcribing as soon as I can find
a ready writer. John Broadbent is only a scrawler.

My brother and you are twin souls.[219] You have all things needful
for life and godliness. You have more friends than come to the share
of one man. You have a loving, a pious, and a sensible wife. What
could you have more? This world has nothing more to give. You
want nothing but a thankful heart. That melancholy turn is directly
opposite to a Christian spirit. Every believer ought to *enjoy life*.

I am, with tender love to Sophy, dear Sammy,

Your affectionate friend and brother,

J. Wesley

Source: holograph; Wesley's Chapel (London), LDWMM 1994/1970/1.

[216] Cf. John 15:19.
[217] Coke had arrived back from North America on June 25, and was with JW in Dublin.
[218] This may refer to Whitehead helping Bradburn regain his health in Feb. 1787, or to
some other benefit. See Bradburn, *Memoirs*, 106–07.
[219] CW and Bradburn were close friends, and shared a tendency to depression.

To Ann Tindall

Dublin
June 29, 1787   5

My Dear Sister,

I know no reason why brother Mill should not stay with you another year. If sister [Isabella] Mill took much of the [Peruvian] bark in the powder, it is no wonder she should turn consumptive. It turned my ague into a consumption in less than eight hours time.   10

I am glad our brethren have agreed upon that method of paying off the debt.

But what is the matter? Have you sent your poetic herd to graze? It is a long time since you sent me any verses! I am, dear Nancy,

Yours affectionately,   15

J. Wesley

Address: 'To / Miss Tindal / in Scarborough / Yorkshire'.
Postmarks: 'JU/30' and 'Ireland'.
Source: holograph; British Library, Department of Manuscripts, Add.   20
   MS. 43695, f. 101.

25

To the Rev. Dean William Digby[220]

[c. July 1787[221]]

Reverend Sir,   30

1. When Dr. Bentley published his *Greek Testament*, one re-marked, 'Pity but he would publish the Old; then we should have

---

[220] William Digby (d. 1812) was a Church of Ireland priest, and Dean of Clonfert from 1766. There is no record of JW meeting Digby, but JW was in Ireland from mid-April through early July 1787, including preaching at Ballinasloe on Apr. 23, about 10 miles north of Clonfert. It was most likely during this time that JW came across Digby's recently published *Twenty-One Lectures on Divinity* (Dublin: W. Watson, 1787). The first thirteen lectures in this volume were intended 'to throw light on the Old Testament in general, but particularly on the first six Books, by Observations drawn from the Hebrew'. As Digby readily admitted (pp. 22ff.), what he presents in these lectures is drawn from and broadly echoes the stance of John Hutchinson.

[221] The manuscript is not dated; nor did Jackson date it in *Works* (3rd), 12:448–49. Telford suggested a date of 1785, unaware that JW was responding to a book published in 1787. His response was likely concluded before he left Ireland in mid-July.

To the Rev. Dean William Digby

two new testaments!²²² It is done. Those who receive Mr. Hutchinson's emendations certainly have two new testaments!²²³

2. But I stumble at the threshold. Can we believe that God left his
whole church so ignorant of the Scripture till yesterday? And if he
5 was pleased to reveal the sense of it now, to whom may we suppose
he would reveal it? 'All Scripture', says Kempis, 'must be understood by the same Spirit whereby it was written.'²²⁴ And a greater
than he says, 'Them that are *meek* will he guide in judgment, and
them that are *gentle* will he learn his way.'²²⁵ But was Mr. Hutchin-
10 son eminently *meek* and *gentle*?²²⁶ So far from it that I cannot hope
he was *taught of God*.

3. However, in order to learn all I could from his *Works*, after first
consulting them, I carefully read over Mr. Spearman,²²⁷ Mr. Jones's
ingenious book,²²⁸ and the Edinburgh abridgement.²²⁹ I read the last
15 with Mr. Thomas Walsh, the best Hebraean I ever knew. I never
asked him the meaning of an Hebrew word but he would immediately tell me how often it occurred in the Bible and what it meant
in each place! We then both observed that Mr. Hutchinson's whole
scheme is built upon etymologies—the most uncertain foundation
20 in the world, and the least to be depended upon. We observed secondly that if the points be allowed, all his building sinks at once;

---

²²² See Richard Bentley (1662–1742), *Dr. Bentley's Proposals for printing a new edition of the Greek Testament, and St. Hierom's Latin Version* (London: J. Knapton, 1721). Bentley proposed to produce a Greek text of the New Testament that was closer to that received by the church at the time of the Council of Nicea—by comparing the text of the Vulgate with that of the oldest Greek manuscripts, particularly Codex Alexandrinus. His *Proposals* included only a brief sample and he never finished the project.

²²³ Hutchinson's proposed emendations are scattered through his writings. JW was referring to Julius Bate (1711–81), who set out to revise the Old Testament on Hutchinson's principles, but made it only through 2 Kings. *A New and Literal Translation from the original Hebrew of the Pentateuch of Moses, and of the historical books of the Old Testament, to the end of the second book of Kings* (London: W. Faden et al., 1773).

²²⁴ Thomas à Kempis, *Imitation of Christ*, I.v.

²²⁵ Ps. 25:9.

²²⁶ Cf. JW to Ann Thornton, Feb. 4, 1787, where he describes Hutchinson as a person of 'uncommon pride and sourness of temper'.

²²⁷ Robert Spearman, *An Inquiry after Philosophy and Theology* (Edinburgh: Kincaid & Donaldson, 1755); cf. JW, *Journal*, Apr. 27, 1758, 21:143–44 in this edn.

²²⁸ William Jones, *An Essay on the First Principles Of Natural Philosophy; wherein the use of natural means, or second causes, in the economy of the material world is demonstrated from reason, experiments of various kinds, and the testimony of antiquity* (Oxford: Clarendon, 1763); cf. JW, *Journal*, Oct. 9, 1765), 22:24 in this edn.

²²⁹ Orig., 'Glasgow'; a misrecollection that appears repeatedly in JW's reference to *An Abstract from the Works of John Hutchinson, Esq.; being a Summary of His Discourses in Philosophy and Divinity*, edited by George Horne and Robert Spearman (Edinburgh: R. Fleming, 1753); cf. *Journal*, Dec. 22, 1756, 21:81 in this edn.

and thirdly that, setting them aside, many of his etymologies are forced and unnatural. He frequently, to find the etymology of one word, squeezes two radices together; a liberty never to be taken where a word may fairly be derived from a single radix.

4. But may I hazard a few words on the [vowel] points? Mr. Hutchinson affirms they were invented by the Masorites, only thirteen or fourteen hundred years ago, in order to destroy the sense of Scripture. I doubt this. Who can prove it? Who can prove they were not as old as Ezra, if not co-eval with the language? Let anyone give a fair reading only to what Dr. Cornelius Bayley has offered in the Preface to his *Hebrew Grammar*, and he will be as sick of reading without [vowel] points as I am—at least, till he can answer the Dr.'s arguments he will not be so positive upon the question.[230]

5. Permit me to add a fews words first on his philosophy, and next his theology.[231] As to his philosophical account of the solar system, it is undoubtedly very ingenious. And I cannot but allow [it] to be in several respects preferable to that of Sir Isaac Newton. But I would be glad to have one difficult removed. If all matter be impenetrable (which I suppose no philosopher now denies), and all the universe be absolutely full of it, I do not ask how a tinker(?)[232] can move but how there can be any movement at all?

6. You say: 'Light and air move, though light springs every way from the sun, [then] returns to it in the form of air. So perpetually light moves outward and air moves inward.'[233] So then light and air are continually moving in opposite directions through every point of space. But how is it that they do not hinder each other? Neither can pass by the other, for every point of space is full. And neither can pass through the other, for matter is impenetrable. 'O but the air is infinitely subtle.'[234] Be it so. But it is matter still, and if ether is matter it is as impenetrable as steel or adamant. Does it not evidentially follow that if neither of these substance can either pass

[230] Cornelius Bayley, *An Entrance into the Sacred Language; containing the Necessary Rules of Hebrew Grammar* ... (London: T. Longman, 1782). JW subsequently published Bayley's comments: 'On the Hebrew Points', *AM* 11 (1789): 150–55.

[231] While JW was earlier drawn to aspects of Hutchinson's philosophy and theology, he began to express reservations by 1770; see JW, *Journal*, Feb. 13, 1770, 22:215–16 in this edn. The comments that follow in this letter enlarge upon those reservations; and balance his continuing recommendation of the *Abstract* of Hutchinson in his letters to [Mary Lewis?], c. Sept. 1778, 29:435–36 in this edn.; and to Sarah Wesley Jr., Sept. 8, 1781, 29:685 in this edn.

[232] *OED*: 'a traveller, itinerant, or vagabond'.

[233] Digby, *Lectures*, 25.

[234] Ibid., 20–21.

through or pass by each other, they cannot pass each other at all? Consequently, this theory is absurd and impossible.

7. As to his theology, I first stumble at his profuse encomiums on the Hebrew language. 'But it may be said, Is it not the language which God himself used?' And is not Greek too the language which God himself used? And did he not use it in delivering to man a far more perfect dispensation than that which he delivered in Hebrew? Who can deny it? And does not even this consideration give us reason at least to suspect that the Greek language is as far superior to the Hebrew as the New Testament is to the Old? And, indeed, if we set prejudice aside and consider both with attention and candour, can we help seeing that the Greek excels the Hebrew as much in beauty and strength as it does in copiousness? I suppose no one from the beginning of the world wrote better Hebrew than Moses. But does not the language of St. Paul excel the language of Moses as much as the knowledge of St. Paul excelled his?

8. I speak this, even on supposition that you read the Hebrew (as I believe Ezra, if not Moses did) with points. For if we read it in the modern way, without points, I appeal to every competent judge whether it be not the most equivocal.[235]

Source: JW's manuscript copy for records; MARC, WCB, D6/1/152b.

To an Unidentified Man

Dublin
July 2, 1787

My Dear Brother,

If *you* can certify for the young man you mention, there is no doubt of his being received on trial at the Conference. And he may be stationed for the first year either at St. Ives or St. Austell.[236]

I was much afraid we should decline at Dublin this year, and not keep up our round thousand. But I was afraid where no fear

---

[235] There is no closing or signature in the manuscript copy.

[236] While the identify of the recommender remains unclear, the young man commended was surely John Sandoe (1755–1810), the only preacher assigned to either of these circuits by the 1787 Conference that was also admitted 'on trial' that year (see 10:623, 625 in this edn.). A native of Gwennap, Cornwall, Sandoe travelled for twenty years until health led him to settle. See *Minutes* (post-Wesley, 1810), 3:135–36.

was. We have now eleven hundred and thirty-seven members in the society.

There are three journeys I would fain take this autumn, if you could tell me how: to Cornwall, to Wales, and to the Isles of Jersey, Guernsey, and Alderney. I am,

Your affectionate friend and brother,

J. Wesley

Source: holograph; Pitts Library (Emory), John Wesley Papers (MSS 153), 3/36.

To Lady Darcy (Brisbane) Maxwell[237]

Dublin
July 4, 1787

My Dear Lady,

Our correspondence, I hope, will never be broken off till one of us be removed into a better world.[238] It is true I have often wondered that you were not weary of so useless a correspondent; for I am very sensible the writing of letters is my brother [CW]'s talent rather than mine. Yet I really love to write to you, as I love to think of you. And sometimes it may please him, who sends by whom he will send, to give you some assistance by me. And your letters have frequently been an encouragement and a comfort to me. Let them never, my dear friend, be intermitted during the few days I have to stay below.

---

[237] Maxwell (influenced by her connections to Ritchie) had recently experienced a distinct manifestation of, and a distinct communion with, *each of the persons of the Trinity*; see Maxwell, *Life*, 247–48, 258, 261–64. While no letter is known to survive, she sought JW's perspective on this. JW had encountered the ideal of 'an experimental verity ... of the presence of the blessed Trinity' in Gaston Jean Baptiste de Renty; see his *Extract of the Life of De Renty* (1741), 5. He began questioning followers whom he believed had received Christian perfection about whether they experienced something similar as early as 1768; see JW to Jane Hilton, July 23, 1768, 28:162 in this edn. JW's interest in this possibility was deepened when he received some papers of Charles Perronet that mentioned such an experience (see Perronet, May 1772, §13 in in-letters); cf. JW to Jane Catherine March, Apr. 26, 1777, 29:340 in this edn.

[238] There is no surviving evidence of correspondence between the two since Maxwell's letter to JW of Jan. 13, 1783.

After Miss[239] [Hester] Roe first and then Miss [Elizabeth] Ritchie had given me so particular an account of that branch of their experience,[240] I examined one by one the members of the select society in London on that head. But I found very few, not above nine
5   or ten, who had any conception of it. I think there are three or four in Dublin who likewise speak clearly and scripturally of having had such a manifestation of the several persons in the ever-blessed Trinity. Formerly I thought this was the experience of all those that were perfected in love; but I am now clearly convinced that it is
10   not.[241] Only a few of these are favoured with it.

It was, indeed, a wonderful instance of divine mercy that, at a time when you were so encumbered with the affairs of this world, you should have so much larger a taste of the powers of the world to come. It reminds me of Brother Lawrence's words: 'When I
15   was charged with the affairs of the convent at Burgundy, I did not understand them; and yet, I know not how, all was well done!'[242] I doubt not you will find the very same experience in everything which God calls you to. His word will be more and more eminently fulfilled, 'In all thy ways acknowledge him, and he will direct thy
20   paths.'[243]

I rejoice to be, my dear Lady,
    Your ever affectionate servant,

J. Wesley

25   *Source*: published transcription; Benson, *Works*, 16:200–01.

---

[239] Orig., 'Mrs. Roe'; a slip, due to Roe now being married to James Rogers.

[240] These detailed accounts may have been verbal. What survives are JW's probing of the experience in letters; see JW to Roe, June 2, 1776 (29:256 in this edn.); JW to Roe, Feb. 11, 1777 (29:323–24); JW to Ritchie, June 16, 1777 (29:346); and JW to Ritchie, Aug. 2, 1777 (29:356). There are also passing comments like in Ritchie to JW, Aug. 15, 1782: 'My soul enjoys sweet communion with the Holy Trinity'.

[241] Cf. Hannah Ball, June 11, 1777, 29:345 in this edn.; and JW to Maxwell, Aug. 8, 1788.

[242] JW knew Brother Lawrence (Nicholas Herman of Lorraine, 1611–91) as one of the items in John Heylyn (ed.), *Devotional Tracts Concerning the Presence of God, and other Religious Subjects, Translated from the French* (London: Joseph Downing, 1724). He records reading this volume in his Oxford Diary, Aug. 4–8, 1732; and later abridged the volume in his *Christian Library*, 38:3–92. The abridgement includes the comment quoted here from the 'Second Conversation' of Brother Lawrence (38:28).

[243] Prov. 3:6.

To Jane (Lee) Freeman

Bethesda
July 8, 1787   5

My Dear Sister,

I have not a moment to spare at this busy time. But I can deny you nothing.[244] I purpose, therefore, to be with you at Ely Place on Monday about one o'clock.

I am   10
　　Yours affectionately,

J. Wesley

Address: 'To / Mrs Freeman / At No. 2 / Ely Place'.
Source: holograph; MARC, MAM JW 3/9.   15

To Samuel Bradburn   20

Dublin
July 10, 1787

Dear Sammy,   25

I desired John Atlay to make up the twenty pounds which I gave Mr. [Levi] Heath [to] fifty.[245] But if he mistook me, and gave him fifty instead of thirty, it will not ruin me. What is still wanting Dr. [Thomas] Coke will supply.

I am glad you have visited the country societies and that you find   30 so much life among them. What we can do for the poor people at Wandsworth I know not. I doubt their case will grow worse and worse.

[244] Freeman had contacted JW, requesting that he perform the marriage of her daughter Elizabeth (b. c. 1764) to George Stacey. Though he was in the middle of his Conference with the Irish preachers, JW took a break on Aug. 9, 1787, to perform the wedding at 5:00 pm. See JW, Diary, 24:214 in this edn.; and *WHS* 23 (1942), 101.

[245] The holograph in MARC begins after the word 'up'. For the financial matter, see JW to John Knapp, June 10, 1787.

If sister Brettel is near lying in, she should in no wise have come to the chapel house, for she cannot lie in there.[246] Therefore I should think the sooner she removes, the better.

I am, with love to sister [Sophia] Bradburn, dear Sammy,

Your affectionate friend and brother,

J. Wesley

Source: holograph; MARC, MAM JW 1/114.[247]

To Rev. Peard Dickinson

Dublin
July 10, 1787

My Dear Brother,

I have hired one of the packets for me and my company, and hope to set out tomorrow for Parkgate.[248] If it please God to give us a prosperous voyage, I shall have a little leisure to write, and to prepare my business for the Conference. The Irish Conference ends this afternoon. The preachers here are wonderfully increased both in grace and gifts, and are a truly respectable set of men. I wish I may find the English like them. My kind love attends yours and my friend.[249] I am,

Your affectionate friend and brother,

J. Wesley

Address: 'To Mr Dickinson'.[250]

Source: holograph; privately held (WWEP Archive holds photocopy of a published facsimile).

[246] Jeremiah Brettel married Rebecca King in July 1786 at Bristol, while stationed there. He was now stationed in London. The Brettels may have lost this pregnancy, as their first child baptized was Maria, on Mar. 3, 1788, in Bristol.

[247] The holograph now in MARC is missing about 1 inch of the top. This portion was still present when Jackson produced his transcription; we draw on that transcription for the missing text—see Jackson, *Works* (3rd), 13:100.

[248] A port city in Cheshire.

[249] I.e., Elizabeth Briggs.

[250] This label is at the top of the page, indicating this was likely part of a double letter (with the main letter possibly addressed to John Atlay, also in London).

To Martha (Wesley) Hall

Dublin
July 10, 1787   5

Dear Patty,

Tomorrow I hope to sail. I am glad you have not forgotten me; and am, with much affection,

Ever yours,

[J. Wesley]   10

Source: published transcription; Jackson, *Works* (3rd), 13:100.[251]

15

To Matthew Stewart

Dublin   20
c. July 10, 1787[252]

[Wesley instructed him to continue travelling in an informal status in the western part of Co. Donegal, enclosed £5, and concluded]

25

When you have spent this, and stand in need of more money, apply to

Your affectionate friend,

John Wesley

30

Source: published summary and excerpt; *Irish Evangelist* 5 (1862), 234.

---

[251] Jackson gives this letter as a portion of that to Samuel Bradburn of the same date; it is missing from the imperfect holograph held in MARC.

[252] Stewart recorded in a manuscript memoir that he was turned down for appointment by the Irish Conference meeting on July 6, 1787, because he was married and had children; but this letter from JW was received about a week later.

To the Rev. Freeborn Garrettson

Macclesfield
July 16, 1787

My Dear Brother,

I have your letter of March the 15th and that of May the 20th.[253]

In the former you give me a pleasing account of the work of God in Halifax and other towns in Nova Scotia; and indeed, everywhere, except at poor Shelburne, from which I had an excellent account a year or two ago. Shall the first be last?[254] What can have occasioned the decrease of the work there?

St. Paul's advice is certainly good for all Methodist preachers: 'It is good for a man not to touch a woman';[255] and 'If thou mayest be free, use it rather'.[256] And yet I dare not exclude those that marry out of our connexion, or forbid to marry. But happy are they, who, having no necessity laid upon them, stand fast in their glorious liberty.[257] I commend you for laying as little burden upon the poor people as possible.[258]

Before I had printing-presses of my own, I used to pay two and thirty shillings to the printers, for printing four and twenty pages duodecimo. The paper was from twelve to sixteen shillings a ream. I do not blame you for printing those tracts.

But you do not send me your journal yet. Surely you have now had time enough to write it over!

Dr. [Thomas] Coke seems to think you are irresolute, and yet not willing to take advice. I hope better things of you. And your heart says to God and man, 'What I know not, teach thou me!'[259]

I am

Your affectionate friend and brother,

J. Wesley

Source: holograph; Wesleyan University Library.

---

[253] See Garrettson to JW, Mar. 10[–15], 1787. The letter of May 20 is not known to survive.

[254] See Matt. 19:30.

[255] 1 Cor. 7:1.

[256] I Cor. 7:21.

[257] See Gal. 5:1.

[258] Garrettson's letter of May 20 may have mentioned his resolve to remain single. He did not marry until 1793.

[259] Cf. Job 34:32.

To Samuel Bradburn

near Manchester
July 17, 1787   5

Dear Sammy,

You should be at Manchester, to meet the Assistants, by 2:00 in the afternoon on the 30th instant.

I have a good letter from William Pitt at Deptford.[260] Pray thank him for it in my name, and tell him I shall take the matter he men-   10 tions into serious consideration.

I desire you to inform Mr. [Josiah] Dornford that I will propose Richard Taylor at the Conference.[261]

I am, with tender love to Sophy, dear Sammy,
    Ever yours,   15

J. Wesley

Source: holograph; MARC, MAM JW 1/115.

20

To Mrs. Jane Armstrong[262]

25
near Manchester
July 19, 1787

Do not think, my dear sister, that I have forgotten you or that I ever can. Did I not tell you when I had the pleasure of sitting by   30 you that

> Mountains might rise and oceans roll
>   To sever us in vain?[263]

---

[260] This letter is not known to survive.

[261] There is no mention of a Richard Taylor in the *Minutes* or Conference Journal for the 1787 Conference.

[262] Little is known of Jane Armstrong (including whether this was her married name, or she was an older single woman), but that her main residence was in Athlone.

[263] Cf. CW, 'At Parting of Friends', st. 4, *Redemption Hymns* (1747), 69.

It is my common rule not to write first to anyone; but I cannot stand on ceremony with *you*. From the time that I first conversed with you at Athlone, ceremony fled away, and I was full as free with you as if I had been acquainted with you many years. Indeed, when
5   you went to Dublin, I was a little afraid that you would be taken up with new things and new acquaintances; but how was I delighted when I found you just the same as I left you![264] You are still aiming at something more excellent than this short-enduring life can give! You cannot be content with the things of earth! Still look up! Set
10 your affections on things above![265] You have already tasted of the powers of the world to come![266] See that you never lose what God has wrought, but that you receive a full reward.[267] And when you have leisure write a line to, my dear Jenny,
       Yours affectionately,

15   J. Wesley

I expect to stay here near three weeks.

20 *Address*: 'To / Mrs Armstrong / 126 Old Church Street / Dublin'.
     Source: (holograph; Drew, Methodist Archives, very fragmentary) published transcription; *Irish Christian Advocate* (Aug. 09, 1895), 381.[268]

25

To Mary (Forrest) Jones[269]

                                                   near Manchester
30   July 24, 1787
Dear Madam,
       There is so great a work of God broke out in the Isles of Jersey and Guernsey, and lately in the Isle of Alderney too, that I must endeavour to visit them as soon as possible. But it cannot be till the

----

[264] JW was in Athlone Apr. 20–22, 1787; then in Dublin June 21–July 10. He is writing after his return to England.

[265] See Col. 3:2.

[266] See Heb. 6:5.

[267] See 2 John 1:8.

[268] We have relied on the published transcription. The holograph is too fragmentary for a flowing text, but the portions that survive fit with the published transcription.

[269] While the address portion is missing, the content and the location of the letter among a set of the Jones family make the recipient clear.

Conference is over. I purpose then with God's assistance to hasten to Southampton, in order to take the packet for Jersey. But as the winds are so uncertain I know not [how] long I may be detained in the islands. Therefore there is no certainty of my being able to visit Wales this year. It would give me much pleasure to see my old 5 friends, but I am not at my own disposal. I am glad to hear that Mr. Jones and Mr. Matthews are well, and wish (as you do) that Mrs. Matthews and her niece would continue in Glamorganshire.[270] If they do, I doubt not it will be for good. May the peace of God rest upon you and them! 10

I am, dear madam,

Yours most affectionately,

J. Wesley

Source: holograph; Cardiff, Wales, Glamorgan Archives, DF/WES. 15

To Arthur Keene 20

Manchester
July 24, 1787

My Dear Brother, 25

It would be strange if I did not write to *you* the first of anyone in Ireland.[271] For is it not natural to take notice first of those whom we love best? Especially when you have my two dear friends—one on one side, and the other on the other side?

You have all need of patience while you hear every day that poor 30 little maid bemoaning herself.[272] She is permitted thus to linger in pain, not only for her own sake (seeing the greater her sufferings

---

[270] These would be Mary's son, Robert Jones Jr.; her son-in-law, Thomas Matthews (b. 1741); her daughter Diana (Jones) Matthews, who married Thomas in 1763; and likely her granddaughter (and Diana's niece), Anna Maria Charlotte Ashby (1768–1837) – the daughter of Thomas and Charlotte (Jones) Ashby.

[271] JW wrote Arthur Keene immediately after arriving at Parkgate in his voyage from Dublin. The letter is not known to survive; but the address portion, with a note from Hester Ann (Roe) Rogers to Isabella (Martin) Keene, is at Duke, Rubenstein, Frank Baker Collection of Wesleyana, Box CO 7, folder 4. It includes Keene's endorsement: '13 July 87 / Revd. J. Wesley / Chester'. Keene apparently replied with surprise at JW's promptness in writing.

[272] The younger daughter of Arthur and Isabella (possibly named for her mother) was sick and would die soon after; see JW to Keene, Aug. 5, 1787.

are here the greater will be her reward); but likewise for your sakes, that your 'wills may be melted down and take the mould divine'.[273] I hope your dear neighbours Mr. and Mrs. D'Olier are likewise profiting by all the providences of God.[274]

5   Peace be with you and yours! I am, dear Arthur,
          Yours most affectionately,

J. Wesley

10   *Address*: 'To / Arthur Keen / near / Dublin'.
Postmarks: 'Manchester' and 'JY/28'.
Endorsement: by Keene, '24 July 87 / Revd. J. Wesley / Manchester'.
Source: holograph; MHS Ireland Archives.

15

To John Ogylvie[275]

20   near Manchester
                                                       July 24, 1787

My Dear Brother,
     As there are so few preachers in the isle I think Mr. [John] Crook's judgment is right. It will not be expedient for you to quit your sta-
25   tion for the present. The work of God would very probably suffer if Mr. Crook and you should be absent at the same time. I believe it may be contrived for you to labour the ensuing year in some part of Yorkshire. Be zealous! Be active for God!
     I am
30   Your affectionate brother,

J. Wesley

Source: holograph; privately held (MARC, MA 2006/004 is a photocopy).

---

[273] Cf. Isaac Watts, 'The Comparison and Complaint', st. 7, in JW, *CPH* (1738), 75.

[274] Richard D'Olier (1737–1816), a grandson of Huguenot refugees to Ireland married Sarah Rosanna Ogle (1736–1816) in 1768. The couple were leaders of the Methodist society in Dublin. They made the unfortunate decision to move back to France in 1791 for Richard's health, and were imprisoned when the Reign of Terror in France began in 1793. They were eventually freed and returned to Dublin. See Crookshank, *Ireland*, 383, 443, 463.

[275] While there is no address portion, John Ogylvie was assigned to the Isle of Man under John Crook as Assistant, and the letter came down through the Ogylvie family.

To Adam Clarke

Manchester
Saturday, July 28, 1787   5

Dear Adam,

On Monday fortnight, if God permit, Dr. [Thomas] Coke, Mr. [Robert] Brackenbury, and I shall set out for Southampton in order to embark for Jersey, on board the first packet. I do not know but we shall bring your friend John King with us.[276]   10

I am, dear Adam,

Yours affectionately,

[J. Wesley]

Address: 'To / Mr Adam Clarke / At Mr [George] Walker's / In St Peter's   15
/ Isle of Guernsey'.

Source: published transcription; Telford, *Letters*, 8:4.

20

To Jeanne Le Gros Bisson[277]

Manchester   25
August 4, 1787

My Dear Sister,

Although it is probable I shall see you in a few days, yet I must write a few lines.[278] I rejoice to hear that you are still happy in God, and trust that happiness will never cease but rather increase more   30
and more till your spirit returns to God. Be assured there is no necessity that it ever should cease. He is willing to give it [to] you always. And he can purify you by the fire of his love, as well as by the fire of affliction. Do not therefore expect or desire affliction, but

---

[276] John King was not assigned to the Channel Islands, but to Thirsk.

[277] Jeanne Le Gros Bisson (1767–1830) was born in St. Martin, Isle of Jersey. Robert Carr Brackenbury sent JW an account of her spiritual experience c. Feb. 10, 1787, and JW's reply to Brackenbury of Feb. 16 drew a letter from Jeanne to JW of July 11, 1787. JW met Jeanne while on a preaching tour to the Isle of Jersey Aug. 20–29, 1787; see *Journal*, 24:53–54 in this edn. They continued to correspond after Jeanne married William Cock (1765–1812) in St. Helier, Isle of Jersey, on Mar. 9, 1788. See the account of her death in *WMM* 9 (1830): 861.

[278] JW was replying to her letter of July 11, 1787.

let the joy of the Lord be your strength.[279] That your joy and peace may flow as a river is the prayer of, my dear sister,[280]

Your affectionate brother,

[J. Wesley]

5   *Source*: published transcription; Jackson, *Works* (3rd), 13:84.

For John Harper
10   ## Testimonial Letter[281]

[Manchester]
[August 5, 1787]

15   Know all men by these presents that I, John Wesley, M.A., late of Lincoln College, Oxford, did on the 4th day of August, in the year of our Lord 1787 (being assisted by other ordained ministers), set apart for the office of an elder in the church of God, by the imposition of my hands and prayer, and with a single eye to the glory of 20   God, John Harper, whom I esteem a fit person to administer the holy sacraments and to feed the flock of Christ; and as such I recommend him to all whom it may concern. Given under my hand and seal the fifth day of August 1787.[282]

John Wesley

25   *Source*: holograph; Library, Wofford College, Spartanburg, South Carolina.[283]

---

[279] See Neh. 8:10.

[280] See Isa. 48:18.

[281] This is one of only two testimonial letters for the four persons that JW ordained first deacon, then elder, on Aug. 3–4, 1787, during Conference, of which there is surviving record of the text (the other is that for Duncan M'Allum below). For background and more details see Appendix B.

[282] John Harper (d. 1815), of Irish descent, was admitted 'on trial' as an itinerant in 1786 (see 10:597 in this edn.) and stationed in Clones. At the 1787 Conference he was ordained by JW for the West Indies. He served there through the early 1790s, marrying Henrietta Hawes, of Antigua. About 1794 he moved to the continental US for his wife's health, but she died soon after. Harper got on well with Francis Asbury and in 1796, after the usual probationary period, he was ordained elder in the Methodist Episcopal Church (neither his time of service in the Caribbean or his ordination by JW were recognized). In 1803 he located in Columbia, SC, where he founded a Methodist church on Washington Street, and in 1805 he took on duties at Mount Bethel Academy until his death. See *MM* 22 (1799), 261–62; and John Garraty and Mark Carnes (eds.), *American National Biography* (New York: Oxford University Press, 1999), 10:130.

[283] The letter was given to the South Carolina Conference by Mrs. William Harper, widow of Chancellor Harper, of South Carolina, son of Rev. John Harper.

To Mrs. H[owton?][284]

Manchester
August 5, 1787

My Dear Sister,

It would have given me pleasure to spend a little time with you. But since it could not be, we are to submit. I am glad you are placed, at least for a season, among them that love and fear God. As you are naturally of an easy, flexible temper, you have great need to converse as often as possible with those that are truly alive to God; which may be a counterbalance to the conversation you will be obliged to have with those of a different character. But perhaps Mr. H. will not always be of the same spirit that he has been in time past. What has hitherto been may have been permitted for the trial of your faith. And if you are like him 'Who ne'er forsook his faith for love of peace',[285] the God of peace will in his own time do great things for you. To his tender care I commit you; and am, my dear sister,

Yours in much affection,

J. Wesley

Source: holograph; MARC, MAM JW 3/67.

To Arthur Keene

Manchester
August 5, 1787

My Dear Brother,

We may see the mercy of God in removing your little one into a better world.[286] It was a mercy for you as well as for her. I was afraid she would have continued in pain long enough to have taken her mother with her. But God does all things well.[287] You must now take care that she may have more air and exercise than she has lately had. Otherwise she may find many ill effects of her late confinement.

---

[284] There is no address portion. It may be Mrs. Howton, as Telford speculates, since JW was able to spend only one day in Worcester after leaving Manchester. But there is no way to confirm this.

[285] Cf. SW Jr., 'The Battle of the Sexes', st. 35, *Poems* (1743), 34; included by JW in *MSP* (1744), 3:32.

[286] Their younger daughter [Isabella Jr.?] had died; see JW to Keene, July 24, 1787.

[287] See Mark 7:37.

I do not wonder that your Dublin newswriters were afraid of stirring up a nest of hornets. Ours in England are not so fearful. They are glad to have anything from *me*; they know how it increases the sale of their paper.

5   May peace be multiplied upon you, and all that are with you! I am, dear Arthur,

Yours most affectionately,

J. Wesley

10   *Address*: 'To / Mr. Arthur Keene / Ranelagh Road / Dublin'.
Postmarks: 'Manchester' and 'AU/10'.
Endorsement: by Keene, '5th Augt. 87 / Revd. J. Wesley / Manchester'.
Source: holograph; MHS Ireland Archives.

15

For Duncan M'Allum
Testimonial Letter

20

[Manchester]
[August 5, 1787]

25   Know all men by these presents that I, John Wesley, M.A., late of Lincoln College, Oxford, did on the fourth day of August, in the year of our Lord 1787 (being assisted by other ordained ministers) set apart for the office of an elder in the church of God, by the imposition of my hands and prayer, and with a single eye to the glory
30   of God, Duncan M'Allum, whom I esteem a fit person to administer the holy sacraments and to feed the flock of Christ; and as such I recommend him to all whom it may concern. Given under my hand and seal the fifth day of August 1787.

John Wesley

35

Source: published transcription; *Methodist Recorder*, March 5, 1869, p. 116.[288]

---

[288] Robert Dugdale of Bristol, the source of this transcription, stated that he had the letter in his possession.

To the Rev. Levi Heath[289]

Birmingham
[August 6, 1787] 5

Dear Sir,

In your way to London I believe you must spend the first night at Oxford. You may inquire at the preaching-house in New Hall Lane for Mr. [Joseph] Harper, who is the Assistant in that circuit. Thence you have then four-and-twenty miles to High Wycombe, where Mr. 10 Batting will entertain you hospitably by a word of recommendation from Mr. Harper. You have then thirty miles to London. At my house near Moorfields I hope you will be at home. And Mr. [Samuel] Bradburn there will recommend you to our friends at Reading, Newbury, Bath, and Bristol. At Bristol I hope you will find your 15 family well, and probably a ship ready to sail.[290]

I commend you to the grace of God, and am, dear sir,

Your affectionate friend and brother,

J. Wesley

20

Source: holograph; Lovely Lane Museum.

25

To the Committee for the Abolition of the Slave Trade[291]

Isle of Guernsey 30
August 18, 1787

Gentlemen,

A week or two ago I was favoured with a letter from Mr. Clarkson, informing me of his truly Christian design to procure, if possible, an Act of Parliament for the abolition of slavery in our plan- 35

---

[289] The letter is mounted, rendering the verso inaccessible, but the content makes the recipient clear.

[290] See JW to Heath, May 18, 1787.

[291] The Committee [later, 'Society'] for the Abolition of the Slave Trade was formed on 22 May 1787. It was established by twelve men; nine Quakers and three Anglicans (Clarkson, Sharp, and Philip Sansom)—the latter being able to lobby Parliament more directly. The Committee's work educating the public about the abuses of the slave trade contributed to passage of the Slave Trade Act of 1807.

tations.[292] I have long wished for the rolling away of the reproach from us, a reproach not only to religion but to humanity itself—especially when I read Mr. [Anthony] Benezet's tracts, and what Mr. Sharp has written upon the subject.[293] My friends in America are
5   of the same mind. They have already emancipated several hundred of the poor Negroes, and are setting more and more at liberty every day, as fast as they can do it with any tolerable convenience. This is making a little stand against this shocking abomination.

But Mr. Clarkson's design strikes at the root of it. And if it can
10   be put in execution will be a lasting honour to the British nation. It is with great satisfaction that I learn so many of you are determined to support him. But, without doubt, you expect to meet with rough and violent opposition. For the slave-holders are a numerous, a wealthy, and consequently a very powerful body. And when
15   you bring their craft into danger, do you not touch the apple of their eye? Will they not then raise all their forces against you, and summon their friends from every side? And will they not employ hireling writers in abundance, who will treat you without either justice or mercy? But I trust, gentlemen, you will not be affrighted at this.
20   No, not when some of your friends turn against you, perhaps some who have made the warmest professions of goodwill, and the strongest promises of assisting you. I trust you will not be discouraged thereby, but rather more resolute and determined. I allow, with men this is impossible; but we know all things are possible with God![294]
25   What little I can do to promote this excellent work, I shall do with pleasure. I will print a large edition of the tract I wrote some years since, *Thoughts Upon Slavery*, and send it (which I have an opportunity of doing once a month) to all my friends in Great Britain and Ireland, adding a few words in favour of your design, which I
30   believe will have some weight with them.[295]

I commend you to him who is able to carry you through all opposition and support you in all discouragements, and am, gentlemen,
    Your hearty well-wisher,
                                                              John Wesley

---

[292] This letter is not known to survive. Thomas Clarkson (1760–1846) took a leadership role in formation of the Society.

[293] For Benezet, see JW's letter c. Mar.–Apr. 1774, 29:22–23 in this edn. For Sharp, see JW's letter of Oct. 11, 1787.

[294] See Matt. 19:26.

[295] In his letter to Thomas Funnell, dated Nov. 24, 1787, JW states that he had completed this task.

Address: 'To / Samuel Hoare, Esq., Banker / in / London'.[296]
Source: published transcription; *Christian Advocate* 79 (Oct. 8, 1931), p. 2.[297]

5

To Jeanne Le Gros Bisson[298]

Penzance   10
September 7, 1787

My Dear Sister,

Almost as soon as we were in the ship the wind entirely died away. But we knew our remedy—we went into the cabin and applied ourselves to him that has all power. Immediately a fair wind sprung up,   15 which never ceased till it brought us to Penzance Bay. Our brethren here were not a little surprised, having given up all hopes of seeing us this year. But so much the more thankful they were to the Giver of every good gift.[299]

I have thought of you much since I had the satisfaction of con-   20 versing with you. And I will tell you every thought that passed through my mind, as I wish always to do. It seems to me that our blessed Lord is willing to show all the power of his grace in you, even his power of saving to the uttermost those that come unto God through him.[300] But there is a mountain that stands in the way; and   25 how you will get over it I know not. I mean pride. O my sister, what can save you from this but the mighty power of God! I almost tremble for you. If you give way to it, yea but a little, your grace will wither away. But still, the God whom you serve is able to deliver you.[301] And he really will, if you continue instant in prayer.[302]   30

---

[296] The letter is addressed to Samuel Hoare (1751–1825), a Quaker banker who was the treasurer of the twelve-member Committee. See the summary of it being read at a meeting on Aug. 27, 1787 in Thomas Clarkson, *History of Rise, Progress, and Accomplishment of the Abolition of the African Slave-Trade by the British Parliament* (London: Longman, 1808), 1:447–48.

[297] This is reported as one of four letters recently purchased in London by E. S. Tipple; its current location is unknown.

[298] JW was writing after having met Jeanne while on a preaching tour to the Isle of Jersey Aug. 20–29, 1787; see *Journal*, 24:53–54 in this edn.

[299] See James 1:17.

[300] See Heb. 7:25.

[301] See Dan. 3:17.

[302] See Rom. 12:12.

That other temptation which did formerly beset you I trust will assault you no more. Or if it should, you are now better prepared for it, and you will know in whom your strength lieth.[303]

When you have opportunity, my dear Jenny, write freely to

Your affectionate brother,

J. Wesley

I hope my dear Miss Lempriere has recovered her health.[304]

Address: 'To / Miss Bisson / In St. Heliers / Isle of Jersey / N.B. Not the Isle of Wight'.
Postmark: 'Bath'. *Charge*: '5'.
Source: holograph; MARC, MAM JW 1/50.

To Mary Cooke

Bath
September 15, 1787

My Dear Sister,

On Monday, the 24th instant, I shall (with God's assistance) be at Bradford. And on Tuesday morning I hope to have the pleasure of waiting upon you at Trowbridge.

Adieu!

On second thoughts I purpose preaching at Trowbridge on Monday noon and Bradford in the evening.

Address: 'To / Miss Cook / In Duke Street / Trowbridge'.
Endorsement: by Cooke; 'Nothing 17th'.[305]
Source: holograph; MARC, WCB, D6/1/338.

---

[303] See Judg. 16:6.
[304] Orig., 'Lampriere'.
[305] There is no record of JW's 16th letter to Cooke.

To James Currie[306]

Bath
September 15, 1787

My Dear Brother,

The account of the dying malefactors which you sent me is exceeding remarkable. I think it is worthy to have a place in the *Arminian Magazine*, and hope it may be of use to others.[307]

You see, God is well pleased with your using the strength you have, and does not send you a warfare at your own cost. Continue to declare the whole gospel and to aspire after all the promises.

I am

Your affectionate brother,

J. Wesley

Address: 'To / Mr. James Curry / At Cottam End / Northampton'.
Postmark: 'Bath'.
Source: holograph; MARC, MAM JW 2/71.

To George Holder

Bath
September 15, 1787

Dear George,

Upon mature deliberation I judge it most advisable that John Barber should remove to Edinburgh (for I can trust him in any part of Great Britain) and that you should supply his place at York.[308] As soon as may be, inform him and Mr. [Thomas] Rutherford of this, that there may be as little delay as possible.

I am, dear George,

Yours affectionately,

J. Wesley

---

[306] James Currie (fl. 1780s) was a schoolmaster in Cotton End, a neighbourhood in Northampton. He was also apparently a lay preacher in the Methodist society there; see JW to Currie, Jan. 24, 1789.

[307] No account like this appeared in *AM* between the date of this letter and JW's death.

[308] John Barber (1756–1816) of Hayfield, Derbyshire, had been converted to Methodism about 1777 and began acting as a local preacher. He was admitted into the itinerant ministry in 1782 and served until his death (twice as President of Conference). See *Minutes* (post-Wesley, 1816), 4:194–95. He was currently stationed at York, where Rutherford was the Assistant. JW needed to fill a position in Edinburgh due to the unexpected death of Joshua Keighley.

Address: 'To / Mr George Holder / Whitby'.
Postmark: 'Scarborough'. *Charge*: '5'.
Source: holograph; MARC, MAM JW 3/48.

5

To Ann Bolton

Bristol
10
September 18, 1787

My Dear Nancy,

Yesterday I received yours of August 24 at my return from a little
tour to the islands of Alderney, Jersey, and Guernsey, where we
were long shut up by contrary winds.[309] At length a ship returning
15
from France and touching at Guernsey took us in and carried us to
Penzance, where we were received as if we had just risen from the
dead, and found God was with us wherever we went. So I pressed
on and will be with *you*.

My Nancy, look up! The Lord of Hosts is at hand![310] He *has* de-
20
livered, he does deliver, and he will yet deliver ! He chastens you
why? *For your profit*, that you may be a partaker of his holiness. He
chastens you also for your profit, that you may be more holy and
consequently more happy. But his ways are in the deep waters and
his footsteps are not known.[311]
25
It is probable I shall see you at Witney in about a month. If I do,
remember you are to tell me all your trials, that we may both grieve
and rejoice together. I cannot well tell you how much I love you—
you are exceeding near and dear to me. But I am sometimes ready
to think that you do not love me so well as you did once. However,
30
I believe you have still some regard for me. Let us still provoke one
another to love and to good works.[312]

The good Lord be ever with you and unite you more and more to
himself! Then you will not forget, my dear Nancy,

Yours in tender affection,
35
J. Wesley

---

[309] Bolton's letter to JW is not known to survive.
[310] See Phil. 4:5.
[311] See Ps. 77:19.
[312] See Heb. 10:24.

Address: 'To / Miss Bolton / In Witney / Oxfordshire'.
Postmark: 'Bristol'. *Charge*: '5'.
Endorsement: by Bolton, 'Sept. [1]8th –87'.
Source: holograph; MARC, MAM JW 1/98.

To Henry Moore[313]

Bristol
September 18, 1787

Dear Henry,

This is nothing strange. Considering the great work of God which has lately been wrought in Dublin, we might reasonably expect Satan would fight in defence of his tottering kingdom. It is our part calmly and steadily to resist him. In such a case as you have mentioned you are justified before God and man for preaching at eleven o'clock on Sunday morning, only earnestly advising them that have heretofore received the sacrament [at] Church to do so still. But I do not imagine any barefaced Calvinism will be *soon* preached at Bethesda.[314]

I am glad sister [Anne] Moore and [Sarah] D'Olier are not idle, and that you preach abroad on Sundays. The death of that sailor may be a warning to others. Tenderly watch over [Rowland Hill?[315]] and his coming to Dublin may be the saving of his soul. Peace be with all your spirits!

I am, with kind love to Nancy, dear Henry,
Your affectionate friend and brother,

J. Wesley

Address: 'To / Mr Henry Moore/ At the New Room in / Dublin'.
Postmarks: 'Bristol' and 'SE/22'.
Source: holograph; MARC, WCB, D6/1/128a.

[313] Moore wrote on the back of this letter: 'Mr. Wesley's answer to my letter informing him of Mr. Hill's arrival, and of the society formed to bring over "gospel ministers".' The visit was by Rowland Hill, the Calvinist evangelist, and the phrase 'gospel ministers' was being used to mean Calvinist preachers (cf. JW, 'Thoughts Concerning "Gospel Ministers"', 13:568–70 in this edn.). Moore's letter to JW is not known to survive. But see JW to Hester Ann (Roe) Rogers, Oct. 12, 1787; and the letter of the Dublin Leaders to JW, Apr. 18, 1789.
[314] Rev. Edward Smyth was now the chaplain at Bethesda Chapel.
[315] The name has been cut out of the holograph.

To Elizabeth Padbury

Bristol
September 19, 1787

My Dear Betsy,

If I do not mistake, one of our preachers desired the justice to give him the oath and was refused.[316] If this is true, I desire as soon as possible to know: Who was the preacher? Who was the justice? On what day did he offer himself to the justice? Was this before or after the prosecution began? Was any distress made, or were the goods sold after he offered to take the oath? I believe your answer to these questions will open a scene which the good justice little expects.

You have lately had a noble exercise of your faith and patience. So have several of your neighbours. This calls you to much and earnest prayer. Then God will arise and maintain his own cause. I advise you all in the meantime to say little. You have better things to talk of. I suppose the rector and the justice are now quiet.[317] Their turn will come by and by.

I am, my dear Betsy,
Yours most affectionately,

J. Wesley

Address: 'To / Miss Padbury / At Whittlebury / near Towcester / Northamptonshire'.
Postmarks: 'Bristol' and 'SE/20/87'. *Charge*: '5'.
Source: holograph; Wesley's Chapel (London), LDWMM 1997/6720.

[316] Likely the 'oath of allegiance' required of dissenting ministers under the Toleration Act of 1688.

[317] Rev. Henry Beauclerk (1745–1817), rector of Whittlebury, was opposing Methodist preaching and the building of a Methodist chapel in the town. JW ended up seeking protection from King's Bench (see JW to Padbury, Oct. 29, 1787).

'To the Trustees of the Preaching[-]house at Dewsbury'[318]

Bristol
September 22, 1787

My Dear Brethren,

Mr. [John] Broadbent informs me that you refuse to settle the house at Dewsbury according to the Articles which we agreed on when I was with you. If you do settle it according to those Articles, well. If not, I have done with you. And I shall give orders today that none of our preachers preach in that house after the twenty-second of October next.

John Wesley

Address: 'To / the Trustees / for the Preaching house / Dewsbury'.[319]
Source: holograph; Drew, Methodist Archives.

To Jonathan Crowther

near Bath
September 25, 1787

Dear Jonathan,

The sum of the matter: you want money and money you shall have, if I can beg, borrow, or—anything but steal. I say, therefore, Dwell in the land and be doing good, and verily thou shalt be fed.[320] I should be sorry for the death of brother Burbeck,[321] but that I know God does all things well.[322] And if his work prospers in your

[318] The heading is in JW's hand; indicating this was part of a double letter sent to John Broadbent. For the beginning of this controversy, see John Atlay (for JW) to John Heald, Feb. 23, 1784; on its conclusion see JW's later circular letter of Aug. 23, 1789.

[319] This address is in the hand of John Broadbent. He added a note to the trustees: 'My Dear Brethren, I hope I have done all in my power to contribute to your happiness and the real good of those connected with us in Dewsbury. I can now do no more. I wish I could prevent this, which I know will distress the souls of many. I wish you had taken the advice of a friend. Ever, John Boadbent.'

[320] See Ps. 37:3; and JW's similar reply to Samuel Bradburn, Aug. 31, 1775, 27:176 in this edn.

[321] Edward Burbeck (d. 1787) was admitted 'on trial' as an itinerant in 1783 (see 10:531 in this edn.). He was assigned to the Inverness circuit (where Crowther was Assistant), along with Joshua Keighley. Like Keighley (assigned to Edinburgh), Burbeck died during this assignment (see 10:645).

[322] See Mark 7:37.

hands, this will make your labours light. Our preachers now find in the north of Scotland what they formerly found all over England; yet they went on. And when I had only blackberries to eat in Cornwall still God gave me strength sufficient for my work.[323]

5   I am, dear Jonathan,
     Your affectionate brother,

J. Wesley

P.S. To Mr. [John] Atlay: Pay to Jonathan Crowther or his order,
10   five guineas.[324]

Source: holograph; privately held (Manchester, Rylands, English Ms 371/127 is a facsimile and transcription).

15

To Robert Barry

near Bath
September 26, 1787
20   My Dear Brother,

I think you misunderstood me.[325] A papist at Lisbon asked a Protestant, 'Do you say I can't be saved in *my* religion?' He replied, 'I say possibly *you* may be saved in *that* religion. But *I* could not.' So
25   I say in the present case to one that asks, 'Can't I be saved if I *dance* or *play* at cards?' I answer, 'Possibly *you* may be saved, though you dance and play at cards. But *I* could not.' So far you may safely speak; but no further. So much and no more I advise our preachers to speak. But I cannot advise them to speak this to unawakened
30   people. It will only anger, not convince them. It is beginning at the wrong end. A plain preacher in London used to say, 'If you take away those rattles from the child, he will be angry. Nay, if he can, he will scratch or bite you. But give him something better first, and he will throw away the rattles of himself.' Yet I do not remember that I
35   call these things 'innocent amusements'. And you know we do not suffer any that use them to continue in our society. Yet I make allowance for *those that are without*. Else I might send my own father

[323] John Nelson records this anecdote in his journal, apparently on Sept. 8, 1743; see Jackson, *EMP*, 1:74.
[324] The facsimile does not contain the address portion, or this postscript. It is reproduced here from Telford, *Letters*, 8:11.
[325] Barry's letter, in which he raised a question about JW's advice in the letter of Sept. 15, 1786, is not known to survive.

and mother to hell, though they not only lived many years, but died in the full assurance of faith.

You do not seem to observe that it has pleased God to give such a measure of light to the Methodists as he has hardly given to any other body of men in the world. And he expects *us* to use all the light we have received, and to deal very tenderly with those who have not received it.

I do not wonder that Dr. [William] Walter is not clear with regard to the doctrine of the new birth. Neither was I when I had been in orders many years. Bear with him, and he may see more clearly by-and-by. I see no reason why you should not communicate with brother [Freeborn] Garrettson and with him too. I receive the Lord's Supper in every Church that I can.

I am

    Your affectionate brother,

                J. Wesley

Endorsement: likely by Barry, 'Revd Jno Wesley / 26th Septr. 1787'.
Source: holograph; Lovely Lane Museum.

To William Black Jr.[326]

near Bath
September 26, 1787

My Dear Brother,

You have great reason to praise God for the great things that he hath done, and to expect still greater things than these.

Your grand difficulty now will be to guard your flock against that accomplished seducer.[327] When you mentioned a person 'came from Scotland', I took it for granted that he was a Calvinist. But I find it is not so well—for I take a Socinian to be far worse than

---

[326] While the address portion is missing, the content and Black's typical endorsement confirm the recipient.

[327] While the letter is not known to survive, Black had clearly sent JW an account of a sermon he heard on June 24, 1787 in Halifax, by a preacher just come from Scotland: 'His text was "Good master, what shall I do to inherit eternal life?" The conditions of salvation, he said, were comprised in the following propositions: I. Those who have been guilty of wilful sin must repent of it, and do so no more; but practice the opposite virtues. II. We must forgive all who have offended us. III. We must make restitution to God, to our neighbour, and to society for the injury we have done them. He then told the congregation that unless these three conditions were complied with, no reasonable hope of mercy could be entertained.' See Matthew Richey, *Memoir of the late Rev. William Black* (Halifax, Nova Scotia: Cunnabell, 1839), 198–200.

even a predestinarian. And such one may easily conclude him to
be from the heads of that miserable sermon. Nevertheless I advise
you and all our preachers never oppose him openly. Doing thus
would only give the unawakened world an advantage against you
5   all. I advise you farther, never speak severely, much less contemp-
tuously, of him in any mixed company. You must use no weapons
in opposing him but only those of truth and love. Your wisdom is:
first, strongly to inculcate the doctrines which he denies, but without taking any notice of him or seeming to know that any one does
10   deny them; secondly, to advise all our brethren (but not in public)
never to hear him at the peril of their souls; and thirdly, narrowly to
inquire whether any one is staggered, and to set such a one right as
soon as possible. Thus, by the assistance of God, even those that are
lame will not be turned out of the way.
15   Peace be with your spirit! I am, dear Billy,
        Your affectionate friend and brother,

J. Wesley

20   *Postmark*: 'NO/7/87'.[328]
Endorsement: by Black, 'Revd J Wesley / Near Bath 26 Sept 1787'.
Source: holograph; UCC Maritime Conference, Archives.

25

To Rev. Joshua Gilpin[329]

Bristol
September 30, 1787

30   Dear Sir,
    I thank you for your copies of verses, several of which I propose
to insert in the *[Arminian] Magazine*. But I know not why you
should not write more. Indeed it is time, when youth is past, to say
with Horace, '*ludicra pono*'.[330] But verses need not be ludicrous. You
35   have a talent for writing serious verses. And why should you bury

---

[328] This was when the letter arrived in North America, likely New York.

[329] Rev. Joshua Gilpin (c. 1755–1828), was vicar of Wrockwardine, Shropshire from 1782, where he befriended John Fletcher in nearby Madeley. JW published poems by 'Rev. G.' that are surely by Gilpin in *AM* 13 (1790), 166–68, 278–79, 391–92; and *AM* 14 (1791), 52–56. Two other poems that may be by Gilpin are found in *AM* 11 (1788), 669–71; and *AM* 12 (1789), 108–10. The only other known published verse of Gilpin is his *Verses Written at the Fountain of Vaucluse* (London: T. Bensley, 1799), which exhibits strong similarity in style.

[330] Horace, *Epistles*, I.i.10.; 'lay aside [my verses and all other] toys' (Loeb).

that talent in the earth?[331] You may preach the gospel in verse as well
as in prose, and sometimes with more effect. For,

> A verse may find him who a sermon flies.[332]

Wishing you a continuance of bodily and spiritual health, I am, dear
sir,
    Your affectionate friend and brother,

                                    J. Wesley

Address: 'To / The Revd Mr Gilpin / To be left at Madeley / near Shifnal
    / Salop'.
Source: holograph; MARC, MAM JW 3/30.

To Henry Moore

                               Bristol
                    September 30, 1787

Dear Henry,
    I know you are a man of feeling. You can sympathize with the af-
flicted. Therefore I employ you in a labour of love. Poor John Bull
is now in the Marshalsea Prison. How far he was formerly to blame
is not now the question. But what can be done for him now? For one
who through a course of many years deserved well of the Methodists? We cannot deliver him from his confinement. That is too hard
for us. But possibly something might be done to make it a little
easier to him. I desire you would go and talk with him. You will find
acceptable words. Tell him I desired you to call upon him in consequence of his letter, and try to make him sensible of the hand of
God in all this.[333] Now especially he stands in need of such a friend.
    I am, dear Henry, with kind love to Nancy,
    Your affectionate friend and brother,

                                      J. Wesley

Pray give him a guinea on my account, and another whenever you
see proper.[334]

---

[331] See Matt. 25:25.
[332] George Herbert, *The Temple*, 'The Church Porch', st. 1, l. 5.
[333] Bull's letter to JW is not known to survive.
[334] Cf. JW to Moore, July 1, 1789.

Address: 'To / Mr Henry Moore / At the New Room, in / Dublin'.
Postmark: 'Bristol'.
Source: holograph; MARC, WCB, D6/3/1/15.

To Sarah (Fownes) Tighe[335]

Bristol
October 2, 1787

Dear Madam,

I have no doubt at all of the uprightness of Mr. Tozer and his wife.[336] But I have more acquaintance with Mr. Harper.[337] He is a truly good man, and has a considerable share of knowledge. So that if he was willing to take the charge of this little school, I know of no one that is more likely to promote the design of it.

I am, dear madam,
Your very affectionate servant,

John Wesley

Next week I expect to be in London.

Address: 'To Mrs Tighe / at Harrow / Middlesex'.[338]
Source: photo of holograph; *Wesleyan Methodist Magazine* 133 (1910): 528.

To Hannah Ball

Bristol
October 4, 1787

My Dear Sister,

You have great reason to praise God, who has kept you for so many years a witness of his great salvation. And you must never be

[335] Sarah Fownes (1743–1821; daughter of Sir William Frederick Fownes) married William Tighe (1738–82) in 1765. William was the son of William Tighe (1710–66) and Lady Mary (Bligh) Tighe (1716–48), and the brother of Dorothea (Tighe) Blachford. So Sarah was the sister-in-law of Dorothea; and like her, was left a widow at a relatively young age. Sarah also emulated her sister-in-law in dedicating herself to charitable ventures. She resided in Rosanna, Co. Wicklow, Ireland. See Harriet K. Linkin, *The Collected Letters of Mary Blachford Tighe* (Bethlehem, PA: Lehigh University Press, 2020), 466–67; and Richard Ludlow, 'Wesley's Friends at Rosanna', *WMM* 133 (1910): 527–33.
[336] Tighe was seeking a master for a small charity school she set up.
[337] This was neither of JW's itinerants, John or Joseph Harper.
[338] She was in Harrow visiting her sons, who were in school there.

afraid or ashamed to declare it, especially to those that love God. Some will believe your report. Some will not, for which they never want pretenses.[339] For it is impossible to cut off occasion of offense from them that seek occasion. When we speak for God, we should speak with all mildness and yet with all earnestness. But by those 5 who do not profit thereby this earnestness will be accounted anger. But still, you have only to go on warily and steadily between the two extremes.

Certainly you may expect to see such a work in High Wycombe as never was yet. On Monday next I expect to set out for London. 10 This winter I shall not have time to take many journeys; but I shall undoubtedly find time to visit you. Peace be with all your spirits!

I am, my dear sister,
Your affectionate brother,

J. Wesley 15

Source: published transcription; Ball, *Memoir*, 168.

20
To Sarah Mallet[340]

Bristol
October 6, 1787
My Dear Sister,
Ever since I saw you I have felt a great love for you and a desire to 25 see you again. When I come to Harwich I hope you will find means to be there.[341] Afterwards probably I may visit you at Long Stratton. I am glad you wrote.[342] I have lately seen a young woman in the Isle of Jersey whose experience is as extraordinary as yours. In one thing 30

[339] Orig., 'patience'; corrected by transcription published in *WMM* 84 (1861): 441–42.

[340] Sarah Mallet (1764–1846), born in Loddon, was niece to William Mallet (1736–1830) of Long Stratton, Norfolk, a Methodist class leader. While staying with her uncle in 1780, she experienced conversion. Over the next few years Sarah felt an urge to preach, but resisted. Then in 1785 Sarah had a series of (epileptic?) fits, during which she often exhorted those around her. Hearing their accounts after she came to herself, and their affirmation of her calling, Sarah began to preach publicly. JW met Sarah in Long Stratton on Dec. 4, 1786 (see *Journal*, 23:426 in this edn.). He became convinced of her call, and offered encouragement of her preaching over his remaining years (see the letter of Oct. 27, 1787 below). In 1793 Sarah married Thomas Boyce (1765–1821), a Methodist local preacher. She continued preaching till her death, despite the ban on female preaching imposed by the Wesleyan Methodist Church in 1803. See Vickers, *Dictionary*, 221; and David East, *My Dear Sally* (World Methodist Historical Society Publications, 2003).

[341] JW does not appear to have made this trip in winter 1787–88.

[342] Sarah's letter to JW is not known to survive.

she seems to be more clear than you—namely, in her communion with the blessed Trinity, with God the Father and God the Son and God the Holy Ghost.[343]

5   It seems to me that no weapon that is formed against you shall prosper if you keep clear of inordinate affection. O keep your heart with all diligence![344] Mark the first risings of desire! Roll yourself (as David speaks) upon the Lord,[345] and he is and always will be your sufficient portion!

    On Monday I am to return to London. Whenever you have lei-
10 sure write freely to, my dear Sally,

      Yours affectionately,

J. Wesley

Address: 'To / Miss Sally Mallitt / At Mr [William] Mallitt's / in Long
15   Stratton / Norfolk'.
Postmark: 'OC/11/87'. *Charge*: '5'.
Endorsement: 'Oct. 6. 1787 / Copied Z. T.'.[346]
Source: holograph; privately held (WWEP Archive holds photocopy).

20

To Isaac Brown

Bristol
25   October 7, 1787
Dear Isaac,

    It was at the request of brother [George] Holder himself that I ordered him to be removed from Whitby, and I have wrote once or twice to that effect.[347] But if his mind is altered, and if *you* judge it
30 safe for him to remain there, I have no objection to it.

    Tomorrow I am to set out for London. When I come thither, I will consider with the preachers what is to be when the circuits *will not* bear the expense allotted to them.

    Peace be with you and yours! I am, dear Isaac,
35   Your affectionate friend and brother,

J. Wesley

---

[343] See Jeanne Le Gros Bisson to JW, July 11, 1787.

[344] See Prov. 4:23.

[345] JW appears to be stressing the literal meaning of the Hebrew verb beginning Ps. 37:5.

[346] I. e., Zachariah Taft, who included in *Holy Women*, 1:85–86.

[347] See JW to Holder, Sept. 15, 1787.

5

To John Heald[348]

London 10
October 10, 1787

My Dear Brother,

My love to you, and my regard for the general work of God, I believe you do not doubt of. I have the case of Birstall house before my eyes.[349] This is a second case of the same kind. It is my duty to 15 prevent a third, if possible. Therefore I answer once for all. If you settle at Dewsbury house on the Conference plan, without any alteration, I shall rejoice. But if this is not done, I dare not suffer any of our preachers to preach in it any longer. I am,

Your real friend and affectionate brother, 20

J. Wesley

No attorney is needed on our case.

25

---

[348] The trustees of the preaching-house at Dewsbury, with John Heald at the head, were still resisting adoption of the 'model deed'. Cf. the earlier letter of Feb. 23, 1784; and JW's circular letter of Aug. 23, 1789.

[349] JW, 'The Case of Birstall House', 9:504–09 in this edn.

To Granville Sharp[350]

London
October 11, 1787

5   Sir,

Ever since I heard of it first, I felt a perfect detestation of the horrid slave trade; but more particularly since I had the pleasure of reading what you have published upon the subject. Therefore I cannot but do everything in my power to forward the glorious de-

10   sign of your society.[351] And it must be a comfortable thing to every man of humanity to observe the spirit with which you have hitherto gone on.

Indeed, you cannot go on without more than common resolution, considering the opposition you have to encounter, all the op-

15   position which can be made by men who are not encumbered by either honour, conscience, or humanity, and will rush on *per fasque nefasque*,[352] through every possible means, to secure their great goddess—interest. Unless they are infatuated in this point also, they will spare no money to carry their cause. And this has the weight of

20   a thousand arguments with the generality of men.

And you may be assured these men will lay hold on and improve every possible objection against you. I have been afraid lest they should raise an objection from your manner of procuring information. To *hire* or to *pay* informers has a bad sound and might raise

25   great, yea unsurmountable prejudice against you.[353] Is it not worth your consideration whether it would not be advisable to drop this mode entirely, and to be content with such information as you can procure by more honourable means?

After all, I doubt the matter will turn upon this: 'Is the slave trade

30   for the interest of the nation?' And here, the multitude of sailors that perish therein will come to be considered.[354]

---

[350] Granville Sharp (1735–1813) was a philanthropist and leading opponent of slavery. JW included extracts from Sharp's *Representation of the Injustice and Dangerous Tendency of tolerating Slavery* (London: White & Horsefield, 1772) in his *Thoughts on Slavery*. See Sharp's letter to JW of Dec. 20, 1773.

[351] The Committee for the Abolition of the Slave Trade, of which Sharp was a founding member (see letter of Aug. 18, 1787). This letter is recorded in their minutes as JW's 'second letter' to the society; see Clarkson, *History of Rise*, 1:451–52.

[352] Lucan, *The Civil War*, v.313; 'through right or wrong' (Loeb).

[353] Likely referring to Thomas Clarkson paying the expenses of former slave ship surgeon Alexander Falconbridge to travel with Clarkson to Liverpool; see *History of Rise*, 1:294.

[354] This was the strategy Clarkson utilized. He did not think the English populace would be motivated by additional accounts of slave deaths and horrors, but they would care about the high rate of sailors dying on these voyages.

In all these difficulties, what a comfort it is to consider (unfashionable as it is) that there is a God! Yea, and that (as little as men think of it!) he has still all power, both in heaven and on earth![355] To him I commit you and your glorious cause; and am, sir,

Your affectionate servant,

John Wesley

Address: 'To / Granville Sharp Esq' [hand delivered].
Endorsement: 'Oct 14. 1787'.
Source: holograph; Cambridge University Library, British and Foreign Bible Society Archives.[356]

To Hester Ann (Roe) Rogers[357]

London
October 12, 1787

My Dear Hetty,

I do not doubt but your calling at Dublin would be in an acceptable time, especially as R[owland] H[ill] was there.[358]

After we left you at Manchester we pushed on and in all haste set out for the Isle of Jersey. But a storm drove us into Yarmouth, in the Isle of Wight. There Dr. [Thomas] Coke and I preached in the market-place, by turns, two evenings and two mornings. A second storm drove us to the Isle of Purbeck, just where the Indiaman was lost.[359] There I had an opportunity of preaching to a little society which I had not seen for thirteen years.[360] We hoped to reach Guernsey the next evening, but could get no further than the Isle of Alderney. I preached on the beach in the morning, and the next afternoon came safe to Guernsey. Here is an open door: high and low, rich and poor receive the word gladly. So that I could not

[355] See Matt. 28:18.
[356] See also the summary of it being read at a meeting of the Committee on Oct. 30, 1787 in Clarkson, *History of Rise*, 1:451–52.
[357] Hester's husband James had been stationed in Dublin 1784 through mid-1787, but was moved to Cork by the 1787 Conference. She and James had come with JW from Ireland to Manchester for the 1787 Conference and were now returned.
[358] The Benson and Jackson edns. give only the initials 'R. H.'. Telford expands as shown, which seem verified by the note in JW to Henry Moore, Sept. 18, 1787.
[359] The *Halsewell*, an East Indiaman, wrecked on the Isle of Purbeck on Jan. 6, 1786.
[360] JW was there Oct. 11–12, 1774; see *Journal*, 22:430–31 in this edn.

regret being detained by contrary winds several days longer than we intended. The same thing befell us in the Isle of Jersey, where also there was an open door, even the governor and the chief of the people being quite civil and friendly.

5   Jane Bisson I saw every day. She is nineteen years old, about the size of Miss [Elizabeth Ritchie], and has a peculiar mixture of seriousness, sprightliness, and sweetness, both in her looks and behaviour. Wherever we were, she was the servant of all. I think she exceeds Madame Guyon in deep communion with God.

10   I hope you will see a revival in Cork also. See that you take particular care of the tender lambs, not forgetting poor P[atty] L[affan].[361] Peace be with all your spirits!

I am, with kind love to James Rogers, my dear Hetty,
Yours most affectionately,

15   J. Wesley

Source: published transcription; Benson, *Works*, 16:266–67.

20

To [Alexander Mather?][362]

London
October 19, 1787

25   My Dear Brother,
You did well in sending Benjamin Leggatt into Epworth circuit.[363] Pray send Michael where you judge proper.[364]
You gave exactly right advice to brother [Parson] Greenwood.[365] And as I can absolutely confide in you, with brothers [John] Pawson, [William] Thompson, [John] Allen, and [John] Goodwin to

---

[361] The Benson and Jackson edns. omit the surname for the first person and give only the initials 'P. L.'. Telford identifies the first as 'Miss Richie' and expands the initials. It is unclear whether he had access to the holograph, or made informed guesses. No records have been found to determine whether 'Patty' (Martha) Laffan is the wife or daughter of Andrew Laffan.

[362] The recipient was likely Alexander Mather, who served as JW's mediator with John Heald and the other trustees of the preaching-house in Dewsbury.

[363] Benjamin Leggatt (1761–1822), a native of Lincolnshire, was converted in 1782 and began serving as a local preacher. This is the first evidence of him making the transition to an itinerant; while he never appears as 'on trial' in the *Minutes*, he received regular appointments starting in 1788 (10:649 in this edn.). Leggatt served for thirty-five years, right up to his death. See *Minutes* (post-Wesley, 1823), 5:381–82.

[364] Likely Michael Fenwick, who was seeking to return to service in some form; cf. JW to Duncan Wright, Jan. 9, 1788.

[365] Greenwood was the Assistant of the Dewsbury circuit.

assist you,[366] what you shall agree with the trustees of Dewsbury I shall make no difficulty to. But remember that this is a *leading case*, and whatever concessions we make here, we must make to all other trustees that shall require them.

I pray consider too what brother Thompson says to me concerning his circuit, and if you think it reasonable that those places should be given back, let them be given back.

I am
Your affectionate friend and brother,

J. Wesley.

I think the contentious spirit in Birstall and Dewsbury circuits is what has hindered the work of God there.

Source: holograph; Wesley's Chapel (London), LDWMM 1997/6718.

To the Rev. Charles Atmore[367]

London
October 20, 1787

Dear Charles,

I am glad to hear so good an account of the work of God in Glasgow. But you must not stay there too long at a time. That is not the Methodist plan. I expect therefore brother [Robert] Johnson and you constantly to change once a quarter.[368]

It does not appear that we have as yet any place in Greenock. But I am glad you have paid a visit to Ayr. Many things have hindered brother [John] Barber, but I hope you will see him soon.[369] It seems brother [Alexander] Suter is in his place.[370]

I am, dear Charles,
Your affectionate friend and brother,

J. Wesley

---

[366] Pawson was the Assistant of the Leeds circuit; Thompson, of Birstall; Allen, of Wakefield; and Goodwin, of Halifax—the four circuits surrounding Dewsbury.

[367] JW ordained Atmore for service in Scotland in July 1786.

[368] Atmore was the Assistant for the Edinburgh circuit (which currently reached over to Glasgow); while Johnson was the Assistant for the Aberdeen circuit.

[369] Barber was being moved to Edinburgh to replace Joshua Keighley; see JW to George Holder, Sept. 15, 1787.

[370] Suter was appointed Assistant for Ayr and Greenock at Conference; but when JW wrote him on Nov. 24, 1787 he was in Aberdeen.

Address: 'To / The Revd Mr Charles Atmore / in / Glasgow'.
Postmarks: 'OC/20/87' and 'OC/23'.
Endorsement: by Atmore, 'Mr. Wesley'.
Source: holograph; MARC, MAM JW 1/6.

5

To Robert Carr Brackenbury

10
London
October 20, 1787

Dear Sir,

It was a good providence which [brought] that Penzance ship to Guernsey, that so seasonably carried us unto Cornwall. We were never more acceptable in the Cornish and Devonshire circuits, or more wanted there. And I am glad we were in the Islands, because very probably it is the last time I shall see them.

Mr. [Jean] De Quêteville is undoubtedly a good young man, and has a tolerably good understanding. But he thinks it better than it is, and in consequence is apt to put himself in your or my place. For these fifty years, if anyone has said, 'If you do not put such an one out of society, I will go out of it,' I have said, 'Pray go. I, not you, are to judge who shall stay.' I therefore greatly approve of your purpose to give Mr. Walker full hearing in the presence of all the preachers.[371] I have often repented of judging too severely, but very seldom of being too merciful. I hope Adam Clarke has now given you the reasons of his long delay.

I was sorry John Atlay had sent your books to Jersey before I returned to London. I had designed to send a few with them, to be presented to some of our friends in Jersey and Guernsey, but must now wait for another opportunity. I enclose a few lines to Miss [Jeanne Le Gros] Bisson, for whom I feel an affectionate concern.[372] I am much afraid the person you speak of does not love Miss Lempriere so well as her fortune.

I think our friends should not refuse to take their share of that nightly labour. It seems to me, if they declined it, they would be wanting in their duty both to their king and country.

15

20

25

30

35

---

[371] The issue concerned George Richard Walker, son of Capt. George Walker, who was in a relationship with Miss Lempriere that would result in their marriage; see the postscript of Adam Clarke to JW, Oct. 29, 1787.

[372] These lines, which Brackenbury would have torn off to give her, are not known to survive.

I am persuaded the heaviness which you feel is partly natural and partly preternatural. On the one side, I believe the corruptible body presses down on the soul;[373] and on the other, Satan labours to distress you. But the God whom you serve is able to deliver you.[374] He will I trust deliver you, and that shortly! I ever am, dear sir,   5
    Your affectionate friend and brother,

J. Wesley

Address: 'To / Robert Brackenbury Esq / In St. Helier's / Isle of Jersey'.
Source: holograph; Wesley's Chapel (London), LDWMM 1994/1986.   10

For Sarah Mallet   15
Testimonial Letter[375]

[Norwich]
October 27, 1787   20

We give the right-hand of fellowship to Sally Mallet, and shall have no objection to her being a preacher in our connexion, so long as she continues to preach the Methodist doctrine and attend to our discipline. You receive this by order of Mr. Wesley and the Confer-   25
ence.

Joseph Harper[376]

Source: published transcription; *Wesley Banner* 3 (1851): 88.[377]

---

[373] See Wisd. of Sol. 9:15.

[374] See Dan. 3:17.

[375] Similar to the testimonial letters JW provided those he ordained, this letter was for Mallet to carry in case her preaching was opposed. Its closest analogy would be the letter JW personally sent to Robert Carr Brackenbury, Nov. 5, 1780, giving him permission to preach in Methodist preaching-houses (29:605 in this edn.). Mallet reported that after she received this letter the resistance to her preaching from only (male) Methodist preachers abated; see Taft, *Holy Women*, 1:84.

[376] Harper was the Assistant for the Norwich circuit, in which Mallet resided.

[377] The first published transcription of this letter (rephrased slightly) was in Taft, *Holy Women*, 1:84 (Taft owned the holograph). We reproduce the text from *Wesley Banner*, which is described as copied from the holograph. The present location of the holograph is unknown.

To David Gordon

London
October 29, 1787

5

My Dear Brother,

When I was there myself, I expected there would be a considerable work of God in the Waterford circuit. So I am not disappointed of my hope. But it will not be easy to secure an additional preacher
10 at this time of the year, as all the preachers are now stationed and we have none to spare.

I hope neither you or your colleague preach too loud or too long; otherwise you will soon do the devil a singular pleasure by disabling yourselves from preaching at all.

15 I never myself bought a lottery ticket; but I blame not those that do.

I am, dear David,

Your affectionate friend and brother,

J. Wesley

20

Address: 'To / Mr David Gordon / At the Preaching house, in / Waterford'.
Postmark: 'OC/31/87'.
Source: holograph; MARC, MAM JW 3/31.

25

To Elizabeth Padbury[378]

30

London
October 29, 1787

My Dear Betsy,

35 I love to see anything that comes from *you*, although it be upon a melancholy occasion.

Nothing can be done in the Court of King's Bench till the latter end of next week at the soonest.[379] And till then I am trying all milder means which may possibly avail. If nothing can be done this

---

[378] The holograph is now mounted in a frame, with the address portion unaccessible, but the content confirms the recipient; as does the record of its donation—see *WHS* 6 (1907): 45.

[379] See note on JW to Padbury, Sept. 19, 1787.

way, we can but fight at sharps then.[380] But prayer and fasting are of excellent use, for if God be for us, who can be against us?[381]

Probably I shall visit you this winter. I always am, my dear Betsy,
Yours most affectionately,

J. Wesley

Source: holograph; Meadville, Pennsylvania, Allegheny College, Pelletier Library, Archives.

To John King

near London
October 31, 1787

My Dear Brother,

A letter directed to London will always find me, in a few days time.

Both in Jersey, Alderney, and Guernsey the fields are white to the harvest.[382] Hitherto there is an open door into every place, without any considerable opposition. And I am not sorry we were detained there by contrary winds far longer than we intended.

There is no need at all that Thirsk circuit should ever be in debt. You have several persons therein that are of considerable ability, and that love the cause of God. Represent things to them in a proper manner, and nothing will be wanting.

If any of the class-leaders teaches strange doctrine, he can have no more place among us. Only lovingly admonish him first.

I am
Yours affectionately,

J. Wesley

Address: 'To / Mr John King / At the Preaching house / In Thirsk / Yorkshire'.
Postmark: 'NO/2/87'.
Source: holograph; Drew, Methodist Archives.

---

[380] I.e., with our swords unsheathed.
[381] See Rom. 8:31.
[382] See John 4:35.

To an Unidentified Recipient[383]

[November 1787?]

5   [...] If you would but consent that the prince of this world should
have *a little* room in your heart, he might perhaps be tolerably contented, and in good measure let you alone. But if you are determined to leave him no place, not for the sole of his foot, if you
resolve to be all-devoted to God, you might expect he would put
10   forth all his strength. And the nearer your full deliverance comes,
the more undoubtedly he will rage. But be nothing terrified by this.
Rather receive it as a token for good. He rages because he knows his
time is short.

15   Help while yet you ask is given[384]

The Lord whom you seek will suddenly come to his temple![385]
      [...] That the God whom you love may stamp his whole image on
your heart, is the continual prayer of, my dear friend,
20   Yours unalterably,

                                                          J. W.

Source: holograph; MARC, WCB, D6/1/92a.

25

To Zachariah Yewdall

30   London
                                            November 1 [1787[386]]

My Dear Brother,
      You send me good news indeed. So even poor Dalkeith will at last
receive the gospel!
35   I have no hope of our doing any good at Preston Pans for the present. Wherever a door is open, there press forward. I do not despair

---

[383] This letter fragment lacks both an opening and the address portion. The suggested
date comes from it being in a folder with that to Adam Clarke of Nov. 9, 1787; and quoting from
the same CW hymn as the letter to Elizabeth Winter, Nov. 1, 1787.

[384] Cf. CW, 'Psalm 121', st. 1, *CPH* (1743), 86.

[385] See Mal. 3:1.

[386] The year is set by Yewdall being assigned to the Musselburgh circuit at the 1787
Conference.

of having some fruit at Musselburgh.[387] If my health is continued, I
hope to pay you a visit in Scotland next summer.

You may have some books to give away. Peace be with all your
spirits! I am

    Your affectionate brother,   5

                                    J. Wesley

Sister [Sophia] Bradburn is alive and well.

Address: 'To / Mr Yewdal / At the Preachinghouse / in / Edinburgh'.
Source: holograph; WTS (DC), Archives, Oxham Collection.   10

To Elizabeth Winter[388]   15

                                  [London]
                          November 1, 1787

My Dear Madam,

    I rejoice to hear that you are not afraid to say, 'My Lord and my   20
God.'[389] Upon this you should meditate day and night.[390] This is
your proper subject; to pore over your own sins and infirmities
would at present hurt rather than help. It is your wisdom, as far as
is possible, to fix your eyes on the joyous side of the prospect. How
gracious and how exceeding great are the promises which God has   25
made to you in the Son of his love, even that you shall be a partaker
of the divine nature, having escaped the corruption that is in the
world.[391] And who knows how soon this promise may be fulfilled.
He is a God at hand, not a God afar off.[392]

                                               30

        See the Lord thy keeper stand
           Omnipotently near;
        Lo, he holds thee by thy hand
           And banishes thy fear.[393]

---

[387] Orig., 'Musselborough'.
[388] The identity of this woman remains uncertain.
[389] John 20:28.
[390] See Josh. 1:8.
[391] See 2 Pet. 1:4.
[392] See Jer. 23:23.
[393] CW, 'Psalm 121', st. 4, *CPH (1743), 86.*

O look up! He is yours! He is all yours. That you may never let him go is the sincere prayer of, my dear Madam,

Your very affectionate servant,

[John Wesley]

Source: holograph; privately held (transcription provided to Frank Baker).

To Adam Clarke[394]

near London
November 9, 1787

Dear Adam,

I am glad to hear that there is a prospect of a good work in the Isle of Alderney, as well as in the Isles of Jersey and Guernsey. I do not despair of seeing our Jersey and Guernsey friends once more, if it should please God to prolong my life. I love them dearly; particularly the family at Mont Plaisir in Guernsey and Jenny Bisson in Jersey.[395] I would take some pains, and undergo some fatigue, were it only to spend two or three days with them.

One would wonder that the prince of this world was so slow and that he did not sooner fight lest his kingdom should be delivered up. He will at length do what he can. But if you continue instant in prayer God will put the bridle in his mouth.[396] It is well we should be convinced that we have need of him. Our safety will we ascribe to him alone.

As the case of sister Horne is too singular to be credited without the fullest evidence, I think you would do well to write the account fair, and have it formally attested by Mrs. Johnson, Mr. Arrivé, and three or four more who were eye-witnesses of the whole.[397]

---

[394] JW was replying to Clarke's letter of Oct. 29, 1787.

[395] Henri De Jersey (b. c. 1735) and his wife Susanne (Le Quesne) De Jersey (1739–1818), lived in Mont Plaisir; they were members of the French class of the Methodist society in St. Peter. See Lelièvre, *Méthodisme*, 215, 253; and *WMM* 16 (1870), 237.

[396] See Rom. 12:12.

[397] Referring to Clarke's account of the miraculous hair-growth and healing of Margaret Horne in his Oct. 29 letter; see Clarke's updated account, c. Feb. 1, 1788. Mrs. Charlotte Johnson was the daughter of Margaret Horne. Pierre Arrivé (d. 1788) was a member of the French class of the society in St. Peter—see Lelièvre, *Méthodisme*, 215; and *WMM* 16 (1870): 145, 237.

You must not believe all you hear concerning the circumstances of Miss Lempriere's marriage.[398] Indeed, you should believe *nothing* about them till you have told it to themselves. Envy will invent a thousand things, and with the most plausible circumstances. Save them if it be possible, which can never be done by harshness. But love will 'break the bone'.[399]

The bailiff was talking of building you an house at St. Peter's. I think it may be done by-and-by.

Be exact in every point of discipline. Keep your rules and they will keep *you*. I am, dear Adam,

> Your affectionate friend and brother,

> J. Wesley

Address: 'To / Mr Adam Clark / At Mont Plaisir / Near St Peters / Isle of Guersey [sic] / N.B. Not Isle of Wight'.
Postmark: 'NO/9/87'.
Source: holograph; MARC, WCB, D6/1/92b.

To Granville Sharp

City Road
November 14, 1787

Sir,

It was from a real desire to promote in whatever way I could the excellent design which you have in hand, that I mentioned to you (not to others) that report which is current in several places, particularly at Bristol.[400] And I am glad I did mention it, because it is now in my power to justify the society from the imputation. To bear the expenses of witnesses coming from distant parts is undoubtedly an act of justice, which is liable to no objection. I believe you judge right in supposing the other report was circulated, if not invented too, by those who leave no means untried to raise prejudice against the institution. These certainly will use every possible method to

---

[398] See the postscript of Clarke's letter.
[399] Prov. 25:15.
[400] The report that Sharp was paying some persons to bear witness against slave traders; see JW to Sharp, Oct. 11, 1787.

blacken your character. Every opportunity of clearing it will be
gladly taken by, sir,

Your obedient servant,

John Wesley

Address: 'To / Granville Sharpe, Esq.'. [hand delivered]
Endorsement: by Sharp, 'Nov 14. 87 / Revd. J Wesley / Read Nov. 22. 87'.
Source: holograph; Drew, Methodist Archives.

To Adam Clarke

London
November 21, 1787

My Dear Brother,

I answer Mr. [Henri] De Jersey and you together.[401] I am unwilling to discourage you in anything. But I really think it would be the
most Christian and the most prudent way to conclude this matter
amicably. I should advise you not to force the course of the river, but
to let the Vale parish alone.[402] Shake off the dust of your feet against
them, and go where you are welcome.[403] The main point seems to
be to remove the prejudice of the bailiff. If possible, this should be
done by fair means. Law is the last and the worst means, though it
is sometimes necessary. But I should expect far more from prayer.

I will order Mr. [John] Atlay today to send the books.

Peace be with your spirits! I am, dear Adam,

Your affectionate friend and brother,

J. Wesley

---

[401] Neither of these letters are known to survive, but they concerned the opposition to
Methodist preaching in the parish of Vale that Clarke had mentioned to JW in his letter of Oct.
29, 1787, saying that they had made a deposition to the royal court, which they hoped would
rule in their favour. Instead, on Nov. 17, 1787 a report was published in the *Gazette de Guernsey*
that the court ordered that if any Methodist attempted to preach in that parish, he should be
seized and brought before the justice. See Lelièvre, *Méthodisme*, 284–85.

[402] Orig., 'Valle parish'.

[403] See Matt. 10:14.

Addresses: 'To / Mr Adam Clarke / At Mont Plaisir / Isle of Guernsey'
   and 'To Mr A Clarke'.[404]
Postmark: 'NO/⟨?⟩/87'.
Endorsement: by Clarke, 'Ans[were]d Dec. 1, 1787'.[405]
Source: holograph; MARC, WCB, D6/1/94a.   5

To Thomas Funnell[406]   10

[London]
November 24, 1787
My Dear Brother,
   Whatever assistance I can give those generous men who join to   15
oppose that execrable trade, I certainly shall give. I have printed a
large edition of the *Thoughts on Slavery* and dispersed them to every part of England.[407] But there will be vehement opposition made,
both by slave-merchants and slave-holders; and they are mighty
men. But our comfort is, he that dwelleth on high is mightier.   20
   I am
      Your affectionate brother,

John Wesley

                                                                            25
Address: 'Thomas Funnell in Lewes Sussex'.
Source: published transcription; *Wesleyan Methodist Magazine* 50 (1827):
   391.

[404] The second address is written at the top of the sheet containing Clarke's letter; the
other portion would have been to De Jersey.
   [405] This letter is not known to survive.
   [406] Apparently the Thomas Funnell who is listed as a linen draper in Lewes, Sussex, in
the 1780s.
   [407] See JW to Samuel Hoare et al., Aug. 18, 1787. No copies bearing this year on the title
page are known to survive; JW may have simply reprinted the last 1774 edn.

To the Rev. Alexander Suter[408]

London
November 24, 1787

My Dear Brother,

It was an idle thing to send cassocks into Scotland, where the ministers do not use them. But a cassock may be easily made into a gown only adding to it a yard or two of stuff.

As we have not yet made a precedent of anyone that was not ordained administering baptism, it is better to go slow and sure.

Our Sunday schools at Bolton contain upward of eight hundred children, and are all taught by our own brethren *without pay*. I love Sunday schools much. They have done abundance of good. I will give you Instructions and Tokens for Children; we are just now printing a large edition.[409] O be zealous for God!

I am

Your affectionate friend and brother,

J. Wesley

Address: 'To / the Revd Mr Al. Suter / in / Aberdeen'.
Postmark: 'NO/24/87'. *Charge*: '5'.
Endorsement: by Suter, 'No. 9'.
Source: holograph; MARC, MAM JW 4/75.

To the Rev. Francis Asbury

London
November 25, 1787

My Dear Brother,

A glorious work indeed God has been working for several years, and is still working in America. But one thing has often given me concern: God is visiting the progeny of Japheth (the English), who

---

[408] JW had ordained Suter on Aug. 3, 1787 for the work in Scotland.
[409] I.e., *Instructions for Children* (1745; *Bibliography*, No. 101) and *Token for Children* (1749, *Bibliography*, No. 175). JW was referring to a printing that bound together a 1787 edn. of *Instructions* with an early 1788 edn. of *Token*.

now 'dwell in the tents of Shem', according to the prophecy of Noah.[410] Nay, he does

> The servile progeny of Ham
> Seize as the purchase of his blood.[411]   5

But in the meantime the progeny of Shem (the Indians) seem to be quite forgotten. How few of these have seen the light of the glory of God since the English first settled among them! And now scarce one in fifty of them among whom we settled, perhaps scarce one in   10
an hundred of them, are left alive! Does it not seem as if God had designed all the Indian nations not for reformation but destruction? How many millions of them (in South and North America) have already died in their sins! Will neither God nor man have compassion upon these outcasts of men? Undoubtedly with man it is impossible   15
to help them. But is it too hard for God?[412] Oh that he would arise and maintain his own cause![413] That he would first stir up the hearts of some of his children to make the conversion of these heathens also matter of solemn prayer. And then
20

> Eternal providence, exceeding thought,
> When none appears will work itself a way.[414]

Pray ye likewise the Lord of the harvest, and he will send out more labourers into his harvest.[415]   25
But beware you do not grudge two brethren out of an hundred to help your northern brethren.[416] It is enough that we send out two to your one, considering the enormous expense. But let us all do what we can, and we do enough. And see that no shyness or coldness ever creep in between you and   30
Your affectionate friend and brother,

J. Wesley

---

[410] Gen. 9:27.

[411] Cf. CW, 'For the Heathen', st. 3, *Hymns of Intercession for all Mankind* (Bristol: Farley, 1758), 28. CW used 'progeny of Ham' for native Americans in this poem; but JW surely intended it for the Africans brought to North America as slaves.

[412] See Jer. 32:27.

[413] See Ps. 74:23 (BCP).

[414] Edmund Spenser, *Faerie Queene*, Bk. I, Canto 6, vii.1–2.

[415] See Matt. 9:38.

[416] I.e., Newfoundland and Nova Scotia.

Address: 'To / The Revd Mr Asbury / At Mr. Wells's, Merchant / No. 11
½ near the Exchange / Charlestown / South Carolina / To be preserved carefully till he arrives'.
Postmark: 'DE/5/87'.
5 *Source*: holograph; Drew, Methodist Archives.

To Robert Dall

10

London
December 1, 1787

Dear Robert,

You have reason to praise God, who has prospered you and
15 given you to see the fruit of your labours. Our all-dispensing God
has called us to preach the plain gospel. I am glad your hands are
strengthened in corresponding with the brethren. I will desire any
to change with you when you see it best, and if I live till spring,
please God, I will visit you at Dumfries.
20 I am, with love to sister Dall,[417]
Your affectionate friend and brother,

J. Wesley

Source: published transcription; Tyerman, *John Wesley*, 3:532.
25

To Adam Clarke[418]

30

London
December 8, 1787

My Dear Brother,

Again and again we have followed our Lord's direction, which is
35 plain and express. You was 'persecuted in one city'; you should then
doubtless have 'fled to another'.[419] The consequences of so doing

---

[417] Dall married Margaret Kayll (c. 1747–1828) in July 1779, while stationed in the Isle of
Man, and took leave of the itinerancy. He was readmitted at the 1787 Conference (see 10:623 in
this edn.) and stationed in Dumfries, Scotland.

[418] This letter reiterates points JW made to Clarke in the letter of Nov. 21, to which Clarke
had replied on Dec. 1, 1787, apparently pushing back against JW's advice concerning the resistance to Methodist preachers in the parish of Vale (the letter is not known to survive).

[419] Cf. Matt. 10:23.

you should have left to our Master. We have followed the direction
over and over, and found no ill consequences at all. If there had
been a society already formed in the place, it had been a very different case. I should have advised you to give no pretense or handle
to the court to intermeddle with your affairs. At present I see no
remedy but prayer.

Peace be with all your spirits. I am, dear Adam,

Your affectionate friend and brother,

J. Wesley

[fly-leaf:]

Brother [Jean] De Quêteville and you do not mind what I say.
I do not wonder at him (he does not know me). But I do at you.
His natural temper is stern: yours is not. Therefore I expect *you* to
regard me, whether he does or no. We have no such custom among
our societies, nor ever had, as for a man to acknowledge his fault
before a whole society. There shall be no such custom while I live.
If he acknowledge it before the preachers, it is enough.[420]

Address: 'To / Mr Adam Clarke / At Mont Plaisir / Isle of Guernsey /
N.B. Not Isle of Wight'.
Postmark: 'DE/10/87'.
Endorsement: by Clarke, 'Recd Decr. 20. 1787 / Ansd ditto'.
Sources: holograph; MARC, WCB, D6/1/94b (body of letter), and Pitts
Library (Emory), John Wesley Papers (MSS 153), 3/38 (flyleaf and
address).

To Thomas Taylor

London
December 11, 1787

Dear Tommy,

Distilled liquors have their use, but are infinitely overbalanced by
the abuse of them. Therefore, were it in my power, I would banish
them out of the world. ...[421]

[420] This likely relates to George Richard Walker. Cf. JW to Robert Brackenbury, Oct. 20,
1787; and JW to Clarke, Oct. 29, 1787.
[421] This ellipsis appears in the published transcription, suggesting that material has been
omitted. It then includes a paragraph on the bill trade that is from JW's letter to Taylor of June
7, 1788 (and can be found there).

Your affectionate brother,

J. Wesley

Source: published transcription; *United Methodist Free Church Magazine* 5 (1862): 360.

To Jeanne Le Gros Bisson[422]

London
December 17, 1787

My Dear Sister,

I feel a great union of spirit with you. I love to think of you. I love to hear from you, especially when you send me that good news that you still stand fast in the liberty wherewith Christ has made you free.[423] I have a good hope that you will never lose any of [the] things which he has wrought in you, but that you will receive a full reward![424]

Do you always find a clear sense of the presence of the ever-blessed Trinity?[425] Are you enabled to rejoice evermore? In what sense do you pray without ceasing? And can you in everything give thanks, seeing it is the will of God concerning you in Christ Jesus?[426] What you speak of your communion with him comforts and warms my heart. I love to read or to hear any part of your experience. If I doubted of anything you say, I would tell you so. I want to be more acquainted with you and to know everything wherein I can serve you.

My dear Jennie, do not forget to pray for
Yours in tender affection,

J. Wesley

Source: holograph; MARC, MAM JW 1/51.

[422] While the address portion is missing, the content makes the recipient clear.
[423] See Gal. 5:1.
[424] See 2 John 1:8.
[425] See Bisson to JW, July 11, 1787; and JW to Mallet, Oct. 6, 1787.
[426] See 1 Thess. 5:16–17.

To Robert Carr Brackenbury[427]

London
December 17, 1787

Dear Sir,

Considering that the god of this world will not fail to fight when his kingdom is in danger, I do not wonder that persecution should come to Jersey and Guernsey, but that it came no sooner. But when it did come, I by no means approved, of appealing to the secular court. It was just such an occasion as they wished for, giving them a fair opportunity of bringing us under their cognizance. But this is what I should have advised them to avoid, with all possible care. I agree with you that the best method to be used in this exigence is fasting and prayer.

Wishing you all every possible blessing, I am, dear sir,

Your affectionate friend and brother,

J. Wesley

Address: 'To / Robert Brackenbury Esq / At Raithby near Spilsby / Lincolnshire'.
Postmark: 'DE/15/87'. *Charge*: '5'.
Source: holograph; Wesley's Chapel (London), LDWMM 1999/7442.

To James Ridall

London
December 17, 1787

Dear James,

If you would not murder yourself, take particular care never to preach too loud or too long. Always conclude the service within the hour. Then preaching will not hurt you.

The doubt whether you are called to preach or not springs wholly from the temptation of the devil. Give not place to his voice; no, not for an hour! Do not reason with him, but look unto Jesus. He will supply all your wants!

[427] For background, see JW to Adam Clarke, Nov. 21 and Dec. 8 above.

I am
>Your affectionate brother,

>>>>J. Wesley

Address: 'To / Mr Ridall / At the Octagon / Chester'.
Source: holograph; MARC, MAM JW 4/51.

To Adam Clarke

>>>London
>>>December 18, 1787

Dear Adam,

I thank you for the use of your books. They contain many ingenious observations. But I think very few of them are solid. Much may be said on both sides.

I am afraid you have been too severe with Mr. Walker.[428] I am persuaded there is much good in him, otherwise he would have washed his hands of the Methodists. Take care you do not contract something of brother [Jean] De Quêteville's temper![429]

I am, dear Adam,
>Your affectionate friend and brother,

>>>>J. Wesley

Address: 'To / Mr Adam Clark'.
Endorsement: by Clarke, 'Rec[eive]d Jan[uar]y 9 88'.
Source: holograph; MARC, WCB, D6/1/96a.

To Robert Green[430]

>>>London
>>>December 20, 1787

My Dear Brother,

I have known you many years. And I always knew you to be an honest man. Therefore I can trust you in greater matters than this.

---

[428] See the postscript of Clarke to JW, Oct. 29, 1787; and JW to Clarke, Jan. 8, 1788.
[429] See flyleaf of JW to Clarke, Dec. 8, 1787.
[430] Robert Green (b. 1733) of Louth, Lincolnshire, was a chair maker and member of the Methodist society.

So I desire brother Longley to give you the ten pounds without delay.[431] I am,

Your affectionate brother,

J. Wesley

Address: 'To / Mr Robert Green / In Louth / Lincolnshire'.
Source: holograph; Drew, Methodist Archives.

To Mary Cooke

London
December 21, 1787

My Dear Sister,

You have unspeakable reason to praise God for his late manifestations to you.[432] And you will generally observe that large consolations are preceded by deep exercises of soul. And we all have reason to praise him for the many tokens we see of his approaching kingdom. It is plain Satan, the murderer and the deceiver of mankind, is in a great measure bound already.[433] He is not now permitted to deceive the nations, as in the past ages. And even in the Romish countries scarce any are now called to resist unto blood. If two or three of you continue instant in prayer, the work will revive at Trowbridge also.[434] When you are met together, boldly lay hold on the promise! His word will speak, and will not lie.[435]

Peace be with all your spirits! I am, my dear sister,

Yours most affectionately,

J. Wesley

Address: 'To / Miss Cook / In Duke Street, Trowbridge / Wilts'.
Endorsements: by Cooke, 'Good' and '18th'.
Source: holograph; MARC, WCB, D6/1/340.

[431] Thomas Longley was the Assistant for the Grimsby circuit, which included Louth.
[432] JW was replying to Cooke's letter of Dec. 11, 1787.
[433] See Rev. 20.
[434] See Rom. 12:12.
[435] See Hab. 2:3.

To Arthur Keene

London
December 21, 1787[436]

5   My Dear Brother,
    It was, I suppose, about the time that you was in the north, I was
in the southern islands, which I think are abundantly the pleasantest part of His Majesty's dominions.[437] And the people in general
are just prepared for the reception of true religion. For with regard
10   to their circumstances, they are in the happy medium, neither rich
nor poor; and with regard to their temper, most of them have the
French courtesy joined to the English sincerity—a great deal resembling many of our friends both in Dublin and in the north of
Ireland.
15   We have reason to be thankful to God on behalf of our poor widows.[438] One thing I cannot but particularly wish, that all their rooms
may be kept as clean as possible.
    I have not had the pleasure of seeing Mr. [Samuel Wesley] Handy.
I suppose he called here when I was out of town.[439]
20   Wishing every blessing to you and your dear family, I am, dear
Arthur,
        Ever yours,
                                                                J. Wesley

25   [on the flyleaf] I have just seen Mr. Handy, who informs me that
James Whitestone is gone hence.[440] Let *us* also be ready!

Address: 'To / Mr Arthur Keen / near / Dublin'.
Postmarks: 'DE/21/87' and 'DE/⟨2⟩6'.
30   *Endorsement*: by Keene, '25 Dec 1787 / Revd. J: Wesley / London'.
Source: holograph; MARC, MAM JW 3/78.

---

[436] Due to JW's unsteady hand, the '21' could be read as '25'; and was read that way by
Keene. However, the postmarks indicate the earlier date.

[437] I.e., the Channel Islands.

[438] The women in the Widows' Home in Dublin; see JW to Keene, Apr. 20, 1787.

[439] JW had been in Stoke Newington Dec. 18–20, 1787; see *Journal*, 24:68 in this edn.

[440] James Whitestone (1760–87), the son of William and Elizabeth (Willson) Whitestone
of Dublin, who had been a student at Kingswood School in 1773; See JW, *Journal*, Sept. 4,
1773, 22:387 in this edn.

To Thomas [Roberts][441]

London
December 22, 1787

My Dear Brother,

Supposing Miss Christian Davenport answers the description of her which you give, and suppose both hers and your parents are now willing,[442] then I do not see that any reasonable objection can be made against your marriage.[443]

I am

Yours affectionately,

J. Wesley

Source: holograph; Duke, Rubenstein, Frank Baker Collection of Wesleyana, Box WF 1.

To Joseph Benson[444]

London
[c. December 27], 1787

Dear Joseph,

I greatly rejoice in the erection of your new preaching-house, and in the tokens of the divine presence with which you and the people

---

[441] [Both this holograph and a followup letter of Jan. 18, 1788 lack the address portion, though the second letter gives the recipient's first name as 'Tommy'. Telford identified the recipient of both as Thomas Roberts, on the assumption that the relationship under discussion is the same alluded to in the first letter of JW to Roberts for which we have an address portion (Feb. 12, 1789). We concur with this judgment, since Roberts was currently stationed in Londonderry, and there was a Methodist family named Davenport in Coleraine nearby.] Thomas Roberts (1765–1832), a native of Bodmin, Cornwall, was converted in early life and began to preach soon after. He was admitted to the itinerant ministry in 1786 (see 10:596 in this edn.) and served his first five years in Ireland. The remainder of his active itinerancy was in England and Wales, until ill health required him to retire in Bristol about 1811. See *Minutes* (post-Wesley, 1832), 7:111; and his memoir in *WMM* 16 (1837): 1–15, 81–95, 161–76.

[442] Orig., 'both yours and your'; a slip by JW.

[443] Christian Davenport was likely a sister of Katherine Davenport of Coleraine; see JW to John Bredin, Apr. 10, 1782. As in Katherine's case, the parents did not approve; see JW to Thomas [Roberts], Jan. 18, 1788.

[444] On Dec. 23, 1787 Joseph Benson presided at the opening of a new chapel in George Yard, Hull, and wrote JW a glowing account of the building; to which this was JW's reply. JW first saw the new chapel on June 20, 1788, whereupon he commented that it was 'nearly as large as the New Chapel in London … well gilt and elegantly finished, handsome but not gaudy'; see *Journal*, 24:94 in this edn.

were favoured at the opening. But if it be at all equal to the new chapel in London, I will engage to eat it.

I am

Yours affectionately,

John Wesley

Source: published transcription; *Wesleyan Methodist Magazine* 59 (1836): 492.

To Zachariah Yewdall[445]

London
December 27, 1787

My Dear Brother,

You are in the right. You can have nothing at all to do with the chapel upon those terms. Nay, a dovecote above it would be an insufferable nuisance, as it would fill the whole place with fleas.

'What is to be done then?' Why, continue instant in prayer, and God will show what you are to do.[446] But he that believeth doth not make haste.[447]

I cannot advise you to set about building an house unless you could find one or two responsible men who would *engage* themselves to finish the building in *such a manner* for an hundred and fifty pounds. Otherwise I think you would be more bold than wise.

I am, with kind love to Mrs. [Agnes] Yewdall,

Your affectionate brother,

J. Wesley

Address: 'To / Mr Zach. Yewdal / in Dalkeith / Scotland'.
Postmark: 'DE/28/87'.
Source: holograph; Drew, Methodist Archives.

[445] The initial preaching house in Dalkeith was woefully small and in bad condition, so Yewdall was mounting a drive to replace it. They would break ground in May 1788, and the new house be opened in Nov. See *AM* 18 (1795), 372–74, 421–22.

[446] See Rom. 12:12.

[447] See Isa. 28:16.

1788

To Adam Clarke

London
January 8, 1788

Dear Adam,

I admired the spirit of young George Walker. All the times that he spent with us I know not that he blamed anyone. He did not tell anything about his father but in simply answering the questions I asked concerning him. I am in great hopes now that his marriage will not do hurt either to him or her.[1]

It is exceeding well that the storm which threatened is so well blown over. It is plain the Lord God omnipotent reigneth and that there is neither counsel nor strength against him.

But you have not sent a plain, full, distinct account of the affair of our old sister, specifying: 1) her age, 2) on what day of the year and month did the first hair shoot out, 3) on what day did she throw it into the fire, 4) on what night did it grow again, [and] 5) who were eyewitnesses of these things?[2] You cannot be too particular.

I do not like your staying so long at a time in Guernsey. I advise you to change islands without fail once a quarter.

Are Mr. and Mrs. De Jersey well, and my two dear maidens?[3] How are Mr. [Pierre] and Mrs. Arrivé?[4] And how does my dear Jenny Bisson go on? She is a letter in my debt.

I wish you all many happy years; and am, dear Adam,

Yours and brother [Jean] De Quêteville's affectionate friend and brother,

J. Wesley

[1] See the postscript of Clarke to JW, Oct. 29, 1787; and JW to Clarke, Dec. 18, 1787.

[2] See the note on JW to Clarke, Nov. 9, 1787, about Margaret Horne.

[3] Henri and Susanne (Le Quesne) De Jersey, their daughter Susanne Jr., and one other daughter. Susanne Jr. would marry Jean De Quêteville in Apr.

[4] Pierre's wife's first name was Elizabeth; see Clarke to JW, c. Feb. 1, 1788.

Address: 'To / Mr Adam Clark / At Mont Plaisir / Isle of Guernsey'.
Postmark: 'JA/8/88'.
Endorsement: by Clarke, 'Rec[eive]d Jany 10th 88 / Ans[were]d ditto 12'.
Source: holograph; MARC, WCB, D6/1/96b.

To Mary (Bosanquet) Fletcher

London
January 9, 1788

My Dear Sister,

I am sincerely glad that you have found an opportunity of trans-
mitting those valuable papers to Mr. [Joseph] Benson.[5] I know no
one in England who is more capable of preparing them for the public view, as there is scarcely any one who better understands the
whole subject of debate. And now I am in hopes both the points will
be carried. On the one hand, Mr. [James] Ireland will be satisfied
(who seems to have, though I cannot tell why, an insuperable prejudice to me); and on the other, justice will be done to the memory of
blessed Mr. [John] Fletcher.

If I live a month or two longer, I shall see you and your relation,
of whom I rejoice to hear so good an account.[6] Who knows what
good things God had in store for him, and for what purposes he has
brought him to England?

Committing you to his care who has kept you from your youth up,
I am, my dear sister,

Most affectionately yours,

J. Wesley

Address: 'To / Mrs Fletcher / At Madeley near Shifnal / Salop'.
Postmark: 'JA/9/88'. *Charge*: '5'.
Source: holograph; MARC, MA 1983/027 (Mather scrapbook).

---

[5] See JW to Benson, Mar. 10, 1787; and Sept. 17, 1788.
[6] Rev. John Fletcher's only nephew (and godson), Jean de la Fléchère (b. c. 1766) had
come from Switzerland in May 1787 to spend some time where his uncle had served. He was
a strong deist, but over some months Mary helped him cultivate openness to Scripture and
spiritual experience. See Moore, *Mary Fletcher*, 206, 210–23.

To Duncan Wright

London
January 9, 1788

Dear Duncan,   5

You send me a comfortable account of the work of God in your
circuit. I cannot doubt but a blessing redounds to you all for the
sake of the poor children.[7] I verily think these Sunday schools are
one of the noblest specimens of charity which have been set on foot
in England since the time of William the Conqueror.   10

If Michael Fenwick has a mind to go to Dumfries and assist Robert Dall, you may give him three guineas, which he must husband
well. He may write to me from thence.

I am, dear Duncan,
 Your affectionate friend and brother,   15

             J. Wesley

Address: 'To Duncan Wright, at Bolton'.
Source: published transcription; Tyerman, *John Wesley*, 3:522.
                   20

To Walter Griffith[8]

                   25

London
January 9, 1788

My Dear Brother,

I do not remember the clergyman you mention, nor the person
whose elegy he writes. But the verses are by no means bad, and   30
probably may have a place in the *[Arminian] Magazine*.[9]

---

[7] See the report, surely from Wright, of the Sunday school for poor children in Bolton,
published in *AM* 11 (1788): 489–90; and JW's record when he visited Bolton months earlier
of 'eight hundred poor children taught in our Sunday schools by about eighty masters, who
receive no pay but what they are to receive from their Great Master'; *Journal*, July 27, 1787,
24:46 in this edn.

[8] Walter Griffith (1761–1825), a native of Ireland, was admitted 'on trial' at the 1784
Conference there (see 10:971 in this edn.), and to full status the following year (10:974). He was
currently the Assistant for the Athlone circuit. Griffith would serve a total of 40 years, be elected President of Conference in 1813, and become the last person interred in JW's tomb at City
Road Chapel. See *Minutes* (post-Wesley, 1825), 6:6–7; and Stevenson, *City Road*, 370, 378.

[9] No elegy matching this description appears in *AM* prior to JW's death.

I am glad to hear that the work of God prospers in your hands. And that neither brother Miller nor you are yet weary or faint in your mind.[10] Press on to the mark![11] This one thing do, save your own soul, and those that hear you.[12] I am, with kind love to sister Griffith,[13]

Your affectionate friend and brother,

J. Wesley

Source: holograph; MARC, MAM JW 3/36.

To Ann Bolton

London
January 10, 1788

My Dear Nancy,

Sometimes it seems a little strange to me that I do not hear from you oftener, considering the union that is between you and me is not a common friendship. No, I have loved you with a peculiar affection almost ever since you was a child. And it has not only remained, but continually increased, during a course of years. I have often seen you tried as by fire.[14] And your faith was purified, but not consumed. But I consider the situation wherein you are. It is in this respect like my own: I am encompassed, and at some times almost overwhelmed, with business. One fruit of which is that I *seem* to forget even my best beloved friends. But I am satisfied, *you* do not forget me, whether I hear from you or no.

'Sir, you are troubled', said Mr. [William] Law to me, 'because you do not *understand how* God is dealing with you. Perhaps if you did it would not so well answer his design. He is teaching you to *trust* him farther than you can *see* him.' He is not teaching *you* the same lesson. Hitherto you cannot understand his ways. But they

---

[10] John Miller (d. 1796), of German ancestry, first appears in the *Minutes* as an itinerant preacher in 1780 (10:510 in this edn.). He was currently stationed with Griffith in Athlone, and would serve in various parts of Ireland up to his death; see *Minutes* (post-Wesley, 1796), 1:347.

[11] See Phil. 3:14.

[12] See 1 Tim. 4:16.

[13] Mrs. Mary Griffith (c. 1760–1827), maiden name unknown, is also buried at City Road Chapel; see Stevenson, *City Road*, 438.

[14] See 1 Cor. 3:13.

are all mercy and truth.[15] And though you do not know now what he does, you shall know hereafter.[16]

I am acquainted with several single women whom I believed [to] be saved from sin. But there is great variety in the manner wherein God is pleased to lead them. Some of them are called to act much for God; some to rejoice much; some to suffer much. All of these shall receive their crown. But when the Son of man shall come in his glory, the brightest crown will be given to the sufferers! Look up, my blessed one! The time is at hand![17]

I am, my dear Nancy,
    Ever yours,

J. Wesley

Address: 'To / Miss Bolton / In Witney, near / Oxford'.
Postmark: 'JA/10/88'.
Source: holograph; privately held (WWEP Archive holds digital copy).

To Jane (Hilton) Barton

London
January 11, 1788[18]

My Dear Sister,

You have indeed had a series of trials one upon the back of another. It is well you know in whom you have believed.[19] Otherwise you would have been weary and faint in your mind. For it is not an easy thing always to remember (then especially when we have most need of it) that 'the Lord loveth whom he chasteneth and scourgeth every son whom he receiveth'.[20] Who could believe it, if he had not told us so himself? It is well that he never fails to give us strength according to our day.[21] And that we know these 'light afflictions,

---

[15] See Ps. 25:10.
[16] See John 13:7.
[17] See Rev. 1:3.
[18] Jackson misread JW's 'Janu' and 'June'.
[19] See 2 Tim. 1:12.
[20] Heb. 12:6.
[21] See Deut. 33:25.

which are but for a moment, work for us a more exceeding and eternal weight of glory'.[22]

I am

    Your affectionate brother,

                             [J. Wesley]

Source: published transcription; Jackson, *Works* (3rd), 12:367–68.

To John Mason

                                   London
                           January 12, 1788

My Dear Brother,

    Proceed with great deliberation. First see that an exact plan be drawn. Secondly give out proposals for the work. And let the lowest bidder do it (we have been used vilely by *Methodist* builders!), provided he be an *honest* and *substantial* man. Thirdly let him be legally bound to do the work at such a price and such a time. Fourthly before a stake is struck procure all the subscriptions you can in the town and for four and twenty miles round about.[23] Lastly let all things be done with much prayer. I am,

    Your affectionate friend and brother,

                              J. Wesley

Address: 'To / Mr. John Mason / At Mr. Richard Vaughan's / In Shepton Mallet / Somersetshire'.

Source: secondary manuscript transcription; MARC, MA 1977/609.

[22] Cf. 2 Cor. 4:17.
[23] Orig. begins 'Thirdly'; a slip by JW or the transcriber.

To [William] Thompson[24]

London
January 12, 1788

My Dear Brother,

I have dispersed a great many of the *Thoughts upon Slavery*, and many of Mr. Clarkson's excellent tracts.[25] It seems as if God had raised him up for this very thing. I wish him success with all my heart.

But there will be vehement opposition. And we may be afraid the slave-merchants will use their whole strength. The comfort is, there is one who is stronger than they.[26]

Wishing sister Thompson and you many happy years, I am,
Your affectionate brother,

J. Wesley

Postmark: 'JA/13/88'.
Source: holograph; University of Cambridge Library, Add. 7674/1/185.

To Joseph Pescod[27]

London
January 13, 1788

Dear Joseph,

Why should you sell the house? Is not the yearly rent of it equal to the interest on the money you would receive for it?

If it wants repairing, the Conference will allow money to repair, and also to renew the lease whenever it expires. By-and-by we should bitterly regret the selling of it.

I am
Your affectionate friend and brother,

J. Wesley

---

[24] While the address portion is missing, the familiar tone of the letter would fit well JW's trusted itinerant William Thompson, who would be elected the first President of Conference in 1791.

[25] Thomas Clarkson had published two tracts at this point: *An Essay on the Slavery and Commerce of the Human Species, particularly the African* (London: J. Phillips, 1786); and *A Summary View of the Slave Trade and of the Probable Consequences of its Abolition* (London: J. Phillips, 1787).

[26] See Luke 11:22.

[27] Pescod, currently the Assistant of the Oxfordshire circuit, added a note to this letter: 'the expense of repairing the house referred to is £25.0.0'.

Address: 'To / Mr Jos. Pescod / At the Preachinghouse / in / Oxford'.
Postmark: 'JA/15/88'.
Source: holograph; MARC, MAM JW 4/40.

To John King

London
January 18, 1788

My Dear Brother,

My illnesses are seldom long; they rarely last above two or three days.

Wherever the preachers are truly devoted to God, his word will surely have free course, and sinners will be converted to him. But what was the matter with Jonathan Peacock? And upon what cause or pretense did he and his class leave the society?[28] Should not you strive to bring them back?

I am

Your affectionate friend and brother,

J. Wesley

Address: 'To / Mr John King / At the Preachinghouse / Ripon'.
Sources: holograph; privately held (WWEP Archive holds photocopy);
[Toase], *Memorials*, 191; cf. *WHS* 25 (1945): 51 (misreads as 'June').

To Henry Moore[29]

London
January 18, 1788

My Dear Brother,

This is an unprecedented thing. I never before saw or heard of such a flow of grace as was seen [in] Dublin three years together without a proportionable ebb succeeding. Whereas to this hour we have no ebb at all. We can only say, 'It is the Lord: let him do what seemeth him good.'[30]

---

[28] The holograph is faded and 'Peacock' is a bit uncertain; he may have been the class leader teaching 'strange doctrine' about whom King had been concerned earlier. See JW to King, Oct. 31, 1787.

[29] Moore's letter to which JW was replying is not known to survive.

[30] 1 Sam. 3:18.

I am glad you have got an house in Marlborough Street. I have appointed a class to meet there.[31] It must needs give much offense. However, give as little as possible. Behave to them with all possible tenderness and courtesy. And do nothing that you foresee will give offense, unless it be a matter of duty.

It is exceeding well that you have made a beginning at Castle Road.[32] I wonder all the villages round Dublin have not been tried before now.

My best love attends my dear Nancy. I am, dear Henry (and Becky too),[33]

Your affectionate friend and brother,

[J. Wesley]

Source: published transcription; Telford, *Letters*, 8:35.

To Thomas [Roberts][34]

London
January 18, 1788

My Dear Brother,

As the matter is now decided, I hope you are able to say, 'Lord, not as I will, but as thou wilt.'[35] I commend you for entirely giving up the matter when you found her parents were absolutely against it. I hope you will think of it no more, but will be now more unreservedly devoted to God than ever!

I am, dear Tommy,

Your affectionate friend and brother,

J. Wesley

I do not see that you [should] quit the circuit.

Source: holograph; Bridwell Library (SMU).

---

[31] The house was apparently the old Lutheran chapel, which the Methodists had been asked to leave after it was ransacked by a mob in 1747. After Methodists became more accepted they used this building off and on again, and classes were meeting there in 1788; see Cooney, 'Dublin Society', 61–62.

[32] Likely means Castle Street.

[33] Referring to Moore's wife Anne, and his sister Rebecca.

[34] See JW's earlier letter of Dec. 22, 1787 to the same person, for identification of the recipient.

[35] Cf. Matt. 26:39.

To William Simpson

London
January 18, 1788

5   Dear Billy,

You did exceeding well to enlarge the number of prayer meetings, and to fix them in various parts of those [places]. I do not know that any means of grace whatever has been more owned of God than this.

10   It is not now, but at the time of Conference, that children are received into Kingswood school.

I am glad sister [Emma] Moon has not forgotten me. I hope sister [Mary] Middleton too thinks of me sometimes. You are welcome to the four volumes of *Sermons*.

15   I am, with kind love to sister [Anne] Simpson, dear Billy,

Your affectionate friend and brother,

J. Wesley

Address: 'To / Mr. Will. Simpson / At the Preaching-house / Stock-
20   ton-upon-Tees'.
Source: published transcription; Telford, *Letters*, 8:35–36.

To John Mann[36]

25

London
January 30, 1788[37]

My Dear Brother,

30   I am greatly concerned for the prosperity of the work of God in Nova Scotia. It seems some way to lie nearer my heart than even that in the United States. Many of our brethren there are, we may hope, strong in the Lord and in the power of his might.[38] But I look upon those in the northern provinces to be younger and tender children, and consequently to stand in need of our most anxious
35   care. I hope all of you that watch over them are all of one mind

---

[36] John Mann (1743–1817) had been part of the John Street society in New York. His Loyalist stance led him to move to Nova Scotia in 1783, where he served as an itinerant and would be ordained in 1789. See Nellie Fox, 'Loyalist Brothers: John and James Mann', *Nova Scotia Historical Review*, 4.2 (1984), 83–89.

[37] Jackson misread JW's 'Janu' for 'June'.

[38] See Eph. 6:10.

and of one judgment;[39] that you take care always to speak the same things and to watch over one another in love.[40]

Mr. Wray is a workman that need not be ashamed.[41] I am glad to hear of his safe arrival. Although he has not much learning, he has (which is far better) uprightness of heart and devotedness to God. I doubt not but he and you will be one, and go on your way hand in hand.

Whatever opposers you meet with—Calvinists, papists, antinomians, and any other—have a particular care that they do not take up too much either of your time or thoughts. You have better work. Keep to your one point, Christ dying for us and living in us. So will you fulfill the joy of, my dear brethren,

Your affectionate friend and brother,

[J. Wesley]

Source: published transcription; Jackson, *Works* (3rd), 14:374.

To Robert Dall

London
February 11, 1788

Dear Robert,

I allow you to build at Dumfries, providing anyone will lend a hundred guineas on interest.[42] I hope to see you, God willing, in May.

I am,

[Your affectionate friend and brother,]

J. Wesley

Source: published transcription; Tyerman, *John Wesley*, 3:532.

---

[39] See Acts 4:32.

[40] See 1 Cor. 1:10.

[41] James Wray (d. 1793) was admitted 'on trial' as an itinerant preacher at the 1781 Conference (see 10:507 in this edn.). After six years serving in England, he was ordained by JW for service in North America in 1787, and appointed as Assistant for the work in Nova Scotia (10:631). Wray was not well received in this leadership role as an 'outsider'; see JW to James Mann, Feb. 27, 1789. He subsequently stepped down to serve under William Black in 1789 (10:683), and relocated to the West Indies in 1791 (10:752). He died at St. Vincent two years later; see *Minutes* (post-Wesley, 1793), 1:275.

[42] By the time JW visited Dumfries in early May, Dall had begun building the new preaching-house, of a size JW judged worried might be too bold; see JW, *Journal*, May 13, 1788, 24:83 in this edn.

To William Holmes

London
February 18, 1788

5   My Dear Brother,
Do right and fear nothing. Exclude every person that will not
promise to meet his or her class, the steward in particular. I require
you to do this. You have no choice. Leave the consequences to God.
I do not advise you to go to the Hay any more, unless they can and
10   will leave you harmless.[43] Now believe, and you shall see better days!
I am
Your affectionate friend and brother,

J. Wesley

Don't regard money. We can supply that.
15
Address: 'To / Mr W. Holmes / At Miss Williams', Milliner / in / Brecon'.
Postmark: 'FE/19/88'. *Charge*: '6'.
Source: holograph; MARC, MAM JW 3/51.

20

To the Rev. Charles Wesley

[London]
February 18, 1788

25   [[Dear Brother,]]
You must go out *every day* or die.[44]
Do not die to save charges. You certainly need not want anything
as long as I live.
[[Adieu!]]

30   *Source*: holograph; MARC, DDWes 3/65b.

To James Currie

35   near London
February 19, 1788
My Dear Brother,
Supposing we could pray in faith for the accomplishment of the
promise which is given in the last chapter of St. Mark, there is no

---

[43] I.e., the preaching house in Hay-on-Wye, Brecon, which had been heavily influenced
by Trevecca College nearby.
[44] CW's health had declined significantly, which would lead to his death on Mar. 29.

doubt but it would be fulfilled now as it was seventeen hundred years ago.[45] And I have known many instances of this both in England and elsewhere.

In fifty years we have been oft(?) molested in field-preaching; and may be so again, those who live fifty years more. Let it be forgotten. Nobody will be fond of following the example of Mr. [Henry] Beauclerk.[46]

I doubt whether the time is come for laying out so much money in building at Northampton. Four hundred pounds! Whence should they come? Stay till providence opens itself. I am, dear James,
  Your affectionate brother,

J. Wesley

Address: 'To / Mr James Currie / in / Northampton'.
Source: holograph; MARC, MAM JW 2/72.

To Henry Moore[47]

near London
February 19, 1788

My Dear Brother,

I am glad the house is opened in Marlborough Street, and that the work of God still prospers among you, particularly among the poor soldiers.[48] You send me likewise good news concerning George Dice.[49] Nurse him tenderly, and he will come to good. Dr. [Thomas] Coke will not fail to rejoice over him.

Not only the devices of the Evangelical Society, but no weapon formed against us shall prosper.[50] Is Bethesda full on the Sunday evenings? Or half full on week days? If it had been in full union

---

[45] See Mark 16:17–18, promising signs like casting out demons and healing the sick to occur, confirming the preaching of disciples.

[46] See JW to Elizabeth Padbury, Sept. 19 and Oct. 29, 1787.

[47] The letter to which JW was replying is not known to survive. On the back of this letter Moore writes: 'In February I asked Mr. Wesley if Dr. Coke would officiate at noon when he came to Dublin. He answered as in the opposite page [i.e., reverse side].' Moore seemed to anticipate that this would raise concern, and it did.

[48] See JW to Moore, Jan. 18, 1788; and Apr. 6, 1788.

[49] Dice had been removed from the itinerant ministry in 1786 (see 10:597, n. 178; and 10:978 in this edn.).

[50] I.e., the society formed to bring over 'gospel ministers' to preach in Dublin, mentioned in the letter by Moore to which JW replied in Sept. 18, 1787.

with the Methodists, I am inclined to think it would have prospered; but it was not likely to stand alone.[51] I do not see how we can go further than to be friends at a distance.

I have referred to Dr. Coke himself in what manner he shall proceed in Dublin. And whatever he and you agree upon, I shall not condemn.

With my tender love to my dear Nancy; nay, and Becky;[52] I am, dear Henry,

Your affectionate friend and brother,

J. Wesley

Address: 'To / Mr Moore / At the New Room / in / Dublin'.
Postmark: 'FE/20/88'. *Charge*: '6'.
Source: holograph; MARC, WCB, D6/1/128b.

To Jeanne Le Gros Bisson

near London
February 20, 1788

My Dear Sister,

Your last letter gave me a very sensible pleasure.[53] Indeed, so do all your letters. And I cannot but acknowledge every letter I receive from you unites you to me more than I was united before. There is something in your spirit that does me good, that softens and quickens me too. But at the same time that melancholy thought occurs, that you are at so great a distance from me, and that it is doubtful whether I shall ever have the satisfaction of taking you by the hand again. Yet I shall, if it be the will of him that orders all things well;[54] who orders all for our profit, that we may be partakers of his holiness.[55] And we know he cannot deny to them that fear him any manner of thing that is good.[56]

---

[51] Actually, Bethesda Chapel, built by William Smyth in 1786, survived into the early twentieth century.
[52] Moore's wife Anne, and sister Rebecca.
[53] This letter is not known to survive.
[54] See Eph. 1:11.
[55] See Heb. 12:10.
[56] See Ps. 84:11.

Your speaking of trials makes me almost ready to cry out in the words of our poet,

> Secluded from the world, and all its care,
> Hast *thou* to joy or grieve, to hope or fear?[57]　　5

Shut up, as you are, in your father's house, and a little, retired, quiet island, and having food to eat and raiment to put on, what can you find to try you? Speak, my dear friend, speak. Surely you will not deny me the pleasure of serving you, or at least of sympathizing　10 with you, if I cannot help you.

One of your trials I can easily foresee. With all your innocence and prudence, you cannot escape censure. In spite of all you can do, the good that is in you will surely be evil spoken of. And it is not unlikely some will join in the cry against you from whom you　15 expected better things. But, as you are just entering into life, one would think you had hardly yet met with any who rewarded you evil for good, and gave you occasion to cry out,

> Ingratitude! Sharp as the viper's tooth![58]　　20

However, you have one friend that never fails and that is always near. What a comfort it is that he is about your bed and about your path, still laying his hand upon you! Does he speak to you in dreams and visions of the night? Or chiefly in your waking hours? I love to　25 hear and to read your experience of his goodness. As soon as you have opportunity, write without reserve to, my very dear sister,

Yours most affectionately,

J. Wesley
　　30

Address: 'To / Miss Bisson / In St Heliers / Isle of Jersey'.
Postmark: 'FE/20/88'.
Source: holograph; MARC, MAM JW 1/52.

[57] Matthew Prior, *Solomon*, ii.386–87.
[58] Cf. Shakespeare, *King Lear* I.iv.302–03 'How sharper than a serpent's tooth it is / To have a thankless child.'

To the Rev. Charles Wesley

February [20?], 1788

I have not one hour to spare from 4:00 in the morning till 9:00 at night. But you may see me on Thursday at Mr. Griffith's, who will come in his coach to fetch you.

O *consent* to be cured![59]

[[Adieu!]]

Endorsement: by CW, '[[My brother]] consent to be / cured! / Febr. 1788 / J. W.'.
Source: holograph; MARC, DDWes 3/65a.

To Ann Bolton

London
February 23, 1788

My Dear Nancy,

You do well to write to me at all times when you are of leisure, but especially when you are in trouble.[60]

It is a just remark of Mr. Addison:

> The ways of heaven are dark and intricate,
> Puzzled with mazes and perplexed with errors.[61]

So it seems at least to our poor, weak understandings, which cannot fathom the deep counsels of God.[62] But what he does now you will know hereafter, and see that he hath done all things well.[63] If you had not seen trouble in the years that are past, you would not have been what you are now. You have fairly profited thereby. You have not suffered so many things in vain, but you have learnt more and more obedience by the things that you have suffered.

---

[59] The underlining for emphasis was likely done by CW.
[60] Bolton's letter to JW is not known to survive.
[61] Joseph Addison, *Cato*, I.i.47–48.
[62] See Job 11:7.
[63] See John 13:7 and Mark 7:37.

On Thursday next I am to leave London. I hope to be at Bristol the Monday following; a fortnight after at Stroud, as usual; and then at Cirencester and Gloucester. Meet me somewhere if you can conveniently. A set of the *[Arminian] Magazine* is not now to be had, but you may have abundance of single ones. 5

And, indeed, you never need want anything that is in the power of,

my dear Nancy,
Yours most affectionately,

J. Wesley 10

Address: 'To / Miss Bolton / In Witney / Oxfordshire'.
Postmark: 'FE/23/88'.
Endorsement: by Bolton, 'Feb 23 88'.
Source: holograph; MARC, MAM JW 1/99. 15

To Robert Carr Brackenbury 20

London
February 27, 1788

Dear Sir,

I cannot exactly agree with your judgment.[64] While there was no 25 preacher in the islands but you, and while the work of God was but just beginning, you was undoubtedly called to spend most of your time there, and then you did right in not being disobedient to the heavenly calling.[65] But the case is very different now. They have now able preachers in French and English; and as they do not do 30 the work deceitfully, it prospers in their hands. Has not the Lord more work for you to do in England? In June (if God permit), I purpose to spend an evening with you at Raithby. Peace be with all your spirits!

I am, dear sir, 35
Your very affectionate friend and brother,

[J. Wesley]

Source: published transcription; Jackson, *Works* (3rd), 13:8.

[64] Brackenbury's letter to JW is not known to survive, but he was questioning whether his ministry should remain primarily in the Channel Islands.
[65] See Acts 26:19.

To Mary (Franklin) Parker[66]

London
February 27, 1788

My Dear Sister,

I loved you from the time I talked with you first, although till that time I was rather prejudiced against you.[67] I thank you for the plain simple account which you gave me of your experience. I cannot at all doubt, but God has indeed purified your heart by faith.[68] Now you are called, to stand fast in the liberty wherewith Christ has made you free.[69] It is his will that you should never more be entangled with either inward or outward sin, but rise up higher and higher, into him that is your head, until you are filled with all the fullness of God.[70]

I am, my dear sister,
Your affectionate brother,

J. Wesley

Source: holograph; Philadelphia, Pennsylvania, Historic St. George's United Methodist Church, Archives.

To David Gordon[71]

Bath
February 29, 1788

My Dear Brother,

I am glad to find that matters are not so bad as they were represented, as to preaching in the morning and meeting the leaders. I hope there has been no blame. And I trust you have not willingly neglected your circuit. It would be worth while to talk at large with

---

[66] While the address portion is missing, this is JW's reply to a letter he received from Mary (Franklin) Parker, dated Feb. 23, 1788.

[67] See JW to Mary Franklin, Mar. 10, 1772, 28:473–74 in this edn.

[68] See Acts 15:9.

[69] See Gal. 5:1.

[70] See Eph. 4:15 and 3:19.

[71] Gordon was currently the Assistant of the Waterford circuit. His letter to JW on these matters is not known to survive.

that young man who neglects the Lord's Supper. But if he obstinately persists in that neglect, you can't give him any more tickets
for our society. Be exact in all things.

I am, dear David,

    Your affectionate friend and brother,   5

                                           J. Wesley

Address: 'To / Mr David Gordon / At the Preachinghouse / in / Water-
    ford'.
Postmarks: 'Bath' and 'Bristol'.   10
Source: holograph; MARC, MAM JW 3/32.

                                                              15

To Sarah Mallet

                                                  Bath
                                 March 2, 1788   20

My Dear Sister,

    I should have been exceedingly glad to see you, for I have a tender
affection for you. And I shall always be well pleased to hear from
you and to know how your soul prospers.[72]

    It is no wonder you should find trials. You may expect them from   25
every quarter. You tread daily on dangers, snares, and death. But
they cannot hurt you whilst your heart cleaves to God. Beware of
pride! Beware of fretfulness! Beware of dejection! But above all beware of inordinate affection! Those who profit by you will be apt
to love you more than enough; and will not this naturally lead you   30
into the same temptation? Nay, Sally, is not this the case already? Is
your heart filled whole with God? Is it clear of idols? I think you can
speak to *me* freely (though on so delicate a subject you can hardly
speak free to anyone else). Is he still the sole object of your desire,
the treasure and joy of your heart? Considering your age, and sex,   35
and situation, what but omnipotence can keep you in the midst of
the fire?

    You will not take it amiss if I ask you another question. I know that
neither your father nor uncle is rich; and in *travelling up and down*

---

[72] The letter to which JW appears to be replying is not known to survive.

you will want a little money. Are you not sometimes straitened?[73]
Only let me know, and you shall want nothing that is in the power
of, my dear Sally,

Yours affectionately,

5   J. Wesley

Address: 'To Miss Sally Mallett / at Mr Mallett's, Staymaker / In Long
Stratton / Norfolk'.[74]
Postmarks: 'Bath' and 'MR/5/88'.
Endorsement: 'March 1788 Copied Z. T.'.[75]
10
Source: holograph; MARC, MA 2008/016.

15   To the Rev. Charles Wesley

Bath
March 2, 1788

[[Dear Brother,]]
20   Hitherto we have had a very prosperous journey. We were just
sixteen hours upon the road. All here are in peace. The little quar-
rels that used to be in the society are dead and forgotten. John
Broadbent has behaved exceeding wisely, and has given less offense
than could have been imagined.[76] The congregations here are sur-
25 prisingly large. Truly the day of God's power has come. Mr. Collins
is in an excellent spirit, and preaches at the chapel three or four
times a week.[77] He did not stay to be asked, but came and offered to
read prayers for me.

Many inquire after *you*, and express much affection and desire
30 of seeing you. In good time! You are first suffering the will of *God*.
Afterwards he has a little more for you to do. That is, provided you

[73] On a back leaf of the letter Mallet writes: 'My way was, wherever I went I work with
my own hands for the poor people where I went to preach, that I might not be chargeable to
any. As I could make men's and women's clothes, I did not want work with the poor, as I gave
them all my labour. And those of my family that were able to help me would not, because they
did not approve of my preaching, nor leaving my business and my home. But I was obliged to
obey God rather than man. Mr. Wesley heard of all this and became a father to me, when my
own father refused to do a father's part.'
[74] Note that JW was writing her via her uncle William.
[75] I.e., Zachariah Taft, who included in *Holy Women*, 1:86–87.
[76] Broadbent was in Bath for his health.
[77] Brian Bury Collins had taken a house on Corn Street in Bath, and was serving Lady
Huntingdon's chapel in Vineyards.

now take up your cross (for such it frequently must be) and go out at least an hour in a day. I would not blame you if it were two or three. Never mind expense, I can make that up. You shall not die to save charges.

I shall shortly have a word to say to Charles and his brother both.[78]   5
Peace be with all your spirits!

[[Adieu!]]

Miss Perrot is gone to rest, so farewell pain![79]

          10

Address: 'To / The Revd Mr C. Wesley / City Road, near Moorfields / London'.[80]
Postmarks: 'Bath', 'MR/5/88', and 'Penney Post Paid'.
Source: holograph; MARC, DDWes 3/68.

          15

To Susanna Knapp[81]

        Bristol   20
       March 4, 1788

My Dear Suky,

That you were at the trouble of sending me a few lines I take exceeding kindly.[82] I was talking with Mr. Eden here a day or two ago, and he said that the roads about Broadmarston are now almost   25
impassable.[83]

On Monday next I hope to be at Stroud, on Tuesday at Gloucester, on Wednesday and Thursday at Worcester, on Friday at Stourport, and on Saturday at Birmingham.

---

[78] See his letters to CW Jr., on Mar. 16; and his nephew Samuel, Mar. 18.

[79] Ann Perrot (1707–88) was buried Jan. 23, 1788 in Bath. She was originally of Bristol and a friend of CW's family, as well as of Mehetabel (Wesley) Wright. See Mehetabel to JW, July 13, 1744.

[80] The address is struck out and replaced with 'Chesterfield Street No 1, Marabone'; hence the penny post marking.

[81] Susanna Knapp (1770–1856) was a daughter of John and Ann (Turner) Knapp. Her parents hosted JW when he was in Worcester, so Susanna came to know and correspond with him. Susanna never married, but became friends with Elizabeth Ritchie, Ann Bolton, and other Methodist women. See Edith Rowley, *Fruits of Righteousness in the Life of Susanna Knapp* (London: Hamilton, Adams & Co., 1866).

[82] Knapp's letter to JW is not known to survive.

[83] Rev. Thomas Eden Jr., now rector of Alvescot in Oxfordshire.

I hope you are making the best use of the vigour of youth in running the race that is set before you.[84] These are precious hours. Improve them to the uttermost, and you will give pleasure to all that love you; in particular to, my dear Suky,

Yours affectionately,

J. Wesley

Address: 'To / Miss Knapp / At Mr [John] Knapp's / In Worcester'.
Source: holograph; Lincoln, Lincolnshire, England, Lincolnshire Archives, LCL/5469.

To the Rev. Charles Wesley

Bristol
March 5, 1788

[[Dear Brother,]]

I hope you keep to your rule of going out every day, although it may sometimes be a cross. Keep to this but one month, and I am persuaded you will be as well as you was this time twelve-month [ago].

If I ventured to give you advice more, it would be this: 'Be *master* of your own house.' If you fly, they pursue. But stand firm, and you will carry your point.

[[Adieu!]]

Endorsement: by Sally Wesley Jr., 'March 5. 1788'.
Source: holograph; MARC, DDWes 3/67.

To Jasper Winscom

Bristol
March 6, 1788

Dear Jasper,

As soon as possible go to the isle and acquaint Thomas Warrick with what is laid to his charge.[85] According to the spirit and manner

---

[84] See Heb. 12:1.

[85] Thomas Warrick was currently stationed at the Isle of Wight. Whatever the issue, Warrick was continued; assigned to the Bristol circuit by the 1788 Conference.

wherein he receives it must our proceeding be. If you see reason to
believe he is truly penitent, we may possibly try him a little longer.
But if he makes light of the matter and braves it out, I am afraid we
must let him drop. Send word of all that occurs to

    Your affectionate brother,

                              [J. Wesley]

Source: published transcription; Telford, *Letters*, 8:42–43.

To Sarah Wesley Jr.

                                  Bristol
                         March 7, 1788

My Dear Sally,

    When my appetite was entirely gone (so that all I could take at
dinner was a roasted turnip) it was restored in a few days by riding out daily, after taking ten drops of elixir of vitriol in a glass of
water. It is highly probable this would have the same effect in my
brother's case. But in the meantime I wish he would see Dr. [John]
Whitehead. I am persuaded there is not such another physician in
England; although (to confound human wisdom) he does not know
how to cure his own wife.[86]

    He must lie in bed as little as possible in the daytime; otherwise it
will hinder his sleeping at night.

    Now, Sally, tell your brothers from me that their tenderly respect-
ful behaviour to their father (even asking his pardon if in anything
they have offended him) will be the best cordial for him under
heaven. I know not but they may save his life thereby. To *know* nothing will be wanting on *your* part gives great satisfaction to, my dear
Sally,

    Yours very affectionately,

                                J. Wesley

Address: 'To / Miss Wesley / In Chesterfield Street, Mary-bone / London'.
Postmarks: 'Bristol' and 'MR/10/88'. *Charge*: '5'.
Endorsement: by Sarah Jr., 'March 7. 1788'.
Source: holograph; MARC, DDWes 5/16.

[86] John Whitehead had remarried; according to his will drafted about 1788 her first name
was Mary.

To the Rev. Charles Atmore

Bristol
March 13, 1788

Dear Charles,

My journeys now grow rather too long to be taken in one year. I am strongly importuned to shorten them by not attempting to journey through Scotland any more. But this I cannot comply with; only thus far, I do not purpose visiting the north of Scotland. I must move in a smaller circle. I intend with God's help to visit first Dumfries, then Glasgow and Edinburgh, and from Edinburgh to return into England—where (even if I reach Newcastle by the end of May) I shall have full as much work as I can do before I return to London to prepare for the Conference.

You must needs pay a short visit to Ayr. That little society must not be neglected. But I cannot imagine what can be done to build up the infant society at Dumfries. If I can find a proper person as I come along, I will bring or send them a preacher.

Charles, be zealous! I am

Your affectionate friend and brother,

J. Wesley

Address: 'To / The Revd Mr Atmore / in / Glasgow'.
Postmarks: 'Bristol', 'MR/14/88', and 'MR/17'.
Source: holograph; MARC, MAM JW 1/7.

To Samuel Bradburn

Bristol
March 13, 1788

Dear Sammy,

With regard to my brother, I advise you:

1.[87] Whether he will or no it be done already, carry Dr. [John] Whitehead to him.

2. If he can't go out, and yet must have exercise or die, persuade him to use a wooden horse thrice a day, and procure one for him.[88]

---

[87] Orig., 'First'; changed to parallel later numbering.
[88] See note on JW to Samuel Bradburn, Apr. 7, 1781, 29:639 in this edn.

3. I earnestly advise him to be electrified; not shocked, but only filled with electric fire.

4. Enquire if he has made his will (though I think it scarce possible he should have delayed it).

The tunes which brother [Benjamin] Rhodes left with you should be immediately printed in the cheap [form].[89]

I am, with kind love to Sophy, dear Sammy,

Your affectionate friend and brother,

J. Wesley

Address: '⟨To / Mr Bradburn / at⟩ new Chappel / ⟨uppe⟩r Moorfields / London'.[90]

Source: holograph; Duke, Rubenstein, Wesley Family Papers, Box 1.

To Charles Wesley Jr.

Bristol
March 16, 1788

Dear Charles,

Before going down to preach I just snatch time to write two or three lines.[91] I think your persuasion is not of man but of God. Let none reason you out of it. But whenever it pleases God to call your father, Sammy and you while I live will find a father and friend in

Your affectionate uncle,

J. Wesley

Address: 'To / Mr C Wesley Junr / In Chesterfield street, Marybone / London'.

Postmarks: 'Bristol' and 'MR/19/88'. *Charge*: '5'.

Endorsement: by Sarah Wesley Jr., 'March 16. 1788'.

Source: holograph; MARC, DDWes 5/17.

---

[89] This was apparently a reprinting of *Sacred Harmony* (1780; *Bibliography*, No. 409).

[90] Half of the address page is torn away.

[91] JW was writing from the New Room in Bristol, where his personal quarters were upstairs from the preaching room. The letter from CW Jr. (or more likely his sister Sarah) describing Charles's 'persuasion' is not known to survive.

To Adam Clarke

Stroud
March 17, 1788

5   Dear Adam,

I immediately answered the letter which brought the account of sister [Margaret] Horne's hair.[92] I am afraid they will make willful mistakes and carry your letters to the Isle of Wight.

I am glad you have spread yourselves through the islands, and
10   that Mrs. De Saumarez has had the courage to join you.[93] I believe she has very good uprightness of heart and (if she go on) will be a burning and shining light.[94] You have reason likewise to praise God on account of Alderney. There is a seed which shall not easily be rooted up.

15   Drink largely when need is of warm lemonade, and no bilious complaint will remain long.

Our Conference deed provided for what brother [Henri] De Jersey desires. I desire the very same things. So I observe Mr. [George] Walker too. The sooner it is done the better.

20   Send your translation to London.[95] My kind love to sister Lempriere,[96] Jenny Bisson (who owes me a letter), and the dear [De Jersey] family at Mont Plaisir. Peace be with your spirits.

I am, dear Adam,
Your affectionate friend and brother,

25   J. Wesley

Direct to me at London, and your letter will come safe.

Address: 'To / Mr Adam Clark / at Mont Plaisir / Isle of Guernsey'.
30   *Source*: secondary manuscript transcription; MARC, MA 1977/502, p. 16.

---

[92] I.e., the more detailed account JW requested in his letter of Jan. 8, 1788, and which Clarke had sent c. Feb. 1, 1788. JW's reply to that second letter apparently never arrived.

[93] The de Saumarez family was a prominent one on the Isle of Guernsey; the specific identity of this person (perhaps an older single woman) has not been located.

[94] See John 5:35.

[95] Clarke was translating Guillaume de Lavaur, *Conference de la fable avec l'historie sainte* (Paris: Cailleau, 1730), which would be serialized in *AM* 14 (1791): 26ff. Cf. Clarke to JW, Oct. 29, 1787.

[96] This may be a sister of the Miss Lempriere who married George Richard Walker.

To the Rev. Charles Wesley[97]

Bristol
March 17, 1788
between 4:00 and 5:00   5

Dear Brother,

I am just setting out on my northern journey. But I must snatch time to write two or three lines.

I stand and admire the wise and gracious dispensation of divine providence! Never was there before so loud a call to all that are un- 10 der your roof. If they have not hitherto sufficiently regarded either you, or the Lord God of their fathers, what was more calculated to convince them than to see you hovering so long upon the borders of the grave? And I verily believe, if they receive the admonition, God will raise you up again. I know you have the sentence of death 15 in yourself.[98] So had I more than twelve years ago.[99] I know nature is utterly exhausted. But is not nature subject to *his* word? I do not depend upon physicians, but upon him that raiseth the dead.[100] Only let your whole family stir themselves up and be instant in prayer; then I have only to say to each, 'If thou canst believe, thou shalt see 20 the glory of God!'[101]

Be strong in the Lord and in the power of his might.[102]

Address: 'To / The Revd Mr C. Wesley / In Chesterfield Street / London'.
Postmarks: 'Bristol' and 'MR/18/88'. *Charge*: '5'. 25
Source: holograph; MARC, DDWes 3/66.

To Samuel Wesley (nephew) 30

Stroud
March 18, 1788

Dear Sammy,

I have long had a great concern for you, but never more than at 35 present. Just now you are in a critical situation, and every hour is of

---

[97] This is the last letter of JW to his brother CW known to survive.
[98] See 2 Cor. 1:9.
[99] See JW, *Journal*, June 13–28, 1775, 22:455–57 in this edn.
[100] See 2 Cor. 1:9.
[101] Cf. John 11:40.
[102] See Eph. 6:10.

importance. Your father is, to all known appearances, just quivering over the grave, and ready to leave you with all the fire and inexperience of youth under your tuition.[103]

5   The time was when you would have taken my advice. But now Miss Freeman has taught you another lesson![104] Alas! What a fatal step was that! I care not a straw for one *opinion* or another. I care not who is head of the church, provided *you* be a *Christian*! But what a grievous loss is it to *you* to be cut off on any pretense whatever from that preaching which is more calculated than any other in England 10 to make you a *real scriptural* Christian. O Sammy, I take upon me to say, if you had neglected no opportunity of hearing your father and me preaching, you would have been another man than you are now.

    But it seems the time is past! Your father is on the wing. You are not likely to see him long; and you know not that you shall see me 15 any more. Whether you do or do not, I earnestly advise you to make a friend of Mr. [Peard] Dickinson. He is a sensible and a pious man, and has a tender regard for you.

    I commit you to him who is able to carry you through all temptations, and am, dear Sammy,

20   Your affectionate uncle,

J. Wesley

Address: 'To / Mr Samuel Wesley / In Chesterfield street Marybone / London'.

Postmarks: 'Gloster' and 'MR/20/88'.

25 *Endorsement*: by Sarah Wesley Jr.(?), 'March 18th 1788 / J.W. to S.W.'.

Source: holograph; MARC, DDWes 5/18.

30   # To William Black Jr.

Gloucester
March 19, 1788

My Dear Brother,

35   I am glad to find you are still going on in the glorious work to which you are called. We have need to make haste therein, to use all diligence. For the work is great, the day is short, and lonely is the night wherein no man can work![105]

---

[103] I.e., under your own instruction.

[104] Mary Freeman Shepherd; see the note on JW's prior letter to his nephew Samuel, Aug. 19, 1784.

[105] See John 9:4.

It is a kind providence which has placed brother Anderson and you in one house.[106] For you may have many opportunities of strengthening each others hands in God.[107]

It is well that Satan is constrained to show himself so plainly in the case of those poor demoniacs.[108] Thereby he weakens his own kingdom and excites us to assault him more zealously. In the beginning of the work in England and Ireland we had many instances of the kind. But he now chooses to assault us by subtlety more than by strength.

I wish you would do all you possibly can to keep our brethren in peace with each other. And your pains will not be lost on poor John McGeary.[109] There is much good in him. Indeed, he is naturally of a bold, forward temper; but I hope his zeal is now according to knowledge.[110]

Undoubtedly you know the objections which John Hoskins makes to John Stretton. If there is any ground for them, should you not freely and lovingly talk with brother Stretton.

Praying that you may increase with all the increase of God, I am
    Your affectionate friend and brother,

                          J. Wesley

Source: published transcription; Richey, *William Black*, 219–21.

To John Stretton

                              Gloucester
                       March 19, 1788

My Dear Brother,

I am glad the little contest between Mr. [James] Balfour and John McGeary is come to a conclusion.[111] It is good advice to every Chris-

---

[106] Alexander Anderson (d. 1833), a recent Scottish immigrant to Nova Scotia who had been a student at King's College, Aberdeen, had been converted by Black. He became a leader in the Methodist society in Halifax. See Richey, *William Black*, 155–56.

[107] See 1 Sam. 23:16.

[108] Black had sent JW some accounts of persons experiencing convulsions, etc., during some services.

[109] See JW to Black, Feb. 20, 1787. Matters were much worse than JW realized, due to McGeary's combative personality. He would end up leaving Newfoundland in Nov. 1788. See John Stretton to Elizabeth (Patten) Bennis, Dec. 7, 1788, Bennis, *Christian Correspondence*, 250.

[110] See Rom. 10:2.

[111] Balfour had been contesting Methodist ministers in his area for some time; see JW to Stretton, Mar. 9, 1786. The current dispute between him and McGeary involved control of the chapel built by the Methodists in Carbonear.

tian, 'If it be possible, as much as lieth in you, live peaceably with all men.'[112] But of all others, the Methodists are concerned carefully to follow this advice. We are a new people, and consequently must expect that many will be prejudiced against us. And there is no way
5   to remove that prejudice but to overcome evil with good.[113]

The experience of Phoebe Bland is an admirably good one, truly consistent both with Scripture and reason; and the account is well drawn up, with good sense, and in remarkably good language.[114]

I have a confused remembrance of some objections against you
10   last year, made I think by John Hoskins. I hope, if there was once some foundation for them, it is now removed. *We* have need to take the utmost care that the good which is in us be not evil spoken of.[115]

I am

Your affectionate brother,

15   J. Wesley

Source: published transcription; Richey, *William Black*, 220–21.[116]

20

To Sarah Wesley Jr.

Worcester
25   March 20, 1788

My Dear Sally,

Mr. [George] Whitefield had for a considerable time thrown up all the food he took. I advised him to slit a large onion across the grain and bind it warm on the pit of his stomach.[117] He vomited no
30   more. Pray apply this to my brother's stomach the next time he eats.

One in Yorkshire who was dying for want of food, as she threw up all she took, was saved by the following means. Boil crusts of white bread to the consistence of a jelly. Add a few drops of lemon juice and a little loaf sugar. Take a spoonful once or twice an hour. By all
35   means let him try this.

[112] Rom. 12:18.
[113] See Rom. 12:21.
[114] Stretton apparently sent JW this account; it never appeared in *AM*.
[115] See Rom. 14:16.
[116] The transcription appears in a footnote; this was surely a double letter with that to Black of the same date.
[117] The leading remedy suggested for vomiting in *Primitive Physic*; see Ailment no. 276, 32:253 in this edn.

If neither of these avail (which I think will not be the case), re-member the lady at Paris who lived several weeks without swallow-ing a grain by applying thin slices of beef to the stomach.

But above all let prayer be made continually; and probably he will be stronger after this illness than he has been these ten years. Is anything too hard for God?[118]

On Sunday I am to be at Birmingham; on Sunday se'nnight at Madeley, near Shifnal, Salop.

My dear Sally,
Adieu!

Address: 'To / Miss Wesley / In Chesterfield Street Marybone / London'.
Postmark: 'MR/24/88'.
Source: holograph; Bridwell Library (SMU).

To Harriet Lewis[119]

Madeley
March 29, 1788

My Dear Sister,

You see I cannot refuse anything that *you* desire; so I write the first opportunity. I was much surprised at the account which you gave of what had lately befallen your friend. But in the whole course of that strange affair one may discover the hand of God. I am per-suaded it was the hand of God for good, both in regard to him and you: to him, that he might learn both more patience and resignation in himself, and more meekness and forbearance toward others; to *you*, that, being cut off from worldly hope, you might simply and nakedly hang upon the living God! You have already tasted that he is gracious. Go on! You are in *his* school, the school of affliction,[120] where you will always find him a present help. But he does not yet clearly point out the way that you should go.

I was greatly pleased with your openness the other day. May there never be any strangeness between you and, my dear Harriet,

[118] See Jer. 32:27.
[119] Little is known of Harriet Lewis (b. c. 1770). JW had just met her in Dudley, Staf-fordshire on Mar. 27, apparently at the home of a Mr. Moon (see JW to Lewis, Apr. 2, 1789). In 1790 she would marry Thomas Cooper in Dudley (Cooper's first wife, Ann Parminter, died in Nov. 1788).
[120] See Ps. 119:65–72.

Yours most affectionately,

J. Wesley

Address: 'To /Miss Harriot Lewis / in / Dudley'.
Postmark: 'Shrewsbury'. *Charge*: '3'.
Source: holograph; MARC, WCB, D6/3/1/20a.

To Thomas Brocas[121]

Madeley
March 31, 1788

My Dear Brother,
  In your little book I do not observe anything amiss, but it contains
many just observations. And many of the arguments in it are strong
and not easy to be answered. But I do not advise you to print by any
means, for you would not sell enough of them to pay the printer.[122]
  I am,
    Your affectionate brother,

John Wesley

Source: secondary manuscript transcription; Drew, Methodist Archives.

To Theophilus Lessey[123]

[c. April 1788]

My Dear Brother,
  That you are slighted in some places ought not to discourage you,
but to humble you, and to put you upon more diligence in search-
ing the Scriptures with more meditation and prayer. As a balance
for the slight you meet with in some places, you see that God gives

---

[121] Thomas Brocas (1756–1818) of Shrewsbury, played a prominent role in the early years
of the Methodist society there, including as a local preacher. See his death notice in *MM* 42
(1819): 143–44; and a biography in *MM* 44 (1821): 481ff.
  [122] There is no record of a publication by Brocas.
  [123] Sometime during the year that Lessey served with Jonathan Coussins (as Assistant) on
the St. Ives circuit (Aug. 1787–July 1788), he wrote JW a dejected letter, wondering if he had
the gifts for ministry. This was JW's reply.

you success in others. And there is no doubt but he gives you as much honour and success as you can bear. Many censures must be expected to follow the expulsion of unworthy members. But this will do you no hurt. The way to the kingdom lies through honour and dishonour.[124]   5

I am in great hopes that sister [Penelope] Coussins will now have better health than she has for some time. And she may say with assurance, 'Health I shall have, if health be best.'[125]

Go on, fulfilling your character, and being 'patient in bearing ill, and doing well'.[126]   10

I am,

Your affectionate brother,

J. Wesley

Source: published transcription; *Wesleyan Methodist Magazine* 45 (1822): 420.   15

To Sarah (Gwynne) Wesley   20

Macclesfield
Friday, April 4, 1788

Dear Sister,   25

Half an hour ago I received a letter from Mr. [Samuel] Bradburn informing me of my brother's death.[127] For eleven or twelve days before, I had not one line concerning him. The last I had was from Charles, which I delayed to answer, expecting every day to receive some further information.[128] We have only now to learn that great   30 lesson, 'The Lord gave, and the Lord hath taken away; blessed be the name of the Lord!'[129] If it had been necessary, in order to serve either him or you, I should not have thought much of coming up to

---

[124] See 2 Cor. 6:8.

[125] Cf. CW, Hymn on Isaiah 40:31, st. 7, *HSP* (1742), 226.

[126] SW Jr., 'The Battle of the Sexes', st. 25, *Poems* (1743), p. 34; reprinted by JW in *MSP* (1744), 3:32.

[127] CW died on Mar. 29, 1788. Samuel Bradburn wrote JW immediately, but sent it to Manchester instead of Birmingham, which resulted in it arriving too late for JW to attend the funeral. See JW to Peard Dickinson, Apr. 8, 1788. Bradburn's letter is not known to survive; but see Sarah Wesley Jr. to JW, Apr. 4, 1788.

[128] This letter from CW Jr., replying to JW's of Mar. 16, is not known to survive.

[129] Job 1:21.

London. Indeed, to serve you, or your dear family, in anything that is in my power, will always be a pleasure to, dear sister,

Your affectionate friend and brother,

John Wesley[130]

Address: 'To / Mrs Wesley / In Chesterfield Street, Marybone / London'.
Postmarks: 'Macclesfield' and 'AP/7/88'. *Charge*: '6'.
Endorsement: by Sarah (Gwynne) Wesley, 'Mr Jn. Wesley / Apr. 4th 1788 / kind'.
Source: holograph; MARC, DDWes 5/19.

To Henry Moore

Macclesfield
April 6, 1788

Dear Henry,

You send me good news. When these soldiers are removed, you must take the more pains with them henceforth.[131]

It is exceedingly strange that the work of God should not yet decay in Dublin. I have not known before a shower of grace continue so long, either in Great Britain or Ireland. And it *will* continue if the people continue genuine Methodists, and do not grieve the Holy Spirit of God.

An organ! *Non [...] defensoribus istis tempus eget*.[132] This will help them just as old Priam helped Troy.[133]

If Mr. [Edward] and Mrs. Smyth are gone to England, I doubt Bethesda will droop.[134] But Dr. [Thomas] Coke will be saved from some embarrassment, and will have a smoother path to walk in.[135]

I am, if possible, more fully employed than before, since my brother's death. Thus far I am come in my way to north Britain, perhaps for the last time. Lately I have been threatened with blind-

---

[130] Note the use of his full name on this 'formal' letter.

[131] Moore's letter is not known to survive; but see JW to Moore, Feb. 19, 1788.

[132] Virgil, *Aeneid*, ii.521–22; 'The hour calls not for such defenders' (Loeb).

[133] Priam was the last king of Troy; who lost the Trojan war.

[134] After the death of Agnes (Higginson) Smyth in 1783, Edward married Elizabeth Dawson (d. 1849) in 1785.

[135] Referring to the tensions between the more Calvinist-leaning Bethesda chapel and the Wesleyan Methodist society in Dublin.

ness.[136] But still you and I have two good eyes between us. Let us use them while the day is![137] I am, with tender love to Nancy, dear Henry,

Your affectionate friend and brother,

J. Wesley 5

My brother fell asleep so quietly that they who sat by him did not know when he died.

J. Wesley[138]

Address: 'To / Mr Moore / At the New Room / Dublin'. 10
Postmarks: 'Macclesfield' and 'AP/10'.
Source: holograph; MARC, WCB, D6/1/130a (letter).[139]

15

To the Rev. Peard Dickinson

near Stockport
April 8, 1788
20
My Dear Brother,

If Mr. [Samuel] Bradburn's letter of March 29 had been directed to Birmingham, where I then was, I should have taken coach on Sunday the 30th and been with you on Monday the 31st. I shall not be at Manchester till the 10th instant. But all is well; by that mistake I am much further on my journey. 25

It is pity but the remains of my brother had been deposited with me.[140] Certainly that *ground* is *holy* as any in England, and it contains a large quantity of 'bonny dust'.[141]

We have all need to stir ourselves up before the Lord and to improve by this providence. And you may improve it much in speak- 30

---

[136] He had 'a pearl in the eye' (likely a cataract); see JW to Hester Rogers, May 28.

[137] See John 9:4.

[138] This note was added on the outside of the sealed letter.

[139] The sheet with the address portion and line on the outside of the sealed envelope is held at Duke, Rubenstein, Frank Baker Collection of Wesleyana, Box WF 1.

[140] Before his death CW requested to be buried in the graveyard of St. Marylebone parish church, as an expression of his loyalty to the Church of England.

[141] JW was protesting that the graveyard behind City Road Chapel was also 'sanctified' ground, because of the mingled dust of those buried there; invoking Thomas Halyburton's image of being buried with his colleagues, so that they may be 'a knot of bonny [i.e., comely] dust'. See *Memoirs of ... Thomas Halyburton* (London: R. Cruttenden, 1718), 226; retained in JW's *Extract of ... Thomas Haliburton* (1741), 91.

ing to the people, as I have done several times. Betsy must accept of my friendship instead of my brother's.[142] I am

Your affectionate friend and brother,

J. Wesley

Source: secondary manuscript transcription; MARC, MA 1977/502/1/49.

To Hannah Ball[143]

Manchester
April 12, 1788

My Dear Sister,

I know not that ever I knew an instance of an English physician curing a dropsy.[144] I have cured several, in defiance of all the [medical] faculty.

I advise you: 1. Use as much exercise as you possibly can.

2. If you have not done it already, eat every morning, fasting, a crust of bread as big as a large walnut.[145]

3. If this does not cure you, try the remedy lately discovered by Dr. Withering, physician to the infirmary at Birmingham, which seldom fails to cure dropsies even of the breast or head.[146] Take one or two of the lower leaves of *foxglove*; dry them before the fire, till they are dry enough to rub into a coarse powder. Take one grain of this, morning and night, three or four or five days, till you find yourself either giddy or sickish. Then take no more. In a day or two it will begin to work, usually both upward and downward, and will operate four or five days. Then the patient is commonly well.

We are sure of one thing, the Lord reigneth.[147] Therefore, 'health we shall have, if health be best.'[148] And choose whatever degree of it we have.

---

[142] I.e., Elizabeth Briggs, who was a favourite of CW's and would marry Peard Dickinson on Apr. 30, 1788.

[143] While the address portion is missing, the recipient is clear from the content.

[144] That is, an edema, or swelling caused by accumulation of water.

[145] See *Primitive Physic*, Ailment #74, receipt 6, 32:166 in this edn.

[146] William Withering FRS (1741–90), whose *Account of the Foxglove, and Some of Its Medical Uses; with Practical Remarks on Dropsy and Other Diseases* (Birmingham: Swinney, 1785), JW read shortly after it was published. See *Journal*, Mar. 21, 1786, 23:387 in this edn.

[147] See Ps. 97:1, etc.

[148] Cf. CW, Hymn on Isaiah 40:31, st. 7, *HSP* (1742), 226.

There are three of you single women in one circuit that breathe one spirit: Patty Chapman and Nancy Bolton and you. But I am afraid you have little intercourse with each other. And I don't see how to help it. It is an mysterious providence which keeps you so far apart. However Nancy Ball and you may quicken each other. I 5
am, my dear sister,
    Your affectionate brother,

                                    J. Wesley

Endorsement: '12th April 1788'. 10
Source: holograph; MARC, MA 2008/013.

To Hugh Moore 15

                                   Manchester
                               April 12, 1788
Dear Hugh,
    I did not question but you would have a comfortable time in the 20
Clones circuit, and the rather because you are a lover of peace and
will promote it by every possible means. You have reason to rejoice
in the exercise of the grace and work of God in the neighbouring societies, and you have encouragement to put forth all your
strength, and to expect to see still greater things than these.[149] 25
    Unless you design to murder yourself you must needs refrain
from speaking loud or long. 'The spirits of the prophets are subject
to the prophets.'[150] Temptations from pleasure are more dangerous
than temptations from pain, but if you watch and pray you will
conquer both. 30
    I am, dear Hugh,
        Your affectionate friend and brother,

                                    J. Wesley

Source: published transcription; *WHS* 29 (1954): 115. 35

---

[149] See John 1:50.
[150] 1 Cor. 14:32.

To Sarah (Gwynne) Wesley

Manchester
April 12, 1788

Dear Sister,

The account which Mr. [Samuel] Bradburn gave me of my brother's removal was very short and unsatisfactory. But the account which Sally has given me is such as it should be, particular and circumstantial.[151] I doubt not but the few solemn words that he spoke before he went hence will not soon be forgotten, but will prove a lasting blessing to all that heard them.

If I may take upon me to give you a little piece of advice, it is to keep little company. You have an handsome occasion of contracting your acquaintance, and retaining only a small select number—such as you can do good to or receive good from.

I am, my dear sister,

Your ever affectionate friend and brother,

J. Wesley

Address: 'To / Mrs Wesley / In Chesterfield Street / Mary-bone / London'.
Postmarks: 'Manchester' and 'AP/14/88'.
Endorsement: 'April 12 / 1788'.
Source: holograph; Pitts Library (Emory), John Wesley Papers (MSS 153), 3/39.

To Sarah Wesley Jr.

Manchester
April 12, 1788

My Dear Sally,

I thank you for the account you have given me.[152] It is full and satisfactory. You describe a very awful scene. The time, I doubt not, was prolonged on purpose that it might make the deeper impression on those that otherwise might soon have forgotten it. What a difference does one moment make, when the soul springs out of

---

[151] See Sarah Wesley Jr. to JW, Apr. 4, 1788.
[152] See Sarah Wesley Jr. to JW, Apr. 4, 1788.

time into eternity! What an amazing change! What are all the pleasures, the business of this world, to a disembodied spirit! Let *us*,
therefore, be ready, for the day is at hand![153]
    But the comfort is, it cannot part you long from, my dear Sally,
        Yours invariably,   5
                                                                J. Wesley

Address: 'To Miss Wesley'.[154]
Source: holograph; Pitts Library (Emory), John Wesley Papers (MSS
    153), 3/40.   10

Circular on Dewsbury[155]

                                                                            15

                                                            Manchester
                                                        April 12, 1788

    Great are the advantages we have reaped for many years from the   20
continual change of preachers. But this cannot subsist any longer
than the places of all the preachers are appointed by one man or
body of men. Therefore wherever trustees are to place and displace
the preachers this change, which we call itinerancy, is at an end.
    It is for *your* sakes, not my own, that I wish this may continue,   25
and the appointment of preachers, which now lies upon *me*, be afterwards executed by the Conference, not the trustees of any of the
houses.
    Is it possible that itinerancy should be continued by any other
means?
                                                            John Wesley   30

This is all the contest, at present, between me and our brethren at
Dewsbury.

Source: printed circular; *Bibliography*, no. 446.[156]   35

---

[153] See Rev. 1:3.

[154] Written at the top of the page, as this was a double letter with that to her mother.

[155] The dispute between JW and the trustees of the preaching-house in Dewsbury (see
his letter to them of Sept. 22, 1787) had garnered larger attention, which would lead to decisive
action at Conference (See JW to the Trustees, Sept. 30, 1788). This circular was to remind
(particularly the preachers) of what JW saw to be at stake.

[156] No surviving copy has been located; this text is taken from Telford, *Letters*, 8:52–53.

To John Atlay

Chester
April 15, 1788

5 My Dear Brother,

My brother never knew the value of Dr. Coke while he lived.[157] I wish I had an hundred preachers like him. If you expected me to die within the year, you should not have printed so large editions; for you know not who will buy them when I am gone. While we live,
10 let us live in earnest.

I have little fear for Sally, much hope for Charles (to whom I wrote lately), and some for Sammy—he certainly fears God.[158]

I *will* have the tunes printed as soon as may be. If the corrected copy is lost, they must be printed from the large copy; but the price
15 must be only two shillings and sixpence.[159]

Pray consult with Thomas Olivers where the additional sermons may be most properly inserted. I have another ready for the press and two more begun.

I am
20   Your affectionate brother,

J. Wesley

Endorsement: by Dickinson(?), 'Mr Wesley April 15 / 1788 / To Mr Atlay, City Road / London'.
25 *Source*: holograph; Huntington Library, Manuscripts, HM 57056.

To Adam Clarke

30 Liverpool
April 17, 1788[160]

Dear Adam,

Is it not a doubt whether you will be suffered to build a chapel so near the chapel-of-ease?[161] I should be afraid one congregation

---

[157] CW was convinced that Thomas Coke was trying to persuade JW of the need to separate from the Church of England. Atlay apparently wrote JW expressing concern about who would resist Coke now that CW was dead.

[158] Referring to CW's children.

[159] See JW to Samuel Bradburn, Mar. 13, 1788.

[160] This is the day Adam Clarke married Mary Cooke in Trowbridge.

[161] Construction on La Chapelle de la Trinite was nearing completion; it opened July 5, 1788. It was a chapel-of-ease for French-speaking persons in St. Peter Port, near what is now Trinity Square.

would hinder the other if ever they meet at the same hour. Then in England, no house of worship must be built within so many yards of any other.

I am glad you have gained Mrs. Saumarez and Miss Lempriere; and I hope Mrs. Walker Jr. is not lost.[162]

When I heard of Jenny Bisson's marriage, I was much afraid she had lost ground.[163] I am glad to hear that you think she is still alive to God, but I shall be surprised if she be as much alive as ever.

So you are a proficient in French. If you come to the Conference, the way will be made plain for you. But if you have not your health in the islands, you must spend part of your time in England. I am, dear Adam,

Your affectionate friend and brother,

J. Wesley

Source: holograph; MARC, WCB, D6/1/98a.

To Thomas Tattershall

Bolton
April 20, 1788

Dear Tommy,

There is work enough for you in England and Ireland, and you have nothing to do with the West Indies.[164] It would be well if someone would ask the rector, now, 'Sir, if Mr. Wesley should come, would you invite him to preach in your church?' What is his name? And where does he live? I am, dear Tommy,

Your affectionate friend and brother,

J. Wesley

Source: published transcription; Byrth, 'Memoir', xxxvii.

---

[162] I.e., the Miss Lempriere who married George Richard Walker.

[163] Jeanne Le Gros Bisson married William Cock in St. Helier, Isle of Jersey, on Mar. 9, 1788. See JW's letter to her with her married name, May 20, 1788.

[164] Tattershall, currently Assistant for the Epworth circuit, apparently volunteered for service in the West Indies.

To Elizabeth Ritchie

Blackburn
April 21, 1788

5 My Dear Sister,

I have been considering at what time I can wait upon Mr. Stones at Rawdon.[165] And the way I can contrive is this: Saturday, April 27 – Sunday, [April 28], Keighley; Monday, [April] 29, Halifax; Wednesday, [April] 30, Huddersfield; Thursday, May 1, Wakefield; 10 Friday, [May] 2, Bradford; Sunday, [May] 4, noon, Birstall; Monday, [May] 5, Leeds; Tuesday, [May] 6, at 11:00, Rawdon, at 6:30, Otley. I hope my dear Miss Richie will be with me, as soon and as much as she can.

Sometime since you was resolved to be altogether a Christian. If 15 your fervour at any time abated, is it not high time that you should set [out] anew? That you should run and never tire![166] I am, my dear sister,

Yours most affectionately,

J. Wesley

20

Source: holograph; Beinecke Library (Yale), Charlton T. Lewis papers.

25

To Sarah (Gwynne) Wesley

Blackburn
April 21, 1788

30

You will excuse me, my dear sister, for troubling you with so many letters, for I know not how to help it. I had you and your family so much upon my heart, both for your own sake and for the sake of my brother.

35 But I am much easier now that I find you are joined with honest John Collinson, whom I know ⟨to⟩[167] be not only a man of probity, but likewise a ⟨man of⟩ diligence and understanding. I am

---

[165] Rev. Samuel Stones (c. 1745–1823), perpetual curate of Rawdon, Yorkshire, welcomed JW to his pulpit on May 6, 1788, at 11:00; see *Journal*, 24:81 in this edn.

[166] See Isa. 40:31.

[167] A small portion is torn from the edge by the wax seal; the missing letters or words are fairly obvious.

th⟨erefore⟩ persuaded he will spare no pains in do⟨ing⟩ what you
wish to be done. So that I shall ⟨not be⟩ wanted among you, as
he will fully supply my lack of service. I only wish both Charles
and Sammy may follow your example and advice in keeping little
company,[168] and those of the best sort, men sound understanding   5
and solid piety—for such only are fit for the acquaintance of men
of sense.

I commit you all to him that loves you and am, my dear sister,
> Ever yours,
>   J. Wesley   10

Address: 'To / Mrs Wesley / In Chesterfield Street / Marybone / Lon-
don'.
Postmark: 'Blackburn'. *Charge*: '6'.
Source: holograph; MARC, DDWes 5/20.   15

To Sarah Wesley Jr.   20

> Blackburn
> April 21, 1788

What a comfort it is, my dear Sally, to think the Lord liveth![169]   25
Nay, and that our union with our human friends will be more perfect hereafter than it can be while we are encumbered with the
house of clay!

You did not send me those verses before. They were very proper
to be his last, as being worthy of one bought by the blood of the   30
Lamb and just going forth to meet him![170]

Now, my Sally, make the best of life. Whereunto you have attained
hold fast![171] But you have not yet received the Spirit of adoption,
crying in your heart, 'Abba, Father!'[172] See that you do not stop

---

[168] See JW to Sarah, Apr. 12, 1788.

[169] See Ps. 18:46.

[170] Sarah Jr. had surely sent JW a copy of the single stanza hymn that her mother copied
down as CW repeated them orally a few days before his death. It was published in *AM* 13
(1790): 672, with the title 'Lines dictated on his Death Bed'. Since JW speaks of verses, Sarah
Jr. may have sent as well one of the other hymns in the folder 'Charles Wesley on His Own
Death' available in the online collection of CW's hymns at Duke.

[171] See Phil. 3:16.

[172] See Rom. 8:15.

short of it! The promise is for you![173] If you *feel* your want, it will soon be supplied. And God will seal that word upon your heart, 'I am merciful to thy unrighteousness, and thy sins and iniquities I remember no more!'[174]

5   Dear Sally,
          Adieu!

Address: 'To Sally Wesley'.[175]
Endorsement: by Sarah Jr., 'April 21. 1788'.
10   *Source*: holograph; Pitts Library (Emory), John Wesley Papers (MSS 153), 4/1.

15   To Susanna Knapp[176]

                                                          Rochdale
20   April 24, 1788
My Dear Suky,
      I hardly expect the young woman will recover, but she should keep to the same regimen. Probably it would save her life if she took three or four times a day the jelly mentioned in the *Primitive Physic*
25   for a consumption.[177]
      It would be well both for her and the young man to continue using the buttermilk to the end of the second month. They might add the use of potatoes, turnips, spinach, or cauliflowers; but no flesh of any kind. He should use every day as much exercise in the open air
30   as he can bear without weariness. I hope in a few weeks he will be a healthy man. Then he may return to the *sparing* use of flesh meat.
      I hope the desire you had when I saw you of being altogether a Christian does not lessen but increase. I love you for your serious-

----

[173] See Acts 2:39.

[174] Cf. Heb. 8:12.

[175] This is written at the top of the page, because (while they are now in separate holdings) it was part of a double letter with that to her mother of the same date.

[176] According to an endorsement on the letter, JW had given health advice to two young persons while in Worcester on Mar. 20–21; and Knapp had written to update him on their current state. Knapp's letter to JW is not known to survive.

[177] The term 'jelly' does not appear among receipts for consumption, but JW was likely referring to either receipt 7 or receipt 13 in *Primitive Physic*, Ailment #49, 32:154–55 in this edn.

ness and was glad of an opportunity of spending a little time in your company, which will always be a pleasure to, my dear Suky,

Yours affectionately,

J. Wesley

My love [to] your dear mamma [Ann].

Address: 'To / Miss Knapp / At the White House / Worcester / +p [i.e., crosspost] Glo'ster'.
Postmark: 'Rochdale'.
Source: holograph; Wesley's Chapel (London), LDWMM 1994/1954.

To William Simpson

near Colne
April 26, 1788

Dear Billy,

You did well to expel those who marry ungodly persons, a real evil which we can never tolerate. You should speak to every believer singly concerning meeting in band. There were always some in Yarm circuit, though not many. No circuit ever did or ever will flourish unless there are bands in the large societies.

It is a good sign that so many of our preachers are willing to contribute to those necessary expenses. They used to be much straitened in their bowels whenever money was wanted.

You have now good encouragement to remain another year in the circuit.[178] But you know two preachers do not remain in the same circuit more than one year. I am, dear Billy,

Your affectionate friend and brother,

J. Wesley

Source: published transcription; Tyerman, *John Wesley*, 3:542.

---

[178] Simpson was returned to the Yarm circuit another year.

To the Rev. Peard Dickinson

Keighley
April 27, 1788

5

My Dear Brother,

I really think it will be proper to publish something in the *Magazine* on that idle popish conceit of 'consecrated ground'.[179] The ground of Bunhill fields is full as well consecrated as that of St.
10   Luke's churchyard.[180]

You should study every means of keeping up your acquaintance with Sammy Wesley. Both Charles [Jr.] and he stand in much need of serious acquaintance, whether men or women. You should introduce our Betsy [Briggs] to Sally Wesley [Jr.]. They are kindred
15   souls, and I think would soon take acquaintance with each other. If I live till the Conference, I will give her another acquaintance that will be after her own heart. Sister Shanell(?)[181] likewise will be a fit acquaintance for her. But let her beware of new acquaintances.

I hope you have found a little house in our neighbourhood. You
20   have both need of much prayer.[182] Peace be with your spirits! I am
Your affectionate friend and brother,

J. Wesley

Source: holograph; Duke, Rubenstein, Perronet Family Papers, scrapbook,
25   p. 22.

---

[179] See JW, 'Thoughts on the Consecration of Churches and Burial Grounds', *AM* 11 (1788): 541–43, 9:531–33 in this edn.

[180] JW was still chafing at CW's rejection of being buried at City Road Chapel, or even across the street in Bunhill fields alongside their mother. Bunhill fields was not formally consecrated; JW likely meant it was so by virtue of the 'saints' buried there (see JW to Dickinson, Apr. 8, 1788). That JW contrasted St. Luke's (Finsbury) churchyard, the parish church nearest City Road Chapel, rather than St. Marylebone, the parish church nearest CW's home, where he was buried, reflects that JW had not been back to London since CW's death to see his grave.

[181] The writing is indistinct, at the end of a line, and no person whose name may fit has been identified.

[182] Dickinson and Elizabeth Briggs were to be married on Apr. 30.

To Henry Moore[183]

Leeds
May 6, 1788

Dear Henry,   5

The Doctor is too warm. He ought to have paid more regard to so respectable a body of men as applied to him. I am a Church of England man. And as I said fifty years ago so I say still, in the Church I will live and die, unless I am thrust out. We must have no more service at Whitefriar's in the church hours. Leave off contention   10
before it be meddled with. Follow after peace!

I am, with kind love to Nancy,

Your affectionate friend and brother,

J. Wesley

15

Address: 'To / Mr Moore / At the New Room / Dublin'.
Postmarks: 'Leeds' and 'MY/11'.
Source: holograph; MARC, DDWes 1/27.

20

To Henry Moore

Whitehaven   25
May 11, 1788

Dear Henry,

Still the more I reflect, the more I am convinced that the Methodists ought not to leave the Church. I judge that to lose a thousand, yea ten thousand, of our people would be a less evil than this.   30
'But many found much comfort in this.'[184] So they would in any *new thing*. I believe Satan himself would give them comfort here-

---

[183] When Thomas Coke arrived in Dublin in the spring of 1788 he unilaterally moved the Sunday service at Whitefriar Street preaching-house to 'church hours'—with the exception that one Sunday out of four, when society members were to attend St. Patrick's Cathedral or another parish of the established Church, to receive the sacrament (see Crookshank, *Ireland*, 442–43. This upset several members of the Dublin society, who saw it as a move toward separation from the established Church. Cf. JW to Brooke, June 14, 1786; JW to Brooke, June 21, 1788; and JW to members of the Dublin society, Mar. 21, 1789. The controversy emerges repeatedly in JW's correspondence over the next several months.

[184] JW's letter of May 6 just reached Dublin on May 11; thus JW was apparently quoting from Moore's letter that drew the earlier response (which is not known to survive).

in—for he knows what the end would be. Our glorying has hitherto been not to be a separate body.

Hoc Ithacus velit.[185]

But (whatever Mr. Smyth does), I am for the old way.[186] I advise you to abide in it till you find another *new event* (although, indeed, you may expect it every day), namely, the removal of
> Your affectionate friend and brother,
>
> J. Wesley

My dear love to Nancy.

Address: 'To / Mr Moore / At the New Room / in / Dublin'.
Source: holograph; MARC, DDWes 1/28.

To the Rev. Dr. Thomas Coke

Glasgow
May 16, 1788

Dear Sir,

I came hither this morning. There is a fair opening at Dumfries and a prospect of much good. I like your proposal concerning Joseph Cownley, and will talk with him about it if I live to see Newcastle.[187]

As I said before, so I say still, I cannot, I dare not leave the Church, for the reasons we all agreed to thirty years ago in the conference at Leeds.[188] Thus far only I could go: On condition that our people would receive the Lord's Supper once a month either at St. Patrick's or their own parish church (the reasonableness of which

---

[185] Virgil, *Aeneid*, ii.104; 'This the Ithacan [i.e., enemy] would wish' (Loeb).

[186] Bethesda Chapel, where Edward Smyth was chaplain, was not officially sanctioned by the Church of Ireland; so in holding services at church hours on Sunday, including the sacraments, he was acting as a quasi-Independent.

[187] Coke had recommended that JW ordain Cownley, now supernumerary in Newcastle, to serve in Scotland (see Coke's letter to Cownley, Apr. 5, 1788, held in the Methodist Archives at Drew). JW did so on June 3–4; see Appendix B. Cownley's health proved too poor for him to serve more than a year in this capacity.

[188] The 1755 Conference; see 10:270–71 in this edn.

should be strongly and largely explained), on this condition I would
allow Henry Moore to read the morning service at Whitefriar's on
the other Sundays.[189]

I wonder at the imprudence of Mr. Edward Smyth, to say nothing of his unkindness.[190]

You did well in changing the stewards at Waterford.

I am, dear sir,

    Yours most affectionately,

               J. Wesley

Address: 'To The Revd Dr Coke / At the New Room / Dublin'.[191]
Postmarks: 'Glasgow' and 'MY/21'.
Source: holograph; MARC, DDWes 5/43.

To Richard Gower[192]

               Glasgow
            May 16, 1788

My Dear Brother,

I hope God will give you more and more happiness in each other.
He surely will if you will seek him with your whole heart. He has
already given you a token for good in the ministration of Mrs. [Eliz-
abeth] Briggs.[193] You can't be too wary in enlarging the number of
your acquaintants. You can enlarge it whenever you please, but you
can't so easily contract it. For the present you have enough. I recommend only one more, Thomas Rankin. He is a rough diamond.

You are quite right in resolving to invite none to dinner. It is a
great expense to little purpose. And whatever you can spare may
answer a much better intention.

---

[189] See the note on JW to Moore, May 6, 1788.

[190] Smyth was drawing those upset with Coke's changes to Sunday services to Bethesda
Chapel; see JW to Adam Clarke, June 25, 1789.

[191] 'Dublin' is struck out and replaced by 'Limerick' in another hand.

[192] Richard Gower (1763–1836) was a single man who was possibly living at the home of
and assisting Elizabeth (Perronet) Briggs, after the death of her husband William in Jan. 1788.
Richard would be admitted into Methodist ministry in 1792 and serve until his death; see
Minutes (post-Wesley, 1841), 8:7–8. While the address portion is missing, the letter was handed
down through the Gower family.

[193] Elizabeth (Perronet) Briggs.

If we live till the Conference, I hope to give my dear Betsy a truly valuable acquaintance: Mrs. [Mary] Blair, Andrew Blair's wife and a fit wife for such an husband.

See that you daily strengthen each other's hands in God,[194] and you will give more and more comfort to, my dear friends,

Your affectionate friend and brother,

J. Wesley

Source: holograph; privately held (WWEP Archive holds photocopy).

To Henry Moore[195]

Glasgow
May 17, 1788

Dear Henry,

I allow two points: 1) that while Dr. [Thomas] Coke is in Dublin he may have service at 11:00 on Sunday as before; 2) that, on condition that our brethren will attend St. Patrick's one Sunday in four, you may read prayers the other three in the room.

When Dr. Coke returns to Dublin, he should immediately send me word who is proper to succeed you there. I shall be glad, if I can contrive it, to have Nancy and you at Bristol next year. It is not unlikely I may finish my course there; and if so, I should love to have her to close my eyes. My brother said I should 'follow him within the year'. But be that as it may, by God's help I will live today.

My dear love to Nancy. I am, dear Henry,

Ever yours,

J. Wesley

Address: 'To / Mr Moore / At the New Room / in / Dublin / +p [i.e., crosspost] Portpatrick'.
Postmarks: 'Glasgow' and 'MY/22'.
Source: holograph; MARC, DDWes 5/42.

[194] See 1 Sam. 23:16.
[195] See JW to Moore, May 6, 1788 for context, where JW instructed Moore to suspend all services at the Methodist preaching-house in Dublin on Sundays at church hours. Moore's reply letter is not known to survive.

To Jeanne (Le Gros Bisson) Cock[196]

Edinburgh
May 20, 1788

My Dear Sister, 5

From my long delay to answer, you might conclude I had forgotten you. But that is impossible. I shall not easily forget the agreeable conversations I had with you at Mont Plaisir and the plain and artless account which from time to time you have given me of your experience.

I shall be glad to know how you have found your soul since you 10 altered your condition. You must needs have abundantly more care now than you had in a single life. And are you able still, among all these cares, to attend upon the Lord without distraction? Does nothing make you unattentive to his presence? Is there no intermission of your communion with the Father and the Son? When you 15 have leisure, you will send a free and full answer to, my dear sister,

Yours very affectionately,

J. Wesley

You may direct to London. 20

Address: 'To Mrs Jane Cock'.[197]
Source: holograph; MARC, MAM JW 2/50.

25

To Jane (Lee) Freeman[198]

[Edinburgh]
May [20], 1788 30

My Dear Sister,

Some years ago, at the Conference in Dublin, this question was debated.[199] Mr. [Edward] Smyth urged several reasons for our sepa-

[196] Jeanne Le Gros Bisson married William Cock (1765–1812) in St. Helier, Isle of Jersey, on Mar. 9, 1788. Her letter to JW informing him of this marriage is not known to survive, but arrived sometime after Mar. 17 (see JW to Clarke, Mar. 17, 1788).

[197] Written at the top of the page; likely sent as part of a double letter (the other portion not known to survive).

[198] Freeman, now residing in Dublin, was one of the members opposed to holding services at Whitefriar Street during church hours. Her letter to JW in this regard is not known to survive.

[199] The Conference for the Irish itinerants held July 7, 1778. See JW, *Journal*, 23:98 in this edn.; and 1778 Irish *Minutes*, Q. 23, 10:965 in this edn.

rating from the Church. But we were all quite of another mind. And I am of the same judgement that I was then. I believe, you need be under no concern on that account, I am, my dear sister,
> Your affectionate brother,

> J. Wesley

I have no fear of your leaving the society, till you leave the body.

Address: 'To / Mrs Freeman'.[200]
Source: holograph; privately held (WWEP Archive holds photocopy).

To William Whitestone[201]

> Edinburgh
> May 20, 1788

My Dear Brother,
From one of Dr. Coke's letters I concluded that you was quite reconciled to the step which he had taken.[202] And I myself can go so far but no further. I will not leave the Church. But on condition that our friends will attend St. Patrick's one Sunday in the month, on the other three I will allow that there should be service at the New Room.
> I am, dear Billy,
> Your affectionate brother,

> J. Wesley

Endorsement: on back in another hand, '20 May 1788 / Revd. Jno. Wesley / Edinburgh / to Mr. Wm. Whitestone'.
Source: holograph; Drew, Methodist Archives.

---

[200] Written at the bottom of the page; part of a double letter, perhaps with that to William Whitestone.

[201] William Whitestone (b. c. 1730) was a stationer in Dublin, who published a few of JW's writings there after 1770. He was in 1788 a member and class leader of the Dublin society (see Cooney, 'Dublin Society', 45, 57). His letter to JW expressing concern about Coke's action in Dublin is not known to survive. In 1755 Whitestone married Elizabeth Wilson, originally of Wheatfield (see Crookshank, *Ireland*, 157).

[202] No letter from Thomas Coke from Apr. through Mar. 1788 is known to survive; but see JW to Coke, May 16, 1788.

To Henry Moore

Newcastle upon Tyne
May 28, 1788 5

My Dear Brother,

I exceedingly approve of your design of enlarging the house.[203]
Let it be done without delay. Only see that your title be good.

I believe whatever Mr. [Edward] Smyth does will do us little hurt.
And if eight hundred are profited by him and Mr. Mann, I shall re- 10
joice therein.[204] You and my dear Nancy are now in particular called
to overcome evil with good.[205] I am, dear Henry,

Your affectionate friend and brother,

J. Wesley

15

Address: 'To / Mr. Henry Moore / At the New Room / Dublin / +p [i.e.,
    crosspost] Portpatrick'.
Source: holograph; privately held (transcription provided to Frank Baker).

20

To Hester Ann (Roe) Rogers

25

[Newcastle upon Tyne]
May 28, 1788

My Dear Hetty,

My not hearing from you for so long a time would have given me
concern, but I knew it was not from want of affection. I am glad to 30
hear you prosper in your soul. Rest in nothing you have attained,
but press on till you are filled with all the fullness of God.[206]

In this day of God's power, I hope many of the backsliders in
Cork will be brought back. There are great numbers of them in
and about the city, and many are of the genteeler sort. It seems 35
you have a particular mission to these; perhaps they will hear none

---

[203] The plan to enlarge the preaching-house on Whitefriar Street was not carried forward.

[204] Rev. William Mann (c. 1759–1843), ordained as priest by the Bishop of York in 1785,
served as curate to Edward Smyth at Bethesda Chapel through 1794; and from 1803 to his
death Mann was a chaplain at St. Saviour's, Southwark. See Seymour, *Huntingdon*, 2:202; and
JW to Adam Clarke, June 25, 1789.

[205] See Rom. 12:21.

[206] See Phil. 3:13–14.

but you. I hope you have already found out Mrs. Forbes (Captain Forbes's wife), and that now she is more than almost persuaded to be a Christian.

The pearl on my eye is but just discernible, and dulls the sight a
5 little, but not much.[207] As it grows no worse, I do not much regard it.

Mr. [Edward] Smyth's society, I verily believe, will do us no harm. And everyone may speak of *me* as he will. I am just flying away as a shadow. It more than makes me amends that James and you still love
10 and pray for, my dear Hetty,

Your most affectionate,

J. Wesley

15 *Source*: published transcription; Benson, *Works*, 16:267.

To Jasper Winscom
20

Newcastle upon Tyne
May 28, 1788

Dear Jasper,

25 It seems to me the most proper Assistant for the Sarum circuit (only do not talk of it yet) will be Jasper Winscom.[208] I am convinced the person whom I had intended for it is not the proper person. It is exceeding well that the warning was given me before the Conference. We have found it so difficult to drive Calvinism out from
30 among us that we shall not readily let it in again. I am, dear Jasper,

Yours affectionately,

[J. Wesley]

Source: published transcription; Jackson, *Works* (3rd), 12:510.

---

[207] I.e., his cataract; see JW to Henry Moore, Apr. 6, 1788.

[208] As a key lay leader, Winscom may have been the one who informed JW of Calvinist leanings of one of the preachers in the circuit. JW was able to persuade to enter the itinerancy at the 1788 Conference, and be assigned—though not as Assistant—to the Sarum circuit; see 10:645–47 in this edn. Winscom withdrew from itinerancy three years later, unwilling to travel too far from Winchester.

To the Rev. Peard Dickinson

Newcastle upon Tyne
May 29, 1788   5

My Dear Brother,

George Clark and his wife are worth your acquaintance.[209] And
you may pick out three or four out of the select society, whose conversation may be profitable. It if be possible, one would not wish
to be intimate with any that had not a tolerable share, not only of   10
grace, but of understanding. I doubt not your wife ⟨could be⟩ of
use to my poor niece [Sarah], who has hardly [any] acquaintance
that are likely to do her good—unless she knows sister Brown at
Warwick Court. She is a valuable woman indeed.[210]

I have received Miss Freeman's letter, enclosed in that of sister   15
Cock's.[211]

I hope both Betsy and you are exact in your hour of going to bed,
in spite of temptations to the contrary. Be steady. Be exact in all
things! I am,

Your affectionate friend and brother,   20

J. Wesley

Endorsement: by Dickinson, 'May 29th –88 / Soon after our mar[riage]'.[212]
Source: holograph; Bridwell Library (SMU).

---

[209] Clark and his wife Adylena (1727–1807) are interred near the east wall of City Road
Chapel close to the altar. Adylena's maiden name is uncertain.

[210] In a letter to her mother dated Aug. 25, 1788, Sarah Wesley Jr. refers to a Mrs. Brown
in Warwick Court, Grays Inn; held at Pitts Library (Emory), Charles Wesley Family Papers
(MSS 159), 1/27.

[211] If this was a letter from Mary Freeman Shepherd, it is not known to survive. Mary
was currently in Paris and her letters back to England were usually carried by hand, so it is very
possible one went through Guernsey and was forwarded on by Jeanne (Le Gros Bisson) Cock.

[212] Dickinson and Elizabeth Briggs were married on Apr. 30, 1788.

To the Rev. William Turner Jr.[213]

May 29, 1788

Reverend Sir,

I exceedingly approve of that excellent institution, and will recommend it to the uttermost of my power. Doubtless inoculation has already preserved thousands of lives, and I trust will preserve thousands more. In your little tract you have given a sufficient answer to the most plausible objections.

Wishing you all success in your undertakings, I am, reverend sir,
Your affectionate servant,

J. Wesley

Source: holograph; Topeka, Kansas, Kansas Historical Society, Menninger Historic Psychiatry Collection, Misc. Box 1-4.

To Sarah Wesley Jr.[214]

Newcastle upon Tyne
May 29, 1788

My Dear Sally,

How often does our Lord say to us, by his adorable providence, 'What I do thou knowest not now, but thou shalt know hereafter!'[215] And how unspeakable is our gain if we learn only this: To *trust* God further than we can *see* him! But this is a stroke that you have long

---

[213] JW was replying to Turner's letter of May 25. Rev. William Turner (1761–1859) was pastor of the Independent (Unitarian) Chapel on Hanover Square in Newcastle. He was active in the anti-slave trade movement and other causes. On learning that JW had just arrived in Newcastle, he wrote asking JW to help remove objections to inoculation while in town. Turner enclosed two pamphlets: Newcastle upon Tyne, Committee for General Inoculation, *Report of the Committee* (s.n., 1786); and William Turner, *An Attempt to Alleviate the Principal Objections to Inoculation; in a Sermon* (Newcastle: T. Saint, 1787). It is unclear whether JW was aware of accusations that Methodists were prone to reject inoculations—like that in the letter of 'Benevolus' to the *Hampshire Chronicle*, Sept. 19, 1787 (see in-letters).

[214] JW is replying to Sarah's letter of May 24, 1788.

[215] John 13:7.

expected. One of fourscore has lived out his date of years.[216] And it is not strange that he is taken away, but that I am still left!

The great lesson which you have now to learn is, 'Take no thought for the morrow.'[217] If you do, your fault brings its own punishment. You are to live today. You have still a friend, the medicine of life! And you have your great Friend always at hand. There is a rule for *you*; 'When I am in heaviness, I will think upon God.'[218] And it is not lost labour.

May the peace of God rest upon you! So prays

  Yours in tender affection,

         J. Wesley

Address: 'To / Miss Wesley'.
Source: holograph; MARC, DDWes 5/21.

To the Trustees of the Millbourn Preaching-House[219]

         Sunderland
         May 31, 1788

My Dear Brethren,

All that you desire (unless I mistake) is the very thing that I desire and design to do. I desire that your house shall be just as the other, and our preachers shall meet the society, hold lovefeasts, and keep watch-nights in them alternately. If in anything I should give the preference to either, certainly I would to the house in Millbourn Place. What do I want but to do you all the good I can in my few remaining days? We have loved one another long, and God forbid that anything should now part you and

  Your affectionate brother,

         John Wesley

Source: published transcription; Coates, *New Portrait*, 29–30.

---

[216] CW was a couple of months past his 80th birthday when he died.

[217] Matt. 6:34.

[218] Ps. 77:3 (BCP).

[219] JW's vacillation between the two preaching houses in Newcastle was continuing, with him suggesting now that preachers would meet in both, but on an alternating schedule (see the note on JW to Edward Coates, Jan. 31, 1787). The trustees of the chapel on Millbourn Place were still balking at adopting the Model Deed unless the Conference paid off their debt.

To Mary Blachford[220]

[Sunderland]
June 3, 1788

I am glad, my dear maid, that you have some remembrance of me.[221] I love you tenderly. And the more, because you are dutiful to your mamma, and willing to be guided by her in all things. The very thought of you is always agreeable to, my dear Mary,

Yours affectionately,

J. Wesley

Address: 'To Miss Blachford'.[222]
Source: holograph; Drew, Methodist Archives.

To Theodosia (Tighe) Blachford[223]

Sunderland
June 3, 1788

My Dear Mrs. Blachford,

You state the case clearly and fairly. And when this is done, there is no great difficulty in it. Many other objections, and plausible

[220] Mary Blachford (1772–1810) was the daughter of Theodosia (Tighe) Blachford. Her mother, a strong advocate of liberal education for women, encouraged Mary to read widely in English, French, and Italian literature, history, and philosophy. In addition to her intellect, Mary was blessed with great beauty. By 15 she was attracting so much attention that her mother was open to an early marriage to a (seemingly) pious man who might enable Mary to pursue a life of study (see JW's attached letter to her mother). Instead, Mary became entangled romantically with her first cousin, Henry Tighe (1771–1836) of Rossana, a son of William and Sarah (Fownes) Tighe. Henry fell madly in love with Mary when he returned from school in England, and drew her away from a contemplative life into the social life of Dublin. Mary wed Henry in 1793, not out of love but because close family connections and his violent passion made refusal difficult. The marriage was unhappy, and childless; but Mary emerged as a leading poet of her time, before dying of tuberculosis. See Linkin, *Mary Blachford Tighe*.

[221] JW had surely seen Mary when he was last in Dublin, in June 1787, as she mentions getting a short letter from him (not known to survive) in mid-Feb. 1788; see ibid., 28.

[222] Written at the top of the page; as part of a double letter to her mother.

[223] In Feb. 1788 Jean de la Fléchère (Rev. John Fletcher's twenty-two year old nephew, who had been visiting Madeley; see note on JW to Mary Fletcher, Jan. 9, 1788) made a visit to Dublin and was enchanted by Mary Blachford—proposing within a month. Theodosia was initially open to this proposal, but this letter highlights the factors that contributed to Mary rejecting the proposal in Jan. 1789, and Jean returning to Switzerland (where he married a Swiss woman in 1792). See Linkin, *Mary Blachford Tighe*, 5–6, 446. An endorsement by an unknown hand on the back of the letter appears to read 'of Fletcher 2'.

ones, might be made to the proposal. But certainly those two are
the strongest of all and the most difficult to be answered: first, her
youth and little experience in the things of the world; and secondly,
his little experience in the things of God. He has made a good beginning. He has set out well. But who can tell what the end will be?   5
By reason of the time, we cannot suppose him to be much established yet. And if he should afterwards relapse into his former state,
what an insupportable trial must it be to her! In a strange country
and separate from all her religious friends! Upon the whole, therefore, I cannot but subscribe to your judgment that you must do   10
nothing suddenly. I am, my dear sister,

  Yours most affectionately,

            John Wesley

Address: 'To / Mrs Blashford / At No. 29, Dominick street / Dublin / +p
 [i.e., crosspost] Portpatrick'.   15
Postmarks: 'Durham' and 'JU/8'.
Source: holograph; Drew, Methodist Archives.

                  20

To Christopher Hopper[224]

           Newcastle upon Tyne
             June 3, 1788   25
My Dear Brother,
 I said nothing, *less* or *more*, in Bradford church concerning the
end of the world; neither concerning *my own* opinion.[225] What I
said was that Bengelius had given it as *his* opinion (not that *the world*
would then end, but) that the millennial reign of Christ would *begin*   30
in the year 1836.[226] I have no opinion at all upon that head. I can

---

[224] On Sunday, May 4, 1788, JW preached in the parish church in Bradford, Yorkshire,
at the invitation of his friend Rev. John Crosse, the vicar. He preached on the epistle reading
assigned in the lectionary: 1 Pet. 4:7, 'The end of all things is at hand' (see *Journal*, 24:80–81
in this edn.). Two weeks later an unsympathetic account of this sermon was published in the
Leeds Intelligencer (see c. May 20, 1788 in in-letters file) and reprinted in other newspapers,
claiming that JW asserted the world would end in 1836, and exhorted his followers to heighten
their evangelistic efforts. When Hopper saw the report, doubting its accuracy, he wrote JW
inquiring what had been said.
 [225] The published versions substitute '… opinion, but what follows: That …' for '…
opinion. What I said was that …'. Some published versions also add italics to several words.
 [226] See JW's acknowledgement of his reliance upon, yet reservations about, Johann Al-
brecht Bengel's scholarship, in the introduction to the book of Revelation in *NT Notes*.

determine nothing about it. These calculations are far above, out
of my sight. I have only one thing to do: To save my own soul and
those that hear me.[227]

I am, with kind love to sister [Ann] Hopper,
5   Yours affectionately,

J. Wesley

Source: holograph; Manchester, Rylands, English Ms 345/122.[228]

10

To Henry Moore

15

near Newcastle
June 7, 1788

Dear Henry,

I incline to think the battle's over, and you will have peace, pro-
20   vided that none of you return railing for railing, but contrariwise
blessing.[229] Beware of showing any coolness to Arthur Keene. You
must conquer him by love. I am glad you have not lost Mrs. [Theo-
dosia] Blachford. She is one of our jewels. I love her much. Only
you will excuse me if I do not love her so well as Nancy and Becky
25   Moore.[230]

Now use all your influence in prevailing on our people to attend
on the sacrament at St. Patrick's monthly. I am, dear Henry, yours
and my Nancy's
Affectionate friend and brother,

30   J. Wesley

---

[227] See 1 Tim. 4:16.

[228] Hopper sent out transcriptions of this letter specifically to the *Manchester Mercury*
(June 17, 1788), p. 4; Felix Farley's *Bristol Journal* (June 21, 1788), p. 1; and the *Leeds Intelligencer* (June 24, 1788), p. 3. Reprints appeared in *Bath Chronicle and Weekly Gazette* (June 19,
1788), p. 3; *General Evening Post* (June 19, 1788), p. 7; *St James's Chronicle* (June 19, 1788), p.
4; *Whitehall Evening Post* (June 19, 1788), p. 1; *Kentish Gazette* (June 20, 1788), p. 4; *Reading
Mercury* (June 21, 1788), p. 4; *Sheffield Register* (June 21, 1788), p. 4; *Aris's Birmingham Gazette*
(June 23, 1788), p. 3; *Hereford Journal* (June 26, 1788), p. 1; and *Chelmsford Chronicle* (June 27,
1788), p. 4.

[229] See 1 Pet. 3:9.

[230] Henry's wife and sister.

Address: 'To / Mr Moore / At the New Room / in / Dublin / +p [i.e., crosspost] Portpatrick'.
Postmarks: 'Newcastle' and 'JW/12'.
Source: holograph; MARC, WCB, D6/1/130b.

To Thomas Taylor

near Newcastle
June 7, 1788

Dear Tommy,

I have no time to spend on controversy about the Church, unless I had leisure to write a folio.

You did well in sending your daughters to Cork.[231] It will very probably re-establish their health.

It is no wonder that everyone should be ruined who concerns himself with that execrable bill trade.[232] In London I expel everyone out of our society who has anything to do with it. Whoever endorses a bill (that is, promises to pay) for more than he is worth is either a fool or a knave. I hope this affliction at Manchester will be the means of saving many souls.

Peace be with you and yours! I am, dear Tommy,
Your affectionate friend and brother,

J. Wesley

Address: 'To / Mr Taylor / At the Preachinghouse / in / Manchester / Crosspost'.
Postmark: 'Newcastle'. *Charge*: '5'.
Endorsement: 'P. Bibles / the Money'.
Source: holograph; MARC, MA 1992/035.

[231] Thomas and Ann (Dupuy) Taylor had two daughters. The eldest was Paulina Horne Taylor (1769–1801), the younger was Ann Dupuy Taylor (see JW's letters to her of Jan. 12, 1787 and Aug. 2, 1788).

[232] See the note on JW to Samuel Bradburn, Nov. 6, 1781; 29:696 in this edn.

To Jane (Lee) Freeman

Whitby
June 13, 1788

My Dear Sister,

If all the members of our society could be persuaded to attend St. Patrick's Church, we should not need the Sunday service at the New Room.[233] I wish you would always attend the Church, except when I am in Dublin; unless you choose to make another [exception], namely when Dr. [Thomas] Coke is in Dublin.[234]

I commend you and yours to him that loves you; and am, my dear Jenny,

Your affectionate brother,

J. Wesley

Source: holograph; MARC, MAM JW 3/10.

To John Francis Valton

Whitby
June 13, 1788

My Dear Brother,

I am [glad] to hear there is one more call to poor Barton(?).[235] It seemed to be a devoted place.

I do not know why Bath circuit may not be one, and Bristol circuit another. But you may be a supernumerary still.

It is not unlikely, if I live till autumn, that I shall accept your kind invitation for a day or two.[236] I shall be glad if I live to finish this Conference. I believe I shall; but I do not depend upon seeing another. I am, with love to sister [Judith] Valton,

Your affectionate friend and brother,

J. Wesley

---

[233] I.e., the preaching-house on Whitefriar Street.

[234] Note that JW's exception is when a Church of England/Ireland clergyman is there to lead the Sunday service, according to the BCP, at the Methodist house.

[235] JW's script is shaky. Barton, Somerset is a possibility.

[236] Valton's letter which invited JW to stay at his house is not known to survive.

Address: 'To / Mr. Valton / At the New Room / Bristol'.
Source: holograph; Duke, Rubenstein, Frank Baker Collection of Wesleyana, Box WF3 (Ann Eliza Fourness autograph book).

To Walter Churchey

Whitby 10
June 14, 1788

My Dear Brother,

Yours of May 24 overtook me here this morning.[237] But I have not received the parcel which you say was sent by the coach.[238] And very probably I shall not receive it, unless it pleases God to bring me back to London.

Health is wonderfully continued. Only I am in the fashion—I have a little of the rheumatism.

The case of that old woman was very remarkable. It is a true saying, 'None are ruined while they are out of hell.'

One would be sorry for the death of George Jarvis, only that we know that God does all things well.[239] If Mr. [William] Holmes has any money of mine in his hands, I desire he would give you a guinea for the widow.[240]

Peace be with you and yours! I am

Your affectionate brother,

J. Wesley

Address: 'To / Mr W-r Churchey / Near the Hay / Brecon'. 30
Postmark: 'Whitby'.
Endorsement: by Churchey, '1788 / 14 June – Mr. J. W. / various'.
Source: holograph; MARC, MAM JW 2/42.

---

[237] This letter is not known to survive.

[238] The parcel contained several of Churchey's poems, in manuscript; see JW to Churchey, July 22, 1788.

[239] See Mark 7:37. George Jarvis (1753–88) was buried May 28, 1788 in Hay, Breconshire.

[240] George Jarvis married Elizabeth Day on May 23, 1779 in Hay, Breconshire.

To Jasper Winscom

Whitby
June 14, 1788

5　My Dear Brother,

Mr. [John] Wesley desires you will call (the first possible opportunity) on Mr. Henry Voysey, in Sarum, and pay him on Mr. Wesley's account twenty pounds, and take a receipt.[241] I am happy to inform you Mr. Wesley is remarkably well. I most cordially wish 10　you every good and perfect gift and am, with love to Mrs. Winscom and yourself,[242]

Yours most affectionately,

Jos. Bradford

Source: published transcription; *WHS* 14 (1924): 135.

15

To an Unidentified Man

20　　　　　　　　　　　　　　　　　　　　　Whitby
June 14, 1788

Sir,

I am afraid there will not be much contributed by the poor congregation at Derby. However, I propose to do what I can in favour 25　of so excellent a charity. Therefore I hope to preach there for the benefit of the General Hospital in my return to London; namely, at 5:00 in the evening, on Friday, the 11th of July.[243] That morning I am to come from Sheffield, and on Saturday to be at Nottingham. I am, sir,

30　　　　Your obedient servant,

John Wesley

Source: holograph; MARC, MA 2005/010 (MARC, MAM JW 1/1A).

[241] Orig., 'Henery Veysey'. Henry Voysey (1753–1829) married Anna Maria Ellison (1753–1836) in 1781. Anna Maria, was another great niece of JW—the daughter of Richard Annesley Ellison (1730–54) and his wife Hannah; the grand-daughter of Susanna (Wesley) Ellison and her husband Richard.

[242] Mary (Butler) Winscom (1744–1809), Jasper's second wife.'

[243] JW fulfilled this pledge—see his *Journal*, July 11, 1788, 24:407 in this edn.; and *Derby Mercury* (July 17, 1778), p. 3 (which says he raised £5). General Hospital in Nottingham, near Derby, had opened in 1782 to serve invalids from any part of England. It was supported by an annual subscription and donations. JW had preached charity sermons for it in 1784 and 1787 in Nottingham; apparently someone in Derby had suggested that they do their part. See *WHS* 5 (1906): 163–64.

To Henry Moore

Scarborough
Monday, June 16, 1788

Dear Henry,

On Saturday next, and on Saturday sennight, I expect to be at Epworth, near Thorne, Yorkshire; on Monday, July 7, at Doncaster, Yorkshire; and on Monday the 14th at London.

These meetings will do you no harm at all. Only go quietly on your way. There should be no delay in enlarging the house if you can get a good title to the ground.[244] As far as is possible I should advise you to take no notice, good or bad, of the warm men. Let them say what they will and do what they can.

Neddy Smyth wrote curtly to me, and I to him; but without a word of dispute.[245] Probably I shall see Mr. William Smyth. But if I do, I will not dispute with him. I am a man of peace.

Peace be with you and yours. I am, dear Henry,
    Your affectionate friend and brother,

J. Wesley

Address: 'To / Mr Moore / At the New Room / in / Dublin'.
Postmarks: 'Scarborough', 'JU/19/88', and 'JU/25'.
Source: holograph; MARC, WCB, D6/1/132a.

To Henry Brooke

Hull
June 21, 1788

Of the Methodists and the Church I think as you do: they *must* not leave the Church, at least, while I live; if they leave it *then*, I expect they will gradually sink into a formal, honourable sect.

Dear Harry,
    Adieu!

Source: secondary manuscript transcription; MARC, MA 1977/489, p. 24.

---

[244] See JW to Moore, May 28, 1788.
[245] Neither of these letters is known to survive.

To the Rev. Peard Dickinson[246]

[Thirsk]
June 24, 1788

5 My Dear Brother,

I do not know any little piece of news which has given me more satisfaction than this, that my sister [Martha] Hall has taken a lodging in Th[omas] Philips' house. I hope to see her and you in about a fortnight, that I may have time to prepare for the Conference.

10 You do well not to indulge your thirst after books, but to confine yourself to a very few. I know no commentator on the Bible equal to Bengalius. His *Gnomon* is a jewel.[247] So is his *Ordo Temporum*: the finest system of chronology that ever appeared in the world.[248]

Now consider with yourself and write down whatever relates to the Conference.

15 Peace be with both your spirits![249] I am

Your affectionate friend and brother,

J. Wesley

Address: 'To / the Revd Mr Dickinson / In the City Road / near
20   Moorfields / London'.
Postmarks: 'Thirsk' and 'JU/27/88'.
Endorsement: by Dickinson; 'June 24th 88 / Mrs Hall's Lodg. / Conference'.
Source: holograph; Godalming, Surrey, Charterhouse School, Archive
     0532/2.

25

To Capt. Richard Williams

near York
30   June 24, 1788

My Dear Brother,

Dr. [Thomas] Coke has been soliciting Joseph Sutcliffe to go to the American islands.[250] But I cannot consent to it in any wise. He has

---

[246] JW was replying to a letter from Dickinson that is not known to survive.

[247] Johann Bengel, *Gnomon Novi Testamenti* (Tübingen: H. Philip Schram, 1742).

[248] Johann Bengel, *Ordo Temporum; a principio per periodos oeconomiae divinae* (Stuttgart: Erhard, 1741).

[249] Dickinson and his wife Elizabeth.

[250] I.e., the West Indies. Orig., 'John' Sutcliff; a slip. Joseph Sutcliffe (c. 1762–1856) entered itinerant ministry in 1786; see 10:597, fn. 172 in this edn.). He was currently stationed on the St. Ives circuit and returned there the following year, to introduce Methodism to the Scilly Isles. Sutcliffe went on to serve seventy years in itinerancy. See Vickers, *Dictionary*, 342–43; *Minutes* (post-Wesley, 1859), 13:211–12; and *WHS* 17 (1930): 123–24.

work enough nearer home. I will send an additional preacher into the St. Ives circuit, and they will go by turns into the Isles of Scilly.

If we live till the Conference, I will talk with George Shadford. And then we shall easily determine where it will be best for him to be?[251] I am,

Your affectionate brother,

J. Wesley

Address: 'To / Capt. R[ichar]d Williams / At Crahaddock[252] / Near Truro / Cornwall'.
Postmark: 'Thirsk'.
Source: holograph; Duke, Rubenstein, Wesley Family Papers, Box 1.

To Walter Churchey

York
June 26, 1788

My Dear Brother,

I answered your last.[253] By what means my letter miscarried I cannot tell.

Above half of that paragraph (which has travelled over most of the kingdom) is very true. The other half is a blunder. What I spoke was a citation from Bengelius, who thought, not that *the world would end*, but that *the millennium would begin* about the year 1836.[254] Not that I affirm this myself, nor ever did. I do not determine any of these things. They *are* too high for me. I only desire to creep on in 'the vale of humble love'.[255]

Peace be with you and yours! I am

Your affectionate brother,

J. Wesley

Address: 'To / Mr Walter Churchey / near the Hay / Brecon'.
Postmarks: 'York' and 'JU/28/88'.
Endorsement: by Churchey, '1788 / June 26 – Mr. J. W. / millenium'.
Source: holograph; Bridwell Library (SMU).

[251] Shadford was currently Assistant of the Redruth circuit; he was appointed Assistant of St. Ives by the 1788 Conference.

[252] Likely means Carharrack.

[253] See JW to Churchey, June 14, 1788.

[254] Churchey's letter to JW about the sermon at Bradford is not known to survive. See JW's earlier response to Christopher Hopper, June 3, 1788.

[255] CW, Hymn on Matt. 5:13, *l.* 8, *Scripture Hymns* (1762), 2:132.

To Adam Clarke[256]

York
June 26, 1788

5   Dear Adam,
I really think the temper and behaviour of the bailiff is little less than miraculous.[257] I will give you ten pounds. Follow those little advices in building which are set down in the *Large Minutes*.[258]
So you stole a match! Mrs. Cooke's not opposing did, indeed,
10   remove the grand hindrance.[259] I pray do not suffer my dear Molly to be idle. Let her active spirit have full employment.
But what becomes of Jenny Bisson (that was)?[260]
I fear your bewitched boy will prove an errant cheat; if not, the French convert too.[261]
15   I am, dear Adam,
Your affectionate friend and brother,

J. Wesley

Address: 'To / Mr Adam Clark / In St. Helier's / Isle of Jersey'.
Postmark: 'York'.
20   *Source*: holograph; MARC, WCB, D6/1/104.[262]

To Sarah Wesley Jr.[263]

25

Grimsby
June 30, 1788

My Dear Sally,
Hemlock I do not at all approve of. It is a very dangerous medi-
30   cine. I doubt whether sea-bathing would reach an internal complaint; I cannot conceive how it should.

---

[256] JW is replying to Clarke's letter of June 2, 1788 (in-files), and (apparently) a second letter not known to survive.

[257] William Le Marchant (1721–1809) was the bailiff of Guernsey (1771–1800). Clarke had informed JW of the financial and other support Le Marchant was providing for building a preaching house in St. Peter Port, Guernsey.

[258] 'Large' *Minutes* (1770), §68, 10:896–97 in this edn.

[259] Clarke had described to JW his marriage to Mary Cooke on Apr. 17, 1788; stressing that her mother, Mary (Pitney) Cooke, now made no objection.

[260] Jeanne (Le Gros Bisson) Cock.

[261] These two accounts were apparently in a separate letter, so the details are unclear.

[262] The holograph that survives is incomplete, beginning with 'I pray do not'. The full text appeared for Dunn, *Clarke* (1863), 63.

[263] The letter from Sarah to which JW was replying is not known to survive.

Although quicksilver compounded with salts is a very strong
poison, yet unmixed it is as innocent as milk;[264] especially when
an ounce of it is taken in the morning and ten drops of elixir of
vitriol in a glass of water at 3:00 or 4:00 in the afternoon. You may
safely use this or the diet drink prescribed in the *Primitive Physic*   5
for 'scorbutic sores'.[265]

The Sunday schools have been of great use in every part of England, and to assist in any of them is a noble employment. But perhaps one less fatiguing would suit you better. Perhaps the being the
leader of a little class, if I can find a few agreeable young women.   10

God does not expect us to be sticks or stones. We may *grieve* and
yet not *murmur*.[266] It is very possible to *feel* and still *resign*. And this
is Christian resignation.

On Monday, July 14, I expect to be in town. If I can, I will endeavour to be in Chesterfield Street on Tuesday.   15

My dear Sally,
    Adieu!

Address: 'To / Miss Wesley / At the Revd Mr Dickinson's / City Road,
    Moorfields / London'.   20
Postmarks: 'Grimsby' and 'JY/3/88'. *Charge*: '6'.
Endorsement: by Sarah, 'June 30. 1788'.
Source: holograph; Garrett-Evangelical, Methodist Manuscripts Collection.

25

To Samuel Bradburn

Epworth
July 6, 1788   30

Dear Sammy,

Tomorrow evening I hope to be at Doncaster; on Wednesday at
Sheffield; and tomorrow se'nnight at London, bringing my daugh-
ter with me.[267] That evening I should not object to preaching at
West Street. On Tuesday morning I would breakfast in Chesterfield   35

---

[264] JW actually tended to avoid prescribing mercury; see *Primitive Physic*, Postscript I,
§3, 32:120 in this edn.

[265] I.e., Ailment §198, receipt #1, 32:226 in this edn.

[266] See 1 Cor. 10:10.

[267] JW was referring to his step-granddaughter, Jane Vazeille Smith (1770–1849), the
daughter of William and Jane (Vazeille / Matthews) Smith, who was travelling with JW from
Newcastle down to London; see *Journal*, July 11, 1788, 24:102 in this edn.

Street, if my sister will be ready at eight o'clock.[268] Then I must
hide myself till Sunday. I will preach at one or the other chapel for
Kingswood.[269]

Peace be with you and yours! I am, dear Sammy,
5   Your affectionate friend and brother,

J. Wesley

Address: 'To / Mr Bradburn / At the New Chapel / Near Moorfields /
London'.[270]
10   *Source*: holograph; Oxford, Lincoln College, Archive, MS/WES/A/9.

To the Rev. Thomas Cursham

Derby
July 12, 1788

Dear Sir,
20   I am glad you sent your sermon and the conditions of your
school.[271] Something of the kind was much wanted among us. Persons are frequently inquiring of me for what school they can send
their children. I judge they may very safely intrust them with *you*.

I wish you good success in all your undertakings, and I am, dear
25 sir,
Your affectionate brother

J. Wesley

Address: 'To The Revd Mr Cursham, Schoolmaster, Sutton in Ashfield,
30   Notts'.
Source: holograph; privately held (WWEP Archive holds digital copy).

---

[268] I.e., his sister-in-law, Sarah (Gwynne) Wesley.

[269] That is, for the annual collection taken to support Kingswood school.

[270] The address is taken from Telford, *Letters*, 7:70; since the holograph is now mounted
and the back not accessible.

[271] The sermon enclosed was Cursham's *Ministerial Reproof and Warning: in a sermon
preached at Ashover Church, June 17, 1787* (Sheffield: J. Brunt, 1788). While Cursham had been
operating his boarding school for a decade, he apparently reached out to JW to recruit Methodist students. He included with the letter a description that read: 'Young gentlemen are genteelly
boarded, and carefully taught the English, Latin, and Greek languages; Writing in all its various
hands, Arithmetic, Merchant's Accounts, the use of the globes, Algebra, etc., for 14 Guineas a
Year and a Guinea Entrance.'

To Henry Moore

London
July 16, 1788

Dear Henry,   5
Take your choice. Either let my dear Nancy Moore come with
you hither, or follow you to Bristol.[272] If not here, I would fain see
her there, because I expect to finish my course within a year, probably either here or there. But to have her with me at the close would
be one of the greatest comforts I could have, next to the favour and   10
presence of God.[273]
I am, my own Henry,
Your ever affectionate,

J. Wesley
15

Address: 'To / Mr Moore / At the New Room / Dublin'.
Postmarks: 'JY/16/88' and 'JY/22'.
Source: holograph; MARC, WCB, D6/1/132b.

20

To Mrs. Martha Ward

London   25
July 6, 1788

My Dear Sister,
You do well in writing freely to me upon whatever occurs to your
mind.[274] And you should lose no time, for probably the time is at
hand when I shall be called to 'arise and go hence'.[275] I hardly expect   30
to see another May, or perhaps the end of another March. But be
that as God pleases.

My remnant of days
I spend in his praise
Who died the whole world to redeem;   35

---

[272] See JW to Moore, May 17, 1788.
[273] Two lines of text here, and a closing postscript, have been thoroughly marked out
(likely in a later hand than JW's).
[274] Ward's letter is not known to survive, but the disagreement over worship during
church hours had found its way to Cork; see JW to Ward, Aug. 2, 1788.
[275] Cf. John 14:31.

> Be they many, or few,
> My days are his due,
> And they all are devoted to him.[276]

5   For upwards of fifty years my language respecting the Church has been just the same as it is now. Yet whenever I am removed, there can be no doubt but some of the Methodists will separate from it and set up independent meetings. Some will accept of livings.[277] The rest (who will, I trust, be the largest third) will continue to-

10   gether on the itinerant plan; and if they abide by their old rules, God will give them his blessing.

     It has been the glory of Methodists to assist all parties without forming any. In so doing, God has abundantly blessed them. What could he have done more for them than he has done? Do not they

15   know when they are well? Mr. [James] Rogers should do all that is in his power to quiet the minds of our people.

     Your son Richard goes on well.[278] He will be a preacher, either regular or irregular. I think we can make room at Kingswood for the children you mention.

20   Peace be with you and yours. I am, my dear sister,
> Yours most affectionately,

[J. Wesley]

25 *Source*: published transcription; Telford, *Letters*, 8:71.

To Jasper Winscom[279]

30

London
July 16, 1788

Dear Jasper,

35   If all our society at Portsmouth or elsewhere separate from the Church, I cannot help it. But I will not. Therefore I can in no wise consent to the having our service in church hours. *You* used to love

---

[276] CW, 'On His Birthday', st. 14, *HSP* (1749), 2:259.

[277] That is, become clergy in the established Church.

[278] Richard Ward was briefly a student at Kingswood school (see Hastling et al., *Kingswood*, Appendix, 117). He never became an itinerant.

[279] Winscom's letter, to which JW was replying, is not known to survive.

the Church; then keep to it. And exhort all our people to do the same.

If it be true that brother Hayter is used to talking against the other preachers, as well as against Thomas Warwick, brother Hayter and I shall not agree.[280] Of dividing circuits we may speak at the Conference.

I am, dear Jasper,
Your affectionate brother,

J. Wesley

Address: 'To / Mr Jasper Winscom / At the Preachinghouse / in / Sarum'.[281]

Source: holograph; WHS Ireland Archives.

To Francis Wrigley[282]

London
July 16, 1788

My Dear Brother,

You judge right. There is a snake in the grass. Some of the preachers are at the bottom of this senseless opposition to that excellent deed. If it be possible, find out who they are. But if you do, *your* name shall never be brought into question concerning it.

You are right likewise concerning this continual dividing and subdividing of circuits.[283] This likewise will come naturally into consideration if we should live till the Conference.

---

[280] George Hayter had been serving as a local preacher since the early 1780s; see Dyson, *Isle of Wight*, 114, 123–25. He was appointed to serve as a travelling preacher, under Thomas Warrick, by the 1787 Conference, but his name was later struck out and he never reappears; see 10:625 fn. 261 in this edn. See also the report of Hayter's attacks upon Warrick in the letter from several members of the society in Newport, July 17, 1788.

[281] The address is revised to forward the letter to Portsmouth.

[282] JW was replying to Wrigley's letter of July 11, 1788, in which Wrigley mentioned that some travelling preachers were encouraging building of preaching houses without use of the 'model deed' approved by Conference; see 'Large' *Minutes* (1763), §67, 10:868–70 in this edn.

[283] Wrigley argued that it made Methodists more dependent on wealthy donors for the required preaching-houses, and encouraged preachers to stay several days in one location (while preaching only every second or third day).

Sister Dillon has no claim to anything from our fund.[284] She knows it well. But we commonly make her a present once a year.

I am, dear Franky,

Your affectionate friend and brother,

5

J. Wesley

Address: 'To / Mr Wrigley / At the Preachinghouse / In Blackburn / Lancashire'.

Postmark: 'JY/17/88'.

10

Source: holograph; New York, Pierpont Morgan Library, MA 516.15.

15

To the Rev. Richard Whatcoat[285]

London

July 17, 1788

20

My Dear Brother,

I am never so busy as not to steal a little time to remember my friends.[286]

I have not heard of your taking any step which I disapprove of. It was not *your* fault that you did not reach the office which I assigned

25

you.

Brother [Thomas] Vasey is very desirous of being stationed either in the English or Irish circuit, and I believe it will be every way for his good. He will be both more holy and more happy than in his American living.[287]

---

[284] Elizabeth Dillon, the widow of the itinerant John Dillon, was receiving yearly support from the designated fund of Conference; this was apparently a different woman.

[285] JW had ordained Whatcoat for service in North America in Sept. 1784. In his letter of Sept. 6, 1786 to Thomas Coke, JW instructed Coke to call a Conference of The Methodist Episcopal Church for May 1, 1787, and announce there that Whatcoat was being appointed as a Superintendent alongside Francis Asbury. When this Conference was held, the American preachers not only refused to accept the appointment of Whatcoat, they voted to remove a paragraph from their initial set of *Minutes* adopted in Dec. 1784 that read 'During the life of Rev. Mr. Wesley, we acknowledge ourselves his sons in the gospel, ready in matters belonging to church government to obey his commands.' See *Minutes of Several Conversations between the Rev. Thomas Coke, LL. D. the Rev. Francis Asbury and Others* (Philadelphia: Charles Cist, 1785), 3; and Lee, *Short History*, 126–27.

[286] Whatcoat's letter to JW is not known to survive.

[287] Vasey's letter to JW expressing this is not known to survive. He returned to England in 1788 and served Methodist circuits, including his last 14 years as a reader at City Road Chapel.

In various parts of England, as well as in America, God has lately raised up many young men who are full of life and fire, and have spread the fire of love wherever their lot was cast.

It was not well-judged by brother [Francis] Asbury to *suffer*, much less *secretly*[288] to encourage that foolish step in the late Conference. Every preacher present ought both in duty and in prudence to have said, 'Brother Asbury, Mr. Wesley is *your* father, consequently ours; and we will affirm this in the face of all the world.' It is truly probable the disavowing *me* will, as soon as my head is laid, occasion a total breach between the English and American Methodists. They will naturally say, 'If they can do without *us*, we can do without *them*.' But they would find a greater difference than they imagine. Next would follow a separation between themselves. Well, whatever may fall out tomorrow, let you and I live today! I am, dear Richard,

Your affectionate friend and brother,

J. Wesley

Address: 'To / The Revd Mr Whatcoat / At Philip Rogers', Esq. / In Baltimore / Maryland / Post p[ai]d to New York'.
Source: holograph; Garrett-Evangelical, Methodist Manuscripts Collection.

To Walter Churchey

near London
July 22, 1788

My Dear Brother,

I am glad you spoke to Mr. Cowper.[289] What pity is it that such talents as his should be employed in so useless a manner![290]

Mr. [Samuel] Bradburn delivered your papers to me a few days ago.[291] But this is so busy a time that I had not time to go through them till today! In the translation of 'The Art of Painting' there

---

[288] The word 'indirectly' is written above 'secretly'. The latter is not struck out, making it unclear if JW intended it as an alternative, or meant '*secretly indirectly*'.

[289] Churchey shared some of his verse with the poet William Cowper (1731–1800), who wrote Churchey on Dec. 13, 1786, commending his talent and encouraging him to publish; see *The Works of William Cowper* (London: H. G. Bohn, 1854), 3:370–71.

[290] JW is referring to Cowper's farcical pieces like 'The Diverting History of John Gilpin'.

[291] The parcel Churchey had sent, containing his poetry; see JW to Churchey, June 14, 1788.

are many very good lines. But there are some that want a good deal
of filing, and many that are obscure. This is the general fault. The
sense is so much crowded that it is not easy to be understood. For
many years I have not had any bookseller but Mr. [John] Atlay, and
5   my Assistants. I doubt whether any bookseller will buy Fresnoy.[292]
Some of the shorter copies are good sense and good poetry.

My brother has left a translation of the Book of Psalms, and verses enough to make up at least six volumes in duodecimo.[293] I could
but ill spare him, now I am myself so far declined into the vale of
10 years. But it is the Lord, let him do what seemeth him good.[294]

Our time is now short. Let my dear sister [Mary] Churchey and
you and I make the best of it. I am

Your affectionate brother,

J. Wesley

15

Address: 'To / Mr Churchey, Attorney at law / Near the Hay / Brecon'.
Postmark: 'JY/22/88'. *Charge*: '6'.
Endorsement: by Churchey, 'Mr J. W. July 22 1788 / Critique on the Mss.'.
Source: holograph; MARC, MAM JW 2/43.
20

To William Kilburn[295]

25

London
July 22, 1788

My Dear Brother,
30   I am glad to receive a letter from *you* on any account, because I
love you and always did. I think you will have reason to praise God
for your preachers the ensuing year.[296] And we shall not be unwill-

---

[292] The poem of which Churchey was apparently most proud was an English translation
of Charles-Alphonse Dufresnoy's *De arte graphica*, published in 1695. It appeared as the first
time in Churchey's *Poems and Imitations of the British Poets* (London: G. Paramore, 1789), with
a dedication to the king and running nearly one hundred pages. JW was suggesting that no
printer would publish it as a stand-alone book.

[293] See MS Psalms, the manuscript collections on each of the four gospels, etc.

[294] See 1 Sam. 3:18.

[295] William Kilburn is listed as one of the lay leaders in Norwich in Thomas Wride's letter
to JW of Dec. 29, 1785.

[296] The 1788 Conference assigned John Poole as Assistant for the Norwich circuit, serving with Richard Reece and Thomas Kelk.

ing to help you a little further. By-and-by you will be able to help yourselves. Only love one another and serve God in earnest. I am
> Your affectionate brother,
>> [J. Wesley]

Address: 'To / Mr W. H. Kilburn / At the Preachinghouse / In Norwich'.
Source: published transcription; Telford, *Letters*, 8:75.

To Catherine Warren

> near London
> July 22, 1788

My Dear Sister,

Our Conference is to begin on the 29th instant, and will continue till the middle of the next week.[297] I purpose, if God continues my life and health, to leave London the Monday following—namely, August the 4th. But I must go round by Portsmouth in order to open the new preaching-house.

So that I expect my little journey through Wales will run thus: Friday, August the 8th, Monmouth;[298] Saturday, 9th, Brecon; Monday, 18th, Carmarthen; Tuesday, 12th, Llangwain;[299] Wednesday, 13th, Haverfordwest; Saturday, 16th, Pembroke; Monday, 18th, Carmarthen; Tuesday, 19th, Swansea; Wednesday, 20th, Cowbridge.

I do not wonder if Mr. [William] Dufton disliked the people, that the people should dislike him. And in this case the work of God must needs be hindered. But I am entirely of your opinion that it will soon revive if you have acceptable preachers. If he does not much object, I will appoint Joseph Cole for one.[300]

Perhaps you could meet me at Llangwain. Peace be with all your spirits! I am, my dear sister,
> Yours very affectionately,
>> J. Wesley

---

[297] It closed on Aug. 6.
[298] JW ended up running a week late, reaching Monmouth on Aug. 15, etc.
[299] I.e., Llwyn-gwair; see *Journal*, Aug. 19, 1788, 24:106 in this edn.
[300] Cole ended up being sent to Scotland. The Pembroke circuit was assigned William Palmer, Charles Bond, and Francis Truscott.

Address: 'To / Miss Wa⟨rren⟩ / H⟨averfordwest⟩'.[301]

Postmark: 'JY/22/88'.

Source: holograph; Pitts Library (Emory), John Wesley Papers (MSS
153), 4/2.

5

To the Rev. Alexander Suter

10

near London
July 23, 1788

My Dear Brother,

As your life is in danger, I think the sooner you are with your
mother the better.[302] And whenever your health will permit, you
need not be idle—there is plenty of employment for you in England.

Eat as many red currants as ever you can. I am
Your affectionate friend and brother,

[J. Wesley]

20

Source: published transcription; Telford, *Letters*, 8:76.

25

To Sarah (Gwynne) Wesley

30

City Road [London]
July 25, 1788

My Dear Sister,

You know well what a regard I had for Miss [Sarah] Gwynne,
before she was Mrs. [Sarah] Wesley. And it has not ceased from that
time till now. I am persuaded it never will. Therefore I will speak
without reserve just what comes into my mind.

---

[301] Most of the address portion has been cut off.

[302] Suter was assigned as a supernumerary in London (where his mother lived) at the
1788 Conference. The following year, his health improved, he was assigned to the St. Ives
circuit.

I have sometimes thought you are a little like *me*. My wife used to tell me, 'My dear, you are too generous. You don't know the value of money.' I could not wholly deny the charge. Possibly *you* may sometimes lean to the same extreme. I know you are of a generous spirit. You have an open heart and an open hand. But may it not sometimes be too open, more so than your circumstances will allow. Is it not an instance of Christian (as well as worldly) prudence to cut our coat according to our cloth? If your circumstances are a little narrower, should you not contract your expenses too?

I need but just give you this hint, which I doubt not you will take kindly from, my dear Sally,

Your affectionate friend and brother,

J. Wesley

Address: 'To / Mrs Wesley / In Chesterfield street / Marybone'.
Source: holograph; Pitts Library (Emory), John Wesley Papers (MSS 153), 4/3.

To John Crook

London

July 27, 1788

My Dear Brother,

Is it not enough that I am alive today? Let God take thought for what is to come.

Ten pounds will be allowed for brother Barrowclough and you; six for you, and four for him.[303]

You did well in sending the collections to the Conference according to our rules. You see you are no loser by it.

If my life is prolonged, I shall probably set out for Ireland at the usual time, namely the latter end of March. But how much grace

---

[303] Crook and Barrowclough had been serving Isle of Man, and were both being moved to Charlemont in Ireland—the funds were likely for the move. David Barrowclough (c. 1767–1844) was admitted 'on trial' as an itinerant in 1787 (see 10:623 in this edn.) and remained under appointment through 1800. He then became pastor of a splinter congregation located ultimately in Stainland, Yorkshire, where he is buried.

may we receive and how much good may we do before that time! I am, with kind love to sister Crook,

> Your affectionate friend and brother,

> J. Wesley

Source: holograph; WTS (DC), Archives, Oxham Collection.

To George Gidley

> London
> July 29, 1788

My Dear Brother,

It is now the fourth year since I visited our friends in Wales, so that I can no longer delay visiting them. But if I should live to see Cornwall again, I will gladly accept of your kind invitation. Peace be with you and yours. I am,

> Your affectionate brother,

> J. Wesley

Address: 'To / Mr Gidley, Supervisor / in / Plymouth'.
Postmark: 'JY/30/88'.
Endorsement: by Gidley, 'ans[were]d Sep. 19th'.
Source: holograph; WTS (DC), Archives, Oxham Collection.

To the Trustees of Dewsbury Preaching-House

> London
> July 30, 1788

My Dear Brethren,

The question between us is, 'By whom shall the preachers sent from time to time to Dewsbury be judged?' You say, 'By the trustees.' I say, 'By their peers, the preachers met in Conference.' You say, 'Give up this, and we will receive them.' I say, 'I cannot, I dare not, give up this.' Therefore, if you will not receive them on these terms, you renounce connexion with

> Your affectionate brother,

> John Wesley

Source: published transcription; Alexander Mather, *A Supplement to the Reverend Dr. Coke's State of Dewsbury-House* (London: T. Chapman, 1788), 21.[304]

To John Heald [via John Atlay]

London
July 30, 1788

My Dear Brother,

I am in great haste, and therefore must write in haste. Last night I had an interview with Mr. Wesley and most of the preachers who have formerly met with you on the settlement of your [preaching-] house. I really believe they much wish for an agreement, and I think what they now request may easily be complied with. It is only that, in case any preacher sent to you should be objected to by you, that you shall not silence him, nor put him away, without your first calling three of the nearest Assistants to hear your complaint. Who, on your *unanimous* evidence against him, *shall agree to put him away*, and the same week provide you with another out of some of the nearest circuits, till a proper preacher can be got to take the place. And the Assistants so called shall, on the first notice given to them, come over to you on the day fixed for that purpose.

This request does not affect your property in the house, your collections, or anything of that kind.

I have no objection to this. John Wesley.[305]

Mr. Wesley desires you will lose no time in your answer to him or Your affectionate,

John Atlay

Address: 'Mr John Heald on Dewsbury-Moor / near Wakefield / Yorkshire'.
Postmark: 'JY/30/88'.
Source: holograph; New Room (Bristol), NR2001.156.

---

[304] By agreement of those who met the evening of July 29, this short letter by JW was sent out the morning of July 30; while that of John Atlay that follows, providing an alternative, was sent later that day (cf. Mather, *Supplement*, 19–21).

[305] This sentence and signature are in JW's hand.

To Catherine Warren

London
August 1, 1788

My Dear Sister,

On Monday the 17th instant (as I observed before) I hope to be at Carmarthen; and on Tuesday, (if I can find my way) at Langwain.[306] The next day you shall dispose of me as you please. I may preach at Trecwn either noon or night. But is it not a pity to take away a night from Haverford, as I can be there no longer than till Saturday night or Sunday morning at furthest; since I am to begin at St. Daniel's at ten o'clock. Consider this and whatever pleases you, my dear Kitty, will please,

Yours affectionately,

J. Wesley

Address: 'To / Miss Warren / in / Haverford West'.
Postmark: 'AU/2/88'.
Source: holograph; Drew, Methodist Archives.

To Sarah Mallet

London
August 2, 1788

My Dear Sister,

Let me know any time what books you wish to have, and I will order them to be sent to you. It is a pleasure to me if I can show in anything the regard which I have for you, as I am firmly persuaded that you have a conscience void of offense toward God and toward man.[307] I do not doubt but you have given God your heart, and do in all things wish to do his holy and acceptable will.

But if so, it is no wonder that you should meet with crosses, both from the devil and his children—especially as you believe you are called of God to bear a public testimony against him. But you are in

[306] I.e., Llwyn-gwair.
[307] See Acts 24:16.

far greater danger from applause than from censure; and it is well for you that one balances the other. But I trust you will never be weary of well doing. In due time you shall reap if you faint not.[308] Whoever praises or dispraises, it is your part to go steadily on, speaking the truth in love.[309]

I do not require any of our preachers to license either themselves or the places where they preach.[310] Indeed, a forward young man in Northamptonshire brought some trouble on himself by preaching in Church time, and so near the Church as to disturb both the minister and the congregation. But that need not fright any other of our preachers. They are just as safe as they were before. Go on, therefore, and fear nothing but sin.

And let me know if there be anything wherein I can assist you, which will be a pleasure to, dear Sally,

Yours affectionately,

J. Wesley

Source: published transcription; Telford, *Letters*, 8:77–78.

To Ann Dupuy Taylor

London
August 2, 1788

My Dear Nancy,

I was well pleased when I heard you were gone to spend a little time in Cork,[311] where you will have an opportunity of conversing familiarly with sister [Martha] Ward and with that blessed woman sister [Hester Ann] Rogers. I do not doubt but you will make the best use of these blessed opportunities. Now, my dear maid, is the time when you may improve your understanding and (what is far better) your heart. Now pray earnestly that you may be enabled to give your whole heart to him who alone is worthy of it.

---

[308] See Gal. 6:9.

[309] See Eph. 4:15.

[310] Indeed, from the outset of the revival JW strongly discouraged his preachers from licensing themselves or their preaching Houses under the Toleration Act. Only in the last year had he begun to recommend such licensing, though without requiring it. See JW, *Journal*, Nov. 1, 1787, 24:64 in this edn.

[311] See JW to Thomas Taylor, June 7, 1788.

I am, my dear Nancy,
    Yours affectionately,

                                                          J. Wesley

Source: published transcription; *Wesley Banner* 1 (1849): 273.

To Mrs. Martha Ward

                                                          London
                                                   August 2, 1788

My Dear Sister,
    The thing has been wholly misrepresented.[312] Dr. [Thomas] Coke
never *designed* any separation. But they urged him to say 'he *wished*
for such a thing', and then faced him down that he *designed* it. He
and I have had much conversation together, and he is now as fully
persuaded as I am that a general separation from the Church either
in England or Ireland would be greatly obstructive of the work of
God.
    I am exceedingly glad that the Dean of Waterford now sees the
Methodists in a true light.[313] It would be a great pity that anything
should impair the good opinion which he now entertains of them. I
have therefore wrote to James Deaves and desired him to bear with
the little oddities of Richard Condy, and to advise all our people in
my name to keep close to the Church and sacrament.[314] I make little
doubt but they will take my advice.
    I am, my dear sister,
        Your affectionate brother,

                                                          [J. Wesley]

Source: published transcription; Telford, *Letters*, 8:79–80.

[312] Ward was receiving reports of the controversy in the Dublin society; see JW to Henry
Moore, May 6, 1788.
[313] Christopher Butson (1747–1836) was the current Dean of Waterford.
[314] This letter to Deaves is not known to survive. Condy was currently the Assistant of
the Waterford circuit.

For Robert Gamble [as deacon]³¹⁵
Testimonial Letter³¹⁶

[London]
[August 3, 1788]   5

Know all men by these presents that I, John Wesley, Master of Arts, late fellow of Lincoln College in the University of Oxford, did on the third day of August, in the year of our Lord one thousand seven hundred and eighty-eight, by the imposition of my hands   10 and prayer, and in the fear of God, set apart Robert Gamble for the office of a deacon in the church of God. Given under my hand and seal the tenth day of August in the year above written.

John Wesley

Source: secondary transcription; MARC, MA 1977/502/3/5.³¹⁷   15

For Matthew Lumb (as deacon)³¹⁸   20
Testimonial Letter

[London]
[August 3, 1788]

25

Know all men by these presents that I, John Wesley, Master of Arts, late of Lincoln College in the University of Oxford, did on the third day of August, in the year of our Lord one thousand sev-

³¹⁵ Robert Gamble (d. 1791) was admitted 'on trial' as an itinerant at the 1785 Conference (see 10:568 in this edn.). Three years later he was one of five preachers ordained by JW to serve in the West Indies (10:668). He died of a fever on the island of St. Vincent in early 1791 (10:746).

³¹⁶ At the 1788 Conference JW ordained six more persons to serve either Scotland or the West Indies (each as deacon, on Aug. 3; then elder on Aug. 5) The text of six of the twelve testimonial letters survives. At the very end of Conference JW also quietly ordained Alexander Mather for service in England (neither testimonial letter survives). For background and more details see Appendix B.

³¹⁷ The original, written on vellum in Thomas Coke's hand and signed by JW sold about 1914 at Sotheby's Auction; the transcription may have been made at that time.

³¹⁸ Matthew Lumb (1761–1847) first appears in the *Minutes*, under appointment in the Dales in 1783 (see 10:534 in this edn.). He served five more years in Scotland, then was one of five preachers ordained by JW to serve in the West Indies (10:668). Lumb returned to England after being imprisoned from preaching to slaves in 1793, and continued itinerating until his retirement in 1826. See *Minutes* (post-Wesley, 1847), 10:455.

en hundred and eighty-eight, by the imposition of my hands and prayer, and in the fear of God, set apart Matthew Lumb for the office of a deacon in the church of God. Given under my hand and seal the tenth day of August in the year above written.

5
John Wesley

Source: holograph; University of York, Borthwick Institute for Archives, MR/Y/CEN 94.[319]

10

For Thomas Owens (as deacon)[320]
Testimonial Letter

15

[London]
[August 3, 1788]

20   Know all men by these presents that I, John Wesley, Master of Arts, late of Lincoln College in the University of Oxford, did on the third day of August, in the year of our Lord one thousand seven hundred and eighty-eight, by the imposition of my hands and prayer, and in the fear of God, set apart Thomas Owens for the
25   office of a deacon in the church of God. Given under my hand and seal the tenth day of August in the year above written.

John Wesley

30
Sources: facsimile of holograph; MARC, WCB, E4/1/4-7, and Duke, Rubenstein, Frank Baker Collection of Wesleyana, Box WF5.[321]

[319] Placed there from Centenary Chapel, York; see *WHS 30 (1955): 24.*

[320] Thomas Owens (d. 1808), of Irish birth, was admitted 'on trial' as an itinerant at the 1786 Conference in Ireland (see 10:978 in this edn.). Two years later he was one of five preachers ordained by JW to serve in the West Indies (10:668). He served there for twelve years, before returning due to health issues. See *Minutes* (post-Wesley, 1808), 3:7.

[321] Text in hand of Thomas Coke, with JW's signature. Also picture in *Methodist Recorder* (Oct. 27, 1898), 11.

For James Bogie (as elder)[322]
Testimonial Letter

[London]
[August 5, 1788[323]]   5

Know all men by these presents that I, John Wesley, Master of
Arts, late fellow of Lincoln College in the University of Oxford, did
on the sixth day of August, in the year of our Lord one thousand
seven hundred and eighty-eight, by the imposition of my hands   10
and prayer, and in the fear of God (being assisted by other ordained
ministers), set apart James Bogie for the office of an elder in the
church of God; whom I recommend to all whom it may concern, as
a proper person to administer the holy sacraments in the congregation, and to feed the church of God. Given under my hand and seal   15
the seventh day of August in the year above written.

John Wesley

Source: holograph; MARC, MA 1977/125.[324]

20

For Robert Gamble (as elder)
Testimonial Letter   25

[London]
[August 5, 1788]

Know all men by these presents that I, John Wesley, Master of   30
Arts, late fellow of Lincoln College in the University of Oxford,
did on the fifth day of August, in the year of our Lord one thousand
seven hundred and eighty-eight, by the imposition of my hands
and prayer, and in the fear of God (being assisted by other ordained
ministers), set apart Robert Gamble for the office of an elder in the   35

[322] On Bogie, see 29:703 in this edn.
[323] JW recorded in his diary that he 'ordained six presbyters' [i.e., elders] on Aug. 5, 1788
(see 24:253 in this edn.). Two of the three surviving letters (Bogie and Lumb) list the ordination
date as Aug. 6, and date the letter itself on Aug. 7. The surviving letter for Gamble has the correct ordination date, but the letter itself is dated Aug. 10. We have placed them together, dated
when the ordination took place.
[324] It was held previously at Richmond College; see transcription in *WHS* 17 (1930): 121.

church of God; whom I recommend to all whom these presents shall come as a proper person to administer the holy sacraments and feed the church of God. Given under my hand and seal the tenth day of August in the year above written.

5

John Wesley

Source: facsimile of holograph, MARC, WCB, E4/1/8-9.

10

For Matthew Lumb (as elder) Testimonial Letter

[London]
[August 5, 1788]

15

Know all men by these presents that I, John Wesley, Master of Arts, late fellow of Lincoln College in the University of Oxford, did on the sixth day of August, in the year of our Lord one thousand seven hundred and eighty-eight, by the imposition of my hands
20 and prayer, and in the fear of God (being assisted by other ordained ministers), set apart Matthew Lumb for the office of an elder in the church of God; whom I recommend to all whom it may concern as a proper person to administer the holy sacraments in the congregation and to feed the church of God. Given under my hand and seal
25 the seventh day of August in the year above written.

John Wesley

Source: published transcription; George Eayrs, *John Wesley* (London: Epworth, 1926), 279-80.[325]

30

To Frances Godfrey

London
35   August 5, 1788
My Dear Sister,
   You have indeed escaped as a bird out of the snare of the fowler; the snare is broken, and you are delivered.[326] Certainly you have great reason to praise him who has brought you to the knowledge

---

[325] Holograph said to be in possession of Edmund Lamplough.
[326] See Ps. 124:6 (BCP).

of his truth; and not only given you to know but to experience the
truth as it is in Jesus. I felt a love for you from the first time I saw
you, when you was under those grievous trials.[327] Now that you have
recovered some measure of health and strength, employ it all to the
glory of him that gave it. Now go on to perfection![328] Hunger and   5
thirst after righteousness, till you are satisfied therewith.[329] Then
you will be more and more near to, my dear Fanny,
    Yours affectionately,

                                 [J. Wesley]

My love to your mother.[330]   10

Address: 'To Miss Frances Godfrey, of Gainsborough'.
Source: published transcription; Jackson, *Works* (3rd), 13:36–37.

                                         15

To Sarah (Gwynne) Wesley

                                 North Green
                         August 7, 1788   20
Dear Sister,
    As the Conference ended yesterday afternoon, my hurry is now
a little abated. I cannot blame you for having thoughts of removing
out of that large house.[331] If you could find a lodging to your mind,
it would be preferable on several accounts, and perhaps you might   25
live as much without care as you did in the great mansion-house at
Garth.
    I was yesterday inquiring of Dr. [John] Whitehead whether Har-
rogate would not be better for Sally than the sea water.[332] He seems
to think it would; and I should not think much of giving her ten or   30
twenty pounds to make a trial. But I wish she could see him first,
which she might do any day between 7:00 and 8:00 in the morning.
    I am, dear Sally,
        Yours most affectionately,

                                  J. Wesley   35

[327] See JW to Godfrey, July 31, 1784.
[328] See Heb. 6:1.
[329] See Matt. 5:6.
[330] Possibly Susannah (Stead) Godfrey; see note on JW to Godfrey, July 31, 1784.
[331] Sarah remained at the house on Chesterfield Street, with Sarah Jr. and Charles Jr,
through 1805; then took a smaller house at 14, Nottingham Street, Marylebone.
[332] Harrogate was known for its spa-water. Sarah Jr. ended up going instead to the coast,
at Ramsgate; see JW to Sarah Jr., Sept. 1.

Address: 'To / Mrs Wesley / In Chesterfield Street / Marybone'.
Postmark: 'Penny Post Paid'.
Endorsement: by Sarah Wesley Jr., 'Aug 7 1788'.
Source: holograph; Pitts Library (Emory), John Wesley Papers (MSS
5   153), 4/4.

To Walter Churchey[333]

London
August 8, 1788

My Dear Brother,
    I think you know that I love you, and that I should rejoice to do
anything for you that is in my power. And one allowed proof of love
is plain dealing. Therefore I will speak to you without any reserve.
    There are many good lines, and some very good, both in the ode
and in the translation of 'The Art of Painting'. And I really think
you improve in versifying. You write a good deal better than you
did some years ago. You express your sense with more perspicuity
than you used to do, and appear to have greater variety of words
as well as more strength. But there is nothing (to use the modern
cant word) 'sentimental' in either the ode or the translation. There
is nothing of tender or pathetic, nothing that touches the passions.
Therefore no bookseller would venture to buy them, as knowing
they will not sell. And they lie utterly out of the way of the Methodists, who do not care to buy or even to read (at least the generality
of them) any but religious books. I do not believe all my influence
would induce them to buy as many copies as would suffice to pay
for the printing.
    I have not yet seen my brother's translation of the Psalms.[334] Nei-
ther, indeed, could I as yet have time to read it, were it put into my
hands.

---

[333] Churchey had clearly pressed JW (in a letter not know to survive) to enlarge upon his
brief critical remarks in the letter of July 22, 1788.

[334] I.e., CW, MS Psalms; containing poetic renderings of the psalms.

If any had asked my advice, they would not have thrust out the account of George Lukins into the world so prematurely.[335] It should have been fully authenticated first.

I am, with love to sister [Mary] Churchey,
Your affectionate brother,

J. Wesley

I expect to be at Brecon on Sunday se'nnight.

Address: 'To / Mr Churchey / Near the Hay / Brecon'.
Postmarks: 'AU/8/88' and 'Brecknock'. *Charge*: '6'.
Endorsement: by Churchey, '1788 / Mr J. W. / Critique on the Mss.'.
Source: holograph; Manchester, Rylands, English Ms 1400/18.

To Arthur Keene

London
August 8, 1788

My Dear Arthur,
Even at this busy time I must snatch a few minutes to write. You have now an easy way to show your affection for me and your willingness to be advised by me. It is the belief of many that you will see me in Ireland no more. But if I should live till spring, I shall endeavour to visit Dublin at the usual time, about the end of March.[336] If then you have a real regard for me, see that your preaching-house be enlarged without delay. Forward the building that it may be ready when I come.

Do this, and I shall know that you have a love for, my dear Arthur,
Your ever affectionate brother,

J. Wesley

[335] George Lukins (1742–1805) had exhibited behaviours for some years that led many to consider him possessed by demons. On June 13, 1788 an 'exorcism' was performed for him at the Temple Church in Bristol, led by the vicar, Rev. Joseph Easterbrook (a graduate of Kingswood school), with John Valton and a couple other itinerants participating, as well as some other Methodist society members; see the published transcription of Valton's diary account of the day in *WHS* 8 (1911):101. Believing Lukins delivered by this service, some participants published an account dated June 18 in the Bath *Journal* (June 23, 1788), p. 2. This sparked a debate over the next weeks, which was picked up in newspapers elsewhere.

[336] JW arrived in Dublin for his last visit on Mar. 29, 1789.

My kind love attend Bella and all the little ones.

Address: 'To / Arthur Keen Esq / near / Dublin'.
Postmarks: 'AU/13/88' and 'AU/17'.
5 *Endorsement*: by Keene, '8 August 1788 / Revd Jno. Wesley / London'.
Source: holograph; MARC, MAM JW 3/79.

10

To Darcy (Brisbane) Maxwell[337]

London
August 8, 1788

My Dear Lady,
15
It is certain many persons both in Scotland and England would be well pleased to have the same preachers always. But we cannot forsake the plan of acting which we have followed from the beginning. For fifty years God has been pleased to bless the itinerant plan, the last year most of all. It must not be altered till I am removed; and I
20 hope will remain till our Lord comes to reign upon earth.

I do not know (unless it unfits us for the duties of life) that we can have too great a sensibility of human pain. Methinks I should be afraid of losing any degree of this sensibility. I had a son-in-law (now in Abraham's bosom) who quitted his profession, that
25 of a surgeon, for that very reason—because he said it made him less sensible of human pain.[338] And I have known exceeding few persons who have carried this tenderness of spirit to excess. I recollect but one who was constrained to leave off in a great measure visiting the sick because he could not see anyone in pain without
30 fainting away.

Mr. Charles Perronet was the first person I was acquainted with who was favoured with the same experience as the Marquis De Renty with regard to the ever-blessed Trinity, Miss [Elizabeth] Ritchie was the second, Miss Roe (now Mrs. Rogers) the third. I
35 have as yet found but a few instances; so that this is not, as I was at first apt to suppose, the common privilege of all that are 'perfect in love'.[339]

---

[337] Lady Maxwell's letter, to which JW was replying, is not known to survive.
[338] JW's only deceased 'son-in-law' was John Matthews (d. 1764), first husband of his step-daughter Jeanne Vazeille. In his later years Matthews was a woolery draper.
[339] See the notes on JW to Maxwell, July 4, 1787.

Pardon me my dear friend, for my heart is tenderly concerned for you, if I mention one fear I have concerning you: lest, on conversing with some, you should be in any degree warped from *Christian simplicity.* O do not wish to hide that you are a Methodist! Surely it is best to appear just what you are. I believe you will receive this as a proof of the sincerity with which I am, my dear Lady,

  Your ever affectionate servant,

                J. Wesley

Source: published transcription; Benson, *Works*, 16:201–02.

To Ann Bolton

                Brecon
            August 15, 1788
Dear Nancy,

Last night I received yours at Monmouth.[340] The same complaint which you make of not receiving an answer to your letter, another person had just been making. But I had answered you both. I cannot therefore but conclude that both my letters had some way or other miscarried.

Since I saw you a young slender girl just beginning to seek salvation I do not remember that you ever offended in anything. But you was always exceeding dear to me. So you are still. And I would show it effectually if my power were equal to my will. I love you the more because you are a daughter of affliction. I suppose you are still in God's school. But you still remember he loveth whom he chasteneth.[341]

If you love me still, write freely to, my dear Nancy,

  Yours very affectionately,

                [J. Wesley]

Address: 'To / Miss Bolton / In Witney / Oxfordshire'.
Source: published transcription; Telford, *Letters*, 8:84.

---

[340] This letter is not known to survive.
[341] See Heb. 12:6.

To John Atlay[342]

Pembroke
August 23, 1788

My Dear Brother,

If you are persuaded that such a promise (which is the whole and sole cause of the breach at Dewsbury) is binding, you must follow your persuasion. You will have blame enough from other persons; my hand shall not be upon you. If I can do you good, I will. But I shall certainly do you no harm.

George Whitfield is the person I choose to succeed you. I wish you would teach him as much as you can without delay.

I am, with kind love to sister [Sarah] Atlay,

Your affectionate brother,

J. Wesley

Address: 'To / Mr Atlay / At the New Chappel / City Road / London'.
Postmarks: 'Pembroke' and 'AU/26/88'.
Endorsement: by Atlay, 'Mr. Wesley Augt. 23'.
Source: holograph; New Room (Bristol), NR2001.226.

To Elizabeth Baker[343]

Carmarthen
August 26, 1788

My Dear Betsy,

Since I had the pleasure of seeing you, I have been thinking much on what you said concerning your loving others too much. In one sense this cannot be. You cannot have too much benevolence for the whole human race. But in another sense you may. You may grieve

[342] JW was replying to Atlay's letter of Aug. 19, 1788; in which Atlay informed JW that he was resigning his position at the book room, and accepting a call from the trustees of the Dewsbury preaching-house to become their preacher.

[343] Elizabeth Baker (1762–1843) was the younger sister of Sarah Baker (of Monmouth and Cowbridge). JW conversed with Elizabeth on Aug. 15, 1788, while in Monmouth (see *Journal*, 24:105 in this edn.). Elizabeth married Edward Jordan of Monmouth in 1792. She was a member of the society for 65 years, and a class-leader for most of those years. See *WMM* 67 (1844), 244.

too much for the distresses of others, even so much as to make you
incapable of giving them the relief which otherwise you should give
them. So I know one that, when he sees any one in strong pain,
directly faints away.[344] Is it something like this which you mean by
feeling too much for others? You can give me two or three instances   5
of it, and then I shall be better able to judge.

Have you a constant witness of the pardoning love of God? And
do you find an abiding love to him? Have you yet been enabled to
give him your whole heart? If so, at what time and in what manner
did you receive this blessing?   10

I think you can speak with all freedom to
    Yours very affectionately,

[J. Wesley]

15

Address: 'Miss Elizabeth Baker of Monmouth'.
Source: published transcription; Jackson, *Works* (3rd), 13:97.

20

To John Atlay[345]

Bristol
August 31, 1788 25

I pray, brother Atlay, do not serve me so. If you will not serve
me yourself, do not hinder others from serving me. Do not fright
George Whitfield from it; but encourage him to it, and instruct him
as quick as possible. My death is nothing to the purpose. I have now   30
nothing to do with the Dewsbury people; go with them and serve
them. But I am still
    Your affectionate brother,

John Wesley

35

Source: published transcription; Atlay, *Letters*, 14.

---

[344] See JW to Lady Maxwell, Aug. 8, 1788.
[345] JW was replying to Atlay's letter of Aug. 28, 1788; in which Atlay reported that he discussed with George Whitfield the possibility of taking over the book room (as JW had requested), and Whitfield demurred.

To Sarah Wesley Jr.

Bristol
September 1, 1788

My Dear Sally,

I received yours yesterday in the afternoon.[346] As Ramsgate is more private, I am not sorry that you are there, and that you have so suitable a companion.[347]

I think it would be expedient for you to bathe every day, unless you find yourself chilled when you come out. But I do not advise you to drink any sea water. I am persuaded it was never designed to enter any human body for any purpose but to drown it.

The great comfort is that you have a good and wise Physician always ready both to advise and to assist. Therefore you are assured, health you shall have if health be best.[348] That all things may work together for your good is the prayer of, my dear Sally,[349]

Your ever affectionate uncle,

J. Wesley

Source: holograph; privately held (WWEP Archive holds photo).

To John Atlay[350]

Bristol
September 4, 1788

My Dear Brother,

I was once afraid that you had dissuaded George Whitfield from taking charge of the books; but I can take your word. Now I am fully satisfied that you did not. And I believe you will teach him everything relating to that charge. But one thing is much upon my mind: I wish you would hire one or two proper persons, and take

[346] This letter is not known to survive.
[347] See JW to Sarah (Gwynne) Wesley, Aug. 7, 1788. Sarah Jr. was accompanied on her visit to Ramsgate by a Miss Mary Ward.
[348] Cf. CW, Hymn on Isaiah 40:31, st. 7, *HSP* (1742), 226.
[349] See Rom. 8:28.
[350] Atlay replied on Sept. 2 to JW's letter of Aug. 31 insisting he had done nothing to dissuade George Whitfield from taking over the book room.

an inventory of all the books that are either in the shop or under the chapel. This will be worth all the pains. Then George will know what he has to do. I am
Your affectionate brother,

J. Wesley 5

Address: 'To / Mr Atlay / New Chappel / London'.
Postmarks: 'Bristol' and 'SE/6/88'.
Endorsement: by Atlay, 'Mr. Wesley Septr. 4th / 1788'.
Source: holograph; MARC, MAM JW 1/4. 10

To Thomas Cooper 15

Bristol
September 6, 1788
Dear Tommy, 20
I will not send any other person into the Derby circuit if you will be there in two or three weeks.[351] Otherwise I must, or the work of God might suffer in a manner not easy to be repaired. You should have told me at first what your disorder was, and possibly I might have saved you from much pain. I am, dear Tommy, 25
Your affectionate brother,

[J. Wesley]

Address: 'To / Mr Thos. Cooper / In Cherry Lane / Birmingham'.
Source: published transcription; Telford, *Letters*, 8:87. 30

---

[351] Cooper had been stationed at Birmingham, and was appointed in early Aug. by the 1788 Conference to the Plymouth circuit. Apparently he resisted this move, appealing to an ailment, and requested instead the Derby circuit. As things turned out, by the time this letter reached Birmingham, Cooper had already left for Plymouth; see JW to Cooper, Feb. 22, 1788.

To Sarah Wesley Jr.[352]

Bristol
September 8, 1788

My Dear Sally,

You shall have just as many friends as will be for you good. And why should not my Betty Ritchie be in the number? I must look to that, if I live to see London again, which will probably be in three weeks.

If sea water has that effect on you, it is plain you are not to drink it.[353] All the body is full of *imbibing* pores. You take in water enough that way. If your appetite increases, so does your strength, although by insensible degrees.

I have seen John Henderson several times. I hope he does not live in any sin. But it is a great disadvantage that he has nothing to do. I hope we shall find him something.[354]

I have a work in hand that will give you pleasure. I have begun to write my brother's life.[355] Now in this you may assist me much. You knew as much of him as most people; and you have the pen of a ready writer. Set down everything you can recollect concerning him. I think between us we shall be able to make something out. You may set down everything you can think of. I can select such a portion as is most proper. You have now leisure for it, and for doing good to any whom providence delivers into your hands.

Peace be with your spirit! I am, my dear Sally,

Yours in tender affection,

J. Wesley

Source: holograph; MARC, DDWes 5/22.[356]

---

[352] JW was replying to another letter from Sarah that is not known to survive.

[353] Cf. JW to Sarah Jr., Sept. 1, 1788.

[354] Henderson had taken his BA degree from Pembroke College, Oxford, in 1786. He was back in the Bristol area with his parents. He would die unexpectedly later this year, being buried on Nov. 18, 1788. This was another blow for Sarah Jr., as she is reported to have said that she and John intended to be married; see Joseph Cottle, *Reminiscences of Samuel Taylor Coleridge and Robert Southey* (London, 1847), 212–13.

[355] JW made little progress on this project before his own death. The first book-length life of Charles Wesley would be by John Whitehead in 1793.

[356] The address portion is not known to survive, but in her reply of Sept. 23, 1788, Sarah Jr. notes that it was misdirected to Margate instead of Ramsgate.

To George Whitfield

Bristol
September 15, 1788   5

Dear George,

A word to the wise. Go on. Learn everything that you can learn. I am not a weathercock. My yea is yea, and my nay is nay.[357]

I am, with kind love to sister Whitfield,[358]

Your affectionate brother,   10

J. Wesley

Address: 'To / Mr Whitfield / In Holywell Street / The Strand / London'.
Postmarks: 'Bristol' and 'SE/16/88'. *Charge*: '5'.
Source: holograph; Bridwell Library (SMU).[359]   15

To Elizabeth Baker   20

Bristol
September 16, 1788

My Dear Betsy,   25

One would be apt to imagine that there could be no ill consequence of the deepest concern for the sin and misery of our fellow creatures. But dear, indisputable experience shows the contrary to a demonstration. Lucretia Smith (to mention only one instance), a young gentlewoman of our society here who found remission of   30 sins long ago and was unblameable in her whole behaviour, reasoned on that question, 'Why does not the God of love make everyone as happy as me?' till she lost all her happiness, all her peace— which she never recovered since.[360] Beware therefore of reasoning on those points which are far too high for you. Such knowledge is   35 too wonderful for us; we cannot attain unto it. His ways are un-

---

[357] See Matt. 5:37.
[358] George Whitfield married Eleanor Ridley (1738–1803) in 1784.
[359] Held previously at WMC Museum, 2002.001.041.
[360] Cf. JW, *Journal*, Dec. 24, 1740, 19:175 in this edn.

searchable and his judgments a great deep.[361] What he doeth thou knowest not now; it is enough that thou shalt know hereafter.[362]

I hope you never will be weary of well-doing.[363] Herein your sister Sally is a pattern. She has done unspeakable good since she came to Cowbridge.[364] God sent her thither to revive his work there. When I first heard of her removal from Monmouth, I could not but be troubled at not seeing by what possible means the want of her could be supplied. But it is done already. God has raised you to supply her place. And he will supply all your wants out of the riches of his mercy in Christ Jesus.[365]

In what sense do you see God? Are you always sensible of his loving presence? How do you 'rejoice evermore' and 'pray without ceasing and in everything give thanks'? It is certain this is the will of God concerning you in Christ Jesus.[366]

Adieu!

Source: published transcription; Jackson, *Works* (3rd), 13:97–98.

To Joseph Benson

Bristol
September 17, 1788

Dear Joseph,

I congratulate you upon the happy increase of your family.[367] And I am glad you have determined to correct Mr. [John] Fletcher's *Letters*.[368] You will observe that it is 'dangerous on such subjects to depart from Scripture either as to language or sentiment' and believe that 'most of the controversies which have disturbed the

---

[361] See Rom. 11:33.

[362] See John 13:7.

[363] See Gal. 6:9.

[364] Elizabeth's sister Sarah Baker had married Isaac Skinner of Cowbridge on Dec. 26, 1786. JW had been in Cowbridge on Aug. 29, 1788; see *Journal*, 24:107 in this edn.

[365] See Phil. 4:19.

[366] See 1 Thess. 5:16–18.

[367] Benson and his wife Sarah had a daughter, Isabella, on Sept. 3. She was baptized on Oct. 20 in Hull.

[368] That is, the manuscript Fletcher had been preparing in response to Joseph Priestley; see JW to Benson, Mar. 9–10, 1787.

Church have arisen from people's wanting to be wise above what is written, not contented with what God has plainly revealed there'.[369]

O Joseph, do not you yourself immediately forget this? And immediately run out in a curious metaphysical disquisition about what God has not *plainly revealed*?[370] What have you or I to do with that 'difficulty'? I dare not, will not, *reason* about it for a moment. I believe just what is revealed, and no more. But I do not pretend to *account* for it, or to solve the difficulties that may attend it. Let angels do this, if they can. But I think they cannot. I think even these

> Would find no end, in wandering mazes lost.[371]

Some years since, I read about fifty pages of Dr. Watts's ingenious treatise upon the glorified humanity of Christ.[372] But it so confounded my intellect, and plunged me into such unprofitable *reasonings*, yea dangerous even, that I would not have read it through for five hundred pounds. It led him into Arianism. Take care that similar tracts (all of which I abhor) have not the same effect upon *you*. Pursue that train of reasoning as far as it will go, and it will surely land you either in Socinianism or deism.

I like your thoughts upon materialism, as I doubt not I should those on the separate existence of the soul.[373] It will be best to print at Hull or York, if you can print almost as cheap and can have as good paper. Should there not be a thousand copies? Then you will reserve an hundred of them for yourself.

The matter of Dewsbury you mistake totally. When I met the trustees at Dewsbury they all promised me to settle the house according to the deed then read. *They* flew off from this, not *I*. I desired no more from the beginning to the end. The sum of all was: If anyone accuses a preacher whom I send, I, not the *accuser*, will be his judge. And *this I cannot give up*.

---

[369] JW uses the quotation marks. There is no known published source. He may be quoting Fletcher's manuscript, but no extended portion of this remains in the form Benson published. More likely he is giving Benson hints about what to emphasize.

[370] JW is responding to the draft of Benson's *Remarks on Dr. Priestley's System of Materialism, Mechanism, and Necessity, in a series of letters to the Reverend Mr. Wesley* (Hull: George Prince, 1788); wherein Benson highlights several 'difficulties' in reconciling Priestley's materialism with prayer, etc. (see pp. 27–28, 35–36, 72–74).

[371] Milton, *Paradise Lost*, ii. 561.

[372] Isaac Watts, *Glory of Christ as God-Man Unveiled* (London: J. Oswald & J. Buckland, 1746).

[373] I.e., Benson's *A Scriptural Essay Towards a Proof of an Immortal Spirit in Man, being a Continuation of Remarks on Dr. Priestley's System ...* (Hull: George Prince, 1788).

I am, with love to sister [Sarah] Benson, dear Joseph,
  Your affectionate friend and brother,

J. Wesley

5   But hold! Does not Mrs. [Mary] Fletcher consider this impression
as *her* property?

Address: 'To / Mr. Benson / At the Preaching-house / In / Hull'.
Postmark: 'SE/18/88'.
10   *Endorsement*: by Benson, 'J. Wesley Sept 1788 / Ans[wer]ed'.
Source: holograph; Duke, Rubenstein, Wesley Family Papers, Box 1.

15

To Francis Asbury[374]

London
September 20, 1788

20   [...]
There is, indeed, a wide difference between the relation wherein
you stand to the Americans and the relation wherein I stand to *all*
the Methodists. You are the elder brother of the American Methodists. I am, under God, the father of the whole family. Therefore
25   I naturally care for you all in a manner no other persons can do.
Therefore I, in a measure, provide for you all; for the supplies
which Dr. [Thomas] Coke provides for you, he could not provide
were it not for me—were it not that I not only permit him to collect, but also support him in so doing.
30   But in one point, my dear brother, I am a little afraid both the
Doctor and you differ from me. I study to be *little*; you study to be
great. I *creep*; you *strut* along. I found a *school*; you a *college*! Nay, and

---

[374] The location (or survival) of the full holograph of this letter is unknown. Henry Moore
had the holograph [or a copy for JW's records] in 1825, and commented that he had been present when JW crafted it. Moore's introduction to the transcription given here makes clear that
it was only an excerpt: 'After speaking on some general subjects, he [i.e., JW] adds' (Moore,
Life, 2:341). The letter did not catch up to Francis Asbury in his perpetual travels until March
15, 1789, in Charleston, SC; drawing this comment in his diary, 'Here I received a bitter pill
from one of my greatest friends. Praise the Lord for my trials also! May they all be sanctified!'
Asbury, *Journal*, 1:594. This is JW's last known letter to Asbury.

call it after your own names![375] O beware, do not seek to be *something*! Let me be nothing, and 'Christ be all in all!'[376]

One instance of this, of your *greatness*, has given me great concern. How can you, how dare you suffer yourself to be called 'Bishop'? I shudder, I start at the very thought! Men may call *me* a knave or a fool, a rascal, a scoundrel, and I am content. But they shall never by my consent call me *Bishop*! For my sake, for God's sake, for Christ's sake put a full end to this! Let the Presbyterians do what they please, but let the Methodists know their calling better.

Thus, my dear Franky, I have told you all that is in my heart. And let this, when I am no more seen, bear witness how sincerely I am

Your affectionate friend and brother,

John Wesley

Source: published excerpt; Moore, *Life*, 2:341–42.

To Henry Moore

Bristol
September 20, 1788

My Dear Brother,

I have taken place in the mail coach for Sunday sennight in the afternoon,[377] so that I shall probably be with you on Monday morning.

Pray tell George Whitfield to settle himself in the book room without delay, as John Atlay has appointed to leave it on the 25th instant.[378] I beg of brother [Thomas] Rankin and you to advise and assist him to the uttermost of your power. Many croakers, no doubt, will strive to discourage him; therefore strengthen his hands all you can.

I am, with much love to my Nancy, dear Henry,

Your affectionate friend and brother,

J. Wesley

Address: 'To / Mr Moore / At the New Chappel / City Road / London'.
Postmark: 'Bristol'. *Charge*: '5'.
Source: holograph; MARC, WCB, D6/1/134a.

---

[375] JW is comparing the preparatory school at Kingswood with the short-lived Cokesbury College.
[376] See CW, 'After a Relapse into Sin', st. 12, *HSP* (1740), 156.
[377] I.e., on Sept. 28, 1788.
[378] See JW to Atlay, Sept. 4 and Sept. 24, 1788.

To an Unidentified Correspondent[379]

Bristol
September 20, 1788

My Dear Friend,

The question properly refers (when we speak of a separation from the Church) to a *total* and *immediate* separation. Such was that of Mr. [Benjamin] Ingham's people first, and afterwards that of Lady [Selina] Huntingdon's; who all agreed to form themselves into a separate body *without delay*, to go to Church no more, and to have no more connexion with the Church of England than with the Church of Rome.

Such a separation I have always declared against; and certainly it will not take place (if ever it does) while I live. But a kind of separation has already taken place, and will inevitably spread, though by slow degrees. Those ministers (so-called) who neither live nor preach the gospel, I dare not say are sent of God. Where one of these is settled, many of the Methodists dare not attend his ministry; so, if there be no other Church in that neighbourhood, they go to Church no more. This is the case in a few places already, and it will be the case in more; and no one can justly blame *me* for this, neither is it contrary to any of my professions.

J. W.

Source: published transcription; *Arminian Magazine* 12 (1789): 45–46.

To Hugh Moore

Bristol
September 21, 1788

My Dear Brother,

If you have not work enough for a month you must alter the circuit,[380] and go through it in two or three weeks—unless you take the advantage of this fine mild autumn to break up fresh ground. I suppose you have already taken in Donard and Baltinglass and

---

[379] Titled: 'Thoughts on Separation from the Church'.

[380] Moore had been appointed Assistant for the Wexford circuit by the 1788 Conference.

the bog of Boira.[381] With faith and prayer you may do great things; these arms are invincible.

It is by no means expedient to make too much haste with regard to the building of [preaching] houses. If we do not take care the Methodists will be destroyed by buildings. If we make rich men *necessary* to us, discipline is at an end. Be bold. Be steady.

I am, dear Hugh,
  Your affectionate friend and brother,

           J. Wesley

Source: published transcription; *WHS* 29 (1954): 115–16 (from transcript in Moore family).

To Thomas Cooper

           Bristol
        September 22, 1788

My Dear Brother,

I have much business to do in London. And as I do not depend upon seeing another year I must be there as soon as possible, and to that end have taken place in the mail coach for next Sunday night. If I should live to see the next autumn, I shall endeavour to see you at Plymouth.

As it was evidently the providence of God which placed you in your present situation,[382] he will doubtless give you grace sufficient for it. Only take care to improve the Sabbath and you will some day stand at the right hand!

I am
  Your affectionate brother,

           J. Wesley

Source: published transcription; *Methodist History* 57 (2019): 172–74.

---

[381] Orig., 'Boiree'. According to Crookshank (*Ireland*, 1:94), the Bog of Boira was 'in the parish of Kiltrisk, Wexford'. All three locations were on the northern edge of the Wexford circuit.

[382] See the note on JW to Cooper, Sept. 6, 1788.

To Peter Mill[383]

[Bristol?]
c. September 22, 1788[384]

5 Dear Peter,

Alter the vile plan of the circuit, [so] that Newcastle may have preaching at 9:00 every Sunday morning.

Stop the chanting at Shields.[385] Show that you regard,
    Your affectionate friend and brother,

10   J. Wesley

Source: holograph; Wilmington, North Carolina, Grace United Methodist Church.

15

To Sarah (Gwynne) Wesley[386]

Bristol
20   September 22, 1788

Dear Sister,

As John Atlay has deserted me, and George Whitfield is but just come into his place, I do not yet know anything of my own circumstances. But I hope to be in town on Monday; and, either for the
25 sake of you or my dear Sally, I shall certainly do anything that is in the power of, dear sister,

---

[383] Mill had been appointed the Assistant of the Newcastle circuit by Conference in early Aug. 1788. Among his other duties, he was charged with bringing to a conclusion the rivalry between the preaching house on Millbourn Place in North Shields, and the 'lower house' on the river bank (see the note on JW to Andrew Inglis, Jan. 20, 1787; and JW to Trustees of the Millbourn preaching-house, May 31, 1788).

[384] The holograph has no date or place of writing. It was surely written before Mill's first meeting with the trustees of the Millbourn Place chapel in early Oct. 1788, where he raised the issue of their practice of 'chanting'.

[385] JW is referring specifically to a practice at the Millbourn Place chapel. He had been there in late May, and became aware that they kept a special pew for 'singers' who apparently led the congregation is some liturgical elements of worship, not limiting themselves to tunes JW had published for Methodist meetings; see Coates, *New Portrait*, 26, 32, 38. The 'singers' did not perform during the service that JW was present, out of respect for his musical preference. But reports JW received led him to assume they were 'chanting the Psalms' as in some large Church of England parishes (see JW to Coates, c. Nov. 5, 1788).

[386] Sarah (Gwynne) Wesley's letter to JW is not known to survive, but it surely contained a request for financial support (likely in addition to the £100 a year agreed to at the time of her marriage to CW; which JW made sure was continued after CW's death).

Your affectionate friend and brother,

J. Wesley

Source: holograph; Drew, Methodist Archives.

To John Atlay[387]

Bristol 10
September 24, 1788

My Dear Brother,

From the time that you gave me warning of quitting my service and informed me you was determined to stay no longer with me (unless upon impossible conditions[388]) than the 25th instant, I re- 15 solved to say nothing more or less about it, but to let the matter go as it would go. Whether you made a wise choice in preferring your present to your former station we shall see, if you and I should live two or three years longer. Meantime I am as ever

Your affectionate brother, 20

John Wesley

P.S. I say nothing about you to the people of Bristol.

Source: published transcription; Atlay, *Letters*, 19.

25

To Sarah Wesley Jr.[389]

Bristol 30
September 26, 1788

Dear Sally,

The reading of those poisonous writers, the mystics, confounded the intellects of both my brother [CW] and Mr. [John] Fletcher, and made them afraid of (what ought to have been their glory) the 35

---

[387] JW is replying to Atlay's letter of Sept. 20, 1788, in which Atlay mentioned that a rumour had reached London from Bristol that JW was saying he had to make a trip to London to remove a recalcitrant Atlay from his position in the book room.

[388] See the conditions stipulated by Atlay in his letter of Aug. 28, 1788. They amounted to JW waiving the conditions of the model deed for the preaching house in Dewsbury.

[389] JW is replying to Sarah Wesley Jr.'s letter of Sept. 23, 1788.

letting their light shine before men.[390] Therefore I do not wonder that he was so unwilling to speak of himself, and consequently that you knew so little about him.

5　The same wrong humility continually inculcated by those writers would induce him to discontinue the writing his journal.[391] When I see those detached papers you speak of, I shall easily judge whether any of them are proper to be published.[392]

On Monday I expect to be in town [i.e., London]. But I shall leave it again on Wednesday and set out for Norfolk and Suffolk.
10　Afterward I shall visit (if God permit) the other northern circuits till the end of October. Then I visit the classes the first two weeks in November. So that I shall not reach Canterbury before November 24.

But do not you want money? You can speak freely to, my dear
15　Sally,

　　　Yours most affectionately,

　　　　　　　　　　　　　　　　　　　　J. Wesley

Source: holograph; MARC, DDWes 5/23.

20

To Walter Churchey

25　　　　　　　　　　　　　　　　　　　　Bristol
　　　　　　　　　　　　　　　　　September 27, 1788

My Dear Brother,

Tomorrow evening I am to set out for London. So I still creep up and down, as I would fain do a little work before the night cometh
30　wherein no man can work.[393] I commend you much for not suffering your daughter [Jane] to go you know not where. What would it profit her to gain a thousand pounds and then lose her soul? Which could scarce fail to be the consequence of placing her in an ungodly family. I do not know anything in Bristol that would suit, but very
35　probably I may find something in London.

---

[390] See Matt. 5:16.

[391] I.e., CW, *MS Journal*.

[392] The scattered manuscript accounts by CW in his later years; found in CW, *Journal Letters*, 416ff.

[393] See John 9:4.

I should be glad if I could have a conversation with Mr. [William] Cowper. I verily think there would be no great difference between us.[394]

September 27, London 5

I think it is a pity to burn the poems. There are many good lines in them. So there are in the dedication, which I thought I had sent you with the rest.[395] I will send two of the Prayer-Books by the first opportunity. Peace be with you and yours. I am
    Your affectionate brother, 10

J. Wesley

Address: 'To / Mr. Churchey / Near the Hay / Brecon'.
Postmark: 'SE/29/88'. *Charge*: '6'.
Endorsement: by Churchey, ' Mr. W. 27. Sepr. 88 / About Jane - op[pose]s 15 burning / the poems'.
Source: holograph; Bridwell Library (SMU).

20

To Darcy (Brisbane) Maxwell[396]

London
September 30, 1788
My Dear Lady, 25
For many years a great person professed, and I believe had, a great regard for me. I therefore believed it my duty to speak with all

[394] See JW to Churchey, July 22, 1788.
[395] The first three sentences are underlined, apparently by Churchey; the reference is to the notebook of poetry Churchey had sent JW; see JW to Churchey, Aug. 8, 1788.
[396] Lady Maxwell was a close friend of Willielma (Maxwell) Campbell, Viscountess Glenorchy (1741–86). They ventured in 1770 to set up a chapel in Edinburgh that they initially intended to be open to gospel preachers of all denominations. However, when Glenorchy met Maxwell's friend JW, she reacted against his Arminianism and stress on Christian perfection. The chapel in Edinburgh was soon restricted to the Calvinist camp, though the relationship between the two women continued. In 1784 Lady Glenorchy and another Calvinist evangelical, Lady Henrietta Hope (c. 1750–86), visited Hotwells spa, near Bristol. They were disappointed to find that the only place of worship was half a mile up a steep hill, at the parish church in Clifton, and decided to fund building a new chapel, near the spa. Lady Hope died before work on the new chapel could start, but she left £2,500 with Lady Glenorchy to ensure it was built. Construction began in 1786, but Lady Glenorchy also died before the year was out. It then became the task of her executrix, Lady Maxwell, to complete the chapel—something that Maxwell admitted left her feeling 'a little awkward' (see Maxwell, *Life*, 266). Maxwell travelled to Bristol for the opening of the chapel in Oct. 1788 (see ibid., 267), and had apparently invited JW to speak there, on the condition he not challenge the Calvinism of the two benefactors.

freedom, which I did in a long letter.[397] But she was so displeased that she said to a friend, 'I hate Mr. Wesley above all the creatures upon earth.'

5 I now believe it my duty to write freely to *you*. Will it have the same effect? Certainly I would not run the hazard, did I not regard your happiness more than your favour. Therefore I will speak. May God enable you not only to pardon it, but to profit thereby! Indeed, unless you profit by it, I do not expect you to forgive.

Be pleased to observe I do not affirm anything. I only beg you
10 calmly to consider, Would it be right for *me* to propagate a doctrine which I believed to be false? Particularly if it were not only false but dangerous to the souls of men, frequently hindering their growth in grace, stopping their pursuit of holiness?

And is it right in *you* to do this? You believe the doctrine of abso-
15 lute predestination is false. Is it then right for you to propagate this doctrine in any kind or degree, particularly as it is not only false but a very dangerous doctrine, as we have seen a thousand times? Does it not hinder the work of God in the soul, feed all evil and weaken all good tempers, turn many quite out of the way of life and drive
20 them back to perdition?

Is not Calvinism the very antidote of Methodism, the most deadly and successful enemy which it ever had? 'But my friend desired that I would propagate it, and lodged money with me for this very purpose.' What then? May I destroy souls because my friend de-
25 sired it? Ought you not rather to throw that money into the sea? O let not any money or any friend move you to propagate a lie, to strike at the root of Methodism, to grieve the holiest of your friends, and to endanger your own soul!

Living or dying, I shall always be, my dear Lady,
30 Your most affectionate servant,

J. Wesley

Source: published transcription; Benson, *Works*, 16:370–71.

[397] The letter was to Lady Huntingdon; it is not known to survive, but some sense of its contents, in which JW 'delivered his own soul' to her, is evident in JW to Joseph Benson, Nov. 20, 1770 (28:326–28 in this edn.).

To Jasper Winscom

London
September 30, 1788

My Dear Brother,

The Conference cannot and will not bear the expense of that foolish lawsuit.[398] I can conceive but one way to pay it. The hundred pounds which you borrowed of me you may pay to the attorney, and his receipt in full shall be your discharge. I am

Your affectionate brother,

J. Wesley

Source: published transcription; Dyson, *Isle of Wight*, 150.

To [Walter Griffith?][399]

London
October 10, 1788

My Dear Brother,

It is certain you cannot preach the truth without offending those who preach the contrary. Nevertheless you must preach it, only in the mildest and [most] inoffensive manner the thing will admit of. And beware that you never return evil for evil or railing for railing, but contrariwise blessing.[400]

You cannot constrain anyone to go to Church; you can only advise them to it, and encourage them by your example.

My kind love to your wife. I am

Your affectionate friend and brother,

J. Wesley

Source: published transcription; *WHS* 10 (1915): 71.

---

[398] It is unclear whether this suit is a continuation of the legal forays sparked by the opposition to Methodist services at Sutton Scotney; see JW to Winscom, May 9, 1785 and June 17, 1786.

[399] The identity of the recipient is listed as probable in *WHS*, but with no indication of the grounds for this judgment. If it was Griffith, his wife's name was Mary.

[400] See 1 Pet. 3:9.

To Mr. _____ in Edinburgh

London
October 10, 1788

5　My Dear Brother,

It is a true saying, and continually fulfilled, that man's extremity is God's opportunity. For at this time we know not which way to turn ourselves between Dumfries and Dalkeith. More money is wanted both for one and the other than we can as yet see any means
10　of procuring. But yet,

> Eternal providence, exceeding thought,
> When none appears, can make itself a way![401]

15　I do not see the way at present. But I know the earth is the Lord's and the fullness thereof.[402] I have no money now, but probably it will not be so long. And I am determined to leave no means untried for setting those two houses out of debt, however it goes with others. Only, in the meantime, we have need of faith and patience.

20　Peace be with you and yours, I am,

Your affectionate brother,

J. Wesley

Source: published transcription; *Wesleyan Protestant Methodist Magazine*
　　4 (1832): 376.

25

To the Rev. James Bogie[403]

30

London
October 11, 1788

My Dear Brother,

It is an excellent plan. The sooner you put it in execution the bet-
35　ter; only see that you be all punctual to follow one another exactly.
Let not a little hindrance or inconvenience put you out of your way;

---

[401] Edmund Spenser, *Faerie Queene*, Bk. I, Canto 6, vii.1–2.

[402] See Ps. 24:1.

[403] JW had ordained Bogie for service in Scotland in Aug. 1788; and he was appointed Assistant for the [North] Berwick circuit. He was proposing a division of southern Scotland into three circuits. The trial run was successful and the division was adopted at the 1789 Conference; see JW to Bogie, Aug. 1, 1789.

suppose a shower of rain or snow. Press on! Break through! Take up your cross each of you and follow your Master.[404] So shall the world and the devil fall under your feet.[405]

I am, dear Jemmy,

Your affectionate friend and brother,

[J. Wesley]

Source: published transcription; Jackson, *Works* (3rd), 12:506.

To Robert Dall

London
October 11, 1788

Dear Robert,

I am glad to see your letter dated from Ayr,[406] and to hear that Joseph Cole is acceptable at Dumfries.

The great difficulty at present is to procure money. If anyone would lend you an hundred pounds, I would take care for the repayment of it; for I am determined you shall not be crushed. Let not the house be seated like a Presbyterian meeting house, but like the New Chapel in London. That at Glasgow is spoiled. I was frighted at it.[407] If the whole expense remaining is but two hundred and fifty pounds, you are a good manager.

You do well to attend the Church every forenoon, and advise all our friends so to do. But I am afraid you undertake too much in preaching twice a day. Pray let the morning preaching never be dropped. I write to Manchester to hasten the collection.

I am, dear Robert,

Your affectionate friend and brother,

J. Wesley

Source: holograph; MARC, MA 1982/001.

[404] See Luke 9:23.
[405] See Rom. 16:20.
[406] This letter is not known to survive. Dall was serving alongside Joseph Cole in the Ayr and Dumfries circuit, and was seeking to build a preaching-house in Ayr.
[407] See JW's comment after preaching for the first time in the chapel on John Street in Glasgow in *Journal*, May 16, 1788, 24:84 in this edn. His objection was that the chapel adopted the layout typical in Scotland of positioning the pulpit in the middle of a long side of rectangular buildings and aligning pews accordingly; instead of at the center of the short side opposite the entrance, with pews facing away from the door (as typical in Church of England buildings and most Methodist preaching-houses).

To the Rev. Joseph Cownley

London
October 12, 1788

Dear Joseph,

I really think you have hardly had so much scandal as one might expect would fall to your share. I have heard very few faults found with you for above these forty years, and I think you and I have not had one quarrel yet. So it is very probable we never shall.

What relates to expense we can set right. But the other evil is more hard to be remedied, because many of the preachers, especially in Scotland, are got above my hand. I never desired them to have service *thrice* a day. I knew it would be too hard for most of them. I never advised them to symbolize with the Scots.[408] I told them, over and over, it was needless. We might have done in Scotland just as we did in England. Dr. [James] Hamilton was already convinced of it. What can be done now I cannot tell. But certainly the preachers must not kill themselves. Retrench what part of the *Sunday Service* you please, and I will not blame you.

I do not see why the collection may not be made at 6:00, with a little preamble telling them the real case. This may answer just as well. Lay it upon me. Say, 'Mr. Wesley charges me not to murder myself.'

Dr. [Thomas] Coke did forget, but is now writing your letters of orders.[409]

I ever am, dear Joseph,
Your affectionate friend and brother,

[J. Wesley]

Address: 'To /Revd Mr Cownley / Minister of the Methodist Church / Leith-Wind / Edinburgh'.
Source: published transcription; Telford, *Letters*, 8:97–98.[410]

---

[408] The preachers JW ordained for Scotland were celebrating the Lord's Supper according to the ritual and gestures of the Church of Scotland, rather than the BCP (or JW's slightly revised *Sunday Service*). See Batty, *Scotland*, 30–31.

[409] JW ordained Cownley as deacon on June 3, and as elder on June 4, 1788, to serve in Scotland (see JW, diary, 24:247 in this edn.). Neither of the letters of orders is known to survive.

[410] The holograph was on the market in 1921; see *WHS* 13 (1921): 86.

To Peter Mill[411]

London
October 18, 1788   5

Dear Peter,

I thank you for the pains you have taken at Millbourn, where you see those good people copy after Dewsbury.[412]

What remains but: 1) To secure Alexander Smith and all the local preachers, that none of them may give any assistance to the sepa- 10 ratists; carefully secure this point. 2) Leave them to themselves, and preach only at the lower house, unless you preach abroad at two o'clock. 3) Speak to as many as you can of the society, taking no notice at all of Edward Coates or his five associates. [4)] Lastly, commend the whole matter to God in prayer. Then he will order all 15 things well.

I am, dear Peter,

⟨Your affectiona⟩te[413] friend and brother,

J. Wesley

20

Address: 'To / Mr Mill / At the Orphan house / Newcastle upon Tyne'.[414]
Postmark: 'Newcastle'.
Source: holograph; Wesley's Chapel (London), LDWMM 1992/121.

---

[411] After his first time preaching in the chapel at Millbourn Place, in early Oct., Mill read to the society a brief note from JW charging them to cease 'chanting' (perhaps just the single line in the letter of c. Sept. 22, 1788). His manner was abrupt, including a warning that if they failed to obey JW would no longer send them preachers. The society was puzzled by the request and refused to accede. Mill wrote JW of their obstinacy, drawing this response. See Coates, *New Portrait*, 37–38.

[412] I.e., they intend to operate as an independent chapel.

[413] A small portion of the lower left side of the sheet is missing.

[414] The last two parts of the address are struck through and replaced with 'at Mr Annett's / Merchant / at Alnwick'. Ralph Annett appears in apprenticeship contracts as a merchant in Alnwick, 1774ff.

To the Rev. Levi Heath[415]

London
October 20, 1788

5   Dear Sir,

I am of the same mind with you that it will be well for you to return to your native country.[416] If you was here, I think we should hardly part again as long as I lived. I have no doubt of finding you employment in England. All the difficulty is, how to get over?

10   Dr. [Thomas] Coke is not pleased with a letter sent to Mr. [Francis] Asbury and transmitted to him, wherein you are charged with neglect of the children—both as to their lessons and behaviour.[417] I can form no judgement at all concerning it till you have an opportunity of answering for yourself. Perhaps you was so unhinged and

15   disconcerted by finding things otherwise than you expected that you had not an heart to apply yourself to anything as diligently as you was used to do.

However that be, I should be right glad to see you well landed in England. And that God may bring you in the full blessing of the

20   gospel of peace is the prayer of, dear sir,

Your affectionate friend and brother,

J. Wesley

Address: 'To / the Revd Mr. Heath / At Cokesbury College / To be left at
        Philip Rogers Esq / In Baltimore / Maryland'.

25   *Source*: holograph; Drew, Methodist Archives.

30   ## To Rachel (Donne) Heath

London
October [20,] 1788

Dear Sister,

35   I cannot say that I was very willing to part from you and my dear children when you left England—especially not an opportunity of taking a long and perhaps a last adieu. It is true I had only had the

---

[415] For details on Levi and Rachel (Donne) Heath, and their daughters Maria and Anna, see the note on JW to Heath, May 18, 1787.

[416] Ultimately the cost of returning proved too great, and the Heaths remained in North America; see JW to Heath, June 26, 1789.

[417] This letter is not known to survive.

pleasure of a very short acquaintance with you. But in that short time I contracted nearer a harmony with you than I had done with others in many years. The sweet hour with you and them at Birmingham will never be effaced from my memory. And how glad should I have been of a few more such hours, before our long separation.

But as it seemed to be the providence of God that called you, I could only say, 'Not as I will, but as thou wilt.'[418] Nevertheless it would give me as heartfelt satisfaction to see you once again in England. I should be glad to contribute a little toward it myself. And I will talk with Mr. Coke upon that head, who will set sail in a few days from the Leeward Islands.

Wishing all blessings, spiritual and temporal, both to you and my very dear children; I am, my dear sister,

Your ever affectionate friend and brother,

John Wesley

Address: 'To Mrs Heath'.
Source: holograph; Drew, Methodist Archives.

To [Jeanne (Le Gros Bisson) Cock?][419]

London
October 24, 1788

My Dear Sister,

It gives me much pleasure to find you are still happy in God, leaning upon your Beloved. O may you increase therein more and more!

---

[418] Matt. 26:39.

[419] There are puzzles with this holograph. To begin, the recipient is not specified. It was apparently included in a package to Adam Clarke which contained the books mentioned and instructed Clarke where to deliver (the note to Clarke is not known to survive). Jackson, *Works* (3rd), 13:86–87 placed it among a set of letters to Jeanne (Le Gros Bisson) Cock; but this faced a second puzzle, as the date on the holograph clearly reads 'Oct. 2?, 1783'. Jackson ignored the one faint number, and changed the year to '1788', since JW did not meet Jeanne until 1786, and Clarke was stationed on the Isle of Jersey 1786–88. The main problem with Jackson's resulting date of Oct. 2, 1788 is that JW was not in London at the time. Telford complicated matters. He had access both to the holograph and to Jackson's *Works*, but did not connect the two. Instead the letter appears twice in his *Letters*: once on Oct. 2, 1783 to Jane Bisson (7:189–90; even though JW had not yet met her); and again dated Oct. 12, 1788 to 'Mrs. Cock' (8:97; inserting a '1' to make a date when JW was in London). But the faint number follows the '2', and most resembles JW's '4'. Therefore we have dated it Oct. 24, 1788, a day JW was in London and writing other letters (assuming the final '3' was a slip on JW's part). The recipient remains a bit uncertain, as there are other possibilities like Mrs. De Saumarez.

May you be more and more holy, and you will be more and more happy! This I long for—even your perfection, your growing up in all things into him that is our head.[420] O may you never endeavour

5
>   Love's all-sufficient sea to raise
>   By drops of creature happiness![421]

I sent you a little book or two by Mr. [Adam] Clarke. If I can be of any service to you in anything, it would be an unspeakable satisfac-
10 tion to, my dear sister,
>   Yours affectionately,

>   J. Wesley

Source: holograph; MARC, MAM JW 1/49.
15

To Edward Jackson[422]
20

>   London
>   October 24, 1788
My Dear Brother,
25   I commend you for denying tickets to all that have neglected meeting their classes, unless they seriously promise to meet them for the time to come. You cannot be too exact in this.

You do well likewise to exhort all the believers that are in earnest, or *would be* in earnest, to meet in band. But the bands in
30 every place need continual instruction; for they are continually flying in pieces.[423]

But the grand means of the revival ⟨of⟩[424] the work of God in Sheffield was the prayer-meetings. There were then twelve of them in ⟨var⟩ious parts of the town every Sunday night. ⟨Keep⟩ up these,
35 and you will keep up the flame. ⟨I am,⟩ with love to sister Jackson, dear Edward,

---

[420] See Eph. 4:15.
[421] CW, 'In Desertion or Temptation', st. 11, *HSP* (1739), 149.
[422] Jackson had been appointed Assistant for the Sheffield circuit at the 1788 Conference.
[423] See JW to Jackson, Jan. 6, 1781, 29:622 in this edn.
[424] The lower left margin is damaged, affecting a few lines (though the absent text seems clear).

Your affectionate friend and brother,

J. Wesley

Address: 'To / Mr Jackson / At the Preaching house / in / Sheffield'.
Postmark: 'OC/24/88'.
Source: holograph; Bridwell Library (SMU).   5

To Thomas Tattershall[425]   10

London
October 24, 1788

Dear Tommy,

Farewell, poor Dr. [John] Hunt! And his shadow, poor Mr. Prand!   15
You may now leave them to themselves. I wish one could borrow an
£100 for Mr. De Curl. I told him, 'I would if I could.' But I know
not when.

I desire you will immediately take any books into your hands, and
be active in performing the whole office of an Assistant. Pray read   20
over the large *Minutes* of the Conference on that head.[426] Seriously
consider every article; and put in execution, as far as is possible,
every one that has not yet been observed.

I particularly desire that the five preachers regularly follow each
other through the whole circuit. Only I allow the following excep-   25
tion (the reasons of which you will easily conceive). Let brother
Woodrow spend a *little* less, and brother Pool[e] a *little* more, time
at Norwich than one of the other preachers.[427] And pray take care:
1) of the morning preaching, 2) of the bands, [and] 3) expel all who
do not meet their bands.   30

I am, dear Tommy,
Your affectionate friend and brother,

J. Wesley

[425] Tattershall had been named Assistant for the Yarmouth circuit at the 1788 Conference,
with John Poole designated Assistant for the abutting Norwich circuit. Poole's health declined,
leading JW to combine the two circuits, with Tattershall overseeing the five total preachers.

[426] See 'Large' *Minutes* (1753–63), §§61–63, 10:865–66 in this edn.

[427] John Woodrow (1762–1850), a native of King's Lynn, Norwich, was admitted 'on trial'
as an itinerant at the 1787 Conference (see 10:623 in this edn.). He served broadly for over sixty
years; see *Minutes* (post-Wesley, 1851), 11:567. John Poole (d. 1801) began itinerating in 1759,
though his first formal appearance in the *Minutes* is in 1765 (see 10:303 in this edn.). Health issues led him to locate in Redruth after his 1789 appointment; see *Minutes* (post-Wesley, 1801),
2:83.

Address: 'To / Mr Tattershall / At the Preachinghouse / Norwich'.
Source: published transcription; Byrth, 'Memoir', xxxvii.

To William Stevens[428]

London
October 31, 1788

My Dear Brother,
You do well to write without disguise.[429] Otherwise I should not be able to judge. As you state the matter I cannot but agree with you that you are called to marry. But it is [a] pity that you had not told me these things as plainly before the Conference. Then I could have made the way plain for you, which now will be attended with some difficulty.
I am, dear Billy,
Your affectionate friend and brother,

J. Wesley

Address: 'To / Mr. Will. Stephens[430] / At the Preaching house / in / Cardiff'.
Postmark: 'OC/31/88'.
Source: holograph; Manchester, Rylands, English Ms 345/122.

To John Francis Valton

London
October 31, 1788

My Dear Brother,
Whoever they were written by, the rules are excellent rules.[431] And I should have no objection to your printing them in the man-

---

[428] William Stevens (1762–1813), a native of Plymouth Dock, was admitted 'on trial' as an itinerant at the 1786 Conference (see 10:596 in this edn.). He served a circuit for 16 years, until asthma required him to desist in 1802; at which point he served 4 years as English master at Kingswood School, then ran his own classical academy. See *Minutes* (post-Wesley, 1814), 4:5.

[429] Stevens's letter to JW is not known to survive. He married Sarah Willis in Bristol on Nov. 24, 1788.

[430] His family name appears as 'Stephens' also in *Minutes* during JW's life; we use the spelling Stevens preferred in his later years.

[431] Valton's letter to JW is not known to survive, leaving unclear the nature of the rules under discussion.

ner you mention. One thing is certain, that it would be some advantage to the poor printer. And it is probable that the rules would be useful to a serious reader.

I think if you used decoction of nettles every morning (if you have not done it already) it might restore your strength. I am, with 5 love to sister [Judith] Valton,

    Your affectionate friend and brother,

                                      J. Wesley

Address: 'To / Mr Valton / At the New Room / Bristol'.
Postmark: 'OC/31/88'. *Charge*: '5'.   10
Endorsement: by Valton, 'Oct 31 1788'.
Source: holograph; New Room (Bristol).

                                         15

To Adam Clarke

                                     London
                          November 5, 1788
My Dear Brother,   20

I am always well pleased to hear from you.[432] I am glad you [have] been to Guernsey. You must in no wise confine yourself to Jersey. It would be a sin against God and the people. You ought not to spend more than twice as much time in Jersey as you do out of it.

It would have been quite wrong to have made a collection for 25 Dr. [Thomas] Coke at this critical time.[433] The Doctor is often too hasty. He does not maturely consider all circumstances.

If you have any money in your hands, you may expend what I subscribed and draw upon me for it.

Probably at the Conference your sphere of action will be enlarged.[434] 30 I hope in the meantime you will not suffer sister [Mary] Clarke to be unemployed. See that she fulfill the office of a deaconess.[435]

Peace be with all your spirits! I am

    Your affectionate friend and brother,

                                      J. Wesley 35

---

[432] Clarke's letter to JW is not known to survive.

[433] Coke was currently trying to raise funds to relieve the residents and promote Methodist work in the West Indies.

[434] Clarke was appointed Assistant for the Bristol circuit at the 1789 Conference.

[435] See Rom. 16:1 (*NT Notes*), where JW defines the office of a deaconess as 'not to teach publicly, but to visit the sick, the women in particular, and to minister to them both in their temporal and spiritual necessities'. The term does not appear (distinct from 'visitor of the sick') in the *Minutes*.

I think it will be well to sell the old chapel.[436]

Address: 'To / Mr Adam Clarke / in / Jersey'.[437]
Source: holograph; MARC, WCB, D6/1/110.

To Benjamin Rhodes

London
November 6, 1788

My Dear Brother,

I am glad to hear that sister Rhodes begins to recover her strength.[438] It has been observed for many years that some at Redruth were apt to *despise* and very willing to *govern* their preachers. But I commend *you* for standing in your place, and changing both general and particular stewards.[439]

The case of Richard Phillips I refer wholly to *you*.[440] But if his gifts be tolerable (as we at London thought), let him not be oppressed.

I am, with love to sister Rhodes,
Your affectionate friend and brother,

[J. Wesley]

Source: published transcription; Telford, *Letters*, 8:102.

---

[436] The old Roman Catholic chapel, Notre Dame des Pas, just outside St. Helier, that had been purchased for Methodist use in 1782. It would be replaced by a house converted into a chapel in downtown St. Helier in 1790.

[437] The terse address and lack of a postmark suggest the letter was sent in a packet.

[438] Rhodes married Elizabeth Brittan (1759–1836) in 1787.

[439] Cf. JW to Rhodes, Jan. 7, 1789.

[440] Richard Phillips had been admitted 'on trial' as an itinerant at the 1784 Conference (see 10:644 in this edn.) and assigned to serve the Redruth circuit in 1788 under Rhodes as Assistant. He never appears again in the *Minutes*.

To John Blunt[441]

City Road [London]
November 7, 1788

Brother Blunt,

I am constrained to tell you you use me ill. Be you ever so great a man and I ever so little, you owe it to me to give me an account at the stated times of those souls I have entrusted you with, for whom I am to give an account to God.

Now I am speaking (perhaps the last time), friendship compels me to speak plain. Of all the men I have conversed with in London or in England, I think you have the most pride. You are above measure self-conceited and full of yourself. Whereas you are by no means equal even in sense to those whom you despise—Mr. [Samuel] Bradburn, [Henry] Moore and John Edwards, for instance.[442] Their natural understanding is stronger than yours, and is likewise far better improved.

O humble yourself before God and man! Despise no man but yourself! Learn to say from your heart, 'Lord, I am not high-minded! I have no proud looks!'[443] Then you will give as much pleasure as you have frequently given pain to

Your affectionate brother,

[John Wesley]

Endorsement: 'Wesley – answers'.
Source: published transcription; Telford, *Letters*, 8:102–03.

To Robert Carr Brackenbury

London
November 7, 1788

Dear Sir,

I snatch a few minutes from visiting the classes to answer your acceptable letter.[444] Mr. [George] Walker, who has been with us two or three weeks, set out for home yesterday. He gave us a very agreeable

---

[441] John Blunt was a merchant in Blackheath who was drawn to JW and the Methodists in the early 1780s. He entertained JW in his home a few times and was apparently appointed a class leader, but this letter marked the rupture of their connection. See JW, *Journal*, Dec. 24, 1783, 23:295 in this edn.

[442] That is, John Edwards of Lambeth; a local preacher.

[443] Ps. 131:1 (BCP).

[444] This letter is not known to survive.

account of the state of religion in Guernsey. The preaching-house is now covering in, at which Mr. [Henri] De Jersey wrought daily as a mason. Mr. [Adam] Clarke gives me a pleasing account of Jersey, complaining only of his want of a larger house at St. Helier's, and
5   of a larger sphere of action, which he may possibly have, if he lives to the Conference.[445]

I exceedingly approve of your spending the winter at Bath.[446] I believe God will make you of use to many there, who are more ripe for your instructions than ever they were before. And I am per-
10 suaded you will yourself profit as much, if not more, by the conversation of a few in Bristol—Mr. [John] Valton and Miss [Elizabeth] Johnson in particular—as by that of any persons in Great Britain.

As you are naturally inclined to a kind of sadness, I could not advise *you* to read books wrote either by Quakers or mystics. I believe
15 they are the very writers that are calculated to do you hurt, to teach you a gloomy religion, instead of the cheerfulness of faith—which surely you should aim at, in and above all things! Wishing you a continual supply of righteousness and peace and joy in the Lord,[447] I am, dear sir,

20   Your affectionate friend and brother,

J. Wesley

Address: 'To / Robert Brackenbury Esq. / At Raithby, near Spilsby / Lincolnshire'.

Postmark: 'NO/7/88'.
25
Source: holograph; Wesley's Chapel (London), LDWMM 1994/1987.

To Charles Bland[448]

30   London
                                                November 8, 1788

Dear Charles,

The *Notes on the New Testament* and the *Appeals* will come with the next Oxford *[Arminian] Magazines*.

---

[445] See JW to Clarke, Nov. 5, 1788.

[446] Brackenbury was struggling with his health, which would lead him to retire from work in the Channel Islands before the 1790 Conference.

[447] Wesley wrote 'God'; then inserted an 'r', apparently trying to alter the word to 'Lord'. See Rom. 14:17.

[448] Charles Bland (d. 1804) was admitted 'on trial' as an itinerant at the 1785 Conference (see 10:568 in this edn.). He was currently assigned to the Oxfordshire circuit, serving under Joseph Pescod as Assistant. Bland would serve until his death, though hampered by asthma much of the time. See *Minutes* (post-Wesley, 1804), 2:221.

If you all exert yourselves, the work of God will prosper throughout the circuit. I pray remember two things: First, bear with Mr.
[Greenaway] Jaques; there is honesty at the bottom. Secondly, let
none of you ever omit the morning preaching at Wycombe, Oxford,
or Witney.   5
    I am, dear Charles,
        Your affectionate brother,

                                  J. Wesley

Address: 'To / Mr C. Bland / At the Preachinghouse / in / High Wycombe'.
Source: holograph; New York, Pierpont Morgan Library, MA 516.16.   10

To Jasper Winscom   15

                                  London
                       November 8, 1788
Dear Jasper,
    William Ashman advised you like an heathen.[449] Mr. [John] Valton   20
deserves pay as well as you do. But he does not want it, and therefore
scorns to take it, knowing the poverty of the land.
    I am glad to hear so good an account of the Isle [of Wight]. The
work of God will flourish there if it be steadily pursued.
    No preacher ought to stay either at Portsmouth, or Sarum, or any   25
other place a whole week together. That is not the Methodist plan
at all. It is a novel abuse.
    I hope you have finished the matter with the attorney;[450] and am,
dear Jasper,
        Your affectionate brother,   30

                                  J. Wesley

Address: 'To / Mr Jasper Winscom / At the Preachinghouse in / Sarum'.
Postmark: 'NO/8/88'. *Charge*: '5'.
Endorsement: by Winscom, 'J. Wesley Nov 8 1788'.[451]
Source: holograph; privately held (WWEP Archive holds photocopy).   35

---

[449] Ashman had been Assistant for the Sarum circuit the prior year.
[450] See JW to Winscom, Sept. 30, 1788.
[451] Winscom also gives a list of seven names on the address page, of unknown purpose.

To Edward Coates[452]

London
5   c. November 10, 1788

My Dear Brother,

My humour was as much out of the question as my stature. My objection to the chanting the Psalms was, we have no such thing among the Methodists. But when I was informed they were not
10 the reading Psalms which were chanted, but only the hymns in the morning and evening service, my objections of course fell to the ground. But as this little dispute is now at an end, there will be no need of saying any more, only that courtesy and brotherly love require it.

15   I am

Your affectionate brother,

John Wesley

Source: published transcription; Coates, *New Portrait*, 39–40.
20

To [Sarah Crosby][453]
25

Lambeth
November 13, 1788

My Dear Sister,

30   I thank you for your account of the death of Miss Corkle(?), which is highly remarkable. It ought not to be hid under a bushel;[454] so I shall order it to be inserted in the *[Arminian] Magazine.*[455]

---

[452] For background, see JW to Peter Mill, c. Sept. 22, 1788; and JW to Mill, Oct. 18, 1788. JW's decision to stop sending itinerant and local preachers to the preaching-house at Millbourn Place sparked letters to JW from both Edward Coates and JW's son-in-law William Smith, seeking to vindicate the worship practice there. In his letter, Coates mentioned that the only reason Mill had given for JW condemning 'chanting' was his 'humour'. This is JW's reply to Coates's letter.

[453] The holograph lacks an address portion, but the most probable recipient in or near Leeds would be Sarah Crosby.

[454] See Matt. 5:14, etc.

[455] There is no such an account in *AM* in the following months.

It is very remarkable that, as brother [John] Peacock has been growing in grace for some years, so God has been increasing his gifts and has been giving him more and more favour among the people to whom he was sent. I know no reason why he may not spend another year at Leeds.[456]

I have had more pain (chiefly rheumatical) within these few months than I had for forty years before. And in September my strength swiftly decayed. But it has pleased God now to restore it, and I am nearly as I was twenty years ago. Probably, if I live, I shall see you at Leeds in summer.

Peace be with all your spirits! I am, my dear sister,

> Your ever affectionate brother,
>
> > J. Wesley

Source: holograph; MARC, MAM JW 2/70.

To William [Butterfield[457]]

London
November 16, 1788

My Dear Brother,

From various parts I have the pleasing account that the word of God prospers in your hands. Go on. Put forth all your strength. The more labour, the more blessing.

I am glad to hear that agreeable man, Mr. [Peter] Lièvre has not forgotten me. I hope to wait upon him again, but not till this tedious work of meeting the classes is over.[458]

I am, dear Billy,

> Your affectionate friend and brother,
>
> > J. Wesley

Source: holograph; privately held (British Library, Western Manuscripts collection, RP 1496 is a photocopy).

[456] Peacock was moved by the 1789 Conference to the Keighley circuit.
[457] William Butterfield was assigned to the Kent circuit, near Deptford where Lièvre was serving as curate.
[458] See JW's *Journal* comment on starting this work 'which usually takes a fortnight' on Nov. 3, 1788; 24:113 in this edn.

To [the Rev.] Joseph Taylor[459]

London
November 16, 1788

5   Dear Joseph,
    I take knowledge of your spirit, and believe it is your desire to do
all things right. Our friends at Newark have forgotten that we have
determined over and over 'not to leave the Church'.[460] Before they
had given you that foolish advice they should have consulted *me*. I
10   desire you would not wear the *surplice*, nor administer the Lord's
Supper any more.
    I am, dear Joseph,
        Your affectionate friend and brother,

J. Wesley

15

Address: 'To / Mr Jos. Taylor / At the Preachinghouse / in / Nottingham'.
Postmark: 'NO/17/88'. *Charge*: '5'.
Source: holograph; MARC, MAM JW 5/13.

---

[459] This is the earliest example among the surviving letters of an anomalous practice (and
point of tension) concerning the preachers that JW ordained for ministry in Scotland. JW had
stressed previously that he ordained persons only for areas not under the immediate control of
the Church of England. This posed an issue when ones he ordained for Scotland subsequently
returned to serve in England. JW's practice was to *stop* using their title of 'Reverend' (see the
address) and to enjoin them from wearing garb or performing roles restricted to those with
ordination while in England. John Pawson was the first to chafe against this injunction; see his
letters to Charles Atmore of Aug. 8 and Oct. 20, 1787, in Pawson, *Letters*, 1:45–46, 50–51. The
anomaly was intensified in this letter to Taylor, as JW had quietly ordained Alexander Mather
for service in England immediately after Conference ended in Aug. 1788 (see Appendix B).

[460] JW wrote 'Newark have forgotten', then appears to insert the word 'should' about
the line. But this reverses JW's point (which is why Telford silently adds the word 'not' after
'should' in his transcription). We retain JW's original text here as most clear.

To William Smith[461]

London
c. November 28, 1788

Dear Billy,

How is this? Do you owe Edward Coates money, or does he owe you money, that you will not break off with that rogue, that knave that is cheating me out of my property? I insist upon your never darkening his doors more, or renounce all connexion with your brother John Wesley. And at the same time give positive orders for the preachers to be withdrawn from Millbourn Place.

Source: published transcription; Coates, *New Portrait*, 42.

To Thomas Carlill[462]

[London]
[November to December] 1788

Dear Tommy,

We have suffered much inconvenience by taking in more preachers than we were able to keep, or indeed to employ, without their staying in one place longer than was good either for *them* or for the *people*. And this is a wrong time of year to send out young preachers, especially into the fens of Lincolnshire. You must therefore make the best shift that you can till towards spring.

I am glad to hear that you go on in love and peace with each other.

All our brethren should pray fervently and continually for the king. Nothing but the mighty power of God can restore him.

I am, dear Tommy,

---

[461] William Smith, the husband of JW's step-daughter Jeanne, was a friend of Edward Coates and supporter of the trustees of the preaching-house in Millbourn Place over the rival house built closer to the river in North Shields. He sent a letter to JW, c. Nov. 5, 1788, that helped induce JW to allow his preachers to resume duties at Millbourn Place by mid-Nov. Then JW received a letter from Peter Mill, c. Nov. 22, 1788, with new charges against the trustees, that led JW to withdraw his preachers again. The present letter was occasioned by JW hearing of Smith's strong opposition to this renewed withdrawal of the preachers.

[462] Carlill was appointed Assistant for the Horncastle circuit in Lincolnshire at the 1788 Conference. King George III suffered various health crises through that summer and fall. At a public event in late Oct. George's behaviour made clear that his sanity was endangered. He was quietly institutionalized in Nov. JW was very concerned because, if George III died or had to abdicate the throne, it would tip the control of government. See fn. 61, 24:122 in this edn.

Your affectionate friend and brother,

J. Wesley

Source: published transcription; Taft, *Original Letters*, 10.

To Henry Moore

Chatham
December 2, 1788

Dear Henry,

You will seal and put Mr. [Francis] Asbury's letter into the post.[463] And pray write strongly to Dr. [Thomas] Coke, begging him to beware of being imposed upon again, as it is plain he has been hitherto.[464] Remind him also that *he* and *I* took Mr. [Levi] Heath from his livelihood, and (whether he has behaved well or ill) are obliged in honour and in conscience to bring him home. I will give fifty pounds towards it.[465] Tell him of 'Caesar and Pompey'.[466]

I am, dear Henry,
Your affectionate friend and brother,

J. Wesley

Direct to Dr. Coke in Charleston, South Carolina.

Address: 'To / Mr Moore / At the New Chappel / near Moorfields / London / Double Letter in his absence to Mr. Whitfield'.[467]
Postmarks: 'Rochester' and 'DE/3/88'.
Source: holograph; MARC, WCB, D6/1/134b.

---

[463] In a momentary slip, JW wrote the name 'AGbury's'; this letter is not known to survive.

[464] Coke was currently at sea, in route to the West Indies; the imposition to which JW objected is unclear.

[465] See JW to Heath, Oct. 20, 1788, and June 26, 1789.

[466] JW had learned that Asbury told George Shadford, 'Mr. Wesley and I are like Caesar and Pompey; he will have no equal, and I will bear no superior.' See JW to Beverly Allen, Oct. 31, 1789.

[467] A separate letter to Whitfield is not known to survive; it was likely a reframed version of this letter.

To the Rev. Charles Atmore[468]

London

December 6, 1788 5

Dear Charles,

Noblemen do not choose to be addressed but by those they have
some knowledge of. Now I have no knowledge of Lord Aylesbury or
he of me.[469] So that I cannot with any decency apply to him. I really
think your best way would be to apply to a greater than him, by ap- 10
pointing a day of fasting and prayer.

I am, dear Charles,

Your affectionate brother,

J. Wesley

15

Source: secondary transcription by James Little; Duke, Rubenstein, Baker
Collection of Wesleyana, VOLS 7, Letter book 10, p. 27.

20

To Walter Churchey

London 25

December 6, 1788

My Dear Brother,

I am glad you wrote to poor Mr. [Richard] Henderson.[470] For certainly he stands in great need of comfort; and he must now needs
seek it in God, for all other streams are cut off. I cannot learn any- 30
thing concerning the manner of John Henderson's death—whether
it was with or without hope—as I cannot find that any of his religious friends were near him at that important season.

The Methodists in general have very little taste for any poems
but those of a religious or a moral kind; and my brother has amply 35
provided them with these. Besides those that are already printed, I

---

[468] Atmore had been named Assistant for the Colne circuit at the 1788 Conference; it is
unclear what request he wanted JW to make of Lord Ailesbury.

[469] Thomas Brudenell-Bruce, 1st Earl of Ailesbury (1729–1814).

[470] Richard Henderson's son John had died in mid-Nov.; being buried on Nov. 18, 1788 in
Bristol. Churchey had a fondness for John, referring to him as 'my lov'd Henderson' in 'Lines
to William Cowper', *ll*. 15ff, Churchey, *Poems*, 794.

have six volumes of his poems in manuscript. However, if you furnish me with the proposals, I will do you what little service I can.[471]

I should be glad to see or hear from Mr. [William] Cowper, but I have no means of access to him at all. I am

5   Your affectionate friend and brother,

[J. Wesley]

Source: published transcription; Jackson, *Works* (3rd), 12:421.

10

To Thomas Cooper[472]

15

London
December 9, 1788

Dear Tommy,

This is a stroke indeed! And will require the exertion of all the
20   resignation which God has ....[473]

You cannot, need not, avoid grieving; but you can and will, by his assistance, avoid mourning.[474] I trust he does enable your heart to say. 'It is the Lord! Let him do what seemeth him good.'[475]

The trials she felt a little before her spirit returned to God were
25   the last battle she had to fight with our great enemy, and she will see him no more. Now giving yourself wholly to him that is ⟨fairer than?[476]⟩ the children of men, now seek happiness in him alone.

I am, dear Tommy,
Your affectionate brother,

30   J. Wesley

Source: published transcription; *WHS* 24 (1944): 73.

---

[471] See JW to Churchey, Aug. 8, and Sept. 27, 1788.

[472] While neither the last name or address appear in the published transcription, this was surely to Thomas Cooper, who buried his wife Ann (Parminter) Cooper in Mistley, Essex, on Dec. 10, 1788.

[473] Ellipses appear in the published transcription, described as places where the writing could not be deciphered.

[474] Likely JW wrote 'murmuring'; see JW to Sarah Wesley Jr., June 30, 1788.

[475] 1 Sam. 3:18.

[476] Published transcription has an ellipsis. See Ps. 45:2.

To Edward Coates[477]

London
c. December 20, 1788

My Dear Brother,

I have all my life been a lover of peace, and am not less so now than I was fifty years ago. Therefore, as to warm words spoken to you or any other, let them pass. They are not worth rehearsing. There is only one charge which is of consequence, that you will not settle the house on the Methodist plan. This is exactly the case of the Dewsbury house; and if you persist in the resolution, you will constrain us to proceed in the same manner.

I am
Your affectionate brother,

John Wesley

Source: published transcription; Coates, *New Portrait*, 44.

To Peter Mill

London
December 20, 1788

My Dear Brother,

It does not appear to me that you have taken any wrong step with regard to North Shields. I think (as you do) that our friend whom you mention is prejudiced in favour of those warm men.[478]

As to Thomas Gibson, you are a little prejudiced against him.[479] He is not a turbulent man. But he sees blots, and would fain cure them if he could. I pray, talk with him alone. You do not know him. However, for the present, the general stewards may stand as they are. But see that they do their duty.

I am, with love to sister Mill, dear Peter,[480]
Your affectionate friend and brother,

J. Wesley

[477] JW is replying to Coates's letter of Dec. 16, 1788.
[478] The friend was surely William Smith.
[479] Gibson was a member of the Methodist society in Alnwick, part of Mill's circuit.
[480] Peter Mill married Isabelle Carnegie (b. 1757) in Scotland, Mar. 1782.

Address: 'To / Mr Mill / At the Orphanhouse / Newcastle upon Tyne'.
Postmark: 'DE/20/88'.
Source: holograph; MARC, MAM JW 4/16.

To Sarah (Gwynne) Wesley[481]

City Road [London]
December 21, 1788

My Dear Sister,

It is undoubtedly true that some silly people (whether in the society or not, I cannot tell) have frequently talked in that manner both of my brother and me. They have said that we were well paid for our labours. And indeed, so we were; but not by man. Yet this is no more than we were to expect, especially from busybodies in other men's matters. And it is no more possible to restrain their tongues than it is to bind up the wind. But it is sufficient for us that our own consciences condemned us not and that our record is with the Most High.

What has concerned me more than this idle slander is a trial of another kind. I supposed, when John Atlay left me, that he had left me one or two hundred pounds beforehand. On the contrary, I am one or two hundred pounds behindhand, and shall not recover myself till after Christmas. Some of the first moneys I receive I shall set apart for you.[482] And in everything that is in my power you may depend upon the willing assistance of, dear Sally,

Your affectionate friend and brother,

J. Wesley

Source: holograph; MARC, DDWes 5/24.

---

[481] JW is replying to Sarah's letter of c. Dec. 18, 1788.

[482] For a detailed account of how JW and the Methodist Conference dealt with monies related to Sarah (Gwynne) Wesley and her children after CW's death, see Clive Norris, 'Untying the Knot: The Afterlife of Charles and Sally Wesley's Marriage Settlement, 1749–1800', *Proceedings of the Charles Wesley Society* 17 (2013): 49–63.

To John Ryley[483]

Coalbrook[e] Row [London]
December 22, 1788   5

My Dear Brother,

What you say is true. There is a grievous neglect. But how shall we remedy it? I will tell you how. Set *your own* shoulders to the work. I will give you a ticket and put you into what office you please. Then you may do essential service to,   10

    Your affectionate brother,

J. Wesley

Address: 'To / Mr John Ryley / in / Tabernacle Road'.
Source: holograph; privately held (WWEP Archive holds photocopy).   15

To Walter Churchey   20

[London]
[December 25, 1788[484]]

25

I have now revised the five volumes of my brother's hymns on the Four Gospels and the Acts of the Apostles.[485] He had himself revised [them] no less than seven times in the space of twenty years.[486] Many of them are little or nothing inferior to the best of them that have been printed. Those of them that savour a little of mysticism I   30
have rather corrected or expunged; but I have no thought or design at all of printing them. I have other work to do which is of more immediate importance. Besides that, I have not two or three hundred pounds to spare.

---

[483] JW mentions visiting a brother John Riley in London in his diary in the 1780s; see Jan. 21, 1784 (23:474 in this edn.), Nov. 22, 1787 (24:228), and Nov. 10, 1790 (24:336).

[484] Date taken from postmark.

[485] Cf. JW to Churchey, July 22, 1788. See CW's MS Matthew, MS Mark, MS Luke, MS John, and MS Acts at https://divinity.duke.edu/initiatives/cswt.

[486] CW created the initial collections between 1764–66, and periodically read through and corrected them until near his death.

I will order my printer to strike off some of your proposals, which I will then occasionally recommend to my friends.[487] Some of them I know will subscribe; and it may be God will incline the hearts of more than I am aware of. But with whom do you agree for paper and printing? Proceed warily, or you may get into much trouble.

That God may bless you and yours, and be your guide in this and in all things, is the prayer of

Your affectionate brother,

J. Wesley

Address: 'To / Mr Churchey / Near the Hay / Brecon'.
Postmark: 'DE/25/88'.
Endorsement: by Churchey, 'Mr. J. W. / re(?) Prop[osals]'.
Source: holograph; Oklahoma City, OK: The Green Collection, GC.PPR.

To Hugh Moore

London
December 25, 1788

Dear Hugh,

You have great reason to praise God who gives you [to] see the fruit of your labour. You say sinners are awakened out of sleep and savingly converted to God, then be thankful. Is not it a good reward for all the pains you have taken? And what if, in the meantime, men say all manner of evil of you?[488] You are never the worse for this. Bear this as the cross which our blessed Lord sees good to lay upon you. A good man says 'David saw God's hand in Shimei's tongue, and therefore he was quiet.'[489] See God's hand in Shimei's tongue!

I am

Your affectionate friend and brother,

J. Wesley

Source: published transcription; *WHS* 29 (1954): 116.

---

[487] For a transcription of the printed Proposals for Churchey's *Poems*, see Mar. 3, 1789, vol. 31 in this edn.

[488] See Matt. 5:11.

[489] Thomas Gouge, *A Young Man's Guide* (London: Neville Simmons, 1676), 73.

To Sarah Mallet[490]

London
December 26, 1788 5

My Dear Sister,

I answered your letter long ago, and desired Mr. [George] Whitfield to send my letter with the *[Arminian] Magazines* which he
was sending to Norwich, desiring withal that the next preacher who
went to Long Stratton would give it [to] you. But for the time to 10
come, whenever I write I will send the letter by post, and I can easily make up the expense.

I am well pleased to find that you have regard for me. So have
I for *you*. And it is therefore a pleasure to me to serve you in anything that is within my power. Indeed I could not so well send the 15
[Explanatory] Notes on the Old Testament, as the edition is nearly
sold off and we have very few of them left, which are reserved to
make up full sets. But any other books are at your service. I want
to forward you in all useful knowledge, which indeed lies in a very
narrow compass. 20

You do not expect to go through life without crosses. And some
will fall upon you on *my* account; for my taking notice of you may
bring envy upon you. But go on your way, and in your patience
possess your soul.[491] Please God, and it is enough. Go steadily and
quietly on, in the way wherein providence leads you. And in every 25
temptation his Spirit will make a way for *you* to escape. If any particular difficulty or trial comes upon you, do not fail to let me know.
None can be more ready to assist you than, my dear Sally,

Yours affectionately,

J. Wesley 30

Address: 'To / Miss Sally Mallet / In Long Stratton / Norfolk'.
Postmark: 'JA/1/89'.
Endorsement: 'Dec 26 - 1788 – Cop[ie]d Z. T.'.[492]
Source: holograph; Bridwell Library (SMU). 35

---

[490] Mallet had apparently informed JW she was not receiving answers to her letters. No
letters from Mallet to JW in 1788 are known to survive. This is explained in part by a note on
the back of this holograph, in Mallet's hand: 'Our letters to each other were stopt [i.e., inter-
cepted]. Some curious minds wished to know what was passing between us. But they found
no evil.'

[491] See Luke 21:19.

[492] I. e., Zachariah Taft, who included in *Holy Women*, 1:88.

To Jeanne (Le Gros Bisson) Cock

London
December 27, 1788

My Dear Sister,

I was glad to receive a few lines from you.[493] From the time I saw you first, and indeed before I saw you, I could not but feel a strong affection for you. And I pray that nothing may abate our affection for each other till we meet in a better world.

When I heard of your marriage it gave me pain. I was afraid least you should have suffered loss. Do you feel as much union with God as ever? As close fellowship with the Father and the Son? And is it as constant as ever? Are you as happy as you was once? And do you ever think of, my dear Jenny,

Your affectionate brother,

J. Wesley

Address: 'To Jeannie Cock'.[494]
Source: holograph; MARC, MAM JW 2/51.

To Sarah [?]

[1788 late?]

⟨...[495]⟩ will be an useful ⟨...⟩ will write to William Palmer and desire him to try Charles a little longer.[496] But in truth the casting voice is in him. For if he insists on the removal, it must take place.

As to the young man, I had much rather *mend* him than *end* him; for he has the fear of God, and not contemptible talents. My dear

---

[493] Her letter to JW is not known to survive.

[494] This appears as a header; meaning that this was almost certainly part of a double letter, with the other portion (not known to survive) likely to Adam Clarke.

[495] The top portion of this holograph, and a couple of words in the next line, are cut away and missing. This renders the addressee and date uncertain. The date is likely during the year (Aug. 1788 to July 1789) that William Palmer was Assistant for the Pembrokeshire circuit, with Charles Bond serving under his direction.

[496] Charles Bond would be laid aside at the 1789 Conference (see 10:677 in this edn.), but reinstated in 1790 (10:715).

Sally, how hard it is for *me*, to refuse *you* anything! But observe; I don't refuse. We compromise the matter.
  Peace be with all your spirits! I am,
    Yours very affectionately,

J. Wesley   5

Source: holograph; privately held (WWEP Archive holds photocopy).

APPENDIX A

List of Wesley's Correspondence (in and out), 1782–88

This Appendix continues the project to compile as complete a listing as possible of the letters known to have been written or received by John Wesley, whether or not the text is extant. Not included are letters that are merely inferred from the existence of a presumed reply. Similarly, references to letters from or to unnamed correspondents are not usually included. For inclusion there must be something specific, at least a clue to the correspondent or an indication of the date or contents of the letter (such as Wesley quoting extracts in his reply).

The columns list in order the date, the writer, the recipient, and details of location where either a transcription of the letter or the evidence for the letter's existence at one time can be found. For surviving letters by Wesley the last column gives where the transcription is published in this edition. For surviving letters written to Wesley, readers are generally directed to the website of The Wesley Works Editorial Project (www.wesley-works.org), where transcriptions are available (the main exception is extended rebuttals of Wesley's published volumes, which are actually books, even if cast in the title as 'letters'). The most common sources of evidence for letters that do not survive during this time period include a specific reference within another letter (abbreviated 'ref.'), quoted extracts in a surviving letter that is replying to the original, or Wesley's notation on a letter received of the date on which he replied.

Date	Writer	Recipient	Location
1782 Jan. 01	John Francis Valton	JW	online
1782 c. Jan. 01	William Watters	JW	ref.; JW reply, Feb. 22
1782 Jan. 04	Rev. Th. Davenport	JW	online
1782 Jan. 05	JW	Ellen Gretton	30:1
1782 Jan. 05	JW	Joseph Thompson	30:2
1782 Jan. 06	Hester Ann Roe	JW	online
1782 Jan. 06	JW	James [?]	30:2
1782 c. Jan. 07	Thomas Tattershall	JW	ref.; JW reply, Jan. 11
1782 Jan. 10	Samuel Bardsley	JW	online
1782 c. Jan. 10	Ann Loxdale	JW	ref.; JW reply, Jan. 18
1782 Jan. 10	Elizabeth Ritchie	JW	online
1782 c. Jan. 10	JW	Rev. Th. Davenport	ref.; Davenport reply, Jan. 15
1782 Jan. 11	JW	Thomas Tattershall	30:3
1782 Jan. 15	Rev. Th. Davenport	JW	online
1782 Jan. 17	JW	Hester Ann Roe	30:3–4
1782 Jan. 18	JW	Ann Loxdale	30:5
1782 Jan. 18	JW	John Francis Valton	30:6
1782 Jan. 19	JW	Rev. Th. Davenport	30:6–7
1782 Jan. 19	JW	Elizabeth Ritchie	30:7–8
1782 c. Jan. 20	Richard Rodda	JW	ref.; JW reply, Jan. 24
1782 Jan. 24	JW	Richard Rodda	30:8–9
1782 Jan. 24	JW	Francis Wolf	30:9–10
1782 Jan. 25	JW	Samuel Bardsley	30:10
1782 Jan. 25	JW	Potential Subscribers	30:11–12
1782 Jan. 26	Sarah (Ward) Nind	JW	online
1782 c. Jan. 26	Ann Tindall	JW	ref.; JW reply, Feb. 1
1782 Jan. 28	Ann Loxdale	JW	online
1782 Jan. 30	JW	Thomas Hanson	30:12–13
1782 c. Feb.	John Pawson	JW	online
1782 Feb. 01	JW	Ann Tindall	30:13
1782 Feb. 05	John Pawson	JW	online
1782 Feb. 09	JW	Alexander Suter	30:14
1782 Feb. 12	Mrs. Dorothy Downes	JW	online
1782 Feb. 12	Thomas Simpson	JW	online
1782 Feb. 12	JW	Ellen Gretton	30:14–15
1782 Feb. 13	'Respectful Reader'	JW	online
1782 c. Feb. 15	James Barry	JW	online
1782 c. Feb. 18	Joseph Benson	JW	online

Date	Writer	Recipient	Location
1782 c. Feb. 20	Joseph Algar	JW	ref.; JW reply, Feb. 24
1782 c. Feb. 20	Robert Leister	JW	online
1782 Feb. 20	JW	John Bredin	30:15–16
1782 c. Feb. 20	George Whitfield	JW	online
1782 Feb. 22	JW	Joseph Benson	30:16–17
1782 Feb. 22	JW	William Watters	30:17–18
1782 Feb. 23	Ann Bolton	JW	online
1782 Feb. 23	JW	'A Respectful Reader'	30:18–20
1782 Feb. 24	Eliz. (Nangle) Bradburn	JW	online
1782 Feb. 24	JW	Joseph Algar	30:20–21
1782 Feb. 26	JW	Ambrose Foley	30:21
1782 Feb. 27	JW	Ann (Turner) Knapp	30:21–22
1782 Feb. 28	Thomas Taylor	JW	online
1782 Feb. 28	JW	Elizabeth Bradburn	30:22–23
1782 c. Mar.	William Ferguson	JW	online
1782 c. Mar.	John Pawson	JW	online
1782 c. Mar.	Richard Swanwick	JW	online
1782 c. Mar. 01	[Thomas Tattersall?]	JW	online
1782 Mar. 02	JW	Robert Costerdine	30:23
1782 Mar. 02	JW	Mrs. Mary Parker	30:24
1782 c. Mar. 06	R. C. Brackenbury	JW	ref.; JW reply, Mar. 9
1782 c. Mar. 06	Ann Loxdale	JW	ref. and excerpts; JW reply, Mar. 9
1782 c. Mar. 07	Hannah Ball	JW	ref.; JW reply, Mar. 10
1782 Mar. 08	JW	Ann Bolton	30:24–25
1782 c. Mar. 09	Thomas Brisco	JW	ref.; JW reply, Mar. 12
1782 Mar. 09	JW	R. C. Brackenbury	30:25–26
1782 Mar. 09	JW	Ann Loxdale	30:26–27
1782 Mar. 10	JW	Hannah Ball	30:27–28
1782 Mar. 12	JW	Thomas Brisco	30:28–29
1782 c. Mar. 15	Thomas Saxton	JW	online
1782 Mar. 16	J. W. Salmon	JW	online
1782 c. Mar. 20	John Francis Valton	JW	ref.; JW reply, Mar. 24
1782 Mar. 22	JW	Robert Costerdine	30:29
1782 Mar. 22	JW	Ann Tindall	30:29–30
1782 Mar. 24	JW	John Francis Valton	30:30–31
1782 Mar. 26	Thomas Carlill	JW	online
1782 Mar. 28	Mrs. K. K[eysell]	JW	online

Date	Writer	Recipient	Location
1782 c. Mar. 30	John Bredin	JW	ref.; JW reply, Apr. 6
1782 Mar. 30	JW	Joseph Benson	30:31
1782 c. Mar. 31	Francis Wrigley	JW	ref.; JW reply, Apr. 4
1782 c. Apr.	[William Collins]	JW	online
1782 c. Apr.	John Furz	JW	online
1782 c. Apr.	Christopher Watkins	JW	online
1782 Apr. 01	unnamed noblewoman	JW	online
1782 c. Apr. 01	Mrs. Davenport	JW	ref.; JW to Bredin, Apr. 10
1782 Apr. 03	JW	Thomas Carlill	30:32
1782 Apr. 04	JW	John Atlay	30:32–34
[1782 Apr. 04]	JW	Francis Wrigley	30:34
1782 Apr. 06	JW	John Bredin	30:35
1782 Apr. 06	JW	Henry Foster	ref.; JW to S. Mitchell of same date
1782 Apr. 06	JW	Samuel Mitchell	30:36
1782 Apr. 07	Hester Ann Roe	JW	online
1782 c. Apr. 08	Thomas Taylor	JW	ref.; JW reply, Apr. 12
1782 c. Apr. 09	John Atlay	JW	ref.; JW reply, Apr. 13
1782 Apr. 10	JW	John Bredin	30:36–37
1782 Apr. 12	JW	Thomas Taylor	30:37–38
1782 Apr. 13	JW	John Atlay	30:38
1782 c. Apr. 14	John Bredin	JW	ref. and summary; Bredin for Adam Clarke, Aug. 13, 1782
1782 Apr. 15	JW	Hester Ann Roe	30:39
1782 Apr. 21	JW	Thomas [Lewis]	30:40
1782 Apr. 24	John Allen	JW	online
1782 c. May	unidentified	JW	online
1782 May 01	JW	Zachariah Yewdall	30:40–41
1782 May 05	JW	[Elizabeth Woodhouse?]	30:41
1782 May 07	JW	Mrs. Nuttal	30:42
1782 May 14	JW	Ann (Dupuy) Taylor	30:42–43
1782 May 16	Capt. Rich. Williams	JW	online
1782 c. May 21	Capt. Thomas Webb	JW	ref.; JW reply, May 25
1782 May 21	JW	William Petty	30:43–44
1782 May 21	JW	Thomas Taylor	30:44–45
1782 May 23	JW	Samuel Tooth	30:45
1782 May 24	JW	Samuel Bardsley	30:45–46

Date	Writer	Recipient	Location
1782 c. May 24	CW	JW	ref.; JW reply, May 28
1782 May 25	JW	Martha Chapman	30:46
1782 May 25	JW	Capt. Thomas Webb	30:47
1782 c. May 26	Mary Clark	JW	ref.; JW reply, June 1
1782 May 28	JW	Charles Atmore	30:48
1782 May 28	JW	CW	30:48–49
1782 June 01	Ann Loxdale	JW	online
1782 June 01	JW	Mary Clark	30:50
1782 c. June 02	Samuel Bradburn	JW	ref.; JW reply, June 7
1782 June 06	James Wood	JW	online
1782 June 07	JW	Samuel Bradburn	30:50–51
1782 June 10	John Baxter	JW	online
1782 June 13	Hester Ann Roe	JW	online
1782 June 16	JW	Jonathan Hern	30:51
1782 c. June 20	Elizabeth Ritchie	JW	ref.; JW to Hester Ann Roe, July 7
1782 June 20	JW	Thomas Tattershall	30:52
1782 June 22	JW	Ellen Gretton	30:52–53
1782 June 25	JW	Hester Ann Roe	30:53–54
1782 June 29	JW	John Francis Valton	30:54
1782 c. July	Freeborn Garrettson	JW	online
1782 c. July 01	John Bredin	JW	ref.; JW reply, July 8
1782 July 07	Mrs. Mary Fletcher	JW	online
1782 c. July 07	Penelope Newman	JW	ref.; JW reply, July 12
1782 July 07	Hester Ann Roe	JW	online
1782 July 08	JW	John Bredin	30:55
1782 July 12	JW	Mrs. Mary Fletcher	30:55–56
1782 July 12	JW	Ann Loxdale	30:56–57
1782 July 12	JW	Penelope Newman	30:57–58
1782 c. July 15	Richard Calcut	JW	ref.; JW to Rutherford, July 29
1782 c. July 15	George Pellat	JW	ref.; JW to Rutherford, July 29
1782 July 15	Mrs. Martha Ward	JW	online
1782 c. July 18	Ellen Gretton	JW	ref.; JW reply, July 23
1782 July 23	JW	Ellen Gretton	30:58–59
1782 July 24	JW	Ann Loxdale	30:59
1782 c. July 29	Joseph Benson	JW	ref.; JW reply, Aug. 3
1782 July 29	Thomas Bond	JW	online

Date	Writer	Recipient	Location
1782 July 29	JW	Thomas Bethell	ref.; JW to Rutherford, July 29
1782 July 29	JW	Thomas Rutherford	30:60
1782 c. July 30	Ann Bolton	JW	ref.; JW reply, Aug. 3
1782 July 30	JW	Alexander Knox	30:60–62
1782 c. July 31	Hannah Ball	JW	ref.; JW reply, Aug. 4
1782 July 31	JW	Mrs. Nuttal	30:62–63
1782 July 31	JW	Catherine Warren	30:63–64
1782 Aug. 03	JW	Joseph Benson	30:64–65
1782 Aug. 03	JW	Ann Bolton	30:65
1782 Aug. 04	JW	Hannah Ball	30:66
1782 Aug. 04	JW	John Bredin	30:66–67
1782 Aug. 05	JW	Ann Tindall	30:67–68
1782 Aug. 06	JW	Francis Wolf	30:68
1782 c. Aug. 10	Rev. Th. Davenport	JW	ref.; JW reply, Aug. 14
1782 Aug. 10	JW	Jasper Winscom	30:69
1782 Aug. 11	JW	William Sagar	30:69
1782 Aug. 12	JW	Harriett Cooper	30:70
1782 Aug. 13	John Bredin	unidentified	online
1782 Aug. 13	JW	Robert Hopkins	30:70
1782 Aug. 14	JW	Rev. Th. Davenport	30:71
1782 Aug. 15	Elizabeth Ritchie	JW	online
1782 Aug. 28	Mr. M. L.	JW	online
1782 c. Aug. 30	JW	William Roberts	ref.; JW to Roberts, Sept. 12
1782 c. Sept.	James Oddie	JW	online
1782 c. Sept. 02	Ellen Gretton	JW	ref.; JW reply, Sept. 7
1782 c. Sept. 06	William Roberts	JW	ref.; JW to Roberts, Sept. 12
1782 Sept. 07	JW	Ellen Gretton	30:72
1782 Sept. 09	Ann Bolton	JW	online
1782 Sept. 09	JW	Richard Rodda	30:72–73
1782 Sept. 09	JW	Joseph Taylor	30:73–74
1782 Sept. 10	JW	Rev. James Creighton	30:74–75
1782 Sept. 12	JW	William Roberts	30:76
1782 Sept. 15	JW	Ann Bolton	30:77
1782 Sept. 16	William Roberts	JW	online
1782 c. Sept. 18	Joseph Andrew	JW	ref.; JW to Joseph Taylor, Sept. 24
1782 Sept. 19	JW	William Roberts	30:78
1782 c. Sept. 23	William Roberts	JW	online

Date	Writer	Recipient	Location
1782 c. Sept. 24	JW	Joseph Andrew	ref.; JW to Joseph Taylor, Sept. 24
1782 Sept. 24	JW	Joseph Taylor	30:78
1782 c. Sept. 25	unidentified man	JW	quoted; JW reply, Sept. 30
1782 Sept. 28	Hester Ann Roe	JW	online
1782 Sept. 30	JW	unidentified man	30:79
1782 c. Oct.	JW	William Ripley	30:80
1782 Oct. 01	JW	Penelope Newman	30:80
1782 Oct. 01	JW	Hester Ann Roe	30:81
1782 Oct. 04	John Trembath	JW	online
1782 c. Oct. 10	Thomas Rutherford	JW	ref.; JW reply, Oct. 19
1782 c. Oct. 12	Zachariah Yewdall	JW	ref.; JW reply, Oct. 21
1782 c. Oct. 14	Alexander Knox	JW	ref.; JW reply, Oct. 22
1782 c. Oct. 15	James Rogers	JW	ref.; JW reply, Oct. 20
1782 Oct. 19	JW	Thomas Rutherford	30:82
1782 Oct. 19	JW	Joseph Taylor	30:83
1782 Oct. 20	JW	James Rogers	30:83–84
1782 Oct. 21	JW	Zachariah Yewdall	30:84
1782 Oct. 22	JW	Alexander Knox	30:85
1782 Oct. 24	JW	Duncan M'Allum	30:86
1782 Oct. 26	JW	Ellen Gretton	30:86
1782 Oct. 28	Mrs. Martha Ward	JW	online
1782 Oct. 30	JW	Elizabeth Bradburn	30:87
1782 Nov. 01	Thomas Taylor	JW	online
1782 c. Nov. 03	Zachariah Yewdall	JW	ref.; JW reply, Nov. 12
1782 c. Nov. 04	William Sagar	JW	ref. and extract; JW to Thomas Hanson, Nov. 9
1782 Nov. 09	JW	Samuel Bradburn	30:88
1782 Nov. 09	JW	Thomas Hanson	30:88–89
1782 Nov. 11	Elizabeth Ritchie	JW	online
1782 Nov. 12	JW	Zachariah Yewdall	30:89
1782 c. Nov. 15	[Mrs. Martha Ward?]	JW	online
1782 Nov. 16	Joseph Benson	JW	online
1782 Nov. 21	Hester Ann Roe	JW	online
1782 Nov. 21	JW	Zachariah Yewdall	30:90
1782 c. Nov. 24	Alexander Knox	JW	ref.; JW reply, Dec. 2

Date	Writer	Recipient	Location
1782 c. Nov. 26	Ann Loxdale	JW	ref.; JW reply, Dec. 1
1782 Nov. 28	Rev. J. Burckhardt	JW	online
1782 Nov. 29	JW	Joseph Benson	30:90–93
1782 Nov. 30	JW	British officer	30:93–94
1782 Nov. 30	JW	John Bredin	30:94
1782 Nov. 30	JW	John Watson Jr.	30:95
1782 Dec.	J. M.	JW	online
1782 c. Dec.	Sampson Staniforth	JW	online
1782 c. Dec. 01	Zachariah Yewdall	JW	ref.; JW reply, Dec. 7
1782 Dec. 01	JW	Hannah Ball	30:95–96
1782 Dec. 01	JW	Ann Loxdale	30:96–97
1782 Dec. 02	JW	Alexander Knox	30:97
1782 Dec. 03	JW	John Francis Valton	30:98
1782 Dec. 05	Samuel Badcock	JW	online
1782 Dec. 07	JW	Zachariah Yewdall	30:98–99
1782 Dec. 14	Joseph Benson	JW	online
1782 Dec. 14	Rev. Th. Davenport	JW	online
1782 Dec. 19	JW	Robert Hall	30:99
1782 Dec. 20	JW	Jonah Freeman	30:100
1782 Dec. 21	JW	William Petty	30:100
1782 Dec. 22	Mrs. Martha Ward	JW	online
1782 Dec. 23	JW	unidentified man	30:101
1782 Dec. [25?]	JW	Matthias Joyce	30:102
1782 Dec. 28	JW	Rev. Th. Davenport	30:102–03
1782 Dec. 31	JW	Ellen Gretton	30:104
1782 Dec. 31	JW	Zachariah Yewdall	30:104–05
1783	JW	Abraham Orchard	30:106
1783 Jan.	William Black Jr.	JW	ref.; JW reply, Feb. 26
1783 Jan 03	JW	on Birstall House	30:106–10
1783 Jan. 03	John Allen	JW	online
1783 Jan. 03	Ann Bolton	JW	online
1783 c. Jan. 03	Ellen Gretton	JW	online
1783 Jan. 05	JW	Ann Bolton	30:110–11
1783 c. Jan. 06	James Oddie	JW	ref.; JW to Brackenbury, Jan. 10
1783 c. Jan. 06	Elizabeth Padbury	JW	ref.; JW reply, Jan. 10
1783 Jan. 10	JW	R. C. Brackenbury	30:111–12
1783 Jan. 10	JW	Elizabeth Padbury	30:113
1783 Jan. 13	Lady Maxwell	JW	online

Date	Writer	Recipient	Location
1783 Jan. 16	JW	Joseph Taylor	30:113–14
1783 Jan. 16	JW	John Francis Valton	30:114
1783 Jan. 18	Ruth Hall	JW	online
1783 c. Jan. 18	Richard Rodda	JW	ref.; JW reply, Jan. 23
1783 Jan. 22	JW	John Francis Valton	30:115
1783 Jan. 23	JW	Richard Rodda	30:115–16
1783 Jan. 23	JW	Thomas Tattershall	30:116
1783 Jan. 25	JW	William Petty	30:117
1783 Jan. 29	Ann Bolton	JW	online
1783 [Feb.]	JW	Miss Fuller	30:117–18
1783 Feb. 01	John Francis Valton	JW	online
1783 Feb. 03	Elizabeth Scaddan	JW	online
1783 Feb. 09	JW	Zachariah Yewdall	30:118
1783 Feb. 10	JW	John Cricket	30:119
1783 Feb. 10	JW	Alexander Knox	30:120
1783 Feb. 13	John Allen	JW	online
1783 c. Feb. 15	Robert Blake	JW	ref.; JW to Rutherford, Feb. 23
1783 c. Feb. 15	JW	Mary Freeman Shephard	ref.; her reply, Feb. 21
1783 Feb. 16	JW	Ellen Gretton	30:120–21
1783 Feb. 18	unidentified	JW	online
1783 c. Feb. 20	Capt. Rich. Williams	JW	ref.; JW to Joseph Taylor, Feb. 25
1783 Feb. 21	Mary F. Shepherd	JW	online
1783 Feb. 23	JW	Rev. J[ames] Bailey	30:121–22
1783 Feb. 23	JW	Thomas Rutherford	30:122
1783 Feb. 24	JW	Ambrose Foley	30:123
1783 Feb. 25	William Collins	JW	online
1783 Feb. 25	JW	George Blackall	30:123
1783 Feb. 25	JW	Joseph Taylor	30:124
1783 Feb. 26	JW	William Black Jr.	30:124–25
1783 Feb. 26	JW	Elizabeth Bradburn	30:126
1783 Feb. 26	JW	Mrs. Elizabeth Carr	ref.; JW to Bradburn, same day
1783 c. Feb. 28	Thomas Hanby	JW	online
1783 c. Mar.	Dorothea (Garret) King	JW	online
1783 c. Mar.	J[ane] T[hornton]	JW	online
1783 c. Mar. 02	John Baxendale	JW	ref.; JW reply, Mar. 7
1783 [Mar. 06]	JW	William Thompson	30:126–27

Date	Writer	Recipient	Location
1783 Mar. 07	JW	John Baxendale	30:127
1783 Mar. 07	JW	John Mason	30:128
1783 Mar. 11	unidentified	JW	online
1783 Mar. 13	Charles Boone	JW	online
1783 Mar. 15	JW	Hester Ann Roe	30:128–29
1783 Mar. 23	JW	unidentified man	30:129
1783 Apr. 01	JW	John Francis Valton	30:130
1783 Apr. 04	JW	CW	30:130–32
1783 Apr. 05	JW	Alexander Knox	30:132–33
1783 Apr. 07	JW	Elizabeth Gibbes	30:133–34
1783 c. Apr. 07	JW	[Abraham Orchard?]	ref.; JW to Eliz. Gibbes, Apr. 25
1783 Apr. 07	JW	Joseph Saunderson	30:134
1783 c. Apr. 07	JW	Mary F. Shepherd	ref.; JW to Eliz. Gibbes, Apr. 25
1783 Apr. 11	Ann Loxdale	JW	online
1783 c. Apr. 20	Agnes Gibbes	JW	ref.; JW reply, Apr. 25
1783 c. Apr. 20	Eliabeth Gibbes	JW	ref.; JW reply, Apr. 25
1783 c. Apr. 20	[John Watson Jr.]	JW	ref.; JW reply, Apr. 25
1783 Apr. 21	JW	Henry Brooke	30:134–35
1783 Apr. 23	JW	Jane (Hilton) Barton	30:135
1783 Apr. 23	JW	Alexander Knox	30:136
1783 Apr. 25	JW	Mrs. Ellen Christian	30:136–37
1783 Apr. 25	JW	Agnes Gibbes	30:137–38
1783 Apr. 25	JW	Elizabeth Gibbes	30:138–39
1783 Apr. 25	JW	[John Watson Jr.]	30:139
1783 Apr. 25	JW	CW	30:140
1783 c. Apr. 26	Thomas Tattershall	JW	ref.; JW reply, May 3
1783 c. Apr. 26	Jasper Robinson	JW	ref.; JW to Tattershall, May 3
1783 Apr. 26	JW	Joseph Taylor	30:140–41
1783 May 02	JW	Rev. John Cricket	30:141
1783 May 02	JW	Mary Smith	30:142
1783 May 02	JW	CW	30:143
1783 May 03	JW	Alexander Knox	30:143–44
1783 May 03	JW	Thomas Tattershall	30:144–45
1783 c. May 10	CW	JW	online
1783 c. May 15	Joseph Benson	JW	ref.; JW reply, Mar. 19

Date	Writer	Recipient	Location
1783 May 19	JW	Joseph Benson	30:145–46
1783 May 19	JW	Agnes Gibbes	30:146–47
1783 May 19	JW	Elizabeth Gibbes	30:147–49
1783 c. May 22	Joseph Benson	JW	online
1783 c. May 22	Catherine Warren	JW	ref.; JW reply, May 26
1783 May 24	unidentified	JW	online
1783 May 24	Edward Dromgoole	JW	online
1783 May 26	JW	Catherine Warren	30:148–49
1783 June 05	JW	Joseph Taylor	30:149–50
1783 June 05	JW	John Francis Valton	30:150
1783 June 07	Jonathan Brown	JW	online
1783 June 07	JW	Hannah Ball	30:151
1783 June 08	Thomas Taylor	JW	online
1783 June 10	JW	Agnes Gibbes	30:152
1783 June 10	JW	Elizabeth Gibbes	30:153
1783 June 12	JW	Elizabeth (Buckley) Ferguson	30:154
1783 June 20	unidentified	JW	online
1783 c. July 01	H. C. Rodenbeeck	JW	online
1783 July 01	JW	Johanna C. A. Loten	ref.; her reply of July 15
1783 July 05	JW	Jane (Hilton) Barton	30:154–55
1783 July 12	JW	Charles Atmore	30:155
1783 July 13	JW	William Black Jr.	30:156–57
1783 July 14	M. H.	JW	online
1783 July 15	Johanna C. A. Loten	JW	online
1783 July 19	JW	John Evan	30:157
1783 July 20	JW	Elizabeth Ritchie	30:158–59
1783 c. July 25	Elizabeth Padbury	JW	ref.; JW reply, Aug. 1
1783 c. July 25	Ann Tindall	JW	ref.; JW reply, Aug. 1
1783 July 30	JW	George Gidley	30:159
1783 July 31	Ann Bolton	JW	online
1783 c. Aug.	John Prickard	JW	online
1783 c. Aug.	Richard Rodda	JW	online
1783 Aug. 01	JW	Elizabeth Padbury	30:159–60
1783 Aug. 01	JW	Rev. Cornelius Winter	30:160–61
1783 Aug. 03	JW	William Roberts	30:161
1783 Aug. 03	JW	Ann Tindall	30:162
1783 c. Aug. 05	John Francis Valton	JW	online
1783 Aug. 06	William Roberts	JW	online
1783 Aug. 08	JW	William Roberts	30:162–63

Date	Writer	Recipient	Location
1783 Aug. 09	JW	Ann Bolton	30:163
1783 Aug. 09	JW	Peter Garforth	30:164
1783 c. Aug. 10	Thomas Tattershall	JW	ref.; JW reply, Aug. 17
1783 c. Aug. 10	Thomas Welch	JW	ref.; MM 40 (1817): 324
1783 c. Aug. 12	William Roberts	JW	ref.; JW to Roberts, Aug. 16
1783 Aug. 15	JW	Thomas Lee	30:164
1783 Aug. 15	JW	Thomas Welch	30:165
1783 Aug. 16	JW	Agnes Gibbes	30:165–66
1783 Aug. 16	JW	Elizabeth Gibbes	30:166–67
1783 Aug. 16	JW	William Roberts	30:167
1783 Aug. 17	JW	Thomas Tattershall	30:168
1783 c. Aug. 18	Thomas Welch	JW	ref.; MM 40 (1817): 324
1783 Aug. 19	JW	Catherine Warren	30:168–69
1783 Aug. 25–31	Francis Asbury	JW	ref; Asbury to JW, Sept. 20, 1783
1783 c. Aug. 25	Thomas Welch	JW	ref.; MM 40 (1817): 324
1783 c. Aug. 28	JW	Thomas Welch	30:169
1783 Aug. 30	JW	Rachel (Norton) Bayley	30:170
1783 c. Aug. 28	John Atlay	JW	ref.; JW reply, Sept. 3
1783 Aug. 31	Thomas Olivers	JW	online
1783 c. Sept.	[Thomas Brisco]	JW	online
1783 c. Sept.	W. A—t S—d	JW	online
1783 Sept. 03	JW	John Atlay	30:170–71
1783 Sept. 05	JW	Sarah Wesley Jr.	30:171–72
1783 Sept. 06	JW	Robert Hall Jr.	30:172–73
1783 Sept. 10	Ann Bolton	JW	online
1783 Sept. 16	Ann Bolton	JW	online
1783 Sept. 17	JW	Edward Dromgoole	30:173–74
1783 Sept. 20	Francis Asbury	JW	online
1783 Sept. 30	JW	Jeremiah Brettel	30:174–75
1783 Sept. 30	JW	Elizabeth Ritchie	ref.; a double letter with next item
1783 Sept. 30	JW	unidentified woman	30:175
1783 Oct. 01	William M'Cornock	JW	online
1783 Oct. 03	JW	Francis Asbury & Preachers	30:176
1783 Oct. 03	JW	Mrs. Howton	30:177

Date	Writer	Recipient	Location
1783 Oct. 03	JW	Hugh Moore	30:177–78
1783 Oct. 03	JW	Richard Rodda	30:178–79
1783 Oct. 13	JW	Jasper Winscom	30:179–80
1783 Oct. 14	Jonathan Hern	JW	online
1783 c. Oct. 15	Francis Asbury	JW	ref.; JW to Richard Williams, Dec. 10
1783 c. Oct. 15	Benjamin Chappell	JW	ref.; JW reply, Nov. 27
1783 Oct. 17	JW	unidentified man	30:180
1783 Oct. 17	JW	unidentified man	30:181
1783 Oct. [18]	JW	Hannah Ball	30:181–82
1783 Oct. 25	unidentified	JW	online
1783 Oct. 26	JW	Jane (Hilton) Barton	30:182–83
1783 c. Nov. 02	Phoebe (French) Nail	JW	ref.; JW reply, Nov. 12
1783 c. Nov. 04	Ann Tindall	JW	ref.; JW reply, Nov. 8
1783 Nov. 04	JW	John Ellison (nephew)	30:183
1783 Nov. 05	Mrs. Dorothy Downes	JW	online
1783 Nov. 05	JW	Thomas Longley	30:184
1783 Nov. 08	JW	Ann Tindall	30:184–85
1783 Nov. 09	JW	Capt. Rich. Williams	30:185
1783 c. Nov. 11	JW	John Pritchard	ref.; JW to Nail, Nov. 12
1783 Nov. 12	JW	Phoebe (French) Nail	30:186
1783 c. Nov. 18	Ann Loxdale	JW	ref.; JW reply, Nov. 21
1783 Nov. 20	Mrs. Mary Gilbert	JW	online
1783 Nov. 21	William Collins	JW	online
1783 Nov. 21	John Haime	JW	online
1783 Nov. 21	JW	Mr. Alexander	30:186–87
1783 Nov. 21	JW	James Alexander	30:187
1783 Nov. 21	JW	Walter Churchey	30:188
1783 Nov. 21	JW	Mrs. Dorothy Downes	30:188–89
1783 Nov. 21	JW	Ann Loxdale	30:189–90
1783 Nov. 27	JW	Elizabeth Bradburn	30:190–91
1783 Nov. 27	JW	Benjamin Chappell	30:191–92
1783 Nov. 29	JW	Isaac Twycross	30:192–93
1783 c. Dec. 05	Ruth Hall	JW	ref.; JW reply, Dec. 9
1783 c. Dec. 05	Ann Loxdale	JW	ref.; JW reply, Dec. 9
1783 c. Dec. 06	Capt. Rich. Williams	JW	ref.; JW reply, Dec. 10
1783 Dec. 07	JW	Alexander Knox	30:193–94

Date	Writer	Recipient	Location
1783 Dec. 09	B. C.	JW	online
1783 Dec. 09	JW	Ruth Hall Jr.	30:194–95
1783 Dec. 09	JW	Ann Loxdale	30:195
1783 Dec. 10	JW	Walter Churchey	30:196
1783 Dec. 10	JW	Capt. Rich. Williams	30:197
1783 Dec. 13	John Pawson	JW	online
1783 Dec. 13	JW	unidentified itinerant	30:198
1783 Dec. 24	JW	Joseph Taylor	30:198
1783 Dec. 25–28	Francis Asbury	JW	ref.; Asbury to JW, Mar. 20, 1784
c. 1784	JW	Joseph Thompson	30:199
1784 c. Jan. 01	Mrs. Mary Parker	JW	ref.; JW reply, Jan. 21
1784 Jan. 04	JW	Isaac Andrews	30:199–200
1784 Jan. 04	JW	R. C. Brackenbury	30:200–01
1784 Jan. 06	JW	John Francis Valton	30:201
1784 Jan. 09	JW	George Davison	30:202
1784 Jan. 10	JW	R. C. Brackenbury	30:202–03
1784 Jan. 10	JW	Rev. Walter Sellon	30:203–04
1784 Jan. 12	George Shadford	JW	online
1784 Jan. 12	JW	Thomas Carlill	30:204
1784 Jan. 12	JW	Joseph Taylor	30:204–05
1784 Jan. 13	Joseph Charlesworth	JW	online
1784 Jan. 14	JW	Ann Tindall	30:205
1784 Jan. 16	JW	Richard Rodda	30:206
1784 Jan. 20	JW	Capt. Rich. Williams	30:206–07
1784 Jan. 21	JW	Mrs. Mary Parker	30:207–08
1784 Jan. 22	William Moore	JW	online
1784 Jan. 22	JW	Robert Hopkins	30:208–09
1784 c. Jan. 25	John Bredin	JW	ref.; JW reply, Feb. 6
1784 c. Jan. 25	Victory Purdy	JW	ref.; JW reply, Feb. 1
1784 Jan. 28	JW	Thomas Hanson	30: 209–10
1784 Feb. 01	JW	Victory Purdy	30:210
1784 Feb. 06	JW	John Bredin	30: 211
1784 Feb. 07	Mrs. Mary Gilbert	JW	online
1784 Feb. 07	JW	Alexander Knox	30:211–13
1784 Feb. 13	JW	Samuel Bardsley	30:213
1784 Feb. 13	JW	R. C. Brackenbury	30:214
1784 Feb. 16	Samuel Bardsley	JW	online
1784 c. Feb. 18	John Heald	JW (via John Atlay)	online
1784 Feb. 19	JW	John Baxendale	30:214–15

Date	Writer	Recipient	Location
1784 c. Feb. 20	Arthur Keene	JW	ref.; JW reply, Mar. 3
1784 Feb. 23	JW (via John Atlay)	John Heald	30:215–16
1784 c. Feb. 25	J. Rogers & H. A. Roe	JW	online
1784 c. Feb. 25	Catherine Warren	JW	ref.; JW reply, Mar. 3
1784 Feb. 25	JW	Samuel Bradburn	30:216
1784 Mar. 03	JW	Rachel Bailey	30:217
1784 Mar. 03	JW	Samuel Bardsley	30:217
1784 Mar. 03	JW	Arthur Keene	30:218
1784 Mar. 03	JW	James Rogers	ref.; address portion of JW to S. Bardsley, Mar. 3
1784 Mar. 03	JW	Catherine Warren	30:219
1784 Mar. 04	JW	William Percival	30:219–20
1784 c. Mar. 10	William Percival	JW	online
1784 Mar. 11	JW	Rev. Brian B. Collins	30:220–21
1784 Mar. 18	JW	Alexander Knox	30:221–22
1784 Mar. 18	JW	Thomas Tattershall	30:222–23
1784 Mar. 20	Francis Asbury	JW	online
1784 Mar. 21	JW	Joseph [Bradford?]	30:223
1784 Mar. 21	JW	[Zachariah Yewdall?]	30:224
1784 Mar. 23	Ann Bolton	JW	online
1784 Mar. 25	S. Saunders	JW	online
1784 Mar. 29	Adam Clarke	JW	online
1784 Apr. 01	JW	Ann Bolton	30:224–25
1784 Apr. 11	JW	Thomas Longley	30:225
1784 Apr. 12	JW	unidentified man	30:226
1784 Apr. 17	Rev. Dr. Thomas Coke	JW	online
1784 Apr. 17	Mrs. Martha Ward	JW	online
1784 c. Apr. 20	Agnes Gibbes	JW	ref.; JW reply, Apr. 28
1784 c. Apr. 20	Elizabeth Gibbes	JW	ref.; JW reply, Apr. 28
1784 c. Apr. 20	unidentified woman	JW	online
1784 Apr. 25	JW	Hannah Ball	30:226–27
1784 Apr. 28	JW	Agnes Gibbes	30:227
1784 Apr. 28	JW	Elizabeth Gibbes	30:228
1784 c. May	Rachel Bruff	JW	online
1784 c. May	unidentified	JW	online
1784 May 02	JW	Charles Wesley Jr.	30:229–30
1784 May 05	JW	James Rogers	30:230–31
1784 May 07	Richard Rodda	JW	online
1784 May 07	JW	Vincent De Boudry	30:231

Date	Writer	Recipient	Location
1784 c. May 10	JW	Mrs. Ellen Christian	ref.; Thomas Wride to JW, June 3
1784 May 11	JW	William Black Jr.	30:232–33
1784 May 12	N. L.	JW	online
1784 May 31	JW	Mary Clark	30:233–34
1784 May 31	JW	Mary (Edwin) Savage	30:234
1784 c. June	James Toole	JW	online
1784 c. June	unidentified	JW	online
1784 c. June	unidentified	JW	online
1784 c. June 1	[Mrs. Sophia Tydeman]	JW	ref.; JW reply, June 18
1784 June 01	JW	Simon Day	30:234–35
1784 June 02	JW	John Broadbent	30:235
1784 June 03	Joseph Entwisle	JW	ref.; JW reply, June 20
1784 June 03	David Gordon	JW	ref.; ibid.
1784 June 03	Thomas Wride	JW	online
1784 June 05	Robert Raikes	JW	online
1784 c. June 06	Lodowick Grant	JW	ref.; JW to Suter, June 13
1784 June 13	JW	Alexander Suter	30:236
1784 June 13	JW	Zachariah Yewdall	30:237
1784 June 18	JW	[Mrs. Sophia Tydeman]	30:237–38
1784 June 20	JW	J. Entwisle & D. Gordon	30:239
1784 June 20	JW	Francis Wrigley	30:239–40
1784 June 21	JW	Mrs. Ellen Christian	30:240–41
1784 June 21	JW	Arthur Keene	30:241–42
1784 June 22	Ann Bolton	JW	online
1784 June 25	JW	John Francis Valton	30:242–43
1784 June 28	JW	Ann Bolton	30:243–44
1784 c. June 29	Alexander Barry	JW	ref.; JW reply, July 3
1784 c. June 29	Elizabeth Gibbes	JW	ref.; JW reply, July 3
1784 [July]	JW	John White	30:244
1784 c. July 01	John Hampson Sr.	JW	online
1784 c. July 01	JW	Mrs. M[arie?] Leuliet	ref.; her reply, July 16
1784 July 03	Thomas Wride	JW	online
1784 July 03	JW	Alexander Barry	30:245
1784 July 03	JW	Robert Barry	30:246–47
1784 July 03	JW	Elizabeth Gibbes	30:247–48
1784 July 16	Mrs. M[arie?] Leuliet	JW	online

Date	Writer	Recipient	Location
1784 July 23	JW	Arthur Keene	30:249
1784 c. July 25	Agnes Gibbes	JW	ref.; JW reply, Aug. 1
1784 c. July 25	Frances Godfrey	JW	ref.; JW reply, July 31
1784 July 26	Thomas Wride	JW	online
1784 July 31	JW	Frances Godfrey	30:250
1784 Aug. 01	JW	Agnes Gibbes	30:250–51
1784 Aug. 09	Rev. Dr. Thomas Coke	JW	online
1784 Aug. 10	Mary Bishop	JW	online
1784 c. Aug. 15	[Rachel Dobinson?]	JW	ref.; JW to Ritchie, Aug. 19
1784 Aug. 18	JW	Mary Bishop	30:252–53
1784 Aug. 19	JW	Elizabeth Ritchie	30:253–54
1784 Aug. 19	JW	S. Wesley (nephew)	30:255–57
1784 Aug. 27	JW	Robert Jones Jr.	30:257
1784 Aug. 30	JW	Joseph Taylor	30:258
1784 Aug. 31	JW	Ann Bolton	30:258–59
1784 Aug. 31	JW	Christopher Hopper	30:259–60
1784 Sept. 01	George Story	JW	online
1784 c. Sept. 01	Ann Tindall	JW	ref.; JW reply, Sept. 4
1784 Sept. 02	JW	Th. Vasey (deacon)	ref.; 30:821
1784 Sept. 02	JW	Rd. Whatcoat (deacon)	ref.; 30:821
1784 Sept. 02	Elizabeth Ritchie	JW	online
1784 Sept. 02	JW	Thomas Coke (supt.)	30:260–61
1784 Sept. 02	JW	Th. Vasey (elder)	30:261–62
1784 Sept. 02	JW	Rd. Whatcoat (elder)	30:262–63
1784 Sept. 04	JW	Ann Tindall	30:263–64
1784 Sept. 06	JW	William Pitt	30:264–66
1784 c. Sept. 07	Christopher Hopper	JW	ref.; JW reply, Sept. 11
1784 Sept. 07	Alexander Knox	JW	ref.; JW reply, Sept. 26
1784 Sept. 07	Christopher Watkins	JW	online
1784 Sept. 08	JW	Sarah Wesley Jr.	30:267
1784 Sept. 09	JW	Dorothea Johnson	30:267–68
1784 Sept. 10	JW	Methodists in America	30:268–70
1784 Sept. 11	JW	Christopher Hopper	30:270–71
1784 Sept. 11–12	JW	[Jonathan Hern]	30:271
1784 Sept. 13	JW	John Francis Valton	30:272
1784 Sept. 17	Dorothea Johnson	JW	online
1784 Sept. 23	Elizabeth Ritchie	JW	online
1784 c. Sept. 25	Agnes Gibbes	JW	ref.; JW reply, Oct. 2
1784 Sept. 26	JW	John Johnson	30:273

Date	Writer	Recipient	Location
1784 Sept. 26	JW	Dorothea Johnson	30:273–74
1784 Sept. 26	JW	Alexander Knox	30:274
1784 c. Oct.	John Stretton	JW	ref.; JW reply, Feb. 25, 1785
1784 Oct. 02	JW	Agnes Gibbes	30:275–76
1784 Oct. 03	JW	Alexander Suter	30:276–77
1784 Oct. 13	JW	Richard Rodda	30:278
1784 Oct. 13	JW	John Francis Valton	30:278–79
1784 Oct. 15	JW	William Black Jr.	30:279–80
1784 c. Oct. 23	Sarah Baker	JW	ref.; JW reply, Oct. 27
1784 c. Oct. 23	Hannah Ball	JW	ref.; JW reply, Oct. 27
1784 c. Oct. 25	John Stonehouse	JW	ref.; JW reply, Oct. 31
1784 Oct. 27	JW	Sarah Baker	30:280–81
1784 Oct. 27	JW	Hannah Ball	30:281–82
1784 Oct. 27	JW	Dorothea Johnson	30:282
1784 c. Oct. 30	John Mason	JW	ref.; JW reply, Nov. 3
1784 Oct. 31	JW	Francis Asbury	30:283–84
1784 Oct. 31	JW	John Stonehouse	30:285
1784 c. Nov.	Mr. Mayo	JW	online
1784 Nov. 02	Christopher Hopper	JW	online
1784 Nov. 03	JW	Martha Chapman	30:285–86
1784 Nov. 03	JW	John Mason	30:286–87
1784 Nov. 07	JW	Sarah Crosby	30:287–88
1784 Nov. 10	Elizabeth Ritchie	JW	online
1784 Nov. 13	JW	John Francis Valton	30:288
1784 Nov. 27	JW	Thomas Tattershall	30:289
1784 Nov. 30	Elizabeth Henson	JW	online
1784 Dec. 04	JW	[John Francis Valton]	30:289
1784 c. Dec. 07	Jonathan Hern	JW	ref.; JW reply, Dec. 11
1784 Dec. 11	JW	Jonathan Hern	30:290
1784 Dec. 11	JW	Ann Tindall	30:290–91
1784 Dec. 17	JW	Samuel Bradburn	30:291
1784 Dec. 24	Joseph Benson	JW	online
1784 Dec. 24	JW	Robert Blake	30:292
1784 Dec. 24	JW	Hugh Bold, Esq.	30:292–93
1784 Dec. 24	JW	Ann Bolton	30:293
1784 Dec. 24	JW	Jeremiah Brettel	30:294
1784 Dec. 24	JW	Thomas Taylor	30:294–95

Date	Writer	Recipient	Location
1784 c. Dec. 26	Ann Tindall	JW	ref.; JW reply, Dec. 30
1784 Dec. 30	JW	Ann Tindall	30:295
c. 1785	unidentified	JW	online
c. 1785	JW	Methodist woman in Bath 30:296	
1785 c. Jan. 01	Mrs. Rebecca Gair	JW	ref.; JW reply, Jan. 5
1785 Jan. 05	JW	Mrs. Rebecca Gair	30:297
1785 c. Jan. 10	Rev. Peard Dickinson	JW	ref.; JW reply, Jan. 15
1785 c. Jan. 10	Agnes Gibbes	JW	ref.; JW reply, Jan. 14
1785 Jan. 11	JW	Patrick Henry Maty	30:297–301
1785 Jan. 14	JW	Agnes Gibbes	30:302–03
1785 Jan. 15	JW	Rev. Peard Dickinson	30:303–06
1785 c. Jan. 16	Dorothea Johnson	JW	ref.; JW reply, Jan. 26
1785 Jan. 17	John Pritchard	JW	online
1785 Jan. 20	Rev. James Creighton	JW	online
1785 c. Jan. 20	Thomas Tattershall	JW	online
1785 c. Jan. 22	Jane (Lee) Freeman	JW	ref.; JW reply, Feb. 1
1785 Jan. 22	Joseph Wells	JW	online
1785 Jan. 25	John Hampson	JW	online
1785 Jan. 26	JW	John Johnson	30:306
1785 Jan. 26	JW	Dorothea Johnson	30:307
1785 Jan. 31	Adam Clarke	JW	online
1785 Feb. 01	JW	Jane (Lee) Freeman	30:307–08
1785 Feb. 02	JW	Robert Barry	30:308–09
1785 c. Feb. 07	Adam Clarke	JW	ref.; JW reply, Feb. 12
1785 c. Feb. 10	John Francis Valton	JW	ref.; JW to Brackenbury, Feb. 15
1785 Feb. 12	JW	Samuel Bardsley	30:309–10
1785 Feb. 12	JW	Adam Clarke	30:310–11
1785 Feb. 15	JW	R. C. Brackenbury	30:311–12
1785 Feb. 15	JW	John Francis Valton	30:312
1785 Feb. 15	JW	Capt. Rich. Williams	30:313
1785 Feb. 16	JW	Ann Bolton	30:313–14
[1785] Feb. 16	JW	Mary Clark	30:314–15
1785 Feb. 17	JW	Arthur Keene	30:315–16
1785 Feb. 18	JW	Ann Tindall	30:317

Date	Writer	Recipient	Location
1785 c. Feb. 20	John Baxendale	JW	ref.; JW reply, Feb. 25
1785 c. Feb. 20	Ann Bolton	JW	ref.; JW reply, Feb. 25
1785 Feb. 23	JW	John Broadbent	30:317–18
1785 c. Feb. 23	JW	Rev. Dr. Thomas Coke	ref.; JW to Stretton, Feb. 25
1785 Feb. 25	Plymouth leaders	JW	JW, *Journal*, Feb. 25, 1785 (*Works*, 23:343)
1785 Feb. 25	JW	John Baxendale	30:318
1785 Feb. 25	JW	Ann Bolton	30:319
1785 Feb. 25	JW	Jonathan Coussins	30:319–20
1785 Feb. 25	JW	John Stretton	30:320–21
1785 Feb. 25	JW	Zachariah Yewdall	30:322
1785 Mar. 03	JW	Methodist Family	30:322–25
1785 c. Mar. 05	Richard Rodda	JW	ref.; JW reply, Mar. 11
1785 Mar. 11	JW	Richard Rodda	30:325–26
1785 Mar. 19	JW	Alexander Knox	30:326–27
1785 c. Mar. 20	Ann Bolton	JW	ref.; JW reply, Mar. 28
1785 c. Mar. 20	Christopher Hopper	JW	online
1785 Mar. 22	Mrs. Mary Fletcher	JW	online
1785 Mar. 25	JW	Barnabas Thomas	30:327
1785 Mar. 28	JW	Ann Bolton	30:328–29
1785 Mar. 30	unidentified	JW	online
1785 c. Apr.	unidentified	JW	online
1785 Apr. 02	Joseph Taylor	JW	online
1785 Apr. 02	JW	Mrs. Mary Fletcher	30:329
1785 Apr. 03	JW	Sarah Crosby	30:330
1785 Apr. 03	JW	Rev. John Fletcher	30:330–32
1785 Apr. 03	JW	[Mary (W / L) Gilbert] 30:332
1785 Apr. 05	unidentified	JW	online
1785 Apr. 07	JW	To Conference	30:332–33
1785 Apr. 07	JW	Joseph Taylor	30:333–34
1785 Apr. 09	JW	Roger Crane	30:334–35
[1785] Apr. 09	JW	George Gibbon	30:335
1785 Apr. 11	JW	CW	30:335–36
1785 Apr. 12	Joseph Pescod	JW	online
1785 Apr. 20	Freeborn Garrettson	JW	online
1785 Apr. 23	JW	CW	30:336–37

Date	Writer	Recipient	Location
1785 c. Apr. 30	CW	JW	online
1785 May 06	JW	Thomas Carlill	30:337–38
1785 May 06	JW	Alexander Knox	30:338–39
1785 c. May 09	JW	Agnes Gibbes	30:339–40
1785 May 09	JW	Jasper Winscom	30:341
1785 May 10	Rev. Samuel Badcock	JW	online
1785 May 12	JW	CW	30:342
1785 c. May 20	CW	JW	ref.; JW reply, June 2
1785 May 24	Joseph Pescod	JW	online
1785 May 30	Thomas Wride	JW	online
1785 c. June	Thomas Tattershall	JW	online
1785 c June	Thomas Wride	JW	online
1785 June 02	JW	CW	30:343
1785 June 08	JW	Alexander Knox	30:344–45
1785 c. June 10	CW	JW	ref.; JW to CW, June 19
1785 June 11	JW	Francis Wrigley	30:345–46
1785 June 14	James Oddie et al.	JW et al.	online
1785 June 15	R. C. Brackenbury	JW	ref.; JW reply, July 23
1785 June 19	JW	CW	30:346–47
1785 June 20	Rev. Dr. Joseph Fisher	JW	online
1785 June 22	JW	Zachariah Yewdall	30:347–48
1785 June 26	JW	Freeborn Garrettson	30:348–49
1785 June 26	JW	Elizabeth Ritchie	30:350
1785 c. July	Samuel Mitchell	JW	online
1785 c. July 01	Joseph Beardmore	JW	ref.; JW to Arthur Keene, July 16
1785 c. July 01	Elizabeth Gibbes	JW	ref.; JW reply, July 17
1785 c. July 01	JW	on Conference	30:351
1785 July 07	JW	Samuel Purvis Jr.	30:351
1785 July 08	JW	Ann Bolton	30:352
1785 July 08	JW	Thomas Wride	30:353
1785 July 10	R. C. Brackenbury	JW	ref.; JW reply, July 23
1785 July 10	JW	Alexander Knox	30:354
1785 July 16	JW	Arthur Keene	30:355
1785 July 16	JW	Lancelot Harrison	30:356
1785 July 16	JW	Alexander Suter	30:356–57
1785 July 17	JW	Mrs. Ellen Christian	30:357–58
1785 July 17	JW	Elizabeth Gibbes	30:358–60
1785 July 17	JW	Ann Tindall	30:360

Date	Writer	Recipient	Location
1780 c. July 20	William Rayner	JW	ref.; JW to Keene, July 31
1785 July 23	Arthur Keene	JW	ref.; docketing on JW to Keene, July 16
1785 July 23	Thomas Wride	JW	online
1785 July 23	JW	R. C. Brackenbury	30:361
1785 July 25	JW	Catherine Warren	30:362
1785 July 30	JW	Sarah Baker	30:363
1785 July 30	JW	Thomas Hanson	30:363–64
1785 July 31	JW	Arthur Keene	30:364–65
1785 c. Aug.	[Richard Rodda?]	JW	online
1785 Aug. 01	JW	Thomas Hanby (deacon)	ref.; 30:821
1785 Aug. 01	JW	John Pawson (deacon)	ref.; 30:821
1785 Aug. 01	JW	Joseph Taylor (deacon)	ref.; 30:821
1785 Aug. 02	JW	Thomas Hanby (elder)	ref.; 30:821
1785 Aug. 02	JW	John Pawson (elder)	ref.; 30:821
1785 Aug. 02	JW	Joseph Taylor (elder)	ref.; 30:821
1785 Aug. 07	William Black Jr.	JW	online
1785 Aug. 07	JW	John Ogylvie	30:365–66
1785 Aug. 14	CW	JW	online
1785 c. Aug. 15	Michael Moorhouse	JW	online
1785 Aug. 18	Mrs. Mary Fletcher	JW	online
1785 Aug. 19	JW	CW	30:366–68
1785 Aug. 22	JW	Thomas Tattershall	30:368–39
1785 Aug. 27	JW	Christopher Hopper	30:369
1785 Aug. 28	Thomas Wride	JW	online
1785 Aug. 30	JW	Agnes Gibbes	30:369–71
1785 Aug. 30	JW	Methodist followers	30:371–73
1785 c. Sept.	JW	Mrs. Mary Fletcher	30:373–74
1785 Sept. 04	JW	Robert Costerdine	30:374
1785 Sept. 05	JW	John Francis Valton	30:374–75
1785 Sept. 05	JW	Thomas Wride	30:375–76
1785 Sept. 07	Thomas Wride	JW	online
1785 Sept. 08	CW	JW	online
1785 Sept. 10	JW	Mary Cooke	30:376
1785 Sept. 10	JW	Michael Moorhouse	30:377
1785 Sept. 10	JW	Mrs. Mary Warrick	30:377–78
1785 c. Sept. 12	Alexander Suter	JW	ref.; JW reply, Sept. 16
1785 Sept. 13	JW	John Atlay	ref.; JW to Winscom, Sept. 13

Date	Writer	Recipient	Location
1785 Sept. 13	JW	John Francis Valton	30:378
1785 Sept. 13	JW	CW	30:379
1785 Sept. 13	JW	Jasper Winscom	30:380
1785 Sept. 15	Mary Cooke	JW	online
1785 Sept. 15	JW	Mrs. Mary Fletcher	30:380–81
1785 c. Sept. 16	Richard Locke	JW	ref.; JW reply, Sept. 19
1785 Sept. 16	JW	Alexander Suter	30:381–82
1785 Sept. 16	JW	Thomas Wride	30:382–83
1785 c. Sept. 18	JW	Mary Cooke	ref.; JW to Cooke, Sept. 24
1785 Sept. 19	CW	JW	online
1785 Sept. 19	JW	Richard Locke	30:383
1785 Sept. 23	Mary Cooke	JW	online
1785 Sept. 23	JW	Richard Rodda	30:384
1785 Sept. 24	JW	Mary Cooke	30:384–86
1785 Sept. 24	JW	Simon Day	30:386
1785 Sept. 26	JW	R. C. Brackenbury	30:386–87
1785 Sept. 29	JW	Richard Rodda	30:388
1785 Sept. 30	John King	JW	online
1785 Sept. 30	JW	Rev. Francis Asbury	30:388–89
1785 c. Sept. 30	JW	Elizabeth Ritchie	30:389
1785 c. Oct. 01	JW	John Burnet	ref.; Burnet reply, Oct. 22
1785 Oct. 02	JW	Mrs. Mary Fletcher	30:389–90
1785 Oct. 03	Thomas Wride	JW	online
1785 c. Oct. 07	JW	Joseph Benson	ref.; Benson to JW, Oct. 15
1785 Oct. 08	JW	Thomas Hanson	30:390–91
1785 Oct. 08	JW	Ann Loxdale	30:391–92
1785 Oct. 08	JW	John Francis Valton	30:392–93
1785 Oct. 08	JW	Thomas Wride	30:393
1785 Oct. 14	Matthias Joyce	JW	online
1785 Oct. 15	Joseph Benson	JW	online
1785 Oct. 15	George Shadford	JW	online
1785 Oct. 15	JW	Charles Atmore	30:394
1785 Oct. 22	John Burnet	JW	online
1785 Oct. 22	JW	Mrs. Mary Fletcher	30:394–95
1785 Oct. 24	Mary Cooke	JW	online
1785 Oct. 25	Joseph Benson	JW	online
1785 Oct. 27	John King	JW	online
1785 Oct. 30	JW	Joseph Benson	30:395

Date	Writer	Recipient	Location
1785 Oct. 30	JW	Mary Cooke	30:396–97
1785 Oct. 31	Dorthy (Furly) Downes	JW	online
1785 Nov. 01	William Boothby	JW	online
1785 Nov. 02	JW	Thomas Wride	ref.; Wride to JW, Nov. 14
1785 Nov. 05	Thomas Wride	JW	online
1785 Nov. 08	JW	William Roberts	30:397
1785 Nov. 08	JW	Thomas Wride	30:398
1785 Nov. 11	JW	Zachariah Yewdall	30:398
1785 Nov. 13	JW	Thomas Tattershall	30:399
1785 Nov. 14	Thomas Wride	JW	online
1785 Nov. 16	JW	John Bredin	30:400
1785 Nov. 16	JW	Matthew Stewart	30:401
1785 Nov. 17	JW	Thomas Wride	30:401–02
1785 c. Nov. 22	Ann Tindall	JW	ref.; JW reply, Nov. 26
1785 Nov. 24	JW	R. C. Brackenbury	30:402
1785 Nov. 26	JW	William Black Jr.	30:402–03
1785 Nov. 26	JW	Mrs. Frances Pawson	30:403–04
1785 Nov. 26	JW	Ann Tindall	30:404
1785 c. Dec.	John Gardner	JW	online
1785 c. Dec.	Jasper Robinson	JW	online
1785 c. Dec. 01	Alexander Knox	JW	ref.; JW reply, Dec. 8
1785 c. Dec. 01	JW	George Snowden	30:405
1785 Dec. 02	JW	John Francis Valton	30:405–06
1785 Dec. 05	Mary Cooke	JW	online
1785 Dec. 06	JW	Walter Churchey	30:406
1785 Dec. 06	JW	William Roberts	30:406–07
1785 c. Dec. 8	Thomas Hanby	JW	ref.; JW reply, Dec. 13
1785 Dec. 08	JW	Alexander Knox	30:407–08
1785 Dec. 09	Thomas Wride	JW	online
1785 Dec. 10	JW	Jane (Cave) Winscomb	30:409
1785 Dec. 13	JW	Thomas Hanby	30:409–10
1785 Dec. 14	JW	Mary Cooke	30:410–11
1785 Dec. 14	JW	J. McKersey & James Byron	30:412
1785 Dec. 14	JW	Thomas Wride	30:412–13
1785 c. Dec. 20	Joseph Benson	JW	online
1785 c. Dec. 20	Mr. Vaughan	JW	online
1785 Dec. [21?]	JW	John Gardner	30:413
1785 Dec. 24	JW	*Gentleman's Magazine*	30:414–15

Date	Writer	Recipient	Location
1785 Dec. 29	Thomas Wride	JW	online
1785 Dec. 29	JW	Thomas Tattershall	30:415–16
1785 Dec. 29	JW	Joseph Taylor	30:416
1785 Dec. 29	JW	Jasper Winscom	30:416–17
1785 Dec. 30	Thomas Wride	JW	online
1785 Dec. 31	JW	Mrs. Mary Fletcher	30:417–18
1786 Jan. 02	JW	James O. Cromwell	30:419
1786 Jan. 02	JW	Freeborn Garrettson	ref.; address portion of JW to Cromwell
1786 Jan. 02	JW	Rev. William Roots	30:420
1786 c. Jan. 07	Samuel Mitchell	JW	ref.; extract in JW reply, Jan. 14
1786 Jan. 07	JW	Mrs. Sarah Wyndowe	30:420–21
1786 Jan. 08	JW	Joshua Keighley Sr.	30:421–22
1786 Jan. 13	JW	Mrs. Mary Fletcher	30:422
1786 Jan. 13	JW	Francis Wrigley	30:423
1786 Jan. 14	JW	Samuel Bradburn	30:423–24
1786 Jan. 14	JW	Samuel Mitchell	30:424–25
1786 Jan. 18	JW	R. C. Brackenbury	30:425
1786 c. Jan. 20	Ann Loxdale	JW	ref.; JW reply, Jan. 26
1786 Jan. 20	Rev. John Pawson	JW	online
1786 Jan. 24	Mary Cooke	JW	online
1786 Jan. 24	JW (by Henry Moore)	Thomas Wride	Wride reply, Feb. 7
1786 Jan. 26	JW	Ann Loxdale	30:426
1786 Jan. 30	Adam Clarke	JW	online
1786 c. Feb.	Matthias Joyce	JW	online
1786 Feb. 02	Samuel Hodgson	JW	ref.; Wride to JW, Feb. 7
1786 Feb. 03	JW	Adam Clarke	30:427
1786 Feb. 07	Thomas Wride	JW	online
1786 Feb. 09	Adam Clarke	JW	ref.; endorsement on JW to Clarke, Feb. 3
1786 Feb. 10	Johanna C. A. Loten	JW	online
1786 Feb. 12	Samuel Bradburn	JW	online
1786 Feb. 12	JW	Mary Cooke	30:427–28
1786 Feb. 14	JW	Samuel Bradburn	ref.; endorsement on Bradburn's letter, Feb. 12
1786 c. Feb. 15	Robert Sydserff	JW	online
1786 Feb. 20	Mary Cooke	JW	online

Date	Writer	Recipient	Location
1786 Feb. 20	JW	Ann Tindall	30:428
1786 Feb. 21	JW	Ann Bolton	30:429
1786 Feb. 21	JW	Adam Clarke	30:429–30
1786 Feb. 21	JW	Thomas Dobson	30:430–31
1786 Feb. 21	JW	John Ogylvie	30:431
1786 Feb. 21	JW	Thomas Taylor	30:431–32
1786 Feb. 21	JW	Peter Walker	30:432–33
1786 Feb. 22	JW	Mrs. Mary Middleton	30:433
1786 Feb. 22	JW	Emma Moon	30:434
1786 Feb. 23	JW	Mary Cooke	30:434–35
1786 Feb. 24	JW	Elizabeth Ritchie	30:435–36
1786 Feb. 24	JW	Thomas Taylor	30:436
1786 Feb. 25	JW	Freeborn Garrettson	30:436–37
1786 Feb. 25	JW	Johanna C. A. Loten	ref.; endorsement on her letter of Feb. 10.
1786 Feb. 25	JW	William Sagar	30:437–38
1786 Feb. 26	JW	James O. Cromwell	30:438–39
1786 Feb. 26	JW	John Stretton	30:439–40
1786 Mar.	Rev. Peard Dickinson	JW	ref.; JW reply, Mar. 1786
1786 Mar.	JW	Rev. Peard Dickinson	30:440
1786 Mar. 02	Hester Anne (Roe) Rogers	JW	online
1786 Mar. 03	JW	Charles Atmore	30:440–41
1786 Mar. 03	JW	Joseph Taylor	30:441–42
1786 Mar. 04	JW	Samuel Bardsley	30:442
1786 Mar. 04	JW	Hannah Bowmer(?)	30:443
1786 Mar. 09	John King	JW	online
1786 Mar. 09	JW	John Stretton	30:444
1786 Mar. 10	Mary Cooke	JW	online
1786 Mar. 10	James Rogers	JW	online
1786 Mar. 12	JW	Rev. Dr. Thomas Coke	30:445
1786 Mar. 14	JW	R. C. Brackenbury	30:445–46
1786 c. Mar. 20	JW	Mary Cooke	ref. and excerpt; Cooke's reply, Mar. 25
1786 Mar. 20	JW	Thomas Tattershall	30:446
1786 Mar. 25	Mary Cooke	JW	online
1786 Mar. 31	JW	Thomas Cooper	30:447
1786 Apr.	Rev. Dr. Thomas Coke	JW	mentioned by Coke in a May 8 letter to Benjamin La Trobe; Herrnhut, Germany,

Date	Writer	Recipient	Location
			Unitätsarchiv der Evangelischen Brüder-Unität, R.13.A.43.a
1786 c. Apr.	[Thomas] Middleton	JW	online
1786 c. Apr.	John Murlin	JW	online
1786 c. Apr	unidentified	JW	online
1786 c. Apr. 01	CW	JW	ref.; JW reply, Apr. 6
1786 Apr. 03	JW	unidentified man	30:447–48
1786 Apr. 06	JW	CW	30:448–50
1786 Apr. 13	'Veritas'	JW	online
1786 Apr. 13	JW	Hannah Ball	30:450
1786 c. Apr. 15	Alexander Mather	JW	online
1786 c. Apr. 15	CW	JW	ref.; JW reply, Apr. 18
1786 Apr. 17	JW	Lancelot Harrison	30:451
1786 Apr. 18	JW	CW	30:451–52
1786 c. Apr. 20	Rev. Dr. Thomas Coke	JW	ref.; JW reply, c. Apr. 25
1786 Apr. 24	Thomas Wride	JW	online
1786 Apr. 25	Freeborn Garrettson	JW	online
1786 c. Apr. 25	JW	Rev. Dr. Thomas Coke	30:452
1786 Apr. 28	JW	Samuel Newham	30:453
1786 Apr. 29	H. D.	JW	online
1786 c. Apr. 29	CW	JW	ref.; JW reply, May 3
1786 c. Apr. 30	James Shacklock	JW	online
1786 Apr. 30	JW	Thomas Carlill	30:453–54
1786 c. May	Andrew Blair	JW	online
1786 c. May	James Rogers	JW	online
1786 c. May	unidentified	JW	online
1786 c. May 01	JW	Mary Cooke	ref.; Cooke reply, May 8
1786 May 03	JW	CW	30:454–55
1786 May 04	J[ohn] F[loyde]	JW	online
1786 May 05	J[ohn] F[loyde]	JW	online
1786 May 06	Rev. Dr. Thomas Coke	JW	online
1786 May 08	Mary Cooke	JW	online
1786 May 09	JW	David Leslie	30:455–56
1786 c. May 10	CW	JW	ref.; JW reply, May 18
1786 May 10	JW	Ann (Bignell) Brisco	30:456
1786 May 14	JW	James Copeland	30:456–57

Date	Writer	Recipient	Location
1786 May 17	JW	Rev. Dr. Thomas Coke	30:457–58
1786 May 18	JW	CW	30:458
1786 c. May 20	JW	Mrs. Hester Rogers	ref.; Ritchie to JW, June 2
1786 c. May 25 June 2	JW	Elizabeth Ritchie	ref.; Ritchie reply,
1786 c. May 30	Rev. Peard Dickinson	JW	ref.; Benson, *Memoirs*, 54
1786 c. June	gentleman in Kent	JW	online
1786 c. June	unidentified	JW	online
1786 June 01	JW	John King	30:459
1786 June 02	Elizabeth Ritchie	JW	online
1786 June 03	Samuel Bradburn	JW	online
1786 June 04	JW	Lancelot Harrison	30:459
1786 c. June 05	Henry Brooke	JW	online
1786 June 08	JW	Catherine Warren	30:460
1786 c. June 10	JW	Rev. Peard Dickinson	ref.; Benson, *Memoirs*, 54
1786 June 14	JW	Henry Brooke	30:461–63
1786 c. June 15	JW	Mary Cooke	ref.; Cooke reply, June 23
1786 June 17	JW	Jasper Winscom	30:463
1786 June 19	Adam Clarke	JW	online
1786 June 20	JW	Samuel Bradburn	30:464
1786 June 20	JW	Sophia Cooke	30:464–65
1786 June 23	Mary Cooke	JW	online
1786 c. July	J. D.	JW	online
1786 c. July	unidentified	JW	online
1786 July 02	JW	Adam Clarke	30:465
1786 July 02	JW	Thomas Rankin	30:466
1786 July 07	JW	Francis Wrigley	30:466–67
1786 July 10	Ann Loxdale	JW	online
1786 July 15	JW	unidentified man	30:467
1786 July 21	JW	Sarah [M'Kim]	30:468
1786 July 21	JW	Catherine Warren	30:468–69
1786 July 22	JW	Edward Jackson	30:469–70
1786 July 22	JW	[Methodist followers]	30:470–71
1786 July 27	CW	JW	online
1786 July 28	JW	Ch. Atmore (deacon)	ref.; 30:822
1786 July 28	JW	John Clarke (deacon)	ref.; 30:822
1786 July 28	JW	Wm. Hammet (deacon)	ref.; 30:822

Date	Writer	Recipient	Location
1786 July 28	JW	Joseph Keighley (deacon)	ref.; 30:822
1786 July 28	JW	Wm. Warrener (deacon)	ref.; 30:822
1786 July 29	JW	James Gildart	30:471
1786 July 30	JW	Richard Terry	30:472
1786 Aug. 01	JW	[Methodist followers]	30:472–73
1786 Aug. 01	JW	Charles Atmore (elder)	30:473–74
1786 Aug. 01	JW	John Clarke (elder)	ref.; 30:822
1786 Aug. 01	JW	Josiah Dornford	30:474
1786 Aug. 01	JW	William Hammet (elder)	ref.; 30:822
1786 Aug. 01	JW	Joseph Keighley (elder)	ref.; 30:822
1786 Aug. 01	JW	William Warrener (elder)	30:475
1786 c. Aug. 02	JW	Mary Cooke	ref.; her reply, Aug. 30
1786 Aug. 02	JW	Elizabeth Davenport	30:475–76
1786 Aug. 07	JW	Ann Bolton	30:476–77
[1786 Aug. 07]	JW	Mrs. Elizabeth Briggs	30:477–78
1786 Aug. 07	JW	Mrs. Mary Fletcher	30:478–79
1786 Aug. 08	JW	Samuel Bradburn	30:479
1786 Aug. 30	Mary Cooke	JW	online
1786 Sept. 06	JW	Rev. Dr. Thomas Coke	30:480
1786 Sept. 06	JW	Mrs. Mary Fletcher	30:480–81
1786 Sept. 06	JW	William Simpson	30:481–82
1786 Sept. 09	Mary (Brooke) Lee	JW	online
1786 Sept. 09	JW	Mary Cooke	30:482–83
1786 Sept. 14	'A. B.'	JW	online
1786 Sept. 15	JW	Robert Barry	30:483–84
1786 Sept. 15	JW	Thomas Longley	30:485
1786 c. Sept. 20	Mrs. Elizabeth Briggs	JW	ref.; JW reply, Sept. 24
1786 Sept. 20	JW	Walter Churchey	30:485–86
1786 c. Sept. 21	William Roberts	JW	ref.; JW reply, Sept. 25
1786 Sept. 24	JW	Mrs. Elizabeth Briggs	30:486–87
1786 Sept. 25	Freeborn Garrettson	JW	online
1786 Sept. 25	JW	Thomas McGeary	30:487–88
1786 Sept. 25	JW	William Roberts	30:488
1786 c. Sept. 30	[R. C. Brackenbury]	JW	online
1786 Sept. 30	JW	Freeborn Garrettson	30:488–89

Date	Writer	Recipient	Location
1786 c. Oct. 01	Sarah Crosby	JW	online
1786 c. Oct. 01	Mary Greenwood	JW	online
1786 c. Oct. 01	Jane Thornton	JW	online
1786 c. Oct. 01	Samuel Webb	JW	online
1786 c. Oct. 01	[Samuel Webb?]	JW	online
1786 Oct. 06	JW	*Leeds Intelligencer*	30:489–90
1786 Oct. 09	JW	George Merryweather	30:490
1786 Oct. 09	JW	John Francis Valton	30:490–91
1786 Oct. 12	JW	Ann Bolton	30:491–92
1786 Oct. 15	JW	Mrs. Elizabeth Briggs	30:492–93
1786 c. Oct. 15	JW	Elizabeth Ritchie	ref.; her reply, Oct. 25
1786 Oct. 17	'C. D.'	JW	online
1786 Oct. 18	JW	Sarah Crosby	30:493
1786 Oct. 21	JW	Thomas Carlill	30:493–94
1786 Oct. 24	Mary Cooke	JW	online
1786 Oct. 25	Elizabeth Ritchie	JW	online
1786 Oct. 25	JW	Rev. Peter Lièvre	30:494–95
1786 Oct. 17–27	Thomas Wride	JW	online
1786 Oct. 27	JW	Jasper Winscom	30:496
1786 Oct. 28	JW	Sarah Crosby	30:496–97
1786 Oct. 29	JW	John Francis Valton	30:497–98
1786 Oct. 29	JW	Thomas Wride	30:498
1786 Nov. 01	Francis Wrigley	JW	online
1786 Nov. 04	JW	Henry Moore	30:499
1786 Nov. 04	JW	'A. B.' Alias 'C. D.'	30:500
1786 Nov. 05	JW	Epworth Circuit	30:500–01
1786 Nov. 09	'E. F.'	*Leeds Mercury*	online
1786 Nov. 11	JW	Richard Rodda	30:501
1786 Nov. 11	JW	William Simpson	30:502
1786 Nov. 11	JW	Rev Joseph Taylor	30:502–03
1786 Nov. 12	JW	Ann Bolton	30:503–04
1786 Nov. 12	JW	Jasper Winscom	30:504
1786 c. Nov. 15	JW	Mary Cooke	ref.; endorsement on Cooke's reply, Dec. 4
1786 c. Nov. 15	James Wood	JW	online
1786 Nov. 16	JW	Thomas Warrick	30:504–05
1786 Nov. 17	JW	John Hollis	30:505
1786 Nov. 23	JW	William Simpson	30:506
1786 Nov. 26	JW	Francis Wrigley	30:506–07
1786 Nov. 28	William Roberts	JW	online

Date	Writer	Recipient	Location
1786 Nov. 28	JW	unidentified	30:507
1786 Nov. 29	Jeremiah Clifford	JW	online
1786 Nov. 30	JW	Freeborn Garrettson	30:508–09
1786 Dec.	JW	Samuel Bradburn	30:509–10
1786 Dec. 03	JW	William Palmer	30:510–11
1786 Dec. 04	Mary Cooke	JW	online
1786 Dec. 09	JW	Mrs. Mary Fletcher	30:511
1786 Dec. 09	JW	William Roberts	30:512
1786 Dec. 10	JW	[John Eggleston]	30:512–13
1786 Dec. 12	JW	Mary Cooke	30:513–14
1786 Dec. 15	JW	Ann Bolton	30:514–15
1786 Dec. 17	JW	Samuel Mitchell	30:515
1786 Dec. 18	William Shepherd	JW	online
1786 Dec. 20	Adam Clarke	JW	online
1786 Dec. 20	JW	William Shepherd	30:516
1786 [Dec. 20]	JW	John Francis Valton	30:516–17
1786 Dec. 20	JW	Zachariah Yewdall	30:517–18
1786 Dec. 22	JW	James Hall	30:518
1786 Dec. 22	JW	John Francis Valton	30:518–19
1786 Dec. 23	JW	unidentified recipient	30:519
1786 c. Dec. 30	William Mallet	JW	online
1787 c. Jan.	unidentified	JW	online
1787 c. Jan.	JW	Theophilus Lessey	30:520
1787 c. Jan. 01	Mattias Joyce	JW	online
1787 Jan. 03	JW	Adam Clarke	30:521
1787 Jan. 02–05	Rev. Dr. Thomas Coke	JW	online
1787 Jan. 08	Robert Scot	JW	online
1787 Jan. 12	E. Vaughn	JW	online
1787 Jan. 12	JW	Ann Dupuy Taylor	30:522
1787 Jan. 13	JW	William Holmes	30:523
1787 c. Jan. 15	J. Morgan	JW	online
1787 Jan. 15	JW	Joseph Algar	30:524
1787 Jan. 17	JW	Richard Rodda	30:524–25
1787 Jan. 17	JW	unidentified	30:525
1787 Jan. 18	unidentified	JW	online
1787 Jan. 15–19	Rev. Dr. Thomas Coke	JW	online
1787 Jan. 20	JW	Andrew Inglis	30:526
1787 c. Jan. 22	Wm. White / J. Pilmore	JW	ref.; JW to White, Jan. 24

Date	Writer	Recipient	Location
1787 c. Jan. 22	William Carne	JW	ref.; JW reply, Jan. 26
1787 Jan. 24	Edward Coates	JW	online
1787 Jan. 24	JW	John Mason	30:526–27
1787 Jan. 24	JW	Rev. William White	30:527–28
1787 Jan. 26	Thomas Taylor	JW	online
1787 Jan. 26	JW	William Carne	30:528
1787 Jan. 31	Rev. Dr. Thomas Coke	JW	online
1787 Jan. 31	JW [via Broadbent]	Edward Coates	30:529–30
1787 Feb. 01	Mary Cooke	JW	online
1787 Feb. 04	JW	Ann (Foard) Thornton	30:530–31
1787 Feb. 07	John Spencer	JW	online
1787 Feb. 09	JW	George Gidley	30:531
1787 c. Feb. 10	R. C. Brackenbury	JW	online (2 items)
1787 Feb. 10	JW	Jonathan Edmondson	30:531–32
1787 Feb. 14	JW	Rev. Thomas Cursham	30:532
1787 Feb. 14	JW	Joseph Taylor	30:533
1787 Feb. 15	JW	Thomas McGeary	30:534
1787 Feb. 16	JW	Abraham Andrews	30:534–35
1787 Feb. 16	JW	R. C. Brackenbury	30:535–37
1787 Feb. 16	JW	John King	30:537
1787 Feb. 17	JW	William Percival	30:538
1787 Feb. 19	JW	John Johnson	30:538–39
1787 Feb. 19	JW	Rev. Joshua Keighley	30:539–40
1787 Feb. 20	JW	William Black Jr.	30:540–41
1787 Feb. 21	JW	William Thompson (?)	30:541
1787 Feb. 22	JW	Rev. Brian B. Collins	30:542
1787 Feb. 23	Adam Clarke	JW	online
1787 Feb. 23	JW	William Holmes	30:542–43
1787 Feb. [24?]	JW	Thomas Cooper	ref.; his autobiography, *WMM* 14 (1835): 82
1787 c. Feb. 25	Arthur Keene	JW	ref.; JW reply, Mar. 3
1787 Feb. 26	Rev. John Pawson	JW	online
1787 Mar. 03	JW	Adam Clarke	30:543
1787 Mar. 03	JW	Arthur Keene	30:543–44
[1787 Mar. 07]	JW	Ann Dupuy Taylor	30:544–45
1787 Mar. 09–10	JW	Joseph Benson	30:546–47
1787 Mar. 10	JW	[George Gidley]	30:547–48
1787 Mar. 13	JW	Samuel Bradburn	30:548
1787 c. Mar. 15	Rev. Dr. Thomas Coke	JW	ref.; JW to Levi Heath, May 18

Date	Writer	Recipient	Location
1787 Mar. 10[–15]	Freeborn Garrettson	JW	online
1787 c. Mar. 15	unidentified	JW	online
1787 Mar. 15	JW	Ann Bolton	30:549
1787 c. Mar. 15	JW	Mary Cooke	ref.; her reply, Mar. 24
1787 Mar. 16	Adam Clarke	JW	online
1787 c. Mar. 20	Samuel Bardsley	JW	ref.; JW reply, Mar. 25
1787 Mar. 24	Mary Cooke	JW	online
1787 Mar. 24	JW	John Francis Valton	30:550
1787 Mar. 25	JW	Samuel Bardsley	30:550–51
1787 Mar. 26	JW	Adam Clarke	30:551
1787 Mar. 31	JW	Mary Cooke	30:552
1787 Mar. 31	JW	Rev. Thomas Hanby	30:553
1787 c. Apr.	John Booth	JW	online
1787 c. Apr.	[William Bulgin]	JW	online
1787 c. Apr.	unidentified	JW	online
1787 c. Apr. 01	JW	Rev. Levi Heath	ref.; JW to Heath, May 18
1787 Apr. 03	JW	John Baxendale	30:553–54
1787 c. Apr. 04	JW	CW	ref.; CW reply, Apr. 9
1787 Apr. 09	CW	JW	online
1787 c. Apr. 10	JW	Mr. Dawson	ref.; JW to Knox, May 16
1787 c. Apr. 15	Benjamin Chappel	JW	ref.; JW reply, June 4
1787 Apr. 18	Samuel Wesley Handy	JW	online
1787 c. Apr. 18	James Rogers	JW	ref.; JW reply, Apr. 21
1787 c. Apr. 20	Mr. Dawson	JW	quoted in JW to Knox, Apr. 23
1787 Apr. 20	JW	Arthur Keene	30:554
1787 Apr. 21	JW	John King	30:555
1787 Apr. 21	JW	James Rogers	30:556
1787 Apr. 23	JW	Alexander Knox	30:556–57
1787 Apr. 27	William Black Jr.	JW	online
1787 c. Apr. 30	Hannah Ball	JW	ref.; JW reply, May 9
1787 c. May	Mrs. Mary Taylor	JW	online
1787 May 02	JW	Arthur Keene	30:557–58
1787 May 04	Alexander Knox	JW	ref.; JW reply, May 16
1787 May 05	Peter Mill	JW	online
1787 May 06	Mrs. Hester Rogers	JW	online
1787 May 06	JW	Rev. Peard Dickinson	30:558–59

Date	Writer	Recipient	Location
1787 May 09	JW	Hannah Ball	30:560
1787 May 09	JW	Joseph Harper	ref.; JW to Ball, May 9
1787 c. May 10	Rev. Richard Whatcoat	JW	ref.; JW reply, c. July
1787 May 13	Adam Clarke	JW	online
1787 May 16	JW	Alexander Knox	30:560–61
1787 May 17	H[enry] B[ennis]	JW	online
1787 May 18	JW	Rev. Levi Heath	30:561–62
1787 May 20	Freeborn Garrettson	JW	ref.; JW reply, July 16
1787 May 20	JW	Joshua Keighley	30:562–63
1787 May 27	JW	Adam Clarke	30:563–64
1787 May 30	JW	Rev. Charles Caufield	ref.; JW to Moore, same day
1787 May 30	JW	Hugh Moore	30:564
1787 May 30	JW	Zachariah Yewdall	30:564–65
1787 c. June	Mrs. Margaret Simpson	JW	online
1787 c. June	[Thomas Taylor?]	JW	online
1787 June 01	William Myles	JW	online
1787 June 03	Rev. Levi Heath	JW	ref.; JW reply, June 10
1787 June 04	JW	Benjamin Chappell	30:565
1787 June 05	JW	Rev. Peard Dickinson	30:566
1787 June 10	Marmaduke Pawson	JW	online
1787 June 10	JW	John Atlay	ref.; JW to Heath, June 10
1787 June 10	JW	Rev. Levi Heath	30:567
1787 June 10	JW	John Knapp	30:568
1787 c. June 15	J[osiah?] D[ornford?]	JW	online
1787 c. June 15	Samuel Webster	JW	online
1787 June 16	A. Brown	JW	online
1787 June 16	Daniel Jackson	JW	online
1787 June 16	JW	Rev. Dr. Henry Leslie	30:568–69
1787 June 18	JW	unidentified clergyman	30:569–72
1787 June 27	JW	Samuel Bradburn	30:572
1787 June 29	JW	Ann Tindall	30:573
1787 c. June 30	Rev. Dr. Thomas Coke	JW	online
1787 c. July	[John Booth?]	JW	online
[1787 c. July]	JW	Rev. William Digby	30:573–76
1787 July 02	JW	unidentified man	30:576–77
1787 July 04	JW	Lady Maxwell	30:577–78
1787 July 08	JW	Jane (Lee) Freeman	30:579

Date	Writer	Recipient	Location
1787 July 10	JW	Samuel Bradburn	30:579–80
1787 July 10	JW	Rev. Peard Dickinson	30:580
1787 July 10	JW	Martha (Wesley) Hall	30:581
1787 c. July 10	JW	Matthew Stewart	30:581
1787 July 11	Jeanne Bisson	JW	online
1787 c. July 12	William Pitt (Deptford)	JW	ref.; JW to Bradburn, July 17
1787 July 13	JW	Arthur Keene	ref.; see note on JW to Keene, July 24
1787 July 14	Mary Cooke	JW	online
1787 c. July 14	John King	JW	ref.; Mary Cooke to JW, July 20
1787 July 16	JW	Freeborn Garrettson	30:582
1787 July 17	JW	Samuel Bradburn	30:583
1787 c. July 17	JW	John King	ref.; Mary Cooke to JW, July 20
1787 July 19	JW	Mrs. Jane Armstrong	30:583–84
1787 July 20	Mary Cooke	JW	online
1787 July 21	Adam Clarke	JW	online
1787 July 24	JW	Mary (Forrest) Jones	30:584–85
1787 July 24	JW	Arthur Keene	30:585–86
1787 July 24	JW	John Ogylvie	30:586
1787 July 28	JW	Adam Clarke	30:587
1787 Aug.	Philip Cox	JW	online
1787 Aug.	Hope Hull	JW	online
1787 Aug.	James O'Kelly	JW	online
1787 c. Aug. 01	Robert Barry	JW	ref.; JW reply, Sept. 26
1787 c. Aug. 01	William Black Jr.	JW	ref.; JW reply, Sept. 26
1787 c. Aug. 01	Thomas Clarkson	JW	ref.; JW to Hoare, et al., Aug. 18
1787 Aug. 01	JW	Mary Cooke	ref.; Cooke to JW, Aug. 6
1787 Aug. 03	JW	John Harper (deacon)	ref.; 30:823
1787 Aug. 03	JW	D. M'Allum (deacon)	ref.; 30:823
1787 Aug. 03	JW	Alex. Suter (deacon)	ref.; 30:823
1787 Aug. 03	JW	James Wray (deacon)	ref.; 30:823
1787 Aug. 04	JW	Jeanne Bisson	30:587–88
1787 Aug. 05	JW	John Harper (elder)	30:588
1787 Aug. 05	JW	Mrs. Howton	30:589
1787 Aug. 05	JW	Arthur Keene	30:589–90

Date	Writer	Recipient	Location
1787 Aug. 05	JW	Duncan M'Allum (elder)	30:590
1787 Aug. 05	JW	Alex. Suter (elder)	ref.; 30:823
1787 Aug. 05	JW	James Wray (elder)	ref.; 30:823
1787 Aug. 06	Mary Cooke	JW	online
[1787 Aug. 06]	JW	Rev. Levi Heath	30:591
1787 c. Aug. 17	JW	Lady Maxwell	ref.; Maxwell, *Life*, 264
1787 Aug. 18	JW	Samuel Hoare et al	30:591–92
1787 Aug. 24	Ann Bolton	JW	ref.; JW reply, Sept. 18
1787 Aug. 24	James Grey	JW	online
1787 Aug. 27	John Dickens	JW	online
1787 Sept. 04	John Walsh	JW	online
1787 Sept. 07	JW	Jeanne Bisson	30:593–94
1787 Sept. 12	Mary Cooke	JW	online
1787 c. Sept. 13	Henry Moore	JW	ref.; JW reply, Sept. 18
1787 Sept. 15	JW	Mary Cooke	30:594
1787 Sept. 15	JW	James Currie	30:595
1787 Sept. 15	JW	George Holder	30:595–96
1787 Sept. 18	JW	Ann Bolton	30:596–97
1787 Sept. 18	JW	Henry Moore	30:597
1787 Sept. 19	Adam Clarke	JW	online
1787 Sept. 19	JW	Elizabeth Padbury	30:598
1787 Sept. 22	JW	Trustees at Dewsbury	30:599
1787 Sept. 25	JW	Jonathan Crowther	30:599–600
1787 Sept. 26	JW	Robert Barry	30:600–01
1787 Sept. 26	JW	William Black Jr.	30:601–02
1787 Sept. 30	JW	Rev. Joshua Gilpin	30:602–03
1787 Sept. 30	JW	Henry Moore	30:603–04
1787 c. Oct. 01	Sarah Mallet	JW	ref.; JW reply, Oct. 6
1787 Oct. 02	JW	Sarah (Fownes) Tighe	30:604
1787 Oct. 04	JW	Hannah Ball	30:604–05
1787 Oct. 06	JW	Sarah Mallet	30:605–06
1787 Oct. 07	JW	Isaac Brown	30:606–07
1787 Oct. 10	JW	John Heald	30:607
1787 Oct. 11	JW	Granville Sharp	30:608–09
1787 Oct. 12	JW	Mrs. Hester Rogers	30:609–10
1787 Oct. 19	JW	[Alexander Mather?]	30:610–11
1787 Oct. 20	JW	Charles Atmore	30:611–12

Date	Writer	Recipient	Location
1787 Oct. 20	JW	Jeanne Bisson	ref.; JW to Bracken-bury, Oct. 20
1787 Oct. 20	JW	R. C. Brackenbury	30:612–13
1787 Oct. 27	JW [via Joseph Harper]	for Sarah Mallet	30:613
1787 Oct. 23	P. Maber	JW	online
1787 Oct. 29	Adam Clarke	JW	online
1787 Oct. 29	JW	David Gordon	30:614
1787 Oct. 29	JW	Elizabeth Padbury	30:614–15
1787 Oct. 31	JW	John King	30:615
[1787 Nov. ?]	JW	unidentified recipient	30:616
1787 Nov. 01	JW	Zachariah Yewdall	30:616–17
1787 Nov. 01	JW	Elizabeth Winter	30:617–18
1787 Nov. 09	JW	Adam Clarke	30:618–19
1787 Nov. 14	JW	Granville Sharp	30:619–20
1787 c. Nov. 17	Adam Clarke	JW	ref.; JW reply, Nov. 21
1787 c. Nov. 17	Henri De Jersey	JW	ref.; JW to Clarke, Nov. 21
1787 Nov. 21	JW	Adam Clarke	30:620–21
1787 Nov. 24	JW	Thomas Funnell	30:621
1787 Nov. 24	JW	Rev. Alexander Suter	30:622
1787 Nov. 25	JW	Rev. Francis Asbury	30:622–24
1787 Nov. 26	Benjamin Rhodes	JW	online
1787 Dec. 01	Adam Clarke	JW	ref.; endorsement on JW to Clarke, Nov. 21
1787 Dec. 01	JW	Robert Dall	30:624
1787 Dec. 08	JW	Adam Clarke	30:624–25
1787 Dec. 11	Mary Cooke	JW	online
1787 Dec. 11	JW	Thomas Taylor	30:625–26
1787 Dec. 17	JW	Jeanne Bisson	30:626
1787 Dec. 17	JW	R. C. Brackenbury	30:627
1787 Dec. 17	JW	James Ridall	30:627–28
1787 Dec. 18	JW	Adam Clarke	30:628
1787 Dec. 20	JW	Robert Green	30:628–29
1787 Dec. 21	JW	Mary Cooke	30:629
1787 Dec. 21	JW	Arthur Keene	30:630
1787 Dec. 22	JW	Thomas [Roberts]	30:631
1787 Dec. 23	Joseph Benson	JW	ref.; JW reply, Dec.
1787 Dec. [27]	JW	Joseph Benson	30:631–32
1787 Dec. 27	JW	Zachariah Yewdall	30:632

Date	Writer	Recipient	Location
c. 1788	Miss A. B.	JW	online
1788	Mrs. A. Brown	JW	online
1788 c. Jan. 01	[Duncan Wright]	JW	online
1788 Jan. 08	JW	Adam Clarke	30:633–34
1788 Jan. 09	JW	Mrs. Mary Fletcher	30:634
1788 Jan. 09	JW	Duncan Wright	30:635
1788 Jan. 09	JW	Walter Griffith	30:635–36
1788 c. Jan. 10	Henry Moore	JW	ref.; JW reply, Jan. 18
1788 Jan. 10	JW	Ann Bolton	30:636–37
1788 Jan. 11	JW	Jane (Hilton) Barton	30:637–38
1788 Jan. 12	JW	John Mason	30:638
1788 Jan. 12	JW	[William] Thompson	30:639
1788 Jan. 13	JW	Joseph Pescod	30:639–40
1788 Jan. 18	JW	John King	30:640
1788 Jan. 18	JW	Henry Moore	30:640–41
1788 Jan. 18	JW	Thomas [Roberts]	30:641
1788 Jan. 18	JW	William Simpson	30:642
1788 Jan. 24	Mrs. Hester Rogers	JW	online
1788 [Jan. 30]	JW	John Mann	30:642–43
1788 Feb.	Richard Garrettson	JW	online
1788 Feb.	[William Collins]	JW	online
1788 c. Feb. 01	Adam Clarke	JW	online
1788 Feb. 04	[John Crook]	JW	online
1788 c. Feb. 08	JW	Mary Blachford	ref.; note on JW to Blachford, June 3
1788 Feb. 11	JW	Robert Dall	30:643
1788 c. Feb. 12	Henry Moore	JW	ref.; JW reply, Feb. 19
1788 Feb. 13	James Currie	JW	online
1788 c. Feb. 15	Jeanne Bisson	JW	ref.; JW reply, Feb. 20
1788 Feb. 18	JW	William Holmes	30:644
1788 Feb. 18	JW	CW	30:644
1788 Feb. 19	James Wood	JW	online
1788 Feb. 19	JW	James Currie	30:644–45
1788 Feb. 19	JW	Henry Moore	30:645–46
1788 c. Feb. 20	Ann Bolton	JW	ref.; JW reply, Feb. 23
1788 Feb. 20	Thomas Dobson	JW	online
1788 Feb. 20	JW	Jeanne Bisson	30:646–47
1788 Feb. [20?]	JW	CW	30:648

Date	Writer	Recipient	Location
1788 c. Feb. 23	R. C. Brackenbury	JW	ref.; JW reply, Feb. 27
1788 Feb. 23	Mrs. Mary Parker	JW	online
1788 Feb. 23	unidentified	JW	online
1788 Feb. 23	JW	Ann Bolton	30:648–49
1788 Feb. 27	JW	R. C. Brackenbury	30:649
1788 Feb. 27	JW	Mrs. Mary Parker	30:650
1788 Feb. 29	JW	David Gordon	30:650–51
1788 Mar. 02	JW	Sarah Mallet	30:651–52
1788 Mar. 02	JW	CW	30:652–53
1788 Mar. 04	JW	Susanna Knapp	30:653–54
1788 Mar. 05	JW	CW	30:654
1788 Mar. 06	JW	Jasper Winscom	30:654–55
1788 Mar. 07	JW	Sarah Wesley Jr.	30:655
1788 Mar. 13	JW	Rev. Charles Atmore	30:656
1788 Mar. 13	JW	Samuel Bradburn	30:656–57
1788 Mar. 16	JW	Charles Wesley Jr.	30:657
1788 Mar. 17	JW	Adam Clarke	30:658
1788 Mar. 17	JW	CW	30:659
1788 Mar. 18	JW	S. Wesley (nephew)	30:659–60
1788 Mar. 19	JW	William Black Jr.	30:660–61
1788 Mar. 19	JW	John Stretton	30:661–62
1788 Mar. 20	JW	Sarah Wesley Jr.	30:662–63
1788 c. Mar. 21	Charles Wesley Jr.	JW	ref.; JW to Mrs. Sarah Wesley, Apr. 4
1788 Mar. 29	Samuel Bradburn	JW (on CW's death)	ref., JW to Dickinson, Apr. 8
1788 Mar. 29	JW	Harriet Lewis	30:663–64
1788 Mar. 31	JW	Thomas Brocas	30:664
1788 c. Apr.	unidentified	JW	online
[1788 Apr. ?]	JW	Theophilus Lessey	30:664–65
1788 c. Apr. 01	unidentified	JW	online
1788 Apr. 04	Sarah Wesley Jr.	JW	online
1788 Apr. 04	JW	Mrs. Sarah Wesley	30:665–66
1788 Apr. 06	JW	Henry Moore	30:666–67
1788 Apr. 08	JW	Rev. Peard Dickinson	30:667–68
1788 Apr. 12	JW	Hannah Ball	30:668–69
1788 Apr. 12	JW	Hugh Moore	30:669
1788 Apr. 12	JW	Mrs. Sarah Wesley	30:670
1788 Apr. 12	JW	Sarah Wesley Jr.	30:670–71
1788 Apr. 12	JW	circular on Dewsbury	30:671
1788 Apr. 15	JW	John Atlay	30:672

Date	Writer	Recipient	Location
1788 Apr. 17	JW	Adam Clarke	30:672–73
1788 c. Apr. 18	Susanna Knapp	JW	ref.; JW reply, Apr. 24
1788 c. Apr. 20	T. B.	JW	online
1788 Apr. 20	JW	Thomas Tattershall	30:673
1788 Apr. 21	JW	Elizabeth Ritchie	30:674
1788 Apr. 21	JW	Mrs. Sarah Wesley	30:674–75
1788 Apr. 21	JW	Sarah Wesley Jr.	30:675–76
1788 Apr. 24	JW	Susanna Knapp	30:676–77
1788 Apr. 26	JW	William Simpson	30:677
1788 Apr. 27	JW	Rev. Peard Dickinson	30:678
1788 c. Apr. 30	Henry Moore	JW	ref.; quote in JW to Moore, May 11
1788 May 06	JW	Henry Moore	30:679
1788 May 11	JW	Henry Moore	30:679–80
1788 c. May 12	Henry Moore	JW	ref.; JW reply, May 17
1788 c. May 15	Jane (Lee) Freeman	JW	ref.; JW reply, May 20
1788 c. May 15	William Whitestone	JW	ref.; JW reply, May 20
1788 May 16	JW	Rev. Dr. Thomas Coke	30:680–81
1788 May 16	JW	Richard Gower	30:681–82
1788 May 17	JW	Henry Moore	30:682
1788 May 18	JW	John Barber (deacon)	ref.; 30:823
1788 May 19	JW	John Barber (elder)	ref.; 30:823
1788 c. May 20	Rev. Edward Smyth	JW	ref.; JW to Henry Moore, June 16
1788 May 20	JW	Jane (Bisson) Cock	30:683
1788 May [20?]	JW	Jane (Lee) Freeman	30:683–84
1788 May 20	JW	William Whitestone	30:684
1788 May 21	Elizabeth Ritchie	JW	online
1788 May 24	Walter Churchey	JW	ref.; JW reply, June 14
1788 May 24	Sarah Wesley Jr.	JW	online
1788 May 25	Rev. William Turner Jr.	JW	online
1788 May 28	JW	Henry Moore	30:685
1788 May 28	JW	Mrs. Hester Rogers	30:685–86
1788 May 28	JW	Jasper Winscom	30:686
1788 c. May 29	'Hocus Pocus'	*St. James's Chronicle*	online
1788 May 29	JW	Rev. Peard Dickinson	30:687
1788 May 29	JW	Rev. William Turner Jr.	30:688

Date	Writer	Recipient	Location
1788 May 29	JW	Sarah Wesley Jr.	30:688–89
1788 c. May 30	Christopher Hopper	JW	ref.; JW reply, June 3
1788 c. May 30	Rev. Thomas Vasey	JW	ref.; JW to Whatcoat, July 17
1788 c. May 30	Rev. Richard Whatcoat	JW	ref.; JW reply, July 17
1788 c. May 30	JW	Rev. Edward Smyth	ref.; JW to Henry Moore, June 16
1788 May 31	JW	Milbourn Trustees	30:689
1788 c. June	'A Constant Reader'	JW	online
1788 June 01	William Black Jr.	JW	online
1788 June 02	Adam Clarke	JW	online
1788 June 03	JW	Mary Blachford	30:690
1788 June 03	JW	Theodosia (Tighe) Blachford	30:690–91
1788 June 03	JW	Joseph Cownley (deacon)	ref.; 30:823
1788 June 03	JW	Christopher Hopper	30:691–92
1788 June 04	JW	Joseph Cownley (elder)	ref.; 30:823
1788 June 07	JW	Henry Moore	30:692–93
1788 June 07	JW	Thomas Taylor	30:693
1788 c. June 8	John Francis Valton	JW	ref.; JW reply, June 13
1788 June 13	JW	Jane (Lee) Freeman	30:694
1788 June 13	JW	John Francis Valton	30:694–95
1788 June 14	JW	Walter Churchey	30:695
1788 June 14	JW	Jasper Winscom	30:696
1788 June 14	JW	unidentified man	30:696
1788 c. June 15	Adam Clarke	JW	ref.; JW reply, June 26
1788 June 16	JW	Henry Moore	30:697
1788 c. June 20	Walter Churchey	JW	ref.; JW reply, June 26
1788 c. June 20	Rev. Peard Dickinson	JW	ref.; JW reply, June 24
1788 June 21	JW	Henry Brooke	30:697
1788 June 24	JW	Rev. Peard Dickinson	30:698
1788 June 24	JW	Capt. Rich. Williams	30:698–99
1788 c. June 25	Sarah Wesley Jr.	JW	ref.; JW reply, June 30
1788 June 26	JW	Walter Churchey	30:699
1788 June 26	JW	Adam Clarke	30:700
1788 June 30	JW	Sarah Wesley Jr.	30:700–01
1788 c. July	John Moon	JW	online

Date	Writer	Recipient	Location
1788 July 06	JW	Samuel Bradburn	30:701–02
1788 July 07	P. T.	JW	online
1788 July 11	Francis Wrigley	JW	online
1788 July 12	JW	Rev. Thomas Cursham	30:702
1788 July 16	JW	Henry Moore	30:703
1788 July 16	JW	Mrs. Martha Ward	30:703–04
1788 July 16	JW	Jasper Winscom	30:704–05
1788 July 16	JW	Francis Wrigley	30:705–06
1788 July 17	Methodists of Newport	JW	online
1788 July 17	JW	Mrs. Ann Joyce	ref.; Joyce reply, Oct. 31
1788 July 17	JW	Richard Whatcoat	30:706–07
1788 July 22	JW	Walter Churchey	30:707–08
1788 July 22	JW	William Kilburn	30:708–09
1788 July 22	JW	Catherine Warren	30:709–10
1788 July 23	JW	Alexander Suter	30:710
1788 July 25	JW	Mrs. Sarah Wesley	30:710–11
1788 July 27	JW	John Crook	30:711–12
1788 July 29	JW	George Gidley	30:712
1788 July 30	Methodists of Newport	JW	online
1788 July 30	JW	Dewsbury trustees	30:712–13
1788 July 30	JW	John Heald [via J. Atlay]	30:713
1788 c. Aug. 01	Walter Churchey	JW	ref.; JW reply, Aug. 8
1788 Aug. 01	JW	Catherine Warren	30:714
1788 Aug. 02	JW	Methodist Societies	10:669
1788 c. Aug. 02	JW	James Deaves	ref.; JW to Ward, Aug. 2
1788 Aug. 02	JW	Sarah Mallet	30:714–15
1788 Aug. 02	JW	Ann Dupuy Taylor	30:715–16
1788 Aug. 02	JW	Mrs. Martha Ward	30:716
1788 Aug. 03	JW	James Bogie (deacon)	ref.; 30:823
1788 Aug. 03	JW	Robert Gamble (deacon)	30:717
1788 Aug. 03	JW	Matthew Lumb (deacon)	30:717–18
1788 Aug. 03	JW	W. M'Cornock (deacon)	ref.; 30:823
1788 Aug. 03	JW	Thomas Owens (deacon)	30:718
1788 Aug. 03	JW	Ben. Pearce (deacon)	ref.; 30:823
1788 Aug. 05	JW	James Bogie (elder)	30:719

Date	Writer	Recipient	Location
1788 Aug. 05	JW	Robert Gamble (elder)	30:719–20
1788 Aug. 05	JW	Matthew Lumb (elder)	30:720
1788 Aug. 05	JW	Frances Godfrey	30:720–21
1788 Aug. 05	JW	W. M'Cornock (elder)	ref.; 30:823
1788 Aug. 05	JW	Thomas Owens (elder)	ref.; 30:823
1788 Aug. 05	JW	Ben. Pearce (elder)	ref.; 30:823
1788 Aug. 06	JW	Al. Mather (deacon)	ref.; 30:824
1788 Aug. 07	JW	Al. Mather (elder)	ref.; 30:824
1788 Aug. 07	JW	Mrs. Sarah Wesley	30:721–22
1788 Aug. 08	JW	Walter Churchey	30:722–23
1788 Aug. 08	JW	Arthur Keene	30:723–24
1788 Aug. 08	JW	Lady Maxwell	30:724–25
1788 c. Aug. 10	Ann Bolton	JW	ref.; JW reply, Aug. 15
1788 Aug. 15	JW	Ann Bolton	30:725
1788 Aug. 19	John Atlay	JW	online
1788 Aug. 23	[John Broadbent?]	JW	online
1788 Aug. 23	JW	John Atlay	30:726
1788 c. Aug. 25	Sarah Wesley Jr.	JW	ref.; JW reply, Sept. 1
1788 Aug. 26	JW	Elizabeth Baker	30:726–27
1788 Aug. 28	John Atlay	JW	online
1788 Aug. 31	JW	John Atlay	30:727
1788 c. Sept.	S[ophia?] B[radburn]	JW	online
1788 Sept. 01	JW	Sarah Wesley Jr.	30:728
1788 Sept. 02	John Atlay	JW	online
1788 Sept. 04	JW	John Atlay	30:728–29
1788 c. Sept. 05	Sarah Wesley Jr.	JW	ref.; JW reply, Sept. 8
1788 Sept. 06	John Atlay	JW	online
1788 Sept. 06	JW	Thomas Cooper	30:729
1788 Sept. 08	JW	Sarah Wesley Jr.	30:730
1788 c. Sept. 15	John Gillis	JW	online
1788 Sept. 15	JW	George Whitfield	30:731
1788 Sept. 16	JW	Elizabeth Baker	30:731–32
1788 Sept. 17	Mrs. Hester Rogers	JW	online
1788 Sept. 17	JW	Joseph Benson	30:732–34
1788 c. Sept. 18	Saarah (Gwynne) Wesley	JW	ref.; JW reply, Sept. 22
1788 Sept. 19	George Gidley	JW	ref.; endorsement on JW letter of July 29
1788 Sept. 20	John Atlay	JW	online
1788 Sept. 20	JW	Rev. Francis Asbury	30:734–35
1788 Sept. 20	JW	Henry Moore	30:735

Date	Writer	Recipient	Location
1788 Sept. 20	JW	unidentified man	30:736
1788 Sept. 21	JW	Hugh Moore	30:736–37
1788 Sept. 22	JW	Thomas Cooper	30:737
1788 c. Sept. 22	JW	Peter Mill	30:738
1788 Sept. 22	JW	Mrs. Sarah Wesley	30:738–39
1788 Sept. 23	Sarah Wesley Jr.	JW	online
1788 Sept. 24	JW	John Atlay	30:739
1788 Sept. 26	JW	Sarah Wesley Jr.	30:739–40
1788 Sept. 27	JW	Walter Churchey	30:740–41
1788 Sept. 29	JW	Mrs. Hester Rogers	ref.; JW endorsement on her letter of Sept. 17
1788 Sept. 30	JW	Lady Maxwell	30:741–42
1788 Sept. 30	JW	Jasper Winscom	30:743
1788 c. Oct.	J. R.	JW	online
1788 c. Oct.	unidentified	JW	online
1788 c. Oct. 08	Robert Dall	JW	ref.; JW reply, Oct. 11
1788 Oct. 10	JW	[Walter Griffith?]	30:743
1788 Oct. 10	JW	Mr. _____ in Edinburgh	30:744
1788 Oct. 11	JW	James Bogie	30:744–45
1788 Oct. 11	JW	Robert Dall	30:745
1788 Oct. 12	JW	Joseph Cownley	30:746
1788 c. Oct. 14	Peter Mill	JW	ref.; JW reply, Oct. 18
1788 Oct. 14	John Francis Valton	JW	online
1788 Oct. 18	JW	Peter Mill	30:747
1788 Oct. 20	JW	Rev. Levi Heath	30:748
1788 Oct. 20	JW	Rachel (Donne) Heath	30:748–49
1788 Oct. 24	JW	[Jane (Bisson) Cock]	30:749–50
1788 Oct. 24	JW	[Edward] Jackson	30:750–51
1788 Oct. 24	JW	Thomas Tattershall	30:751–52
1788 c. Oct. 25	William Stevens	JW	ref.; JW reply, Oct. 31
1788 c. Oct. 28	Adam Clarke	JW	ref.; JW reply, Nov. 5
1788 Oct. 31	Mrs. Ann Joyce	JW	online
1788 Oct. 31	JW	William Stevens	30:752
1788 Oct. 31	JW	John Francis Valton	30:752–53
1788 c. Nov. 01	R. C. Brackenbury	JW	ref.; JW reply, Nov. 7
1788 Nov. 05	JW	Adam Clarke	30:753–54
1788 c. Nov. 05	Edward Coates	JW	online (summary)

Date	Writer	Recipient	Location
1788 c. Nov. 05	William Smith	JW	online (summary)
1788 Nov. 06	JW	Benjamin Rhodes	30:754
1788 Nov. 07	JW	John Blunt	30:755
1788 Nov. 07	JW	R. C. Brackenbury	30:755–56
1788 Nov. 08	JW	Charles Bland	30:756–57
1788 Nov. 08	JW	Jasper Winscom	30:757
1788 c. Nov. 10	JW	Edward Coates	30:758
1788 c. Nov. 10	JW	William Smith	ref.; Coates, *New Portrait*, 39
1788 Nov. 13	JW	[Sarah Crosby]	30:758–59
1788 Nov. 16	JW	William [Butterfield?]	30:759
1788 Nov. 16	JW	[Rev.] Joseph Taylor	30:760
1788 c. Nov. 22	Peter Mill	JW	online
1788 c. Nov. 28	JW	William Smith	30:761
1788 c. Dec.	Joseph Cownley	JW	ref.; Coates, *New Portrait*, 45
1788 c. Dec.	JW	Thomas Carlill	30:761–62
1788 Dec. 02	JW	Henry Moore	30:762
1788 Dec. 06	JW	Rev. Charles Atmore	30:763
1788 Dec. 06	JW	Walter Churchey	30:763–64
1788 c. Dec. 08	William Smith	JW	ref.; Coates, *New Portrait*, 43
1788 Dec. 09	Rev. Dr. Thomas Coke	JW	online
1788 Dec. 09	JW	Thomas Cooper	30:764
1788 Dec. 16	Edward Coates	JW	online
1788 c. Dec. 18	Mrs. Sarah Wesley	JW	online
1788 c. Dec. 18	JW	William Smith	ref.; Coates, *New Portrait*, 48
1788 Dec. 19	Rev. Dr. Thomas Coke	JW	online
1788 c. Dec. 20	Jane (Bisson) Cock	JW	ref.; JW reply, Dec. 27
1788 c. Dec. 20	JW	Edward Coates	30:765
1788 Dec. 20	JW	Peter Mill	30:765–66
1788 Dec. 21	JW	Mrs. Sarah Wesley	30:766
1788 Dec. 22	JW	John Ryley	30:767
1788 Dec. 25	JW	Walter Churchey	30:767–68
1788 Dec. 25	JW	Hugh Moore	30:768
1788 Dec. 26	JW	Sarah Mallet	30:769
1788 Dec. 27	JW	Jane (Bisson) Cock	30:770
[1788–1789]	JW	Sarah [?]	30:770–71

APPENDIX B

John Wesley's Ordinations
and the Accompanying 'Testimonial Letters'

From its outset John Wesley understood the mission of the wing of Methodism in which he took leadership as 'to reform the nation, and *in particular* the Church, to spread scriptural holiness over the land'.[1] Through the first decade 'the nation' encompassed in this mission was England, Wales, and Ireland—with their shared episcopal 'Church'. Commitment to this mission led Wesley to avoid actions in these areas that might suggest Methodists were a separate Dissenting church.

In the 1750s Wesley extended 'the nation' of the Methodist mission to include Scotland—where he faced the *established* Church of Scotland, which was presbyterian in structure and Reformed in theological stance; and the *episcopal* Church of Scotland, a much smaller 'tolerated' body that was not overly welcoming of the Methodists. This greatly reduced focus on 'the Church' in particular to the Methodist mission in this setting.

In the late 1760s Wesley was persuaded to extend 'the nation' again, sending lay-preachers to British-related colonies in North America. Here too focus on 'the Church' was less central—both because the Church of England was not formally *established* in some colonies, and due to the sparsity of churches served by ordained clergy in colonies where it had this status. This sparsity troubled Wesley because many Methodists lacked availability to liturgical forms of worship and the Lord's Supper—which he esteemed as central 'means of grace'. Wesley's concern was heightened with outbreak of rebellion among the colonists in the 1770s, because it led to the withdrawal of a significant portion of Church of England clergy from the most affected areas. Indeed, Wesley pleaded (unsuccessfully) with bishops in the Church of England to ordain some of his lay preachers to help fill this gap.[2]

---

[1] See the 'Large' *Minutes* (1763), §4, 10:845 in this edn.; emphasis added.
[2] Cf. JW to Brian Bury Collins, Aug. 1, 1780, 29:586–87 in this edn.; and JW to Robert Lowth, Aug. 10, 1780, 29:589–91 in this edn.

Wesley's concern for Methodists in the (eventual) United States of America grew as the rebellion ended in independence of the colonies from British rule and the Church of England. This left the majority of his American followers without access to, or uncomfortable attending, churches with (episcopally) ordained priests, where they could receive sacraments. Francis Asbury underlined this situation in a letter to Wesley of March 20, 1784, appealing for him to send not only 'such preachers as you can fully recommend' but also 'a minister'. In response to this appeal, John Wesley finally took an action that his brother Charles and others had feared (and helped dissuade him from) at earlier junctures.

In his public letter to 'Our Brethren in America' of September 10, 1784, justifying the action he took the preceding week, John noted that he had been convinced since at least the mid-1740s, from a book by Peter King, 'that bishops and presbyters are the same order, and consequently have the same right to ordain'.[3] He attributed his previous hesitance to act upon this conviction—by ordaining at least some of his lay preachers as priests—to a determination to transgress the polity of the Church of England 'as little as possible'. But he insisted that this constraint did not apply in relation to his followers in the newly independent colonies, since (through a divinely overseen set of 'providences') they were no longer subject to the Church of England. Indeed, Wesley seemed to judge it his providential *duty* at this juncture to provide them the resources needed to establish a new 'Church' in their new nation. These resources included a revised version of the Articles of Religion and the *Book of Common Prayer*.[4] But more crucial, Wesley provided them with ordained priests to preside over the full forms of worship laid out in their Articles and *Sunday Service*—and a model for extending and continuing the ordained offices.

Discussions leading up to provision of these resources began at the Conference in late July 1784 (although there in no mention of it in the official *Minutes*, likely because it took place only among 'the cabinet'[5]). At the forefront of this discussion was how to provide American Methodists with ordained clergy, since no Church of England bishop was willing to ordain their lay preachers. Wesley decided to act on the conviction that his status as an ordained 'presbyter' (or elder) included authority to ordain others as deacons and elders. Thereby he transgressed the polity of the Church

---

[3] See above in this volume. See also JW, *Journal*, Jan. 20, 1746, 20:112 in this edn.; and JW to CW, June 8, 1780, 29:574 in this edn.

[4] See *The Sunday Service of the Methodists* (1784, *Bibliography*, No. 433), vol. 8 in this edn.

[5] See 10:549–50 in this edn.

of England. But a letter of Thomas Coke to Wesley shortly after Conference (dated August 6–9, 1784) makes clear a shared concern to honor 'the practice of the primitive churches'. An important dimension of this concerned the number of persons to be ordained. It had been a long-standing practice for three bishops to participate in ordaining a new bishop. Analogously, Wesley had two elders join him in ordaining the lay preachers being set apart as elders for the American Methodists, *and* he sent to America a cohort of three elders, who could jointly ordain others judged worthy of the role. The more peculiar (and later debated) act which Coke convinced Wesley to take was to lay hands on Coke (who was already an ordained Church of England elder). For Wesley this was to recognize Coke as a 'superintendent' of Methodist clergy in America. But Coke's letter indicates that he understood it as bestowing '*the power of ordaining others, … received by me from you*'—an understanding that would lead Coke eventually to assume the title of 'bishop'.[6]

In his August 6–9 letter Coke also commended to Wesley the suggestion (originally made by John Fletcher) that Wesley provide for each of those he ordained 'letters testimonial of the different offices with which you have been pleased to invest us'. While these were analogous in function to 'certificates' of ordination, they are worded as public letters. Accordingly, we include in this collection of Wesley's letters transcriptions of all the testimonial letters of ordination for which there is surviving evidence of their wording.

Since less than half of these 'testimonial letters' survive in some form, the remainder of this appendix will be devoted to identifying *all* of the persons for whom there is evidence that they were ordained by John Wesley—and thus who would have received a testimonial letter.[7]

Ordinations in 1784[8]

The first ordinations by Wesley took place at the beginning of September 1784, in Bristol, in a room maintained for Wesley's use

[6] See the discussion in A. Raymond George, 'Ordination in Methodism,' *London Quarterly and Holborn Review* 176 (1951): 156–69, pp. 160–62.

[7] This summary is informed by John S. Simon, 'Wesley's Ordinations', *WHS* 9.7 (1914): 145–54; Frank Baker, 'Wesley's Ordinations', *WHS* 24.5 (1944): 76–80; H. Edward Lacy, 'John Wesley's Ordinations', *WHS* 33.6 (1962): 118–21; and John C. Bowmer, 'Wesley's Ordinations: An Elucidation', *WHS* 34 (1964): 99.

[8] Technically, JW's testimonial letters speak of 'setting apart' persons as deacons or elders, but this is parallel language for 'ordaining' in the Church of England and beyond.

at the home of John Castleman.[9] On September 1 Wesley (assisted by Thomas Coke and James Creighton, both elders) laid hands on Thomas Vasey and Richard Whatcoat, ordaining them as deacons. The next day the same three elders ordained Vasey and Whatcoat as elders.[10] Then Coke was 'set apart' as superintendent, with Creighton and the newly ordained Vasey and Whatcoat joining Wesley in the act.[11] If Wesley gave Vasey and Whatcoat testimonial letters of their ordination as deacons, they are not known to survive; unlike the surviving text of all three letters on Sept. 2, 1784.

Ordinations in 1785

Having made the decision to ordain to address the providential situation in North America, Wesley next turned his attention to Scotland—another setting not under the jurisdiction of the Church of England, and where his Methodist followers had very limited access to the sacraments.[12] After conferring with 'a few select friends', during the 1785 Conference Wesley 'set apart' Thomas Hanby, John Pawson, and Joseph Taylor as deacons on August 1; and the following day, as elders. None of the testimonial letters for these ordinations are known to survive.

By contrast, a testimonial letter, signed by Thomas Coke, ordaining Robert Johnson as a deacon to serve in Scotland on October 24, 1785, was present at one time in the collection of the Methodist Book Room in London.[13] It appears that Coke ordained William Hunter a deacon at this same time; and that he had *not* received approval from Wesley to do so.[14]

---

[9] See *WHS* 2 (1900): 99–110.

[10] It was typical in the Church of England for at least a year to elapse between these ordinations. Thus JW was ordained deacon on Sept. 19, 1725 and priest on Sept. 22, 1728. But in extraordinary circumstances the ordinations could take place closer together—witness the case of CW, ordained deacon on Sept. 21, 1735 and priest on Sept. 29, 1735.

[11] See JW, Diary, Sept. 1–2, 1784, 23:497 in this edn.; JW to 'Our Brethren in America, Sept. 10, 1784; and *WHS* 7 (1909): 8–11.

[12] JW published a defense of his 1784 ordinations, with an addendum defending his ordinations for Scotland, in the 1785 Minutes; see 10:615–17 in this edn.

[13] See John Alfred Sharp, *A Catalogue of Manuscripts and Relics … belonging to the Wesleyan Methodist Conference* (London: Methodist Publishing House, 1921), 3.

[14] See CW to JW, Apr. 9, 1787.

Ordinations in 1786

While Wesley makes no mention of it in his diary or *Journal*, we know from a letter of John Pawson that JW ordained William Hunter and Robert Johnson as elders to serve in Scotland when he visited Edinburgh on May 27, 1786.[15] Hunter's testimonial letter is not known to survive, but Johnson's was at one time in the collection of the Methodist Book Room in London.[16]

When gathered with his preachers in Bristol at Conference in late July 1786, JW ordained five more men to serve in Scotland and British portions of North America. While the ordinations are again not mentioned directly in the published *Minutes*, nor in JW's *Journal*, he lists 'ordaining' in his diary on both July 28 and 29, 1786 (see 23:567–68 in this edn.; based on earlier precedent, this would be each person as deacon the first day, as elder the second). JW also names in his diary on July 28 three of those ordained: William Hammet [for Newfoundland], Joshua Keighley [for Scotland], and William Warrener [for Antigua]. Charles Atmore recorded in his diary that he was another one of those ordained [for Scotland], and that there were five in total.[17] The fifth was almost certainly John Clarke [for Newfoundland].[18] Of these five, the only known surviving testimonial letters are for Atmore and Warrener (both as elder; and both dated Aug. 1, though listing the ordination as on July 29). Significantly, according to Charles Wesley, JW was encouraged at the 1786 Conference to ordain as well a preacher for a remote area in Cornwall, but this was rejected.[19]

Ordinations in 1787

At the 1787 Conference in Manchester JW ordained four persons. Again, there is no direct mention of this in the *Minutes* or his

[15] See transcription of John Pawson to Charles Atmore, June 2, 1786, in *WHS* 12 (1920): 107–09; and the clarification of Hunter's name in *WHS* 34 (1964): 99.

[16] See Sharp, *Catalogue*, 15; and Lacy, 'Wesley's Ordinations', 119.

[17] See Baker, 'Wesley's Ordinations', 79–80.

[18] John Clarke, an Irish itinerant, appears in the *Minutes* first in 1784 (see 10:556 in this edn.). He is listed along with Hammet as elders being assigned to Newfoundland in the 1786 *Minutes* (10:605 in this edn.). The ship carrying Hammet and Clarke to their assignment was driven off course to in the West Indies, where they remained. Clarke served until 1790 before disappearing from the stations. His name reappears as a member of the St. Vincent society in 1806. Cf. George G. Findlay and W. W. Holdsworth, *The History of the Wesleyan Methodist Missionary Society* (London: Epworth, 1921), 2:50.

[19] CW to Rev. Benjamin La Trobe, July 30, 1786, MARC, DDWes 4/43.

Journal; but in his diary JW records 'ordained four' [as deacons] on August 3, 1787, and names Duncan M'Allum as one 'ordained' [as elder] on August 4 (see 24:217 in this edn.). From various sources the four ordained can be identified as John Harper [for St. Eustatius in the West Indies], Duncan M'Allum [for Scotland], Alexander Suter [for Scotland], and James Wray [for Nova Scotia].[20] Of these four, the only known surviving testimonial letters are for Harper and M'Allum (both as elder; and both dated Aug. 5, though listing the ordination as on Aug. 4).

Ordinations in 1788

In 1788, while in Glasgow, JW ordained John Barber as deacon on May 18, and as elder on May 19, to serve in Scotland.[21] A couple of weeks later, while in Newcastle, JW ordained Joseph Cownley as deacon on June 3, and as elder on June 4, also to serve in Scotland.[22]

At the Conference in London in early August, JW ordained six more persons to serve either Scotland or the West Indies (according to his diary the ordination as deacon took place on August 3; the ordination as elder on August 5[23]). These included: James Bogie [Scotland], Robert Gamble [West Indies], Matthew Lumb [West Indies], William M'Cornock Sr. [West Indies],[24] Thomas Owens [West Indies], and Benjamin Pearce [West Indies].[25] We know the names of these six either from surviving testimonial letters or from their listing in the column of elders being sent to the West Indies.[26]

[20] John Pawson names M'Allum and Suter in a letter to Charles Atmore, Aug. 8, 1787; while Wray is listed as an elder appointed to Nova Scotia in the *Minutes* of the 1787 Conference (10:631 in this edn.).

[21] See JW, Diary, 24:245 in this edn.; no mention is made in the *Journal*.

[22] See JW, Diary, 24:247 in this edn.; no mention is made in the *Journal*.

[23] See JW, Diary, Aug. 3, 1788 (24:253 in this edn.), 'ordained six'; and Aug. 5, 1788 (ibid.), 'ordained six presbyters'.

[24] William M'Cornock (1746–89), a native of Ireland, first appears in the *Minutes* in 1779, stationed on the Enniskillen circuit (see 10:488 in this edn.). He served several circuits in Ireland before being sent by the 1788 Conference as a missionary preacher in the West Indies (10:668). He died there the following year; see John Crump to JW, Aug. 12, 1789.

[25] Benjamin Pearce (d. 1795) was admitted 'on trial' as an itinerant at the 1784 Conference (see 10:553 in this edn.). He served appointments in England, Ireland, and Wales, before being ordained by JW in 1788 to serve in the West Indies (10:668). He served there seven years, before dying of a fever during a voyage from Grenada to Barbados. See *Minutes* (post-Wesley, 1795), 1:317.

[26] See 1788 *Minutes*, 10:651–52 in this edn.

One more ordination took place at the 1788 Conference, separate from the previous six. JW records in his diary that he 'ordained Alexander Mather' on the morning of August 6, the last full day of Conference; and again the next morning, as Conference was breaking up.[27] This ordination was separate, and possibly clandestine, because it was the first time JW ordained someone to serve in *England* (note that he waited to do this until after the death of his brother Charles in March). JW's reason for this action was to provide continuity for Methodists in England in the event of his death—in part by insuring there would be *three* elders in London (counting James Creighton and Peard Dickinson; Thomas Coke was departing for his third visit to North America) to insure the possibility of further ordinations on the now common model, if desired. By some accounts JW not only ordained Mather, but set him apart as a 'superintendent' (or bishop).[28]

Ordinations in 1789

Having crossed the bridge of ordaining lay preachers for service in England at the 1788 Conference, JW added two more the following year, before he set out for his annual preaching tour (again reflecting concern for continuity in case of his death). On February 25, 1789 he ordained Henry Moore and Thomas Rankin as deacons; and on February 27, as elders.[29] The testimonial letter for Moore's ordination as elder survives; as *may* that of Thomas Rankin.[30]

---

[27] See JW, Diary, Aug. 6–7, 1788, 24:253 in this edn.

[28] See Samuel Bradburn, *The Question, are the Methodists Dissenters?* ([Liverpool?], 1792), 14; George Smith, *History of Wesleyan Methodism*, 2nd edn. (London: William Nichols, 1862), 2:97–98; and the discussion in George, 'Ordination', 163.

[29] See JW, Diary, 24:273–74 in this edn.; neither are included in the published *Journal*.

[30] Simon, 'Wesley's Ordinations', 153, reports that in 1914 it was in a safe of a stockbroker in London; and Sharp, *Catalogue*, 16, lists it as in the Methodist Archives in 1921. Its current location (or survival) is unknown.

Index of Recipients of Surviving Letters

Printed in the USA
CPSIA information can be obtained
at www.ICGtesting.com
CBHW070847051224
18396CB00001B/1/J